Praise for *After Enlightenment*

"Simply put, Betz's accomplishment is s̶
entire span of Hamann's work in its theological and philosophical significance ...
though much remains to be done in thinking with Hamann, Betz's work is a major
accomplishment that deserves wide readership."

Lutheran Quarterly

"This is an important book for at least two reasons. On the one hand, it is a complete,
reliable, and agreeably written introduction to Johann Georg Hamann's life, work
and world. On the other hand, it contributes substantially to the ongoing discussion
in contemporary theology and philosophy about the seemingly ineradicable tension
between modernity and Christianity."

Modern Theology

"After Enlightenment has much to offer those who are familiar with Hamann, as
well as those who are not. The way Betz handles Hamann's difficult writings and
communicates his thought is a clear and precise manner is praiseworthy ... The
comprehensiveness of the study is enhanced by the ease of Betz's prose, offering a
tremendous tool for understanding the enigmatic yet fruitful 'Magus of the North'."

Journal of the Evangelical Theological Society

"[Betz] has produced the best and fullest survey of the life and writings of Johann
Georg Hamann in a generation, helpfully including many passages from Hamann's
letters and publications and commenting intelligently on the style, theology,
philosophy, and (to a lesser extent) historical context of Hamann's notoriously
obscure oeuvre; second, he has written an intellectual history covering Hamann's
relation to the major figures of his time as well as his subsequent influence on and
reception by philosophers and theologians down to our own day."

Church History

"John Betz' book is arguably the single best work on Hamann in the English speaking
world and the most informed recent work on Hamann in any language. Hamann is
as profound as he is obscure; hence a comprehensive interpretation of Hamann in
relationship to the philosophers, theologians, and literati of his own time with an eye
constantly upon our own intellectual context, is a rare achievement. I warmly
commend After Enlightenment to a wide readership."

Reinhard Huetter, Duke University

Illuminations: Theory and Religion

Series editors: Catherine Pickstock, John Milbank, and Graham Ward

Religion has a growing visibility in the world at large. Throughout the humanities there is a mounting realization that religion and culture lie so closely together that religion is an unavoidable and fundamental human reality. Consequently, the examination of religion and theology now stands at the centre of any questioning of our western identity, including the question of whether there is such a thing as "truth."

ILLUMINATIONS aims both to reflect the diverse elements of these developments and, from them, to produce creative new syntheses. It is unique in exploring the new interaction between theology, philosophy, religious studies, political theory and cultural studies. Despite the theoretical convergence of certain trends they often in practice do not come together. The aim of ILLUMINATIONS is to make this happen, and advance contemporary theoretical discussion.

Published:

Sacrifice and Community: Jewish Offering and Christian Eucharist
Matthew Levering

The Other Calling: Theology, Intellectual Vocation, and Truth
Andrew Shanks

The State of the University: Academic Knowledges and the Knowledge of God
Stanley Hauerwas

The End of Work: Theological Critiques of Capitalism
John Hughes

God and the Between
William Desmond

After Enlightenment: The Post-Secular Vision of J. G. Hamann
John R. Betz

The Theology of Food: Eating and the Eucharist
Angel F. Mendez-Montoya

After Enlightenment

The Post-Secular Vision
of J. G. Hamann

John R. Betz

Nothing was shining through to them except a dreadful, self-kindled fire.

Wisdom 17: 6

A John Wiley & Sons, Ltd., Publication

This paperback edition first published 2012
© 2012 John R. Betz

Edition History: Blackwell Publishing Ltd (hardback, 2009)

Blackwell Publishing was acquired by John Wiley & Sons in February 2007. Blackwell's publishing program has been merged with Wiley's global Scientific, Technical, and Medical business to form Wiley-Blackwell.

Registered Office
John Wiley & Sons Ltd, The Atrium, Southern Gate, Chichester, West Sussex, PO19 8SQ, UK

Editorial Offices
350 Main Street, Malden, MA 02148-5020, USA
9600 Garsington Road, Oxford, OX4 2DQ, UK
The Atrium, Southern Gate, Chichester, West Sussex, PO19 8SQ, UK

For details of our global editorial offices, for customer services, and for information about how to apply for permission to reuse the copyright material in this book please see our website at www.wiley.com/wiley-blackwell.

The right of John R. Betz to be identified as the author of this work has been asserted in accordance with the UK Copyright, Designs and Patents Act 1988.

Library of Congress Cataloging-in-Publication Data

Betz, John R.
After Enlightenment : the post-secular vision of J. G. Hamann / John R. Betz.
    p.   cm. – (Illuminations)
  Includes bibliographical references and index.
  ISBN 978-1-4051-6246-3 (hardcover : alk. paper) – ISBN 978-0-470-67492-5 (pbk. :alk. Paper)
1. Hamann, Johann Georg, 1730–1788. I. Title.
  B2993.B48 2008
  193–dc22

                                                    2008004418

A catalogue record for this book is available from the British Library.

Set in 10/11.5pt Sabon by SPi Publisher Services, Pondicherry, India

1   2012

For Laura

He was not the light, but came to bear witness to the light. The true light that enlightens every man was coming into the world.

John 1: 8–9

And we have the prophetic word made more sure. You will do well to pay attention to this as to a lamp shining in a dark place, until the day dawns and the morning star rises in your hearts.

2 Peter 1: 19

Contents

Preface

The purpose of this book is twofold. On the one hand, it seeks to illuminate the life and writings of a notoriously obscure figure, Johann Georg Hamann (1730–88), who was widely influential in his own day – even revered as the "Magus of the North" – but tends to be known today, if it all, only indirectly by way of association with his protégé Johann Gottfried Herder (1744–1803), the Counter-Enlightenment, and the literary movement known as the *Sturm und Drang*. In short, it seeks to recover an important but neglected figure – also in the hope of correcting a common miscon- ception of Hamann, namely, that he was an "irrationalist," or even (as some have suggested) the founder of modern irrationalism. On the other hand, more constructively, it seeks to draw out the implications of Hamann's "metacritical" engagement with his friends and contemporaries, who included some of the leading lights of the German Enlightenment, such as Kant, Lessing, and Mendelssohn. Specifically, it seeks to show that his arguments against the Enlighteners (the *Aufklärer*), while delivered in an intentionally obscure form, are nevertheless, upon closer examination, lucid, penetrating, and ultimately so prescient as to anticipate (from a decidedly Christian perspective) postmodern readings and deconstructions of the Enlightenment. Indeed, inasmuch as Hamann prophesied the end of the Enlightenment, foreseeing what Frederick Beiser has called the "fate of reason," this book presents him as a kind of postmodern prophet, i.e., as someone who was already, however anachronistically, in conversation with postmodernity. And herein especially, it is argued, lies his uncanny, prophetic relevance beyond his time to our own.

To the extent that this book places Hamann in conversation with postmodernity (which shares Hamann's lack of confidence in the power of autonomous reason, divorced from tradition, to determine an ultimate meaning or even the nature of reason itself), it in some respects represents a continuation of the author's disserta-tion. Aside from this thematic similarity, however, the present book is an entirely new and different work. It was conceived out of a sense that what was needed, given the peculiar and (arguably) unparalleled hermeneutical challenges posed by Hamann's allusive, enigmatic style, was a comprehensive introduction to his life and works as the sine qua non for understanding him; and that no work on Hamann that would hope to make him comprehensible to readers today – or hope to provide anything more than a loose collection of quotations and aphorisms – can dispense with a sustained treatment of his writings and the particular circumstances that occasioned them.

Therefore, in an attempt to present, as far as possible, the whole of Hamann – both the man and his work – the author has taken an approach similar to that of Gwen Griffith-Dickson's groundbreaking translation-commentary, *Hamann's Relational Metacriticism* (1995), which provides detailed exposition and insightful analysis of some of Hamann's most important writings. The main difference between this study and that of Griffith-Dickson, aside from the expressly post-secular theme and having more explicitly theological concerns, is that the present book is more comprehensive (including treatment of additional, hitherto untranslated texts, chiefly from Hamann's London Writings and his so-called Mystery Writings), but also, necessarily, more selective with regard to the passages that are translated and the level of commentary it provides. In any event, the author owes much to Griffith- Dickson's work, which remains an invaluable resource for Hamann studies. It should by all means be consulted for what is lacking in the present volume – as should the very good and richly annotated translations by Kenneth Haynes, which have appeared more recently under the title *Hamann: Writings on Philosophy and Language* (2007).

As for the main title of the book, perhaps a few remarks are in order. For titles of this sort are by now, of course, something of a cliché, recalling titles of other books, most notably, Alasdair MacIntyre's *After Virtue* (1981) and, more recently, Catherine Pickstock's *After Writing* (1998). With *After Virtue* the present book shares the conviction that the effort of the Enlightenment to ground morality in reason alone has failed, and that the only way forward is in some way to "get over" and beyond the cherished illusion that reason alone is able to provide a sufficient basis for morality or culture. In *After Virtue* it was also proposed as a way forward that we look again to tradition (which the Enlighteners for the most part spurned as a source of wisdom), specifically to the example of St Benedict – whose example, among others, stands as a reminder that through Christ extraordinary virtue and holiness are possible. In the present book, following Hamann, who prophesied the nihilistic destiny of the Enlightenment more than two centuries ago, a similar but explicitly "metacritical" argument is made: namely, that any notion of *secular* reason that would claim to be pure of tradition is an illusion, since both how we reason and what we reason about are a product of tradition; and that, for this reason, given this *a priori* dependence, reasonable persons would do well to heed the *inspired* tradition of the prophetic word (and the Word to which it points), which comes to the aid of reason like "light shining in the darkness," and is *more sure* (2 Pet. 1: 19) and ultimately *more fruitful* (Isa. 55: 11) than the principles and works of reason alone. Likewise, in keeping with Hamann's view of language as the "mother" of reason (and, as such, the focal point of his debate with the Enlighteners), the present book shares with Pickstock's *After Writing* the desire to get beyond the deadening effects of modern-instrumental and postmodern-deconstructive conceptions of it – ultimately, to a more vital, a more inspired, a more Christological conception of language as a dynamic medium of divine descent (revelation) and human ascent (transformation), in short, as prophecy (which, following Hamann, one might define as "a speech to the creature through the creature").

Finally, the present work may evoke comparisons with John Gray's *Enlightenment's Wake* (1995) or Graeme Garrard's *Counter-Enlightenments, From the Eighteenth Century to the Present* (2006); and rightly so. There is, however, at least this difference: that in the conclusion, after a brief rapprochement with the "postmodern triumvirate" of Nietzsche, Heidegger, and Derrida, the present book steers a decidedly *post-secular* course (and thus an implicitly eschatological course) beyond postmodernity (inasmuch as the latter is simply the logical, nihilistic surd of secular modernity) toward Christ. But what, one might well ask, could possibly justify making such audacious claims on the basis of the witness of so obscure and seemingly unimportant a figure? The reason for doing so is elaborated in the rest of this book.

Inasmuch as the present book seeks to retrieve Hamann from relative obscurity, to push him to the forefront of relevance, and to place him in conversation with contemporary issues and concerns, it also, necessarily, bears certain limitations. For it is intended as a comprehensive introduction to Hamann and his writings (with particular attention to his post-secular relevance), and not to the substantial body of secondary literature on him. What is cited in passing from other Hamann scholars, generally for the purpose of illuminating a difficult text, should therefore in no way be taken as an exhaustive representation of the scholarship on Hamann that has been done in the past century, beginning more or less with Rudolf Unger's two- volume work, *Hamann und die Aufklärung* (1911). The author has learned from many more than can be acknowledged here. For further study of the relevant scholarship the reader is therefore referred to the online bibliography of Hamann literature at http://members. aol.com/agrudolph/bib.html.

As for the text itself, it should be noted that Chapter 2 is a revised version of an article that originally appeared in *Pro Ecclesia* 14 (Spring 2005). As for the translations included in this volume, they are always based upon the best available critical edition – the standard edition of Hamann's works being that of Josef Nadler, 6 vols. (1949–57); the standard edition of Hamann's correspondence being that of Walther Ziesemer and Arthur Henkel (1955–75). While the translations of O'Flaherty, Griffith-Dickson, and Haynes were occasionally consulted, unless otherwise indicated all translations are my own. As for Hamann's prolific and somewhat idiosyncratic use of dashes, which bear some analogy to other literature from this period, e.g., Laurence Sterne's *Tristram Shandy,* they have been retained as in the original texts. Given the highly rhetorical, passionate, and energetic nature of Hamann's style, they tend to be used either for elocutionary value, as pauses or breaks, or to communicate intensity of feeling or sublimity of content. Other unusual emphases, such as the use of capitals or italic (e.g., GOd for *GOtt,* or GOD for *GOTT*), have also been retained.

And one last note, an apology of sorts: It is possible that I have done Hamann a disservice by writing this book, for I have done what he explicitly asked not be done: I have written what, in some respects, could be considered a hagiography. As he says in one of his last works, in typical humility, "Do not worry about adding an ell to me or my stature. The measure of my 'greatness' is neither that of a giant nor an angel, no hand broader than that of a common human ell. Please do not paint any moustaches on my life, unless I can still laugh with you, so that the world is not forced to invest and transfigure a rotten sinner with the nimbus of a 'saint.'" So, too, in his first publication, the *Socratic Memorabilia,* he says that he is merely a "signpost" and "too wooden to accompany his readers in the course of their reflections" – an authorial decision that he rigorously carried out to the end of his *pseudonymous* authorship, strictly adhering to the words of the Baptist: *Illum oportet crescere, me autem minui* (John 3: 30). But signposts – especially in a time of great intellectual and moral confusion, when the age of reason, having proudly refused the gift of the *light* of faith, has run its inevitable course into nihilism – deserve to be seen. And it is ultimately to this end, as a sign for the times, that this book is proposed.

Baltimore
July, 2008

Acknowledgments

As with any book, there are many – family, friends, mentors, and colleagues – who have either been formative influences or have contributed in one way or another to this book's completion, and whom I wish specifically to thank. Firstly, I wish to express my gratitude to three scholars who mentored my work at various points, whose love for Hamann, like an animating influence, brought him to life, and who instilled in me a sense of his lasting importance; to each of them I remain deeply indebted. The first is James C. O'Flaherty, the dean of American Hamann scholars, who introduced me to Hamann while I was an undergraduate at Wake Forest University. Though by training a theologian who received his degree from Chicago Divinity School, O'Flaherty was also a distinguished man of letters. He was, moreover, a Virginia scholar-gentleman of the kind that seems to have faded from the world, and – by those who were privileged to know him – is sorely missed. I also wish to express my profound gratitude to the Tübingen systematic theologian, Oswald Bayer, who graciously took me under his wing at a difficult time, gave me my first footing in Lutheran theology in 1991–2, guided my dissertation research, held a valuable seminar on Hamann's *Metakritik* in the spring semester of 1997, and provided helpful counsel at various stages of this book. Finally, I wish to express my thanks to John Milbank, whom I fortuitously met in Marburg nearly ten years ago, who steered my dissertation into a conversation with postmodernity, and has incalculably enriched my sense of Hamann's importance to an engagement with modern (and postmodern) secular reason.

Among others whose suggestions for the book have been helpful – and who are valued still more for their friendship – I wish to thank David Hart and Grant Kaplan. I would also like to thank my colleagues in the Theology Department at Loyola University in Maryland – especially Stephen Fowl, Frederick Bauerschmidt, and Trent Pomplun for nearly a decade of stimulating conversation and sound advice. Thanks also to Graham McAleer for great philosophical conversation, and to Paul Richard Blum for kindly answering occasional translation queries. Among others who have taken the time to read this work in an early form, or in one way or another have been of supererogatory support, I wish to thank Reinhard Hütter of Duke Divinity School and Cyril O'Regan of the University of Notre Dame. Thanks also to the Fulbright Program for a scholarship to study in Tübingen in 1996–7, and to the Loyola College Center for the Humanities for a Junior Faculty Sabbatical in 2003. Thanks as well to Claire Mathews McGinnis for being a wonderful colleague and neighbor – and, not least of all, for a recent refresher course in Hebrew.

Among other friends and family near and far, I also wish to thank Vitold Jordan, who opened my eyes one day in Tübingen; Hank Hilton, SJ and Peter Ryan, SJ, true companions of Jesus; Jeff Perry of SLFC, who knows what enlightenment is all about and (without knowing it) has been a great support; and Jim Murphy and other friends at CCSFX. In all of these cases, Hamann's maxim holds true: "God speaks to the creature through the creature." Thanks also to my immediate family: to my mother and father, Katherine A. Betz and Charles S. Betz, for more than I can express; to my brother David S. Betz; to my mother- and father-in-law, Janet Wells and R. Michael Wells; to my brothers- and sisters-in-law, Michael and Heather, Christopher and Mary Eileen; and to the rest of my extended family stretching from Salem, Oregon to Cambridge, England. Thanks also to Emma for putting up with a distracted father for so many months. And thanks, above all, to my wife, Laura, the brightness of my life, who is a daily reminder that there is a "Father of lights," who gives "good and perfect" gifts (Jas. 1: 17) to those who trust in him. Her love and support have been without fail, a daily image of the love that never ends, and it is to her, it goes without saying, that I dedicate this book.

And thanks, finally, to Rebecca Harkin, Karen Wilson, Bridget Jennings, Annette Abel, Zeb Korycinska, Sally Cooper, and Mary Dortch for their abundant help in seeing this book through to publication – especially to Mary, both for her careful redaction of the text and her consistently sound advice. Thanks also to Susan Szczybor for her regular help on any number of things, to Peggy Feild for kindly processing so many ILL requests, and, last but not least, to Anne and Gerard Dolan, God-given friends from Rodgers Forge, whose backyard is a small Eden and whose prayers uphold more than we know.

Abbreviations

The following abbreviations are used in the notes for frequently cited works:

G-D   Gwen Griffith-Dickson, *Hamann's Relational Metacriticism* (Berlin: de Gruyter, 1995).

HH   *Johann Georg Hamanns Hauptschriften Erklärt* (Gütersloh: Bertelsmann, 1956–63), vol. II, ed. F. Blanke and L. Schreiner; vol. V, ed. E. J. Schoonhoven and M. Seils; vol. VII, ed. L. Schreiner

HMK   Oswald Bayer, *Verunft ist Sprache. Hamanns Metakritik Kants* (Stuttgart-Bad Cannstatt: Fromann-Holzboog, 2002).

JGH   James C. O'Flaherty, *Johann Georg Hamann* (Boston: Twayne, 1970).

JP   Søren Kierkegaard, *Journals and Papers*, 7 vols., ed. and tr. Howard V. Hong and Edna H. Hong (Bloomington: Indiana University Press, 1967–78).

KSA   Friedrich Wilhelm Nietzsche, *Kritische Studien Ausgabe*, ed. G. Coli and M. Montinari (Berlin: de Gruyter, 1988).

LS   Johann Georg Hamann, *Londoner Schriften*, ed. Oswald Bayer and Bernd Weissenborn (Munich: C. H. Beck, 1993).

N   Johann Georg Hamann, *Sämtliche Werke*, 6 vols., ed. Josef Nadler, Historical-critical edn. (Vienna: Herder, 1949–57).

NB   Josef Nadler, *Johann Georg Hamann 1730–1788: Der Zeuge des Corpus mysticum* (Salzburg: Otto Müller Verlag, 1949).

SM   James C. O'Flaherty (ed.) *Hamann's Socratic Memorabilia: A Translation and Commentary* (Baltimore, MD: Johns Hopkins University Press, 1967).

ZH   Johann Georg Hamann, *Briefwechsel*, 6 vols., ed. Walther Ziesemer and Arthur Henkel (Wiesbaden: Insel, 1955–75).

Introduction

... Hamann – born, as it were, with an eternity – anticipated every time ...

Jean Paul[1]

With the confusion caused by Kantianism we have wasted years that will never return ... This immensely wise and profound thinker, this seer, we did not recognize and heed.

Friedrich Schlegel[2]

... Hamann lives on, indeed, has greater prominence than before. He is one of the most profound Christians and defenders of Christianity in our century.

Wilhelm Dilthey[3]

The German author and critic, Johann Georg Hamann (1730–88), revered by contemporaries as the *Magus in Norden* or "wise man of the North," tends to be known today, if at all, either for his importance to the so-called Counter-Enlightenment, or for his influence upon the proto-Romantic literary movement known as the *Sturm und Drang*, or for his influence upon Johann Gottfried Herder, who in turn influenced the development of post-Kantian philosophy. In short, he tends to be known today more by association than for anything he himself said or wrote. For many reasons, however, this circumstance must be considered unfortunate – given that Hamann's fascinating pseudonymous writings, which abound in hermetic allusions and learned wit, are utterly unique in all of German literature; given his equally fascinating personality, which Kierkegaard admiringly described as "the *hyperbole* of all life";[4] given, furthermore, the richness of his theological aesthetics, and – herein lies the timeliness of his thought today – the profundity of his insights as a critic of secular reason.

But if Hamann has not received the attention he perhaps deserves, on at least one occasion, on November 18, 1993, he broke through to a wider audience when the *New York Review of Books* featured a debate between two distinguished scholars: the well-known historian of ideas, Isaiah Berlin (more of a fox than a hedgehog), and James C. O'Flaherty, the dean of American Hamann studies (more of a hedgehog than a fox). The proximate cause of their debate was the publication earlier that year of Berlin's provocative monograph on Hamann, based upon an early study, titled *The Magus of the North: J. G. Hamann and the Origins of Modern Irrationalism.*[5]

[1] Jean Paul, *Vorschule der Ästhetik*, ed. Wolfhart Henckmann (Hamburg: Felix Meiner Verlag, 1990), p. 379.

[2] Friedrich Schlegel, *Deutsches Museum* III, p. 51, in *Kritische Neuausgabe*, vol. 6, ed. Hans Eichner (München: Verlag Ferdinand Schöningh, 1961), p. 628: "Mit der Kantischen Verwirrung haben wir Jahre, die für Deutschland unwieder-bringlich wichtig waren, verschwendet. Diesen großen *weisen* Tiefdenker, den Hellsehenden haben wir nicht gekannt und beachtet."

[3] Wilhelm Dilthey, *Gesammelte Schriften* (Leipzig and Berlin: B. G. Teubner, 1936), vol. 17, p. 102.

[4] *JP* II 1543 (n.d., 1837), (*Pap.* II A 623).

[5] Isaiah Berlin, *The Magus of the North: J. G. Hamann and the Origins of Modern Irrationalism*, ed. Henry Hardy (New York: Farrar, Straus, & Giroux, 1993); repr. in Isaiah Berlin, *Three Critics of the Enlightenment: Vico, Hamann, Herder* (Princeton, NJ: Princeton University Press, 2000).

In this study Berlin makes a bold claim: Hamann is one of "the few wholly original critics of modern times."[6] But this claim is bound up with another that is as tendentious as it is problematic: Hamann is not only an "irrationalist," but "the pioneer of anti-rationalism in every sphere."[7] Hence, as directly follows from Berlin's own commitments and corresponding genealogy of modernity, his inevitable conclusion: Hamann is an anti-modern obscurantist whom the advance of secular reason has rightly left behind.

While one must admire Berlin for the breadth of his erudition, in this particular matter one must regret that he does not plumb the depths of Hamann's concerns or take into account nearly fifty years of scholarship, which has come to very different conclusions. For, rather than seeing Hamann as an irrationalist or as simply a reactionary thinker, modern Hamann scholarship has come to see that he was, in some sense, radically progressive – in fact, as Oswald Bayer has put it, a "radical Enlightener."[8]

Accordingly, following more recent scholarship, the present work seeks to show some of the ways that Hamann was ahead of his time – more specifically, how he saw through and past the Enlightenment's claims regarding the nature and scope of autonomous reason to its problematic philosophical, religious, political, cultural, and aesthetic consequences.

It is rare, of course, that a prophet receives widespread recognition in his own time, except perhaps from a small coterie of followers; and, in keeping with the gospel axiom (Mark 6: 4), as far as we know, no one from Hamann's home town of Königsberg regarded him as one – though Kant, a personal friend, and most nearly Hamann's opposite, had great respect for him. What no one assessing Hamann's significance can overlook, however, is that his admirers included some of Germany's most prominent poets and philosophers; nor can one ignore the extraordinary degree of importance they attached to him. To Goethe, who was an avid collector of Hamann's writings, he was not only original (*cette tête unique*),[9] but "the brightest mind of his day" (*der hellste Kopf seiner Zeit*);[10] indeed, he goes so far as to identify Hamann as the "literary father" of the German people.[11] To Herder and Jacobi, his closest disciples, Hamann was not just a friend and mentor, but someone they downright revered. To Friedrich Schlegel, Jean Paul, and F. W. J. Schelling, Hamann stood above his age as a prophet and seer. To Hegel, who wrote the first review of his collected writings in 1828, he possessed a "penetrating genius."[12] And, last but not least, there is Kierkegaard, who not only "rejoices" in Hamann, but suggests that Hamann, together

---

[6] Berlin, *Three Critics*, p. 257.

[7] Ibid.

[8] Oswald Bayer, *Zeitgenosse im Widerspruch: Johann Georg Hamann als radiklaer Aufklärer* (Munich: Piper Verlag, 1988).

[9] As Goethe puts it in French to Charlotte von Stein, September 17, 1784, in *Werke*, vol. 4 (Weimar, 1890), sect. 6, pp. 359f.: "J'ai toujours aimé beaucoup les feuilles Sybillines [sic] de ce mage moderne et cette nouvelle production ... Il y a des bons mots impaiables, et des tournures tres sérieuses qui m'ont fait rire presque à chaque page ... Je me trouve très heureux d'avoir le sens qu'il faut pour entendre jusqu'à un certain point les idées de cette tête unique, car on peut bien affirmer le paradox qu'on ne l'entend pas par l'entendement." Quoted in *HH* I, p. 20.

[10] Kanzler Friedrich von Müller, *Unterhaltungen mit Goethe*, ed. R. Grumach (Weimar, 1982), p. 109 (from December 18, 1823). See also the collection titled, *Johann Georg Hamann: "Der hellste Kopf seiner Zeit,"* ed. Oswald Bayer (Tübingen: Attempto Verlag, 1998).

[11] As Goethe put it upon discovering the writings of Vico, "It is truly a beautiful thing if a people can claim such a literary father; one day Hamann will become a similar codex for the Germans." See *Italienische Reise* (Weimar, 1890) (letter from Naples, March 5, 1787), sect. 1, p. 31.

[12] G. W. F. Hegel, "Hamanns Schriften," *Jahrbücher für wissenschaftliche Kritik* (1828); reprinted in *Berliner Schriften, 1818–1831*, vol. XI of *Werke*, ed. E. Moldenhauer and K. M. Michel (Frankfurt am Main: Suhrkamp Verlag, 1986), p. 325.

with Socrates, was one of the "most brilliant minds of all time."[13] But if this is so, if such unanimous testimony is any indication of Hamann's true stature, it would appear that in the age of the Enlightenment it was ironically Hamann, by all accounts the *darkest* author in the history of German letters, who was truly *enlightened* – making it all the more preposterous that today so few in the modern academy have even heard of him. As Kierkegaard, sensible to such ironies, poignantly put it:

> the originality of his genius is there in his brief statements, and the pithiness of form corresponds completely to the desultory hurling forth of a thought. With heart and soul, down to his last drop of blood, he is concentrated in a single word, a highly gifted genius's passionate protest against a system of existence. Poor Hamann, you have been reduced to a subsection by Michelet. Whether your grave has ever been marked, I do not know; but I do know that by hook or by crook you have been stuck into the subsection uniform and thrust into the ranks.[14]

But if Hamann's fate has been unjust, the recovery of his thought is timely. For it is only now, one could argue, after the ideals of the Enlightenment have run their course for more than two hundred years and the theoretical and moral foundations of secular humanism have collapsed in ways that Hamann predicted, that the full range and prophetic importance of his post-secular vision can begin to be appreciated. This is especially true of his devastating "metacritique" of Kant and the Enlightenment's *faith* in reason, which makes him in many ways a Christian precursor of postmodern philosophy – ultimately, I argue, to the point of forcing a choice between secular postmodernity and a "post-secular" theology. In order to get to this point, however, one must first get past the "Enlightenment" itself – a term that is taken in the present context, notwithstanding the diversity of its proponents' views, to describe a period of thought characterized by "a consistently rational approach to the great questions of religion and ethics, of theology and philosophy."[15] Specifically, it will require engaging the thought of such well-known *Aufklärer* as Kant (arguably the Enlightenment's most important philosopher), J. D. Michaelis (the father of modern biblical criticism), Lessing (the German Enlightenment's most important dramatist and critic), and Mendelssohn (arguably its most important theorist concerning the relationship between Church and state). What distinguishes the present work from other critical assessments of the Enlightenment, however, is that it engages the Enlightenment not from a remote perspective, but from the perspective of an extremely cultured contemporary, who, in the case of Kant and Mendelssohn, was also a personal friend.

Of course, given how thoroughly the principles of the Enlightenment continue to animate public discourse, to the point of being virtually unquestioned at the level of popular culture, getting past the Enlightenment cannot be taken for granted. Indeed, as Charles Taylor has suggested, it involves engaging nothing less than a fortress of established ideas that he calls the "citadel of secular reason,"[16] which dominates

---

[13] Søren Kierkegaard, *The Concept of Anxiety,* ed. and tr. with introduction and notes by Reidar Thomte (Princeton, NJ: Princeton University Press, 1980), pp. 178, 198; *JP* II 1555 (n.d., 1844), (*Pap.* V B 45); (n.d., 1844), (*Pap.* V B 55:14).

[14] Søren Kierkegaard, *Concluding Unscientific Postscript,* trans. Howard Hong and Edna Hong (Princeton, NJ: Princeton University Press, 1980), p. 224. The reference is to Karl Ludwig Michelet, a Hegelian who wrote an entry on Hamann in his *Geschichte der letzten Systeme der Philosophie in Deutschland* (1837).

[15] *JGH,* p. 150.

[16] See the postscript by Charles Taylor, in Paul J. Griffiths and Reinhard Hütter (eds.) *Reason and the Reasons of Faith* (New York and London: T. & T. Clark, 2005), p. 23. See also Charles Taylor, *A Secular Age* (Cambridge, MA: Belknap Press, 2007).

from a seemingly impregnable position the entire landscape of modern society, for which the imperative to "question authority," especially that of religious tradition (and to replace it with the authority of one's own opinion as an infallible guide, regardless of one's moral formation), is a matter of uncritical acceptance. All of which is given its philosophical mandate in Kant's revolutionary essay from 1784, which hails the Enlightenment as an unprecedented advance in the history of the human race: the advance of reason beyond ignorance, superstition, uncritical deference to authority, and the immaturity of "self-incurred guardianship."[17] And so it was marketed, as successfully as any ideology ever has been: rational persons (and who would not want to be numbered among them?) no longer need to be guided by the heteronomy of faith and tradition, but can be guided by – and place their trust in – reason alone.

One can hardly dispute the success of these doctrines, which so readily appeal to human pride (recalling the first temptation), and whose trans-national expansion has been so swift and wide-reaching as to rival that of any universalistic religion.[18] Indeed, they form the touchstone of modern western civilization, informing everything from a widespread distrust of "organized religion" to a radical "separation of Church and state," deriving from a tendentious reading of the "establishment clause" of the United States Constitution (namely, as implying a mandated inadmissibility of any form of natural law or natural theology, i.e., atheism as the de facto state religion, which would have been as unthinkable and unadvisable to the ancients as to the vast majority of the *Aufklärer* themselves). All of which derives from the Enlightenment's radical doctrine, formulated in light of the so-called "wars of religion,"[19] the dark background against which the Enlightenment is ever proposed, that religion should be a private affair, restricted to the interiority of the believing individual, and without political expression – against which, out of devotion to the *purity* of secular space (where secular opinions alone are welcome and allowed to hold sway), one must ever be on guard.

Of course, few serious critics, not even Hamann, would reject the principles of the Enlightenment *tout court* – say, the principles of popular representation or free- dom of religion. Inasmuch, however, as the Enlightenment proposed a doctrine of reason that required no faith, a vision of society that required no tradition, and a politics that required no God (the source of all light and being), in Hamann's view the "Enlightenment" was a misnomer, resting upon principles that were both

---

[17] See Kant, "What is Enlightenment?" in James Schmidt (ed.) *What is Enlightenment?: Eighteenth-Century Answers and Twentieth-Century Questions* (Berkeley: University of California Press, 1996), pp. 58–64.

[18] In this regard the ideology of the Enlightenment – to the degree that its doctrine of freedom has gradually devolved into purely subjective voluntarism and is no longer bound to universal standards of rationality (as was still the case with Kant) – represents the modern antithesis of Islam: whereas the latter promotes universal submission at the expense of individual freedom, the former propagates itself by flattering the freedom of the individual and his or her "right to choose" as the highest imaginable authority, *id quo maius cogitari nequit*. The one is driven at root by a doctrine of imperial freedom *from above* (namely, that of the infinitely determining power of the divine will); the other, by a doctrine, ultimately, of anarchic, chthonic freedom *from below* (namely, the infinite plasticity of the human will). In short, the one is a doctrine of divine voluntarism, the other, its inversion, a human voluntarism; while the one gives all the glory to God, arguably at the expense of the creative dignity and freedom of the *imago Dei*, the other gives all the glory to man at the expense of God. Such is the fateful dialectic of our times, with no redemption in sight as long as one fails to see in Christ the glory *of God* in the glory of the perfection *of man* (2 Cor. 4: 6).

[19] For an account of the so-called "wars of religion" as, in fact, wars of modern nation-states, see William Cavanaugh, " 'A fire strong enough to consume the house': the wars of religion and the rise of the state," *Modern Theology* 11/4 (October 1995), pp. 397–420.

philosophically and theologically defective. Moreover, it was seen to represent not the dawning of a bright new age, but a deceptive "northern light," which would bring about a new age of spiritual darkness. To be sure, the *Aufklärer* thought of themselves as guides, "guardians" to the "dependents" who had not yet been liberated from the ignorance of superstition and the heteronomy of tradition. In Hamann's view, however, they were nothing of the kind: they were not messianic saviors to a world lying in darkness, in a secular parody of religious expectation, but hypocritical demagogues masquerading as angels of light (cf. 2 Cor. 11: 14).[20]

The source of the hypocrisy, in Hamann's view, lay in the Enlighteners' doctrine of reason, specifically their claim that reason is free – "pure" – of the contingencies of history and tradition. To Hamann, simply from a philosophical perspective, this was nonsense. For reason, he argued, is not accidentally but essentially a matter of language; and language, in turn, is obviously bound up with history and tradition. And yet it was precisely upon such dubious grounds that the Enlighteners presumed to dispense with tradition, indeed to arrogate for themselves the authority hitherto afforded historical revelation – whereby the run-of-the-mill *Aufklärer* could suddenly regard himself as a greater authority than Moses. Moreover, as Hamann prophetically perceived, it was upon this dubious foundation that the Enlighteners sought to advance a specific political agenda, to inaugurate a new, essentially ahistorical and therefore purely secular society, one that could function not only without divine revelation, but as if there were no God (*etsi Deus non daretur*). In other words, Hamann foresaw in the Enlighteners' political dream a society that would be for all intents and purposes atheistic – a society for which any revelation, however true, and any prophetic testimony, however saintly, would be fundamentally irrelevant, extrinsic to the concerns of government, allowed perhaps at the margins as a matter of subjective, merely personal opinion, but deprived of any objective legitimacy in matters of state and public policy.

As Hamann anticipated, however, the price of so strict a separation of reason from religious tradition (of philosophy from theology) would be reason's own demise, and with it the creation of a moral vacuum, inasmuch as for him reason has no integrity apart from history and tradition (reason too, he argued, has a genealogy), and can attain no *enlightenment* apart from grace and revelation. Indeed, admitting only the dim light of reason alone, refusing to admit the clarifying, supernatural light of faith, the Enlighteners would bring about no "cosmopolitical chiliasm," but rather, as Hamann prophesied five years prior to the French revolution, new forms of violence perpetrated by those ostensibly under their "tutelage." As he put it in response to Kant's famous essay,

> The enlightenment of our century is a mere northern light, by virtue of which no cosmopolitcal chiliasm can be prophesied except one that can be prophesied in a sleeping cap and behind the stove. All the empty talk and reasoning about liberated dependents, who pose as guardians to guardians who are themselves dependents but equipped with *couteaux de chasse* [hunting knives] and daggers, is a cold, unfruitful moonlight without enlightenment for the lazy understanding and without warmth for the cowardly will – and the whole answer to the posed question is a *blind illumination* for every dependent who strolls along at noon.[21]

[20] Cf. Isa. 58: 6; 60: 1–2; 61: 1.
[21] My emphasis. Hamann to Christian Jacob Kraus, in ZH V, p. 291. Cf. Garrett Green's translation and notes in Schmidt, *What is Enlightenment?*, pp. 145–53.

In Hamann's vocabulary, therefore, the word "enlightenment" is always loaded with irony, arising from the contrast between his contemporaries' secular and his own theological understanding of the term. For his contemporaries it meant an awakening through reason to the immanent "natural light" of reason, typically conceived in *univocal* terms, i.e., in the absence of any analogical relation to, or dependence upon, a divine light or Logos. For Hamann, on the other hand, the term "enlightenment" meant the supernatural light of transcendence shining in the darkness, like the star of Bethlehem; in any event, it meant something *more* than reason alone. In sum: to his contemporaries it meant the light of an "auto-illumination"; to him, the illuminating presence of the *gift* of the Holy Spirit (Luke 11: 13), apart from whom our reasonings are proportionately dark, debilitated, and confused. As the Psalmist says, "In thy light we see light" (Ps. 36: 9).

Of course, *if* the light of reason is understood not in secular, but in theological terms, namely, as a divine gift (as something that is one's own only as something given) and thus as the obscure beginning of an incremental sharing in the light of God, which cannot be completed apart from the light of faith, *then* there is no need to see the light of faith in dialectical opposition to the light of reason. Rather, as with the relation between nature and grace (which is the ontic correlate of the noetic relation between reason and faith), the light of faith could then be understood as the perfecting *illumination* of what reason dimly discerns, according to what de Lubac, in keeping with ancient and medieval tradition, calls "the twofold relation of the *datum optimum* of creation to the *donum perfectum* of divinization."[22] In short, as two different gifts, reason and faith, like nature and grace, might then be understood analogically, which has the advantage of preserving some sort of relation, without collapsing the interval of difference between them.

But this, one must be clear, is *not* the modern doctrine of reason, and it was not to this carefully balanced doctrine, which recognized reason's limitations and need for faith and revelation, that Hamann was opposed. On the contrary, the Enlightenment's doctrine of reason was characterized precisely by the collapsing of any analogical interval between nature and grace, reason and faith. Whereas the ancient and medieval doctrine of reason was one of reason's analogical participation in a divine light or Logos, the modern doctrine of reason is that of an autonomous rationality, which admits no light beyond its own and no authority beyond the private volitions into which it inevitably resolves. If, therefore, Hamann tends to oppose faith to reason, one must emphasize that he is not critical of reason per se, which he regarded as a divine gift and essential part, together with language and religion, of the "bond of society,"[23] but only of reason's misuse, i.e., when it is presumptuously and hypocritically made "absolute" and as a consequence, in the absence of any higher ordination, given its cultural-linguistic dependence, ultimately resolves into the tastes and prejudices of the time. It is in this light, therefore, as a form of ironic protest against *this* particular doctrine of reason, that one should understand the obscurity and dialectical form of Hamann's authorship – from his cryptic oracles to his "clouds" of learned laconisms – namely, as a way of saying, of reflecting in an outwardly facing mirror, that his contemporaries, the *lumières* of the Enlightenment, are "in the dark."

But if the obscurity of Hamann's indirect, allusive style is a function of his protest against his contemporaries' claim to give light *directly*, without any historical mediation, apart from any tradition or revelation, purely by the accessing of one's own native

---

[22] See Henri de Lubac, *A Brief Catechesis on Nature and Grace* (San Francisco: Ignatius Press, 1984), p. 50.
[23] N III, p. 231.

powers, it is also a positive function of the tradition in which he stands. Whereas the *Aufklärer* purveyed their doctrines according to the Cartesian model of clear and distinct ideas, he spoke according to an entirely different model, a biblical, prophetic model: from the darkness preceding creation, out of which God said, "'Let there be light'" (Gen. 1: 3); to the darkness and thick clouds atop Mt Sinai from which Moses emerged, his face illuminated, to deliver the Law (Exod. 20: 21; 34: 29ff.); to the light of the Word made flesh, which shines in the darkness (John 1: 5ff.); to the sure prophetic word, "which shines in a dark place" (2 Pet. 1: 19), etc. Indeed, the whole of Hamann's authorship can be understood as playing upon the contrast between secular and theological notions of light, darkness, and what passes for genuine illumination. All of which is summed up in a late unpublished writing where he quotes Horace, saying: "Non fumum ex fulgore, sed ex fumo dare LUCEM."[24] In other words, whereas the *Aufklärer* claimed to give light – in the words of *The Baltimore Sun*, "Light for All" – in Hamann's view they merely produced darkness and smoke. He, on the other hand, produced darkness, and did so intentionally, in the hope of giving light, since in a fallen world genuine spiritual illumination presupposes the recognition of a need, a lack, indeed, a confession that one has hitherto been intellectually and spiritually "in the dark" (cf. Isa. 9: 2; Matt. 5: 3).

The following chapters are thus concerned with a figure who took an exceedingly ironic and prophetic stand against his age, and who did so in a way that continues to challenge what passes for "enlightenment" in our own. To be sure, postmodern philosophy eventually caught up with Hamann's metacritique of "pure reason," which leaves modern secularism without any foundation in something called "reason alone," and thus without the same degree of faith in reason that once was so confidently espoused. But even if secular *reason* has collapsed – in fulfillment of Hamann's prophecies – *dogmatic* secularism, even in the absence of compelling reasons, remains. This can be seen in the strident debates, especially in America, between the adherents of religious tradition and those who, in the name of a purely secular state, would expunge every trace of religious influence from the public sphere and public policy, demanding an absolute separation of the inner from the outward, religious conviction from political obligation – all of which is enshrined in the mantra that "religion is best kept out of politics."

What is rarely asked in these debates, however, is whether such demands are even coherent – whether a political order based upon a tradition-free rationality is even philosophically defensible. Hamann argued that it was not. Indeed, from his perspective, seeing the void looming behind it – *in fugam vacui* – the notion of a secular rationality that is thought to exist independently of tradition is vacuous, something that can be maintained only as a willful fiction or fabrication – a modern myth – which reduces to what Nietzsche would call the "will to power." Accordingly, Hamann prophesied that the Enlightenment, theoretically unable to support itself, being based upon illusions regarding its own rationality, would end in nihilism. In the view of partisans of the Enlightenment, this may make Hamann an "irrationalist"; in view of the developments of philosophy and culture in our time, however, it makes Hamann uncannily prophetic. And for this reason – not to mention his insightful views on a range of topics, including biblical exegesis, faith, reason, history, revelation, language, poetry, artistic genius, human sexuality, paganism, Judaism, and the mysteries of Christianity, all of which will be treated in the chapters that follow – he speaks beyond his age to our own.

---

[24] N III, p. 347. From Horace, *Ars Poetica*: "Not smoke from lightning, but from smoke to give *light*" (Hamann's emphasis).

NOTORIOUS DARKNESS: READING SIBYLLINE LEAVES[25]

While a discussion of style may be superfluous in the case of other authors, for whom style is more or less accidental to the content that is conveyed, in the case of Hamann it is unavoidable. As O'Flaherty observes, "Whoever deals with Hamann's thought must perforce come to terms with the difficult but fascinating subject of his style."[26] On the one hand, this is due to the extraordinary importance Hamann himself attached to the question of style. Following Buffon, he says, "Le style est l'homme même."[27]

On the other hand, the necessity of discussing Hamann's style is due to the fact that in the history of German letters no writings, with the possible exception of Jacob Böhme's hermetic corpus, are more readily regarded as dark, obscure, and even unintelligible. As Bayer acknowledges, "The prejudice has stubbornly persisted to this day that Hamann is dark. Everyone who has heard of him or his sobriquet, the *Magus in Norden,* associates it with a mysterious darkness."[28] What is more, as H. A. Salmony claims, "no work in the German language is as difficult to understand as every one of Hamann's writings."[29]

Such a view of Hamann is by no means peculiar to modern-day readers, however. As Eckhard Schumacher observes, "from the first reviews in the 1760s to the literary histories of the nineteenth century to today's lexical entries, Hamann's texts have been variously characterized as the superlative of darkness, the paradigm of unintelligibility."[30] As a Hamburg reviewer of Hamann's *Socratic Memorabilia* unsparingly put it, "No *alchemist,* no *Jacob Böhme,* no *mad enthusiast* could say or write anything more *unintelligible* and *nonsensical* than one may read here."[31] Similarly, the first lexicon article on Hamann from 1811 speaks of "the dark chaos of his mystical and unnatural style ... his mysterious allusions, his fanatical excurses, his affected *bon mots,* his puzzling citations, his exaggerated use of biblical texts, and his disconnected, unbalanced, metaphorical manner of expression, which are merely a few of the errors that he gladly heaps upon his readers as though they were ornaments."[32] And a century later, Ludwig Reiners concludes: "In comparison to Hamann's writings, Hegel's *Phenomenology of Spirit* is ... perfect vacation reading.

---

[25] A fuller account of Hamann's style and the history of his reception can be found in my article "Reading 'Sibylline Leaves': J. G. Hamann in the History of Ideas," in *Hamann and the Tradition,* ed. Lisa Marie Anderson (forthcoming, Northwestern University Press).

[26] *JGH,* p. 100.

[27] N IV, p. 424. At the same time, as he says to his son, there are specifically "evangelical" reasons bound up with it. "My dear child, I commend to you the *evangelical law of economy* in speaking and writing: Accounting for every *vain, superfluous* word – and *economy of style.* In these two mystical words lies the whole art of thinking and living. Everything that Demosthenes was thinking of when he repeated a single word three times is for me contained in the two words *economy and style.*"

ZH V, p. 88; cf. ZH V, p. 177. Demosthenes is supposed to have said that the most important element in the art of speaking is, "firstly, the performance [*hypokrisis = actio*], secondly, the performance, and thirdly, again the performance." The phrase "economy of style" is a reference to Matt. 12: 36f. See Bayer, *Zeitgenosse im Widerspruch,* p. 41.

[28] Bayer, *Zeitgenosse im Widerspruch,* p. 20.

[29] H. A. Salmony, *Hamanns metakritische Philosophie* (Zollikon: Evangelischer Verlag, 1958), pp. 15–16.

[30] Eckhard Schumacher, *Die Ironie der Unverständlichkeit: Johann Georg Hamann, Friedrich Schlegel, Jacques Derrida, Paul de Man* (Frankfurt: Suhrkamp Verlag, 2000), p. 89. The following account of Hamann's style and the history of its reception follows that of Schumacher, pp. 89–102.

[31] From the *Hamburgische Nachrichten aus dem Reiche der Gelehrsamkeit,* vol. 57 (1760), p. 452.

[32] Schumacher, *Die Ironie der Unverständlichkeit,* citing the *Lexicon deutscher Dichter und Prosaisten,* ed. Karl Heinrich Jördens, vol. VI (Hildesheim, 1811).

For with Hamann something new appears: intentional, created darkness."[33] Such conclusions might seem exaggerated were it not for Hamann's own statements to this effect. For example, in his own pseudonymous review of his own *Socratic Memorabilia* he not only quotes the Hamburg review with approval, but even refers to himself as "unintelligible," "dark," "cryptic," even "deranged"; and to his writing as "comparable to a *Japanese* or *Chinese* picture, in which one can perceive *wild* and *dreadful* figures, but whose significance no *rational* person can understand."[34]

Given such a self-portrait, one can hardly be surprised at the familiar accusations of "darkness" and unintelligibility; nor can one be surprised at Berlin's thesis of Hamann's irrationalism. Indeed, given Hamann's apparent intention *not to be understood,* it is a legitimate question whether any effort to understand him is doomed from the start. As even so learned a critic as Lessing put it to Herder, "I would not [presume] to understand [Hamann] in all respects; at least I would not be able to be sure whether I understood him. His writings seem to be tests of manhood for those who claim to be polyhistorians. They truly require a little knowledge of everything [*Panhistorie*]."[35] If this was true for Lessing, whose erudition and familiarity with the debates of the time was virtually unmatched, readers of today cannot hope to fare better. Nor is it promising to know that Hamann was often not even understood by his friends. Thus the *Teutsche Merkur* refers to him in 1775 as the leader of a sect, "who has succeeded in gaining many admirers, who revere him without understanding him."[36] And true enough, the very one who first hailed him the *Magus in Norden,* Friedrich Carl von Moser, confesses to Herder: "I admire the visionary Hamann without understanding him."[37] Similarly, Jacobi confesses to Hamann, "I have not been able to come to the bottom of your dark method ..."[38] And, adding to the absurdity, on several occasions Hamann even admits that he no longer understands himself.[39]

As O'Flaherty has pointed out, however, noting the existence of several collections of Hamann's sayings, such perceptions "must be immediately qualified by the fact that scattered throughout his generally obscure prose are many succinct, epigrammatic, and very quotable expressions."[40] As Jean Paul put it to Friedrich Schlegel, "I read a sentence [of Hamann] and put it away and have enough eggs to brood over in my mind."[41] And, true enough, amid the thick darkness of his style, one will find here and there many wonderful aphorisms, which shine forth, as it were, out of the darkness. As Matthias Claudius observes, "he has wrapped himself in a midnight robe, but the golden little stars shining from it here and there betray him, and allure, so that one does not regret the effort [required to understand him]."[42] Likewise,

---

[33] Ludwig Reiners, *Stilkunst: Ein Lehrbuch der deutscher Prosa,* newly edited by Stephan Meyers and Jürgen Schiewe (Munich: C. H. Beck, 1991), p. 265.

[34] N II, pp. 86ff; cf. his remark to Herder, ZH III, p. 38, "Ha! Ha! Such crumpled, confusing and anomalous allegorical figures have become my *element,* without them I can neither breathe nor think."

[35] Letter from Lessing to Herder, January 25, 1780, *Lessings Briefe* (Berlin and Weimar: Aufbau Verlag, 1967), p. 463.

[36] *Fortsetzung der kritischen Nachrichten vom Zustande des teutschen Parnassus.* In *Der Teutsche Merkur,* 18/2 (December 1774), pp. 174f.

[37] ZH IV, p. 480.

[38] ZH VI, pp. 233f. (January 17, 1786).

[39] See, for example, ZH IV, p. 202 (July 2, 1780); ZH V, p. 358 (February 11, 1785); ZH VI, p. 269 (February 15, 1786); and ZH VII, p. 157 (April 22–3, 1787).

[40] *JGH,* p. 100.

[41] Jean Paul, *Sämtliche Werke,* ed. Eduard Berend (Berlin: Akademie Verlag, 1952), vol. 6, pp. 258f.

[42] Matthias Claudius, *Sämtliche Werke* (Munich: Winkler Verlag, 1968), p. 23.

Mendelssohn issues the following advisory to prospective readers in his review of Hamann's *Crusades of the Philologist*: "Since you might be tempted against your will to throw away this strange little volume and will not have the patience to search the desert for the genuinely pleasant spots it affords, allow me to charm your attention with a few examples."[43]

This is not to say that Hamann was incapable of limpid prose, or that he only occasionally stumbled upon a felicitous phrase. On the contrary, in order to begin to understand the originality of his style, one must appreciate the fact that its difficulties are in large part intended. Admittedly, this is something of a *novum* in the history of western literature: an author who would seem intentionally to defy any attempt to understand him. Without presuming to get to the bottom of Hamann's style, however, which may very well be impossible, one may at least venture the following preliminary explanation.[44] On the one hand, negatively, it should be seen as a calculated attempt to show up the *Aufklärer*, i.e., to show that they are not as bright as they think they are, indeed, to force upon them a confession of ignorance, in order that they might thereby be made more disposed to the light of faith they (in Hamann's view) sorely lack. At the same time, it is almost certainly an attempt to reinstate the distance, which the *Aufklärer* had collapsed, between reason and the mysteries of the faith – an attempt, in short, to safeguard the mysteries of the faith *as* mysteries, which defy reduction to "reason alone." On the other hand, positively, the difficulty of Hamann's writings is bound up with what could be described as an intentionally "sublime" style – a style that seeks to produce light out of darkness, and impresses almost to the degree that one has first experienced a corresponding degree of interpretive pain.[45] As Goethe explains,

> In order to achieve the impossible he lays hold of all elements; the profoundest, most mysterious perceptions, where nature and spirit meet in secret, illuminating lightning flashes of understanding, which beam forth from such an encounter, images laden with significance suspended in these regions, provocative sayings from sacred and profane authors, and whatever else might be added in the way of humor – all this constitutes the wonderful totality of his style, his communications.[46]

Clearly, Goethe was fascinated by Hamann's style; and, given phrases like "lightning flashes of understanding," he more than suggests that reading him was a kind of "sublime" experience.[47] But what he equally perceived, and what warrants equal consideration, is that Hamann's oracular utterances "from on high," as it were, tend to go hand in hand with a notorious, and down-to-earth sense of humor. Indeed, what makes Hamann's style more original still is his tendency to bathos, i.e., his tendency precisely at the most sublime moments of his texts to indulge in the comical,

---

[43] Moses Mendelssohn, "Rezensionsartikel in *Briefe, die neueste Literatur betreffend (1759–1765)*, ed. Eva J. Engel, in *Gesammelte Schriften: Jubiläumsausgabe*, vol. 5/1 (Stuttgart-Bad Cannstatt: Friedrich Frommann Verlag, 1991), p. 559.

[44] For more on Hamann's style, see especially O'Flaherty's introduction to the *SM*, pp. 61–85.

[45] To this extent it is also an intentionally parabolic style, which purposely keeps a vain, unsympathetic, or otherwise preoccupied reader at bay, but yields an unexpected return for those properly disposed to the message it contains (cf. Mark 4: 1–20).

[46] Goethe, *Dichtung und Wahrheit*, book XII, in *Werke*, 14 vols., ed. E. Trunz (Hamburg: Christian Wegner Verlag, 1961), vol. 9, p. 515.

[47] Cf. N II, p. 208, where Hamann speaks of "monosyllabic lightning," as though producing it were the sublime vocation of poetry.

the trivial, the fatuous, or even the obscene, thereby effecting an intentional "break of style" or *Stilbruch*.[48] At one level, this would seem to contradict the claim that Hamann sought to achieve a kind of "sublime style." For what, one will ask, does the sublime, the elevated, have to do with the trivial and the base? At another level, however, as we shall see, Hamann is simply following theological precedent. To be sure, we are no longer dealing here with a classical conception of the sublime, as in Longinus. Rather, with Hamann we are dealing with a specifically Christian style – a "style" he found characteristic of the triune God in the economy of salvation, a "style" in which the "highest" shockingly appears in connection with the "lowest," the offensive, and even the contemptible, to the point of appearing interchangeable with it.[49]

Admittedly, the foregoing explanations, which suggest that there is a hidden "logic" to Hamann's style, will not allay the inevitable frustration of reading him and trying to understand him. As Jean Paul reminds us, "The great Hamann is a deep heaven full of telescopic stars, with many a nebula that no eye will resolve."[50] Similarly, Friedrich Schlegel observed, "With his divinatory profundity he stood alone in the literature of his time, for which his peculiar religious orientation was already alienating and all the more inaccessible given that his sibylline leaves and hiero-glyphic intimations are even more veiled in the dark raiment of symbolic allu-sions."[51] Goethe, too, was keenly aware of the hermeneutical challenges posed by every one of Hamann's publications, which require one completely to "forgo what is ordinar-ily called understanding":

> If now one is not able to approach him in the depths or stroll with him in the heights, or seize upon the figures he has in mind, or from an infinite scope of literature find out the exact sense of a reference to which he merely alludes, things only become cloudier and darker about us the more we study him, and with the years this darkness will con-tinue to grow, because his allusions were directed to an exceptional degree at the spe-cific, prevailing circumstances of the life and literature of the time. In my collection I have some pages of printed text where in his own hand he cited the passages to which his allusions refer. If one looks them up, they again give off a double light, which appears highly agreeable, though one must completely forgo what is ordinarily called understanding. For this reason too such leaves deserve to be called sibylline, because one cannot treat them in and of themselves, but must wait for an opportunity when one might by chance have recourse to their oracles.[52]

---

[48] As O'Flaherty puts it, *SM*, p. 78: "The more elevated the concept ... the more he seems to delight in juxtaposing to it that which is lowly, eccentric, or even trivial. For instance, in referring to the Virgin Birth of Christ he invokes the name of a notorious English quack doctor who had propounded an absurd theory of virgin birth." See N II, p. 75. Cf. N II, p. 213, where, immediately after quoting Luther's translation of the *Te Deum*, "O King of Glory, *Lord Jesus Christ*! You are *God the Father's* eternal Son," Hamann says, "One would pronounce a judgment of blasphemy, if one chided our witty sophists as stupid devils, who value the Lawgiver of the Jews as much as an *ass's head*, and the proverbs of their mastersingers as *dove droppings*."

[49] Thus, understood in such terms, following also Luther's understanding of the divine *sub contrario*, Hamann's style reflects the shocking, rationally incomprehensible style of a God who not only becomes flesh, but sin itself (see John 1: 14; 2 Cor. 5: 21).

[50] Paul, *Vorschule der Ästhetik* I, §14; *Sämtliche Werke*, vol. 4, p. 220.

[51] Friedrich Schlegel, "Geschichte der alten und neuen Literatur," in Hans Eichner (ed.) *Kritische Neuausgabe* (Munich: Verlag Ferdinand Schöningh, 1961), vol. 6, p. 378.

[52] Goethe, *Dichtung und Wahrheit*, vol. 9, p. 515.

Nevertheless, along with Goethe, the greater lights of the age clearly recognized genius in Hamann's style, and not, as the lesser lights and commentators would have it, the ravings of an abstruse or irrational enthusiast. In accordance with the sublime effect Hamann sought to produce, they experienced lightning flashes of understanding amidst the darkness of ignorance, and thus a corresponding degree of pleasure amidst interpretive pain.[53] As Goethe described the experience, "Every time one opens [Hamann's works], one discovers something new, given that the meaning inhabiting every passage touches us and excites us in a manifold way."[54] They also appreciated the irony of Hamann's magi-cal [sic] authorship – his attempt to give light out of darkness – in the age of facile and fatuous "enlightenment" in which he was living. As Goethe points out, in reference to one of Hamann's own maxims, "Clarity is a proper distribution of light and shadow," to which he adds the words, "Note well!"[55]

There is, then, something to Hamann's notorious "darkness" that has nothing to do with an inability to write clearly. Firstly, it marks a conscious departure from the literary standards of French neoclassicism (herein lay his immediate importance to Goethe and the *Sturm und Drang*). Secondly, given its oracular quality, and the pleasure within the "pain" it affords, Hamann's style should be understood in the context of a general interest during this period in the sublime as a literary topos, beginning most notably with Boileau's French translation of Longinus' *Peri Hypsous*, which appeared in 1672. Indeed, given Hamann's familiarity with Longinus as well as with Lowth's *Lectures on the Sacred Poetry of the Hebrews* (1753), with their emphasis upon the sublimity of Hebrew poetry, Hamann was arguably the first to introduce into German letters an intentionally "sublime style," characterized like Hebrew poetry by elevated themes, a proliferation of symbolic figures, gnomic allusions, darkness, terseness, and vehemence of expression.[56] Accordingly, the sublime quality of his style must ultimately be understood as a function of his imitation of the Word of God itself, the *light* that "shines in the *darkness*" (John 1: 5), the "*prophetic* word," which "shines in a *dark* place" (2 Pet. 1: 19). In order, therefore, to penetrate the veils of his style and come to discern its inner logos, one must probe the depths of the divine style of the Logos of which it is an imitation, which tends to provoke its audience (cf. John 6: 60ff.) and defy rational comprehension (see 1 Cor. 1: 18ff.), being clothed in a mysterious parabolic form, but becomes intelligible to those of sympathetic disposition who are willing to follow closely (Matt. 13: 10ff.), like the disciples, who are able to discern "in such disguise," as Hamann puts it, "the beams of heavenly glory."[57]

A BRIEF HISTORY OF SCHOLARSHIP

The effort to publish a complete edition of Hamann's works began toward the end of his life with his friends, most notably, Herder, Jacobi, Hippel, and Kraus, and also with Goethe. But their efforts were plagued by difficulties, the first of which was how to get around Hamann's humility, which balked at the idea, not to mention his humorous and off-putting responses to their proposals. For example, when Herder

---

[53] Cf. N II, p. 208, where Hamann speaks of "monosyllabic lightning," as though producing it were the sublime vocation of poetry.

[54] Goethe, *Dichtung und Wahrheit*, in *Werke*, vol. 9, p. 515.

[55] Goethe, *Maximen und Reflexionen*, in *Werke*, vol. 12, p. 412; see. ZH VI, p. 235.

[56] For more on the Hamann–Lowth connection, see Chapter 5.

[57] N II, p. 171.

asked him about it he suggested that they call the edition "Bathhouse quackeries" (*Saalbadereien*), and the initial volume, "First little tub" (*Erstes Wannchen*).[58] Needless to say, Herder dismissed these suggestions.[59] Whether or not Hamann made these suggestions in jest (there is good reason to believe that he was quite serious), he realized that his own writings were perhaps too difficult to be worth publishing; that he never wrote for the public anyway, except ironically, having written for individual readers who "knew how to swim" (in reference to his "archipelagic" style); and that a *collected* edition of such occasional and "flying leaves" was in itself almost a contradiction in terms.[60]

These difficulties were not lost on Hamann's friends and admirers as they continued to plan an edition after his death. They themselves were well aware of the serious hermeneutical challenges any future readership would have to face. As we have seen, they also realized that the notorious darkness of his style, which even they had great difficulty penetrating, would only thicken with time. All of which made the question more pressing whether one could publish any edition without extensive commentary – not to mention the question of who could be found and persuaded to undertake so Herculean a task.

In the meantime, with no edition forthcoming, some of Germany's brightest lights were growing impatient. As Jean Paul lamented, Hamann remained "a great sphinx, like the Egyptian, half buried in the sand."[61] Thus in 1804 he pressed the matter with Jacobi, asking, "What will happen with Hamann? [i.e., the publication of his works] – Say something definite! I can see everything die – for it will come again – but not a genius."[62] Similarly, in 1807 Schelling thanks Jacobi for having acquainted him "with the writings of this powerful and original mind" [*urkräftigen Geistes*], encouraging him either to publish Hamann's writings himself or at least continue to promote the endeavor by word of mouth.[63] By 1813, however, there was still no edition, and not wanting Hamann to sink further into oblivion, Friedrich Schlegel wrote to Jacobi to request a selection of Hamann's writings to publish in his journal, *Deutsches Museum*. In response, Jacobi sent him Hamann's early confessional work, *Biblische Betrachtungen,* which Schlegel then published along with the following introduction, in which he explains to his readers why someone as profound as Hamann could, regrettably, continue to be so obscure:

> Hamann is less well known than [Lessing and Lavater]. He was utterly unconcerned with the glories of being an author. Entirely concerned only to seek and discover truth and true wisdom, he communicated what his perceptive spirit had investigated and found, writing for the most part anonymously in individual humorous tracts, as in dispersed sibylline leaves, which here and there seem dark due to the fullness of his learning and wit, and their deep meaning ... For this reason only very few were able to understand and appropriate the value of Hamann's spirit. His writings have even remained partly unknown, and a complete collection is a literary rarity. In recent years, however, the wish has often been expressed for a new edition of his works. And yet it is hard to believe that such a special effort should be required for *Hamann* ...; for an

---

[58] ZH V, p. 204. For more on the significance of these titles, see Chapter 10.
[59] ZH V, p. 248.
[60] See N II, p. 61.
[61] Paul, *Sämtliche Werke*, vol. 3, 4, p. 45 (January 2, 1801).
[62] Paul, *Sämtliche Werke*, vol. 3, p. 274 (Letter of January 30, 1804).
[63] F. W. J. Schelling, *Sämtliche Werke*, ed. K. F. A. Schelling (Stuttgart and Augsburg: J. G. Cotta'scher Verlag, 1856–61), I, vol. 7, p. 293.

author, who was perhaps the most original, and unquestionably one of the most profound and erudite that the eighteenth century produced in Germany! – But one knows the *stream* of German literature and what drives it; how all light things float to the top and the best and noblest are so easily forgotten and pulled down into the vortex of general thoughtlessness.[64]

The decision to publish selections from Hamann's *Biblische Betrachtungen,* the largest work among Hamann's "London Writings," was a prudent choice, since it contains the core of his theological vision; unlike Hamann's later "authorship," it also has the advantage of being written in clear, accessible prose. It was a modest beginning, to be sure, but significant advances were soon to follow. In 1816 a friend of Jacobi and fellow member of the Academy of the Sciences, Friedrich Roth, published a two-volume edition of selections from the London Writings, titled *Johann Georg Hamanns Betrachtungen über die Heilige Schrift* [Johann Georg Hamann's meditations on Holy Scripture]. Three years later, in 1819, Friedrich Cramer published a collection of aphorisms titled *Sibyllinische Blätter des Magus in Norden (Johann Georg Hamann's), Nebst mehrern Beilagen.* The decisive turn of events, however, came with Roth's first edition, *Hamanns Schriften,* which appeared in seven volumes between 1821 and 1827 and included a modest selection of Hamann's correspondence.[65] Finally, Hamann's writings were available to the public; and one can gauge something of the intellectual and cultural significance of the achievement from the fact that the first edition was reviewed by none other than Hegel in a substantial two-part review, roughly seventy-five pages in length, which marks the proper beginning of Hamann scholarship.[66]

With the deaths of Hegel in 1831 and Goethe in 1832 the great age of German classicism and philosophy came to a close, and with their passing Hamann's literary and philosophical testament once again threatened to recede into oblivion. Less than ten years later, however, Hamann came to the attention of Kierkegaard (quite possibly by way of Hegel's review), whose journal entries, especially between 1836 and 1837, contain many references to Hamann, in whom he found a model for his own religious philosophy and experiments as a humorist.[67] Indeed, throughout his works and journals Kierkegaard praises no other modern author as much as Hamann, not only for his "profound sensibility and enormous genius," and not only for being "the greatest humorist in Christendom," which is to say, "the greatest humorist in the world," but also for the depth of his personality, which he admiringly describes as "the *hyperbole* of all life."[68] That Hamann could be admired by such different thinkers as Hegel and Kierkegaard is remarkable enough (and in many ways they represent precisely the difference between Hamann's own very different disciples, Herder and Jacobi.) What is even more remarkable is that all of them – Herder, Jacobi, Goethe, Schelling, Hegel, and Kierkegaard – in one way or another made claims to being Hamann's heir or definitive interpreter, as though their literary,

---

[64] Friedrich Schlegel, "Hamann als Philosoph," *Deutsches Museum* III (1813), pp. 33–52.

[65] *Hamanns Schriften,* 7 vols. (Berlin: Reimer, 1821–7). The eighth and final volume, edited by G. A. Wiener, containing an appendix and concordance, did not appear until 1842.

[66] Hegel, "Hamanns Schriften," pp. 275–352. For a treatment of Hegel's review, see Stephen N. Dunning, *The Tongues of Men: Hegel and Hamann on Religious Language and History* (Missoula, MT: Scholars Press, 1979), especially pp. 103–36.

[67] See John R. Betz, "Hamann before Kierkegaard: a systematic theological oversight," *Pro Ecclesia* 16 (Summer 2007), pp. 299–333.

[68] *JP* II 1681 (n.d., 1837), (*Pap.* II A 75); II 1543 (n.d., 1837), (*Pap.* II A 623).

philosophical, or spiritual credentials somehow depended upon it. Such is the obscure but powerful influence, which is more felt than seen – like a black hole operating behind or between the familiar stars – that shows him *ex negativo* to be one of the dark, mysterious centers of gravity of the intellectual life of his age.

If today, however, Hamann remains an obscure figure, this is entirely understandable. Firstly, this circumstance is due to the fact that he defies any single classification, so that it is difficult to say whether he is a philosopher, a theologian, a prophet, a humorist, an eccentric genius, a man of letters, a literary critic, or perhaps all of these at once. Thus, falling through the cracks between the disciplines, he is generally studied by none of them. Secondly, it is due to Hamann's own intention not to write for the public and not to make a name for himself, the story of Babel being all too familiar to him.[69] Thirdly, as we have seen, it is largely due to the occasional and exceedingly obscure nature of his writings, which even in his own day were considered the epitome of "dark and puzzling" (in Mendelssohn's phrase), and today are all the more difficult – if not impossible – to understand.

But this has not kept him from being assimilated in reference and survey works, in which he is variously described as a proto-Romantic,[70] a forerunner of Herder (or perhaps Schleiermacher),[71] an "irregular dogmatician,"[72] a forerunner of dialectical theology,[73] or, occasionally, a mystic.[74] While some of these classifications are more or less accurate, others can be very misleading. The connection between Hamann and Schleiermacher, for example, would require immediate qualification, given that for Hamann faith remains a creature – an effect – of the external Word (*fides creatura verbi*), along the lines of Romans 10: 17, rather than vice versa (*verbum creatura fidei*).[75] Surely the most mistaken classfication, however, as touched upon above, is that of Isaiah Berlin, namely, that Hamann was an "irrationalist," indeed, the "founder of modern irrationalism."

For all of Berlin's distinction as a historian of ideas, this classification is particularly wide of the mark – unless Hegel is to be regarded as irrational for his own critique of the Enlightenment, or Schelling and Kierkegaard are irrational for attacking Hegel's own brand of rationalism, or Wittgenstein is irrational for critiquing the

---

[69] See Kierkegaard's keen observation, *JP* II 1700 (n.d., 1837): "Now I perceive why genuine humor cannot be caught, as irony can, in a novel and why it thereby ceases to be a life-concept, simply because not-to-write is part of the nature of the concept, since this would betray an all too conciliatory position toward the world (which is why Hamann remarks somewhere that fundamentally there is nothing more ludicrous than to write for the people). Just as Socrates left no books, Hamann left only as many as the modern period's rage for writing made relatively necessary, and furthermore only occasional pieces"; cf. *JP* II 1701 (n.d.): "For how could Hamann ever think of publishing the whole body of his works – he who, completely in agreement with Pilate, whom he declares to be the greatest philosopher, said: What I have written I have written."

[70] See, for example, M. H. Abrams's classic studies, *The Mirror and the Lamp: Romantic Theory and the Critical Tradition* (New York: Norton, 1958) and *Natural Supernaturalism: Tradition and Revolution in Romantic Literature* (New York: Norton, 1971). See also Isaiah Berlin, *The Roots of Romanticism*, ed. Henry Hardy (Princeton, NJ: Princeton University Press, 1999).

[71] Wilhelm Dilthey, "Vom Aufgang des geschichtlichen Bewusstseins. Jugendaufsätze und Erinnerungen," in *Gesammelte Schriften* (Leipzig and Berlin: B. G. Teubner, 1936), vol. 11, pp. 1–39.

[72] Karl Barth, *Kirchliche Dogmatik* (Zurich: Theologischer Verlag, 1986), I/1, p. 294.

[73] See, for example, H. E. Weber "Zwei Propheten des Irrationalismus: Joh. G. Hamann and S. Kierkegaard als Bahnbrecher der Theologie des Christusglaubens," *Luthertum* [*Neue Kirchliche Zeitschrift*] 28 (1917), pp. 23–58, 77–125.

[74] Such was the view, for example, of Ludwig Giesebrecht. See *HH* VII, p. 40.

[75] For the difference between Luther and Schleiermacher in this regard, see Oswald Bayer, *Autorität und Kritik* (Tübingen: Mohr-Siebeck, 1991), pp. 156–68.

positivism of G. E. Moore; unless, that is, the rationality of a given age, in this case the secular rationality of the Enlightenment, is an authority so universal and self-evident as to be beyond interrogation and criticism. For that matter, one must reiterate that Hamann's occasionally vitriolic rhetoric is never directed at reason per se, which he considers a gift of God, but only at its idolatrous misuse and transgressing of its proper limits, as when it encroaches upon the mysteries of faith or attempts to reduce these mysteries to rational terms. To be sure, in defending the mysteries of the Trinity, Christ, and Scripture, Hamann tends in the direction of fideism (like any Christian writing in the middle of the Enlightenment, he tended to stress the *difference* between faith and reason), but even he affirms, in keeping with the majority of the Christian tradition, that "*Faith* has need of *reason* just as much as reason needs faith."[76] Indeed, following Oswald Bayer, one could even say that Hamann was *more* rational than his contemporaries, a kind of "radical *Aufklärer*," in that, like Kant, but going *beyond* him, he subjected reason to *metacritical* scrutiny, laying bare the presuppositions – the "articles of faith"– latent but denied by every dogmatic a priori rationalism, however "self-evident" or transcendentally refined it may claim to be.

Specifically, Hamann calls attention to what the *Aufklärer* virtually ignored, namely, the historical contingencies of tradition and the "impurities" of language and metaphor pervading all putatively "pure" thought. And in this respect, I argue, post-modern "deconstruction" is but a continuation of the kind of metacriticism Hamann introduced two centuries before – with this all-important difference, that Hamann's deconstructive metacriticism has a teleological point. As a humbling of autonomous reason and all proud systems of thought (in the sense of 2 Cor. 10: 5), it is meant not to leave reason in a state of despair, but to prepare it for faith, thereby saving reason from theoretical suicide and providing it with its ultimate object, an object that can only be *given*. To be sure, precisely because Hamann foresaw that *secular* reason, left to its own devices, would end in nihilism, he wished to accelerate its demise; but he did so in order to bring reason to the point of a more radical understanding of its limits, so that reason could be born again, as it were, through the humble admission of the light of faith and a corresponding life-giving sense of reason's ordination to revelation. None of which (unless one is a secular dogmatist and happy to maintain theoretical illusions about the autonomy of reason for the sake of a secular politics) makes Hamann an "irrationalist."

The most provocative and unwarranted aspect of Berlin's thesis, however, is his suggestion that Hamann is the "forgotten source of a movement that in the end engulfed the whole of European culture," i.e., Hamann, as the founder of modern irrationalism, stands at the beginning of a causal chain that culminated in the atrocities of National Socialism.[77] Just in case one is talking about the same Hamann, and not confusing him with *Haman* from the book of Esther, let it be stated at the outset that Hamann was a friend of the Jewish philosopher Moses Mendelssohn; that he denounced the persecution of the Jews;[78] that he called Judaism the "bodily mother of evangelical Christianity";[79] and that he passionately defended the election of Israel against what he considered to be the anti-Semitic implications of the natural religion *of the Enlightenment*. No doubt, there was an element of *Blut und Boden*, a touch

---

[76] ZH VII, p. 165.

[77] Isaiah Berlin, "The Magus of the North," *New York Review of Books* (October 21, 1993), p. 64.

[78] See, for example, N I, p. 319: "Has Jesus ceased being the king of the Jews. Has the inscription on his cross been changed? Do we not persecute him in his people?"

[79] N III, pp. 356f.

of the dark irrationalism of German Romanticism running through the torch-lit rallies of the Nazis at Nuremberg, and perhaps Hamann's emphasis upon the senses and the passions against a rationalist aesthetic canon can *remotely* be connected to this. But the "final solution," let us not forget, was a cold-blooded *rational* calculation, a demonic *syllogism* of the kind that Hamann says "crawl on their belly or go on four legs."[80] In other words, the horrors of Nation Socialism can just as easily be attributed, according to a different genealogy, to the impersonal, bureaucratic *arithmetique politique* of Berlin, which Hamann passionately decried, not to mention the rise of modern secularism itself.

Fortunately, as a corrective to such misreadings, from the mid-twentieth century onwards there has been a boom in scholarship, beginning with Josef Nadler's six-volume critical edition (1949–57), an ambitious but incomplete five-volume commentary (1956–63), titled *Johann Georg Hamanns Hauptschriften Erklärt*, and the first studies and translations of Hamann in English by Walter Lowrie, Ronald Gregor Smith, William Alexander, and, most notably, James C. O'Flaherty.[81] This renaissance has continued in Germany under the banner of the Tübingen systematic theologian, Oswald Bayer, who has produced, next to a monograph, *Zeitgenosse im Widerspruch* (1988), several new editions and commentaries, including a new edition of Hamann's earliest writings, the *Londoner Schriften* (1993), and more recently an edition of Hamann's "metacritical" writings on Kant's philosophy, which appeared in 2002 under the title *Vernunft ist Sprache: Hamanns Metakritik Kants*.[82] Since the 1990s there has also been a revival of interest in Hamann in Britain and the United States due to the theologians John Milbank, Catherine Pickstock, and Graham Ward, who have found in Hamann (together with Jacobi) a unique source of "Radical Orthodoxy."[83] And now there is even greater access to Hamann's writings through Gwen Griffith-Dickson's translation-commentary, *Hamann's Relational Metacriticism* (1995), and, more recently, Kenneth Haynes annotated translation, of *Hamann: Writings on Philosophy and Language* (2007).[84]

HAMANN AND MODERN THEOLOGY

Given that Hamann writes, above all, as a Christian, indeed as a kind of modern-day prophet, it may be helpful briefly to situate him within a larger theological context. According to Karl Barth, for example, he figures in the history of theology, together

---

[80] N III, p. 218.

[81] Among the works in English, see Walter Lowrie, *Johann Georg Hamann: An Existentialist* (Princeton, NJ: Princeton Theological Seminary Press, 1950); Ronald Gregor Smith, *Johann Georg Hamann: A Study in Christian Existence, With Selections from his Writings* (London: Collins, 1960); W. M. Alexander, *Johann Georg Hamann: Philosophy and Faith* (The Hague: Martinus Nijhoff, 1966); James C. O'Flaherty, *Unity and Language: A Study in the Philosophy of Johann Georg Hamann* (Chapel Hill: University of North Carolina Press, 1952), *Hamann's Socratic Memorabilia: A Translation and Commentary* (Baltimore: Johns Hopkins University Press, 1967), *Johann Georg Hamann* (Boston: Twayne, 1979), to this day, the best brief introduction to Hamann's thought, and , *The Quarrel of Reason with Itself: Essays on Hamann, Michaelis, Lessing, Nietzsche* (Columbia, SC: Camden House, 1988).

[82] See Bayer, *Zeitgenosse im Widerspruch*; see Oswald Bayer and Christian Knudsen, *Kreuz und Kritik: Hamanns Letztes Blatt: Text und Interpretation* (Tübingen: J. C. B. Mohr, 1983); see Johann Georg Hamann, *Londoner Schriften*, ed. Oswald Bayer and Bernd Weissenborn (Munich: C. H. Beck, 1993); Oswald Bayer, *Vernunft ist Sprache: Hamanns Metakritik Kants* (Stuttgart-Bad Cannstatt: Frommann Holzboog, 2002).

[83] John Milbank, Catherine Pickstock, and Graham Ward (eds.) *Radical Orthodoxy: A New Theology* (London: Routledge, 1999); see also John Milbank, *The Word Made Strange: Theology, Language, Culture* (Oxford: Blackwell, 1997).

[84] Gwen Griffith-Dickson, *Hamann's Relational Metacriticism* (Berlin: de Gruyter, 1995) (G-D); Kenneth Haynes, *Hamann: Writings on Philosophy and Language* (Cambridge: Cambridge University Press, 2007).

with Luther, as an "irregular dogmatician."[85] And, to be sure, he is not a theologian in any ordinary sense of the term. "I am no theologian," he says, likening himself to the prophet Amos, "but a herdsman who picks wild figs" (Amos 7: 14).[86] But neither, as we have seen, is he simply a literary critic, or a philosopher, or a humorist, being uniquely all of these at once. Thus, defying strict classification, he has come to escape the attention of most disciplines, including theology.

For those theologians who have studied him, however, like Hans Urs von Balthasar, who dedicates a full chapter to Hamann (the only Protestant) in his theological aesthetics, *The Glory of the Lord,* this must be considered unfortunate. As he poignantly puts it,

> At the threshold of modernity stands a uniquely tragic figure ... because in this figure all lines seem to converge – the concerns of strict Lutheranism, of classical education and culture, and of a theological aesthetics that would embrace them both in a genuine encounter – and yet, he remained a figure out of joint with his times and his thought never came to fruition.[87]

Indeed, von Balthasar goes on to say, Hamann stood "alone in seeing that the real problem was how to construct a theory of beauty in such a way that in it the total aspiration of worldly and pagan beauty is fulfilled while all glory is at the same time given to God in Jesus Christ."[88] And so, thinking of the fate of modern theology, he laments, "How little was needed and [Hamann] could have become the theological mentor and 'familiar spirit' of German Idealism (instead of Schleiermacher), exceeding his actual historical influence, and so determined the theological climate for more than a century."[89]

While one could certainly debate the extent of Hamann's actual historical influence, especially upon post-Kantian philosophy,[90] it is doubtless true that his influence upon modern theology, excepting certain Lutheran circles, has been negligible. For what was briefly and singularly united in Hamann (both a full-blooded theological aesthetics, which sought to take in the whole of human history, literature, and culture, and an uncompromising Christocentrism) eventually split off into two antithetical directions: on the one hand, a subjective theology of feeling and culture in the Romantic spirit of Schleiermacher; on the other hand, an objective, dogmatic, dialectical theology in the tradition of Kierkegaard and the early Barth. If the one direction takes in too much of the world, to the point of being conflated with the world, the other, it could be said, takes in too little of it, i.e., too little of the analogical witness of nature and history, to the point that the fullness of the Christian

---

[85] Karl Barth, *Kirchliche Dogmatik* (Zurich: Theologischer Verlag, 1986), I/1, p. 294.

[86] N II, p. 115.

[87] Hans Urs von Balthasar, *The Glory of the Lord: A Theological Aesthetics,* vol. 1: *Seeing the Form* (San Francisco: Ignatius, 1982), p. 80 (revised translation).

[88] Ibid., p. 81.

[89] von Balthasar, *The Glory of the Lord,* (San Francisco: Ignatius, 1985), vol. 3, p. 277.

[90] Following Frederick Beiser and John Milbank, I would argue that his influence on the history of philosophy, while obscurely mediated, was, in fact, profound. See John Milbank, "The theological critique of philosophy in Hamann and Jacobi," in Milbank et al. *Radical Orthodoxy,* p. 23: "it is not ... that Hamann *might* have been, instead of Schleiermacher, the pivotal figure for the nineteenth century, or that Hamann and Jacobi are neglected because they sadly had little influence. Rather ... their influence was tremendous: subterranean and concealed perhaps, yet still objectively traceable." See also Frederick Beiser, *The Fate of Reason: German Philosophy from Kant to Fichte* (Cambridge, MA: Harvard University Press, 1987), pp. 16–43.

faith is reduced to what Pannenberg calls a "subjective wager."[91] In short, what was lost from view was a genuine synthesis of Protestant Christocentrism (with all its feeling and subjective passion) and Catholic universalism (with all its objectivity and sacramental vision of reality). And looking back to Hamann's theological aesthetics, it was this synthesis that von Balthasar sought to reclaim for his own analogical, Christocentric theology of history and culture.

After von Balthasar (a Catholic), two of the most significant theological recoveries of Hamann have been made by Oswald Bayer (a Lutheran) and John Milbank (an Anglican); and it is in large measure owing to their efforts that Hamann has made a modest comeback in theology – with each of them pointing the way to a recovery of a particular aspect of his thought. Through von Balthasar, for example, one can rediscover Hamann's importance to a theological aesthetics; through Bayer, his importance as a metacritic of modernity and a source for contemporary Lutheran theology; through Milbank, his relevance as a forerunner of "Radical Orthodoxy" and a source for theological engagements with all forms of secular reason, but especially those permutations of it that one finds in postmodern (but by no means post-secular) philosophy.

OVERVIEW

Following in this tradition of scholarship and seeking to synthesize its varied and important insights, the present work has two distinct aims. On the one had, it attempts to present Hamann's relevance to the history of theology and his theological views on a range of topics – from creation, to history, to biblical exegesis, to the Trinity, to the relationship between faith and reason, to language, to poetry, to human sexuality, to pagan religion, to the relationship between Judaism and Christianity. On the other hand, given that Hamann was a highly engaging and prophetic thinker, who seems uncannily to have seen into our own time, the present work seeks to put his ideas in a contemporary light, specifically for the powerful theological response he offers to modern and postmodern philosophy and culture. Indeed, my final aim is to present Hamann as the founder, in the middle of the Enlightenment, of a distinctly postmodern, post-secular theology.

Given Hamann's obscurity in the English-speaking world, however, the present work is also intended to provide a comprehensive introduction to his life and writings – including treatment of texts like the London Writings and his *Mysterienschriften*, which are fundamental to his Christian vision of reality, but have never or only partially been translated into English. Accordingly, the book is divided into five parts, each of which focuses on a set of writings from a given period of his life and begins with a biographical chapter that puts these writings in their context. While in the case of other authors, the inclusion of biographical chapters would be unnecessary and even tedious, in this case it is indispensable: firstly, because there is no substantial biography of Hamann in English; secondly, given that his writings are simply unintelligible apart from the particular circumstances

---

[91] Indeed, the ironic result of Barth's theology, in his otherwise noble efforts to safeguard Christianity from historical criticism, is that he not only unmoors biblical faith from objective history, but takes subjectivism in theology to new extremes, whereby the proclamation of the Gospel reduces to a "saga," something between history and mythology, and faith reduces to a *subjective* wager. For a penetrating critique of Barth in this regard, see Wolfhart Pannenberg, *Wissenschaftstheorie und Theologie* (Frankfurt am Main: Suhrkamp Verlag, 1973), pp. 266–77.

that occasioned them; and, finally, following Hamann's own maxim, given that one cannot understand the work apart from the man (and in his case this applies to an almost unparalleled degree).

Part I, "The Making of a Christian Socrates," begins with a biographical chapter on Hamann's conversion and his post-conversion dealings with Kant. Chapter 2 then focuses upon Hamann's confessional texts from 1758, which are a record of his conversion, which took place in London, and are therefore commonly known as his "London Writings." These texts are crucial to understanding the rationale of Hamann's subsequent publications, because it is these directly personal, *private-lyric* writings that set the stage for his subsequent exceedingly indirect, *public-dramatic* "authorship"; indeed, the former are in many ways the key to the latter. Chapter 3 then treats Hamann's first major work, the *Socratic Memorabilia* (1759), which is arguably the second great assault on the Enlightenment, after Rousseau's *Discourse on the Sciences and the Arts* (1750), and is essentially an "apology" for Christian faith before the court of reason. It is directed at two of Hamann's friends who tried to "bring him back to his senses" and reconvert him from his new "enthusiasm" to the cause and ideals of the Enlightenment: Christoph Berens and Immanuel Kant. At the conclusion of this chapter, I also discuss a pair of Hamann's so-called "love letters" to Kant, which were composed around the same time and concern Kant's amusing proposal that he and Hamann collaborate on a physics book for children. This never came to pass, however, mainly owing to the irresistible irony that Hamann found in the proposal, which he did not hide from Kant, and so the entire affair has come to be known as the "*Kinderphysik* fiasco."[92]

Part II, "Crusades of the Philologist," centers on (in Chapter 5) a sundry collection of works bearing this title, which includes Hamann's influential proto-Romantic manifesto, *Aesthetica in nuce* (1762), and continues his literary "crusade" against his contemporaries, most notably, the Göttingen Orientalist and biblical critic, J. D. Michaelis. In a nutshell, these writings present Hamann's "aesthetics," given their concern with the "perception" of the Word of God in creation and Scripture, and to this extent they resume the original theme of the "London Writings." They also place the entire concept of art and literary criticism in an ironic light, posing it over against the eschatological judgment of Christ, the ultimate "art critic," to *whom* (borrowing Kant's phrase, but turning it on its head) "all must submit." Concerning similar themes, Chapter 6 deals with Hamann's so-called *Herderschriften*, which were occasioned by Herder's prize essay on the origin of language, which was published in 1772, and represent Hamann's response to every immanent and autonomous theory of language, stemming from his – on this point at least – renegade disciple. As such, these writings not only develop the linguistic anthropology of the *Aesthetica in nuce*, but are pivotal, I argue, to a theological response to postmodern theories of language.

Part III is concerned with Hamann's so-called *Mysterienschriften*. As their designation would suggest, and as accords with the sublimity of the mysteries they treat, these works tend to be even more cryptic and difficult than Hamann's other writings. Chapter 8, for example, treats the mystery of marriage, following Paul, as a protological prefiguration of the cosmological-eschatological mystery of Christ and his Church. It also treats a mystery of surprising importance to Hamann's thought: the

---

[92] See Beiser, *The Fate of Reason*, pp. 32–3.

mystery of shame and what is "shameful" to reason. The works treated in Chapter 9, including the mysteriously titled *Konxompax,* are more directly concerned with history, as Hamann responds, on the one hand, to a revival of interest in pagan religion and, on the other hand, to the popularity of Freemasonry among his contemporaries – most notably, Johann August Starck and Gotthold Ephraim Lessing. In these works in particular Hamann highlights the difference he sees between the fullness of the mystery of Christianity and the ultimate poverty of the natural religion and esoteric pseudo-religion of the Enlightenment.

Part IV includes, in Chapter 10, a discussion of *Divestment and Transfiguration,* the work in which Hamann finally reveals the true nature and purpose of his authorship. The focal chapters here are his late metacritical writings against Kant and Moses Mendelssohn. Accordingly, Chapter 11 will be of especial interest to those interested in Kant's philosophy, treating Hamann's review – the very first! – of the *Critique of Pure Reason* (1781), and his *Metakritik über den Purismum der Vernunft* (1784). These texts contain incisive criticisms of Kant's philosophy and, by implication, of all forms of transcendental idealism. Chapter 12 is concerned with a text that Hegel considered to be the most important of Hamann's writings. Written in the same year as the *Metakritik* and conceived as its twin, *Golgotha and Scheblimini* is essentially a metacritical mosaic of Mendelssohn's *Jerusalem oder über religiöse Macht und Judentum,* which had been published the previous year, 1783. While Hamann greatly valued Mendelssohn's friendship and did not wish to offend him, he was deeply concerned that his version of *Jerusalem* threatened to dissolve Judaism into the terms of a purely natural religion – indeed, to confuse Jerusalem itself with the modern secular state. Thus he speaks to his friend as a prophet, calling him to return to the true spirit of Judaism as a prophetic religion.

Part V begins with a final biographical chapter concerning the last three years of Hamann's life, beginning with his preparations for a journey into a circle of Catholic intellectuals and admirers in Münster, centered on the figure of the Princess Amalia von Gallitzin. It is in these years, through the observations of others, that we finally see Hamann's true spiritual stature emerge, having been hidden for so many years behind so many masks and pseudonyms. The focal point of this chapter is a text written shortly before his death that was to be his final literary testament, his so-called "final page." Fittingly, it is the most intricate of all his works, an extremely dense, cryptic monument to his self-understanding as a Christian author. On the basis of the other chapters, the conclusion, "After Postmodernity: Hamann before the Postmodern Triumvirate," makes a case for Hamann as a thinker who in many ways strikingly anticipates the thought of Nietzsche, Heidegger, and Derrida, but does so as a compelling Christian alternative to them.

While the present work is conceived as a whole and is intended to be read continuously, it is also structured in such a way that one may begin at any point, depending upon one's interest. For example, those interested chiefly in the fundamentals of Hamann's Christian vision might simply read Chapters 2 and 9. Given their lyric quality, the writings treated in Chapter 2 also have the virtue of being the most accessible. For those interested in Hamann's radical, Lutheran use of Hume or his doctrine of Socratic ignorance, Chapters 1 and 3 will be most relevant. For those interested in his theological aesthetics, Chapters 2 and 5 will be most relevant; for those interested in his biblical hermeneutics as an alternative to merely rational or historical-critical approaches to Scripture, Chapters 2, 5, and 12 will be most relevant; for those interested in Hamann's view of language, Chapters 5 and 6; for those interested in his critique of Kant, Chapter 11; for those interested in his understanding of the relationship between Judaism and Christianity and the possibilities he offers for Jewish-Christian dialogue, Chapter 12; for those interested in his spiritual life, teaching, and influence as a spiritual father, Chapter 13.

Part I

The Making of a Christian Socrates

1

Life and Writings 1730–1788

My mother is an unrefined peasant, and I, as you know, a Sauvage du Nord sans rime et sans raison, who understands neither rhymes nor syllogisms, neither manners nor maxims.

Hamann to Jacobi[1]

Hamann ... a true παν *of harmony and discord, light and darkness, spiritualism and materialism.*

Schelling[2]

The inscription on a tile stove in Kold's Tavern in Fredensborg applies to Hamann: allicit atque terret.

Kierkegaard[3]

Hamann was born on August 27, 1730 in the east Prussian port city of Königsberg (now Kaliningrad).[4] His father, Johann Christoph Hamann, hailed from Lausitz and was a beloved bather-surgeon in the old city; his mother, Maria Magdalena Nuppenau, was a pious woman of poor health from Lübeck. The elder of two sons, Hamann was named after his paternal uncle, Johann Georg (1697–1733), who was an author of some repute, having produced a poetry lexicon, which was reprinted as late as 1765, a sequel to a popular Baroque novel, and a collection of hymns, some of which were set to music by Georg Philipp Telemann and, in one case, by Georg Friedrich Händel.

Raised, prophetically enough, in the old-city bathhouse in the street of the Holy Ghost, Hamann speaks happily of his childhood and glowingly of his parents. In a fragment dated 1778, *Apologie meines Cretinen*, he relates a story in which his father was once asked by a certain chancellor whether he did not wish to have the title doctor or counselor, to which his father replied, "Your excellence, I already have a title ... a few weeks ago I was a lead pallbearer at my brother-in-law's funeral, and I heard the people behind me exclaim: 'That's *the old town bather!*' A few days ago, at the funeral of one of my patients, I was in the last pair of the procession, and heard people around me saying: 'That's *the old town bather!*' Thus, whether in the first or last pair, my title is 'the old town bather,' and as such I wish to live and die."[5]

---

[1] ZH V, p. 463.
[2] F. W. J. Schelling, *Sämtliche Werke*, ed. K. F. A. Schelling (Stuttgart and Augsburg: J. G. Cotta'scher Verlag, 1856–61), I, vol. 10, p. 171.
[3] *JP* II 1546 (*Pap.* II a, 442) (May 22, 1839).
[4] The present chapter is based upon the following sources: Hamann's autobiography in *Londoner Schriften*, ed. Oswald Bayer and Bernd Weissenborn (Munich: C. H. Beck, 1993) (*LS*), pp. 313f.; C. H. Gildemeister, *Johann Georg Hamann's des Magus in Norden, Leben und Schriften*, 6 vols. (Gotha: Friedrich Andreas Perthes, 1857–1873); Josef Nadler, *Johann Georg Hamann 1730–1788: Der Zeuge des Corpus mysticum* (Salzburg: Otto Müller Verlag, 1949) (NB); and James C. O'Flaherty, *Johann Georg Hamann* (Boston: Twayne, 1979) (*JGH*).
[5] N III, p. 324. The title of this text refers to Hamann's younger brother, who suffered and died prematurely from mental illness.

His father's humility, occupation and, above all, his therapeutic tub left a deep impression on him. "Wonder not," he says, "if that tub, whose impartiality was once sung by an old poet, is as holy [to me] as the midwife arts of Phainarethe ... were to the son of Sophroniscus [i.e., Socrates]."[6] And again, years later he remarks to Jacobi that he venerated his father's tub like Socrates his mother's midwife's stool, adding lines from a Greek poem he had envisioned as an epigraph: "The bather and the ... always bathe / The worst and the best man / In the same tub."[7] As it happens, these seemingly incidental remarks are highly significant to Hamann's self-understanding as an author; for it is in this light that he understood his own vocation as a Christian Socrates, seeing his own literary productions as "metacritical tubs" in which to wash the feet of his age (see John 13: 5f.).

THE MAKING OF A PHILOLOGIST

Though Hamann's parents were of modest means, they did everything they could to promote his education; and so he was tutored from an early age in various subjects, especially languages, among them Greek, French, and Italian, acquiring a proficiency in philology that would decisively influence his intellectual development and interests. The nature of his instruction was haphazard, however. For instance, his first teacher ran the bizarre experiment of teaching him Latin without grammar, and it is to this that Hamann would later attribute the unsystematic nature of his own reading and writing. Even so, he managed to become a remarkably good translator of classical texts – so good, in fact, that his second teacher regarded him as a Greek and Latin prodigy. His progress in languages was countered, however, by setbacks in such basic studies as history, geography, and writing, similarly contributing, he suggests, to a difficulty organizing and expressing his thoughts that he never entirely overcame.

Eventually, after the brief employment of a tutor, the last of many, Hamann's father sent him to a public school, where he met with success, finishing first in his class. It was during this period that he was introduced to philosophy, theology, mathematics, and Hebrew, and his head became "a fair booth full of wholly new goods."[8] With an encyclopedic curiosity, which he later equated with dissipation, he then matriculated at the University of Königsberg in the spring of 1746. Though he initially considered a vocation to theology, he soon abandoned the idea, feeling drawn instead to classical and belletristic literature, and in particular to all things French. As he puts it,

> What kept me from having a taste for theology and all serious disciplines was a new inclination that had awakened in me for things ancient, for criticism – then for the so-called beautiful and fine arts, for poetry, novels, philology, for French authors and their talent for poetic composition, for painting, depicting, for pleasing the imagination, etc."[9]

A more immediate reason he cites for not taking up theology, however, was a speech impediment, in addition to his poor memory, the corruption of the clergy, his high estimation of this vocation, and his sense of hypocrisy – though afterwards he confesses a lack of faith in the "source of all good," from whom he could have expected to receive what he lacked, and with whose help he could have overcome any obstacles.[10]

---

[6] N III, p. 324.
[7] ZH V, p. 331.
[8] *LS*, p. 321.
[9] *LS*, p. 323.
[10] *LS*, p. 322.

While at the university, Hamann (like Kant before him) was a student of Martin Knutzen (1713–51), the professor of logic and metaphysics, who was well known throughout Europe for his particular combination of pietism and Wolffian rationalism. The professor who elicited his greatest respect, however, was the Wolffian professor of physics and member of the Berlin academy, Karl Heinrich Rappolt (1702–53), whom he admired for his humor, his knowledge of Roman authors, his poetry, and, notwithstanding his outspoken opposition to pietism, the simplicity of his Christian wisdom.[11] While at the university he also formed many friendships, most notably, with Samuel Gotthelf Hennings (1725–87), Johann Gotthelf Lindner (1729–76), and Johann Christoph Berens (1729–92), collaborating with the latter two on a weekly periodical for women, which was modeled on the English *Tatler* and ran for nearly a year, called *Daphne*.[12] Whether or not *Daphne* "belongs to the best weekly publications of the century," as Nadler claims, it was Hamann's first venture as an author; and though the overall style of the publication was "light and pleasant," in keeping with the general optimism of the Enlightenment, his pseudonymous contributions clearly "sound the more serious ethical and religious notes of the publication."[13]

At some point in his studies, Hamann took up law and for a time seems to have envisioned a legal career; by 1752, however, he left the university without a degree as a self-designated *atrium liberalium cultor* and *homme de lettres* to find a job as a *Hofmeister* (a private tutor), among the minor nobility of the Baltic.[14] Partly through family connections, he managed to secure posts in Livonia and later in Courland. His main objective, however, was to find employment in Riga, where he hoped to rejoin his friends Berens and Lindner. (Berens was a native of the city, where his family owned a trading house; Lindner began teaching at the cathedral school of Riga in 1753, becoming rector in 1755.) In the meantime, given ample time for leisure, he indulged his intellectual curiosity to the point of gluttony, virtually bankrupting himself on books and employing his friends, especially Lindner, in the service of procuring them. Among the authors he read during this period were Descartes (on whom he wrote an essay), the historian Chladenius, the French Jesuit Rapin, and the English Shaftesbury.[15] Of the latter two, Hamann also made translations: of Rapin's *Réflexions sur l'Eloquence, la Poètique, l'Histoire et la Philosophie* (1686), and of the first two essays in Shaftesbury's three-volume *Characteristics of Men, Manners, Opinions, Times* (1711); the first of these concerned religious enthusiasm, the second, among other things, common sense and the right of reason to scrutinize the claims of tradition.[16]

As these translations suggest and Hamann's notebooks from this period confirm, Rapin and Shaftesbury had a decisive influence upon his intellectual development. Rapin, whose collected works Hamann owned, provided the basis for his knowledge of the

---

[11] *LS*, p. 322.

[12] For Hamann's contributions to *Daphne*, see N IV, pp. 15ff.

[13] See NB, p. 43; *JGH*, p. 20. For further treatment of Hamann's contribution to *Daphne*, see Bernhard Gajek, "Hamanns Anfänge," *Eckart* 29 (1960), pp. 113–18. See also Wolfgang-Dieter Baur, "Johann Georg Hamann als Religionspublizist," *Neue Zeitschrift für systematische Theologie*, 31 (1989), pp. 141–64.

[14] NB, p. 43.

[15] For Hamann's study of Descartes, see N IV, pp. 221ff.

[16] For Hamann's translations of Rapin and Shaftesbury, see N IV, pp. 45–91. See also Nadler's textual notes, pp. 466f., 473f.

history of philosophy and the Church Fathers. He also provided a bibliographical source for Hamann's growing library, which included works of Cornelius Agrippa von Nettesheim, Albertus Magnus, Francis Bacon, Tommaso Campanella, Copernicus, Galileo, Gassendi, Hobbes, Giordano Bruno, Machiavelli, and Raymond Lull.[17] Moreover, according to Nadler, Hamann found in the writings of the Jesuit not only a favorable portrait of Socrates (the subject of Hamann's first major work) and a critical and religiously motivated reserve *vis-à-vis* dogmatic rationalism, but also the notion of divine condescension (*Herunterlassung*), which is arguably the most important theme of Hamann's thought and authorship.[18] The influence of Shaftesbury, on the other hand, was (if not initially, then ultimately) negative, inasmuch as he represented the very deism that Hamann would spend his life combating. Indeed, Shaftesbury is typically mentioned in Hamann's works in connection with Voltaire, Diderot, and Bolingbroke as an enemy of faith and revelation. Nevertheless, Hamann could request as late as 1766 that Herder send him as many of Shaftesbury's works as he could acquire, finding in Shaftesbury a model for his own evocative, satirical style.[19]

In addition to his translations of Rapin and Shaftesbury, Hamann made two other translations during this period that are worth noting. The first signals his preoccupation with (and, for the time being, apparently sympathetic attitude toward) the "free thinkers" of the Enlightenment: his translation of a short, inflammatory work by the Italian Count Alberto Radicati (1698–1737) titled *La Religion Muhammedane compare à la paienne de l'Indostan par Ali-Ebn-Omar, Moslem*.[20] The work feigns to be a translation from the Arabic of a letter written by a certain Muslim, Ali-Ibn-Omar, to a certain Brahmin named Cing Kniu [*sic*], and includes, curiously enough, the following epigraph from Lactantius: "Is it not better to live like cattle than to worship deities so impious, profane, and sanguinary?"[21] Why Hamann should have been so interested in the work is unclear. In any case, it represented a direct challenge to his at this point nominal Christian faith – one that eventually led him to study the Koran in Arabic. For not only does the work exalt Islam as approximating a natural religion of reason, it directly implies that the Hebrew (and Christian) Scriptures, like the Vedas, are a "collection of ill conceived fables that are without connection, without order, as outlandish as they are depraved, which offend the senses as well as reason,

---

[17] N IV, p. 466. Needless to say, some of these authors were more influential than others. For the time being, one might simply note the importance of the Renaissance philosophers Bruno (1548–1600) and Campanella (1568–1639). Of the former, Hamann claimed that his principle (originally in Cusa) of the *coincidentia oppositorum* was worth more than all of Kant's critique (ZH IV, p. 462); with regard to Campanella one might note his doctrine, which one finds earlier in Raymond Sabundus and was fundamental to Hamann's Christian vision, that God reveals himself through the analogous books of nature and Scripture.

[18] N IV, p. 467. See also NB, pp. 59f.

[19] N IV, pp. 474f.

[20] Before Voltaire, Radicati was one of Europe's most hostile opponents of traditional Judaism and Christianity. In 1726, under suspicion by the Inquisition, he took refuge in England, where he became friends with Anthony Collins and Matthew Tindal, two of the most outspoken English deists. In 1733, after a brief imprisonment, he fled to Paris and then to Holland, where he died, apparently after recanting. The work under discussion was published in London in French in 1737. See Nadler's notes, N IV, pp. 480f.

[21] From Lactantius, *The Divine Institutes*, I, 21, in *Ante-Nicene Fathers*, vol. 7 (Peabody, MA: Hendrickson Publishers, 1994). The point of the letter, which contains an introductory biography of Mohammed, is to convince Cing Kniu that his prejudice against Islam is wholly unjustified given the preposterousness of his own beliefs, i.e., his willingness to believe certain incredible, indeed, scandalous stories about the divine in the Vedas. The author then claims that the religion of Mohammed and the testimony of the Koran are, by comparison, the picture of sound reason.

and are utterly insulting to the Godhead."[22] In this regard Radicati draws a parallel between a story in the Vedas, which he lampoons and judges to be blasphemous, and the biblical account of Exodus, both of which, he implies, portray a God who unjustly punishes people for the very things God causes in them (e.g., Pharaoh's hardened heart). Whatever Hamann may have thought of Radicati's work at this point in his life, it revealed that the Enlightenment had a favorable attitude toward Islam (as approximating a religion of reason) and a corresponding hostility toward Judaism (arguably even an anti-Semitism) and Christianity (inasmuch as it rests upon Judaism), thus setting the stage for Hamann's conversion and passionate defense of the Hebrew Bible against the "enlightened" critics of the age. Indeed, whereas the *Aufklärer* strove to *separate* Christianity from Judaism, and to clarify Christianity into a natural religion, as we shall later see, Hamann sought both to defend the positive revelation given to Israel, and to reaffirm as *indissoluble* the prophetic bond between them.

Although Hamann was chiefly engaged with intellectual subjects during this time, he also immersed himself in the study of trade and commerce, in part because of the influence of his friend Berens, who had hopes of recruiting him for his family's trading firm. In fact, the last translation of this period, and the only one to be published, is a translation of Plumard de Dangueil's *Remarques sur les avantages et les desavantages de la France et de la Grande Bretagne, par rapport au commerce et aux autres sources de la puissance des etats* (1754). The translation was solicited by Berens for the purposes of increasing trade in the Baltic and popularizing the interests of a growing merchant class. It was also appended with a substantial essay by Hamann himself (his first published work), which extols the merchant as the soldier of the future, whose "weapon of trade" promises an end to war and a new era of peace; and who, as the nobleman of the future, promises an end to social injustice and the establishment of a genuine commonwealth.[23] Although this was Hamann's first and last substantial foray into economic theory, his views in this regard never seem to have changed, and would later be brought to bear in his critique of the economic policies of Frederick the Great.

HAMANN'S CONVERSION

During his *Hofmeisterzeit* (1752–6) Hamann thus acquired a vast knowledge of the intellectual cross-currents of his day, and on this basis would soon emerge as an important mediator within Germany (especially to Kant) of contemporary philosophers such as Rousseau and Hume. The immediate course of his life, however, was determined by his friendship with Berens. Berens had recently returned from Paris full of Enlightenment ideas and had plans for Hamann as a kind of press secretary for his family's firm. The initial plan was for Hamann to attend Berens on trips to Petersburg and London, ostensibly for trade negotiations on behalf of the city of Riga. Matters developed more quickly than expected, however, in all likelihood

---

[22] N IV, p. 202. The positive valuation of Islam as a religion of reason, requiring no appeal to anything beyond reason, such as miracles, the Trinity, or Christ's resurrection, was a commonplace during the Enlightenment.

[23] N IV, pp. 225–42. See also NB, pp. 65f. Hamann had already read Rousseau's *Discours sur l'origine et les fondements de l'inégalité parmi les hommes*, and his essay represents, in some measure, a response to it.

because of the imminent European outbreak of the Seven Years War (1756–63), and so Hamann was dispatched to London alone, stopping in Königsberg for some time to care for his ailing mother until her early death.[24] On October 1, 1756 he set off for London, apparently in no haste (perhaps foreseeing the folly of trade negotiations during the war), making lengthy stops in Berlin, where he made the acquaintance of prominent *Aufklärer,* including Moses Mendelssohn, with whom he was soon to engage in a lively correspondence; and then in Lübeck, where he tarried for nearly two months with his mother's family. Finally, he arrived in London, via Bremen, Amsterdam and Rotterdam, late in the evening on April 18, 1757.

Unfortunately, Hamann left no details concerning the specific nature of his mission (whether it was primarily commercial or also involved a diplomatic component).[25] What we do know is that it involved contact with the Russian embassy and was a complete failure. As Hamann puts it,

> When I disclosed the nature of my business to those I was appointed to meet, they marveled at the importance of my affairs, even more at the manner in which they were carried out, and perhaps most of all at the choice of the person with whom such matters were entrusted. After they recovered from their initial amazement, they began to smile – unabashedly revealing their opinion of those who had sent me …[26]

Disconcerted, Hamann wrote a brief letter to the Russian ambassador, whose reply, for all its graciousness, only confirmed the pointlessness of the mission. Thus began the downward spiral that ended in Hamann's conversion: "I went about depressed, staggering to and fro, without a soul with whom to share my burden, who could give me advice or help."[27]

With no further reason to be in London and little money to spare, Hamann reports being near "desperation" and seeking to allay his troubles through "empty amusements." At this point it occurred to him to procure a lute, the one instrument he played, and try to make his living as a musician. Soon thereafter he came into the company of a wealthy English lute player, and for a time enjoyed his patronage: "I ate for free, I drank for free, I made love for free, I raced around for free; I fruitlessly alternated between gluttony and reflection, between reading and knavery, between industriousness and complete inactivity …"[28] And, at least temporarily, he thought he had found what he was looking for, assuring himself, "he can make you famous, you now have at least one person with whom to socialize, you have a house where you can amuse yourself, you can practice the lute, you can assume his profession and be as happy as he is."[29] And yet he admits that he nowhere found rest, moving as many as twelve times within the year. Things finally fell apart when he discovered that his patron was having a homosexual affair, at which point he moved

---

[24] Upon her death, Hamann composed an effusive memorial, *Denkmal,* which he included in his *Kreuzzüge des Philologen* (1762). See N II, pp. 233–8.

[25] O'Flaherty's conjecture (*JGH,* p. 22), following Nadler, is that it was both, and thus *handelspolitisch*. Accordingly, Hamann was sent to London in order to secure a trade agreement on behalf of the Baltic port cities that were seeking greater independence from Prussia. Hamann's and Berens's assumption, which turned out to be correct, was that the Seven Years War would leave Russia in control of East Prussia (including Königsberg). Apparently, what they did not foresee was that England would shift its alliance to Prussia, *ipso facto* forestalling relations with the Baltic cities now under Russian occupation. See NB, p. 22.

[26] LS, p. 337 (N II, pp. 34f.).

[27] LS, p. 338 (N II, p. 35).

[28] LS, p. 339 (N II, p. 37).

[29] LS, p. 339 (N II, pp. 36f.).

to a coffeehouse, and from there to a room in a home on Marlborough Street, where he resided from February 8, 1758.[30]

It was here, with no money, a £300 debt, and failing health that he began an intensive reading of the Bible. As he puts it,

> I wanted to seclude myself in this house, and sought to comfort myself with nothing but all my books, quite a few of which I had not yet not read or at least read without much consideration or putting them to proper use. At the same time, God inspired me to obtain a Bible ... having previously been indifferent to it.[31]

Having finally found one to his liking (most likely the Oxford Bible of 1755), he began his reading on March 13, but to no great effect. Six days later, however, on Palm Sunday, he began his reading anew and gradually began to perceive that God was somehow speaking *to him* and that the same one who authored the Bible was also the author of his life.[32] A few weeks later, on the evening of March 31, as he was reading the fifth chapter of Deuteronomy, he "fell into deep reflection, thought about Abel, of whom God said: the earth *opened its mouth* to receive the *blood* of your brother –"[33] and suddenly

> I felt my heart beat, I heard a voice sighing and wailing in its depths as the voice of blood, as the voice of a murdered brother, who wanted to avenge his blood if I did not at times hear it and should continue to stop up my hears to its voice. – that precisely this made Cain a restless fugitive. I felt at once my heart swelling, it poured itself out in tears, and I could no longer – I could no longer hide from God that I was the murderer of my brother, that I was the murderer of his only begotten Son.[34]

Herein lies the heart of Hamann's conversion, beginning with a sense of guilt ("I too am Cain") and ending with a profound sense of forgiveness and peace (essentially following the pattern of Matt. 5: 3–4). For no sooner do "we hear the blood of the redeemer crying out in our heart than we feel that its ground has already been sprinkled ..., that the same avenging blood cries grace to us."[35] Similarly, he speaks of his conversion in terms of an exchange:

---

[30] The third party in question was a rich "baron" named Senel, and so the whole matter of Hamann's falling out with him is known as the "Senel affair." There has been some speculation that Hamann himself had become sexually involved with his patron, and that he left out of jealousy. See H. A. Salmony, *J. G. Hamanns metakritische Philosophie* (Basel: Zollikon Verlag, 1958). But this is not supported by the evidence. See Wilhelm Koepp, "Hamanns Londoner Senelaffäre, Januar 1758" in *Zeitschrift für Theologie und Kirche* 57 (1960), pp. 92–108; 58 (1961), pp. 68–85. Indeed, Hamann's view of homosexuality is quite clear: while he excuses Socrates' homoerotic tendencies on account of his pagan context and his aesthetic sensibility, i.e., a desire to see a harmony of inner and outward beauty (see N II, pp. 67f.), he consistently impugns the court of Frederick the Great for its "tolerance" and homosexual license. For an example of his sharp rhetoric in this regard, see N III, p. 30. Moreover, as we shall see in Chapter 8 *vis-à-vis* modern *Scheidekunst*, Hamann's vision of reality is fundamentally nuptial, even at the level of philosophy, as expressed in terms of a coincidence of opposites (*coincidentia oppositorum*), whereby marriage points typologically to the central mystery of the hypostatic union of divine and human natures in Christ, and ultimately to the eschatological mystery of the union of Christ and his Church, along the lines of Paul (Eph. 5: 31f.). See also ZH VII, p. 158: "What God has joined together, no philosophy can separate; just as little unite, what nature has separated. Divorce and sodomy sin against nature and reason [–] the elemental philosophical forms of original sin, dead works of darkness [–] with the *Organis* of our internal and external life, our physical being = nature and metaphysical being = reason."

[31] *LS*, p. 342 (N II, p. 39).

[32] *LS*, p. 59 (N I, p. 4).

[33] *LS*, p. 343 (N II, p. 41).

[34] Ibid.

[35] *LS*, pp. 138f. (N I, p. 78).

My son! Give me your heart! – Here it is my God! You demanded it, as blind, hard, rocky, misguided, and stubborn as it was. Purify it, create it anew, and let it become the workshop of your good Spirit. It deceived me so many times when it was in my own hands that I no longer wish to recognize it as my own. It is a leviathan that you alone can tame – – by your indwelling may it enjoy peace, comfort, and blessedness.[36]

In short, he says that God poured him "from one vessel into another" (cf. Matt. 9: 17).[37] And afterwards, The Spirit of God continued, in spite of my great weakness, in spite of the long resistance that I had previously mounted against his witness and his stirrings, to reveal to me more and more the mystery of divine love and the benefit of faith in our merciful and only Savior.[38]

The immediate consequence of Hamann's conversion was a lyrical outpouring of meditations on the Bible, which he originally titled *Tagebuch eines Christen* (Diary of a Christian), but which have come to be known collectively as the "London Writings." As Nadler poignantly puts it, "They are ... the diary of a soul concerning the greatest experience it could possibly have: [becoming] a child of God."[39] At the same time, however, their content is, in Nadler's words, "the whole of creation, nature, and history, the kingdom of God and the kingdom of man."[40] Indeed, what is so interesting about Hamann's conversion is that, rather than leading to a pietistic withdrawal from the world, it led precisely to a more intensive engagement with it. Thus, having completed the London Writings in only a few months, and with no further reason to stay in England, Hamann set sail for Riga on June 27, 1758, fittingly enough, aboard a warship.

HAMANN'S FALLING OUT WITH BERENS

Upon returning, in spite of the failure of his mission, Hamann received a warm welcome from the Berens family; it was understood that the mission's failure was not his fault. And so he quickly resumed work, corresponding with Berens, who was still in Petersburg, and assuming the familiar role of a house tutor to some of the younger members of the family. But if things had superficially returned to normal, Hamann himself had clearly been changed. As he put it to his brother around this time, summing up his new attitude after his conversion:

God does not wish to hear us, to receive us, and to know us except in his Son ... I write to you not as an enthusiast [*Schwärmer*], not as a Pharisee, but as a brother, who could not love you as long as he did not know and love God; but who now wishes you well with all his heart, and since he has learned to pray, will not forget to pray for you too. ... One's heart loves one's brothers through God alone ... If we do not know Jesus, we have come no further than the pagans. As the apostle James says, all miracles, all mysteries, and all works of faith and true religion are united in the worthy name by which we are called Christians. This worthy name, by which we are called, is the only key of knowledge, which opens the heaven and the hell, the heights and the depths, of the

---

[36] *LS*, p. 345 (N II, pp. 42f.).
[37] Ibid.
[38] *LS*, p. 343 (N II, pp. 40f.).
[39] NB, p. 76.
[40] N II, p. 198; NB, p. 78.

human heart. ... Now I live in the world with pleasure and with a light heart, and know that godliness holds promise for this life and the life to come, and that it is useful for all things (1 Tim. 4: 8). Since I have come to know God's Word as the medicine, as the wine, which alone is able to make our heart glad and our face to shine with oil, as the bread that strengthens the heart of man, I am neither a misanthrope, nor a hypochondriac, nor an accuser of my brethren, nor an Ishmael of divine providence ...[41]

While at the Berens home, he continued to indulge his intellectual curiosity, reading, among others, Batteux, Kant, Klopstock, Lessing, Ramler, Wieland, and Winckelmann, whose *Gedanken über die Nachahmung in der Malerei und Bildhauerkunst* had appeared in 1756.[42] His chief interest at the time, however, was Catharina Berens (1727–1805), his friend's sister, whom he considered to be the spouse God intended for him.[43] Since Christoph was still in Petersburg, he wrote to ask for his permission to marry her.[44] The surprising response, which arrived in early January, 1759, was an unequivocal "No." Presumably, Hamann had shared with Berens some of the details of his conversion in London, knowing very well his friend's antipathy toward all forms of "enthusiasm"; possibly he also communicated his waning interest in a commercial vocation. Nevertheless, he was shocked and deeply hurt, and soon thereafter returned to Königsberg.

The nature of Hamann's falling out with Berens becomes clearer in light of a letter to their common friend Lindner in March of the same year. In it Hamann identifies the source of the problem: Berens's disgust over his conversion, his fear of losing a friend and fellow laborer in the cause of the Enlightenment, and his corresponding, patronizing counsel that Hamann "keep only as much religion as is necessary."[45] To which Hamann wryly responds, "This is prudent advice, like that of Job's wife, who did not intend to curse God, but to *bless* him."[46] He then goes on to say,

> If our friend sees my current state of mind as one greatly to be pitied, do not let him look upon my enthusiasm [*Schwärmerey*] as an *alienum quid* that could not befall him [as well ...] I am a leopard, and his soap will not change my spots. ... All his flattering hurts me more than his most caustic remarks. They are the probes by which he wants to sense whether I am still possessed of sound reason and ambition. If an enthusiast is a fool, ask him ... whether in view of his goals ... he would not have to recognize himself as one. ... If he wants to know what I do now, tell him that I *Lutherize*; for something must be done. This adventuresome monk said in Augsburg: here I am – I cannot do otherwise. God help me. Amen.[47]

Clearly, Berens, an enthusiastic entrepreneur, was troubled by Hamann's lack of ambition; as Hamann saw it, however, he could not go back to laboring for "the god of this world" (2 Cor. 4: 4). He had made a break: instead of working for men, he now aimed to work for God: "The best side one can take [in this life] is to work for

41 ZH I, pp. 242f.
42 Gildemeister, *Johann Georg Hamann*, vol. 1, pp. 155f.
43 See *LS*, p. 435 (N II, pp. 52f.).
44 See *LS*, pp. 434f. (N II, pp. 52f.).
45 ZH, p. 306.
46 Ibid.
47 ZH, p. 307.

the sake of God; to live because he wills it, to work because he wills it, to rest."[48] And so he says, "My vocation is neither to be a businessman, nor a civil servant, nor a man of the world.... Reading the Bible and praying are the work of a Christian ..."[49] But if Hamann's relationship with Berens had soured, it was not broken, as each amicably continued his efforts to convert the other. As Hamann puts it to Lindner,

> I do not recognize the vehement tone that you detect in our friend's letters. I see every-thing as an effect of his friendship, and this itself I see as a gift as well as a test from God. He warns or promises that he will not lose sight of me; and I shall certainly not lose sight of him and his family. But he should worry about me as little as I about him. I grant him his business; and he should grant me my leisure ...[50]

HAMANN'S RELATIONSHIP WITH KANT

That Hamann's falling out with Berens was not the end of their friendship is clear from the fact that in June Berens no sooner returned to Riga from Petersburg than he set out for Königsberg to check on him. As Nadler puts it, for Berens it was no longer a question about Catharina or the family firm, but about a friend he clearly loved and did not want to lose.[51] And in his noble attempt to "save" his friend he recruited none other than the distinguished professor, Immanuel Kant. Berens was acquainted with Kant, as was Hamann, and he calculated that Hamann's respect for the elder professor could be of use.[52] Indeed, it seems that Kant was the ace in the hole in his plan to bring Hamann back to his senses, to curb his unfortunate "enthu-siasm," and to re-employ him in the service of the Enlightenment. Thus he arranged that they all meet one evening in early July for supper at the "Windmill," a rural inn outside of Königsberg. The evening was by all accounts awkward. Kant scarcely knew what he was getting involved in (which was something approximating a lovers' quarrel), and Hamann, for his part, was in no way prepared to abandon his faith, which could not be squared with the fundamental principles of the Enlightenment (of which Kant was its philosophical, and Berens its commercial representative). Afterwards he described the occasion to his brother as follows:

> At the beginning of the week I was in the company of Herr B. and Master Kant at the inn at the Windmill, where we had a rustic meal together. We have not seen each other since. Confidentially – our relationship still does not have the intimacy it once did, and we impose upon ourselves the greatest restraint in order to avoid the appearance of it.

---

[48] ZH, p. 307.

[49] ZH, p. 309.

[50] ZH I, pp. 303f. That Hamann refers to his leisure is significant as a reaction to the purely commercial aims of his friend. It is also reflected in the subtitle of his first major publication, the *Socratic Memorabilia*, and in the fact that, after returning to Königsberg to care for his ailing father, he did not have a steady job for four years. At the same time, as O'Flaherty points out, there were other factors contributing to Hamann's unemployment, most notably the Russian occupation of Königsberg throughout this four-year period. See *SM*, p. 30.

[51] NB, p. 95.

[52] As early as April, 1756, Hamann calls Kant "a man of superior intellect" (*ein fürtrefflicher Kopf*), and in a letter to Lindner written shortly thereafter speaks of Kant's dissertation with evident approval. See ZH I, pp. 191, 198. That Hamann knew Kant personally at this point is clear from other letters written at this time. See ZH I, pp. 224, 226, where on two different occasions he mentions meeting him in the company of other friends. See NB, p. 96.

I commend the development of this game to God, whose providence I trust, and ask and hope [to receive] from him the necessary wisdom and patience.[53]

A few weeks later, Berens and Kant, later simply "the two," made another attempt, this time dropping by Hamann's house. Kant proposed that Hamann translate part of Diderot's *Encyclopédie*, and they agreed to take up matters again at Kant's house a few days later. The scheduled meeting never took place, however. Instead Hamann penned a letter to Kant that Nadler calls a "historical moment" in the intellectual life of the eighteenth century.[54] Hamann begins the letter by excusing Kant for his unwitting involvement in the whole affair. He then says that Berens is to blame; that he should not have tempted him to unleash his feelings – of irritability, rage, and envy – upon Kant as well, indeed, for having exposed Kant "to the danger of coming so close to a man invested by the sickness of his passions with a power to think and to feel that a healthy person does not possess."[55] "This," he says, "is what I wanted to whisper in your suitor's [Berens's] ear, when I thanked you for the honor of your first visit."[56]

Thus began Hamann's from the start awkward relationship with Kant; and it is from this initial correspondence that the Socratic motif would arise. In the letter Hamann dares to suggest that if Kant is Socrates, and Berens is Alcibiades, then Kant would need the voice of a genius (i.e., a Socratic *daimon*) for his instruction, namely, Hamann himself. Hamann admits that this role suits him, thereby showing a remarkable degree of confidence in his intellectual powers, given the stature of his correspondent. At the same time, he wishes to dispel any suspicion of pride, asking Kant to bear with him for the duration of the letter and to hear him "as a genius speaking out of a cloud." Undoubtedly, Kant's patience was being put to the test, especially given the impertinence of Hamann's language: "I write epically because you are not yet able to read lyric language."[57] Moreover, Hamann ridicules the very articles Kant had suggested he translate, making it clear that he had no interest in providing this kind of service for the cause of the Enlightenment in the future. Finally, dismissing Kant's role in the whole affair, he says, "I have to laugh at the *choice of a philosopher* for the purpose of bringing about a conversion in me. I view the best demonstration the way a reasonable girl views a love letter; and a Baumgartian explanation as an amusing *fleurette*."[58]

One can only wonder how Kant received such comments; indeed, one must see it as a testament to Kant's generous and magnanimous character that they remained lifelong friends. But if Kant had managed to get involved in a quarrel between friends, it was not without intellectual benefit for Kant himself. For in his emotionally-driven letter Hamann not only raised pertinent questions about the unreliability of reason but, most importantly, he provided Kant with what may have been his first exposure to Hume. In fact, Hamann draws upon Hume precisely to defend the embattled principle of faith: "The Attic philosopher Hume has faith necessary if he should

---

[53] ZH I, p. 362. See *SM*, p. 56.

[54] ZH I, p. 373.

[55] ZH I, p. 373. As Nadler points out, priding himself over his new friendship with Kant (with whom he spent a great deal of time in between visits with Hamann), Berens undoubtedly provoked Hamann's envy. See NB, p. 99.

[56] ZH I, p. 373.

[57] ZH I, p. 374.

[58] ZH I, p. 378.

[merely] eat an egg and drink a glass of water."[59] Furthermore, he uses Hume to draw a radical Pauline (and Lutheran) parallel between the purpose of reason and the purpose of the law. "Reason," he says, "is not given to make us wise, but to convince us of our folly and ignorance; just as the Mosaic law was given to the Jews not to make them righteous, but to make them more conscious of their sins."[60] Finally, he adduces a quotation from Hume's *Enquiry Concerning Human Understanding* in which Hume, a "Saul among the prophets," unwittingly speaks the truth:

> that the *Christian Religion* not only was at first attended with miracles, but even at this day cannot be believed by any reasonable person without one. Mere reason is insufficient to convince us of its veracity: And whoever is moved by *Faith* to assent to it, is conscious of a continued miracle in his own person, which subverts all the principles of his understanding, and gives him a determination to believe what is most contrary to custom and experience.[61]

One can only assume that such observations made an impression on the pre-critical Kant, including Hamann's off-hand remark that he has to arm the "feeble eyes" of his reason with the glasses of an "aesthetic imagination."[62] Indeed, inasmuch as he mediated Hume, Hamann may have proved to be the genius behind Kant's critical philosophy after all, with its critical assessment of reason's limits. That being said, such skepticism regarding the capacities of reason is about the extent of any similarity between them: whereas Hamann views Hume's skepticism as an opportunity for faith, along the lines of Philo at the conclusion of the *Dialogues Concerning Natural Religion*, Kant redoubles his efforts to ground the postulates of faith in practical reason. But for all their intellectual differences, they remained on friendly terms (as did Hamann and Berens), and so, towards the end of October, it was Kant himself who stopped by Hamann's home to convey the news of Berens's departure. As Hamann put it to Lindner, "From the way things stand between me and [Kant], I expect soon to have either a very close or a very distant relationship with him."[63]

It was in the middle of all this, during the last two weeks of August, 1759, that Hamann issued his response to Kant and Berens in the form of his first major work, the *Socratic Memorabilia*. Given the lack of an in-town publisher, however, it would not appear for several months, and in the meantime Kant had proposed that he and Hamann write a physics book for children. The suggestion could not have been more suited to Hamann's sense of humor: the distinguished professor, who writes for the learned, now wishes to write for children; and so he took the opportunity to write to Kant about his own views concerning pedagogy and the proper way to

---

[59] ZH I, p. 379.

[60] Ibid.

[61] ZH I, p. 180. David Hume, *Enquiries Concerning Human Understanding and Concerning the Principles of Morals*, ed. P. H. Nidditch (Oxford: Clarendon Press, 1995), p. 131.

[62] ZH I, p. 380. Cf. Hamann's remark to Lindner about Kant from October, 1759 (ZH I, p. 425): "He appeals to the *whole* in order to make judgments about the world. But this requires a knowledge that is no longer *patchwork*. To deduce the fragments from the whole is like deducing the known from the unknown. A philosopher who asks me to see the *whole* makes as difficult a request as one who would ask me to see the *heart* with which he writes. The whole is precisely hidden to me, as is your heart. Or do you suppose that I am a god?" And, true enough, as Kant's thought matured into its "critical" phase, he came to adopt precisely Hamann's view of the limits of theoretical knowledge.

[63] See ZH I, pp. 425, 440. As a further gesture of good will, Kant also began sending Hamann some of his lecture notes.

communicate a theory of nature.[64] Specifically, he reminds Kant of the necessity of condescending to the level of children if one wishes to be their teacher, and points directly to divine condescension in nature and Scripture – the theme of his London Writings – as an appropriate model. Nothing came of the project, however. For one thing, Kant was undoubtedly tired of being lectured to; for another thing, he must have realized that Hamann was, in worldly terms, useless.

In the meantime the *Socratic Memorabilia* appeared, "compiled" by an anonymous "lover of boredom for the boredom of the public," and dedicated, curiously, both to "nobody" and to "two." By "nobody" Hamann meant the "no particular person" of the public, for whom, the work was, in a sense, written, but which would undoubtedly get nothing out of it and hence be bored with it. The real addressees of the work, however, were Kant and Berens; and at least they, Hamann hoped, might get his message (which, as he rightly calculated and even intended, would be more or less inscrutable and stupefying to the anonymous public). And his message to them, wrapped behind many veils and symbolic allusions was simple: he was not to be reconverted to the ideals of the Enlightenment. On the contrary, he held out the hope that his friends would experience a similar conversion to orthodox Christianity, which would "liberate" them from their unwitting "bondage" to the ideology of the age.

Needless to say, Kant never recanted his allegiance to the Enlightenment (nor, so far as we know, did Berens), and to this extent, aside from having powerfully defended the principle of faith, the *Socratic Memorabilia* was a failure. But for all that, it had a *Wirkungsgeschichte,* having been reviewed by none other than Mendelssohn in Nicolai's and Mendelssohn's influential journal, *Briefe, die neueste Literatur betreffend.* Aside from the review, which was largely positive, Nicolai and Mendelssohn subsequently tried to recruit Hamann as a contributing editor for their journal.[65] The offer must have been tempting, for Hamann desperately needed employment and would have enjoyed the stimulating intellectual company. On the other hand, it would have meant moving to Berlin, the hated center of the German Enlightenment and the seat of Frederick the Great, the philosopher king of Sans Souci, which he symbolically identified wth Babel and against which his budding authorship was directed. As he put it to Jacobi years later, "My hatred of Babel – that is the true key of my authorship …"[66] As a matter of principle, therefore, he turned down the offer and stayed in Königsberg, whose publishing capacities were for the time being limited to a modest weekly called the *Wochentliche Königsbergische Frag- und Anzeigungs-Nachrichten.*

---

[64]   ZH I, pp. 444–53.

[65]   See Thomas Abbt's letter to Mendelssohn (April 28 [July 21], 1762): "Your idea that he [Hamann] should be employed is excellent. In one of H[amann's] letters there are ideas suitable to at least ten letters [i.e., *Briefe die neueste Litteratur betreffend*]."

[66]   ZH VI, p. 235. Similarly, around the same time, he speaks of Berlin as a "French Bedlam or Chaldean Babel," and says that he would not exchange all the glory of Solomon for the lot of Lazarus" (ZH VI, p. 259); cf. ZH III, p. 124. More generally, for Hamann's understanding of Berlin as Babel, see Gildemeister, *Johann Georg Hamann,* vol. 1, p. 199, and *JGH,* p. 136.

2

The London Writings: On the Glory of Trinitarian Condescension

What a twofold drama of majesty and abasement, of Divinity and the profoundest level of human misery – What a drama for the Creator and all the host of creation; the world, angels and men all take part in this mystery: as observers, actors, and sponsors. It is finished – this password, which the man of God called out on Golgotha, deafened all of nature, created a new heaven and a new earth, transfigured God, transfigured man, and revealed to all the world, angels and men, that God is just and that all should be justified who would come to believe in him.

"Reflections on church hymns"[1]

Following Hans Urs von Balthasar's reading of Hamann, the present chapter is concerned with Hamann's theological aesthetics, whose defining mark is his understanding of glory in terms of *kenosis,* i.e., as the radiance of divine condescension (making him an important source for von Balthasar's own theological project). While it would be typical to treat Hamann's aesthetics in light of his *Aesthetica in nuce* (1762), here I will be concerned with his early so-called "London Writings," which were composed at a furious pace after his conversion in London in 1758. For it is here that Hamann first articulates what one might call a "hermeneutics of condescension," beginning with meditations on Scripture and leading to a Trinitarian vision of all things in terms of the *kenotic presence of transcendence.* And, in this respect, for all its historical importance and epigrammatic power, the *Aesthetica in nuce* is essentially a condensed manifesto of ideas first penned in London.

Beyond their relevance to Hamann's theological aesthetics, the London Writings are of interest for a number of reasons. Firstly, his radical intuition of divine condescension, as lyrically expressed in these writings, is the source of his profoundly anti-Gnostic sensibility, informing everything from his aesthetics (including his view of creation and language) to his late "metacritique" of pure reason; consequently, these writings are indispensable to understanding everything he subsequently wrote. Secondly, as a series of meditations on Scripture, they exemplify his practice of allegorical-typological interpretation, which singles him out not only *vis-à-vis* the rationalist biblical criticism of the Enlightenment, but also with regard to his own Lutheran tradition, which was generally less inclined to figurative exegesis; moreover, his practice of allegorical interpretation here anticipates his own prophetic, typological understanding of history throughout his subsequent publications.

---

[1] *LS*, p. 373 (N I, p. 270). Although the following chapter and any additional references to the London Writings are based on this edition, I include parenthetical references to Nadler's edition.

Thirdly, these writings challenge modern notions of subjectivity inasmuch as, for Hamann, the individual subject is not a pre-given identity or *cogito* but linguistically constituted – ideally, by the biblical texts, such that one's subjective identity is constituted, so to speak, *ex auditu* by the Word of God. Fourthly, they are the first writings to distinguish Hamann, the former advocate and failed entrepreneur of the Enlightenment, from Hamann, the *Magus in Norden,* and thus constitute a rich document in the history of conversions. Indeed, as Bayer and Weissenborn have noted, they represent a cultural and literary deposit of the first rank, comparable in spirit and scope to Augustine's *Confessions.* For after much searching in the books of classical and modern wisdom and finding them ultimately "comfortless," Hamann similarly turns to Scripture, is seized by its hidden depth, and encounters therein the spiritual allegory of his life. In fact, the whole of Hamann's thought, particularly as centered upon a defense of the inspiration and allegorical depths of the Hebrew Bible against the neologians, is in many ways a modern reprise of Augustine's struggle with the Manichees – just as Hamann's argument with the deists in many ways recapitulates Augustine's argument with the Platonists. For like Augustine *vis-à-vis* the Platonists, what Hamann found so astonishing about Christianity was the radical humility that Christianity proclaims – whereby God not only becomes incarnate, but is always already, as the Logos, intimately and (as we shall see) kenotically present to his creation. And, finally, there is an undeniable advantage in beginning with these writings, which, unlike Hamann's later authorship, are direct and personal, written in clear, accessible prose.

The London Writings were composed between March and July, 1758, at which point Hamann returned to Riga and, eventually, to Königsberg. They include a small piece titled *Ueber die Auslegung der heil. Schrift* [On the interpretation of Holy Scripture]; an extensive lyrical commentary on Scripture titled *Biblische Betrachtungen eines Christen* [Biblical Meditations of a Christian]; an autobiographical account of Hamann's conversion, *Gedanken über meinen Lebenslauf* [Reflections on the course of my life]; *Gedanken über Kirchenlieder* [Reflections on church hymns]; a small collection titled *Brocken* [Fragments]; *Betrachtungen über* Newtons *Abhandlung über die Weissagungen* [Observations about Newton's treatise on prophecies];[2] and a lengthy concluding prayer. With the exception of the first text, "On the interpretation of Holy Scripture," and the "Observations about Newton's treatise," both of which are undated, all of the writings were composed in this order. I begin, however, with Hamann's autobiography, which he began midstream on April 21, the same day he concluded his *Biblical Meditations.* I then treat in the following order, "On the interpretation of Holy Scripture," *Biblical Meditations,* "Reflections on church hymns," "Fragments," and "Observations about Newton's treatise."

NIGHT THOUGHTS: ON THE INTERPRETATION OF SCRIPTURE

We have already sketched the course of events that led to Hamann's conversion, and so we know that he went to London in 1757, presumably to negotiate a trade agreement on behalf of Christoph Berens's trading firm in Riga. We also know that soon thereafter, having failed in the venture for reasons unknown, he fell into desperate poverty and wantonness, moving restlessly from one place to another for nearly a

---

[2] This is not Newton the physicist, but Thomas Newton (1704–82), the Bishop of Bristol. The full title of Newton's treatise is *Dissertations on the Prophecies, Which have remarkably been fulfilled, and at this time are fulfilling in the world* (London, 1754–8).

year. At a certain point, however, he began a conscientious reading of Scripture and "descended," as he would later describe it, "into the hell of self-knowledge."[3]

> My loneliness, the prospect of absolute poverty and of being a beggar ... in short, the barrenness of my circumstances and the magnitude of my worries took away my taste for my books. They were poor consolation, these friends, which I deemed necessary for my existence and by whose company I was so taken that I viewed them as the only support and ornament of human destiny. Under the tumult of all my passions, which overwhelmed me ... I always asked God for a friend, for a wise, sincere friend, whose image I no longer recognized ... a friend who could give me a key to my heart, the thread that would lead me out of my labyrinth. Praise God! I found this friend in my heart, who crept into it right when I most felt its emptiness, darkness, and desertedness. By this time I had read through the Old Testament once in its entirety and the New [Testament] twice ... Because I wanted to make a new beginning, it seemed as if I began to perceive a cover over my reason and my heart, which had kept the book closed to me the first time. I thus set out to read it with more attention, in a more orderly fashion, and with more hunger; and to write down my thoughts as they would occur.[4]

Thus began the *Biblical Meditations,* the scriptural commentary comprising several hundred pages that would occupy him for the next month. At the beginning of the *Meditations,* Hamann notes that he was influenced in his undertaking by James Hervey (1714–58), who himself produced a popular biblical commentary titled *Meditations and Contemplations* (1748), and which Hamann had read as early as 1756.[5] He also mentions being influenced by the author of *Night Thoughts,* that "venerable swan," Edward Young (1681–1765); and, in fact, no other author is cited more frequently throughout the London Writings. But if these authors were an encouragement to his faith, their works paled in comparison to the Scriptures themselves. As he puts it,

> I forgot all my books about [the Scriptures], I was even ashamed ever to have compared them to the book of *God,* ever to have placed them side by side, and ever to have preferred another. I found the unity of the divine will in the redemption of Jesus Christ; that all history, all miracles, all the commandments and works of God lead to this central point, to lead the human soul out of slavery, servitude, blindness, folly and death to the greatest happiness, to the highest blessedness and to an accepting of such goods, whose greatness, when they are revealed, must shock us more than our own unworthiness or the possibility of making ourselves worthy of them.[6]

Having begun to perceive the allegorical depth of the Hebrew Scriptures Hamann then proceeds to identify himself with the people of Israel: "I recognized my own crimes in the history of the Jewish people, I read my own life's story, and thanked God for his long-suffering with this his people, because nothing but such an example could justify a similar hope." And again he says, "Whoever would compare my life with the travel log of Israel would find that they exactly correspond."[7]

The central account of Hamann's conversion, however, as we have seen, concerns the story of Cain and Abel. For just as David recognized his own crime in Samuel's parable (2 Sam. 12: 7), Hamann recognized in the murder of Abel his own guilt in

---

[3] N II, p. 164.
[4] *LS,* p. 342 (N II, p. 39f.).
[5] See *JGH,* p. 25; Oswald Bayer and Bernd Weissenborn's commentary, *LS,* p. 452; ZH I, p. 134.
[6] *LS,* p. 343 (N II, p. 40).
[7] *LS,* p. 345 (N II, p. 42).

the spilling of Christ's blood. In other words, through a sudden, uncanny transposition accomplished on the part of Scripture itself (and for which he would later employ the term "metaschematism"),[8] Hamann discovered that Scripture was "living and active" (Heb. 4: 12), that in some strange way it was also addressed to him. Thus he was fond of holding up to scoffing critics the line from Horace, "Quid rides? mutato nomine de te fabula narratur": "Why do you laugh? Change but the name and the story speaks of *you*."[9] Specifically, he came to experience that the Hebrew Bible had an uncanny power to strip away pretensions, even to the dividing of "soul from spirit, joints from marrow" (Heb. 4: 12), thereby proving its authority as the Word of God even as the rationalist critics of the age were calling its authority and historical authenticity into question – unable to see themselves as already interpolated into Scripture and judged *by it,* whether in the person of Cain, as Hamann found *himself* described, or in the person of Adam seeking knowledge apart from obedience, or in the builders of the tower of Babel trying to "make a name" for themselves. What is more, inasmuch as it was able to create unity out of the formlessness, the nothingness, of his life, he is happy to speak of the work of the Holy Spirit in the writing of Scripture as a similar *creatio ex nihilo,* which parallels the work of the Father in creation and the work of the Son in redemption (see 1 Cor. 4: 6).

Following Oswald Bayer, one is thus presented with a hermeneutics that is squarely opposed to the interpretive practices of the modern subject, indeed, a hermeneutics that fundamentally overturns modern accounts of subjectivity altogether, be they Cartesian, Romantic, or transcendental. For it is no longer a question of how can I (viewed as a complete, self-present, pre-textual identity) understand the text, but rather a question of how *the text* understands and constitutes *me*.[10] Indeed, as Bayer puts it, "Scripture interprets me and not I scripture."[11] Accordingly, priority shifts from the modern subject, which constitutes *itself* (e.g., through Descartes's radical doubt or Kant's transcendental unity of apperception), to the text, which *represents* the subject to itself in a new light, metaschematically constituting (or reconstituting) its identity by means of the figures and parables in the story that is told. Thus Hamann inverts the motto from Albrecht Bengel (which Eberhard Nestle later placed at the beginning of his edition of the Greek New Testament): "*Te totum applica ad textum: rem totam applica ad te.* There is a ὕστερον πρότερον in this sentence. The first must be the last. The more the Christian recognizes that in this book *his own* story is told, the more the zeal grows for the letter of the Word."[12] In other words, biblical exegesis is first and foremost not about applying one's effort to the interpretation of Scripture as to an object of historical-critical investigation, as if the uncovering of its meaning depended upon the intellectual resources that one could bring to bear on it (this would be a kind of exegetical Pelagianism). Rather, one applies oneself and one's intellectual gifts to Scripture because one is *first* addressed by it and *its* authority over

---

[8]   Hamann's use of this term derives from Paul's first letter to the Corinthians (4: 6), where Paul says that he has "figuratively applied" (μετεσχημάτισα) his words to Apollos and himself – not for his own benefit, but so that through indirect means the Corinthians will come to the realization that his message (about not boasting in human leaders, vv. 3: 5–4: 5) applies specifically *to them.*

[9]   Hamann's emphasis. See ZH VI, p. 272 (to Jacobi): "Quid rides? de TE fabula narratur." See Horace, *Satires* I/1, 69f.: "Quid rides? mutato nomine de te fabula narratur," in *The Complete Odes and Satires of Horace,* tr. with introduction and notes by Sidney Alexander (Princeton, NJ: Princeton University Press, 1999), p. 193. See also ZH I, p. 396 (to Lindner): "Why are you laughing? You yourself are the man of the fable." See Bayer's discussion in *Autorität und Kritik: Zur Hermeneutik und Wissenschaftstheorie* (Tübingen: Mohr-Siebeck, 1991), p. 20.

[10]   See Bayer, *Autorität und Kritik,* pp. 19f.

[11]   Bayer, *Autorität und Kritik,* p. 22.

[12]   ZH II, p. 9.

the interpreting subject has been established – when one recognizes that Scripture is, so to speak, its own interpreter (*sacra scriptura sui ipsius interpres,* as Luther puts it), interpreting those who would presume from a superior vantage to interpret it.[13] Accordingly, Hamann concludes his brief autobiography with heartfelt thanks for the treasure he came to find in the Word of God (cf. Matt. 13: 44):

> I conclude, with a proof [based on] my own experience, with heartfelt and sincere thanks to God for His saving Word, which I have found tested as the only light not only to come to God, but to know ourselves[;] as the most valuable gift of divine grace, which surpasses nature and all its treasures as far as our immortal spirit surpasses the lime of flesh and blood[;] as the most astonishing and venerable revelation of the most profound, most sublime, most marvelous mysteries, whether in heaven, on the earth [or] in hell, of God's nature, attributes, [and] great, bounteous will chiefly toward us miserable human beings ... as the only bread and manna of our souls, which a Christian can no more do without than the earthly man can do without his daily necessities and sustenance – – indeed, I confess that this Word of God accomplishes just as great wonders in the soul of a devout Christian, whether he be simple or learned, as those described in it [;] that the understanding of this book and faith in its contents can be attained by no other means than through the same Spirit, who inspired its authors[;] that his inexpressible sighs, which he creates in our hearts, are of the same nature as the inexpressible images, which are scattered throughout the Holy Scriptures with a greater prodigality than all the seeds of nature and its kingdoms.[14]

From this passage it is clear that, methodologically, Hamann's hermeneutics is based upon the *claritas interna Spiritus Sancti*: in order to understand Scripture one must be enlightened by the same Holy Spirit who originally inspired it. In fact, properly speaking, there is no understanding of Scripture outside of this circle that is anything but a confirmation of one's prejudices, a *Gaukelspiel* of reason with itself – and, as we shall see, Hamann maintains the same view with regard to the books of nature and history, both of which are closed, sealed, to a purely rational understanding. Within the circle of understanding, however, i.e., once one has submitted oneself to *its* scrutiny, Scripture becomes "living and active," capable of accomplishing miracles in those who read it; and it is in this way that it shows itself to be the Word of God, i.e., the same effective Word of the Creator, who said, " 'Let there be light,' and there was light" (Gen. 1: 3). As Hamann notes, reflecting with Longinus on the sublimity of the Word of God, "Longinus found it marvelous that Moses would have the highest God speak and that what he speaks happens."[15] And, as we shall see, it is to this sublimely creative power of the Word that all of the *mimetic* actions of Hamann's own dramatic Christian authorship ultimately refer. But, as the above quotation attests, Hamann leaves even the comparison to creation behind, for Scripture is as superior to nature as the spirit is superior to flesh and blood: "Nature is glorious, who can overlook it, [yet] who understands its language[;] for the natural man it is mute and lifeless. But Scripture, the Word of God, the Bible, is more glorious, is more perfect [; it is] the wet nurse that gives us our first food, the milk that makes us strong ..."[16] Moreover, he says that it is "the tree of life, whose leaves heal the people and whose fruits are there to nourish our souls."[17]

[13] See Luther, *Werke. Kritische Gesamtausgabe* (Weimar: H. Böhlaus, 1906–61), vol. 7, p. 97.

[14] *LS,* pp. 345–6 (N II, p. 43).

[15] *Biblical Meditations,* in *LS,* p. 73 (N I, p. 15).

[16] *LS,* p. 152 (N I, p. 91); see also p. 109 (N I, p. 49): "Nature vanishes before your Word. Here is the holy of holies[;] the whole of creation is but an a forecourt in comparison to what we see in your Word."

[17] *LS,* p. 152 (N I, p. 92). See Rev. 22: 2.

Needless to say, such convictions regarding the authority of Scripture and the scriptural constitution of the self placed Hamann in direct opposition to his age, the age of "reason" and "criticism" to which, in the words of Kant, "everything," including Scripture, "must submit."[18] And so it is with good reason that Dilthey described Hamann as the Pascal of the eighteenth century, whose conversion experience *vis-à-vis* Kant and the Enlighteners is not unlike the conversion experience of Pascal *vis-à-vis* Descartes and the beginnings of modern rationalism. For here too the God of the philosophers is not the God of Abraham, Isaac, and Jacob; nor is there any proper knowledge of the Scriptures or of God apart from the Spirit, who is given by Christ. Thus Hamann claims in words reminiscent of Pascal "that without faith in Jesus Christ it is impossible to know God [and] what a loving, inexpressibly good and beneficent being he is."[19] What most distinguishes the God of Christianity from the God of the philosophers, however, is the astonishing extent of his love for human beings. Thus he says that God's "wisdom, omnipotence, and all other attributes seem to be, as it were, but the instrument of his love for man."[20] Similarly, he says, "The pagan, the philosopher, recognizes the omnipotence, majesty, holiness, and goodness of God; but of the *humility* of his *love for man* he knows nothing."[21] Accordingly, for Hamann, "This preference for human beings, the insects of creation, belongs to the most profound [truths] of divine revelation," which reason in no way can fathom – just as it *a fortiori* cannot fathom "that Jesus Christ would not simply be content to become a man, but [would condescend] to become a poor and most pitiable one."[22]

Admittedly, such views are hardly unique to Hamann. But arguably nowhere else in the history of Christianity, not even in Irenaeus, does one find so profound an emphasis on humility as an attribute of the divine nature, and nowhere else does one find this attribute extended with such impeccable logic to *all* the persons of the Trinity. Thus Hamann speaks in striking terms, in addition to the humility of the Son, of the humility of the Holy Spirit, "who, in the face of our proud little mare of reason, produced a book as his Word, in which, like a foolish and crazy [spirit], what is more, like an unholy and unclean spirit, he made small, contemptuous events into the history of heaven and of God (1 Cor. 1: 25)."[23] And on the following day he adds, "Indeed, the entire Bible seems to have been written for just this purpose, to teach us the kingdom [*Regierung*] of God by way of trivialities ... Everything that appears to earthly reason as improbable and absurd is, for the Christian, invariably and undeniably certain and comforting."[24]

GLORY IN THE "RAGS" OF SCRIPTURE

In view of the foregoing, we may identify at least two lasting effects of Hamann's conversion: on the one hand, a profound sense for the allegorical depths and critically transforming "metaschematic" power of Scripture as a work of the Holy Spirit (in comparison to which human criticism pales); on the other hand, a radical personal commitment to Christ, who is now the center of his life, for "when our soul first finds its center in him, it no longer leaves him in its movements; as the earth is

[18] Kant, *Critique of Pure Reason,* tr. Norman Kemp Smith (New York: St Martin's Press, 1965), p. 9.
[19] *LS,* p. 346 (N II, p. 43).
[20] *LS,* p. 346 (N II, p. 43).
[21] *ZH* I, p. 394.
[22] *LS,* p. 346 (N II, p. 43).
[23] Ibid.
[24] *LS,* p. 349 (N II, pp. 45f.).

true to the sun, so it remains true to him ..."[25] And, true enough, as von Balthasar observes, "Hamann never deviated one iota from this consistent and unbroken Christocentrism."[26]

But again, what makes Hamann relatively unique in the history of Christianity, is the degree of emphasis he places upon divine humility – to the point that humility becomes the lens through which he understands the entire economy of salvation, from the work of the Father in creation, to the work of the Son in redemption, to the work of the Spirit in the inspiration of Scripture. Accordingly, he begins his hermeneutical preface, "On the interpretation of Scripture," by saying: "God an author! – – <The Creator of the world and Father of human beings is denied and reproved, the God-man was crucified, and the inspirer of God's Word is ridiculed and blasphemed.> The inspiration of this book is just as great an act of abasement and condescension as the creation of the Father and the incarnation of the Son."[27] Hamann employs dashes here, as he does throughout his works, for added emphasis, in this case in order to highlight the mystery of divine condescension – as if to suggest that Christianity itself is a kind of mystery religion, which is literally "closed off" (μύω) to the uninitiated, in this case to proud rationalists who stand "before the temple" (*pro-fanum*) of the Christan mysteries (including its Scriptures, doctrines, and sacraments) in contemptuous unbelief. Indeed, by his dashes and by the *stylus atrox* of his subsequent "authorship," he means precisely to "fend off" Christianity's "cultured despisers," who presume to judge its mysteries on the basis of reason alone. And so he goes on to say,

> As little as an animal is capable of reading the fables of Aesop, Phaedrus, and *la Fontaine* – or, even if it were it able to read them – it would not be able to make such bestial judgments regarding the sense of the stories and their justification as human beings have made in criticizing and philosophizing about the book of God.[28]

Thus, once again we see that for Hamann, far from being immediately accessible to reason or modern biblical criticism, there is no fathoming of Scripture apart from the Spirit of humility in which it was written: "Humility of heart is the one required disposition and most indispensable preparation for the reading of the Bible."[29] For it is humility that first enables one to see in the humble form of the "old rags" of Scripture, which rationalists are wont to despise or treat as merely human, a divine means of salvation and enlightenment:

> We all find ourselves in a swampy dungeon like the one in which Jeremiah found himself. Old rags served as ropes to pull him out; to them he owed his gratitude for saving

---

[25] *LS*, p. 349 (N II, p. 46).

[26] Hans Urs von Balthasar, *The Glory of the Lord: A Theological Aesthetics* (San Francisco: Ignatius, 1985), vol. 3, p. 246 (modified translation). See, for example, *LS*, p. 431 (N II, p. 48), where Hamann says: "It would be more possible to live without one's heart and head than to live without him. He is the head of our nature and all our powers, and the source of movement, which can no more stand still in a Christian than the pulse can stand still in a living man. Yet the Christian alone is a living human being, moreover, an eternally immortal living being, because he lives and moves and has his being in God ..." Cf. Hamann's remark to Lindner, ZH I, p. 341: "the Christian does everything in God; eating and drinking, traveling from one city to another, residing there for a year ... are divine matters and works."

[27] *LS*, p. 59 (N I, p. 4) (the angle brackets enclose text scratched out but included here nevertheless); on the same page, see also: "The Word of this Spirit is just as great a work as creation, and just as great a mystery as the redemption of human beings[;] indeed, this Word is the key to the works of the former and the mysteries of the latter."

[28] *LS*, p. 59 (N I, p. 4).

[29] Ibid.

him. Not their appearance, but the services they provided him and the use he made of them, redeemed his life from danger. (Jer. 38: 11–13)[30]

And, of course, for Hamann it is the same with Christ, who is likewise clothed in a humble form, the form of a servant (and for this reason likewise rejected), but whom the poor in spirit are able to see as the savior. As von Balthasar observes,

> The same wonder that fills Hamann at the depletion of God in the servant figure of Christ fills him when he contemplates it in the Holy Scriptures, for there 'old rags' are twisted into ropes to pull man out when he lies trapped like Jeremiah in the miry pit, and one must, with Paul, venture to speak of the foolishness and infirmity of God.[31]

After meditating on the similarly humble materials Christ used to heal the blind man (John 9: 6), Hamann then considers the description of David's behavior before the court of Gath: "So he changed his behavior before them; he pretended to be mad when in their presence. He scratched marks on the doors of the gate, and let his spittle run down his beard" (1 Sam. 21: 13–14). What Hamann finds of particular interest here is the response that this behavior elicits from Achish (vv. 14–15): "Achish said to his servants, 'Look, you see the man is mad; why then have you brought him to me? Do I lack madmen, that you have brought this fellow to play the madman in my presence? Shall this fellow come into my house?' " Hamann then asks, "Who can read the story of David without a trembling of reverent fear [*Zittern der Ehrfurcht*], [the story of one] who distorted his gestures, played like a fool, painted the doors of the gate, [and] slobbered on his beard, without hearing in the judgment of Achish an echo of the thinking of an unbelieving joker and sophist of our time."[32]

What is immediately striking here is the language of fear and trembling that Hamann adopts in view of this passage; for in the story of David before Achish, which is presented *as the Word of God*, one is presented with a story that defies rational comprehension, indeed, a story that flatly contradicts rational notions of what should pass as divinely inspired. And here already one can see a few of the reasons why Kierkegaard begins his study of Abraham, *Fear and Trembling,* with a quotation from Hamann. What Hamann finds most interesting in this story, however, is how Achish's judgment is reflected in the judgment of the critics of God in every age, and particularly those of the Enlightenment, who dismiss Scripture in the same way that Achish dismisses David. And, for Hamann, the passage is doubly fearful given that this gesture amounts to blasphemy (cf. Matt. 12: 24–31). Yet it is precisely such an improbable story and, in general, such an improbable *style* that God has chosen (in Scripture, in Christ, and in a Church founded by fishermen), and so he concludes his reflections, fittingly, with a quotation from Paul on the ironic form of divine election (1 Cor. 1: 18, 26–8).

BIBLICAL MEDITATIONS

If "On the interpretation of Holy Scripture" is a brief statement of method, Hamann's *Biblical Meditations* is its application in the form of a lengthy biblical commentary.

---

[30]   *LS*, p. 59 (N I, p. 4). Cf. ZH I, p. 341, where Hamann says to Lindner: "Allow me my pride in these old rags. These old rags have saved me from the pit, and I pride myself in them like Joseph in his colored coat."

[31]   von Balthasar, *The Glory of the Lord,* vol. 3, p. 251.

[32]   *LS*, p. 61 (N I, p. 5).

But here too he prefaces his meditations with hermeneutical reflections on the proper way to understand the Bible, as when he says: "The necessity of putting ourselves as readers into the disposition of the author we have before us ... is a rule that is as necessary here as in the case of other books."[33] As difficult or impossible as this may be in the case of a human author, for Hamann it is not impossible in the case of God, "because the Holy Spirit is promised to all who petition the heavenly Father."[34] And, once again, it is in this way that one enters the circle of understanding. For Hamann, however, the circle is not limiting, as a kind of pietistic reading might suggest, but opens everything. Indeed, for him the Bible is the key to understanding the larger books of nature and history. As he puts it in the "Fragments," "Nature and history are ... the two great *commentarii* on the divine Word; and the latter, on the other hand, the only key that unlocks our knowledge of both."[35] Similarly, he says,

> God revealed himself to human beings in nature and in his Word. One has not yet discerned the similarities and the relationships [that obtain] between these two revelations; nor has one sufficiently explained them or penetrated to [their] harmony, which could open a wide field [of investigation] for a healthy philosophy.[36]

Whether or not this passage would have been included in the collection of Hamann's writings that Schelling received on loan from Jacobi (when Schelling was a member of the Academy of the Sciences in Munich, and Jacobi was its president), it clearly suggests the path of Schelling's late philosophy. The same holds true of the following passage: "Both revelations explain [and] support one another, and cannot contradict one another, as much as the interpretations of reason concerning them might. It is, on the contrary, the greatest contradiction and misuse of reason, if it should wish to reveal *itself*."[37] In other words, for Hamann, it is the greatest misuse of reason if it should wish to find *itself* revealed in nature. And herein lies the crux of Hamann's (and by extension the late Schelling's) difference from Kant, Hegel, and all forms of transcendental philosophy, for which reason is not so much a faculty that interprets reality as one that lays down its rules, that *constitutes* it. Indeed, rather than displaying a greater worldliness by making reason rather than revelation the measure of reality, Kant and German Idealism precisely shut out the world, so that one no longer encounters in it anything other than reason, anything foreign to reason and its domain except, in the case of Kant, a "transcendental = x," about which one can know nothing and which (as Hamann, Jacobi, and John Milbank all point out) might as well "be nothing."[38]

Hamann's reading of Scripture is therefore anything but a narrow biblicism; on the contrary, it was precisely this reading that opened the otherwise "sealed" books of nature and history.[39] As Joachim Ringleben puts it, "The Bible was to him precisely

---

[33] *LS*, p. 66 (N I, p. 8).

[34] Ibid.

[35] *LS*, p. 411 (N I, p. 303). Whereas Hamann here speaks of Scripture as the key to nature and history, he also speaks of faith in such terms, as we shall see in the *Socratic Memorabilia*. Cf. *LS*, p. 307 (N I, p. 246): "Without faith we cannot even understand creation and nature ..."

[36] *LS*, p. 66 (N I, pp. 8f.).

[37] *LS*, p. 67 (N I, p. 9). My emphasis.

[38] See John Milbank, "The theological critique of philosophy in Hamann and Jacobi," in John Milbank, Catherine Pickstock, and Graham Ward (eds.) *Radical Orthodoxy: A New Theology* (London: Routledge, 1999), p. 26.

[39] See *LS*, p. 209 (N I, p. 148): "What a sealed book is nature itself without the interpretation of its Spirit and creator."

the book above all books, the book *of* books: *liber instar omnium*. What was said there opened his eyes to all speech; and the very one whom the Bible revealed he saw again everywhere."[40] In short, "The Bible was his *Hen* because it disclosed the *Pan*."[41] It is in such terms, then, that one must understand the intimate connection in Hamann between Scripture and aesthetics, between a hermeneutics of the Word and a hermeneutics of the world. It is also in such terms that one should understand his later self-designation as a "philologist," as a "lover of the Word," in the narrowest *and* broadest sense of the term, as well as his astonishing remark shortly after his conversion: "To me every book is a Bible."[42]

But if the Word of God "opens" the otherwise "sealed" books of nature and history, for Hamann the converse is also true: a vision of the world apart from the eyes of faith, apart from the lens of the Word, in short, a vision of the world according to reason alone, will have difficulty making anything out, much less discerning any meaning or Logos in what it sees. Indeed, unable to substantiate the phenomena, much less hear the Logos speaking through them, everything becomes illusory:

> What a Nothing, what a smoke, what a pestilent Nothing are [our days] in our eyes when reason counts them! What an All, what a treasure, what an eternity, when they are counted by faith ... All is wisdom in your order of nature when our spirits are opened by the Spirit of your Word. All is labyrinth, all disorder, if we wish to see by ourselves. If we despise your Word, [we are] more miserable than blind ... [Yet] our eyes see as sharply as the eagle, receive the light of angels, when we see all things in your Word, loving God![43]

Already in the London Writings we thus see a fundamental conviction of Hamann's thought: that a genuine aesthetics depends upon faith in the creative Word; that in its absence reason is unable to substantiate or hold together the reality, much less appreciate the providential tapestry, of what it perceives – to the point that one is ultimately presented with a choice between faith or nihilism, an aesthetic of the All or an aesthetic of the void.[44]

A further aspect of Hamann's aesthetics is that he not only sees all of nature and history in light of the Word (of Scripture), but extending the rule of Scripture – the whole of which is about Christ (Luke 24: 27) – he sees the whole economy of nature and history as a similarly mysterious and wonderfully manifold witness to the Word made flesh.[45] To be sure, this witness is more transparent in the history of Israel and the prophecies and allegories of the Hebrew Bible, which announce the coming of the Word with increasing clarity from the Torah to the minor prophets. But the

---

[40] Joachim Ringleben, " 'Rede, daß ich dich sehe': Betrachtungen zu Hamanns theologischem Sprachdenken," in *Neue Zeitschrift für systematische Theologie und Religionsphilosophie* 27 (1985), p. 222.

[41] Ringleben, "Gott als Schriftsteller: Zur Geschichte eines Topos," in Oswald Bayer (ed.) *Johann Georg Hamann: 'Der hellste Kopf seiner Zeit'* (Tübingen: Attempto Verlag, 1998), p. 37. See *LS*, p. 132 (N I, p. 72): "God has revealed everything in his Word"; p. 136 (N I, p. 75): "What mysteries of our nature are clarified in God's Word. Without it, the whole human being seems to be nothing but earth, formless and void, darkness over the surface of the deep."

[42] *ZH* I, p. 309.

[43] *LS*, p. 131 (N I, pp. 70f.). For more on this see Georg Baudler, *"Im Worte Sehen." Das Sprachdenken Johann Georg Hamanns* (Bonn: H. Bouvier Verlag, 1970).

[44] For a thorough development of Hamann's insights in this regard, see Conor Cunningham, *Genealogy of Nihilism: Philosophies of Nothing and the Difference of Theology* (London: Routledge, 2002).

[45] To this extent his understanding of history is fundamentally guided by the principle of analogy. See *LS*, p. 106 (N I, p. 47), where Hamann says, "The truth is single; yet it has countless analogies and expressions." Cf. *SM* (N II, p. 61), where he quotes from Young: "*Analogy*, man's surest guide below."

generosity of Hamann's vision of history is such that the witness to the Word includes for him, as for Photius, even "the flowery language and phrases of the pagans."[46] In this respect he could be said to fulfill Paul's command to take all things captive in obedience to Christ (2 Cor. 10: 5). Accordingly, Hamann takes particular delight in the *unwitting* prophecies of history, whether they be uttered by a high priest like Caiaphas, who thought it better for one man to die for the people (John 18: 14), or a skeptic like Hume, who could provide an altogether legitimate definition of faith, saying of Christianity that a continuous miracle is required in order "to believe what is most contrary to custom and experience."[47]

For Hamann, then, Christ is the prophetic content and ultimate meaning of history and, as such, the key to the propaedeutic mysteries of paganism and Judaism. As von Balthasar puts it, for Hamann, "both Judaism and paganism are oriented towards this one Word, which fulfills them both by revealing through the mystery of [his] own lowliness, the primal glory of God's self-abasing love ..."[48] Indeed, the whole of history is understood here as a single economy of divine condescension, pointing to the central mystery of the servant-form of Christ, the servant-king. This mystery is revealed more clearly in some of the Psalms and in the suffering servant of Isaiah, but for Hamann any philologist, i.e., any lover of the Word, can also find it in the mythology and poetry of the pagan authors of antiquity, as when, to note but one example, Odysseus, the king of Ithaca, appears in his own court, disguised by Athena (i.e., Wisdom), in the form of a beggar.[49] As he puts it in a striking passage in which he compares the God of Israel to the gods of Greek mythology:

> Do we not find in Hosea: "I am like a moth to Ephraim, like rot to the people of Judah (5: 12)." Does he not often change himself into a golden rain in order to win the love of a people and a soul. Is his justice not jealous about the bowels of his mercy and his love for the children of men. And what great projects did he have necessary in order to blind – that I should speak so humanly – the first [his justice]. How many amorous pursuits does he engage in to make us sensitive and to keep us faithful. Must he not abduct us, must he not often use force against his will – Tell me, how could it have occurred to the pagans to convert the glory of Olympus into the image of an ox, which eats grass?[50]

Thus, where Plato sees corrupting lies, Hamann sees a veiled understanding of divine condescension; where modernity sees little but ridiculous anthropomorphisms, Hamann sees allusions to the incredible measures, and apparent *folly*, of God's love. Indeed, he does not hesitate to compare Zeus' "self-emptyings," as so many dream-like anticipations, with the historical facts of what "our religion has revealed to us" (see Phil. 2: 7).[51] Thus he says,

---

[46] N II, p. 172. See also Ringleben, "Rede daß ich dich sehe," p. 222.

[47] See David Hume, *Enquiries concerning Human Understanding and Concerning the Principles of Morals*, ed. P. H. Nidditch (Oxford: Clarendon Press, 1995), p. 131.

[48] Hans Urs von Balthasar, *The Glory of the Lord: A Theological Aesthetics*, vol. 1 (San Francisco: Ignatius, 1982), pp. 80f.

[49] N II, p. 211; cf. N II, p. 68: "The pagans were accustomed to such contradictions [i.e., divine love *sub contrario*] from the *clever fables* of their poets; until their sophists, like ours, damned them as they would a parricide, which one commits against the basic principles of human knowledge."

[50] ZH I, p. 352. The "golden rain" is an allusion to the story of Danaë and the manner of Zeus' entrance into her chamber; the reference to God's righteousness is an allusion to Zeus' wife Hera, who represents justice and order and whom Zeus deceived by his transformations; the reference to the ox is to the rape of Europa. See Harry Sievers, *Johann Georg Hamanns Bekehrung* (Zurich: Zwingli Verlag, 1969), pp. 126–35.

[51] ZH I, p. 352.

Even the pagans knew to weave a little word of these mysteries into their mythology. Jupiter transformed himself into a miserable, shivering, and half-dead cuckoo dripping with rain in order to enjoy the favor of his lawful wife – And the Jew, the Christian rejects his king because he coos like a hen around his chicks, contending in a meek and lowly form for the rights of his love.[52]

Here we stand at the source of Hamann's authorship and his opposition to the rationalism of the Enlightenment: the "folly" of divine condescension, which is a "stumbling block to Jews and foolishness to Gentiles" (1 Cor. 1: 23). What is particularly noteworthy, however, is that, for Hamann, it is an apparent folly that applies not only to the servant-form (*Knechtsgestalt*) of the Son, but equally to the humility of the Holy Spirit, who adopts a similar *Knechtsgestalt* in the writing of Scripture, lowering himself to speak through human beings and, what is more, through the history and stories of an ancient people that, in some cases, no rational or even moral person could hope to understand. The only difference in this regard is that whereas in the incarnation and crucifixion the Son offends what counts as "good logic" and "good philosophy," the Spirit offends "good taste" and what counts as "good style." Indeed, for Hamann, one must marvel that the Spirit, like the Son, submits the work of his inspiration to the scrutiny and judgment of the world – in this case, to the judgment of literary critics, whom Hamann wryly calls "high priests in the temple of good taste."[53] "The talk," he says, "is not of a revelation that a Voltaire, a Bollingbroke, a Shaftesbury would find acceptable [nor one might add, more recent critics of Christianity, such as Christopher Hitchens]; that would most satisfy their prejudices, their wit, their moral and political fancies ..."[54] Indeed, "The notion that the highest being himself would honor human beings with a special revelation seems to these jokers so alien and extraordinary that they inquire with Pharaoh what this God wants ..."[55] For the kind of people "who trust their insights enough to dispense with divine instruction would have found mistakes in any other revelation and [hence] need no revelation. They are the healthy ones who have no need for the physician" (cf. Luke 5: 31).[56]

Yet all of this, for Hamann, belongs to the mysterious, ironic judgment of providence.[57] For those who, like Pharaoh, would snub divine revelation and presume to pass judgment on Scripture precisely thereby confirm the truth of Scripture: that "God opposes the proud, but gives grace to the humble" (Jas. 4: 6) – just as Scripture

---

[52] See Matt. 23: 37. ZH I, p. 394. It is noteworthy here and in many places throughout the *Biblical Meditations* that Hamann never faults the Jews for rejecting Christ without faulting Christians themselves. See, for example, LS, p. 125 (N I, p. 65): "How can we [speak] of the blindness of the Jews and their stubbornness without shame, without blasphemy, without fear, in view of our own – we Christians, to whom God has revealed infinitely more, do we not live in the same idolatry to which the Jews succumbed; in the same unbelief, in which they were stuck; in the same blindness, notwithstanding the testimony of their senses, the testimony of Moses and the express will of God as revealed through commandments, blessings, and chastisements. Oh God! If their judgment was so terrible, how [terrible] will ours be [?]. If Jerusalem came to such an end, what will be the fall of Babel?"

[53] See N II, p. 205.

[54] LS, p. 68 (N I, p. 10). The sentiment of Voltaire, and much noxious hostility to traditional Judaism and Christianity in general, is notably expressed in his *Sermon of the Fifty*, ed. J. A. R. Séguin (New York: R. Paxton, 1962), pp. 11f.: "If one can dishonor the Deity with absurd fables, then let those fables perish forever . . . You know, my brethren, what horror took hold of us when we read together the writings of the Hebrews, concentrating only on all those features offensive to purity, charity, good faith, justice, and universal reason – features found not only in every chapter, but, to crown it all, also consecrated . . . Happily enough, absurdity here outdoes barbarism; but, once more, it is not here that I wish to examine what is ridiculous and impossible. I confine myself only to that which is execrable."

[55] LS, pp. 67–8 (N I, pp. 9–10).

[56] Ibid. My emphasis.

[57] Ibid.

itself is "sealed" against rational exegesis, and just as the rock of Christ (1 Cor. 10: 4), foreshadowed in the Torah (Exod. 17: 6; Num. 20: 11), is "resistant and hard" to unbelievers, but to them that tap into him in faith is the source of "living water" (John 4: 10, 7: 38).[58] Indeed, for Hamann, God is pleased to appear foolish in the eyes of the world, in keeping with what Paul says about the irony of divine election (1 Cor. 1: 18ff.). And, as we have seen, he finds a striking example of this in the account of David's behavior before Achish, the king of Gath, in 1 Samuel 21:

> The Holy Spirit has become an historian of human, foolish, indeed, even sinful deeds in order to dupe Achish like David. David disguised himself[;] the Spirit of purity and wisdom – – he makes signs on the doors of the gates – – – – – – – The Holy Spirit is not satisfied to speak and write like a man – – but as less than a man – – as a foolish, raving madman – – but he poses this way only in the eyes of God's enemies – – he paints the *doors* of the *gates* with signs that no Achish could make any sense of, signs people took for the handwriting of an idiot – – what is more, he lets his spittle run down onto his beard. He seems to contradict and pollute himself by what he inspired as the Word of God. He has the lies of an Abraham, the bloodguilt of Lot, he distorts the man pleasing to God into the figure of one who, as is thought, lies under God's greatest punishment.[59]

What is most shocking here is that, according to Hamann's allegorical interpretation, what is ultimately being said in this biblical passage is said not simply about David, but about the Holy Spirit and the "style" of Holy Scripture – which would explain his otherwise excessive use of dashes. And this, in turn, provides one of the keys to the peculiar semiotics of Hamann's *own style*, i.e., his subsequent authorship, and *its* reception. For like the Spirit of God, he too puts on faces and masks; he too hides behind the appearance of a madman, painting the doors of his writings with bizarre signs, allusions, and ciphers – not out of mere eccentricity, but as an appropriate, calculated posture before a proudly rational audience, as a *mimetic* performance, an "aesthetic imitation," a faithful enacting of divine folly in an age that proudly considered itself the age of "Enlightenment." In fact, so far does Hamann's imitation eventually go that he wishes to incur the same judgment that Christ himself received from the teachers of the law (cf. Mark 3: 20f.). As he shockingly puts it to Herder years later, "The ideal of my embryo [here his "Aprons of fig leaves"], in case it should be born, will draw upon itself the unavoidable judgment: *He has an unclean spirit.*"[60]

In any case, for Hamann, the "folly" of the humility of Scripture, which his own authorship will imitate, is calculated to offend proud rationalists, and to this extent the form of Scripture is a matter of divine election, of God's pleasure in hiding the kingdom from "the wise and learned" and revealing it to mere children (Matt. 11: 25f.) – who are *wiser* than the average *Aufklärer* in that they at least know that they are *dependents,* and have not forgotten to ask for their daily bread:

> For ... we see that it pleased God to hide his counsel [from] us human beings ... in such a way so as to go behind the wise of the world, the LOrds [sic] of the world; thus did God make the lowly, the despised, indeed, the things that are not, as the apostle says, into instruments of his secret counsel and hidden will.[61]

---

[58]   See Gregory of Nyssa, *The Life of Moses* (Mahwah, NJ: Paulist Press, 1978), p. 87.

[59]   *LS*, p. 160 (N I, p. 99).

[60]   *ZH* III, p. 305. Cf. N II, p. 200.

[61]   *LS*, p. 219 (N I, p. 158).

At the same time, however, for Hamann the humility of Scripture has another, plainly practical purpose, being suited precisely to accommodate our sensible nature and our intellectual weakness. This is why Scripture is written in a narrative form, and why Christ himself speaks in parables. "Scripture," he says, "can speak to us in no other way than in parables, because all our knowledge is sensible, figural, and because the understanding and reason everywhere transform the images of external things into allegories and signs of abstract, spiritual, and higher concepts."[62] Indeed, for Hamann, even as a matter of philosophical principle, there is no such thing as a purely rational approach to truth; rather, reason itself operates in the light of a sensible communication, in terms of figures. And this is why he later rejects as misguided from the start the transcendental methodology of Kant's critical philosophy. Yet, Hamann observes, this providential wisdom of God in condescending to communicate to the senses by means of stories and parables in a way that could be understood by all persons – and not just by scholars or scientists – is something proud critics cannot seem to comprehend:

> God condescended as much as possible to accommodate human inclinations and concepts, indeed, even prejudices and weaknesses. This marvelous characteristic of his love, of which Holy Scripture is full, is ridiculed by weak minds, who prefer a human wisdom or a satisfaction of their curiosity ... an agreement with the taste of the time ... to the divine Word. No wonder ... if the Spirit of Scripture is dismissed with just the same indifference, indeed, if the Spirit seems just as mute and useless as the savior did to Herod, who, notwithstanding his great curiosity and expectation to see him, readily sent him ... back to Pilate. (Luke 23: 7–11)[63]

Once again Hamann is amazed that the Son's treatment at the hands of his judges should be repeated in the case of the Holy Spirit, whose writings were dismissed by Voltaire as absurd fables offensive to reason and therefore worthy of his ridicule and contempt. As Hamann sees it, however, this mysterious pattern does not stop with the rejection of the Son and the Holy Spirit, but extends even to the rejection of creation as the self-abasing declaration of the Father's love.

In any case, in view of these mysterious correspondences, Hamann realized that the operations of the economic Trinity call for an entirely new understanding of beauty and glory: "Glory," as von Balthasar explains, "as *kenosis*, not only of the incarnate Son, but also of the [Father], who by creating reaches into nothingness, and of the Holy Spirit, who conceals himself, as Hamann strikingly puts it, 'under all kinds of rags and tatters,' 'under the rubbish' of the letter of Scripture."[64] In other words, Hamann perceived that this coincidence of opposites – of glory and *kenosis*, majesty and abasement – which is found in Christ, is mysteriously proper to *all* the persons of the Trinity: that their shared glory consists precisely in their shared humility, their reciprocal *kenosis*, which could be said to provide a speculative glimpse of the "perichoretic" life they share in eternity. Moreover, following Hamann, one could say that this reciprocal *kenosis* of the divine persons testifies in

---

[62] *LS*, p. 219 (N I, pp. 157f.). Cf. p. 173 (N I, p. 112): "Finite creatures are able to see the truth and the essence of things only in parables."

[63] *LS*, pp. 68f. (N I, pp. 10f.).

[64] von Balthasar, *The Glory of the Lord*, vol. 1, pp. 80f. Cf. *LS*, p. 251 (N I, p. 190): "Next to the wealth of God in nature, which arose out of nothing, there is no greater creation than the transformation [in Scripture by the Holy Spirit] of human concepts and impressions into heavenly and divine mysteries; this omnipotence [which transforms] human language into the thoughts of the Cherubim and Seraphim."

a special way to the *unity* of the divine nature, as though it is in some sense due to the shared *humility* of the divine persons, as much as to any other divine attribute, that the Trinity is *one*. As he strikingly puts it, speaking of the *unity* of the operations of the Trinity *ad extra*: "It belongs to the unity of divine revelation that the Spirit of GOd [sic] should have lowered himself and emptied himself of his majesty just as the Son of God did in assuming the form of a servant, and just as the whole of creation is a work of the greatest humility."[65] This, one might say, is the fundamental intuition of Hamann's thought – so much so that the *Biblical Meditations* are essentially a series of observations, occasioned by a particular verse or story, in light of this one theme:

> How much did God the Father humble himself when he not only formed a lump of clay, but also animated it with his breath. How much did God the Son humble himself: he became a man, he became the least among men, he took upon himself the form of a servant [*Knechtsgestalt*], he became the unhappiest of men, he was made sin for us ... How much did God the Holy Spirit humble himself when he became a historian of the most particular, contemptible, and insignificant events on earth in order to reveal to man in his own language, in his own history, in his own ways the plans, the mysteries, and the ways of the Godhead?[66]

Accordingly, throughout the *Biblical Meditations,* almost in the form of a mantra, one will find expressions like the following: "Who is not amazed by God's condescension, when ..."[67] Indeed, Hamann marvels everywhere over the *depth* of God's love, which causes him to deny – or so it would seem – his own divinity.[68] For example, while the creation of Adam is already an act of condescension (Gen. 2: 7), whether understood according to the literal sense or not (for the literal sense serves precisely to underscore his point), Hamann goes further to note the way God condescends to the *fallen* Adam. As he poignantly puts it, "God conceals from the man the very attribute that could terrify him as a sinner. He denies here his omniscience; he condescends to the blindness of Adam. [He asks,] 'Adam, where are you?'"[69] And even in God's banishing of Adam and Eve from the garden he finds traces of God's loving condescension, when God clothes their shame with "garments of skin" (Gen. 3: 21), as a "prophetic comfort" that one day human beings will be clothed with the Holy Spirit.[70]

But if the first principle of Hamann's hermeneutics is an understanding of divine condescension, the second principle, which he shares with the Church Fathers, is that what is hidden in the Old Testament is revealed in the New ("vetus in novo

---

[65]   N II, p. 171.

[66]   *LS*, pp. 151–2 (N I, p. 91). Hamann was well aware, of course, and would have affirmed that creation is a cooperative work of all the persons of the Trinity (in light of Gen. 1: 2 and John 1: 3, etc.); nevertheless, he attributes creation in a special way to the Father, who similarly "comes down," as it were, by "reaching into nothingness." See in this regard p. 196 (N I, p. 135): "In order to indicate the unity of the divine persons we always find in Scripture a confusing [*Verwechselung*] of the works by which they reveal themselves. The triune God created the world, but the work of creation is attributed in a special way to the Father; the triune God was the redeemer of the world, [yet] the blessed Son alone became a human being and suffered on our behalf – without excluding the fellowship of the other two persons in the work of our redemption ..."

[67]   *LS*, p. 96 (N I, p. 37).

[68]   See *LS*, p. 144 (N I, p. 83): "God feels a human sympathy when human beings wrestle with him; he forgets that he is God, he forgets his omnipotence ..."

[69]   *LS*, p. 77 (N I, p. 18).

[70]   *LS*, p. 78 (N I, p. 19).

patet, novum in vetere latet"). Thus he says that "The entire law of Moses was simply a figure of the knowledge and the truth that would be revealed in Christ."[71] Likewise, he says, quoting Revelation, '*The Spirit of prophecy is the testimony of Jesus*' (Rev. 19: 10). Throughout all of Holy Scripture, this rule serves as the cornerstone and must be the touchstone for all exegetes."[72] Thus he marvels over the story of Abraham's obedience (Gen. 22) and the mystery hidden therein that God, the Father, would one day imitate Abraham, the father of faith; over the story of Joseph, whose life is virtually a transparent allegory of Christ; over Joshua, who is likewise a type of Christ; over the book of Ruth, which by itself is rich enough to preserve the entire Bible; and over Samuel, whose apparition prefigures Christ's resurrection (1 Sam. 28: 13).[73] But "in no story," according to Hamann, "did it please the Holy Spirit to reveal himself so much as in that of David," for here "every chapter is a story of human redemption."[74]

"REFLECTIONS ON CHURCH HYMNS"

Turning now to Hamann's "Reflections on church hymns," we come to understand that the ultimate aim of divine condescension is our deification. For

> Just as God condescended to us, in order to be like us in all things ... so should man be exalted, rapt above all finite creatures and transfigured into God himself. God became a son of man and heir to the curse, death, and fate of human beings; so should man become a son of God, a sole heir of heaven, and be as closely united with God as the fullness of divinity dwelled bodily in Christ."[75]

Similarly, Hamann says,

> How human, how weak, how lowly does God make himself on our account? ... He himself became a human being in order to transform us into gods. – – He gives us everything that he has – – What could be more dear to him than his Son and his Spirit – – Everything that God possesses is mine – – and for what in return? Give me, my son, your heart."[76]

It is notable that Hamann does not hesitate to use precisely the language of divinization, of *theosis,* that one finds in early Church Fathers like Irenaeus and Athanasius. But what is most interesting here, and arguably most profound about Hamann's early thought as a whole, is that he combines this patristic emphasis upon *theosis* with his own emphasis upon *kenosis,* and that he does so in Luther's felicitous image of a marvelous exchange (*commercium mirabile*): "Is it possible to conceive of a greater exchange, a greater trade. Is anything more amazing than the union of Jesus Christ and of God with us, since he made himself nothing [*sich vernichtigt*] in order to exalt us to the throne and seat of God ..."[77]

---

[71] *LS*, p. 291 (N I, p. 230).

[72] *LS*, p. 97 (N I, p. 39).

[73] *LS*, p. 94 (N I, p. 35); pp. 98–100 (N I, pp. 41–3); p. 121 (N I, p. 60); p. 146 (N I, p. 85).

[74] *LS*, p. 164 (N I, p. 103); p. 163 (N I, p. 102).

[75] *LS*, p. 375 (N I, p. 272).

[76] *LS*, p. 356 (N I, p. 253); see Prov. 23: 26.

[77] *LS*, p. 103 (N I, p. 40).

For Hamann, therefore, Luther's understanding of exchange, *commercium*, need not be limited to the exchange that takes place between *homo peccator* and *Deus iustificans*, whereby God's righteousness becomes our own, but may also, in its most proper mystical depths, be understood in terms of our participation in the divine nature (2 Pet. 1: 4). For, as Hamann naturally concluded, only this astonishing height of glory properly corresponds to the depth of divine condescension: "Who would have thought that God would find his honor in our obedience and the pleasure of his glory in our fellowship and participation [?]."[78] Indeed, Hamann not only says that "this participation in the divine nature was the ultimate purpose of the incarnation," but that it is prefigured in the relation between the body and the soul.[79] The difference is that the union of the soul with God – which Scripture indicates as the purpose of creation already through Adam's direct animation by the breath of God (Gen. 2: 7) – is "incomparably more perfect."[80] As Hamann puts it, "Let us never forget that the nature, whose existence we receive from the breath of life, belongs intimately to God, is closely related to him, that it therefore can reach perfection and happiness in no other way than that it return to its origin, its source ..."[81] Similarly, he says:

> If [the soul], in comparison with God, is itself nothing but a breath of God, how great must we become through him, how blessed in him ... As the limits of our members and organs of sense, together with their sensations, compare to the flight of which our souls here already are capable, what excessive imaginations must we have of a being – that is to be One in God, as the Father is in the Son, and the Son in the Father. (John 17: 21)[82]

Whether or not Hamann could be considered a mystic – if he was, he was certainly not one of the monastic variety – such statements raise questions about Hamann's knowledge of or relation to the mystical tradition.[83] Here, however, it is not a question of mysticism *à la* Schleiermacher (as Dilthey argued), but of mysticism in the tradition of the early Church, e.g., in Paul and Ignatius of Antioch, continuing through the Byzantine period (e.g., in Gregory Palamas) and the Spanish golden age

---

[78] *LS*, p. 74 (N I, p. 16).

[79] *LS*, p. 370 (N I, p. 268).

[80] *LS*, p. 73 (N I, p. 15).

[81] Ibid. For all his emphasis upon divine condescension, Hamann is, therefore, not opposed to notions of mystical ascent as such; he is opposed only to an ascent that is not borne on the wings of divine condescension, i.e., a theology of glory in Luther's sense of the term. In fact, one could say that he affirms as one and the same the mystery of divine *kenosis* and human *theosis*, i.e., of God's temporal journey into our humanity and our eternal journey (*epektasis*) into the divine infinite. See p. 363 (N I, p. 261): "By a mysterious, more intimate relationship with the highest being, the smallest, most finite, and weakest creature is thus capable of becoming happier and greater than the cherub or seraph, which makes itself into God."

[82] *LS*, p. 370 (N I, p. 268).

[83] Lutheran scholarship, in keeping with its own tradition, has for the most part tended to deny such claims, if not to ignore them altogether, pointing precisely to Hamann's doctrine of divine condescension and to his own "sensualism." See, for example, Helmuth Schreiner, *Die Menschwerdung Gottes in der Theologie Johann Georg Hamanns* (Tübingen: Katzmann Verlag, 1950), pp. 46–7. Thus Schreiner can say, "Absorption of humanity into divinity, the dissolution of divinity in the human soul ... identity of God and soul – of all this there is not a trace to be found in Hamann." No doubt, this is a correct assessment *if* mysticism is taken to mean absolute identity, which orthodox mystics of the Christian tradition, despite the suggestiveness of their language, have never maintained. (For the analogical interval is never removed; the creature never becomes the Creator.) At the same time, it leaves aside the question of whether Hamann's "sensualism" is not first and foremost a product of *his mysticism*; and also whether his notion of exchange is not fundamentally related, beyond Luther, to the tradition of mystical marriage. Indeed, Hamann raises questions as to whether Luther's own theology of *commercium demands* to be taken in this direction, beyond – without displacing – the language of justification, as Tuomo Mannermaa and other Finnish Lutherans have suggested.

(e.g., in Teresa of Avila). Of course, it would be difficult to say whether Hamann had much awareness of these later figures, and given the disparity of contexts (Hamann, a Lutheran, writing in the middle of the Enlightenment), even their association seems odd. Yet one should not be surprised that he should speak of such mystical *topoi* of the Eastern Church as the indwelling of God in the soul (John 14: 23) and the transfiguration of Christians in Christ (Matt. 17: 1f.); or that he should address God in the language of mystical marriage more common in the West: "Without You I am nothing; You are my entire self [*mein ganzes Ich*]."[84] Indeed, while he more often speaks of divine adoption, it is notable that he also speaks of himself as the "treasure and bride of Christ."[85]

But again, what makes Hamann such a powerful spokesman of the Lutheran tradition is his insistence that none of this is possible apart from the grace of God's prior condescension, in the absence of which Christianity is easily distorted into a kind of Promethean asceticism. Commenting on Genesis 11, he writes, "Come, says God, let us come down from heaven. This is the means by which we have come closer to heaven. The condescension of God to the earth; no tower of reason whose spire reaches to heaven ..."[86] In short, one might say that for Hamann there is no Scheblimini (Ps. 110: 1) apart from Golgotha (Matt. 27: 33), no glory apart from abasement (cf. John 12: 24), just as there is no exaltation of the creature apart from Christ's humility, which is the key to the economy of salvation and the logic of every ascent (see Phil. 2: 6–11 and Eph. 4: 10).

"FRAGMENTS" AND "PROPHECIES"

Aside from being numbered one through ten, Hamann's "Fragments," fittingly enough, lack any obvious organization. Instead, he begins his prefatory reflections *in medias res* with the story of the feeding of the five thousand and the words of Christ to the disciples: "Gather up the fragments left over, so that nothing may be lost" (John 6: 12). As with everything in Hamann, the title and the pericope are laden with significance. The title points to the form of all his future publications, which will likewise be small, seemingly insignificant, indeed a mere collection of fragments; at the same time, however, the pericope points to his hope that his own fragments will produce a similarly surprising yield: that his own "authorship," which reasonable persons will likewise look upon as insignificant, even contemptible, might nevertheless, with God's help, produce a surprisingly robust defense of the Christian faith. And, it almost goes without saying, the citation of this particular story says something about his peculiarly Christian sense of humor, which delights in how divine providence contradicts rational calculations and expectations: "There is a boy here who has five barley loaves and two fish. But what are they among so many people?" (John 6: 9).

For Hamann, however, the story has yet another layer of allegorical significance: the five barley loaves are a figure for the five senses, and their multiplication is the miraculous yield of the arts and sciences over time. "What a storehouse of knowledge," he says, "is the history of learning ... Is it not a wonder of our spirit that it is able to transform the poverty of the senses into such great wealth that one must

[84] *LS*, p. 157 (N I, p. 96); p. 390 (N I, p. 287). Cf. Gal. 2: 20.
[85] *LS*, p. 358 (N I, p. 255).
[86] *LS*, p. 89 (N I, p. 30).

marvel over it [?]."[87] Clearly, Hamann recognizes the dignity of the arts and sciences and in this respect stands *with* his contemporaries. At the same time, however, he refuses to entertain such exalted notions of reason as were common in his day, e.g., notions of reason as a faculty independent of the senses. For "Upon what [are all the sciences] founded? Upon five barley loaves, upon five senses; and *these* we share with the non-rational animals. Not only the entire warehouse of reason, but even the treasury of faith rests upon this stock."[88]

The significance of these statements lies in what they say about Hamann's anthropology and epistemology, which carries over into all his later works: human beings may very well share in the world of ideas as the image of God, but the very power of reason, which distinguishes us from the animals, is nevertheless based upon the information of the senses – with this difference, that it transfigures the information of the senses "into allegories and signs of abstract, spiritual, and higher concepts."[89] In other words, we are not angels; we have, save for the workings of grace, no pure intuitions; and reason cannot be divorced from the senses or from its interpretive role *vis-à-vis* the texts of nature, history, and tradition without spinning its wheels in the fabrication of *entia rationis*. In this respect Hamann's position is not all that different from Kant's later critique of pure reason (*genetivus objectivus*!) and the dialectical illusions to which it is prone. Indeed, he suggests *before* Kant (though in a reversal of his friend's famous maxim) that apart from the testimony of the senses, reason is blind: "Our reason is like that blind Theban prophet, Tiresias, to whom his daughter, Manto, described the flight of the birds, and who [then] prophesied on the basis of her report."[90]

To be sure, at one level, Hamann's empiricism is simply a continuation of the classical Aristotelian axiom that nothing is in the intellect that was not previously in the senses ("nihil in intellectu quod non prius fuerit in sensu").[91] But his empiricism also derives from Paul's teaching on faith and the overall implications of the incarnation. Thus he refers to the apostle's words, "Faith comes by hearing, and hearing by the Word of God" (Rom. 10: 17); and to the words of Christ to the disciples of John the Baptist, "Go and tell John what you *hear* and *see*" (Matt. 11: 4).[92] Indeed, herein, in the incarnation, lies the source of his profoundly anti-Gnostic sensibility; and it is ultimately upon this incarnational, theological basis that he carries out his later "metacritique" of Kant's transcendental philosophy. In particular, he criticizes the Gnostic tendency, which resurfaces in modern rationalism, to spurn the senses and, as in Plato's *Phaedo*, even the body itself:

> How much more does man sin in his complaints over the prison of the body, over the limits imposed by the senses, over an insufficiency of light ... In the eyes of a spirit made for heaven, *the visible* world may be ever so desolate, the bread that God serves us here may be ever so meager and poor, [yet] *they are blessed*, and along with

[87] *LS*, pp. 406f. (N I, pp. 298f.).

[88] *LS*, p. 406 (N I, p. 298).

[89] *Biblical Meditations*, in *LS*, p. 219 (N I, p. 158).

[90] See Kant, *Critique of Pure Reason*, B 75: "Concepts without content [of the senses] are empty; intuitions without concepts are blind." Since this section of the *Critique* pertains to the concepts of the understanding, it would be more accurate to speak here, as Kant does in the transcendental dialectic, of transcendental illusion, since this is proper to the misuse of reason. Tiresias is a figure of Greek mythology, who, among other things, prophesied the patricide of Oedipus. See *LS*, p. 539.

[91] See ZH VII, p. 166.

[92] *LS*, p. 406 (N I, p. 298).

them we too are blessed by an omnipotent, wonder-working, mysterious God, whom we Christians call our own; because he has revealed himself in the greatest humility and love.[93]

It is not, then, because Hamann disparages reason per se that he contends with the rationalists of the age. Rather, it is because of their *misuse* of reason, which prevents them from seeing the revelation afforded to the senses in creation, in Christ, in the sacraments, and, as we have already seen, in the text of Scripture. Of course, at a certain level this is understandable; for, apart from the light of faith, reason would never expect to find the *ens infinitum* in the finite, the Holy Spirit in the "rags" of the Old Testament, the glory of God in the *forma servi* of Christ, much less the whole of God in the fragments of the Eucharist. But while reason in its quest for unity and totality is almost naturally disposed to despise the *manifold* of the senses,[94] in Hamann's view reason errs in assuming that it can attain to some kind of unity on its own. Glossing the words of Paul (1 Cor. 13: 12), he says, "*We live here on scraps. Our thoughts are nothing but fragments. Indeed, our knowledge is patchwork.*"[95]

The individual fragments that follow are a sundry collection, though loosely analogous to Kierkegaard's own *Philosophical Fragments*, inasmuch as they deal with questions that are more philosophical in nature – in this case questions regarding self-love, self-knowledge, human freedom and happiness, the problem of evil, and the relationship between the body and the soul. But their content is equally theological, inasmuch as, aside from touching upon topics like prophecy and providence, the philosophical questions Hamann poses ultimately require theological answers.

In the first and longest fragment Hamann addresses the topic of freedom, which he understands as a function of self-love: "This self-love," he says, "is the heart of our will, from which all inclinations and desires, like the veins and the arteries, arise and to which they return. We can just as little *think* without self-consciousness, as we can *will* without it."[96] Almost incidentally, Hamann anticipates here the "I think," which, for Kant, accompanies all our representations. He also touches upon the intimate connection between thought and will, *intellectus* and *voluntas*. What is most interesting, however, is the quasi-Augustinian argument he makes about the nature of freedom: that it exists, paradoxically, for the sake of an *involuntary* desire, i.e., self-love, and that this *necessity*, in which we find our *freedom*, is a natural desire that ultimately leads us to God. In the words of Edward Young, whom Hamann cites in this context, "Man love thyself / In this alone free-agents are not free."[97] In other words, if freedom necessarily serves self-love, this natural desire of self-love cannot be fulfilled apart from self-knowledge; for one must know oneself in order to love oneself. But here is the catch: since we precisely *do not* know ourselves (*contra* Rousseau), and indeed *cannot* know ourselves apart from God, since we are the *imago Dei* (Gen. 1: 26), we cannot properly love ourselves without knowing God. Hence the law of self-love leads us naturally beyond ourselves to God. "*From this,*" Hamann says, "*one can see* how necessarily our self is grounded in its Creator,

---

[93] *LS*, p. 406 (N I, p. 299).

[94] As Aristotle puts it in book XII of the *Metaphysics* (1076a), quoting the *Iliad*, "The rule of many is not good; one ruler let there be."

[95] *LS*, p. 407 (N I, p. 299).

[96] *LS*, p. 407 (N I, pp. 299f.).

[97] *LS*, p. 408 (N I, p. 300).

that the knowledge of ourselves is not in our power, *that in order to measure it out we must penetrate to the seat of the Godhead, which alone can ascertain and resolve the mystery of our nature.*"[98]

In the third fragment he continues his meditations on God's profound condescension to human affairs, which extends even to the spinning of goats' hair (Exod. 35: 25f.). "In the histories, laws, and customs of all people," he says, "we find, if I may say so, the *sensum communem* of religion. Everything ... winks to us of our vocation and the God of grace."[99] And if this is true even of the smallest blade of grass, Hamann asks, should the most minor of human actions be any less significant? Indeed, in Hamann's view everything is significant, especially the symbolic actions of one's life:

> An English divine first attempted to introduce the unction of grace into the doctrine of nature; we are still waiting for a Derham who would reveal to us in the kingdom of nature not the God of naked reason, if I may say so, but the God of Holy Scripture, who would show us that all its treasures are nothing but an allegory, a mythological painting of heavenly systems – just as all historical events are the shadow-images of secret deeds and revealed wonders.[100]

Taken by itself, this passage could give the impression that Hamann was a kind of Platonist. In point of fact, however, it is based upon Hamann's understanding of divine condescension, which leaves nothing mundane and everything a potential sign of God's presence. As Hans-Martin Lumpp put it, contradicting caricatures of Christianity as a form of otherworldly Gnosticism, "because God enters the world and human history and *there* speaks to human beings, this world [*das Diesseitige*] is of unsurpassable importance and significance."[101] Indeed, precisely because of divine condescension, there is no Platonic divide, no χωρισμός, fixed between the finite and the eternal, this world and another; rather, heaven *and earth* declare the kenotic presence, the immanent glory, of transcendence.

Admittedly, the above passage could also be taken to deny any real distinction between natural and revealed theology; and, doubtless, Hamann lends himself to this impression when he discovers none other than "the God of grace" throughout nature and history. But once again any coincidence of the two is strictly speaking a matter of grace, a matter of an aesthetics that is *given* by the Spirit of Christ, in whom alone such a reconciliation is accomplished. As Hamann puts it in the eighth fragment, "*All* the appearances of nature are dreams, faces, riddles, which have their meaning, their secret sense. The book[s] of nature and history are nothing but *ciphers*, hidden signs, which require [for their understanding] the same key that

---

[98] *LS*, p. 409 (N I, p. 301). Thus the very self-love, which is the ground of the possibility of concupiscence, naturally and, as it were, inevitably (in the presence of faith and the absence of sin) unites the creature to God. Indeed, the very self-love which makes sin possible is also, almost ironically, the natural motor of ecstasy. Thus, in *On Loving God* Bernard of Clairvaux not only begins his stages of love with self-love but in the end returns to it, albeit in a transfigured form: to a love of *oneself* for the sake of God.

[99] *LS*, p. 411 (N I, p. 303).

[100] *LS*, p. 412 (N I, p. 304). The reference here is to William Derham (1657–1735), an English divine whose work, *Physico-Theology: A Demonstration of the Being & Attributes of God, from His Works of Creation*, appeared in 1712. The popular work was translated into German in 1764 and is, undoubtedly, one of the targets of Kant's refutations of the physic-theological proof in his *Critique of Pure Reason*. See *LS*, p. 540.

[101] See Hans-Martin Lumpp, *Philologia Crucis: Zu Johann Georg Hamanns Fassung von der Dichtkunst* (Tübingen: Max Niemeyer, 1970), p. 135.

interprets Holy Scripture and is the point of its inspiration."[102] Indeed, apart from the illumination of the Holy Spirit, the books of nature and history, like the Bible itself, remain "sealed." Thus he concludes:

> What is the difference between natural and revealed religion? If I understand it properly, it is the difference between the eye of a man who sees a painting without understanding the least about painting, drawing or the history that is represented and the eye of an artist, between the natural and the musical ear.[103]

The fourth fragment concerns the problem of evil, and for the most part Hamann's account is not particularly original: good is what maintains or restores the health of the body, the soul, and their connection; evil, on the other hand, is what vitiates or destroys them. What is more notable, however, is his reversal of the standard question. For "rather than asking: where does evil come from? we should ... reverse the question and marvel that finite creatures are capable of being good and happy. In this consists the true mystery of divine wisdom, love, and omnipotence."[104] But, importantly, Hamann does not gloss over the reality of evil or the difficulty of explaining it, and so he concludes the fragment with an allegory of the Christian life as the only way to make sense of the matter.[105]

Among the rest of the fragments, the sixth is particularly significant given the way in which it anticipates Kierkegaard, especially his lyric memorial to Abraham in *Fear and Trembling*. Indeed, here in a nutshell one arguably finds the seed of Kierkegaard's famous work and his corresponding understanding of the "knight of faith." The fragment consists of a single pithy sentence: "When one considers how much strength, presence of mind, and speed, of which we are otherwise incapable, the fear of an extraordinary danger inspires in us: then one can understand why a Christian is so superior to the natural, secure man, because he seeks his blessedness with constant fear and trembling."[106] In addition to this passage, which undoubtedly caught Kierkegaard's attention, there is another from the third fragment concerning unwitting prophecies that provoked his consideration:

> Could one not say of Socrates, when he refers to his guardian spirit, what [Scripture] says of Peter: he did not know what he said [see Mark 9: 6]; or of Caiaphas, who prophesied and proclaimed divine truths without himself or his listeners having the slightest perception of what the Spirit of God spoke through him. This point is illustrated in the strange story of Saul and Balaam; that even among the idols, indeed, in the very instruments of hell, the revelation of God is manifest; and that he himself uses them as his servants, like Nebuchadnezzar.[107]

As we have already seen from the *Biblical Meditations*, the theme of unwitting prophecies goes hand in hand with Hamann's radical understanding of divine condescension, which is so profound as to exclude the possibility that anything could escape God's ultimate designs, in other words, that all things testify, despite themselves, to divine truth (in radical application, as it were, of the doctrine of the *privatio boni*).

[102] *LS*, p. 417 (N I, pp. 308f.).
[103] *LS*, p. 411 (N I, pp. 303f.).
[104] *LS*, p. 413 (N I, p. 305).
[105] The allegory is of a monarch and his favorite child, who is temporarily abandoned to a realm of foes, but indelibly bears the royal seal and is rescued in every danger by an unseen friend, who will render justice at the appointed time.
[106] *LS*, p. 416 (N I, p. 308).
[107] *LS*, p. 412 (N I, p. 304).

But while Kierkegaard was generally enthusiastic about Hamann, he thinks that this passage from the third fragment goes too far, even to the point of blasphemy.[108] Whether or not Kierkegaard's judgment is fair cannot be decided here.[109] But if this passage is, in Kierkegaard's view, seen to derive from Hamann's excessive humor, it is noteworthy that Hamann is quite serious: that all things serve God, whether consciously or not. And if even the enemies of God unwittingly speak the truth, how much more, Hamann suggests, are God's willing servants prophets of divine things. As he puts it in the eighth fragment, "We are all capable of being prophets."[110] Indeed, for Hamann, the vocation of the human being in Christ is quite simply *to reveal God*. And given this emphasis of his thought, it is not surprising that he should have been interested in Thomas Newton's *Dissertations on the Prophecies*, which he read during this time.

Hamann begins his "Observations" by restating what he discovered through personal experience: "Every biblical story is a prophecy – which is fulfilled in every century, and in every human soul. One need only open the Bible to believe in and feel the omnipresence and omniscience of the Spirit of God." He then goes on to make a striking connection between the dual (literal-spiritual) senses of Scripture and the composite nature of the human being, so that Scripture, as the work of God, is oddly analogous to the *imago Dei*: "Every story bears the image of the human being, a body, which is trivial, composed of earth and ashes, the sensible letter, but also a soul, which is the spirit of God, the breath of his mouth, the light and the life, which shines in the darkness and cannot be comprehended by it."[111] On the one hand, Hamann means to indicate here the obtuseness of rational exegesis when it comes to Scripture, which escapes its comprehension just as Christ eluded the crowd (Luke 4: 30). On the other hand, he again emphasizes the humility of the Holy Spirit, who is, as it were, incarnated, hidden beneath the form of the sensible letter. As he puts it, "The Spirit of God reveals himself in his Word ... in the form of a servant [*Knechtsgestalt*] – is flesh – and dwells among us full of grace and truth."[112]

Hamann thus returns to the same theme that fascinated him from the beginning of his *Meditations*: the condescension of the Holy Spirit, whose work in the writing of Scripture is analogous to the condescension of the Son. For just as one can find in the flesh of Christ "all the treasures of wisdom" (Col. 2: 3), one finds a similar wealth in the "flesh" of the stories of the Holy Spirit. In the story of Noah, for example, he finds hidden as in a seed, "the mysteries of the kingdom of heaven."[113] Thus the patriarch himself is an image of God (see Ps. 78: 65), whose drunkenness points to the mystery of the vine (John 15: 1). Ham laughing at his father's nakedness is a type of the same spirit that ridiculed the disciples on the day of Pentecost. By walking backwards in order honorably to cover their father (Gen. 9: 23), both Shem and Japheth represent the noble attempts of the Jew (through the law) and the Greek (through philosophy) to restore the human condition from its fallen condition. But

---

[108] See *JP* II 1693, p. 257: Humor can therefore approach blasphemy; Hamann would rather hear wisdom from Balaam's ass or from a philosopher against his will than from an angel or an apostle.

[109] For more extensive treatment of the relation between Hamann and Kierkegaard, see John R. Betz, "Hamann before Kierkegaard: a systematic theological oversight," *Pro Ecclesia* XVI (Summer 2007), pp. 299–333.

[110] *LS*, p. 417 (N I, p. 308).

[111] *LS*, p. 421 (N I, p. 315). See John 1: 5.

[112] *LS*, p. 421 (N I, p. 315). See John 1: 14.

[113] *LS*, p. 421 (N I, p. 315).

"they did not know of the corruption of their nature – and so they did no more than to spread a cover over it, like a cloak. This was all that their shoulders were able to bear. Their righteousness, their strength, their wisdom could do nothing more."[114] And, it almost goes without saying, the ark is a type of salvation through Christ. Hamann then discusses the prophecies concerning Ishmael, who is simply "a name, a shadow, a type, a sign, which God has posited,"[115] reiterating a notion that occurs with some frequency throughout the *Biblical Meditations*: that the human race ultimately divides into two according to God's initial prophecy in Genesis 3: 15. This division is not limited to Isaac and Ishmael, but, following Augustine, can be found in types already in Cain and Abel, in the blessing of Shem and Japheth and the cursing of Ham (and Canaan), etc.: a division that is reflected not merely in the history of nations but in the history of every individual person, inasmuch as the dual destinies of the human race are reflected in and brought about by the choices individual human beings make.

The final section of the *Observations,* which skips over the bulk of Newton's *Treatise,* is titled "Prophecies concerning the Jews." And it is here that Hamann makes some of his most striking observations about the election of Israel and the relationship between Jews and Christians. In the *Biblical Meditations* he had already affirmed Israel's election:

> God undeniably found it most suited to his wisdom to bind this greater revelation of himself first to a particular human being, then to his offspring, and then to a particular people ... We can no more fathom the reasons for this election than we can know why it pleased him to create [the world] in six days, which his will could just as easily have accomplished in a moment.[116]

Accordingly, "the history of this people is in itself of greater importance with regard to our religion than that of any other."[117] And for Hamann this is particularly so inasmuch as the history of Israel is a running type of human redemption. "The Jews," he says, "will always remain a mirror in which we see, as in an enigma, the mystery of God in the redemption of the human race."[118] But, for Hamann, as for Paul, whom he faithfully follows (Rom. 9–11), Israel is not simply a type of redemption, nor is it merely a type of the Church (as a strict supersessionism would have it); rather, it is the historical reality of the people of God, the olive tree onto which the Gentiles are grafted (Rom. 11: 17f.). Indeed, the mystery of the salvation of the Gentiles is uniquely bound up with the destiny of this particular people. Furthermore, to Christians who would arrogantly boast, Hamann counters: "Have we not crucified the Son of God just as they [?] Do we not dig the graves of the prophets, whom they have killed [?] Can we Christians read Obadiah without alarm [?] Is not the same end threatened to us Gentiles, to us who are grafted onto the olive tree [?]."[119] And, finally, prophesying against his own people nearly two centuries into the future, he says: "Has Jesus ceased to be the king of the Jews [?] Has the

---

[114] *LS*, pp. 422f. (N I, pp. 316f.). Needless to say, Hamann does not mean to say that the law is not divinely revealed or that it is a merely human invention.

[115] *LS*, p. 424 (N I, p. 318).

[116] *Biblical Meditations*, in *LS*, p. 68 (N I, p. 10).

[117] *LS*, p. 69 (N I, p. 11).

[118] *LS*, p. 425 (N I, p. 319).

[119] *LS*, p. 425 (N I, p. 319).

inscription on his cross been changed? Do we not persecute him in his people?"[120]
Needless to say, Hamann was all too prophetic, and in this regard one might regret
that his full-blooded *historical* faith, which professed Judaism to be "the bodily
mother of evangelical Christianity,"[121] did not prevail over the *abstract* religion of
the Enlightenment (which in the name of religious pluralism and tolerance radically
undermined all notions of Israel's election), but was instead shunted to the margins
of relevance.

---

[120]   Ibid.
[121]   N III, pp. 356f.

3

A Typological Re-reading of Socrates: On Faith, Reason, and History

[Hamann] has said the best that has been said about Socrates.

Kierkegaard[1]

Hamann found a real delight in inviting his knowledge-greedy contemporaries, platter-lickers, to his long-necked stork flask.

Kierkegaard[2]

But perhaps all of history is ... a riddle that will not be solved unless we plow with another heifer than our reason.

Hamann[3]

Composed within the last two weeks of August, 1759, the *Socratic Memorabilia* is the first salvo of Hamann's "authorship" (to distinguish it from the London Writings). We have already discussed the context of its genesis: how it was written in response to Kant's and Berens's efforts to curb Hamann's "enthusiasm" and re-enlist him in the cause of the Enlightenment. But it was not simply Hamann's personal faith that was being scrutinized; it was also, by implication, the Christian faith itself to which he had newly and fervently returned. Thus the *Socratic Memorabilia* represents both a spirited defense of his personal faith (the *fides qua*) and at the same time a defense of creedal Christianity (the *fides quae*) in view of the *Religionskritik* of the *Aufklärer*. Needless to say, given the intellectual prejudices of the age, the chances of mounting a successful self-defense were slim, and the chance of converting Kant and Berens to orthodox Christianity next to nil. If, therefore, Hamann was to have any hope of success, he would have to communicate with them indirectly, and how better, he reasoned, than through the figure of Socrates, to whom the *Aufklärer* commonly appealed as a proto-rationalist, forerunner of the Enlightenment, and overall champion of their cause.[4]

Hamann's portrait of Socrates was not the first, of course; nor was it the only one from this period.[5] What is unique about the *Socratic Memorabilia*, however, is a perspective informed by Hamann's conversion experience and a corresponding skepticism toward the rationalism of the age. Thus, whereas the Socrates of the *Aufklärer*

---

[1] *JP* II 1555 (n.d., 1844), (*Pap.* V B 45).

[2] *JP* II 1681 (n.d., 1837), (*Pap.* II A 75).

[3] N II, p. 64.

[4] For further discussion of the Socrates cult of the Enlightenment, see Benno Böhm, *Sokrates im achtzehnten Jahrhundert. Studien zum Werdegange des modernen Persöhnlichkeitsbewußtseins* (Leipzig, 1929). See HH, p. 17.

[5] At the time of its composition, Hamann had been reading a popular French rendering of Xenophon's *Memorabilia*, which had been translated into German several decades ago, titled *The Likeness of a True and Non-Pedantic Philosopher, or the Life of Socrates*. See SM, p. 59.

tends to be a reflection of their rationalist prejudices, Hamann's Socrates is oddly biblical, even proto-Christian. Accordingly, the entire work is governed by an explicit analogy between paganism and Christianity – as "type" and "fulfillment" – which *eo ipso* calls into question the claims of the *Aufklärer* to represent the renewal or fulfillment of classical wisdom. Indeed, following the same method of allegorical and typological exegesis he practiced in the London Writings, he reads Socrates in terms of multiple typologies, each of which not only contradicts a specific conceit of the *Aufklärer*, but smuggles in right under their noses a particular content of the Christian faith.[6] For example, against their proud rationalism, he appeals to Socrates' profession of ignorance as a prefiguration of the humility of faith (1 Cor. 8: 2f.); against their prized autonomy, he appeals to Socrates' deference to his *daimon* as a prefiguration of the guidance of Christians by the Holy Spirit; against their vanity, he appeals to Socrates' humble appearance as a prefiguration of the *Knechtsgestalt* of the Son of Man (see Isa. 53: 2); and, finally, he appeals to Socrates' unjust death as sharing in the fate of the prophets and martyrs, moreover, as a pagan anticipation of the unjust sentencing and death of Christ. In sum, so completely does he contradict his contemporaries and reclaim Socrates for his own purposes that the latter, rather than being a patron and forerunner of the Enlightenment, turns out to be a patron and forerunner of orthodox Christianity.[7]

If one angle of indirection is through the figure of Socrates, the other is through the renowned skeptic and "enemy" of Christianity, David Hume, and Hamann's use of him is arguably just as ironic as his use of Socrates. For, picking up on Philo's remarks at the conclusion of the *Dialogues Concerning Natural Religion,* Hume is transfigured into a John the Baptist among the philosophers, whose skepticism points the way to faith by exposing the ultimate groundlessness – and hence hypocrisy – of the Enlightenment's dogmatic rationalism. For, as Hamann reasoned, if Hume's skepticism could be brought to bear against metaphysics, why should it not apply with equally devastating force against the dogmas and varnished self-certainties of the Enlightenment? Indeed, precisely by showing the tenuous status of any dogmatic rationalism, Hume's skepticism had the virtue of demonstrating the philosophical legitimacy of "belief," which Hamann naturally translates into German as "faith" (*Glaube*). Whether or not Hume would have authorized such a translation is beside the point, for Hume's skepticism suffices to show that some kind of natural faith (which is to be distinguished from supernatural faith) is at work in everyday experience, and that reason – for all its alleged autonomy and pre-eminence over faith – cannot do without it. In other words, in the absence of faith not only is it "impossible to please God" (Heb. 11: 6) or be "credited with righteousness" (Rom. 4: 3), for Hamann it is impossible to *know* anything with any degree of certainty at all – beyond, say, the truths of mathematics or the analytic judgments of logic. Thus, in a novel epistemological twist on Luther's *sola fide,* for Hamann there turns out to be no *knowledge* except "by faith."

But not only is faith indispensable to reason, e.g., as far as trusting the veracity of the senses, the phenomenal world, or even reason itself; Hamann's further claim is

---

[6] Although allegory and typology may loosely be classed together in that both point to a meaning beyond the literal sense, one might distinguish them as follows: whereas in the case of allegory the particular historical form in which it is clothed tends to be irrelevant to the moral or spiritual content being conveyed, in the case of typology a given historical content is precisely what is being signified. See *HH* II, p. 14.

[7] See *SM*, p. 6: "This thought is, of course, not original with Hamann. It had been held by many of the Church Fathers, including Justin Martyr, Lactantius, Minutius Felix, and others." See also p. 83.

that faith, objectively the Christian faith, is also the key to understanding history itself as revelation, and it is this idea that subsequently gets developed *mutatis mutandis* in the philosophies of Schelling and Hegel. For just as reason needs a natural faith to ground its own investigations and heuristically to support its natural desire to know the truth (which is otherwise subject to suspicion, as Marx, Nietzsche, and Freud have shown), it also needs the illumination of supernatural faith both to understand *that* history is an unfolding revelation and to understand *what*, as revelation, it reveals. And in this respect the *Socratic Memorabilia* recalls the London Writings. What clearly distinguishes it from them, however, is that while the London Writings were private, lyric, and never intended for publication, the *Socratic Memorabilia* is defined by a highly stylized public, dramatic, gnomic, allusive, oblique, ironic, pseudonymous, prophetic form: the same curious form that marks all of Hamann's so-called "authorship." In other words, while it is inspired by the same vision, the *Socratic Memorabilia* represents Hamann's first experiment in indirect communication, deriving ultimately from his conviction that faith "cannot be communicated like merchandise."[8]

Most obviously, the indirect communication consists in Hamann's attempt to speak through a published work and through the mask of Socrates with Kant and Berens, who indirectly appear as Sophists. But this is not all, since the entire work is replete with oblique expressions, following the same pattern of indirection. For example, Christ, who is nowhere named directly, is "the Gallilean of the schemer Julian"; similarly, Paul is "the great teacher of the Gentiles," and so on. Indeed, Hamann even uses the same devices of periphrasis and antonomasia to refer to classical, modern, and contemporary figures. Thus the Sophists are "polyhistorians"; the *Aufklärer* are "Cretans"; Peter the Great is "the Scythian"; a skeptic is "a Hume"; Kant is, curiously enough, the "Warden of the Mint"; and Kant and Berens together are simply, "the two."[9]

THE PROPHET AND THE IDOL

As with all of Hamann's publications, his intention in the *Socratic Memorabilia* is cryptically folded into the title page. As he puts it to Jacobi, "For me the title is not simply a sign to hang out, but the *nucleus in nuce,* the mustard seed of the whole growth."[10] And, similarly, in one of his last works, he refers to the title as a "microcosmic seed, an Orphic egg," again referring to it in organic terms as that from which something is produced, only now in the language of the mysteries.[11] In any event, he means more than that his works unfold organically, like a shoot from a seed; he means that they possess a vital power to transform those who have properly digested them (cf. Ezek. 3: 1f.), precisely along the lines of the parable of the sower (Mark 4; Matt. 13). As for the title itself, its profounder significance is bound up with the teasing subtitle, which contains the only clue to the work's author: "Compiled for the boredom of the public by a lover of boredom." Here already one sees something of the irony that drives the work: a "lover of boredom," i.e., one seemingly

---

[8]   ZH VII, p. 176.

[9]   See *HH* II, p. 18; see *SM*, pp. 70f.

[10]   ZH VI, p. 137; cf. C. H. Gildemeister, *Johann Georg Hamann's des Magus in Norden, Leben und Schriften*, 6 vols. (Gotha: Friedrich Andreas Perthes, 1857–73), vol. 5, p. 501: "For me the title is the face and the preface, the head on which I spend the most time."

[11]   N III, p. 373.

ill-equipped for the job, is going to drive away the "boredom of the public." While the self-designation is certainly a comical allusion to Hamann's unemployment at this time, it also masks his very serious intentions *vis-à-vis* Kant and Berens and, more mockingly, *vis-à-vis* an insatiable public, which is driven from one empty amusement to another, indeed "always learning" but "never able to come to the knowledge of the truth" (2 Tim. 3: 7).

Then there is the curious "double dedication to nobody and to two." "Nobody" here means the "nobody in particular" of the anonymous public; "the two," once again, are Kant and Berens. To which Hamann adds the following epigraph from Persius, completing the title vignette: "O the cares of mankind! How much emptiness there is in things! Who is going to read this? – – Are you talking to me? – – Nobody, by Hercules! – – Nobody? – Perhaps *two*, or maybe *nobody*."[12] The fact that this epigraph from Persius begins with an obscure quote on the part of Persius from another Roman satirist, Lucilius, and continues with a feigned dialogue about a prospective readership, says something upfront about Hamann's profoundly indirect style, his satirical bent, his intended audience, "the two," and his anticipation of the limited reception his work would receive. The title page then concludes with a spurious place of publication, Amsterdam, which is yet another device of indirection, but perhaps also a veiled suggestion that things are not always what they seem (as is the case with the common misconception regarding Socrates' supposed rationalism).[13]

Turning now to the first dedication, "to the public or nobody, the well-known," we find that it is immediately followed by a quotation in Greek from Euripides' satirical drama, *Cyclops*, "Where's *nobody*?" (οδ' ΟΥΤΙΣ, ποῦ 'στιν;). What this is meant to suggest about Hamann's relationship to the public is unclear: Is he siding with the Cyclops against the "nobody-in-particular" of the public? Hamann's procedure is as typical as it is (for unintended readers like Hegel) infuriating, requiring the pontifical labor, to which he subsequently refers, of methodically connecting a historical or classical reference with a contemporary significance – a connection that will most likely be lost on an unintended reader, but whose sudden combination is meant to generate a "prophetic word," like a spark from two sticks, for the particular reader or readers he has in mind, in this case Kant and Berens.[14] But if it is impossible for Hamann's text to have the same pyrotechnic effect on readers today, the original Homeric context to which the quotation refers is illuminating. It refers to the exchange between Odysseus and Polyphemus, the king of the Cyclops, in book IX of the *Odyssey*, where Odysseus, who is trapped in the monster's cave, inebriates him with an offering of wine, strategically tells him that his name is "nobody," blinds him in his one eye while asleep, and subsequently escapes. When the other Cyclopes, upon hearing Polyphemus scream, come to ask him what is wrong and whether someone is trying to kill him, the dumb monster replies "'nobody' is killing me ..." Hamann would thus seem to be representing himself as Odysseus against the one-eyed Cyclops, i.e., against the myopic and ultimately fatuous philosophy of the *Encyclopédie*. For like the Homeric hero he presents an offering, in this case to the curious, easily duped public of the Enlightenment, and by it he hopes to defeat

---

12   Persius, *Satires* I, lines 1–3, in Auli Persii Flacci, Satirarum Liber cum scholiis antiquis edidit, Otto Jahn (Hildesheim: Georg Olms Verlagsbuchhandlung, 1967), p. 6.
13   Nadler, however, one should note, attributes the fictitious place of publication to an error in work's publication history. See N II, p. 383.
14   See *HH* II, p. 11.

the monster (i.e., the ideology of the Enlightenment) and free two of his friends, two individuals, who, like Odysseus' companions, have been devoured by it, i.e., who have unwittingly been drawn into and assimilated by the ideology of the age.

The first dedication is thus a ruse: Hamann offers the public a treatise on Socrates in order to drive away its boredom, to amuse its insatiable, encyclopedic curiosity, knowing all the while that it will not be able to digest his little offering, since it does not accord with the tastes and prejudices of the time. Yet all of this is as is intended. Indeed, the *Socratic Memorabilia* is meant precisely to be an emetic: both for Kant and Berens, and for the public, which he hopes will cough up his friends who have been consumed by the service of its vanity. (Therein lies the Christian existential motivation of the work and its importance as a model to Kierkegaard.) If, therefore, Hamann mocks the public, he does so in the voice of a prophet out of contempt for a monstrous idol-ology, which has claimed the individuality of two of his friends. As he puts it in the opening of his dedication:

> *You* make a name for yourself, and need no proof of *your* existence; *You* find faith, and do no miracles to merit it; *You* receive honor, and have neither any conception or feeling of it. *We know that no idols in the world exist.* Nor are *You* a man; but of necessity *You* are [fashioned in] a human image, which superstition has made into a god. *You* are not wanting for eyes and ears, but they neither see nor hear; and the artificial eye that *You* make, and the artificial ear that you plant, are, like *Your* own, blind and deaf (Prov. 9: 13). *You* have to know everything, and learn nothing; *You* have to judge everything, and understand nothing; you learn constantly, [but] can never come to the knowledge of the truth (2 Tim. 3: 7); *You* are dreaming [*dichtest*], have work to do, are abroad, or per-haps you are sleeping when *Your* priests loudly call out [to you], and *You* are expected to answer them and the one mocking them with fire. Sacrifices are brought to *You* on a daily basis, which others consume on *Your* account, in order to make *Your* existence seem probable in view of *Your* heavy diet. As loathsome as *You* are, *You* nevertheless endear yourself to all, so long, that is, that one does not appear before *You* empty-handed. I throw myself like the philosopher at the hearing feet of a tyrant. My gift consists in nothing but little cakes from which a god like *You* once *burst*. Leave it, there-fore, for a pair of *Your* devotees, whom, by means of these pills, I wish to purify from the service of *Your* vanity.[15]

The point, then, of the *Socratic Memorabilia,* next to providing an apology for Hamann's faith, is to free Kant and Berens from their unwitting devotion to a stupid, insensate idol, in this case, the "enlightened," but nevertheless myopic ("one-eyed") public, which commands their allegiance and consumes their offerings in return for its approbation and applause – be the offerings, in Kant's case, public lectures or published works, or, in Berens's case, his labor to manufacture greater wealth for the merchant class. As for the allusions to Elijah and Daniel, they make clear that Hamann understands himself in similar terms: he is a prophet contending with an idol, a false "god," and a widespread cult of false prophets, the *Aufklärer,* among

---

[15] N II, p. 59. The first reference is to 1 Corinthians 8: 4, where Paul quotes an unknown source, saying "we know that 'no idol in the world really exist.'" The second is to 1 Kgs. 18: 27ff., where Elijah is engaged with the prophets of Baal. The third is to the philosopher Aristippus, who had pleaded for something from the tyrant Dionysius, was rejected, subsequently subjected himself to the ridicule of a bystander by throwing himself at the tyrant's feet, and uttered the comical reply: "Do not blame me; blame Dionysius who has ears in his feet" (See *HH* II, p. 68). The fourth refers to the apocryphal book, *Bel and the Dragon,* where Daniel "took pitch, fat, and hair, and boiled them together and made cakes, which he fed to the dragon. The dragon ate them and burst open. And Daniel said, 'See what you have been worshipping!'" (v. 27).

whom he numbers his friends as two unwitting devotees. In any event, in Hamann's view, the Enlightenment, far from being purely rational, is itself a kind of religious cult, with its own priests, dogmas, slogans, and daily communicants who feed at the altar of reason.[16] As for the allusion to Daniel bursting the dragon with an offering of "pitch, fat, and hair," it corresponds to Odysseus' offering to the Cyclops. Finally, as for the comical reference to Aristippus throwing himself at the "hearing" feet of Dionysius, the tyrant – not to mention Daniel's lampooning of the Babylonian "gods" – one sees here both Hamann's own sense of humor and his conviction that Christian humor is the appropriate response to the fundamentally ludicrous nature of idolatry, however refined and "rational" its permutations may be.

FROM SOCRATIC IRONY TO CHRISTIAN HUMOR

The second dedication, "to the two," begins with another epigraph, now from Sophocles' *Electra*: " – It is a small offering, to be sure, but all that I have" (σμικρα μεν ταδ᾽, αλλ᾽ ομως ἁ ᾽χω).[17] Along with the double dedication, this offering carries a double intention: just as Hamann hopes to burst the idol, i.e., to deconstruct the ideology of the Enlightenment, he also hopes to "purify" his friends from the "service" of its "vanity." Hamann could not be sure, of course, whether Kant and Berens would take his "medicine" (one will recall that he conceived of his texts as therapeutic devices along the lines of his father's occupation, i.e., as "little tubs" in which to give his contemporaries a much needed metacritical bath). Nevertheless, he hoped that he could appeal to their friendship, and so the second dedication begins with an elliptical allusion to the friendship between Alexander and Aristotle: "The public in Greece read the memorabilia of Aristotle on the natural history of animals, and Alexander understood them. Where a common reader might see nothing but *mold,* the feeling of friendship, gentlemen, might help you to discover a little microscopic forest in these pages."[18]

Here again we see that the *Socratic Memorabilia* is not really for the public at all, but for "the two," whose friendship might help them to see that there is more going on here than meets the eye. Indeed, though the work may strike them as "nothing but *mold,*" like a microscope their friendship will magnify miniature worlds of meaning that the public, not knowing the personal circumstances of the work's composition, will neither see nor understand.[19] In any case, Hamann means to say that the *Socratic Memorabilia* is a far more intricate text than one might at first think,

---

[16] Cf. *HH* II, pp. 63f.

[17] N II, p. 61.

[18] Ibid. The reference to Alexander and Aristotle derives from Bacon (*De dignitate et augmentis scientiarum*, 1623), who seems to have been slightly mistaken. In the classical sources, it seems that Alexander expressed his displeasure at his teacher for having disseminated among the people, not his history of the animals (περὶ τὰ ζῷα ἱστορίαα), but his *Metaphysics*. See *HH* II, p. 72.

[19] In this respect, the *Socratic Memorabilia*, and Hamann's "authorship" generally, may formally be considered kind of "mystery writing," which cannot be understood apart from a secret initiation into the peculiar interpersonal circumstances that occasioned it. To this extent it is patterned upon the "mystery writing" of God himself (as he saw it in Scripture and creation), whose meaning is "hidden from the wise and learned," i.e., the *Aufklärer*, "but revealed to little children" (Matt. 11: 25). Accordingly, the same hermeneutics that arose out the London Writings is at work here. As Hamann later puts it with regard to the style of Scripture, which he imitates: "If the divine style elects the foolish – the trivial – the base – in order to put to shame the strength and ingenuity of all profane authors: then eyes that are illumined, inspired, armed with the jealousy of a friend, a confidant, a lover are required to recognize in such disguise the beams of heavenly glory" (N II, p. 171.).

containing multiple layers of microscopic meaning, and that friendship is the hermeneutical key to understanding it – just as a sympathy which comes from the Holy Spirit is the key to understanding Scripture.

That being said, just as profounder understanding of Scripture occasionally requires that one penetrate the rough exterior of the letter to discover the *sensus spiritualis* it contains, Hamann suggests that understanding his text will similarly require that one penetrate the thick irony in which it is veiled: "I have written about Socrates in a Socratic manner. *Analogy* was the soul of his inferences, and he gave them *irony* for a body. Uncertainty and confidence may be as characteristic of me as they will; here, though, they must be considered aesthetic imitations."[20] What Hamann means by analogy here is essentially the art of drawing comparisons, of which we have already seen several examples, most centrally the example of Socrates himself as a "type" of Christ, and Socrates' teachings as "analogous" to the teachings of Paul. What he means by irony, however, is more complex. On the one hand, it refers to Socrates' art of questioning (from εἴρομαι); on the other hand, it refers to the art of dissembling (from εἴρων, a dissembler), as when one seems to mean one thing, but means precisely the opposite. And it is in this sense, above all, that the *Socratic Memorabilia* is ironic, given that Hamann clothes himself in the figure of the "rational" and "learned" Socrates only to remind the *Aufklärer* of Socrates' professed *ignorance*.

At the same time, it is important to note that Hamann indulges in irony because in his view Christianity not only commends irony, but is *essentially* ironic. This is true, for example, at some level, of the Lutheran doctrine of *simul iustus et peccator*. It is also true inasmuch as, for Hamann, God appears throughout the economy of salvation *sub contrario,* as is especially manifest in the Cross (see 1 Cor. 1: 18ff.; 2 Cor. 5: 21). For here worldly wisdom is shockingly contradicted, even "made foolish," since everything is the opposite of what it seems to be and – for a pagan sensibility, like Nietzsche's – is supposed to be. For here "folly is wisdom," "weakness is strength," "humility is glory," "the least is greatest," to which one could add, "the broken makes whole," etc. Indeed, from Hamann's perspective, the entire economy of salvation could be said to be ironic – even humorous – to the extent that the "gods" of the world are "outwitted."[21] And for him this is especially true of the devil, whose own words are turned against him when, in the first unwitting prophesy, he tells Adam and Eve, whom he intends permanently to corrupt, that they will be "like God" (Gen. 3: 5), which is precisely what happens to their descendents in Christ, who are made "participants in the divine nature" (2 Pet. 1: 4).[22] All of which is famously summed up by Augustine in the ironic phrase *felix culpa*. Thus Hamann says, "The Christian needs irony in order to humiliate the devil. This figure was the first in Paul's rhetoric; and with this figure God conducted our first parents out of paradise; not in order to mock them, but their tempter."[23] Another example of irony he finds in Scripture is David's slaying of Goliath *with his own sword* (1 Sam. 18:

---

[20] N II, p. 61.

[21] See ZH I, pp. 344f.

[22] Of course, the way to deification is not that prescribed by the devil and taken by Adam and Eve, an attempted seizing of divinity through disobedience, but rather the way of Christ, "who did not think equality with God something to be grasped at" (Phil. 2: 6), and who thereby shows the way to deification (cf. John 10: 34f.) for all who would follow him (Phil. 2: 7–11).

[23] ZH I, p. 339.

50–1), which is a defining rhetorical device of Hamann's publications. And, as we have already seen, he clearly associates irony with the prophets: "the irony that one finds among the children of unbelief seems weak to me compared to the use the prophets make of it."[24] In any case, for Hamann, it is clear that Socratic irony (ignorance = wisdom) is fulfilled in Christian irony (the folly of the Cross = divine wisdom). And it is in this ultimate sense that analogy was the "soul" of Socrates' inferences.

The rest of the dedication concerns the difference between Hamann's portrait of Socrates and those of Xenophon and Plato, who treat Socrates, respectively, with a "superstitious" and "enthusiastic" reverence. Indeed, for Hamann, they clothed Socrates with a beauty inappropriate to his peculiar appearance and manner of expression: "In comparison with that of *Xenophon* and *Plato,* Socrates' style might have seemed wrought by the chisel of a sculptor, and his manner of writing would perhaps have been more plastic than *picturesque.*"[25] By contrast, Hamann suggests that his "mimic" work is a more faithful representation, given that it does not follow the "straightforward" approaches of Xenophon and Plato, but instead seeks to reproduce Socrates' own indirect style of communication: "It would have been easiest for me to approximate these *pagans* more closely in their straightforwardness."[26] In demonstration of his own indirect method, Hamann then makes an oblique reference to two contemporary English authors, Henry St John Viscount Bolingbroke and Shaftesbury, which provides a further clue to his intentions: "But I have had to content myself with borrowing for the veil of my religion that which a patriotic *St. John* [i.e., Bolingbroke] and a Platonic *Shaftesbury* have woven, respectively, for their unbelief and misguided faith."[27] In other words, whereas Bolingbroke and Shaftesbury had to dissemble their irreligion, their apostasy from orthodox Christianity, Hamann feels compelled to do the opposite, namely, conceal his traditional faith in an age of unbelief.

Hamann then concludes with a word of caution, telling "the two" that "Socrates was no average critic," as if to say that, if they want to understand the meaning of Hamann's text, they would do well to follow Socrates' example, who was an admirable reader of the similarly unsystematic and famously obscure writings of Heraclitus:

> He distinguished in the writings of Heraclitus between what he understood and what he did not understand, and drew a very proper and modest inference from the comprehensible to the incomprehensible. On this occasion Socrates spoke of *readers* who could *swim.* A confluence of ideas and sensations in that living *elegy* of a philosopher made his maxims into a group of small islands, lacking the *bridges* and ferries of method that would have established a community among them.[28]

Hamann's description of the writings of Heraclitus is, of course, an elliptical way of describing his own style and the kind of readers he requires: readers who will be able to make the connections on their own. Thus, Ernst Jünger speaks of Hamann as thinking "in archipelagos with submarine connections."[29] But this should not lead one to think

---

[24] ZH II, p. 23.

[25] N II, p. 80.

[26] N II, p. 61.

[27] Ibid. See *SM*, p. 192, and *HRM*, p. 402.

[28] N II, p. 61.

[29] Ernst Jünger, *Blätter und Steine*, 3rd edn. (Hamburg: Hanseatische Verlagsanstalt, 1942), Aphorism no. 87, quoted in *SM*, p. 74.

that Hamann was disorganized or incapable of systematic expression (though he seems to suggest as much in his early autobiography). On the contrary, following the example of Socrates, he purposely leaves the connections up to his readers in order not to interfere with their reflections, but maieutically to assist them in their labor of understanding. As he put it in a letter to Kant around this time, "My mimic style is governed by a stricter logic and closer connections than in the concepts of livelier minds."[30]

TOWARD A PHILOSOPHY OF HISTORY

If ever an author began *in medias res,* forcing his readers to swim, it was Hamann, and his so-called "introduction" is no different. It begins with an obscure anecdote, which ostensibly has something to do with the history of philosophy, about Peter the Great falling at the feet of a statue of Richelieu and offering "the dumb stone half of his vast kingdom":

> The history of philosophy has suffered a fate like that of the statue of the French minister of state. A great artist showed what his chisel could do with it; a monarch, the *name* of an entire century, covered the expenses for it and admired the creation of his subject; the Scythian, on the other hand, who traveled in his trade and, like Noah or the Galilean of the visionary Julian, became a *carpenter* in order to be the God of his people – this Scythian indulged in a weakness, the memory of which alone could immortalize him. He ran to the marble and generously offered the dumb stone half of his vast kingdom, if only he would teach him how to rule the other half. Should our history become mythology, this embracing of a lifeless teacher, who selflessly performed wonders of fulfillment, will be transfigured into a fairytale that will resemble the relics of Pygmalion's life. At some point beyond reckoning, the *creator of his people,* in the language of our wit, will have to be understood just as poetically as a *sculptor of his wife.*[31]

Now we know why Hamann requires "readers who can swim": not only is this passage full of puzzling allusions; it is initially unclear, what, if anything, they have to do with the history of philosophy. If, however, after no small amount of exegetical labor, one makes the "submarine" connections, it begins to become clear that Hamann is elliptically criticizing what his contemporaries have made of the history of philosophy. For, like Girardon's statue of Richelieu, they have turned the living testament of history, which Hamann saw as the unfolding drama of God's self-communication *to* human beings *through* human beings, into a mute, lifeless artifact – an idol fit to adorn the "temple of learning," but unable to convey true wisdom, because it is used more than anything as a means to display their own learning, just as Girardon's statue is a demonstration of the artist's skill. When, therefore, Hamann's refers to "our history becoming mythology," he would seem to be saying that his contemporaries threaten to turn history into a merely poetic construction, like Pygmalion's wife, something refashioned according to their own tastes and prejudices, without any sense of the meaning of history *qua* revelation. As he puts it,

> Truly, there is an idol in the temple of learning, which bears beneath its image an inscription to the *history of philosophy*; and one that has not lacked high priests and Levites. *Stanley* and *Brucker* have given us colossi that are just as strange and incomplete as the image of beauty that a Greek composed from the charming qualities of all the beautiful maidens, whose impressions provided him with a purpose and an occasion.

---

[30] ZH I, p. 378 (O'Flaherty's translation); see also N IV, p. 423.
[31] N II, p. 62.

They are always greatly admired and *sought* by *learned* connoisseurs of the arts, who regard them as masterpieces; sensible people, on the other hand, either silently ridicule them as fantastic growths and chimeras or pass the time by parodying them in theatrical sketches.[32]

To be sure, many politically-minded Enlighteners, would-be "creators of their people," have been impressed by these "fantastic" works, and like Peter the Great, have turned to them as oracles for their grand cosmo-political programs; and it is along these lines that they appeal to Socrates as a reformer and icon of reason in order to gain a certain historical credibility. But at the end of the day, Hamann suggests, these histories are as lifeless and incommunicative as the statue made by Pygmalion, who fell in love with his own creation; they are chimerical compositions, bizarre reflections of the time, that do not reveal history for what it is, i.e., a drama of divine self-communication, but obscure it. What is needed, therefore, is not a "colossal" multi-volume *history of philosophy* like those produced by Stanley and Brucker – who are no more able to interpret their colossi than the diviners of Babylon are able to interpret the colossus of Nebuchadnezzar's dream (Dan. 2) – but a *philosophy of history* that would open our eyes to what the *mystery* of history *reveals*.

From the foregoing we may thus draw two basic conclusions. First, that for Hamann, the study of history, like the study of Scripture, is a hermeneutical science; in other words, history is significant, it reveals something, and as such stands in need of interpretation – but not a strictly rational interpretation, which would foreclose the possibility of it revealing something *more* than reason. Rather, here again, as with Scripture, the best hermeneutics will be one that shares in the genius of the Holy Spirit. Second, if all of history is significant, paganism too, however obscurely, will bear traces of God's self-revelation. Thus the significance of history turns out to be both profounder than reason alone can fathom (against secular historiography) and broader than a narrow fundamentalism would expect. As Hamann puts it,

> Just as Caesar sheds tears at the statue of the Macedonian youth, and the latter, [standing] at the grave of Achilles, jealously calls to mind a herald of glory like that of the blind *Minnesänger*: so too an Erasmus bends his knee in jest before the saintly Socrates, and the Hellenistic muse of our von Bar is compelled to disturb the comical shade of a *Thomas Diafoirus,* in order to preach to us the subterranean truth: that there have been godly men [*göttliche Menschen*] among the pagans; that we should not despise the cloud of these witnesses; that heaven anointed them to be its messengers and translators; and that they were consecrated precisely to that vocation among their peoples which the prophets had among the Jews.[33]

Having issued his call for a genuine philosophy of history, Hamann proceeds to suggest that, in this respect, the methods of modern science will be of no avail. As he puts it, in one of his many aphorisms, "Just as nature is given to us to open our eyes,

---

[32] N II, p. 62. References are to Thomas Stanley (1625–78), who produced a four-volume *History of Philosophy* (1655–62), and to Johann Brucker (1696–1770), a Wolffian who produced a five-volume *Historia critica philosophiae a mundi incunabilis ad nostrum usque aetatem deducta* (1742–4). The other reference is to the famous Greek painter, Zeuxis, whose "Helen," commissioned by the city of Croton, was a composite of the traits of five beautiful maidens. See *SM*, pp. 114–15.

[33] N II, p. 64. References are to Erasmus who, upon reading and admiring Socrates' last words, is supposed to have exclaimed in jest, "holy Socrates, pray for us!"; to Georg Ludwig von Bar (1702–67), a Greco-Francophile German poet, who wrote in French, and among his works composed a poem in the voice of Thomas Diafoirus, a ridiculous character from Molière's *Malade imaginaire*, who, in Bar's poem praises the great pagans of Greece and Rome as "divine men" whom heaven chose to be its "translators," like the prophets among the Jews. See *HH* II, p. 95.

so history is given to open our ears," adding, "To analyze a body and an event down to its primary elements means to want to catch sight of God's invisible nature, his eternal power and divinity."[34] In other words, if Hamann criticized modern secular historiography for being deaf to history, i.e., deaf to the Logos who speaks through it, here he criticizes the analytic method of modern science for presuming to penetrate the secrets of nature and history without reverence for God's "eternal power and divinity" (see Rom. 1: 20). His point is not to denigrate modern science, however, but to say that its method, not content with things as they appear to the senses, fails to perceive God's self-revelation through them. Indeed, it treats the phenomena as untruth (as Nietzsche too points out in his critique of the concept of "appearance"); thus, as the grand result of its search for a bare super-sensible truth, it will eventually arrive at nothing at all. Hamann expresses something along these lines to Kant in the following parable, "Truth did not allow herself to be approached too closely by highway bandits; she wore layer after layer of clothing so that one doubted one would ever find her body. How terrified they were when they had their way and saw before themselves that terrifying ghost, the truth."[35]

Hamann's point, in other words, is that if one dispenses with nature, history, and God's self-revelation through them, on the way to some bare metaphysical truth, the result will be, as Hamann's writings increasingly predict, a spectral reality of ghostly landscapes (Descartes), insular illusions (Kant), and, ultimately, ontological nihilism (Heidegger). As a result, once the sensible world comes to seem illusory, because it no longer "speaks," because it is no longer seen as a divine revelation, any reality it may possess comes to depend increasingly upon the ability of the modern subject poetically to "back it up." As Hamann puts it, "Whoever does not believe Moses and the prophets ... will always be a poet against his knowledge and will, like *Buffon* on the history of creation and *Montesquieu* on the history of the Roman empire."[36] In other words, the Logos of creation, no longer perceived by faith, is reduced to the *mythos* of our making. More than a century later, Nietzsche will say much the same thing, though in his case fully embracing the poetic nihilism the death of God entails. As he dramatically puts it, "All possible superstitions are posited into the void."[37]

A further problem besetting secular historiography, as Hamann sees it, in spite of the colossal histories already mentioned, is the question of completeness. In other words, in what sense can modern historiography be called a science if it is based upon a merely fragmentary record of the past, if its very object is fundamentally incomplete? And what, for that matter, are we to make of the fact that so many religious texts, like those of the third-century Gnostics, have been lost? This last question may be vexing to those looking for evidence of "alternative Christianities," but Hamann, interestingly enough, was blithely unconcerned by it. For if *all* things are governed by divine providence, including the hairs on our heads, then this certainly applies to the collection and tradition of a canon of Scripture. Indeed, if the Holy Spirit is able to call to mind all that is necessary (John 14: 26), then a Christian has no cause to fret over what of history has been lost or forgotten:

> If no young sparrow falls to the ground without our God, then no [literary] monument of ancient times has been lost that we should lament. Should his providence not extend

---

[34] N II, p. 64.
[35] ZH I, p. 381.
[36] N II, p. 64.
[37] See Nietzsche, "Nachgelassene Fragmente," in *Kritische Studienausgabe,* ed. G. Coli and M. Montinari (Berlin: de Gruyter, 1988), vol. 7, p. 466.

to writings, since He Himself became an author, and since the Spirit of God was so exact as to record the value of those first forbidden books, which a pious zeal, on behalf of our religion, committed to the fire? We admire Pompey for disposing of the writings of his enemy, Sertorius, and consider this to be a prudent and noble action; why then should we not admire the Lord for allowing the writings of a Celsus to perish? It is not without reason, then, when I say that, regarding all the books that should be of any concern to us, God showed at least as much care as Caesar did for the inscribed scroll when he jumped into the sea, or Paul did for his parchment at Troas (2 Tim. 4: 13).[38]

Such, presumably, would have been Hamann's response to the quest for a lost canon of Gnostic texts and "gospels": had they been of any profound spiritual significance or provided any necessary supplement to those we already possess, the Holy Spirit would have preserved them as jealously as the far older canonical gospels and New Testament epistles. Indeed, according to this exalted view of divine sovereignty, any zealous destruction of Gnostic texts on the part of the early Church, if it ever occurred, would have to be reckoned a judgment of providence.

But what, then, according to Hamann, is one to make of the historical fragments that remain? In any case, it is clear that for him one should not follow the example of modern historians, who know ever so many facts and record them ever so dutifully, but do not have the slightest idea of what their larger significance might be. And it is in this connection that Hamann makes a comical allusion to the talents of a legendary "artist" who managed after some practice to throw a lentil through the eye of a needle:

> For the artist who succeeded in throwing a lentil through the eye of a needle, was not a bushel of lentils enough to practice the skill he acquired? One would like to put this question to all persons of learning who do not know what to do with the works of the ancients any more than our artist knew what to do with his lentils. If we had more than what time has seen fit to give us, we ourselves would be compelled to throw our cargoes overboard, to set fire to our libraries, or to do what the Dutch do with their spices.[39]

The point of this passage, which Nietzsche, incidentally, cites approvingly, is this: modern historians have no better sense of the purpose of history, i.e., what to do with so many facts, than the legendary artist did with his lentils.[40] Nor would a more extensive knowledge of the past make any difference. For the problem is that no one has fundamentally addressed the question of history as a matter of philosophy; in other words, no one has come up with a satisfactory *philosophy of history*. This is not to say that the *Aufklärer* did not have a doctrine of history, which, of course, they did: namely, as progress, as an emergence out of the darkness of ignorance and superstition into the light of reason, which they (as proto-Hegelians) uniquely

---

[38] N II, p. 64. Apparently, at some point in the siege of Alexandria, Caesar was forced to abandon ship and leapt into the sea, swimming with one hand and holding important military papers above water in the other. See *HH* II, p. 99.

[39] N II, p. 65. In order better to control market value in their trade, the Dutch were wont to dump excess spices overboard.

[40] Nietzsche, in *Die Philosophie im tragischen Zeitalter der Griechen* (1873), says: "Rarely does the human race produce a good book in which the battle song of truth, the song of philosophical heroism, is intoned with intrepid freedom – and, as often happens, these books pass away rather quickly. Be that as it may, we should not complain about this, but rather allow ourselves to hear the expeditious words of consolation, which Hamann directs to those persons of learning who complain about lost works. For the artist who succeeded in throwing a lentil through the eye of a needle, was not a bushel of lentils enough to practice the skill he acquired? One would like to put this question to all intellectuals who do not know what to do with the works of the ancients any more than our artist knew what to do with his lentils" (my translation). See *KSA*, vol. 1, p. 811.

possessed (in a secular parody of Col. 1: 13). It was also in the name of their doctrine of progress that history's "irrational" elements, e.g., visions, oracles, in short, any special miracles or unusual revelations, were treated as nothing but mythology and superstition, once again revealing the Enlightenment's penchant for pure secularism.[41]

From Hamann's perspective, however, this is precisely why the Enlightenment's conception of history is so inadequate: not only does it run roughshod over anything that does not fit the mold of progress, anything that an eighteenth-century person cannot understand – supernatural oracles, visions, miracles, special revelations – it mistakenly assumes that *reason* is the measure of all things, including the measure of history itself (again anticipating Hegel). Thus Hamann laments the absence of a genuine philosophy of history, of the kind the late Schelling, in many ways inspired by Hamann, variously attempted, which would realize that history is a revelation of something *more* than reason and therefore requires *more* than reason, namely, faith – faith that something super-rational has in fact been revealed – as the principle and *sine qua non* of its interpretation:

> I am amazed that, as of yet, no one has ventured to do as much for history as *Bacon* has done for physics. *Bolingbroke* advises his student to study ancient history as one would study the pagan doctrine of the gods or a lexicon of poetry. But perhaps all of history is more mythology than this philosopher thinks, and like nature a sealed book, a concealed witness, a riddle that will not be solved unless we plow with another heifer than our reason.[42]

The importance of Hamann's call for a philosophy of history at this juncture in the history of ideas almost goes without saying, preparing the way for more serious philosophical consideration of history qua revelation (even if in Hegel the revelation turns out to be wholly rational). It also represents a watershed moment in our understanding of history: between a Christian understanding of history as the "age" between fall and *eschaton* (according to the original meaning of secular as "*saeculum*") and a modern secular view of history as so many univocal instances of "progress as such."[43] More concretely, the choice is between a multi-dimensional Christian understanding of history as a "diachronic chain of allusion and reference,"[44] i.e., as an extended prophecy played out between "type" and "fulfillment," with all the shadows and excesses of meaning that this implies, and a uni-dimensional secular view of history, which has no fulfillment but the social and technological progress that every subsequent moment supposedly brings (as an advance upon the one preceding it). In short, the choice is between a Christian view of history as a kind of unfinished divine poem, whose meaning can be grasped only in part, and a secular

---

[41] As Hamann puts it, "The transmission of a divine oracle says as little to a philosopher of modern taste as [would] the appearance of a comet. In his opinion, as soon as it comes to oracles, apparitions, dreams, and similar meteors [i.e., omens], [of the kind one finds] in the book handed down to us by that most foolish of people and in the remnants of the Greeks and Romans, one should either excise these fairy tales of our children and wet nurses (since all past centuries are, compared to our present one, but children and wet nurses in the art of *experience* and *thought*) or admire them the way one admires the literary flourishes of our Alpine poets" (N II, p. 69).

[42] N II, p. 65. Hamann has in mind here Bolingbroke's *Letters on the Study and Use of History* (1738; 2nd edition, 1752). See *HH* II, p. 100.

[43] See John Milbank, *Theology and Social Theory: Beyond Secular Reason* (Oxford: Blackwell, 1990), pp. 9ff. From a Christian perspective, therefore, the word "secular" in modern usage should really be placed in quotation marks, since a corruption of its original meaning has occurred.

[44] See Milbank, *The Word Made Strange: Theology, Language, Culture* (Oxford: Blackwell, 1997), pp. 278f.

view of history as a series of discrete moments which, having no part to play in any larger poem or unfolding drama, expressing nothing but the banality of "progress as such," are equally meaningful and meaningless.

In any case, given Hamann's prophetic view of history, it is now clear why he does not treat Socrates merely as a figure of the past, whose significance is limited to the culture of ancient Greece. Still less does he view him as the *Aufklärer*, the "modern-day Athenians," do: "If they seriously believe in Socrates, then his sayings are witnesses against them. These new Athenians are the progeny of his accusers and the mixers of the poison [that killed him], and even more fatuous slanders and atrocious murderers than their fathers."[45] Rather, he views him, as he views all of history, in the light of faith, which reveals a prophetic dimension and a prophetic significance to Socrates' life that is unavailable to reason alone.

A PROPAEDEUTIC TO REAL ENLIGHTENMENT

As we have already seen, for Hamann the prophetic dimensions of Socrates' life and thought include, among other things, his ignorance, his tutelary spirit, and his unjust death, all of which Hamann sees as pointing to Christianity. At the same time, however, Socrates continues to be a mask for Hamann himself in his dealings with Kant and Berens. For example, Hamann mentions an early benefactor of Socrates named Crito, who, seeing promise in the young man, in the best of intentions procured a series of Sophists to be his tutors. Of course, given what we know about Socrates' later attitude toward the Sophists, the effort plainly had an unintended result. As Hamann puts it, "The succession of men and women assigned to Socrates to be his teachers, and whom Crito doubtless had to pay off, is impressive enough; yet Socrates remained *ignorant*."[46] Hamann's point in including this biographical detail is clear: Crito is the wealthy benefactor Berens; Socrates is the promising young Hamann; and Kant is one of the Sophists who has been assigned to Hamann's re-education program. In other words, we see here a perfect example of Hamann's use of "metaschematism," where his interlocutors are represented parabolically in a different light – in the way that David appears, to dramatic effect, in Nathan's parable in 2 Samuel 12.

Doubtless, "the two" would not have taken kindly to the comparison; but Hamann no sooner acknowledges the insult than he asks for their forgiveness, for he, more than they, will have to bear the burden of his ignorance: "The impertinent confession this implied was to a certain extent an insult, but one seems to have forgiven the upright client and candidate for it since he himself was the one most burdened by it."[47] In other words, Hamann foresees that his commitment to Christian orthodoxy and his skepticism toward the Enlightenment will be ill-received; but he takes heart that this is precisely how Socrates' contemporaries reacted to him on account of his professed ignorance:

> The opinion of Socrates can be reduced to these harsh tones, when he said to the Sophists, the intellectuals of his time: I know nothing. Thus it came about that these words were a thorn in their eyes and a scourge on their backs. All Socrates' *intuitions*,

[45] N II, p. 67.
[46] N II, p. 70.
[47] N II, p. 70.

which were nothing but the *expectorations* and *secretions* of his *ignorance*, seemed as frightening to them as the hair on the head of the Medusa, the navel of the Aegis.[48]

In other words, far from confirming his interlocutors in their established conceptions, Socrates' ignorance, like an unsolicited oracle of introspection, was precisely what most confounded them. Thus Hamann concludes that, ironically, far from being the historical champion of rationalism, few thinkers would have been more dreadful to the *Aufklärer*, the modern-day Athenians, than Socrates. Hamann's profounder point, however, is that Socrates' profession of ignorance was not a guise adopted in order simply to infuriate the Athenians (as Nietzsche's reading of him suggests), but a kind of feeling by which he himself was profoundly affected. Indeed, according to Hamann, it was the source of Socrates' teaching and preternatural wisdom, and can be fathomed only in the way that one fathoms a particular malady by having suffered from it oneself:

> Socrates seems to have talked as much about his ignorance as a hypochondriac about his imagined illness. Just as one must know this malady in order to understand a hypochondriac and make sense of him, so too a sympathy with ignorance would seem to be required in order to have a conception of Socratic ignorance.[49]

Yet it is precisely this sympathy with ignorance that the *Aufklärer*, given their thirst for "encyclopedic" knowledge (the kind of knowledge that Hamann compares to the dimwitted Cyclops),[50] are unable to fathom or understand. For they are proud, unwilling to humble themselves and make a similar confession, namely, that, at the end of the day, for all the volumes of the *Encyclopédie*, they know next to nothing. Therein lies the comical element. This is also why they must forgo any claims to being Socrates' true, modern-day disciples. To be sure, from their own "enlightened" perspective, wisdom consisted in the recognition of one's autonomy as a rational agent – *sapere aude!* ("dare to think for yourself!") Kant will later say, and, by implication, "have every bit of confidence in your own opinions." For Socrates, on the other hand, it consisted in precisely the opposite. And Hamann finds it particularly noteworthy that this *reversal* of conventional wisdom should have been anticipated by the oracle of Apollo at Delphi:

> *Know thyself!* the door of that famous temple proclaimed to all who entered to offer a sacrifice to the god of wisdom and to consult him concerning their trivial affairs. Everyone read, admired, and knew this saying *by heart*. They wore it upon their foreheads like the stone in which it was engraved, without comprehending the meaning of it. The god doubtless laughed behind his golden beard when, during the time of Socrates, the ticklish [question] was put to him as to who among all those living at the time was the wisest. *Sophocles* and *Euripides* would never have become such great models for the theater were it not for their art of analyzing the human heart. But *Socrates* surpassed them both in wisdom since he had come further in self-knowledge than they had, and knew that he knew nothing.[51]

In other words, the wise know that they know nothing. Such is the irony, the divine joke, at the origin of western philosophy: the god laughs because Socrates, though

---

[48] N II, p. 73.
[49] N II, p. 70.
[50] Cf. N III, pp. 72f.; Nadler's note under "encyclisch" (N VI, p. 113).
[51] N II, p. 71.

he professed to be ignorant, was in fact the wisest of all. And Hamann laughs too, given that this judgment, though it appears foolish, in fact makes foolish and puts to shame all the pompous erudition and conventional wisdom of the world (see 1 Cor. 1: 18ff.). Moreover, Hamann relishes not only the irony, but that one sees here the trumping of reason by prophecy, which is precisely the point of his own prophetic authorship: that there are some things that reason alone is too dumb, too dimwitted, too uninspired, indeed too *unenlightened* to understand, but are nonetheless essential to what it means to be a human being.

But if Hamann delights in the god's comical judgment, for him self-knowledge remains a profoundly serious matter. As he puts it to Kant around this time, trying, it would seem, to convey something of the depths of his conversion experience, "Self-knowledge is the most difficult and the highest, the easiest and the most base natural history, philosophy, and poetry."[52] Similarly, he says, "No amount of aesthetic thaumaturgy suffices to replace an immediate feeling, and nothing but the *descensus ad inferos* [*Höllenfahrt*] of self-knowledge paves the way for our deification."[53] In any event, for Hamann self-knowledge is not a byword; nor can it be defined as an awakening to one's own potential as a rational agent (*à la* Kant). On the contrary, it is a profound sensation which he associates with a kind of rebirth:

> The ignorance of Socrates was *sensation* [*Empfindung*]. Between a sensation and a doctrine, however, there is a greater difference than that between a living animal and its anatomical skeleton. However much the ancient and modern skeptics wrap themselves in the lion's skin of Socratic ignorance, they nevertheless betray themselves by their *voice* and their *ears*. If they know nothing, why does the world need a learned demonstration of it? Their hypocrisy is ludicrous and shameless. Whoever has need of so much acumen and eloquence to convince himself of his ignorance must harbor within his heart a powerful antipathy toward the truth of it.[54]

Thus far Hamann has already indicated one analogical connection between paganism and Christianity, namely, the way in which its irony (seen in Apollo's judgment) points to Christian folly. Now, in view of Socrates' ignorance, understood as a profound feeling or sensation (for which the *Aufklärer* have as little sensibility as the ancient Athenians did), Hamann draws a further analogy between Socrates' ignorance and the Christian virtue of humility. What is most wonderful to Hamann about Socrates' profession of ignorance, however, is that it leads to his *being known* by the god, anticipating yet another teaching of Christianity, as stated by Paul in 1 Corinthians 8: 2–3:

> For the testimony that Socrates gave of his ignorance I know of no more honorable seal and at the same time no better key than the oracle of the great *teacher of the Gentiles*: Ει δε τις δοκει ειδεναι τι ουδεπω ουδεν εγνωκε καθως δει γνωναι˙ Ει δε τις αγαπα ΘΕΟΝ ουτος εγνωται υπ αυτου. 'If anyone thinks that he knows something, he does not yet know as he ought to know. But if a man loves God, he is known by him' – just as Socrates was known by Apollo to be a *wise man*. But as the seed of all our natural wisdom must decay and perish into ignorance, and as from this *death*, from this *nothing*,

---

[52] ZH I, p. 374.
[53] N II, p. 164.
[54] N II, p. 73.

the *life* and *nature* of a higher knowledge must spring forth newly created – thus far the *nose* of a Sophist does not reach.[55]

In other words, the *Aufklärer*, like the Sophists, think they know something. In point of fact, however, they have not yet begun to know as they ought; if they had, they would humble themselves and confess their ignorance like Socrates. Instead, as Hamann sees it, they are proud and, as a result, blind to one of the profoundest revelations of paganism, which coincides with the teaching of the apostle (and also Origen): that true wisdom consists not in *knowing* and knowing how much one knows, but in loving God, humbly confessing one's ignorance (one's sins), and thereby *being known*. All of which accords with the words of the Psalmist, "For though the Lord is high, he regards the lowly; but the haughty he knows from afar" (Ps. 138: 6; see Matt. 7: 23).

The contrast, then, which Hamann would have Kant and Berens consider, is between a worldly way of knowing, which merely "puffs up" (1 Cor. 8: 2) and redounds to the glory of the knowing subject, and a higher, Socratic-Christian way of knowing, which neither grasps acquisitively after knowledge, as paradigmatically represented in (Genesis 3), nor does anything out of "selfish ambition" (Phil. 2: 3), but glories *ironically* in weaknesses and limitations (2 Cor. 12: 9), whereby the intellect is made receptive of divine light and wisdom. Herein, and not in any proud rationalism, lies the true path to enlightenment. Thus Hamann says in a later work that "the true genius knows only his dependence and weakness, or the limits of his gifts."[56] But here again, Hamann points out, the *Aufklärer* fail to follow Socrates' example, even as they boast of being his modern-day disciples:

> The many imitators of Socrates in our age, and the canonical teachers of the public and patron saints of unjustly famous arts and merits, have not yet succeeded in living up to their model in all his lovely shortcomings. Given that they infinitely depart from the testament of his ignorance, one has to marvel at all the inventive readings and glosses of their anti-Socratic demon regarding our master's teachings and virtues as the embellishments of *free* translation; and it is just as dangerous to trust them as to follow them.[57]

Such is the discrepancy between Hamann's Socrates and that of the *Aufklärer*. And along with it comes a radically different estimation of the purpose of reason. For the *Aufklärer* the purpose of reason is to question the authority of tradition in the name of free inquiry, thereby de facto replacing the authority of tradition with that of the autonomous individual, regardless of his or her moral formation. For Hamann, on the other hand, the purpose of reason is precisely to deconstruct all proud knowledge falsely so called, the kind of knowledge which is really *doxa* but nevertheless opposes itself to faith, so that true knowledge can begin: the kind of knowledge that is born of humility and leads to love (1 Cor. 8: 1f.). Indeed, for Hamann it is only through a *suffering* of reason's limitations that philosophy properly begins, having been prepared by a kind of *docta ignorantia* for the light of faith; and to this extent what he proposes as a model of epistemological rebirth follows the same pattern as

---

[55] N II, p. 74.
[56] N II, p. 260.
[57] N II, p. 260.

that laid down for spiritual rebirth in the gospel of John: "Unless a grain of wheat falls to the ground and dies, it remains alone, but if it dies, it bears much fruit" (12:24). In any event, Hamann means to suggest that whereas the way of rational autonomy popularized by the Enlightenment is ultimately dead and *unenlightened,* the way foreshadowed by Socratic ignorance and fulfilled in Christian humility is *fruitful,* because it is alive to the *illuminating* presence of the Holy Spirit.

Such, then, is the irony attending all modern talk of "enlightenment"; and such is the radical misconception of Socrates on the part of the *Aufklärer,* who fail to appreciate not only Socrates' ignorance, but that this ignorance went hand in hand with a kind of inspiration, "as if he, among all the night-owls of his fatherland, was the only one to perch upon the helmet of Minerva."[58] Along these lines Hamann then makes a further typological connection, reminiscent of early Christian apologists, like Justin Martyr, comparing Socrates' tutelary spirit, his *daimon,* to the genius of the Holy Spirit:

> What is it in *Homer* that makes up for his ignorance of the rules of art, which Aristotle invented after him, and what is it in *Shakespeare* that makes up either for his ignorance of these critical laws or his transgression of them? *Genius* is the unanimous answer. Clearly, Socrates could well afford to be ignorant; he had a genius upon whose science he could rely, whom he loved and feared as his god, whose *peace* meant more to him than all the reason of the Egyptians and the Greeks, whose voice he trusted, and whose *wind* (as the experienced quack-doctor Hill has proven to us) can make the empty understanding of a Socrates as fruitful as the womb of a pure virgin.[59]

On the one hand, Hamann anticipates here a theme that he will develop in his *Aesthetica in nuce,* the theme of genius and true creativity, as contrasted with a merely rational approach to nature and the arts, which in his view characterizes the Enlightenment. The one approach is dictated by rational rules; the other, while not antinomian, is guided by genius. On the other hand, what is noteworthy here is that Hamann again enlists Socrates as a witness to the Christian faith, noting not only a connection between the fruitful humility of Socrates and that of Mary, but a further connection between Socrates and Paul: that Socrates' genius, his "god," meant more to him than all reason and provided him with a "peace" that "surpasses all understanding" (Phil. 4:7).

In light of the foregoing typological connections, the main point of the *Socratic Memorabilia* is now clear: Socrates is more of a proto-Christian than a proto-Enlightener; and thus, *vis-à-vis* the *Aufklärer,* Hamann can claim to be the more genuine disciple of Socrates. For just as the *Aufklärer* have failed to appreciate Socrates' ignorance as a type of sensation (adumbrating the feeling or subjective passion of faith), they have also failed to appreciate his undeniably religious devotion to his *daimon* (foreshadowing the guidance of Christians by the Holy Spirit). Moreover, they utterly fail to perceive the point of Socrates' dialectic, which is precisely not to flatter one's sense of autonomy as a rational agent, but, on the contrary, to bring about the recognition of one's epistemological weaknesss and a corresponding sense of dependence (which is precisely the opposite of what Kant will propose twenty-five years later in his 1784 essay). As Hamann puts it, identifying the *Aufklärer* with

---

[58] N II, p. 76.
[59] N II, p. 75. Cf. Phil. 4:7. John Hill (1716?–75): pharmacist, botanist, physician, and writer, who proposed a theory of virgin birth through the effect of the wind. See *SM,* pp. 78f.

the Athenians (as if to say that the *Aufklärer,* far from being Socrates' modern-day disciples, are in fact the modern-day heirs of those who killed him):

> The Athenians were curious. An ignorant person is the best physician for this satyriasis. Like all inquisitive persons, they were inclined to *communicate*; and so they had to go along with being asked questions. But they possessed more the gift of invention and delivery than of retention and judgment; thus Socrates always had opportunity to make up for their lack of memory and judgment, and warn them against frivolity and vanity. In short, Socrates lured his fellow citizens out of the labyrinths of their learned Sophists to a *truth* that *lies in a hidden place,* to a *secret wisdom*, and away from the idol-altars of their devout and politically shrewd priests to the worship of an *unknown God.*[60]

Clearly, Hamann sees himself in a similar light; for just as Socrates stands in relation to the Athenians, he stands in relation to the *Aufklärer*. As Kierkegaard observed, "Hamann's relationship to his contemporaries [parallels] Socrates' [relation] to the Sophists (who could say something about *everything*)."[61] And this comparison applies as much to the method as to the intent of their communications. For just as Socrates' ignorance (and apparently ugly appearance) provoked greater reflection on the part of his interlocutors, so too Hamann's writings, while outwardly having the form of folly and offense, are carefully crafted mirrors of introspection. Furthermore, just as Socrates seeks to lead his interlocutors by way of ignorance to a "secret wisdom" that surpasses rational comprehension, Hamann's aim is that, having similarly brought about a confession of dependence, "the layman would fall on his face, pray to God, and confess that God is truly in us."[62] Therein lies the secret wisdom that is unavailable to proud secularists, precisely because it cannot be found except by way of humility. As the Psalmist says, notably in the context of a confession of guilt, "You desire truth in the inward parts; therefore teach me wisdom in my secret heart" (Ps. 51: 6).

In sum, *vis-à-vis* his contemporaries, Hamann saw himself as a genuinely Christian Socrates – and, as such, as a more genuine disciple of Socrates. Accordingly, his entire authorship was conducted (by way of an explicitly Socratic-Christian dialectic) for the sake of leading his readers to a humble confession of ignorance and dependence, thereby to a genuine form of self-knowledge, and thence to a secret and *mysterious* wisdom inaccessible to the kind of *pro-fane* [sic] secular reason proudly espoused by the *Aufklärer*. Furthermore, as a *Christian* Socrates, he showed that Socrates' life points to Christ, both in his humble appearance and his unjust death, and that his teaching is analogous to and fulfilled in the Christian wisdom of Paul (Acts 17: 22f.; 1 Cor. 8: 2–3). But if this is so, if Socrates may be considered a prophetic figure of Christ and a herald of Christian wisdom, then, Hamann reasons, Socrates deserves to be numbered among the prophets. Indeed, for Hamann, as for many of the early Christian apologists, one may speak in this regard of an analogical community between Jew and Gentile:

> Plato told the Athenians to their faces that Socrates was given to them by the gods in order to convict them of their folly and to encourage them to emulate him in virtue. Should anyone not wish to suffer Socrates among the prophets, one must ask him: *Who is the father of prophets?* and whether our God has not called himself and shown himself to be a *God of the Gentiles?*[63]

60 N II, p. 76.
61 *JP* II 1547 (*Pap.* III B 17).
62 ZH I, pp. 396.
63 N II, pp. 76f.

At the conclusion of the work Hamann then brandishes a sword of ultimate division between himself and the *Aufklärer*, hoping against hope to liberate Kant and Berens from their bondage to the ideology of the age. Should they side with him, he warns, they must be prepared for the offense it will cause; for never was there a servant of truth who did not end up offending the one-eyed Cyclops of the public, as the example of Socrates shows. If, however, they are not fit for the ascetical service of truth, if they lack the courage necessary to break free from the dominant ideology of the age, if they do not wish to participate as prophets in the prophetic testimony of history, then they will perforce have to renounce any similarity to Socrates and content themselves with "licking the plates" of the gods of this world:

> Whoever is not prepared to live on *crumbs* and *alms*, or on *stolen goods*, or to go without everything for the sake of a *sword*, is not fit for the service of truth. May he, earlier rather than later! become a reasonable, useful, well-mannered man of the world, or learn how to bow and lick plates: thus will he insure himself, for the rest of his life, against hunger and thirst, the gallows and the rack. And if it is true that GOD Himself, as we read in the *good confession* that he made before Pilate; if it is true, I say, that God Himself *thus* became a man and *thus* came into the world, *in order that he might testify to the truth*: then no omniscience is needed to foresee that he would not come away from the world as well as Socrates, but would die a more shameful and cruel death than the *parricide of the most Christian king*, Louis the *Beloved*, who is a great-grandchild of Louis the *Great*.[64]

CONVERTING HUME: KNOWLEDGE "BY FAITH ALONE"

There is, then, something novel and subversive in Hamann's reading of Socrates as a forerunner of Christianity: for not only does he deprive the Enlighteners of their favorite champion, but he sets them on a course to embrace the very faith they, in the name of reason and the Socratic spirit, thought they had to reject. What makes the *Socratic Memorabilia* even more subversive and ironic, however, is that Hamann does the same thing with David Hume, the other philosopher with whom the work is principally, albeit briefly, engaged. The most obvious connection between Socrates and Hume is, of course, the ignorance of the one and the skepticism of the other. And yet, as the foregoing would suggest, Hamann is compelled to deny that Hume's skepticism represents a genuine fulfillment of Socratic ignorance. Indeed, he faults the skeptic for hypocrisy and vain insolence, which has little in common with the humility of Socratic ignorance, authentically understood.

Nevertheless, in the context of a critical reception of Hume, he identifies the moment of truth in modern skepticism, which makes it too an unwitting ally of Christianity: namely, that many of the things we take for granted, say, our own existence and the reality of an external world, are *credenda*, i.e., things that in themselves cannot be rationally demonstrated and are therefore, strictly speaking, proposed for our *belief*:

> Our own existence and the existence of all things outside us must be believed and can be made out in no other way. What is more certain than the end of a man's life, and of what truth do we possess a more universal and attested knowledge? Yet no one is so wise as to believe this except one who, as Moses gives us to understand, is [specially]

---

[64] N II, p. 82. As O'Flaherty notes, in January 1757 Robert François Damiens attempted to assassinate Louis XV (*Le Bien-Aimé*) and was tortured for several months before he was finally executed (*SM*, p. 204).

instructed by God himself to realize that he must die. What one believes, therefore, does not have to be proven, and a proposition can be ever so incontrovertibly proven without on this account being believed.[65]

With typical brevity Hamann makes two points here of great consequence. The first is that some things not only require no rational demonstration, but are not even susceptible of it; and this is how it is with our knowledge of the external world. We know it not by reason – in the way that one knows the answer to a syllogism – but by faith. In fact, the more we might try rationally to demonstrate its reality – say, after the manner of Descartes – the more we find that we are strikingly unable to do so, that its very existence (which is something other than its essential structures) eludes our grasp. That is the first point, which highlights not only the *difference* between faith and reason (as distinct modes of knowing), but also the *primacy* of faith with regard to the most basic forms of knowledge. Indeed, for Hamann, reason needs faith, or at least some rudimentary form of faith, in order to "know" anything with any degree of certainty at all.[66] Hamann's second point again highlights the difference between faith and reason in that those things that *can* be demonstrated sufficiently, or which we would never dream of contradicting, do not on this account necessarily elicit our belief. Such is the case, for example, with one's own death: we know that we are mortal, but we tend not to believe it. Thus, according to Hamann, reason is not only generically different from faith, but fundamentally incapable of accounting for it. And given this inability of reason to account for faith, which arises on an entirely different basis, faith is not susceptible to any criticism on the part of it. As he puts it,

> There are proofs of truths that are as worthless as the application that can be made of the truths themselves; indeed, one can believe the proof of a proposition without approving of the proposition itself. The reasons of a *Hume* may be ever so convincing, and the refutations of them based merely on derivative principles [*Lehnsätze*] and doubts; yet faith wins and loses equally, whether one is dealing with the ablest pettifogger or the most honorable attorney. Faith is no work of reason and therefore cannot succumb to any attack by it; for *faith* arises as little from reasons as *tasting and seeing* do.[67]

The historical significance of this statement to someone like Kierkegaard is obvious. Writing in the middle of the Enlightenment, Hamann shows not only that faith is different from reason and irreducible to it, but that it is in no way bound to rational requirements that it be demonstrable or even probable. Furthermore, because faith arises on an entirely different basis from reason, no proof of reason can be brought to bear against it. Thus "faith wins and loses equally" in the face of arguments both for and against it.

But if Hamann hereby secures the legitimacy of faith *vis-à-vis* reason, none of this should lead to the impression that he was an irrationalist, or that he was somehow against reason, or even that he was a fideist, in the way that this is normally understood. For if Hamann is in any sense against reason, he is against only a puritanical

---

[65] N II, p. 73. Deut. 31: 14ff.
[66] See Hamann's letter to Kant, quoted above, "Hume has faith necessary if he should [merely] eat an egg and drink a glass of water" (ZH I, p. 379).
[67] N II, pp. 73f.

form of secular rationality, summed up in the phrase "pure reason," that hypocritically presumes to do without faith. For that matter, one could legitimately regard him as a defender of reason, given his insight that, apart from faith, reason itself and the entire enterprise of human knowledge is ultimately defenseless against skepticism and nihilism. And it is in this sense, in radical epistemological application of Luther's doctrine of salvation, that one may legitimately speak, following John Milbank, of knowledge – and not just salvation – "by faith alone."[68]

KANT, HAMANN, AND THE SO-CALLED *"KINDERPHYSIK* FIASCO"

The brief correspondence that took place during the late fall of 1759 between Kant and Hamann – the one, arguably, the greatest of German philosophers, the other the only serious contender for the title of "the German Socrates" – is doubtless one of the more interesting in the history of German letters. Among the attending circumstances, Kant had recently sent Hamann a copy of his short essay on theodicy, "Versuch einiger Betrachtungen über den Optimismus."[69] And in the meantime Hamann was awaiting the arrival of the first published copies of the *Socratic Memorabilia* in Königsberg. One may presume that Kant had not yet read Hamann's Socratic "apology"; and what he ever made of it we do not know. In any case, their correspondence at this time represents a continuation of their heated dialogue that began when Kant tried to "reconvert" him to the Enlightenment back in July of the same year, having suggested, among other things, that Hamann translate portions of Diderot's *Encyclopédie*, a suggestion Hamann roundly dismissed. Now, several months later, Kant suggested that they collaborate, curiously enough, on a physics book for children. In response Hamann penned three ironic and somewhat bitter "love letters"; and thus began what has come to be known as the "*Kinderphysik* fiasco," with Germany's greatest philosopher playing right into the hands of its greatest Christian humorist.[70]

The first letter begins with an epigraph from Horace and more or less continues where the *Socratic Memorabilia* left off:

> – – ah! miser,
> Quanta laboras in Charybdi
> Digne puer meliore flamma!
> *Horat.*[71]

In other words, the suggestion is that Kant is a poor soul, whose philosophical labors are in vain, because he is being sucked in by a monstrous whirlpool, in this case the fashionable ideology of the age. Kant is worthy of a better fate, of course, but his current intellectual course is doomed to shipwreck. In the proper opening of

---

[68] See Milbank, "The theological critique of philosophy in Hamann and Jacobi," in John Milbank, Catherine Pikstock, and Graham Ward (eds.) *Radical Orthodoxy: A New Theology* (London: Routledge, 1999), p. 23.

[69] See Frederick Beiser, *The Fate of Reason: German Philosophy from Kant to Fichte* (Cambridge, MA: Harvard University Press, 1987), p. 30.

[70] In 1763 Hamann included the first two of his three letters to Kant as a published supplement to his *Five Pastoral Letters on School Drama*, titling them, "*Zugabe zweener Liebesbriefe an einen Lehrer der Weltweisheit, der eine Physick für Kinder schreiben wollte*" (N II, pp. 369–74).

[71] ZH I, p. 444. Oh! Poor soul / How much you labor in Charybdis / Youth worthy of a better flame!

the letter, Hamann writes: "The benefactors who [boast of] your merits would shrug their shoulders in pity if they knew that you were going around pregnant with a *physics book for children* ... so I take it for granted ... that you have spoken earnestly with me about it." The rest of the letter is interlarded with similar sarcasm, as when Hamann notes the audacity of Kant's proposal:

> You [must] have certain reasons to suppose that you will have the good fortune of succeeding where so many others have failed. Otherwise you would not have the heart to set upon this course when the fate of your predecessors could frighten you from it. You are in truth a master in Israel if you think it a small thing to transform yourself into a child, notwithstanding your erudition! Or do you have more confidence in children, when your adult audience has difficulty keeping up with you in the patience and speed of thought? Since, moreover, your proposal requires an exceptional knowledge of the *world of children*, which is acquired neither in gallant nor academic [circles], all of this seems to me so fanciful that, simply out of an inclination to the fantastic, I would already risk a black eye for so dashing and imprudent a ride.[72]

Perhaps Hamann was right that Kant had not sufficiently considered the difficulties involved in writing for children, however noble his intentions may have been. As Hamann goes on to say, "Preaching to intellectuals is as easy as deceiving honest people ... [but] a baptized philosopher will know that more is involved in writing for children than a Fontenellian wit and a seductive style."[73]

Hamann's profounder point, however, is that Kant has unwittingly stumbled upon the mystery of divine condescension, to which the proposal of writing something so lofty in content for children bears a fitting analogy:

> To manage to receive praise from the mouth of children and infants! – To take part in such an honor and taste is no *ordinary* business: one must begin not by *stealing colored feathers*, but with a voluntary self-emptying of all one's superiority in age and wisdom, and with a renunciation of all vanity. A philosophical book for children, therefore, would necessarily appear as simplistic, foolish, and tasteless as a *divine* book written for human beings. Test yourself then: Do you have enough heart to be the author of a simplistic, foolish, and tasteless theory of nature? If you do, then take heart, for you are also a *philosopher for children*. Vale et sapere *AUDE*![74]

Thus ends the first letter. That Kant should have proposed something so close to Hamann's heart and provided him with so ripe an opportunity to spell out his understanding of Christianity is rather extraordinary; for if the mystery of Christianity is essentially the mystery of the folly of God's loving condescension to man, then how better to present these mysteries than by way of the very discussion Kant had proposed. If at this point, however, Kant should fail to see that the language of divine condescension – of creation, of the economy of salvation, of the Scriptures – could never be simply the language of reason, then there would essentially be nothing more to say, and they would amicably have to part ways.

To judge from the sarcasm of Hamann's first letter, it would seem that he never had any intention of taking up Kant's proposal. From the second letter, however,

---

[72] ZH I, p. 445.
[73] Bernard le Bovier de Fontenelle (1657–1737).
[74] The phrase *sapere aude*, of which Kant makes particular use twenty-five years later in his essay, "What is Enlightenment?," comes originally from Horace, *Odes* I, 27. Needless to say, for Hamann, it never had quite the meaning Kant attributed to it.

having had more time to think about it, he seems at least briefly to have entertained the idea: they would simply have to come to terms about the proper content and method. But here again, whether or not he was serious about the project, what most interested Hamann was the suitability of the proposal as an allegory by which to convey his understanding of Christianity, as when he gives the following suggestion about how they should proceed:

> The great law of method for children consists, then, in this: that one condescend to their weakness; that one become their servant if one would be their master; that one follow them if one would govern them; that one learn their language and what animates them if we should want to move them to imitate our own. And yet it is possible neither to *understand* this practical principle, nor to *fulfill* it in practice, unless, as one says in the idiom of everyday life, one is crazy about kids and loves them without quite knowing why. Do you feel among your deep-seated inclinations the weakness of this kind of love for children? If so, then the *Aude* will come to you very easily, and the *sapere* too will flow; and within a period of six days you can become the author of an honest, useful, and handsome work for children – not that any T – –, much less any courtier or Phyllis will, out of gratitude, congratulate you for it.[75]

On the one hand, as Beiser notes, Hamann is picking up on Rousseau's program of education in *Émile*: "the proper method of education is to put oneself in the position of the child."[76] At the same time, however, Hamann clearly means to indicate here, through an allegory, something about God's radical love for human beings, which causes him to condescend to our weakness, to become our servant, to learn our language, etc. – all for the sake of raising human beings to the heights of participation in the divine nature. Of course, as Hamann recognizes, any author who would dare to imitate the style of God, who clothes himself in humility and accommodates himself to human weaknesses and limitations, cannot expect to receive the praise of supercilious intellectuals (such as Celsus, Porphyry, Nietzsche, et al.). On the contrary, for Hamann, anticipating Kierkegaard, it is almost axiomatic that the *truer* the imitation, the greater the offense it will cause.

With the humble language of Scripture as his model, Hamann then proceeds to suggest that Kant take the "rejected cornerstone" of the Mosaic creation account as his point of departure, "since it contains the origin of all things," and since "an historical approach to science is always better than a logical one."[77] Furthermore, it would be useful to begin with something the children would be familiar with. But for all that, Hamann does not deny the apparent inconsistencies in the account. On the contrary, for him it is almost axiomatic that Scripture will not measure up to rational expectations, no more than the Cross satisfies philosophical prejudice. "A person of conventional wisdom," he says, "will read the first three chapters of Genesis with the same eyes with which the celebrated astronomer [i.e., Galileo] gazed upon the heavens. Naturally, it will appear to him full of eccentric concepts and anomalies."[78] Even so, Hamann counsels, Kant "should not be ashamed to ride the wooden horse of Mosaic history," and to present natural history according to its terms.[79]

---

[75] ZH I, p. 446.

[76] Beiser, *The Fate of Reason*, p. 32.

[77] Ibid. In view of Hamann's reference to the "rejected cornerstone," one will note once again the symmetry Hamann perceives between the rejection that the Son suffers (in the flesh) and the Spirit suffers (in the letter).

[78] ZH I, p. 446.

[79] Ibid.

To judge from the content of Hamann's third letter, it seems that, in the previous two, he must have offended Kant after all, who in all likelihood took Hamann's ironic tone as a rejection of the proposal. Thus, as in the *Socratic Memorabilia*, Hamann begins his third letter with an appeal to their friendship: "Honored friend, this title is not an empty word for me, but a source of duties and delights that mutually correspond. May you judge what is enclosed from this perspective."[80] Hamann makes plain that, in his view, a true friendship occasionally requires the seasoning of salt; and so he says to Kant, instead of being offended, "You need to repel me as energetically as I attack you; and as forcefully stand up to my prejudices as I attack yours: otherwise your love of truth and virtue will, in my view, be as contemptible as a paramour's arts."[81] As the letter progresses, however, it is clear that the project will not amount to anything. Hamann is frustrated over Kant's silence and irritated that he did not take his previous letters seriously. "If we wish to pull from the same yoke," he says, "we have to be of the same mind. The question is whether you will raise yourself to my pride or I will lower myself to your vanity?"[82] To be sure, the impertinence of Hamann's remarks would suggest that he never took Kant's proposal seriously. But by now his reasons are also clear: not only do they have very different methodologies; they also have very different conceptions of nature – of creation – as such. As Hamann puts it,

> Nature is a book, a letter, a fable (in the philosophical sense) or however you want to call it. Assuming that we knew all its letters to the best possible degree; that we could make out the syllables and pronounce all the words; that we even knew the language in which it was written – – Is all of that by itself enough to understand a book, to make judgments about it, to extract its character? In other words, the interpretation of nature involves more than physics. Physics is nothing but the Abc. Nature is an equation of an unknown quantity, a Hebraic word written with nothing but consonants to which the understanding must supply the [vowel] points.[83]

Whether or not Kant took any of this to heart – whether he understood that, for Hamann, the book of nature is in the final analysis unintelligible apart from the Holy Spirit, who is poured into the hearts of those who believe in Christ (Rom. 5: 5) – is impossible to say. What is important here is simply that his suggested project of a physics book for children – a book, that is, about nature – furthered Hamann's seminal reflections about the nature of creation in general, which soon developed into his influential manifesto, the *Aesthetica in nuce*. One could even say that Hamann's understanding of creation as developed in the *Aesthetica in nuce* is already contained "in a nutshell" at the conclusion of this letter, where he says that "creation is not a work of vanity, but of humility, of condescension."[84]

---

[80] ZH I, p. 448.
[81] Ibid.
[82] ZH I, pp. 449f.
[83] ZH I, p. 450.
[84] ZH I, p. 452.

Part II

Crusades of the Philologist

4

Life and Writings 1760–1774

In a wonderful, profound, and obscure way Hamann penetrated the ultimate depths in which language, religion, and poetry hold together.

Dilthey[1]

If Königsberg was a relatively humble East-Prussian port city – though it could boast of its Albertina University and Kant – to an active religious imagination like Hamann's its name undoubtedly carried overtones of Zion, i.e., "the mountain of the king"; and it was from here, rather fittingly, armed with a sense of providential commission, that he conducted his lifelong literary campaign against the Enlightenment, as embodied in the "enlightened" despot of Sans Souci, Frederick the Great, and his court of "enlightened" architects and master builders, the "pyrgotects," of Berlin-Babel. What is especially noteworthy about Hamann's "crusade," however, is that he conducted it as a philologist – as a lover of the Word, in both the literary and theological senses of the term. Indeed, inspired precisely by the Word (in the Johannine sense), he came to have an even deeper love of the languages and literatures of the world. Thus, in addition to the languages he already knew (Latin, Greek, Hebrew, English, French, and Italian), he began to immerse himself in Arabic in order to read the Koran, eventually adding to his repertoire Spanish, Portuguese, Latvian, and even Chaldaic.[2]

AGAINST THE PURIFICATION OF LANGUAGE

Hamann's literary "crusade" began in earnest in 1760 with contributions to an obscure weekly called the *Wochentliche Königsbergische Frag- und Anzeigungs-Nachrichten*, among them his *Essay on an Academic Question* (*Versuch über eine akademische Frage*), *Miscellaneous Notes on Word Order in the French Language* (*Vermischte Anmerkungen über Wortfügung in der französischen Sprache*), and, appropriately, around Christmas, *The Magi from the East, at Bethlehem* (*Die Magi aus Morgenlande, zu Bethlehem*). Although Kant himself occasionally wrote for the publication, Hamann's highbrow contributions were scarcely fitting in what amounted to a tabloid; indeed, as Nadler suggests, it was as if Hamann's writings themselves "lay in a manger."[3]

The first two essays are significant inasmuch as they testify to Hamann's philosophical empiricism and corresponding views on language. In the *Essay*, for example, following Locke and Hume, he says, "The nature of our thought is grounded upon sense impressions and the sensations bound up with them."[4] And from here, given the sensory aspect of language, it is but a step to his statement in the *Miscellaneous*

---

[1] Wilhelm Dilthey, *Gesammelte Schriften* (Leipzig and Berlin: B. G. Teubner, 1936), vol. 11, p. xvi.

[2] For references, see Rudolf Unger, *Hamanns Sprachtheorie im Zusammenhang seines Denkens* (Munich: C. H. Beck, 1905), p. 131.

[3] NB, p. 120.

[4] N II, p. 123.

Notes: "The wealth of all human knowledge rests upon the exchange of words [*Wortwechsel*]."[5] Aside from drawing attention to the importance of language to thought – quoting Edward Young he says, "Speech, thought's canal! Speech, thought's criterion too!"[6] – it is in this connection that he also makes a striking comparison between the nature of finance and the "currency" of language:

> Money and language are two things, whose investigation is as profound and abstract as their use is universal. Both stand in a more proximate relation to one another than one might expect. The theory of the one explains the theory of the other; and so they would seem to flow from common principles. The wealth of all human knowledge rests upon an exchange of words; and it was a theologian of penetrating wit, who called theology – this eldest sister of the higher sciences – a grammar of the language of Holy Scripture. On the other hand, all the goods of civic or societal life refer to money as to their universal measure, as, according to some translations, even Solomon is already supposed to have realized.[7]

Presumably, among the things Hamann means to say here (taking his other works on language into account) is that just as monetary units, coins for example, can be worn down by use and must be minted anew, so too language can lose its profounder significance, as when a metaphor becomes hackneyed and trite; in which case language must be stamped anew by the power of poetic genius. While in other works, especially his *Aesthetica in nuce,* Hamann treats the topic of poetic genius directly, in these two essays his concern is to identify what it is that wears a language down and calls for its renewal: namely, an excessively rational approach to language that he identifies with the influence of the French Academy.[8] For Hamann, examples of such an overbearing rational approach include invasive orthographical reforms, which presume to tamper with the matrix of natural language, "cleansing" it of supposed "errors" (a practice Hamann especially deplores), a preference for artificial terms and abstract concepts, and a stultifying adherence to rational canons of artistic expression – in short, everything that conspires to "rob a language of its pristine power."[9] Accordingly, in his *Essay* he speaks of "the mischief of muddling up languages and the crude faith in certain symbols and formulas" as having gained predominance over "the most powerful, freshly dug root of a word or the infinite genealogy of a concept."[10]

Hamann's *Miscellaneous Notes*, published toward the end of 1760, continues in the same vein. As the title indicates, it is concerned with the subject of French word order. Whereas French syntax is relatively rigid, he argues, German syntax is capable of great variation, like Latin. Hamann adduces the following example, "Er hat mir das Buch gegeben," and notes its multiple variations, each of which has a particular emphasis: "Mir hat er das Buch gegeben," "Das Buch hat er mir gegeben," and

---

[5] N II, p. 129.
[6] Ibid.
[7] Ibid. The "theologian of penetrating wit" is Luther. In a footnote Hamann refers to Eccles. 10: 19: "and money meets every need"; and to Aristotle, both *de Moribus*, V, 8 and *de Republica*: στοιχεῖον καί πέρας τῆς ἀλλαγῆς.
[8] Such influence is evident, for example, in that the president of the Berlin Academy was the French rationalist, Pierre Moreau de Maupertuis, who in 1754 had proposed a purely utilitarian theory of the origin of language, a theory that would eventually provoke Hamann's own contribution to the topic when the Academy raised the question again in 1770. See *JGH*, pp. 123f.; see, more generally, pp. 112–22.
[9] *JGH*, p. 114.
[10] N II, p. 126.

"Gegeben hat er mir das Buch."[11] The point of his comparison is not to denigrate French, in which he was perfectly fluent; rather, it is to say that the power of any given language is to some extent a function of the freedom of expression it allows. By the same token, excessive regulation, i.e., the imposition of aesthetic norms or politically correct language by rational or ideological decree, deprives a language of its primal power; in short, it emasculates it of its poetic potential. To illustrate his point, on the verso of the title page, Hamann printed an illustration of a rooster with a baton in one claw and a musical score in the other attempting to direct two cockerels, presumably capons, in the singing of church music.[12] His point, which is more explicitly and passionately propounded in the *Aesthetica in nuce,* is that an overly rational approach to language renders one incapable of speaking with the kind of creative authority with which he himself speaks. And in this connection he concludes his essay, by way of reference to two French financial geniuses, Maximilien de Béthune Sully and Jean Baptiste Colbert, picking up on the same analogy between language and money he made at the beginning:

> The purification of a language strips it of its wealth, just as a correctness that is too fastidious strips it of its strength and manhood. – In a city as large as Paris it would be no trouble finding in any given year forty learned men who infallibly understand what is pure and good in their mother tongue, and necessary for the monopolization of such second-hand rubbish. – Once in any number of centuries, however, it so happens that a gift of Pallas – a human image – falls from heaven, fully authorized to govern the public treasury of a given language with wisdom – like a Sully, or shrewdly to increase it, like a Colbert.[13]

THE *MAGI* AND "THE KNIGHT OF FAITH"

Among Hamann's initial contributions to the *Wochentliche Königsberische Frag- und Anzeigungs-Nachrichten, The Magi from the East, at Bethlehem,* in reference to the gospel account of the wise men (Matt. 2: 1–12), is important for an altogether different reason: namely, that it contains ideas of germinal significance to Kierkegaard's philosophy, bearing, in particular, upon such important Kierkegaardian concepts as the "knight of faith" and the "teleological suspension of the ethical." It was occasioned by the coincidence of two contemporary events: the first, a Danish expedition to the Middle East to study oriental languages (1761–7), which was led by Karsten Niebuhr and funded by the King of Denmark at the behest of the Göttingen orientalist, Johann David Michaelis (1717–91), ostensibly for the sake of illuminating the biblical text; the second, Captain Cook's voyage to the South Seas to observe a rare passage of Venus past the sun.[14]

Aside from Hamann's own interest in oriental languages and literatures, the coincidence of these two events would have been significant to him for a number of reasons. Above all, they would have indicated to him a fundamental trust in the

---

[11] N II, p. 131.

[12] See *JGH,* p. 113.

[13] N II, p. 136.

[14] James C. O'Flaherty, "East and West in the thought of Hamann," in *The Quarrel of Reason with Itself: Essays on Hamann, Michaelis, Lessing, Nietzsche* (Columbia, SC: Camden House, 1988), pp. 63, 109, 113. The essays in this collection shed invaluable light on Hamann, his contemporary context, and his importance to German letters (and philosophy) in general.

ability of reason (whether through modern historical criticism or modern astronomy) to bring about "enlightenment," in this case, to "illuminate" the nature of things (whether this be the ancient languages of the biblical texts or the nature of the physical universe); all of which was portentously symbolized in the quest for the "morning star," understood as a metaphor for the Enlightenment as such.[15] In any case, for Hamann, who was already disposed to an ironic and humorous view of the Enlightenment and its understanding of "illumination," the coincidence of these two events presented a prophetic opportunity laden with symbolic meaning. Thus, over against his rationalist contemporaries, who were fascinated by the "morning star," Venus, and scientific advances resulting from their devotion to the light of reason, he entertains his readers with reflections about the portentous significance of another star, namely, the star of Bethlehem, and its witness to *the* "morning star," which is Jesus (Rev. 22: 16). Whereas the former is discovered along the highway of reason or scientific research, the latter is discovered by keeping to the narrow, obscure, and seemingly irrational way of faith. Indeed, according to Hamann, as the example of the wise men would suggest, the way of faith, far from being rationally transparent, often defies rational calculation:

> My present reflections will come to rest where the little child lay, whose mysterious birth occupied the curiosity of the angels and the shepherds, and whom the magi of the Orient, under the guidance of an extraordinary sign, made haste to Bethlehem to worship. Upon finally reaching the goal of their pilgrimage, they doubtless expressed their joy in solecisms, as is often the case with violent and sudden passions. If the muse of so felicitous a poet and no less sharp-witted an art critic dared to celebrate the visitation of the shepherds at the manger in a comic opera, then perhaps I may be allowed to commemorate the wise men with some reflections by lighting a few grains of Socratic frankincense.[16]

One can see here what would have interested Kierkegaard: faith is more a matter of passion than of reason, and, from a rational perspective, tends to express itself in solecisms. The rest of the text is still more pertinent. Hamann says that he does not intend to investigate the magi's teachings or origin, but simply to make a few observations about, interestingly enough, the *morality* of their pilgrimage; and it is in this context that he says, "Human life seems to consist in a series of symbolic actions by which our soul is able to reveal its invisible nature …"[17] But because "the mere body of an action can never disclose to us its worth," we naturally end up judging its worth according to imagined motivations and consequences.[18] And it is precisely with respect to "this law of experience and reason" that the decision of the pilgrims to make their journey does not appear in a favorable light:

> To judge from their own words, the motive that brought them thus far gives us the impression of a delusion that has long set in, a myth to which they held as to a sure prophetic word – not to mention the trouble they, as citizens, caused and the injustice they

---

[15] It is not that Hamann was opposed to such investigations; for he too accords reason its proper domain. Rather, here and throughout his writings, he wished to challenge an overweening confidence in the power of reason to disclose either the *ultimate* nature of things or the *ultimate* meaning of the biblical texts, beyond what light modern natural science or modern historical criticism might, respectively, be able to shed.

[16] N II, p. 139. The poet and critic here is Klopstock.

[17] Ibid.

[18] Ibid.

committed against their homeland by virtue of such extravagant reverence for a foreign king. As for the consequences of their undertaking, it stands to reason that the mothers who had to bewail the bloodbath of their children would likewise have sighed over the rashness and impertinence of these strangers. Even the newborn king of the Jews himself was forced to flee because his worshippers had betrayed [the time and place of his birth] to Herod, the reigning Anti-Christ, who is a liar and murderer from the beginning. Tremble! deluded mortals, who make claims to your righteousness on the basis of the nobility of your intentions![19]

In other words, according to Hamann, one's righteousness does not come from good intentions, since they may lead unwittingly to catastrophic results (according to what we might call a "law of unintended consequences"), as in the case of the magi. Nor, for similar reasons, can one bank on the success of one's "system" (in the sense here of a construct by which one is guided), since others may one day judge it harshly as a product of fantasy (as today we might judge the astronomy of the magi). Nor, certainly, should one be guided by popular opinion or seek one's righteousness by following conventional wisdom (of which the magi are precisely a counterexample). Rather, for Hamann, the righteousness of any given action springs from an altogether different source, namely, from faith (see Gen. 15: 6; Rom. 4: 3), and so Hamann goes on to say, in what amounts to a formula for life, "Take heart! deceived [*betrogne*] mortals who despair over the painful aftereffects of your good works and feel the heel pricks of your victory! The will of providence must be more urgent to you than the conceits of your contemporaries and generations to come."[20]

For Hamann, then, the life of a Christian is something generically different from the life of an unbeliever; it is guided neither by reason – at least not by reason alone – nor by popular opinion; nor does it concern itself with the judgment of posterity. Rather, it is a doubly hidden existence: hidden, firstly, "with Christ in God" (Col. 3: 3) as the interior subjective principle of one's symbolic actions; hidden, secondly, with regard to the objectively unforeseeable results of one's actions, which one hopes to be contributions (perhaps a mere two mites) to the kingdom of God (1 Pet. 2: 4f.). In other words, since we cannot foresee the results of our actions, since we, so to speak, weave only on "the underside of the carpet," as Hamann puts it in the *Aesthetica in nuce*, never seeing the ultimate effect of our weaving, the life of a Christian is necessarily a life of faith, repeated ever anew, in the workings of providence (Rom. 8: 28).[21] And in this context he goes on to say, anticipating the pith of Kierkegaard's memorial to Abraham:

> There are actions of a higher order which bear no analogy to the elements (the statutes) of this world ... Not only the end, but the entire journey [*Wandel*] of a Christian is the masterpiece (Eph. 2: 10) of the unknown genius, whom heaven and earth have known and will recognize as the one creator, redeemer and sustainer in transfigured human form."[22]

---

[19] N II, p. 140.
[20] Ibid.
[21] See N II, p. 199; see John Milbank, *The Word Made Strange: Theology, Language, Culture* (Oxford: Blackwell, 1997), p. 74.
[22] N II, p. 140.

The work then concludes with a cento of scriptural passages, which testify to the contrast between the life of faith as currently hidden and the transfiguration of this life in glory:

> Our life, it is said, is hidden with Christ in GOD. But when Christ – our life – reveals himself, then we too will be revealed with Him in glory. And elsewhere: for this reason the world does not know you, because it did not know Him. What we will be has not been revealed. But we know that when [He] is revealed we will be like Him, for we will see Him as He is. Indeed, indeed. He will come in such a way that He will appear glorious with His saints, and wondrous with all who believe in Him. How infinite will be the pleasure of those who long for His appearing, surpassing the great joy of our enthusiasts from the Orient upon seeing the star! As the original scripture of our faith says, full of emphasis and simplicity: "They rejoiced with exceedingly great joy" (εχαρησαν χαραν μεγαλην σφοδρα).[23]

In sum, in view of *The Magi from the East* and Hamann's sixth fragment (which was discussed in Chapter 2), it is no wonder that Kierkegaard quotes Hamann in the motto to *Fear and Trembling* (though this particular quote concerns yet another aspect of Hamann's authorship, namely, his practice of indirect communication). For in multiple ways Hamann is an unrecognized source of Kierkegaard's philosophy: from his understanding of the "knight of faith," to his notion of the "teleological suspension of the ethical," to his practice of indirect communication, to his doctrine of the "paradox," to his anti-systematic, anti-Hegelian "fragments." As Hamann wonderfully puts it in "The Magi from the East," in proto-anti-Hegelian fashion, "The system of today, which provides the proof of your presuppositions, will be the fairytale of tomorrow."[24]

CRUSADES OF THE PHILOLOGIST

Hamann's fortunes took a turn for the better when a talented young publisher, Johann Jakob Kanter, arrived in town and in 1761 published Hamann's next set of writings. Among them was his "Elegy, in the form of a circular on church music" (*Klaggedicht, in Gestalt eines Sendschreibens über die Kirchenmusick*), which may be an indirect communication to his one-time fiancée, has almost nothing to do with church music, and deals chiefly with his understanding of the connection between the sacred and the profane. He also published, at about the same time, "French project" (*Französisches Projekt*), a translated satire of the current state of French philosophy, which Hamann suggests is in need of an "inoculation du bon sens";[25] *Clouds* (*Wolken*), whose title alludes both to Aristophanes' comedy and to Christ's second coming (Mark 13: 26), and is a comical response to reviews of the *Socratic Memorabilia*; and *Chimerical Ideas* (*Chimärische Einfälle*), which is a response to a critical review of Rousseau's *Julie, or the New Héloïse* that was published in Nicolai's and Mendelssohn's *Briefe* and signals Hamann's increasing opposition to the journal that earlier tried to recruit him.

In the following year, 1762, Hamann continued his polemic against contemporary literary criticism with a pair of texts titled "Authors and art critics" (*Schriftsteller*

---

[23] N II, pp. 140f. Col. 3: 3; 1 John 3: 2.
[24] N II, pp. 140f.
[25] The author of the original text, *L'Inoculation du bons sens*, was a Frenchman, Nicholas Josef Selis. See NB, p. 139; *JGH*, p. 139.

und Kunstrichter) and "Readers and art critics" (*Leser und Kunstrichter*). As their respective titles suggest, these texts provide many insights into Hamann's self-understanding as an author and his understanding of the dynamic that obtains among author, reader, and critic. Specifically, they suggest how this dynamic is, for the most part, a fallen one (which mirrors the "mis-relation" between the author of creation and human readers of this text); how the true author writes with the reader in mind, to the point of self-denial; and how the role of the modern critic is, by contrast, too often a presumptuous exercise in judgment, when judgment should ultimately be reserved for *the* eschatological critic, who is none other than Christ.

By far the most important publication of 1762, however, was a sundry collection titled *Crusades of the Philologist* (*Kreuzzüge des Philologen*). As Nadler rightly observes, whereas the *Socratic Memorabilia* provided a propaedeutic to a philosophy of history (i.e., a way to read history through the eyes of faith), the *Crusades of the Philologist* sketches out nothing less than a Christian philosophy of all languages, literatures, and poetries.[26] As far as first impressions go, the collection is striking: on the title page the "philologist" (i.e., Hamann) depicts himself in effigy in the form of the horned head of the god Pan.[27] As for the title itself, both "crusades" and "philologist" have multiple meanings. By "crusades," Hamann certainly indicates a continuation of his literary campaign against the Enlightenment – a campaign conducted under the sign of the Cross. Indeed, if anything, the work promises an intensification of hostilities, as the epigraph from Virgil's *Eclogues* would suggest: – – – *erunt etiam altera bella, atque iterum ad Troiam magnus mittetur Achilles.*[28] At the same time, however, the word says something about the "cruciform" style in which the work itself is written; and in this regard Hamann speaks elsewhere of "disarming" his readers through "aesthetic obedience to the Cross."[29] Finally, as Hamann explains in a letter to Nicolai in 1763, shedding some light on his labyrinthine style, the title is a "provincial joke." It refers, he says, to the "craftiness" of the Teutonic Knights in Prussia, who constructed elaborate labyrinths near their fortresses (each serving as a mock "Jerusalem") and entertained themselves after hangovers – *post pocula et crapulas* – by running through them, presuming by such games, such mock "crusades," to absolve themselves from any further obligation to defend the actual city of Jerusalem.[30]

As for the word "philologist," it refers most obviously to Hamann's interest in classical languages and literatures; hence the nearly constant references throughout the collection to Roman and Greek poets, orators, and philosophers, among them, Horace, Persius, Ovid, Lucretius, Cicero, Quintilian, Pindar, Plato, Porphyry, and Demosthenes, to name some of the better known. The etymological meaning of the term, however, which is so important as fundamentally to determine both the form and content of all of Hamann's publications, is that Hamann is not simply a "lover

---

[26] NB, p. 126.

[27] See ZH II, p. 125. Needless to say, if the pious nature of earlier writings, such as *The Magi from the East, at Bethlehem*, had caused Hamann to be celebrated by the Pietists, this gesture was sure to offend them. As with all of his other masks and guises, however, the illustration of Pan is a case in point that Hamann's intention was precisely not to have devotees, not to be the founder of a school, but to be a fool for Christ. Why he chose to depict himself specifically in the form of a truncated image of Pan, i.e., Pan without the lower parts, is bound up with the theme of the *Aesthetica in nuce*: its polemic against the truncated, excessively rational hermeneutics of his Enlightenment contemporaries and its Pandean ode to the senses and passions.

[28] N II, p. 113. "There will be other wars, and once again the great Achilles will be sent to Troy."

[29] N III, p. 234.

[30] ZH II, p. 195. See also G-D, p. 77.

of words," but a "lover of *the* Word" in the Johannine sense, i.e., a lover of the Logos, who "was made flesh and dwelt among us" (John 1: 14). Finally, as both a "critic" and a lover of Scripture, he is a "lover of the Word" in the particular sense of Hebrews 4: 12–13:

> The word of God is living and active, sharper than any two-edged sword, piercing until it divides soul from spirit, joints from marrow; it is able to judge the thoughts and intentions of the heart. And before him no creature is hidden, but all are naked and laid bare to the eyes of the one to whom we must render an account.

It would be impossible to exaggerate the importance of this verse to Hamann's self-understanding as a Christian author. In his view, it is not simply a statement about the critically transforming power of Scripture, as he himself experienced it in London; it is the very essence of criticism (in the sense of κρίνειν as "to separate") and the point of everything he wrote: that his own inspired words might share in this critical, penetrating power of the Word; that he himself, as a "meta-critic," might be an instrument of the ultimate, end-time critic, which is Christ, who judges the "work" of one's life (2 Cor. 5: 10) and to whose infallible "critique," *pace* Kant, "all must submit."[31] As he puts it in a farcical palinode to Mendelssohn's review of the *Crusades*:

> Now what should we say of the taste of the philologist? Firstly, his name signifies a lover of the living, powerful, double-edged, penetrating, marrow-dividing, critical Word, before whom no creature is hidden, but all is equally patent to his eyes; next, gleaming in the banner of his flying collection is that sign of offense and foolishness by which the most insignificant art critic triumphs with Constantine and conducts the oracle of judgment to victory.[32]

Thus, whereas in the *Socratic Memorabilia* Hamann sought through an aesthetic imitation of Socrates to become an oracle of introspection, i.e., to lay bare his friends' hypocrisy, mediate a feeling of their own ignorance, and thereby prepare them for the message of Christianity, here, in *Crusades of the Philologist*, he undertakes an explicitly Christian form of criticism, one conducted under the sign of the Cross and hence in the guise of folly and offense (1 Cor. 1: 18f.). In this way, by kenotically taking himself out of the equation through the appearance of folly, he hopes to leave his readers room for reflection and, if at all possible, to convey the critical, transforming power of the Word of God. The last clue to Hamann's intentions is given on the verso, which features a fragment from Ecclesiastes in Hebrew: "given by one shepherd" (12: 11). The rest of the verse and its context are illuminating: "The sayings of the wise are like goads, and like nails firmly fixed are the collected sayings that are given by one shepherd. Of anything beyond these, my child, beware." One may therefore gather that Hamann's own sayings are of this nature: they are inspired by the one Shepherd, who is Christ (John 10), and "like nails firmly fixed" are meant to be goads to his unbelieving contemporaries, until the true "morning star," which brings *true* enlightenment, "rises in their hearts" (2 Pet. 1: 19).

In keeping with the "folly" of Hamann's witness, the assortment of texts in this sundry collection is similarly baffling. Among them one will find reprints of several shorter pieces from 1760 and 1761, some early (perhaps intentionally) unflattering

---

[31] Kant, *The Critique of Pure Reason*, tr. Norman Kemp Smith (New York: St Martin's Press, 1965), A xi, p. 9.
[32] N II, p. 263.

poems, a eulogy for his mother, an early Latin essay on sleep and dreams, some "Nibblings," which is a satirical critique of Robinet's recently attempted theodicy in *De la nature,* and an "index for the single letter p," which contains such hilarious entries as the following:

> Paul, a dark author, whom a *doctor iuris* from Padua wanted to prostitute on account of his infamous darkness (p. 148); *philologist* took a trip and made observations among the Latvian peasants (p. 215); wishes for a winnowing-shovel (p. 197); by means of examples and parables warns a little nibbler in the Elysian fields against *aliena cornua fronti addita* (p. 197); compares himself to the horse of Alexander the Great (p. 174); to a Margot la Ravadeuse (p. 215); to a bird (p. 148); has damaged books in his library (p. 212); speaks in prosopopeias with his mother's dead body (p. 235); with an archangel (p. 201); is angry about aesthetical Spinozism (p. 177); about exegetical materialism (p. 203); edifies himself with an Arabic dictionary as an antidote for boredom (p. 183); affects a gibberish style and nevertheless speaks of classical perfection (p. 215); *philologists* are bankers (p. 130); *philosophers* are saucy suitors (p. 211); *prophets* include Herod and Caiaphas (p. 205); a *Pythian* prophetess' hairs stand on end (p. 189). *Cetera desunt.*[33]

Needless to say, this comical "index" would itself require some deciphering; in any case, it shows that Hamann is not simply a pious tractarian, but one who, as Kierkegaard profoundly appreciated, unfailingly delivers his utterly serious message as a Christian *humorist,* in keeping with Paul's understanding of folly as *the* form of true wisdom. But if much in the collection, between the bookends of a fictional editor's preface and this comical index, is a compilation of warmed-over material, one may gather that this was precisely Hamann's intention, as though all of this was included in order to set off two new works, which form the work's core: Hamann's *Cloverleaf of Hellenistic Letters (Kleeblatt hellenistischer Briefe)* and perhaps his most influential work, *Aesthetics in a Nutshell: A Rhapsody in Kabbalistic Prose (Aesthetica in nuce: Eine Rhapsodie in Kabbalistischer Prose).*[34] These two works continue his reflections on the nature of style, authorship, and art criticism, though now his focus is more upon an aesthetics (or hermeneutics) of creation and Scripture.[35] Chief among his concerns is to emphasize the prophetic dimensions of these twin texts against the obtuse rational critics of the Enlightenment, whose Stoic sensibility has deadened them to the testimony of the senses and the passions (the very language, according to Hamann, whereby God condescends to speak to his creatures), and who fail to see that creation, history, and Scripture are, in any case, *more* than a mirror of rational verities and therefore cannot be understood, much less fathomed, by reason alone.

As for the titles of these works, the first of the two, *Cloverleaf of Hellenistic Letters,* is more or less self-explanatory. The work comprises three letters: the first concerns the *koine* or common dialect in which the New Testament was written; the second critiques the uninspired classical philology of Hamann's contemporaries; the third is concerned with biblical exegesis and marks the beginning of Hamann's

---

[33] N II, pp. 239–40. Pagination is Hamann's and refers to the original edition of 1762.

[34] See ZH II, pp. 125, 128. See Hans-Martin Lumpp, *Philologia Crucis: Zu Johann Georg Hamanns Fassung von der Dichtkunst* (Tübingen: Max Niemeyer, 1970), p. 20.

[35] I use the terms "aesthetics" and "hermeneutics" here as more or less interchangeable, inasmuch as creation is, for Hamann, similarly a matter of interpretation, and since the understanding of Scripture similarly requires a certain kind of perception.

debate with J. D. Michaelis, the founder of modern biblical criticism, who started the first journal in the field, *Orientalische und exegetische Bibliothek.*[36] In fact, just as Kant and Berens are the key to the *Socratic Memorabilia,* here, and even more so in the *Aesthetica,* the key is Michaelis. And it is to him that the otherwise cryptic epigraph from Lucretius, with which the *Cloverleaf* begins, is ironically addressed: "TU mihi supremae praescripta ad candida calcis currenti spatium praemonstra, callida musa, Calliope, requies hominum divomque voluptas, te duce ut insigni capiam cum laude coronam."[37] In other words, Michaelis is Hamann's Calliope, the muse who has inspired him to write ultimately both the *Cloverleaf* and the *Aesthetica.* While the praise for Michaelis is not altogether disingenuous, since Hamann respected Michaelis's philological talents, it is clearly offered tongue-in-cheek, since Hamann has every intention of winning the philological contest.

The title of the second work, *Aesthetica in nuce: Eine Rhapsodie in Kabbalistischer Prose,* is more intriguing. The first thing to note in this regard is that "aesthetics," as an independent discipline, first gained currency through the unfinished work, titled *Aesthetica,* of the Wolffian philosopher, Alexander Gottlieb Baumgarten (1714–62); and Hamann's understanding of the term is very much in keeping with the word's original acceptation as a science dealing with sensation or perception (αἴσθησις).[38] At the same time, the title alludes to the work of Christoph Otto Schönaich, whose *Die ganze Aesthetik in einer Nuss, oder neologisches Wörterbuch,* a satirical work against Klopstock, was published in 1754.[39] But if the title is borrowed, in Hamann's hands it assumes multiple additional meanings, signifying "in a nutshell" both the outward form of his writing (the rough exterior of his own *stylus atrox*) and its inner content (the edible prophetic message, which is meant to be digested).[40] And what is the work's prophetic message? And what is the particular "aesthetics" it offers its readers? This too is cryptically signified in the title: it is a perception of the dialectical form of revelation, which conveys the exalted in the lowly, the sublime in the humble, wisdom in folly, etc. In other words, Hamann's title is a gnomic allusion to what his contemporaries, owing to their rationalist prejudice, were precisely *unable to see:* namely, the glory of God hidden within the *kenosis* of creation; the glory of God hidden within Christ, who "had no form or comeliness that we should look at him, and no beauty that we should desire him" (Isa. 53: 2); the glory of God hidden, above all, in the "*grandiose* paradox"[41] of the Cross; and the glory of God hidden, finally, within the humble letter of Scripture, often enough under a similarly offensive form. And, certainly, the title is a comical allusion to Hamann himself, who is a "hard nut to crack," with whom one must be patient if one is to get past the rough, offensive exterior of his style (*stylus atrox*) and digest the sublime content of the message he conveys.

The title, then, is at least crackable; and the same is true for the subtitle, in which we are told that this aesthetics will be a "rhapsody in kabbalistic prose." Of course,

---

[36] See Lumpp, *Philologia Crucis,* p. 20.

[37] N II, p. 168. Trans: "Do you go before and show me the course as I run my race to the white line of my final goal, clearly marked out before me, yes you, Calliope, Muse all-skillful, man's repose and god's delight, that led by you I may win the crown with illustrious praise," Lucretius, *De rerum natura,* book 6, vv. 92–5, trans. W. H. D. Rouse (Cambridge, MA: Harvard University Press, 1982).

[38] For more on the connection between Hamann and Baumgarten, see G-D, pp. 79ff.

[39] G-D, p. 432.

[40] Cf. Ezek. 3: 1f., where Ezekiel eats the scroll "and it was in my mouth as sweet as honey."

[41] See Nietzsche, *Nachgelassene Fragmente* (Frühjahr, 1884), in *KSA,* vol. 11, p. 86. Cf. *Jenseits von Gut und Böse,* §46, in *KSA,* vol. 5, p. 67.

how a pithy summary, contained in a nutshell, could at the same time be a rhapsody is anybody's guess; and therein lies something of Hamann's humor. That being said, "rhapsody" and "kabbalistic" have, in addition to their original meanings, connotations specific to Hamann's polemic against Michaelis. By "rhapsody" he means the art of the ancient Greek rhapsodes (ῥαψῳδοι), who sang recitations of epic poetry, often in a disconnected style with great fervor. In other words, they did not convey anything new so much as give extemporaneous interpretations of traditional verse. This is why at the conclusion of the work, finally providing a clue to the title, Hamann cites Plato's *Ion*, where Socrates refers to the rhapsodes as interpreters of interpreters, "οἱ ῥαψῳδοι – ἑρμήνεων ἑρμενείς."[42] It is also why in the same context he says that his "newest aesthetics" is also the "oldest." Hamann's point, then, is that he too will speak as a rhapsode: he will not speak on his own but as an "interpreter of interpreters." At one level, this self-understanding goes along with his view that all science is essentially a matter of hermeneutics, of interpretation, and that any philosophy that would claim to begin a priori, apart from a textual tradition, is either hypocritical or deceived. More specifically, however, he will speak as an "interpreter of interpreters" in two senses: both as an interpreter of Scripture (as a self-interpretation of God), and as an exegete of the leading exegete of Scripture, namely, Michaelis.[43] And then there is the etymological root of the word, "ῥάπτειν," which means "to sew or stitch together" as an appropriate description for Hamann's consciously hyper-textual style. And, finally, the word bears an ironic reference to a passage in one of Michaelis's works, where he criticizes certain New Testament epistles traditionally attributed to Paul for lacking "strict demonstration" and being mere "rhapsodies" constructed out of earlier compositions.[44] Thus, in writing a "rhapsody," Hamann is consciously imitating and implicitly defending what Michaelis considers unworthy of sacred Scripture.

In keeping with its meaning, the word "kabbalistic" is more cryptic and therefore has the potential to be more misleading. The first thing to be noted here is that the word is perfectly suited to Hamann's sense of humor, evoking such notions, so antithetical to his "enlightened" contemporaries, as "hermeticism," "esotericism," "cryptography," and, above all, "darkness." The most obvious meaning, then, aside from what it says about the obscurity of Hamann's style, is that his writing has a secret, mystical sense, like the hidden sense the kabbalists presumed to find in the Torah, which is unavailable to profane and unenlightened readers.[45] Secondly, there is the original meaning of the word "kabbalah," namely, "transmission" or "translation," which echoes what Hamann means by "rhapsody" as "interpretation." Thirdly, the word suggests the extraordinary, mystical importance that Hamann, like the kabbalists, attaches to human language, Hebrew in particular, as reflective of the original "creative language of God."[46] And, finally, in adopting this word Hamann is intentionally, if somewhat facetiously, contesting the opinion of Michaelis, who explicitly rejected kabbalism as nonsense. As Michaelis put it in

---

[42] A key point of Plato's discussion (535a) is that the poets are interpreters of God, which means here that Hamann is an interpreter of the interpreters of God, who are in this case, most specifically, the authors of Scripture.

[43] See G-D, p. 82.

[44] See Lumpp, *Philologia Crucis*, p. 31. The passage comes from Michaelis's *Einleitung in die Göttlichen Schriften des neuen Bundes* (Göttingen, 1750), p. 289.

[45] See Lumpp, *Philologia Crucis*, p. 31.

[46] See Gershom Scholem, *Major Trends in Jewish Mysticism* (New York: Shocken Books, 1946), p. 17.

his *Beurtheilung der Mittel, welche man anwendet, die ausgestorbene Hebräische Sprache zu verstehen* from 1757,

> The Jews consider the Hebrew language to be especially sacred and completely divine in origin, applying this even to the minute characteristics of the letters, to say nothing of the Cabbalist who seeks in them various idle mysteries. They reckon it a divine virtue on their part that they express the essence of things; and an entire heap of credulous Christians have repeated this principle after them.[47]

Clearly, then, Hamann means to come to the defense of these "credulous" Christians, since for him, as for Paul (2 Tim. 3: 16), all Scripture is inspired and holy, down to the last dot and tittle (see Matt. 5: 18).[48] Of course, for a modern exegete like Michaelis, this is precisely the problem: from his "rational" perspective he cannot fathom how historically contingent, evolving languages – much less individual strokes on a page – could be vehicles of eternal truth.

Upon closer examination, the subtitle of the *Aesthetica in nuce* is thus a cryptic declaration of Hamann's polemic against Michaelis; and it is in this light that one should understand the work's two mottos. The first is taken from Judges 5: 30: "Spoil of dyed stuffs embroidered, two pieces of dyed work embroidered for my neck as spoil." The verse is part of Deborah's song, one of the most ancient passages in the Old Testament and, to a modern sensibility, surely one of the most abhorrent. It features that "most blessed of women," Jael, who under the cover of hospitality offered refuge to the Canaanite general, Sisera, in order to drive a peg through his skull while he slept (4: 17ff.), at which point the Israelites emerge victorious over the Canaanites. In short, it is the very kind of passage that the Enlighteners were wont to excise (like Thomas Jefferson) or condemn (like Voltaire). What the verse might mean in the present context is hopelessly obscure. We can be sure, however, that Hamann was not shy about offending the "enlightened" sensibility of his contemporaries; indeed, for him, even this verse must be reckoned an instance of the condescension of the Holy Spirit, who did not shy away from revealing the mysteries of God even through such troubling details of Israelite history as these. But if Lumpp is right, the specific reference is again to Michaelis: like the women awaiting the spoil of victory, Hamann is awaiting the second part of Michaelis's edition of Lowth's *Lectures on the Sacred Poetry of the Hebrews* (the first appeared in 1758, with ample commentary by Michaelis).[49] The problem, however, is that there will be no spoil because the Canaanite general is dead; and so too, Hamann suggests, is Michaelis's reading of the Old Testament, because it is devoid of the life-giving Spirit who alone opens the meaning of Scripture. The second motto is more transparent. It comes from the Book of Job, where Elihu says to Job,

> Behold, my heart is like wine that has no vent; like new wineskins, it is ready to burst. I must speak, that I may find relief; I must open my lips and answer. I will not show partiality to any person or use flattery toward any man. For I do not know how to flatter, else would my Maker soon put an end to me. (32: 19–22)

---

[47] Cited in Lumpp, *Philologia Crucis*, p. 31.
[48] Cf. N III, p. 105.
[49] See Lumpp, *Philologia Crucis*, p. 33.

ON "SOLOMON OF PRUSSIA" AND HIGH SCHOOL DRAMA

The ultimate target of Hamann's philological crusade, however, was the Prussian king, Frederick the Great (1712–86).[50] The Francophile philosopher of Sans Souci had assumed power in 1740 and before long had surrounded himself with French courtiers, including for a time his "grand vizier," Voltaire.[51] In response to the king's "enlightened" despotism, and in an act of some political daring, in 1761 Hamann had anonymously published as a separate work a pair of satirical essays in French under the title *Mosaic Essays* (*Essais à la Mosaique*). Apparently, the king refused to read German and could not speak it very well, and so these essays would have been more likely to catch his attention. The first was titled, "A neological and provincial letter on the inoculation of good sense" ("Lettre néologique et provincial sur l'inoculation du bons sens") and picks up on the theme of Hamann's earlier essay, titled "French project." The second, titled "Philippic gloss" ("Glose Philippique"), aside from being a gloss on the first essay, refers to the "Philippics" of Demosthenes, and specifically to an anecdote about King Philip of Macedon, who upon refusing to honor a poor woman's request, supposedly received the tart reply: "Then cease to be king!" ("Desine ergo rex esse!").[52]

As one might gather, the overall tone of these "letters" is one of impertinent defiance – as in Hamann's provocative suggestion that Voltaire is a member of the "academy of Satan." And it is in the same spirit that he ferociously satirizes Frederick a decade later in an unpublished letter "To Solomon of Prussia" ("Au Salomon de Prusse"), and in a final cryptic letter from 1773 with the curious title, "Lost letter of a northern savage to a Peking financier" ("Lettre perdue d'un sauvage du nord à un financier de Pe-Kim").[53] The principal aim of these prophetic letters, which never came to the attention of the king, is to recall Frederick to Christianity from his idolatrous and adulterous affair with French philosophy (whereby he repeats the sin of Solomon); and to this end Hamann even suggests (in jest?) that the king recruit Jesuits to rid Prussia of pagan influences.[54]

The majority of Hamann's battles, however, did not involve the king directly, but rather the literary critics in his capital. In 1763, for example, Hamann was again provoked to respond to Nicolai's journal, this time in defense of his friend Lindner, the rector of a school in Riga. In 1762 Lindner had published a book on school drama, containing many "truly inferior pieces," which the editors of the *Briefe* were quick to lampoon.[55] The pedagogical issues involved, and their implicit connection to the grand Christian theme of divine condescension, were familiar to Hamann from the "*Kinderphysik* fiasco," and so he responded with *Five Pastoral Letters on School Drama* (*Fünf Hirtenbriefe das Schuldrama betreffend*), to which he appended

---

[50]   For further discussion of Hamann's relationship to Frederick the Great, see *JGH*, p. 136ff.

[51]   N II, p. 281.

[52]   N II, p. 278.

[53]   N II, p. 297, p. 299; N III, pp. 55ff. Hamann addresses the king as Solomon, following Voltaire's ode to the "Solomon of the North," who "brings light," but also to indicate his adulterous affair with foreign gods. As Hamann puts it in the *Glose Philippique*, "It is not permitted for you to foreswear the faith of the fathers and your nephews with the *bon sens* of the whores of Ashdod, Ammon, and Moab. It is not fitting to take the bread from the children and cast it to the little dogs, to neglect your vineyard in Baalhamon, and to dally with foreign muses (whose mouths bring forth mere froth and whose right hand is one of lying and deception). – Solomon, the king of Israel, did he not sin in this way?" (N II, p. 293, O'Flaherty's translation).

[54]   N II, pp. 304f.; NB, p. 179.

[55]   NB, p. 122.

the first two letters of his earlier correspondence with Kant. He begins by quoting John 6: 9, which he had earlier quoted in his "Fragments": "One of his disciples, Andrew, Simon Peter's brother, said to him, 'There is a boy here who has five barley loaves and two fish. But what are they among so many people?'" Hamann's point, as the subsequent miracle of the feeding of the five thousand attests, is that, from a divine perspective, a child's meager contribution not only matters, but is capable of confounding the expectations of a reasonable adult (or, in this case, an enlightened literary critic). Accordingly, one must not despise the folly of children or their school productions; for

> every school is a mountain of GOd [sic], like Dothan, full of horses and chariots of fire all around Elisha. Let us, therefore, open our eyes and take heed that we not despise one of these little ones, for theirs is the kingdom of heaven and their angels continually see the face of the Father in heaven – –[56]

In other words, not only do children stand under the protection of heaven, however much learned criticism may be arrayed against them, for Hamann, they themselves can be prophets of divine things. Indeed, "their school stages," he says, "will one day serve as a model for the temples of the Muses"; for their humility is the measure of God's future "dramatic tabernacle."[57] All of which goes to say that the kingdom of God demands a change of perspective: for not only must one learn to condescend to the level of children, which is in itself "an *examen rigorosum*," one must also learn to see in their burlesque performances, which an *Aufklärer* like Diderot would be inclined to ridicule, an image of divine election, which delights in the foolish and the lowly and the things that are not, in order to confound the "wise" and the things that are (1 Cor. 1: 27–8).[58] Such is the Christian irony and humor that guides Hamann's own literary productions, which are small, seemingly insignificant, even contemptible in the eyes of the lesser lights of his day, but which, with God's blessing – like the fragments of the Gospel – he hopes will produce a greater yield than any rational critic would have anticipated, as he triumphs *through the folly* of the Cross.

THE HAMANN–HERDER CONNECTION

The year 1764 marked a new phase in Hamann's literary production. The Russians had finally left Königsberg after the Peace of Hubertusburg, and Hamann's publisher, Kanter, received permission from the Prussian authorities to start a new periodical. The paper was called *Königsbergsche Gelehrte und Politische Zeitungen*, and Hamann became its editor and chief review writer.[59] The year also marked the beginning of a new and – for German intellectual history – immensely consequential friendship: that between the German "Socrates" and his disciple, the German "Plato."[60] In 1762 Johann Gottfried Herder (1744–1803) had arrived in town as the charge of a Russian army doctor, who was grooming him for a medical career; his

---

[56] N II, p. 356. Hamann's text is a cento, a patchwork, of passages from Scripture. See 2 Kgs. 6: 11–17; Matt. 18: 1–11.

[57] N II, p. 356.

[58] N II, pp. 358, 367.

[59] NB, pp. 123f. Among the many books he reviewed were Robinet's *De la nature*, Michaelis's *Erklärung des Briefes and die Hebräer*, and Kant's *Beobachtungen über das Gefühl des Schönen und Erhabenen*. See N IV, pp. 257–435.

[60] See ZH V, p. 217.

interests quickly gravitated to philosophy and theology, however, and somewhere in between Kanter's publishing house (which had published one of his early poems) and meeting the town surgeon (Hamann's father) he made Hamann's acquaintance.[61] By late 1764 Hamann had become Herder's tutor in English and Italian, and before long they became intimate friends. But if their respect for one another was mutual, as Hamann clearly recognized Herder's gifts, their relationship remained that of a mentor and his admiring disciple. For example, Herder writes,

> Dearest Hamann, if you only knew how I view every little scrap [*Flick und Zettel*] I receive from you, surely you would tear none up … Moreover, in every one of your letters is a *single* word that speaks so deeply to me … Again, I ask for your glowing sparks, and promise as soon as possible my drops of water in return.[62]

Similarly, of his perceived role *vis-à-vis* Hamann, Herder refers to himself as "a Turkish camel-driver, who travels ahead to gather sacred apples for his ambling holy beast, which bears the Koran."[63] And regarding their common connection to Kant, he writes, "Kant seems wholly *retiré* with me! But of you he speaks with respect [*Achtung*]."[64] By the end of the year, however, at Hamann's recommendation, Herder received a position at Lindner's school in Riga. In subsequent years they would occasionally see each other, but for the most part after 1769 their friendship was to be carried on in a lifelong correspondence, which Nadler calls "one of the most treasured examples of personality and humanity in the eighteenth century."[65]

In the meantime, on the home front, Hamann's father's health had been steadily declining, and so had his brother's. With the onset of what appeared to be temporary depression, and later turned out to be a more serious case of mental illness, Hamann's brother had resigned from his position at the cathedral school and returned home. For Hamann, this was a source of great concern. Initially, he seems not to have understood the serious nature of his brother's illness and had hopes that he would soon resume his vocation as a teacher; and for a time his brother did take a position as a *Hofmeister*. But things gradually worsened, to the point that his brother too was in need of care; and it was amid these circumstances, in order to procure further household assistance, that Hamann's father employed a young woman named Anna Regina Schumacher (1736–89). She was neither educated nor from the same social class as Hamann, but they soon became intimately involved, without, however, getting engaged or consummating their relationship in marriage; instead, they maintained a so-called "marriage of conscience" (*Gewissensehe*). Whatever Hamann's reasons may have been, this arrangement was a cause of consternation to friends and critics alike, and to this day remains one of the strangest aspect of his life.[66] Questions of moral probity aside, however, one should bear in mind that Hamann still felt inwardly betrothed to Catharina Berens, his "Aspasia," the wife he believed God had ordained for him, and thus, according to Nadler,

---

[61] NB, pp. 150ff.

[62] ZH III, pp. 60–1. At the conclusion of the letter, Herder even goes so far as to say, "Greetings and a kiss to your two children, and you, Magus of the North, speak only a word, that my wife might soon bear one too."

[63] NB, p. 153; ZH II, p. 315.

[64] NB, p. 153; ZH II, p. 265.

[65] NB, p. 154; cf. p. 193: "Hamann's letters to Herder are by themselves enough to justify a life and commemoration by posterity. Hardly ever has one genius so candidly, so benevolently, so strictly educated another. Rarely has one genius more willingly, more sensibly, and on such equal footing, allowed himself to be educated by another."

[66] See *JGH*, pp. 26f.

could see his renunciation of marriage as a form of self-denial.[67] In a later work Hamann also suggests reasons enunciated by Paul (1 Cor. 7: 26), and that his refusal to marry is to be seen in terms of an "apocalyptically" legitimate defiance of an illegitimate Prussian state, whose king was a secularist and whose marriage laws, as embodied in the *Codex iuris Fridericiani*, he refused to recognize. Given, further- more, their difference in social standing, Hamann confides to Herder that he was "inwardly convinced" that a marriage would be ill-suited both to Regina's happi- ness and the happiness of their children.[68] Admittedly, none of this fully allays the offense; but, as we shall see, one of the peculiar characteristics of Hamann's piety was that he did not want to allay it. On the contrary, he in many ways intentionally sought to appear worse than he actually was (hence his self-portrait as Pan), seeing this as more appropriate to genuine Christianity and discipleship than the bour- geoise norms of a hypocritically Christian state.

If Hamann's life had been rather topsy-turvy until now, after a failed trip to find employment as a house tutor for the princess of Hessia in 1763 and a brief stint as a secretary and translator for a friend in Mitau from 1765 to 1766, things finally set- tled down in 1767. For it was in this year, as a result of Kant's direct help, that he gained his first steady job as a translator with the Königsberg General Excise and Customs Administration. Given Hamann's earlier polemics against the Prussian state, this position was as ironic as it was disagreeable: working under the supervi- sion of imported French bureaucrats, the new oppressors, he was not only working for the king, but even helping to collect taxes on his behalf. That being said, the posi- tion was a blessing, providing enough income for him to buy a house on the out- skirts of town, where he and Regina could begin their household, together with Hamann's brother, for whom they cared until his premature death in 1778. After a few years they had a son, Johann Michael (b. 1769), and then three daughters, Elisabeth Regina (b. 1772), Magdalena Katharina (b. 1774), and Marianne Sophie (b. 1778). To judge from Hamann's correspondence, their home seems to have been a very happy one. Since it was situated far from work, however, Hamann acquired a small place *am alten Graben*, which was closer to his office; and it was here, for the most part, that he resumed his "authorship."

Though busy as never before, Hamann continued as editor of Kanter's journal until 1776, writing many more reviews. As far as the history of ideas is concerned, perhaps his most significant contribution to the journal was a partial translation of Hume's *Treatise of Human Nature,* which was published in 1771 under the title *Night Thoughts of a Doubter (Nachtgedanken eines Zweiflers).*[69] Its significance lies in the fact that Kant would almost certainly have read it, a full ten years prior to the publication of the *Critique of Pure Reason.* And this, together with Hamann's *Socratic Memorabilia* and their correspondence during this period (in which Hume's skepticism played a prominent role), doubtless contributed to Kant's famous "awak- ening" from his "dogmatic slumbers." Indeed, Hamann was probably the most important source for Kant's knowledge of Hume, from his early correspondence

---

[67] NB, p. 160.

[68] See N III, pp. 199f.; ZH III, p. 263. For further discussion, see G-D, pp. 248ff. The most idealized interpretation, in any case, is that of Nadler: "The new attraction to Anna Regina did not replace the old one to Catharina, but melted with it into a single melody, almost as a harmony of heavenly and earthly love" (N IV, p. 485).

[69] N IV, pp. 364–70. The translation of Hume's *Treatise* is of the so-called "conclusion of the book," section I, 4, 7. See Oswald Bayer, *Vernunft ist Sprache: Hamanns Metakritik Kants* (Stuttgart: Frommann-Holzboog, 2002), p. 44.

with Kant in 1759 to a partial translation in 1780 of Hume's *Dialogues Concerning Natural Religion,* which Kant read and greatly appreciated, to the point of encouraging its publication.[70] In addition to his work for the journal, Hamann also undertook several other translations during this period, including a study of gout published in 1770 and three essays published together in 1774 on: Bolingbroke's "Letters on the study and use of history," Hervey's "Remarks on Lord Bolingbroke's letters," and Thomas Hunter's "Observations on Tacitus."[71]

The most significant of Hamann's writings during this time, however, are his so-called *Herderschriften,* which concern the subject of language and, in particular, the question of its origin. The subject had been of widespread interest during the Enlightenment, involving intellectuals across Europe. For example, William Warburton, the Bishop of Gloucester, had written on the topic in *The Divine Legation of Moses* (1738), in which he affirmed a divine origin of language.[72] The French Abbé Condillac, on the other hand, argued for an origin in the cries of animals in his *Essai sur l'origine des connaissances humaines,* which was published in 1746. Along somewhat similar lines, in his *Essai sur l'origine des langues,* written between 1749 and 1755 (but unpublished until 1782), Rousseau had argued that language's origin was to be found in the passions: "It is neither hunger nor thirst but love, hatred, pity, anger, which drew from them the first words."[73] Rejecting the so-called "higher" hypothesis (i.e., of a divine origin), the French president of the Berlin Academy, Maupertuis, attempted a synthesis of rational and empirical approaches in his *Dissertation sur les différens moyens, dont les hommes se sont servis pour exprimer leurs idées,* published in 1754.[74] And this, in turn, elicited a response from Johann Peter Süßmilch, another member of the Academy, who defended the "higher" hypothesis in his *Versuch eines Beweises, daß die erste Sprache ihren Ursprung nicht von Menschen, sondern allein vom Schöpfer erhalten habe,* which was composed in 1756, but not published until 1766.

By 1769 the Berlin Academy was clearly seeking a resolution to the debate when it announced a prize competition, calling for essays in response to the following two-part question: "Supposing that human beings were left to their own natural faculties, would they be in a condition to invent language? And, if so, by what means would they manage to invent it?"[75] The question could not have been more opportune for Herder, who had been contemplating the topic for some time, and he took the prize with his last-minute submission, *Abhandlung über den Ursprung der Sprache,* which was completed in December 1770 and subsequently published by the Academy in 1772. Hamann, however, did not greet his disciple's prize-winning essay with the same degree of enthusiasm, but feared that he had gone "whoring after the

---

[70] N III, pp. 245–74. As it happens, this last translation was never published, since another translation had already appeared. Even so, it was the first translation of the *Dialogues* that Kant would have read (just prior to the appearance of his *Critique of Pure Reason*).

[71] NB, p. 342.

[72] For a contemporary discussion of Warburton's ideas on language, see Milbank, *The Word Made Strange,* pp. 55–63.

[73] J.-J. Rousseau, *Essay on the Origin of Languages,* tr. John H. Moran, in *On the Origin of Language,* introd. by Alexander Gode (Chicago: University of Chicago Press, 1986), p. 12.

[74] In 1755 Maupertuis published another work on the same topic, *Refléxions philosophiques sur l'origine des langues et sur la signification des mots.*

[75] For more on this topic and the background of Hamann's *Herderschriften,* see G-D, pp. 154ff., and Frederick C. Beiser, *The Fate of Reason: German Philosophy from Kant to Fichte* (Cambridge, MA: Harvard University Press, 1987), pp. 130ff.

beautiful spirits of his century and their *bon ton.*"[76] Therein lay the circumstances of Hamann's so-called *Herderschriften*, commencing with a pair of reviews that originally appeared in the *Königsbergische gelehrte und politische Zeitungen,* and which Hamann subsequently published with a pseudonymous supplement in 1772. The first was a review of another anonymous submission to the Academy by Dietrich Tiedemann, titled "Attempt at an explanation of the origin of language" (*Versuch einer Erklärung des Ursprungs der Sprache*); the second, was a review of Herder's *Preisschrift.*[77]

Whether or not Hamann's review does justice to Tiedemann's *Versuch* (Beiser, for one, considers it a noteworthy contribution), his review is damningly brief.[78] Tiedemann defines language as an instrumental "collection of tones" for the purpose of communicating pre-linguistic thoughts. And so Hamann bitterly asks, "Why not go ahead and call it a machine?"[79] Clearly, Hamann has little regard for materialist explanations of language, either as a function of the parts of speech or as arising from a logical "necessity of connecting tones with representations."[80] Regarding the former, he says, with apparent irony, "The *origin of human language* and the *invention* of the *Partium Orationis* are as different from one another as reason, logic, and Barbara Celarent."[81] The problem with the other explanation is not only that there are no such things as pre-linguistic concepts that, once they are formed, subsequently have to be connected to visible or audible signs – since concepts are a function of language to begin with – but that the so-called "explanation" begs the question of the mysterious relationship between thought and language in the first place. Thus Hamann "leaves it to readers, who have gotten beyond *middle school [die mehr als Primaner sind]*, and are no bribed journalists, to see for themselves how vapid and banal the author's philosophy is." Adding insult to injury, he then says, "Aside from the fact that he [Tiedemann] can conceive of language only from the standpoint of *grammar,* he seems not even properly to have mastered the latter in his own mother tongue."[82] Hamann thereupon concludes the review expecting that he will have more and presumably better things to say about Herder's *Preisschrift.*

As it turned out, Hamann was bitterly disappointed. He had expected Herder to trounce Tiedemann's naturalism and successfully defend Süßmilch's "higher" hypothesis. Instead, his own disciple ended up deriding the "higher" hypothesis and espousing the very naturalism that Hamann despised. Although Hamann begins to state his case against Herder in his review, his full-scale response was carried out in two independent works that were composed around the same time: *The Knight of the Rose-Cross' Last Will and Testament concerning the Divine and Human Origin of Language (Des Ritters von Rosencreuz letzte Willensmeynung über den göttlichen und menschlichen Ursprung der Sprache*), which presents Hamann's own views on the origin of language, and his *Philological Ideas and Doubts concerning an Academic Prize Essay (Philologische Einfälle und Zweifel über eine akademische Preisschrift*),

---

[76] ZH III, pp. 16f.
[77] N III, pp. 13–24.
[78] See G-D, p. 164; and Beiser, *The Fate of Reason,* p. 135.
[79] N III, p. 15.
[80] N III, p. 16.
[81] Ibid. "Barbara Celarent" was from the first line of a famous syllogistic poem, and thus had everything to do with reason and logic.
[82] N III, p. 16.

in which he corrects Herder's *Preisschrift* like a schoolboy composition.[83] The first text, whose title alludes both to the Lutheran coat-of-arms (which depicts a cross in a rose) and to the Rosicrucianism of a contemporary, Johann August Starck (1741–1816), presents Hamann's mature views on language as at once natural and supernatural, human and divine. The second is, in the words of von Balthasar, "a devastating caricature" of Herder's naturalism.[84] But even if Hamann presumes to correct his former student's essay, according to Nadler it was as if the right hand were correcting the left; indeed, so closely did they work together that Hamann remained Herder's teacher, while Herder continued to be Hamann's counselor and spokesman to the next generation.[85]

A SATIRICAL MASTERPIECE AND OTHER WRITINGS

That Hamann and Herder remained on intimate terms can be seen from their subsequent correspondence. For example, toward the end of 1773 Hamann wrote to his friend to announce the publication of his comic masterpiece, *New Apology of the Letter h* (*Neue Apologie des Buchstaben h*).[86] Though the title would not suggest as much, the *New Apology* was occasioned by a recent work on religion, *Betrachtungen über die Religion*, by a contemporary rationalist, Christian Tobias Damm. The latter work was only partially concerned with orthography, but given Damm's sensibility as a zealous rationalist, having little patience for the contingent and arbitrary aspects of language or religion, the silent terminal h (as in words like *Rath* or *Muth*), which in his view had no ostensible phonetic purpose, had to go.[87] Few occasions could

---

[83] As it happens, *Philological Ideas and Doubts* was never published, ultimately it seems out of respect for Herder (see their exchange in this regard, ZH III, pp. 36–42). Initially, however, Hamann had sought to publish it with his scathing attack on Frederick, *Au Salomon de Prusse*. Having been turned down by Kanter, Hartung, and, oddly enough, the local lodge of the Freemasons (see N III, pp. 61–5), Hamann even tried to publish it through Nicolai in Berlin. Having received no reply from the latter, he then had published, in the form of an appeal, his almost impenetrable *Monologue of an Author* (*Selbstgespräch eines Autors*) under the ludicrous Chinese pseudonym Mien-Man-Hoam (N III, pp. 67–79). Upon being turned down by Nicolai, he then had published another farce, *To the Witch at Kadmonbor* (*An die Hexe zu Kadmonbor*), in which Nicolai, lacking a *museus sinicus*, allegedly asks a witch to help him translate the Mandarin's (i.e., Hamann's) correspondence, at which point his letter is suddenly transformed into a monologue, and the addressee into a two-faced Alecto (one of the Furies) with a "Juno-like eye of a calf and a watering eye of an owl" (N III, pp. 81–6). Hamann, speaking as Nicolai, then ends the letter with the suggestion that Mien-Man-Hoam (i.e., Hamann) follow the example of his ancestor Haman to the gallows (Esther 7: 10), in one of many comical plays on his own bad name (see N III, p. 173). Of course, all absurdity aside, had Nicolai published Hamann's work, it almost certainly would have met with the censors and possibly had serious consequences for Hamann himself. NB, pp. 203ff.; N III, pp. 423f.

[84] Hans Urs von Balthasar, *The Glory of the Lord: A Theological Aesthetics* (San Francisco: Ignatius, 1985), vol. 3, p. 248. This is not to say that Hamann rejects the natural hypothesis altogether, but only a natural hypothesis that would exclude the supernatural (as the origin of the natural).

[85] NB, p. 195. Cf. p. 194: "It was truly a spiral in which their shared intellectual life circled ever higher from the one to the other. All of Hamann's and Herder's writings, especially during this period, developed out of mutual interaction and coordination with one another."

[86] The "new" in the title is feigned, as is the stated place of publication, Pisa. Kant, for his part, enjoyed the piece so much that he hoped Hamann would continue to write in this vein. See *JGH*, p. 120; NB, p. 214.

[87] Thus Damm prescribes against this "barbaric," "useless," and "unfounded" practice, which he considers an international embarrassment, "that no letter be written that cannot be pronounced, and, consequently, that the pronunciation of letters be the sole and highest judge in matters of orthography …" For, "Whoever is unfaithful in the orthography of the little letter h is willingly unfaithful and unjust in the great revelations and mysteries of universal, sound and practical human religion" (quoted by Hamann, N III, pp. 91, 93). In other words, Damm viewed writing as a pristine mirror of speech, and in this regard, as we shall see, Hamann's critique of Damm and defense of "writing" bears some comparison to Derrida's deconstruction of the purity of "speech."

have been so suited to Hamann's sense of humor, irony, and righteous indignation, and so he leapt to the poor letter's defense: first in the guise of "Heinrich Schröder," an old Königsberg schoolteacher, who purports to know something about orthography, and then in the voice of the letter h itself.

In the first part of the work Hamann makes mincemeat of Damm's claims, especially those regarding the clarity and consistency of his position. Among other things, Hamann points out that Damm would by the same token have to get rid of all double consonants, e.g., "ll, the ß, tt, mm, nn," which are yet more difficult if not impossible to pronounce.[88] He also points out Damm's hypocrisy, given that he *arbitrarily* exempts the double consonants in his own name. So why, Hamann asks, this idiosyncratic, *fanatical,* and indeed *irrational* hostility toward the little letter h? Furthermore, Hamann predicts that if Damm's reforms should succeed, if our pronunciation should meet with the same fate as our religion, whereby both are made to conform to the Procrustean bed of an imperious, supposedly universal "rational" standard,

> then the fate of our mother tongue is easy to foresee. What divisions! What Babylonian confusion! What muddling of letters! [*Buchstabenmengerey*]. All the diversity of dialects and their *siboleths* [*sic*] would pour into the books of every province, and what *dam* [punning on *Damm*] would be able to stop this orthographical flood?[89]

In other words, aside from the butchering, emasculation, and enervation of language that would ensue, no amount of rational orthography could handle the sheer mass of arbitrary elements of which language is comprised, or suffice to impose universal norms on something that is through and through determined by history, tradition, and etymology, by idioms and dialects that are always particular and contingent. Thus Hamann at once damningly and comically says in view of Damm's incomprehension of this fact,

> I would ten times over rather talk to a blind man about the *first* and *fourth* days of the Mosaic creation account, or lose my breath to the wind talking to a deaf man about the harmony of a little nightingale and a French castrate than dispute any longer with an opponent who is not even able to see that a universal, sound, practical human language, human reason, and human religion, without *arbitrary* principles, is its own *oven of ice*.[90]

That is to say, for Hamann, the notion of a universal, essentially ahistorical language, the *desideratum* of the rational orthographers, is a *contradictio in adjecto* – as is the notion of a universal, ahistorical rationality and the notion of a universal, ahistorical, but supposedly "natural" religion.

The combination of the terseness of Hamann's language and the expansiveness of his point here is striking; indeed, one sees in this last quotation a perfect example of how, contra the Enlighteners, he strove to achieve a sublime style in imitation of the allegorical profundity and parabolic power of the Word of God – a style that could be described as "elastic grain," hard to chew and at first digest, but containing

---

[88]   N III, p. 94.
[89]   Ibid.
[90]   N III, p. 97.

depths of potential meaning that have yet to unfold and appear. For in so few words about so seemingly narrow and incidental a subject as orthography, one can find essentially the whole of his critique of the Enlightenment.[91]

The wide-ranging implication here is that, for Hamann, the fanatical attack of the orthographers on the little letter h perfectly represented the spirit of the age and its attack upon everything that is offensive to "reason," and which it therefore similarly sought to excise, be it the mystery of the incarnation, the mystery of the Cross, or the mystery of a God who is one yet three. Accordingly, the first part of the work concludes by inveighing against Damm's hypocrisy, the poverty of pure reason, and the murderous stupidity of the age, which would presume to eliminate from natural language a mysterious image of the Spirit of the invisible God.

In a satirical postlude the letter h then begins to speak for itself in its own voice. Prophesying against the reformers, it says: "You little prophets of Bohemian-Breda! Do not wonder that I speak in a human voice, like that mute beast of burden [i.e., Balaam's ass], in order to punish you for your transgression. Your life is what I am – a breath."[92] Indeed, for Hamann, the silent letter h, which is an offense to reason, is symbolic not only of life and soul and the invisible creative human spirit, but ultimately of the creative breath of God, whose humble, kenotic presence in Scripture, creation, and the lives of inspired Christians the "enlightened" reformers similarly cannot comprehend.[93] Moreover, in his view, the attempt to excise the letter h was symptomatic of the larger attempt, in the name of the establishment of a purely secular state, to excise the very Spirit whose invisible presence is the origin of all human language and society – leaving the rump of an artificial language and an artificial society that are *eo ipso* devoid of spirit and life (John 6: 63). Accordingly, the *New Apology* expresses Hamann's call for a poetic restoration of language as a vehicle of inspiration, as a medium of things human and divine, upon which anycultural renewal would also depend. For, as he keenly recognized, as it goes with a language, so it goes with a people, given that the culture of a people is *essentially* and not arbitrarily a function of its language, its forms of discourse. By the same token, this is why, in Hamann's estimation, the tampering of the *Aufklärer* with language, this sacred matrix, was no minor affair. Rather, given what it represented, it threatened to enervate the whole of European culture – at least inasmuch as, in the name of secular reason, the spirit of God, the source of all creativity and inspiration (symbolized by the silent h), is fanatically excised from public discourse.

Following Nadler's classification, the next group of Hamann's writings comprises three texts, beginning with his *Supplement to the Memorabilia of the Blessed Socrates* (*Beylage zun Denkwürdigkeiten des seligen Sokrates*), which was written toward the end of 1772 and is a reprise of the original theme of his authorship. The work was occasioned by Johann August Eberhard's *New Apology of Socrates* (*Neue Apologie des Socrates*), in which the author, a liberal theologian from Halle (and later teacher

---

[91] As O'Flaherty rightly observes regarding the *New Apology*, this work is not only the best sustained example of Hamann's irony and humor but is at the same time remarkable for its combination of micrological detail with the broadest of metaphysical principles. Nowhere else has Hamann so successfully balanced so weighty a topic on so narrow a base. (*JGH*, p. 120).

[92] N III, p. 105. The epithet, "little prophets of Bohemian Breda," derives from Friedrich Melchior Grimm's polemic, *Le Petit Prophète de Böhmischbroda* (1753).

[93] N III, p. 106.

of Schleiermacher), argued against the damnation of the pagans. It was not this aspect of Eberhard's argument, however, that Hamann found provocative, given his own positive treatment of Socrates in the *Socratic Memorabilia* and his own largesse toward paganism in general (deriving from his understanding of divine providence and the prophetic working of the Holy Spirit throughout human history). Rather it was Eberhard's purely rational presentation of Socrates as a "proselyte of our modern jokers and moralists," stripped of the religious and prophetic aspects that Hamann had earlier emphasized. For that matter, Hamann realized that Eberhard's apology was not so much a defense of paganism as it was an attack upon traditional Christianity, whereas his own treatment of Socrates was intended precisely as a *praeparatio evangelica.*[94] Thus, in the form of a comical review written in the voice of "a cleric from Swabia," he comes to the defense both of Christian orthodoxy and, incidentally, the Herrnhuter brethren.

Hamann's *Prolegomena on the Newest Interpretation of the Oldest Document of the Human Race* (*Prolegomena über die neueste Auslegung der ältesten Urkunde des menschlichen Geschlechts*) belongs to this same group. Written in early 1774 in the voice of "Christianus Zacchaeus" to a certain "Apollonium philosophum," the *Prolegomena* is a recommendation to Kant (Apollonius philosophus) of Herder's *Oldest Document of the Human Race.*[95] The two had previously corresponded about Herder's work, and Hamann was now proposing to publish it.[96] Aside from stating his agreement with Herder, in whom he takes pride as Isaac in Esau, as well as vouching for the importance of Genesis as an "historical document," Hamann makes some striking observations regarding language and Scripture, among them the following: "*language* and *Scripture* [*Schrift*] are the most inescapable *organs* and conditions of all human learning, more essential and absolute than the eye to seeing and sound to hearing."[97] (From here, as we shall see, it is but a step to Hamann's later "metacritique" of the "purisms" and a priori method of Kant's critical philosophy.) The main theme of the work, accordingly, as the title and references to Church Fathers such as Cyril of Alexandria and Lactantius suggest, is a return to origins, "to the basic elements of the oracles of God" (Heb. 5: 12).[98] But as with all of Hamann's works, this one too had a particular motivation, in this case the dubious doctrines of his contemporary, Johann August Starck. Indeed, just as Herder had renewed Hamann's interest in primordial history, it was Starck's pronouncements concerning the origins of Christianity that led Hamann to a more intensive study of the early Church.[99] And it was largely in response to Starck that Hamann's next and most cryptic set of writings, his so-called *Mysterienschriften,* were conceived.

---

[94] N III, p. 114.
[95] N III, pp. 123ff; see NB, p. 224. The pseudonym and the epithet for Kant refer to a text from the early Church titled, *Consultationum Zacchaei Christiani et Apollonii Philosophi.*
[96] Cf. ZH III, pp. 82–90.
[97] N III, p. 130.
[98] N III, p. 125.
[99] Hamann already had a knowledge of the Fathers through his early study of Rapin, as well as of the ancient philosophies of Plato and the Neoplatonists, e.g., Plotinus, Porphyry, and Iamblichus. According to Nadler, however, none was as important to him as "the wise man," Philo, whose works he had acquired no later than 1763. See NB, p. 253. In any event, guided by Johann Lorenz Mosheim's *De rebus Christianorum ante Constantinum Magnum Comentarii,* which were published in 1753, he now quotes freely from Justin, Minutius Felix, Clement, Origen, and Cyril of Alexandria, from Lactantius, Irenaeus, Photius, Tertullian, Eusebius, et al. See N III, p. 152; see also NB, pp. 187f., 197.

5

Toward a Christological Poetics: A New Aesthetics of Scripture and Creation

With his theological Aesthetica in nuce, *Hamann stands in the background of the whole idealist movement, mysteriously over-shadowing it, but at the same time just as mysteriously surpassing it …*

Hans Urs von Balthasar[1]

Neither the dogmatic soundness of orthodox Pharisees, nor the poetic extravagance of free-thinking Sadducees will renew the sending of the Spirit who drove the holy men of GOd (ευκαιρως ακαιρως) to speak and to write.

Aesthetica in nuce[2]

… Christian or poet. *Do not be surprised that these are synonyms.*

Hamann to Lindner[3]

Hamann's *Aesthetica in nuce: Eine Rhapsodie in Kabbalistischer Prose,* the central text in his collection *Crusades of the Philologist,* has long been regarded as a manifesto of the proto-Romantic movement known as the *Sturm und Drang,* and there is much truth to this.[4] Thus Hamann is rightly described as a defender of the "man of feeling" (to borrow the title of Henry Mackenzie's famous work), the individual artist, and the rights of genius over against an excessively rational approach to nature and human creativity. As Hamann strikingly puts it, "Nature works through the senses and passions. How could one sense anything who has mutilated her instruments?"[5] Accordingly, the *Aesthetica* may legitimately be read as an excoriating critique of the dispassionate and therefore jejune art and literary criticism of the age, which is unable to see that creation itself is a work of genius (contra Descartes, it is more than a machine or a system of vortices), and that every individual feat of creative genius is likewise something that reason alone, having stoically disabused itself of the senses and the passions, is impotent to fathom or reproduce.

By extension, the *Aesthetica* may also be read as a prophetic indictment of modern philosophy in general, with its dubious anthropological starting point (in Descartes)

---

[1] Hans Urs von Balthasar, "Laikale Stile," in *Herrlichkeit: Eine Theologische Ästhetik* II/2 (Einsiedeln: Johannes Verlag, 1962), p. 603.
[2] N II, p. 211. One might render ευκαιρως ακαιρως as "in season and out of season." Cf. 2 Tim. 4: 2.
[3] ZH I, p. 367.
[4] See, for example, M. H. Abrams's classic study, *Natural Supernaturalism: Tradition and Revolution in Romantic Literature* (New York and London: Norton, 1971), pp. 400ff.
[5] N II, p. 206.

and its corresponding anaesthetic *insensibility* for anything outside of or beyond the control of the modern subject. For once the assumptions of modern philosophy are accepted and the finite rationality of the modern subject becomes the measure of all reality, the invisible things of God no longer *appear* in and through the "things that have ·been made" (Rom. 1: 20). In other words, once the analogical community between the visible and the invisible is broken, and God no longer appears within the horizon of theoretical philosophy, the possibility of a theological *aesthetics* – of a seeing of the infinite in the finite – is foreclosed. Moreover, once the mysterious bond between the visible and the invisible is severed (according to what Hamann identified as the characteristic *Scheidekunst* of modernity), and once all mystery disappears into either the "otherworldly" (for those still possessed of a religious imagination, however impoverished) or the "unreal" (for those lacking it altogether), the only reality that is left inevitably reduces to what is either a priori or technologically "in our power."[6] All of which is inaugurated in Descartes's fantasy of self-mutilation in the opening of his *Meditations* – "I shall consider myself as not having hands or eyes, or flesh, or blood or senses, but as falsely believing that I have all these things. I shall stubbornly and firmly persist in this meditation; and, even if it is not in my power to know any truth, I shall at least do what is in my power ..." – which heralds both the pathology and, arguably, the violence of modern philosophy in general.[7]

The only problem with this reading, at least when it is taken as a sufficient summary of Hamann's text, is that it tends to neglect not only his specifically Christian view of how the senses and passions are to be restored, but also the exegetical debate between him and J. D. Michaelis, the father of modern biblical criticism, apart from which the work as a whole is unintelligible. Indeed, even Hamann's paean to poetry and poetic genius must be understood in the context of his response to Michaelis's historical-critical approach to Scripture – especially the latter's heavily annotated 1758 edition of Lowth's lectures on the sacred poetry of the Hebrews, originally delivered in Latin in 1753 (*De sacra poesi Hebraeorum praelectiones academicae*)[8] – and his denial of a mystical, typological sense of Scripture, which both Hamann and Lowth affirmed.[9]

Admittedly, a debate about biblical exegesis might seem too narrow a concern for a text that deals with such wide-ranging topics as creation, human creativity, the origin of language, and the canons of poetry. One will recall, however, that in the wake of his conversion Hamann viewed the Bible as a mystical key to all reality, revealing the extra-biblical world of nature and history to be, analogous to the Bible itself, a book full of signs and prophetic typologies of the ever-speaking Logos. Accordingly, rather than limiting one's perception, for Hamann the Bible opened mysterious dimensions of meaning that are otherwise "sealed" to the rationalism of supposedly "enlightened" modern exegetes (in the sense of Matt. 11: 25). As Joachim

---

[6] See in this regard, von Balthasar's discussion of the "halving of the mystery" in *Cordula oder der Ernstfall* (Einsiedeln: Johannes Verlag, 1987), pp. 64ff.

[7] *Descartes, The Philosophical Writings*, vol. 2, trans. J. Cottingham, R. Stoothoff, D. Murdoch (Cambridge: Cambridge University Press, 1984), p. 15. See in this regard Max Horkheimer and Theodor W. Adorno, *Dialectic of Enlightenment*, trans. John Cumming (New York: Continuum, 1994).

[8] As it happens, much of Michaelis's commentary was included in the English translation of Lowth of 1787. See Robert Lowth, *Lectures on the Sacred Poetry of the Hebrews*, trans. G. Gregory, FAS (Boston: Joseph T. Buckingham, 1815).

[9] Given Michaelis's status as commentator, one might think that Hamann's dispute with him would also, implicitly, be a dispute with Lowth; in point of fact, however, Hamann not only shares many of Lowth's positions, but in the opening of the *Aesthetica* makes a point of distinguishing between them, as between the wheat and the chaff.

Ringleben puts it, "The Bible was his *Hen* because it disclosed the *Pan.*"[10] Indeed, for Hamann the Bible contained, in a loosely kabbalistic sense, the elemental principles of all things, the ABCs in which all things are written, and this is why exegetical errors here (of the kind he finds in Michaelis) are so grievous. For to the extent that they distort one's understanding of the biblical text, they invariably distort one's perception of everything. The ultimate reason, then, why Hamann needs to "clear the threshing floor of holy literature" – and why he needs to separate the "wheat" of Lowth's lectures from the "chaff" of Michaelis's commentary – is so that, like his contemporary William Blake, with whom he bears some comparison, he can "cleanse the doors of perception."[11]

If one approaches the *Aesthetica* in this light, Hamann's seemingly abrupt transitions from the topic of biblical exegesis to the subject of creation and human creativity (which from the underside of the carpet, so to speak, seem abrupt and disjointed) suddenly appear seamless. The same applies to Hamann's transition to the topic of human language as an interpretive response to the language of creation (see Gen. 2: 20), and to his transition from language to poetry, since for him, as for Lowth, the two were originally one and the same: "Poetry is the mother-tongue of the human race."[12] Moreover, for Hamann, following Lowth, inasmuch as it involves a question of origins, the question of language qua poetry is also a question of religion.[13] Indeed, for Hamann, all language, and poetic language in particular, betrays a common religious root, being fundamentally – however distorted or jumbled it now may be – an utterance of the *imago Dei* in response to the Logos – the Word in the words – of creation (John 1: 3; Col. 1: 16).

Therein lies the theological basis of Hamann's "philo-logical" investigations, which allows him to treat pagan poetry as a subclass of prophetic literature. It is also why he can say in all seriousness, in the name of a radical Christian worldliness, "To me, every book is a Bible."[14] But inasmuch as the Bible remains the *liber instar omnium,* the "book of books," moreover the most poetic of books, as Hamann following Lowth contends, it necessarily comprises a kind of aesthetic canon. In other words, the Bible is for Hamann in some mysterious sense the measure of all poetry and literature. On the one hand, this allows him to escape the confines of a narrow biblicism and make an effortless transition from the Bible to the world of literature, from the sacred to the profane.[15] On the other hand, it allows him to *prove* all things in light of Scripture, which remained for him the mysterious final Word among the words of the world.

Accordingly, the guiding thread of the *Aesthetica,* which weaves all of Hamann's reflections together, is analogy: an analogy between the interpretation of Scripture and the interpretation of creation; an analogy between the poetic language of creation

---

[10] Joachim Ringleben, "Gott als Schriftsteller: Zur Geschichte eines Topos," in *Johann Georg Hamann: 'Der hellste Kopf seiner Zeit,'* ed. Oswald Bayer (Tübingen: Attempto Verlag, 1998), p. 37. Cf. *LS,* p. 132 (N I, p. 72): "God has revealed everything in his Word."

[11] N II, p. 197. See *The Complete Poetry and Prose of William Blake,* ed. David V. Erdman (London: Doubleday, 1988), p. 39: "If the doors of perception were cleansed every thing would appear as it is: infinite." For an illuminating recent study, see Matthew J. A. Green, *Visionary Materialism in the Early Works of William Blake: The Intersection of Enthusiasm and Empiricism* (New York: Palgrave Macmillan, 2005).

[12] N II, p. 197.

[13] See Lowth, *Lectures on the Sacred Poetry,* p. 26, "Thus if the actual origin of poetry be inquired after, it must of necessity be referred to religion ..."

[14] ZH I, p. 309.

[15] James C. O'Flaherty, "East and West in the thought of Hamann," in *The Quarrel of Reason with Itself: Essays on Hamann, Michaelis, Lessing, Nietzsche* (Columbia, SC: Camden House, 1988), p. 110.

and the poetic language of human beings; an analogy, furthermore between the poetry of Scripture and the poetries of world literature; and, finally, an analogy between divine and human criticism, which points to the ultimate, eschatological "criticism," i.e., the judgment (from κρίνειν), of Christ. Admittedly, on a first reading, the *Aesthetica* would seem to belie any strict organization; closer examination, however, shows it to be a highly intricate and organized *text* (as are, for that matter, all of Hamann's publications), revealing a clear logic to the weave of its overlapping progression: from Scripture, to creation, to poetry. In the following, therefore, I will first discuss Hamann's understanding of Scripture *vis-à-vis* Michaelis, focusing on the *Cloverleaf of Hellenistic Letters* as a propaedeutic to the concerns of the *Aesthetica*; then, in the context of a discussion of the *Aesthetica*, we will see how a distinctive biblical exegesis broadens into and blends with a distinctive exegesis of nature; finally, I will sum up Hamann's aesthetics of Scripture, creation, and poetry in terms of a properly Christological poetics.

If the foregoing helps to untangle some of the threads of the *Aesthetica*, suggesting that they are ultimately part of an intricate, overlapping design, a few additional observations may also be helpful regarding its style. For if there is an intricate, "beautiful" pattern to the text, as I have suggested, then it is hidden from view beneath the tempestuous waves, the Dionysian dithyrambs, of Hamann's "sublime," oracular style. We have already discussed this style in general and in the *Socratic Memorabilia*. The difference here is that Hamann's style becomes still more prophetic, energetic, and declamatory, in keeping with Lowth's observations regarding the sublimity of Hebrew poetry. Indeed, Lowth's observations apply so readily to Hamann's own style as to be worth quoting at length:

> These observations are remarkably exemplified in the Hebrew poetry than which the human mind can conceive nothing more elevated, more beautiful, or more elegant; in which the almost ineffable sublimity of the subject is fully equaled by the energy of the language, and the dignity of the style. And it is worthy [of] observation, that as some of these writings exceed in antiquity the fabulous ages of Greece, in sublimity they are superior to the most polished productions of that polished people. Thus if the actual origin of poetry be inquired after, it must of necessity be referred to religion; and since it appears to be an art derived from nature alone, peculiar to no age or nation, and only at an advanced period of society conformed to rule and method, it must be wholly attributed to the more violent affections of the heart, the nature of which is to express themselves in an animated and lofty tone, with a vehemence of expression far removed from vulgar use. It is also no less observable, that these affections break and interrupt the enunciation by their impetuosity; they burst forth in sentences pointed, earnest, rapid, and tremulous; and in some degree the style as well as the modulation is adapted to the emotions and habits of the mind ... Is it not probable, that the first effort of rude and unpolished verse would display itself in the praise of the Creator, and flow almost involuntarily from the enraptured mind?[16]

To be sure, since the eighteenth century not one reader of Hamann has failed to appreciate or lament or at least comment upon the eccentricity of his style: for some he is dark and cryptic, but profound; for others, modern-day heirs of the *Aufklärer*, his style is a case in point of his irrationalism. But, as Lowth's description reveals,

---

[16] Lowth, *Lectures on the Sacred Poetry*, pp. 25f. Cf. John Milbank, *The Word Made Strange: Theology, Language, Culture* (Oxford: Blackwell, 1997), p. 65: "Hence Lowth emphasizes what he calls (borrowing from Cicero) the *sententious* style of Hebrew poetry: exemplified most of all in its 'brevity', supplying 'a more energetic and pointed effect', which is simple and direct and yet just for that reason results in fascinating 'obscurity' ..."

Hamann's style is more than anything a self-conscious imitation of the sublime, oracular style both he and Lowth attributed to the sacred poetry of the Hebrews.

CLOVERLEAF OF HELLENISTIC LETTERS: ON THE STYLE OF SCRIPTURE

A further indication that Hamann's style is modeled on the inspired, and therefore sublimely energetic style of Scripture can be gleaned from the epigraph to his *Cloverleaf of Hellenistic Letters*, which comes from Romans 15: 15: τολμηρότερον δὲ ἔγραψα ("I have written more boldly"). Though the target of the comparison is unnamed until the third letter, for reasons noted in the previous chapter, it is clearly directed against Michaelis, especially in light of the quotation on the verso, where Hamann ironically addresses Michaelis as his "muse" Calliope through the mouth of Lucretius: "Do you go before and show me the course, as I run my race to the white line of my final goal, clearly marked out before me, yes you, Calliope, Muse all skillful, man's repose and god's delight, that led by you I may win the crown with illustrious praise."[17] As usual, the irony is thick. Hamann has no intention of winning the "crown" of an academic reputation; from the outset of his authorship he has spurned such motivations. And if Michaelis is his "Calliope," then this too is to be taken ironically, in the sense that Michaelis has merely provoked his "bolder," i.e., more inspired, response.

The first letter begins by responding to a contemporary work of biblical scholarship by the Königsberg Orientalist, Georg David Kypke, published in 1755, *Observationes sacrae in novi foederis libros*. Hamann suggests that the title of the work is a misnomer since the author's observations are nothing but "a picnic of profane authors," and adduces a verse from Haggai satirizing the presumption that the mere treatment of a sacred text makes that treatment itself in some way sacred: " 'If one carries holy flesh in the skirt of his garment, and touches with his skirt bread, or pottage, or wine, or oil, or any kind of food, does it become holy?' The priests answered, 'No!' " (Hag. 2: 12).[18] By implication, therefore, the question he raises is what kind of exegesis is appropriate in the case of a sacred text, in other words, by what criterion is exegesis itself to be judged sacred and not profane?

A further concern of the first letter is the style of the New Testament; and it is in this context that he takes the philological debate of his day to a higher level:

> The debate concerning the language and style of the New Testament is not entirely unknown to me; accordingly, I doubt whether the art of philology alone is sufficient to resolve the contradictory opinions on this matter. One should not only know what good Greek is, as the reviewer says, but also what language as such is; not only what defines the eloquence of a classical author, but what style as such is. Philosophical insight concerning both of these matters is sorely lacking ... for this a higher philosophy is truly required.[19]

Whether or not Hamann himself delivers this kind of "higher philosophy" – one searches in vain in his writings for anything like a systematic treatise on

---

[17] Lucretius, *De rerum natura* VI, 92–5, trans. W. H. D. Rouse, 2nd edn. (Cambridge, MA: Harvard University Press, 1982), pp. 498f.
[18] N II, p. 169.
[19] Ibid.

anything – he clearly points in this direction, calling attention to the need for a philosophy (and ultimately a theology) of language. And to this end, in his view, even the "common tongue," the *koinē* of the New Testament, is revealing. Firstly, it tells us something about the circumstances in which the New Testament was written: in Hellenized Palestine under Roman occupation by people who were by no means the "*literati* of their *seculi*."[20] Indeed, for Hamann, it is precisely our ability more or less to determine the time and place of the New Testament writings that makes them all the more dependable and believable. Secondly, it tells us that "these books were not written for Greeks (1 Cor. 1: 22–3) and for those of learning" in the language of pure reason (for which abstract clarity is a *desideratum*). On the contrary, they are historically "impure," characterized by the different perspectives and prejudices of their authors. And yet, as discomfiting as this may be to a die-hard rationalist (for whom the external, sensible, historical form is separable from, and ultimately irrelevant to, a purely rational content), from Hamann's theological perspective it is precisely this impure material, this mass of historical contingencies, that constitutes the sacred treasury of Scripture.[21] Accordingly, he says that Christianity is distinguished by "a new tongue and a holy style":

> Go into whatever community of Christians you will, the language at the holy place will betray their fatherland and genealogy – that they are παρά φύσιν pagan branches grafted onto a Jewish trunk. The more edifying the speaker, the more we will hear his Galilean shibboleth; the more fire, the more that sect of the Canarese whom the Ishmaelites (the children of our Church according to the flesh) ridicule (as it is written, χλευαζοντες ελεγον, οτι γλευκους μεμεστωμενοι εισι); the more of the dew of the morning in whose womb the sun of righteousness rises with healing in its wings – – in short, the element of the Orient in our official style leads us back to the cradle of our race and our religion, so that one should by no means be astonished at the aesthetic taste of some Christian authors, *si aures* (as a Latinist of our time with fine Hispanic taste has put it) *perpetuis tautologiis, Orienti iucundis, Europae invisis laedant, prudentioribus stomachaturis, dormitaturis reliquis.*[22]

Hamann's profounder point in the letter, however, is that the common tongue of the New Testament, and the medium of the different personalities of its authors, is an example of the Holy Spirit's kenotic condescension to the idiosyncracies of human history; and this, in turn, exemplifies the unity of divine revelation throughout the economy of salvation. Indeed, as we have seen, it signals the mystery of divine humility proper to all the persons of the Trinity (which also explains the profounder significance of the word "cloverleaf" in the title of Hamann's triptych). As he puts it, essentially summing up the theme of his London Writings, "It is proper to the unity of divine revelation that the Spirit of GOd [*sic*] should have lowered himself and emptied himself of his majesty through the style of the holy men he inspired, just as the Son of God did by assuming the form of a servant, and just as the entire creation

---

[20] N II, pp. 169f.

[21] N II, p. 170: "Every manner of thought that begins to be somewhat fashionable, every unnoticeable transition in one's passions, affects the expression of one's concepts."

[22] N II, pp. 170f. The Latinist here whom Hamann quotes happens to be Michaelis: "If they batter one's ears with perpetual tautologies, to the Orient they are pleasant, to Europe they are odious, to the more discriminating they are an irritant, and to everyone else a soporific." For the supposed source of the quotation in Michaelis's commentary on Lowth, see N II, p. 406.

is a work of the greatest humility."[23] And for this reason, in view of such extraordinary humility, he says, "Merely to admire God ... in nature is perhaps an affront similar to that shown a sensible man, whose worth the rabble presumed to judge by [the quality] of his coat."[24]

And yet, in Hamann's view, it is precisely this mistake that rational exegetes like Michaelis typically make in their profane reading of Scripture, when, failing to appreciate this "mystery," which is by definition "closed" to the "pro-fane," they either dismiss the writings of the Old Testament as "absurd fables" unworthy of the supreme being[25] or like the neologians (or later Rudolf Bultmann) seek to separate the "mythological" form of Scripture from a certain moral or existential content. In other words, just as reason cannot fathom the mystery of the incarnation or see the Son of God in his lowliness, neither can it see the glory of the Holy Spirit in the *Knechtsgestalt* of Scripture. This is why Hamann is happy to admit that, from a purely rational perspective, the spiritual sense of Scripture, which is "hidden from the wise and learned" (Matt. 11: 25), cannot help but appear outwardly to a profane reading, i.e., to those lacking faith, in a way analogous to the Word of the Cross (1 Cor. 1: 18f.), as "foolishness," indeed as full of contradictions and apparent malapropisms:

> If the divine style elects the foolish – the trite – the ignoble – in order to put to shame the strength and ingenuity of all profane authors: then it almost goes without saying that eyes that are illumined, inspired, and armed with the jealousy of a friend, an intimate, a lover are required in order to see in such disguise the beams of heavenly glory. As a well-known exegete puts it, *DEI Dialectus, Soloecismus*. – The same applies here: *Vox populi, vox DEI*. – The emperor says schismam [*sic*], and the gods of the earth rarely bother to be masters of language. What is sublime in Caesar's style is its carelessness.[26]

This passage indicates at least three things. Firstly, for Hamann the humble form of Scripture, indeed, the humility of all the works of the economic Trinity, cannot be appreciated apart from a corresponding humility and sympathetic disposition, whether this be understood as an effect or precondition of illumination, i.e., genuine enlightenment, by the Holy Spirit. Secondly, it indicates that the divine style has complete disregard for the "grammatologies" of the world, i.e., that God is in no way obliged to fit the bearings of a transcendental logic or what any finite consciousness presumes to delimit as possible. Thirdly, it indicates Hamann's profound admiration for Paul, and especially his discourse on the folly of the Cross: "But God chose what is foolish in the world to shame the wise ... what is weak in the world to shame the strong ... what is low and despised in the world, things that are not, to reduce to nothing things that are" (1 Cor. 1: 27f).

---

[23] N II, p. 171.

[24] Ibid.

[25] See Voltaire, *Sermon of the Fifty*, ed. J. A. R. Séguin (New York: R. Paxton, 1962) p. 11.

[26] N II, p. 171. The allusion is to Emperor Sigismund, who is supposed to have said at the council of Constance (1411–37): "We don't want any schismam," i.e., schism, in the Church. When the correct spelling was pointed out to him, namely, "schisma," he replied: "Well, I am an emperor and have greater authority than the grammarians. I can even make another grammar." Quoted in Martin Seils, *Johann Georg Hamann: Eine Auswahl aus seinen Schriften* (Wuppertal: Brockhaus Verlag, 1987), p. 268.

Fittingly, therefore, Hamann continues his letter with a reference to Paul's famous dictum in 2 Corinthians 4: 7, only now as applied to the earthen quality of the divine style: "We have this treasure of divine documents, as Paul says, ἐν ὀστρακίνοις σκεύεσιν, ἵνα ἡ ὑπερβολὴ τῆς δυνάμεως ᾖ θεοῦ καὶ μὴ ἐξ ἡμῶν," adding, "we can be sure that the *stylus curiae* of the kingdom of heaven, especially when compared with that of the Asian courts, remains the meekest and humblest."[27] Indeed, he says, "the external appearance of the letter bears a greater resemblance to the untamed foal of an ass, that beast of burden, than to the proud stallions that spelled Phaeton's demise – *nec nomina novit equorum*."[28] If, therefore, one is to judge the style of the New Testament, one must do so in light of divine humility:

> According to all the textbooks of rhetoric, both journalistic and epistolary styles belong to the *humili generi dicendi*, of which class there remain few analogies in ancient Greek. And yet it is with just this kind of taste that one must judge the books of the New Testament, and in this respect they are to a certain extent original.[29]

The letter then concludes with an amusing story that Hamann picked up from his reading about the Ottoman empire, which aptly sums up his understanding of divine inspiration and his corresponding view of Scripture:

> Lately, for a change of pace, I have been reading Prince Dimitri Kantemir's history of the Ottoman Empire and yesterday came across some reports concerning Misri Efendi, the Shaw of Persia under Achmet II and Mustafa II. The fresh memory of these passages and my pleasure in them leads me to conclude [my observations] with this extraordinary man, who is said to have been a gifted poet and, secretly, a Christian. The mufti, not presuming to judge his songs, apparently said: "The meaning and the sense of them is known to no one but GOd and Misri" – – The mufti also ordered that his poetry be collected in order to examine it. He read it – threw it into the fire – and issued the following fatwa: "Whoever speaks like Misri Efendi and shares his beliefs shall be burned, except for Misri Efendi himself, and him alone; for no fatwa can be issued against those who are taken up with inspiration." What do you think, dear sir, of the mufti? Does he not put many popes and reviewers to shame?[30]

In a concluding remark Hamann then puts himself in Misri's shoes, suggesting that he himself, for all the nonsense of his own writing, is similarly inspired, and thus deserves to be spared a fatwa on the part of the critics of the Enlightenment: "Do whatever you want with this awful mishmash, just no fatwa ..." Thus the letter comes full circle, returning to Hamann's initial point about Kypke's *Observationes sacrae*: for here what is judged to be common, namely, the style of the New Testament (and, by implication, his own mishmash writing) is, in fact, sacred, whereas what his contemporaries call sacred, namely Kypke's *Observationes sacrae,* is in fact common and profane.

---

[27] N II, p. 171.
[28] Ibid. Aside from the reference to the brazen Phaeton, son of Helios, who could not manage his father's horses and, as a result, nearly scorched the earth before being struck down by Zeus, the allusion is to the ass's colt upon which Christ rode into Jerusalem (Matt. 21: 1ff.).
[29] N II, pp. 171f.
[30] N II, pp. 172f.

Hamann's second letter is concerned less with biblical exegesis, and more with the exegesis of classical pagan authors, among them Homer, Pindar, Euripides, Quintilian, Plato, and Aristotle.[31] But here again, with respect to classical letters, he is concerned with the matter of proper interpretation, and his ire is reserved in particular for the sterile intellectualism and jejune philology of his day, which fails to appreciate the spirit of genius of the ancient writings themselves:

> Anger robs me of all reasoning, dear sir, when I think of how such a noble gift of GOd as the sciences has been devastated, torn to pieces by strong spirits in coffee houses and trampled under foot by lazy monks in academic congresses [*Messen*]; – and how it is possible that young people can fall in love with that old fairy, lacking teeth and hair – or perhaps has fake teeth and hair – which goes by the name of erudition.[32]

The zeal of Hamann's charge against the sciences of his day bears some comparison to Rousseau's *Discours sur les sciences et les arts,* which was published just a decade earlier in 1750; and Hamann certainly shares some of Rousseau's concerns. His complaint here, however, is directed more specifically at the uninspired way his contemporaries tend to approach history, without a living sense of time or what Heidegger would call *Zeitlichkeit*; and in this regard, *mutatis mutandis,* he could be said to anticipate Heidegger's similar criticisms of modern historicism. Thus Hamann asks,

> Can one understand the past without for a moment understanding the present? – – And who would presume to derive adequate conceptions of the present without a knowledge of the future? The future determines the present, and the latter the past, just as the end determines the nature and use of means.[33]

Indeed, he suggests that without the synthetic power of poetic (and ultimately divine) inspiration, history will resemble the valley of dry bones descried by Ezekiel:

> The field of history has always seemed to me like that wide valley full of bones – – And behold! they were very dry. None but a prophet can prophecy that these bones will grow veins and flesh and be covered with skin. – – As of yet there is no breath in them – – until the prophet prophecies to the wind, and speaks to it the word of the Lord.[34]

Such, then, is the importance of poetic (and ultimately divine) inspiration, without which history itself (and the books of the ancients) will be like a valley of dry bones, which are dead and unable to speak. And this is why Hamann says with regard to history that a kind of divination, *vis divinandi,* is required to understand it, to fathom its future aspect and thereby bring its meaning for the present to life.[35]

---

[31] Of the last two, Hamann observes: "In my opinion, Plato and Aristotle should be read and compared as models, respectively, of eclectic and encyclical philosophy. Here we have Scylla and Charybdis, which, as Ulysses was instructed, we should be happy to navigate past – Leibniz is said not to have been systematic enough, and Wolff not eclectic enough. All too often, however, closer examination reveals things to be quite the reverse of what initially appeared to be the case. – Aristotle is model of illustration; Plato of color" (N II, p. 175).

[32] N II, p. 177.

[33] N II, p. 175.

[34] N II, p. 176. See Ezek. 37.

[35] N II, p. 175.

The first and second letters set the stage for the third, where it first becomes clear that his target all along has been Michaelis. To be sure, Hamann admires him for his philological gifts:

> Germany has few authors like Herr Michaelis who have achieved so much and are capable of achieving so much more, whose works one can receive with thanks and whose promises or their fulfillment one must greet with anticipation. His extensive and intensive insights are something rare; and the gift to impart them goes along with this.[36]

But

> for all this author's merits I detect a πρωτον ψευδος in the oldest and most recent writings I have received from him, and which, in view of his assessment of the improper [methods employed] in teaching the Hebrew language, made a stronger than usual impression upon me. It is so intimately bound up with his entire way of thinking that I find it just as impossible to put my finger on it as one in the field of Jezreel could say: there is Jezebel![37]

In other words, indirectly Hamann means to identify Michaelis with Jezebel, the arch-nemesis of Elijah and the prophetic spirit in general; at the same time, by the darkly comical reference to 2 Kings 9 concerning her death and the unsuccessful attempt to bury her, he means to say that Michaelis's *proton pseudos* is so endemic that no part of his work is left unaffected by it.

Unfortunately, what Hamann means by this *proton pseudos* is not entirely clear; as he himself says in jest, in reference to Jezebel's scattered remains, he cannot put his finger on it. That being said, it certainly has to do with Michaelis's "quixotic" crusade to "revive the dead language of Hebrew" by attending to its philological roots, which involves painstaking philological scrutiny of Arabic and Semitic languages in general. This is not to say that Hamann, a philologist himself, considered knowledge of ancient languages unimportant. On the contrary, it was due in part to Michaelis, Hamann's "Calliope," that Hamann was inspired to begin his own study of Arabic. Nor, for that matter, does he fail to appreciate Michaelis's intention to revive the language of Scripture, since this too is his own concern. Rather, their difference lies in what constitutes a proper method of biblical exegesis, which will "revive" the "dead languages" of the Bible; and in Hamann's view Michaelis's rationalistic methods by themselves are woefully inadequate for bringing about the resurrection he seeks. As he puts it, clearly with Michaelis in mind:

> For all the artificial means one might employ [namely, to revive the Hebrew language], it could very well amount to this: You understand neither the scriptures nor the power of GOD, neither its inspiration nor its interpretation, which does not depend upon philosophical principles. The origins of the Hebrew dialect may therefore be as dead as the uterus of Sarah: – the most wonder-working linguists are sometimes the most impotent

---

[36] N II, p. 179.

[37] Ibid. In a footnote Hamann also refers to Rev. 2: 20–3. Among the works targeted here by Hamann are Michaelis's Hebrew grammar and his *Beurtheilung der Mittel, welche man anwendet, die austestorbene Hebräische Sprache zu verstehen*. See G-D, p. 432.

exegetes; – the strictest law-givers the breakers of their tablets, or they may also come to be one-eyed through the guilt of their children.[38]

In short, no amount of philological method can make up for a lack of inspiration. Without it, the language of the Hebrew Bible will be lifeless and barren, and any critical investigation of it will be powerless to penetrate the many veils of its meaning.[39]

AESTHETICA IN NUCE: ON THE LANGUAGE OF CREATION

Hamann's *Aesthetica in nuce* is many things. For one thing, in a hilarious piece of prosopopeia, it is a discourse on the part of a "nut" (i.e., Hamann himself), who at one point in his passionate diatribe interrupts himself in an apostrophe to Michaelis, in which he sarcastically hails him as a "highly- and indeed most-learned Rabbi!"[40] All of which attests to Hamann's sense of humor. For another thing, as the subtitle of the work says, it is a "Rhapsody in kabbalistic prose." In the previous chapter I suggested some of the plainer meanings of this phrase, among them, that Hamann's prose, like that of the kabbalists, is similarly dark and hermetic, containing layers of unexpected significance. For all its mysterious meanings, however, one must emphasize that the *Aesthetica* is first and foremost a continuation of Hamann's exegetical debate with Michaelis and therefore must be understood in this context. Whereas in the *Cloverleaf* Hamann identifies Michaelis as his philological rival, here he properly launches his own opposing philological crusade; and whereas in the *Cloverleaf* he merely adumbrates the connections among Scripture, poetry, and creation (and how best to interpret them), here these connections become more apparent.

---

[38] N II, pp. 182f.

[39] This is not to say that a historical-critical method is pointless, since it can be historically illuminating. But for Hamann (following Bacon), it cannot serve as an exclusive basis for interpreting the biblical text, firstly, because Scripture's divinely inspired perspective – which at some level comprehends all times and ages – explodes all finite historical perspective (making purely historical determinations of the meaning of Scripture to a certain extent irrelevant). As Bacon puts it, whom Hamann cites (N II, p. 202), because Scripture's dictates "comprehend the vicissitudes of all ages; with an eternal and certain foreknowledge of all heresies, contradictions and differing and changing estates of the Church ... they are not to be interpreted only according to the latitude and obvious sense of the place; or with respect to the occasion whereon the words were uttered; or in precise context with the words before or after; or in contemplation of the principal scope of the passage; but we must consider them to have in themselves, not only totally or collectively, but distributively also in clauses and words, infinite springs and streams of doctrines, to water every part of the Church and the souls of the faithful. For it has been well observed that the answers of our Savior to many of the questions which were propounded to Him do not appear to the point, but as it were impertinent thereto. The reason whereof is twofold; the one, knowing the thoughts of his questioners not as we men do by their words, but immediately and of himself, he answered their thoughts and not their words; the other, that He did not speak only to the persons then present, but to us also now living, and to men of every age and nation to whom the Gospel was to be preached. And this also holds good in other passages of Scripture" (*De augmentis scientiarum*, book IX, in *Works* IV, pp. 116–18). Secondly, as Hamann puts it, Michaelis's historical-critical method fails to appreciate that "the literal or grammatical, the carnal or dialectical, the Capernaitic or historical senses are all, to the highest degree, mystical, and depend upon such fleeting, spiritual, arbitrary, and incidental determinations and circumstances that one cannot draw down the key to their understanding without ascending to heaven ..." (N II, p. 203). To be sure, Hamann says in reference to Michaelis's promoted philological expedition to the Middle East, "one must not shy away from traveling across the sea or into the regions of such shadows, which since yesterday or the day before, for hundreds or thousands of years – mysteries! – have believed, spoken, and suffered," but of these shadows, he wryly continues, "the broad sweep of world history can tell us scarcely as much as can fit onto the narrowest tombstone, or Echo, that nymph known for her laconic memory, can retain at any given time" (ibid.).

[40] N II, p. 201.

The text of the *Aesthetica* begins with an epigraph from Horace, in whose voice Hamann indirectly rebukes Michaelis, other neologians, and the general confidence of the age in the power of reason by means of historical-critical research to explain the mysteries of the biblical text:

> I loathe the profane crowd and repel it. Hold your tongues! I, priest of the muses, sing to maidens and youths of songs not heard before. And of kings to be feared by their own flocks. But the dominion of Jove is against these kings, glorious in his triumph over the giants, moving all things by his brow.[41]

And it is in this vein that he calls for a "shovel" for his muse to cleanse the "threshing-floor" of Scripture from the dross of Michaelis's criticism: "Not a lyre! – nor a paint brush! – but a winnowing-shovel for my muse to cleanse the threshingfloor of sacred literature!"[42] Aside from the comical image of Hamann's muse wielding a shovel, the allusion here is to the words of John the Baptist: "His winnowing-shovel is in his hand and, and, and he will clear the threshing floor and gather his wheat into the granary, but the chaff he will burn with unquenchable fire" (Matt. 3: 12). Accordingly, it is precisely this that Hamann intends to do in the *Aesthetica*, namely, separate the wheat of Lowth's lectures from the chaff of Michaelis's commentary. And lest we fail to recognize the chief target of his criticism, he goes on to greet Michaelis with a pun on his name: "Hail the archangel over the relics of the language of Canaan! – he wins the contest riding on fair little asses; – but the wise idiot of Greece borrows Euthyphro's proud stallions for the philological debate."[43]

As Lumpp points out, it is notable that Michaelis is depicted as sitting not upon the living Word of God, but (in reference to the title of one of Michaelis's own works, *Beurtheilung der Mittel, welche man anwendet, die ausgestorbene Hebräische Sprache zu verstehen*) upon the relics of an ancient language that, from a purely rationalist-historicist perspective, cannot help but seem dead.[44] He presides, in other words, not over a living treasury, but over the dry bones of the letter of Scripture, unable to draw from them anything but the meager results of his philological research. The further allusion to Michaelis riding on fair asses, in reference to Judges 5: 10, is more opaque; but, if Lumpp is correct, it contains the whole of Hamann's critique of Michaelis *in nuce*. At one level, Hamann doubtless means to say that Michaelis's public reputation has been achieved not by his own inspiration, but by riding the "fair ass" of Lowth's lectures; or, what is worse, in order to win a prize in a philological contest.[45] More importantly, however, Michaelis fails to recognize that the language of the Hebrew Bible is not dead – *ausgestorben* – but precisely that into which the Spirit of God enters as his very own tabernacle and chariot-throne. As the letter to the Hebrews puts it, the language of Scripture is "living and active" (4: 12). Yet it is precisely this that Michaelis cannot see: lacking the inspired gift of interpretation (cf. 1 Cor. 12: 10), he cannot see the prophetic Spirit of God tabernacling within the contingent and seemingly arbitrary elements of human language.

---

[41]   Horace, *Odes* III, 1. My translation.

[42]   N II, p. 197.

[43]   Ibid.

[44]   Hans-Martin Lumpp, *Philologia Crucis: Zu Johann Georg Hamanns Fassung von der Dichtkunst* (Tübingen: Max Niemeyer, 1970), p. 43.

[45]   Lumpp, *Philologia Crucis*, p. 44.

For Hamann, therefore, the most indispensable element of biblical exegesis is inspiration; and here again, as before, he appeals to his old model Socrates, the "wise idiot of Greece," citing Hermogenes in Plato's *Cratylus:* "Indeed, Socrates, you do seem to me to be uttering oracles exactly like an inspired prophet."[46] Socrates responds that his inspiration must have come from Euthyphro, the inspired priest, possessed of "superhuman wisdom," with whom he had just been conversing; and that they might at a later time try to conjure his inspiration away, once "we have found someone, whether priest or sophist, who is skilled in that kind of purifying." Presumably, by way of this comparison, Hamann means to suggest that he too is inspired, that he too speaks prophetically in oracles, and that this makes him a better exegete than Michaelis. As for Euthyphro's horses, which Hamann will borrow in his debate, we are given a further clue to their significance from a subsequent footnote, where Hamann cites Bacon, "my Euthyphro," saying, "as hieroglyphs are older than letters, so are parables older than arguments."[47] In other words, if Hamann's inspiration is superhuman, it is also derived from Bacon.

From here Hamann goes on to suggest that the problem with modern biblical criticism is that it fails to appreciate the nature of poetry and inspired writing in general, obtusely applying rational canons of exegesis to inspired texts that flow from a source that is older than abstract reasoning. As he famously puts it, "Poetry is the mother-tongue of the human race; just as gardening is older than the cultivated field; painting – than writing; song – than declamation; parables – than syllogisms; barter – than trade."[48] And it is in this primordial context, in which the "senses and the passions speak and understand nothing but images" – and when "the entire wealth of human knowledge and blessedness consists in images" – that our first parents initially opened their mouths, uttering "winged oracles."[49] Indeed, the oracles of our first parents, he suggests, are properly understood as a response to the first oracle of creation, "Let there be light!" For it is with these words that "the sensation of the presence of things begins."[50] All of which goes to say that, for Hamann, human language, having its origins in an inspired response to the divine language of creation, i.e., in an oracular response to an oracular God, is fundamentally poetic. Indeed, this is what constitutes the dignity of human beings as the crown of God's creation: our ability to express an invisible nature through a visible form and, in some way, like God himself, to shape the world by the words of our mouths. Quoting Manilius, he says, "Each is a little image and likeness of GOD" (*Exemplumque DEI quisque est in imagine parva*).[51]

Hamann's understanding of language thus goes hand in hand with his understanding of poetry, and this, in turn, is bound up with his understanding of creation: not merely as a sensible manifestation of divine glory, but as a kenotic address "to the creature through the creature":

---

[46] Plato, *Cratylus*, tr. H. N. Fowler, Loeb Classical Library (London, 1926), 396d–397a. For translation of the Greek and Latin notes to the *Aesthetica*, see G-D, pp. 409–31, or J. M. Bernstein (ed.) *Classic and Romantic German Aesthetics* (Cambridge: Cambridge University Press, 2003), pp. 1–23.

[47] N II, p. 197. As Lumpp points out (p. 46), Bacon is Hamann's "Euthyphro" in several senses: by virtue, among other things, of his decidedly empiricist perspective, his corresponding rejection of abstract scholasticism and rationalism, his aphorisms, and his affirmation of a double and harmonious revelation in nature and Scripture. Indeed, "both understand history as an action of God, as prophecy and fulfillment" (p. 47). For a study of Hamann and Bacon, see Sven-Aage Jørgensen, "Hamann, Bacon, and tradition," *Orbis Litterarum* 16 (1961), pp. 48–73.

[48] N II, p. 197.

[49] Ibid.

[50] Ibid.

[51] N II, p. 198.

Speak, that I may see you! – – This wish was fulfilled by creation, which is a speech [*Rede*] to the creature through the creature; for day to day pours forth speech, and night to night declares knowledge. Its password [*Losung*] can be heard across every climate and in every dialect to the ends of the world.[52]

Aside from the reference to Psalm 19, this passage bears comparison to received notions, typical in the Middle Ages and Renaissance, for example, in Alan of Lille and Raymond Sabundus, of the so-called *liber naturae* or book of nature.[53] In the famous verses of Alan of Lille, *Omnis mundi creatura / Quasi liber et pictura / Nobis est et speculum*.[54] Furthermore, following Bayer, it comprises a felicitous formula for a Christian doctrine of creation, given that it does justice both to God's immanence (his nearness to the creature) and his transcendence (his freedom with regard to the creature). For, on the one hand, by virtue of the *freedom* by which he addresses the world (creation as "an address *to* the creature"), God stands at a distance from the world; on the other hand, by virtue of his *love*, he intimately relates himself to it, to the point of entering into it and speaking through it (creation as "an address to the creature *through* the creature"). Accordingly, following Bayer, creation itself is ultimately to be understood in terms of Christ as *Schöpfungsmittler*, in whom both moments are perfectly expressed: both the divine freedom and authority by which God speaks *to* the creature and the humanity by which he speaks "to the creature *through* the creature" – an identity that Luther summed up in his disputation on the divinity and humanity of Christ (1540), "Ibi creator et creatura unus et idem est."[55]

But if the foregoing provides a foundation for a Christian doctrine of creation, Hamann recognizes that, as a consequence to our fallen condition, we do not necessarily experience creation as he describes it:

Wherever the guilt may lie (whether outside us our in us): nature leaves for our use nothing but jumbled verse [*Turbatverse*] and the *disiecti membra poetae*. It is the task of the scholar to collect them; of the philosopher, to interpret them; for the poet, to imitate them – or more boldly still! – – to bring about their destiny.[56]

In other words, from our fallen perspective, we no longer necessarily experience creation as God speaking "to the creature through the creature." Instead, all that we perceive are the fragments of an original poem, which we no longer know how to

---

[52] Ibid. Cf. ZH I, p. 393: "Creation is a speech, whose thread stretches from one end of heaven to the other." The first part is more obscure and refers to a story about Socrates, which has come down to us from Erasmus and, earlier, from Apuleius. See Erasmus, *Apophthegmata* III, 70. See Lumpp, *Philologia Crucis*, p. 55. As the story goes, Socrates at some point addressed the son of a wealthy man in just these words, *loquere igitur, adolescens, ut te videam* – namely, in order to "see" his talent. Hence, what Hamann means in the present context is that creation similarly fulfills (or, more precisely, has always already fulfilled) the creature's desire to see God's "invisible nature" (see Rom. 1: 20).

[53] See especially Oswald Bayer, *Schöpfung als Anrede: Zu einer Hermeneutik der Schöpfung*, 2nd edn. (Tübingen: Mohr-Siebeck, 1990). See also Joachim Ringleben, "'Rede, daß ich dich sehe': Betrachtungen zu Hamanns theologischem Sprachdenken," *Neue Zeitschrift für systematische Theologie und Religionsphilosophie* 30 (1988), pp. 209–24.

[54] Quoted in Bayer, *Schöpfung als Anrede*, p. 5.

[55] Bayer, *Schöpfung als Anrede*, p. 18; cf. Oswald Bayer, *Zeitgenosse im Widerspruch: Johann Georg Hamann als radiklaer Aufklärer* (Munich: Piper Verlag, 1988), pp. 96f; for Martin Luther's disputation, see *Werke. Kritische Gesamtausgabe* (Weimar: H. Böhlaus, 1906–61) vol. 39/II, pp. 105f.

[56] N II, pp. 198f. By the phrase *disiecti membra poetae* ("the members of the dissected poet"), which comes from Horace (*Satires*, I, 4, v. 62), Hamann is alluding to the fate of Orpheus who was torn to pieces by the Maenads, and who therefore metonymically stands in the present context for the jumbled and fragmentary verse of creation.

read. Indeed, no amount of labor on the part of the scholar or scientist will avail to do anything more than, so to speak, assemble the letters. As Hamann put it to Kant, "Physics is nothing but the Abc. Nature is an equation of an unknown quantity, a Hebraic word written with nothing but consonants to which the understanding must supply the [vowel] points."[57] To be sure, the philosopher may try to interpret them, but it is the poet alone, Hamann here suggests, who can hope to restore the poem to its original integrity and thereby fulfill its original intention.

One might think that Hamann means here any poet in whose words the world is seen and heard anew; and, however unwittingly, and however expressionistic its forms might be, poetic language in general certainly shares in the attempt to translate the original text, so that the world might once again strike us as significant, indeed, as a divine revelation "to the creature through the creature." But given the context of the Fall, it is clear that for Hamann even the best poetic "translations" will be poor and partial; for after Babel language itself is fallen, having lost something of its original disclosive power, i.e., its power to "translate" the "angelic tongue" of creation and thereby reveal the divine in and through the human. Thus arise the various truncated forms of language by which we try to make sense of the world. As he puts it in a notoriously difficult passage,

> Speaking is translation – from an angelic into a human tongue, i.e., thoughts into words, – things into names, – pictures into signs, whether they be poetic, kyriological, historical, symbolic, or hieroglyphic – – and philosophical or characteristic. This kind of translation (by which I mean speaking) corresponds more than any other to the underside of a carpet. "And shows the stuff but not the workman's skill"; or to a solar eclipse that is observed in a vessel full of water.[58]

Hamann's first point here is that all language is invariably a kind of translation – whether it be of one's own thoughts, or whether of the "angelic tongue" of creation, or whether simply, and more prosaically, of the impressions of one's immediate environment. In short, for Hamann there is no such thing as purely spontaneous language. Rather, language is that whereby we mysteriously translate either thoughts into words or pictures into signs. His second point, which pertains to the text of creation as a manifestation of the thoughts of God, is that not all "translations" are equally inspired. Thus, following Wachter's classification, language can assume any number of forms: poetic, kyriological, historical, symbolic, hieroglyphic, etc.[59]

---

[57] ZH I, p. 450.

[58] N II, p. 199. For a source for the various kinds of signification Hamann has in mind, see the first section of J. G. Wachter's *Naturae et Scripturae Concordia. Commentatio de literis ac numeris primaevis aliisque rebus memorabilibus cum ortu literarum coniunctis* (Copenhagen, 1752). The quotation, 'And shews the stuff ..." comes from the Earl of Roscommon's *Poems* (London, 1717), p. 9. For the most detailed investigation of this passage, which summarizes previous scholarship, see Xavier Tilliette, "Hamann und die Engelsprache: Über eine Stelle der Aesthetica in nuce" in *Acta des Internationalen Hamann-Colloquiums*, ed. Bernhard Gajek (Frankfurt: Vittorio Klostermann, 1979), pp. 66–77.

[59] According to Lumpp, *Philologia Crucis*, p. 57, Hamann's appropriation of Wachter's classification can be understood, in provisional terms, as follows: by poetic and kyriological, he means language that images the things themselves (citing Wachter, "non ... signa ... sed rerum ipsarum imagines"); by symbolic, an allegorical sense that is "between the thing and the sign," hidden, as it were, beneath the forms of the things themselves ("sub ... rerum naturalium formis ... allegoricum sensum recondere, ... ingenii ... solertia cognoscibilem"); by historical, a relation between thing and sign that is qualified by an etymological reference; by hieroglyphic, a form of typology; and by philosophical and characteristic, conceptual and alphabetical languages that no longer reflect, but are arbitrarily and artificially applied to the things themselves. Whether or not Hamann fully subscribed to Wachter's thesis, the latter understood these forms in terms of a historical development.

According to Lumpp, what Hamann means by "shows the stuff but not the workman's skill" would seem to apply to the last-named forms of language, i.e., characteristic or abstract philosophical languages, which say something about the text of creation, but, like the "underside of a carpet," are incapable of revealing its true intent and "artistry." Indeed, as the image of a solar eclipse reflected in water would suggest, these forms of language are the most inept of translations, providing only the dimmest reflection of the things themselves.[60]

Now it is clear why in subsequent sections of the *Aesthetica*, following Bacon, his "Euthyphro," Hamann inveighs against the proliferation of abstract philosophical terms and concepts as against so many "idols," which are mute and lifeless and effectively obscure any perception of the Creator speaking through his works. This is also why, against the abstract reasoning of his day, whose conceptions have "overrun the text of nature like the Flood,"[61] he appeals to "the torch of Moses," i.e., the light of the Torah, which "illuminates even the intellectual world" with "its own heaven and earth"[62] – as if to say that the inspired language of Scripture reveals what abstract philosophical language cannot, being of all poetic works the most adequate translation of the text of creation. To put it in a nutshell, Hamann's philological crusade is thus carried out on two different but complementary fronts: on the one hand, against the abstractions of modern philosophy, which effectively obscure the Logos speaking in and through creation; on the other hand, against modern biblical criticism, which would similarly obscure the allegorical depths of the Logos speaking through the biblical text.

THE DITHYRAMBS OF A CHRISTIAN DIONYSUS

Aside from Hamann's self-depiction as the lusty, horned satyr-god Pan on the title vignette of the *Crusades*, one of the most striking aspects of the *Aesthetica* is his invocation of Dionysus in order to castigate his contemporaries for their sterile rationalism, which, in his view, has made them unfit critics of the arts. As he hyperbolically puts it to them, "Do not venture into the metaphysics of the fine arts without being fully initiated into the orgies and Eleusinian mysteries. The senses are Ceres, and Bacchus the passions; – the ancient foster-parents of beautiful nature," adding from the Roman poet, Tibullus, "Bacche! veni dulcisque tuis e cornibus vua / Pendeat, & spicis tempora cinge Ceres!" ("Come Bacchus! with your sweet grapes dangling from your horns & wreathe your head, O Ceres, with ears of corn!").[63] Needless to say, Hamann is not invoking pagan gods; nor is he condoning sexual license. Rather, he invokes Ceres and Dionysus as figurative representations of the senses and the passions, whose dignity he seeks to restore. Avenging their denigration at the hands of a "murderous" and "lying" philosophy, which has sought truth *apart* from them – a philosophy that, in effect, has "cleared nature out of the way," even as, paradoxically, it enjoins the classical imitation of it, he says in typically imagistic and passionate invective:

> Nature works through senses and passions. How can you sense anything if you have mutilated her instruments? Can it be that even benumbed veins [*Sennadern*] are fit for movement? – – Your murderous, lying philosophy has cleared Nature out of the way, so

[60] See Lumpp, *Philologia Crucis*, p. 58.
[61] N II, p. 207.
[62] N II, p. 199.
[63] N II, p. 201.

why do you demand that we should imitate it? ... Yes, you fine critics! You are ever asking what truth is, and reach for the door, since you cannot wait for any answer to this question – Your hands are always washed, whether you want to eat bread or even when you have just passed a death sentence. – Do you not even want to know how you have gotten rid of Nature? – – – Bacon accuses you of flaying it with your abstractions. Does Bacon testify to the truth? Well then! Cast stones at him – and chase after his shade with snowballs and clumps of clay.[64]

Once again Hamann calls upon Bacon, his "Euthyphro," thereby signaling his stand with the British empiricist tradition against the Cartesianism and Stoicism of the modern Continental tradition, for which nature, the senses and passions, rather than being sources of knowledge and creativity, are always already deceptive and problematic, leading to ever more transcendentally refined forms of idealism (from Descartes to Kant to Husserl). Indeed, such is the "puritanical" and, in Hamann's view, fundamentally Gnostic tendency of modern Continental philosophy, which is wont to recoil and abstract from the senses and the passions, from the truth right there *in* the senses. All of which Hamann fittingly captures in the image of Pilate washing his hands of Christ, in whom, right before Pilate's eyes, the ideal and the real are one and the same. Thus, once again, we see the Christological basis of Hamann's critique of the abstract rationalism of the age – the fact that in Christ the divine is at one with the human, the spiritual is at one with the sensible and material. For that matter, for Hamann, following Bacon, the senses are *more* to be trusted than abstractions, since, in his view, the latter are arbitrary, whereas the former are the immediate impression of divine ideas, "the creator's own stamp upon creation, impressed and defined in matter by true and exquisite lines."[65] As he puts it, "Every impression of nature in the human being is not only a memorial, but a pledge of the fundamental truth: Who the LORD is."[66]

In any case, Hamann agrees with Bacon that the "natural" use of the senses has been perverted by the "unnatural" use of abstractions, i.e., by a kind of philosophy that can find no certainty in the senses but seeks truth in abstraction from them.[67] And it is against this "unnatural" use of abstractions that he declares:

Oh for a Muse like the fire of a goldsmith, and like the fullers' soap! (Mal. 3: 2) – – She will dare to purify the natural use of the senses from the unnatural use of abstractions, whereby our conceptions of things are just as mutilated as the name of the Creator is suppressed and blasphemed. I am speaking to you, Greeks! because you think yourselves wiser than the chamberlains with the Gnostic key; – Try for once to read the *Iliad*

---

[64] N II, p. 206.

[65] See Bacon, *Novum organum* I, Aphorism 124: "But I say that those foolish and apish images of worlds which the fancies of men have created in philosophical systems must be utterly scattered to the winds. Be it known then how vast a difference there is between the Idols of the human mind and the Ideas of the divine. The former are nothing more than arbitrary abstractions; the latter are the creator's own stamp upon creation, impressed and defined in matter by true and exquisite lines. Truth therefore and utility are here the very same things: and the works of nature themselves are of greater value as pledges of truth than as contributing to the comforts of life" (Francis Bacon, *Novum Organum, with Other Parts of the Great Instauration*, Paul Carus Student Editions, vol. 3 (Chicago and LaSalle, IL: Open Court, 1994).

[66] N II, p. 207.

[67] Essentially, he means here the kind of philosophy that seeks a "'unity in the universal concept' by means of abstraction 'from the contingent and particular.'" See Oswald Bayer, "Die Geschichten der Vernunft sind die Kritik ihrer Reinheit," in *Acta des vierten Internationalen Hamann-Kolloquiums* (Frankfurt am Main: Peter Lang, 1987), pp. 26f.

if you have beforehand sifted out by abstraction the two vowels α and ω, and tell me your opinion of the sense and euphony of the poet: Μηνιν ·ειδε Θε· Πηλι·δε· ·Χιληος [Sing, -G-ddess -f the wr-th -f -chilles s-n -f Peleus].[68]

Here again Hamann invokes his muse, this time, however, not to ask for a shovel, but for a purifying fire (cf. Matt. 3: 11f.). What is striking here, as Griffith-Dickson points out, is that Hamann completely transvalues received philosophical notions of purification (whether Platonic, Stoic, or Cartesian), since "abstractions are not to be purified from the senses, but rather the other way around: the *natural* use of the senses must be purified from the abuse, indeed, the violence of abstractions."[69] This kind of purification is called for, Hamann proceeds to explain, because the denigra- tion of the senses not only mutilates our powers, but blasphemes the Creator, who created them in the first place. And those he singles out for censure are "the Greeks," i.e., his rationalist contemporaries who have imbibed too much of the asceticism and Gnosticism of Greek philosophy. For even if they have not sought Gnosis by literally castrating themselves (see Matt. 19: 12), the violence of their abstraction from the senses and passions has effectively castrated the lower powers of their souls, leaving themselves eunuchs, as it were, who may pride themselves in being "rational," but are impotent to understand the poetic genius of Homer, who sings of the legendary wrath of Achilles.

But as the final part of the passage suggests, the main reason why they have no sense for the poetic language of Homer, and why above all they have no sense for the poetic language of creation and the Hebrew Bible, is that, according to their own purely rational canon of exegesis, they have no sense for Christ, who is the key to their intelligibility. Thus Hamann extracts from the Homeric text precisely the alpha and omega, as if to say that the poetry of Scripture and creation will be similarly meaningless once one takes away Christ, *the* Alpha and Omega (Rev. 1: 8). "All the colors of the most beautiful world grow pale," he says, "as soon as you extinguish that light, the firstborn of creation."[70] Hamann makes a similar point when he alludes to the "great and small" (*masora magna et masora parva*) scribal additions made by Masoretes to the text of the Hebrew Bible during the eighth century, which included notes and, famously, vowel points: "Behold! The great and small Masorah of the world's wisdom has overrun the text of nature like the Flood. Were not all its beauties and riches bound to turn into water?"[71] To be sure, here it is not a case of what is taken away from the text but rather of what is added to it. Yet Hamann's fundamental point is the same; for while the Masoretes are known for what they *added* to Scripture with all their points, glosses, and annota- tions, what from a Christian perspective they notoriously *left out* was, of course, Christ, the *res significata* – and with him, ironically, the only thing indispensable to an understanding of the Hebrew scriptures they assiduously sought to elucidate (cf. Luke 24: 27; Gal. 4: 2ff.).

Having defended the senses and indicated the necessity of Christ for a full-blooded aesthetic (of Scripture and creation), Hamann then gives a full-blown defense of the passions, resuming his diatribe against the fundamentally prudish and masochistic

---

[68] N II, p. 207. The full Greek text reads: μῆνιν ἄειδε θεὰ Πηληιάδεω' Αχιλῆος.
[69] G-D, p. 114.
[70] N II, p. 206. Cf. Col. 1: 15; 2 Cor. 4: 6.
[71] N II, p. 207. See G-D, p. 439.

nature of modern philosophy, for which knowledge is a function of epistemic abstention (looking back to Descartes and ahead to Kant and Husserl), and even a form of self-inflicted violence (as in Descartes's opening meditation: "I shall consider myself as not having hands or eyes, or flesh, or blood or senses …"). And again he points out the absurd irony that his contemporaries continue to call for the artistic imitation of nature along classical lines even as their epistemological prejudices call for the denial of it, i.e., an ascetical-methodological turning away from the natural testimony of the senses and passions:

> You make nature blind precisely in order that she might be your guide! Or rather you yourselves have put out your eyes with your Epicureanism so that people might take you for prophets, who dream up their own inspiration and interpretations. – You want to rule over nature, and bind your own hands and feet through Stoicism, so that in your assorted poems you can pipe all the more movingly of the diamond fetters of fate. If the passions are members of dishonor, do they on this account cease being weapons of manhood? Do you understand the letter of reason better than that allegorical chamberlain of the Alexandrian church understood the letter of Scripture, who made himself a eunuch for the kingdom of heaven? Those who commit the greatest evils against themselves are the favorites of the prince of this age; – – his court jesters are the worst enemies of beautiful nature; she may very well have Corybants and Galli for pot-bellied priests, but strong spirits are her true devotees.[72]

Once again Hamann uses sexual metaphors to castigate the Stoicism of his contemporaries, whom he equates with castrati. They claim to rule over nature, but ironically they have merely bound their "own hands and feet," i.e., the senses and the passions, the very things with which we feel. Thus, instead of being truly free, all they can do is pipe in high-pitched tones of the "diamond fetters of fate." The reference to "members of dishonor" is another reference to their sexual impotence; instead of coming of age and recognizing the passions as "weapons of manhood," they are ashamed of them. The third reference is, of course, to Origen, the Church Father who is supposed to have castrated himself; and Hamann accuses his contemporaries of understanding the role of reason about as well as Origen understood the letter of Scripture. Origen thought he was doing a service to God; the *Aufklärer* think they are doing a service to reason. In point of fact, however, in denigrating their own nature they are simply playing into the hands of the prince of the age (cf. 2 Cor. 4: 4; Eph. 2: 2). True, the Phrygian goddess Cybele (at some level a personification of Nature) may have been worshiped by castrated priests called Galli, but these are not nature's true devotees. Those who truly imitate her and do her justice are not to be found among the life-denying castrati, but among strong inspired spirits, who draw upon and make use of the senses and passions. Herein, Hamann avers, and not in a misguided form of pagan asceticism, lies the wellspring of human creativity, as he goes on to say,

---

[72] N II, p. 208. Hamann does not mean here Epicureanism in the popular sense of hedonism, but the popularity in his day of the Epicurean poet Lucretius, who sings in *De rerum natura* of the emasculated priests, known as Galli, of the "great mother" goddess, Cybele; the Corybants were her dancing worshipers. At the same time, by "Galli" Hamann doubtless intends the double entendre of the Gallic, i.e., French philosophers in the court of Frederick, the prince of the age, as a vicar for *the* prince of the age (see 2 Cor. 4: 4; Eph. 2: 2; 1 John 5: 19). And, in general, as Kenneth Haynes notes (*Writings on Philosophy: Johann Georg Hamann*, ed. and trans. Kenneth Haynes (Cambridge: Cambridge University Press, 2007), p. 80), and as the connection to Lucretius would suggest, Epicureanism was associated in Hamann's day with atheism.

A philosopher like Saul sets up monastic laws (1 Sam. 14: 24) – – Passion alone gives to abstractions and hypotheses hands, feet, wings; – to images and signs, spirit, life, and tongue – – Where can you find more rapid inferences? Whence is the rolling thunder of eloquence engendered, and its companion – monosyllabic lightning.[73]

At this point, it is worth asking why Hamann, as a Christian, should have such an investment in the senses and the passions. After all, the passions, and to some extent even the senses, are the very things from which, according to many Church Fathers, Christians are expressly enjoined to flee for the sake of genuinely spiritual know-ledge. Furthermore, what could Hamann possibly mean by his apparent endorsement of paganism and libertinism, when he says, "Do not venture into the metaphysics of the fine arts without being fully initiated into the orgies and Eleusinian mysteries"? The first thing to note here, aside from the obvious hyperbole, is Hamann's under-standing of knowledge in sexual terms as involving a *coincidentia oppositorum* of form and matter, concept and intuition – the very kind of "sexual" knowledge (in the Hebrew sense of *yada*) his contemporaries have forsaken, having shunned "inter-course" with the senses and passions in the name of *pure* reason. Hence Hamann's persistent association of modern philosophy with a kind of epistemological prudery. Another thing to note here is that Hamann does not mean passions in the sense of vices "suffered," but the vital parts of the soul which can be thus affected (one might say the "spirited" and "appetitive" parts, according to Plato's psychology), without which we would not be human beings capable of high degrees of emotion, but angels; and in this regard he could accuse his contemporaries of embracing a deceptive form of angelism (cf. 2 Cor. 11: 14).

The main reason, however, why Hamann is so hostile to the *proud* rationalism of his day is that for him the senses and the passions, which his contemporaries in one way or another despise, are the "sacred language," the chosen site, to which God *condescends* to speak "to the creature through the creature" – and not just to super-cilious intellectuals, who would have preferred a language more suited to their prej-udices. As he puts it, "He may speak through creatures – through circumstances – or through blood and fire and billows of smoke, wherein the language of the sanctuary [*Heiligthum*] consists."[74] The fact that Hamann uses the word "sanctuary" here is surely no coincidence, but an indication that for him the senses, rather than being opposed to the things of the spirit or reason, are precisely the way to the Holy of Holies. Indeed, as von Balthasar points out, Hamann's entire aesthetics is centered upon the *fleshliness* of God in Christ and the *wonder* that it is precisely through the *flesh* that the *spirit* is saved.[75] Thus Hamann's celebration of the senses and the pas-sions (i.e., the sub-rational depths of the human soul) turns out to be precisely a function of his faith in Christ, who speaks to and redeems the human being entire (body, soul, and spirit). By the same token, it is ultimately due to his incarnational and thoroughly anti-Gnostic perspective – as Irenaeus *redivivus* – that he is so pas-sionately opposed to the jejune rationalism of the age. As he puts it, summing up the contrast between his own full-blooded Christian aesthetic and the typical aesthetic and art criticism of the Enlightenment, which in his view is unable to ground either a genuine sensualism or a robust doctrine of the arts,

---

[73] N II, p. 208. In a footnote, Hamann cites Shakespeare's *Midsummer-Night's Dream*, "Brief as lightning in the collied night, / That (in a spleen) unfolds heav'n and earth / And ere a man has power to say: Behold! / The jaws of darkness do devour it up. (I. i. 145–8).

[74] N II, p. 204. See Joel 2: 30; Acts 2: 19.

[75] von Balthasar, "Laikale Stile," p. 611.

When talking to blinking art critics ... I have to use what they give me, an aesthetic language of their own, only with this difference: to their characteristically dried-up fibers I oppose the better characteristics of fresh green wood; to their trees, which are bare, unfruitful, twice-dead, and plucked up by the roots (Jude 12), those that are planted by streams whose water flows from the sanctuary.[76]

SEEING ALL THINGS IN CHRIST

For Hamann, then, it is now clear that the key to a full-blooded aesthetics is Christ, who establishes the *dignity* of the senses by his incarnation (John 1: 14; 1 John 1: 1), and the *dignity* of the passions, one could add, by fully assuming a passionate human soul (contra Apollinarius!). At the same time, however, one must not neglect to point out that for Hamann the senses and the passions are fallen, and, like reason, stand in need of *redemption* through Christ, in whom one is able to perceive anew the Logos speaking in and through creation and Scripture.[77] In short, whereas without Christ we can neither fully see nor fully feel, with Christ "the more we are able to see and taste and behold and touch His loving condescension [*Leutseligkeit*] in his creatures."[78] Indeed, when we see all things in Christ, "Every impression of nature in the human being is not only a memorial, but a pledge of the fundamental truth: Who the LORD is. Every counter-effect of the human being upon creatures is a letter and seal of our participation in the divine nature, and that we are His offspring [*Seines Geschlechts*]."[79]

For Hamann, then, Christ not only renews our aesthetic sensibility, helping us to see nature *as* creation, indeed as a kind of divine poem; he also renews our feeling of intimacy with the Creator, our sense that we are made in his image and likeness, in short, that we too are poets called to shape the world by the words of our mouths (albeit, in this case, the world to be shaped is a *pre-existent* world; therein lies the *maior dissimilitudo* of the analogy between us and the Creator *ex nihilo*). As he puts it,

This analogy between the human being and the Creator lends all creatures their content and character, and on this the bonds of trust and faith in all of nature depend. The more we are animated by this idea of the image of the invisible GOd, the more we are able to see his friendliness in his creatures; and to taste it, look upon it, and touch it with our hands.[80]

The reason the "bonds of trust and faith" throughout nature depend upon this analogy between the *imago Dei* and the Creator, between ourselves as poets and the

---

[76] N III, p. 378; von Balthasar, "Laikale Stile," p. 605.

[77] But this should not be taken to mean that God leaves nothing for the creature to interpret, as though, once the text of creation is purified of abstractions, as from a palimpsest, its original meaning will suddenly appear so clearly as to require no labor of interpretation. On the contrary, for Hamann the mystery of creation consists partly in what God leaves to the *imago Dei* as God's poetic "other" to interpret, almost in the form of an unfinished poem, as Adam's naming of the animals would suggest (Gen. 2: 19). Hence the human being is not a slavish mime, but a genuinely creative "other" who is called by God precisely to shape the world by the word of his mouth; therein, for Hamann, lies the essence of the human being as a linguistic being, and with it the essence of human freedom. But again, it is not a radical freedom *in abstracto*, but rather an analogous freedom, rooted in a sense of our connection and likeness to God, which "lends all creatures their content and character," and upon which "trust and faith throughout nature" depend (N II, pp. 206f.).

[78] N II, p. 207. Cf. Col. 1: 15; 2 Pet. 1: 4; Rom. 8: 29.

[79] N II, p. 207.

[80] N II, pp. 206f.

"Poet in the beginning of days," is that, apart from this analogy, there is no assurance that our own linguistic constructions are anything but arbitrary impositions upon a reality ultimately alien to us. In short, our words could no longer be taken to be the words of creation. Accordingly, from Hamann's perspective the *proton pseudos* of modern philosophy lies in that it does not begin with this analogy, this creative connection between ourselves and the Creator, but instead with the abstract contents of consciousness, and from this dubious starting point seeks impossibly to bridge the gap between the concepts of the mind and the impressions of the world. As a result, once the anthropocentric starting point of modern philosophy is accepted, the world no longer has anything to say; it no longer speaks, but falls eerily silent (cf. Ps. 19: 1). In Christ, on the other hand, who renews the analogy between God and human beings, we are enabled once again to *hear* the Logos in the *visible* work of creation – as though perception were meant to be, from the beginning, a synaesthetic *religious* experience, and all art were meant to be an innovative *poetic* response to it.

For Hamann, then, Christ is the key to nature and Scripture, such that when one is "in Christ" these "books," which previously had little or nothing to say, as if being written in a coded, hermetic language, suddenly begin to *speak* (cf. 2 Cor. 3: 15). What is more, their speech begins to reveal the same *dialect* – the same "style" – by which creation was first spoken, Scripture was written, and to which Christ's entire life is one dramatic testimony: one "dialect," which is essentially a "coincidence of opposites," of majesty and abasement, glory and *kenosis* (cf. Phil. 2: 6f.). As Hamann puts it, more or less putting "in a nutshell" the aesthetics of his London Writings:

> The book of creation contains examples of universal concepts that GOD wished to reveal to the creature through the creature; the books of the covenant contain examples of secret articles that GOD wished to reveal to the creature through the creature. The unity of the author is reflected in the dialect of his works; – in all *one* tone of immeasurable height and depth! A proof of the most glorious majesty and of the most complete self-emptying! A marvel of such infinite quiet [*Ruhe*] that makes GOD seem like nothing, so that as a matter of conscience, one is forced either to deny his existence, or be a beast (Ps. 73: 21–2); but at the same time of such infinite power, which fills all in all, that one does not know how to save oneself from his most penetrating activity![81]

Once again Hamann employs the formula "to the creature through the creature," signaling that divine revelation does not occur directly, but *through* the "books" of creation and Scripture (in keeping, on the one hand, with God's characteristic humility, and, on the other hand, with the sensible nature of the creature). And, once again, the key to these two books is Christ, who shows them to be intimately related "texts." Indeed, not only do both speak to the senses (in the way, for example, that the Bible similarly speaks through figures and parables); more importantly, both point to Christ, witnessing formally to the same "dialect" and hence to a *common*, ultimately *triune* authorship.

To be sure, in the case of the "books" of nature and Scripture, this "dialect" is less perceptible, if not, from a purely rational perspective, totally imperceptible. Seen in Christ, however (in whom we see a striking coincidence of height and depth, glory and shame, majesty and abasement, the fullness of Deity and "the most complete self-emptying"), nature and Scripture suddenly give off a strangely similar double light. Thus, for example, nature can lend proof simultaneously to the theist and to

---

[81] N II, p. 204.

the atheist, to the most dreamy-eyed idealist and to the crassest materialist (as the unending debates over arguments from design attest); it can inspire worship of the Creator, who is revealed in his works (see Wisd. 13: 5; Rom. 1: 20), and at the same time leave one despairing that a world seemingly driven by natural selection, "the blind watchmaker" in Richard Dawkins's phrase, has any meaning at all. So too the starry host: the vastness of the heavens can inspire at once wonder over their grandeur and nausea over our seeming insignificance; indeed, they can either turn one into a philosopher like Aristotle (*Metaphysics* 982b) or, as Hamann puts it, "a beast" (Ps. 73: 22). In sum, the physical universe can seem both full of God's glory and at the same time curiously bereft of it. As Shakespeare, well aware of the contradiction, put it, the firmament can seem a "majestical roof fretted with golden fire" and at the same time as *nothing but* "a foul and pestilent congregation of vapors" – just as the human being can appear at once "like a god! the beauty of the world" and, at the same time, as nothing but the "quintessence of dust."[82]

Curiously enough, as Hamann perceived, something similar can be said of Scripture. To the Church Fathers it contained the "oracles of God"; to Luther it was the "divine *Aeneid*"; and to the bitter Voltaire, on the other hand, speaking of the Old Testament, it revealed nothing divine but, on the contrary, "disgusting and abominable fancies" offensive to any person of reason.[83] To be sure, at one level, whether one is speaking of nature or Scripture, this discrepancy can be explained as a function of the subjective mode of the perceiver (according to the scholastic maxim, "quidquid cognoscitur per modum cognoscentis cognoscitur"), or, as Christ himself more succinctly puts it, "Whoever has ears, let him hear" (Matt. 13: 9). For Hamann, however, it is also due, objectively, to the parabolic form or "style" of divine revelation in general, whether in creation, in Scripture, or in Christ himself. For it is a language, a Logos, that characteristically appears at once common and elevated, trivial and profound, high and low: "*one* tone," as he puts it, "of immeasurable height and depth." So too, as an example of this dialectic, the Athenians could say of the *lofty* Paul, " 'What would this *babbler* say?' " (Acts 17: 18); and, quoting his critics, even Paul could say of himself, " 'His letters are weighty and strong, but his bodily presence is weak, and his speech of no account' " (2 Cor. 10: 10).

But nowhere is this dialect heard so loudly and clearly, and nowhere is this striking *coincidentia oppositorum* so evident, as from the Cross of the Son of God: the *crucified Lord of glory*. This is why, for Hamann, Christ, the Logos, *in this double aspect* of height and depth, majesty and abasement, is the philological and exegetical key to the "language" of nature and Scripture; and why the whole of nature, however eloquent, pales by comparison. As he poignantly put it to his brother,

> Do not run to men, even if they should be high priests like Eli; it is the voice of God. Hear what he says. The rolling thunder, the whispering spring, and the cool evening breeze in the midst of the garden are the tongues of his attributes. [But] what are all the suns and earths with their harmony; and what is all the language of the morning stars among angels and men: A sounding gong – compared to the love that speaks from the blood of his Son, Our brother, the lamb that was slain for Us from the foundation of the world.[84]

---

[82]   *Hamlet*, II. ii. 307–8.

[83]   Luther, *Werke*, TR 1, p. xviii; cf., TR 5, p. 168. For an in-depth analysis of Luther's last note, from which this appellation derives, see Oswald Bayer, *Gott als Autor* (Tübingen: Mohr-Siebeck, 1999), pp. 280–301. Cf. Voltaire, *Sermon of the Fifty*, p. 23.

[84]   ZH I, p. 401.

As in the London Writings, which speak of God's self-emptying love in Christ as the heart and measure of all things, here too we are given to understand that all the works of God – from the "book" of nature, to the book of Scripture, to the continuing "book" of history – are so many revelations, so many tongues, whose interpretation is found in Christ (cf. 1 Cor. 12: 10; 14: 10f.). Indeed, continuing with the biblical metaphor, one could say that the entire book of creation is folded into the infinite "book" (or "library," as John Milbank has sublimely put it), which is Christ himself (cf. John 21: 25).[85] Accordingly, the one who is versed in this "book" and has entered into its pages (Rev. 21: 27) is able to read all things (cf. Col. 2: 3); just as the one who hears his voice (John 10: 4) is able to hear in all things one dialect of majesty and abasement (Eph. 4: 8–10), glory and humility (Phil. 2: 6ff.): one dialect revealed in Christ, to whom all of nature (Luke 19: 40), Scripture (Luke 24: 27), and the saints (Rev. 5: 11ff.) bear witness; and to whom Hamann himself testifies with the dialectical title of his late work, *Golgotha and Scheblimini*, which refers at once to "the place of the skull," Calvary, and to the intra-Trinitarian declaration of the Father to the resurrected Son, " 'Sit at my right hand,' until I make your enemies a footstool for your feet" (Ps. 110: 1).

TOWARD A CHRISTOLOGICAL POETICS

Thus far in this chapter we have been circumscribing two principal questions. The first, initially raised by Michaelis, was how to revive the dead, ancient language (or languages) of the biblical text; and the irony of Hamann's response to it consisted chiefly in the suggestion that Michaelis's own *uninspired* criticism was responsible for any death the *inspired* language of the Bible may have suffered. His further point was that whatever meager fruits Michaelis's philological expedition to the Middle East may yield, historical criticism alone can never hope to determine the meaning of the biblical text, which depends, as Hamann puts it, "upon such fleeting, spiritual, arbitrary, and incidental determinations and circumstances that one cannot draw down the key to their understanding without ascending to heaven …"[86] Indeed, whatever can be determined historically regarding the genesis, context, forms, and redactions of Scripture, can for Hamann, following Bacon, never exhaust a text that prophetically encompasses all times and ages, the past as well as the future – a text that is inspired by a perspective that is, at the end of the day, eternal (Ps. 119: 89; Matt. 24: 35). The second question is a corollary of the first and concerns the modern insensibility for the language of nature as such. "By what means," Hamann asks, "shall we resurrect the extinct language *of nature* from the dead? – – By means of pilgrimages to Arabia Felix, by means of crusades to the lands of the East and the rehabilitation of their magic"?[87] This question follows from the first because here too we are concerned with hermeneutics, in this case, a hermeneutics of creation,

---

[85] As Milbank has suggested in this regard (echoing Hamann's and Bacon's understanding of the prophetic multi-dimensionality of Scripture, which always thwarts historical criticism's feeble efforts to determine biblical content and meaning), efforts to understand the "historical Jesus" apart from genuine inspiration are similarly futile, since "The world is but a few books in the library that is Christ." Indeed, for Milbank, Christ's infinity breaks down any ultimate separation between "fact and fiction," the real and the imagined, since the world could not possibly contain all the books that could be written of him (John 21: 25). From a paper at The World and Christian Imagination National Research Conference, November 9–11, 2006, at Baylor University.

[86] N II, p. 203.

[87] N II, p. 211. My emphasis.

and because what is problematic here is likewise an obtusely "rational" approach to the text of nature, which forecloses any genuine experience of God speaking to the creature through it.

We have also seen that for Hamann the answer to both questions is Christ. As the Alpha Christ stands at the beginning of creation as its archetype (John 1: 3; Col. 1: 16); as the Omega, he is also its guiding *telos* and judge. "The poet in the beginning of days," Hamann says, "is the same as the thief at the end of days."[88] In short, Christ is the protological and eschatological Logos, the first and final Word of creation, and therefore the answer to the hermeneutical riddle it poses. Whereas, apart from Christ, creation threatens to become mute and meaningless, in Christ it speaks anew and is perceived once again as a "speech to the creature through the creature." The same is true of Scripture: whereas apart from Christ it is full of riddles and apparent contradictions, in Christ its pages come alive (Luke 24: 27) and its language is shown to be a still more intimate and personal "speech to the creature through the creature" (as Hamann himself experienced in London). In response, therefore, to Michaelis's question about how to revive the dead languages of Scripture, he asks:

> How, then, shall we consume the death in the pots in order to make the added vegetables palatable for the children of the prophets? By what means shall we propitiate [*versöhnen*] the embittered Spirit of Scripture? "Do you think I want to eat the flesh of bulls and drink the blood of goats?" Neither the dogmatic soundness of orthodox Pharisees, nor the poetic license of free-thinking Sadducees will renew the sending of the Spirit who drove the holy men of GOd (ευκαιρως ακαιρως) to speak and to write.[89]

In other words, if the added vegetables represent the fruit of Michaelis's historical criticism, which by itself is unable to make Scripture palatable, the additional ingredient that will make it so is the Holy Spirit, the Spirit of Christ, through whom the depths of Scripture are revealed (see 1 Cor. 2: 10). But the Spirit is amenable neither to the hypocritical orthodox, who may be true to the letter of Scripture but inside are "full of dead men's bones" (Matt. 23: 27f.), nor to free-thinkers, who run roughshod over the letter of Scripture or even discount it altogether.

So what, then, will renew the sending of the Spirit? Hamann does not say so here in so many words, but it clearly involves the confession of Christ, the Giver of the Spirit (John 4: 10). As he puts it,

> The beloved disciple of the only-begotten [Son], who is in the father's bosom, has declared it to us: that the spirit of prophecy inhabits the testimony of the *one* and only Name by which we are blessed and can inherit the promise of this and the future life; the name which no one knows but him who receives it, which is above all names, that at the name of JESUS every knee shall bow, of all who are in heaven and on the earth and below the earth, and every tongue confess, that JESUS CHRIST is LORD to the glory of GOd! – the Creator, who is praised in eternity! Amen![90]

In other words, the only thing that will call down the Spirit and renew the text of Scripture is the confession of Jesus as Lord; for the Spirit of Scripture, the Spirit of

---

[88] N II, p. 206.

[89] N II, p. 211. See 2 Kgs. 4: 38–41 and Ps. 50: 13. One might render ευκαιρως ακαιρως as "in season and out of season."

[90] N II, p. 212. See John 1: 18; Acts 4: 12; Rev. 2: 17; Phil. 2: 9–10.

the prophets, is none other than the Spirit who testifies to Jesus (Rev. 19: 10). Indeed, when one reads the prophetic books in this light, with Christ in mind, Hamann says, quoting Augustine, "it will intoxicate you":

> The spirit of prophecy is the testimony of JESUS; this first sign, whereby he revealed the majesty of his *Knechtsgestalt*, transfigures the holy books of the covenant into good, old wine, which confounds the stewards' judgment and strengthens the weak stomach of the art critics. *Lege libros propheticos non intellecto CHRISTO*, says the Punic Church father, *quid tam insipidum & fatuum invenies? Intellege ibi CHRISTUM, non solum sapit, quod legis, sed etiam inebriat* ["If you read the prophetic books without understanding CHRIST, what exceedingly insipid and fatuous things you will find! But if you perceive Christ in them, what you read will not only be to your taste, but will also intoxicate you"].[91]

Once again Hamann refers to the majesty *in* the form of a servant, as if to remind us that there can be no true perception of Christ, indeed no genuine faith, that does not at least cognize the offense, that does not at least recognize, in Paul's words, the "folly" and the "stumbling block" of the Word of the Cross (1 Cor. 1: 18f.). All of which points to Kierkegaard, especially the Kierkegaard of *Practice in Christianity*. By the same token this is what allows Hamann to sympathize with his unbelieving contemporaries, inasmuch as they profoundly feel the offense, as in their reaction to certain unsavory and on the face of it, morally problematic stories in the Old Testament (e.g., Gen. 22 or Judg. 4), or in the way that Goethe or Nietzsche were sorely offended by the Cross. Hamann's aesthetics does not gloss over the offense. He knows very well where his contemporaries are troubled. What he proposes to them, however, is that the offense they perceive is the outward form of a mystery, whether one is speaking of the lowly, outward form of Scripture or the lowly, outward form of Christ; and that when one gets over the offense of Christ, and comes to see all the riches that are in him (Col. 2: 3), one will likewise come to discover all the riches of Scripture itself, which are similarly concealed from the "wise and learned" but revealed to mere children (Matt. 11: 25). That being said, Hamann warns his readers that his aesthetics lies on the other side of a death: that the perception of which he speaks lies on the other side of a suffering, namely the suffering of a death to oneself in baptism (see Rom. 6: 3f.). Quoting Luther, he says, "Adam must first be dead before he [can] experience [*leide*] this thing and drink the strong wine. Therefore, see to it that you do not drink wine when you are still an infant; every doctrine has its measure, time, and age."[92]

Toward the end of the *Aesthetica,* Hamann finally turns to the question of poetry as a literary genre, comparing Homer's "monotonous meter" to Klopstock's free verse. At first one might think that this subject is tangential to his leading questions concerning Scripture and creation, but as we have seen, for Hamann all of these questions are, in fact, intimately related: since Scripture is a kind of poetry (as in the "Sacred poetry of the Hebrews"), since creation itself is a kind of poetry (of which the Fall has left us only "jumbled verse"), and since all human poetry is in some sense an imitation of nature ("Poetry is an imitation of beautiful nature"),[93] indeed, a poetic response to a divine poem. No doubt, many a poet may fancy himself or

---

[91] Ibid. The quotation from Augustine's commentary on John, *In Ioannis tractatus*, IX, 3.
[92] N II, p. 213. From Luther's *Vorreden zur Heiligen Schrift*. The context is Luther's discussion of predestination and grace.
[93] N II, p. 205.

herself an "original," and in a sense, according to Hamann's own terms, such originality is precisely the birthright of human beings as the *imago Dei*. For Hamann, however, such originality is *radically* original only when it is understood that one's own poetic and symbolic actions are an analogical response to "the Poet in the beginning of days."

Accordingly, Hamann's aesthetics steers a middle course between classicism and subjective expressionism. For, on the one hand, like the classicists (Boileau, Batteux, Gottsched, et al.), he understands poetry as an "imitation of nature." "Nature and Scripture," as he puts it, "are the materials of the beautiful, creative, imitative Spirit."[94] On the other hand, for Hamann such imitation, being a "creative" imitation, does not entail a slavish adherence to objective rules or "rational" standards. On the contrary, genuine art and poetry is an effect of genius. "What is it in *Homer*," he asks, "that makes up for his ignorance of the rules of art, which Aristotle invented after him, and what is it in *Shakespeare* that makes up either for his ignorance of these critical laws or his transgression of them? *Genius* is the unanimous answer."[95] For this reason, Hamann's understanding of imitation must not be confused with a slavish reproduction of the past. As he puts it, clearly taking aim at Winckelmann:

> As though our learning were merely a matter of recollection, we are always being referred to the monuments of the ancients, in order to form the spirit by means of memory. But why do we remain standing at the hole-ridden fountains of the Greeks and abandon the most living springs of antiquity? Perhaps we ourselves do not even know what it is that we admire in the Greeks and Romans to the point of idolatry ... Salvation comes from the Jews ...[96]

In other words, why do his contemporaries gawk at the monuments of the Greeks and Romans when they could draw endless inspiration from the most living fountain of antiquity, which comes from the Jews, namely, Christ himself (John 7: 37f.)? As it is, like Narcissus, whose story Hamann recounts at length from Ovid, they have fallen in love with a deception. And so he chides them, saying, "I expected to find healthier concepts in your philosophical writings – to your shame – Christians! – But, of course, you feel the prick [*Stachel*] of the good name by which you are called as little as the honor that GOD did himself in assuming the loathsome name of the Son of Man."[97] Thus, once again, as with the philosophers (regarding nature) and the biblical critics (regarding Scripture), the ultimate problem with the aesthetic theorists of the Enlightenment is that they have forsaken Christ, the ever-living fount of creation (Rev. 21: 5–6).

In sum, on the one hand, given his emphasis upon the "creative" element, Hamann is clearly a defender of the genius against the dictates of reason (as in his defense of Klopstock's "unbounded" verse" as contrasted with Homer's comparatively "monotonous meter"); on the other hand, given the "imitative" element, it is equally clear that he does not endorse a pure subjectivism. As Frederick Beiser observes:

> If we were to sum up *Aesthetica in nuce*, then we would have to single out two doctrines: that art ought to imitate nature and reveal the word of God; and that art ought to

[94] N II, pp. 205, 210.

[95] N II, p. 75.

[96] N II, p. 209. Cf. Jer. 2: 13: "for my people have committed two evils: they have forsaken me, the fountain of living water, and dug out cisterns for themselves, cracked cisterns that can hold no water." Cf. Isa. 55: 1. As the rest of the *Aesthetica* makes clear, the Jewish source of Hamann's living aesthetic is Christ. See John 4: 13f. and 7: 37f.

[97] N II, p. 210.

express the innermost personality of the artist. What is central to Hamann's aesthetics, however, is precisely the combination or intersection of these doctrines. It is a seemingly paradoxical fusion of an extreme subjectivism, which insists that the artist express his innermost desires and feelings, and an extreme objectivism, which demands that the artist strictly imitate nature and surrender to its effects upon him.[98]

As Beiser rightly points out, the resolution of this apparent paradox between subjective freedom and objective imitation is to be found in Hamann's understanding of the human being as the *imago Dei*. For it is precisely, and most especially, through the poetic freedom of the human being that God himself, as the *original poet,* is revealed in his image. Thus, the maximum of human freedom and creativity, rather than being an instance of pure subjectivism, is simultaneously the maximum of God's self-revelation. As we saw above, "Every counter-effect of the human being upon creatures is a letter and seal of our participation in the divine nature, and that we are His offspring [*Seines Geschlechts*]."[99] Accordingly, human *poesis* is never something purely subjective, but always already a participation in the expressive language of creation; and as such it provides "a metaphysical insight," as Beiser points out, into the nature of reality itself.[100]

What, then, is the summa of Hamann's aesthetics and the key to a proper perception of everything? At this point we should not be surprised given the centrality of Christ. As he puts it in his concluding apostil, where he refers to himself as the "oldest reader of this rhapsody in kabbalistic prose": "Let us now hear the final sum of his newest aesthetics, which is the oldest: Fear GOd and give Him the glory, for the time of his judgment is come, and worship Him who made heaven and earth, the sea and the fountains of water!" (Rev. 14: 7).[101]

---

[98]   Frederick C. Beiser, *The Fate of Reason* (Cambridge, MA: Harvard University Press, 1987), pp. 36f.
[99]   N II, p. 207.
[100]   Beiser, *The Fate of Reason*, p. 37.
[101]   N II, p. 217.

6

Correcting a Disciple: Hamann and Herder on the Origin of Language

Dearest Hamann, if you only knew how I view every little scrap I receive from you, you would surely tear none up ... Moreover, in every one of your letters is a single *word that speaks so deeply to me ... Again, I ask for your glowing sparks, and promise as soon as possible my drops of water in return.*

Herder to Hamann[1]

For me it is a matter neither of physics nor of theology, but of language, *the* mother *of reason and its revelations, its A and Ω. It is the double-edged sword of all truths and lies; and do not laugh if I must attack the* matter *from this* angle. *It is my old lyre, but by* it all things *are made.*

Hamann to Jacobi[2]

If the relationship between Hamann and Herder is "one of the most treasured examples of personality and humanity in the eighteenth century," as Nadler suggests – a relationship that could be characterized as one between the German Socrates and his disciple, the German Plato – it was also a relationship that was put to the test by Herder's prize-winning submission to the Berlin Academy on the question of the origin of language, his *Abhandlung über den Ursprung der Sprache* (1772), and Hamann's bitterly ironic response to it.[3] The reasons for Hamann's reaction are complex and will require some sorting out. The first thing to consider, however, is his longstanding antipathy toward the Berlin Academy, which he viewed as an intellectual front for the detested regime of Fredrick the Great. Furthermore, having long forsworn any direct engagement with the *Aufklärer*, he would never have dreamed of entering a prize competition at their behest. Naturally, therefore, he thought that his disciple had gone "whoring after the beautiful spirits of his century and their *bon ton.*"[4]

In any event, whatever one makes of Herder's "adulterous affair" with the Berlin Academy, the content of his *Preisschrift* would seem on the face of it rather sensible. His intention had been to steer a middle course between the extreme supernaturalism of Süßmilch (whose understanding of the origin of language involved divine instruction on the order of a *deus ex machina*) and the extreme naturalism of Condillac and Rousseau (who argued that the development of language was more or less natural to any creature of feeling). The problem, as Herder saw it, was that neither

---

[1] ZH III, pp. 60–1.
[2] ZH VI, p. 108.
[3] NB, p. 154.
[4] ZH III, pp. 16f.

explanation did justice to the dignity of the human being: Süßmilch made human beings into passive recipients, neglecting to appreciate the creativity implied in Adam's naming of the animals (Gen. 2: 19), whereas Condillac and Rousseau failed to appreciate the qualitative difference between animals and human beings. As Herder puts it in a memorable *bon mot,* "Condillac and Rousseau necessarily erred concerning the origin of language, because they erred so famously and so differently concerning this difference: the former made animals into men, the latter made men into animals."[5]

That being said, Herder did not want to deny the role of feeling in human language, as something to some extent shared with the animals; and this is why he opens his essay with a concession to Condillac: "Already as an animal, man possesses language" ("Schon als Tier hat der Mensch Sprache"). But this alone, he argued, could not account for the qualitative difference between the language of human beings and the instinctive cries of animals. In fact, human language, he argued, is not a function of instinct at all, but of a "totally unique orientation and development of all powers," which he calls reason or "reflection" [*Besonnenheit*].[6] To give his own example, whereas from a vast "ocean of sensations," from a more or less *unlimited* horizon – a horizon that is precisely *undetermined* by strong instinct – human beings are capable of stopping the flood of sensations, reflecting upon a sheep, and identifying it as the particular animal that "bleats," a wolf goes through no such process of "reflection." The sheep appears on the wolf's *limited* horizon either as something of no concern or simply as food. By contrast, given that human beings *are* naturally reflective, Herder says that we can account for the origin of human language as something concomitantly "invented" along with reflection "as naturally and necessarily as human beings are human beings."[7]

On the face of it, it is difficult to see what Hamann found so problematic in such claims. For his own theory of language, as we shall see, falls neither on the side of an extreme naturalism, nor on the side of an extreme supernaturalism. The matter is all the more confusing given that Herder clearly continued to think of himself as Hamann's disciple. In fact, he considered their positions so similar that, in an apologetic and deferential letter of August 1772, he could claim to be mystified by Hamann's reaction.[8] One could even say that Hamann owed Herder a debt of gratitude for clarifying and popularizing many of the ideas in the *Aesthetica* that had been left woefully unclear owing to Hamann's intentionally dark, hermetic style. Before sorting out the subtle but important differences between them, it will therefore be important to consider some of the fundamental ideas they continued to share, ideas that would profoundly affect the course of post-Kantian philosophy.

For one thing, and most importantly, against the dominant rationalism of the day both held that reason was *unthinkable* apart from language, and that language, in turn, was unthinkable apart from a given cultural context. In this regard, they relativized the claims of the *Aufklärer* regarding the universality of reason and heralded a suspicion of transcendental epistemology that today is so common as to

---

[5] Johann Gottfried Herder, *Abhandlung über den Ursprung der Sprache* (Stuttgart: Reclam, 1966), p. 20. Cf. Herder, *Essay on the Origin of Language,* tr. Alexander Gode, in *On the Origin of Language,* introd. by Alexander Gode (Chicago: University of Chicago Press, 1986).

[6] Herder, *Abhandlung,* pp. 26f.; *Essay on the Origin of Language,* p. 110.

[7] Herder, *Essay on the Origin of Language,* p. 34.

[8] ZH III, pp. 10ff.

be taken for granted.[9] For another thing, like Rousseau, both held that the original language was poetry and, hence, older than prose. As Herder puts it, echoing Hamann's *Aesthetica,*

> For what was *this first language but a collection of elements of poetry?* An imitation of the stirring and acting and sounding of Nature! Enlivened by the interjection of all beings and the interjection of human feeling! The natural language of all creatures poetically formed by the understanding into sounds, into images of action, passion, and living influence! A dictionary of the soul that is at the same time mythology and a marvelous epic of the actions and speech of all beings! Which is to say, a continuous fabulation [*Fabeldichtung*] informed by passion and interest! – What else is poetry but that?[10]

For Herder, then, language is not an invention of reason *in the abstract*, i.e., it is not something that comes forth from reason as the mere instrument for communicating its concepts (as was commonly held by the *Aufklärer*); rather, it arises as a result of a response, charged with feeling, to the living language of nature. To be sure, for Herder, language emerges from reason qua reflection, which can give the impression that language is a kind of derivative construction. Yet it is equally clear that for him reason does not have priority over language, but that both arise together, indeed, imply one another: "Without language man has no reason, and without reason, no language."[11] And in this respect, like Hamann, he plays upon the ambiguity of the Greek word *logos,* as meaning both "reason" and "word."[12] Other similarities include a shared stress upon the importance of the senses and the passions; a shared conviction that the original, expressive, poetic language of nature has been obscured by the distorting effects of abstract philosophical terms and concepts (which bear no similarity to the passionate language of nature); a shared sense that nature can once again speak through the vital, expressive spirit of the poet;[13] and in general a shared sense that art is fundamentally an expression of the life, vitality, energy, in short, the *spirit* of the artist.[14]

What, then, given all these similarities, was the cause of Hamann's ire? And why, for that matter, should this seemingly antiquated debate over the origin of language be of interest today? The briefest answer to these questions is that, in Hamann's view, Herder had willy-nilly reduced the *theologoumenon* of language to a matter of anthropology. In other words, sharply stated, he had profaned the theological *mystery* of language, which for Hamann is always already an analogue of the divine Logos and the most privileged aspect of the human being as the *imago Dei*, by presenting it in purely naturalistic terms. It was bad enough that he had scornfully

---

[9] Indeed, both advocated a theory of language that, in the words of Charles Taylor, "totally upsets the outlook of the mainstream epistemological tradition." See Charles Taylor, *Philosophical Arguments* (Cambridge: Harvard University Press, 1995), p. 13.

[10] Herder, *Abhandlung*, pp. 50f.; *Essay on the Origin of Language*, pp. 135f.

[11] Herder, *Abhandlung*, p. 37; *Essay on the Origin of Language*, p. 121.

[12] This ambivalence traces back to Aristotle's understanding of the human being in the *Politics* (λόγον δὲ μόνον ἄνθρωπος ἔχει τῶν ζῴων (1253a)), where the uniqueness of the human being can consist either in the possession of reason or language.

[13] See Herder, *Abhandlung*, pp. 6f.; *Essay on the Origin of Language*, pp. 88f.

[14] See in this regard, with particular reference to Herder, Werner Strube, "Vom ästhetischen Umgang mit poetischen Texten. Ein Beitrag zu Poetik und Hermeneutik des 18. Jahrhunderts," in Jörg Schönert and Friedrich Vollhardt (eds.) *Geschichte der Hermeneutik und die Methodik der textinterpretierenden Disziplinen* (Berlin: de Gruyter, 2005).

treated Süßmilch's supernaturalistic hypothesis, thereby satisfying the vanity of the secularists in Berlin. Worse still, he had trampled upon the heart of Hamann's understanding of original *and* redeemed language as a prophetic speech "to the creature through the creature" – a formula that prohibits any reduction of language to exclusively natural *or* exclusively supernatural terms. So too, therefore, he had failed to appreciate the irreducibly Christological, i.e., human *and* divine, character of language. Moreover, he had left out of the picture, in a matter of such immense importance to Hamann as language, the very touchstone of Hamann's thought: his understanding of all things, *especially* language, in terms of divine condescension. Finally, when one considers the centrality of the relationship between thought and language to Hamann's thought, the insufferable theological consequences of Herder's position are clear. For if reason is constituted by language, but language itself is a purely natural "invention," then reason itself can likewise be understood in purely naturalistic and therefore purely secular terms. In short, Herder had made any theological understanding of language – and with it any notion of language as prophetic or inspired speech – superfluous, since the human logos could be satisfactorily explained apart from a divine Logos. And to this extent, given that culture is essentially a function of language, as Hamann and Herder both profoundly grasped, Herder's naturalistic explanation had unwittingly opened the floodgates to a purely secular understanding not merely of language, but also of reason, culture, and indeed everything.

Admittedly, from today's perspective, the debate over the origin of language may seem antiquated, at least if we no longer think of it as a question for which scientific answers are pending. As Charles Taylor observes, no one has come even close to explaining it.[15] Yet somehow, as Hamann profoundly realized, this curious debate managed to touch upon everything: for if language is lost to secularism, everything is lost. And it is in this light, finally, that one can begin to appreciate his harsh reaction to Herder's *Preisschrift*. Indeed, from Hamann's perspective, it merely shored up the very rationalism and secularism his entire authorship was intended to combat. In the same letter in August, Herder seems to have got Hamann's point. He tells him not to worry, that in a future work, his *Älteste Urkunde des Menschengeschlechts*, he "will show precisely the opposite," i.e., defend a position more in keeping with Hamann's own.[16]

HAMANN'S REVIEW OF HERDER'S *PREISSCHRIFT*

If there is otherwise much to appreciate in Herder's *Preisschrift*, Hamann's incisive review quickly reveals the distance in genius between them. Hamann's first sentence plays on Herder's last sentence. Herder had in jest sought to excuse his "disobedience" *vis-à-vis* the Academy for not having delivered a "hypothesis" in accordance with its precise instructions. To this act of deference, Hamann wryly responds, "As a result of his 'disobedience' the author has merited the attainment of the Academy's prize."[17] The ironic use of "disobedience" here is obvious. Instead of disobeying the Academy, Hamann's own "disobedient" disciple had given it precisely what it was looking for. "In *'compensation'* for this discrepancy," Hamann continues, "Herr Herder has, instead of delivering an hypothesis, sought to banish an *hypothesis* [namely,

---

15 Taylor, *Philosophical Arguments*, p. 83.
16 ZH III, p. 11.
17 N III, p. 17.

Süßmilch's "higher" hypothesis], which he considers " 'in every respect unworthy of the human mind ...' "[18]

Herder lampoons Süßmilch's theory, firstly, because of its crude anthropomorphism: human beings, Süßmilch had argued, could not have learned language unless God had essentially come down and taught it to them. To be sure, Süßmilch's theory was not as crude as Herder makes it out to be. His reason for insisting on the "higher" hypothesis was that human language is always already marked by a beautiful order and syntactical structure (anticipating, in a way, Saussure's understanding of *langue,* as opposed to *parole*); and this network, he argued, given its complexity, cannot have evolved, but must have been given. According to Herder, however, Süßmilch's theory leaves us not only with an unworthy conception of God, who is belittled by such anthropomorphisms, but also with an unworthy conception of human beings. And here again Herder appeals to Genesis 2: 19.[19] In sum, Herder considers Süßmilch's hypothesis "unworthy of the human mind" because it amounts to what today we would call a "God of the gaps" theory. In other words, Süßmilch affirmed a divine origin simply because he could not conceive of a plausible natural explanation. And in this regard, Herder's debate with Süßmilch strikingly prefigures more recent debates concerning evolution and the so-called "intelligent design" hypothesis.

Seen in this light Herder's position seems quite plausible, and Süßmilch's, by contrast, somewhat naïve, if not crassly anthropomorphic. And yet, wonder of wonders, Hamann leaps to Süßmilch's defense. For *if* one is forced to make a choice between a natural and a supernatural explanation, he feels compelled to defend the "higher" hypothesis. But, importantly, he does not defend the hypothesis wholesale, certainly not in the form of a "God of the gaps" theory. Drawing ironically upon quotations from the *Preisschrift,* he sums up Herder's critique of Süßmilch as follows:

> "If you cannot explain language on the basis of human nature, then it [must be] divine." – –
> The nonsense in this conclusion is neither *concealed nor subtle* – – Herr *Herder* says:
> "I can fully explain it on the basis of human nature." Who has said more? The former
> hides behind a cover and cries from it: *"Here* is *God!"* The latter presents himself visibly
> on the stage, and in a dramatic performance says, *"Behold! I am a man."*[20]

In other words, Herder and Süßmilch are involved in an absurd dialectic: the one says the origin of language must be divine because he cannot explain it naturally; the other says it must be natural because he can. Neither explanation, in Hamann's view, is satisfying. Süßmilch makes the mistake of assuming that a divine explanation cannot include a natural one; Herder, on the other hand, comes close to making the opposite mistake of assuming that a natural explanation cannot include one that is divine. In any case, for Hamann there is no need to think of the natural and supernatural explanations as mutually exclusive.

But, in all fairness, Herder is somewhat more subtle than Hamann makes him out to be. In fact, he seems very close to Hamann when he says that his naturalistic explanation "presents God in the best light," namely, as having created the human soul in such a way as to be able to "create and perpetuate language" by its own means.[21] Indeed, he says, "The origin [of language] is worthily said to be divine only

---

[18] N III, p. 17.
[19] Herder, *Abhandlung,* p. 123.
[20] N III, p. 17.
[21] N III, p. 18.

insofar as it is human."[22] It is by no means transparent, therefore, that Herder's naturalistic explanation necessarily excludes the divine. On the contrary, the natural explanation, whereby human beings come up with language on their own, is the only explanation that he thinks worthy of God in the first place. And Herder is not far from Hamann on this point, especially given Hamann's kenotic understanding of creation and corresponding understanding of the freedom and archontic dignity of the human being as the *imago Dei*, which is expressed pre-eminently in Adam's naming of the animals (Gen. 2: 19). As Hamann put it in the *Aesthetica*:

> The creation of the stage compares to the creation of man as epic to dramatic poetry. The former took place by a Word; the latter by action. Heart! Be still as the sea! – – Hear the counsel: Let us make men [*Menschen*] in our image, after our likeness, and let them have dominion! – – Behold the deed: And GOD the LORD made man from a lump of clay – – Compare the counsel and the deed; worship! the mighty speaker with the Psalmist (Ps. 33: 9); the supposed gardener with the evangelist [*Evangelistin*] of the disciples (John 22: 15–17); and the free potter (Rom. 9: 21) with the apostle to Hellenistic philosophers and Talmudic scribes.[23]

For all their notable similarities, however, Hamann proceeds to highlight the difference between them, saying: "Here! Here! (by the life of Pharaoh!) here is *God's finger!* This *apotheosis,* Αποκολοκυντωσις, or, as the case may be, *apophtheirosis* smacks perhaps more of Galimatias than the most debased and unworthy, but nevertheless *privileged* anthropomorphism."[24] In other words, Herder's apotheosis of the human being is worse – more nonsensical and more pernicious – than Süßmilch's anthropomorphism. For the latter, however disagreeable it may be to Herder, is "privileged" in that God himself, according to Hamann, in creation, in Scripture, and in Christ himself, speaks precisely *in anthropomorphisms,* i.e., in speech that is shockingly adapted to the sensible nature of the creature. As Hamann bluntly puts it some years later to Jacobi, "Without anthropomorphism no revelation is possible …"[25] Indeed, in this respect, as Hamann sees it, Herder has precisely failed to grasp the depths of divine condescension, whereby human language, however naturally it may have arisen, is at the same time assumed and dignified as the chosen vehicle, indeed the mobile throne, of divine self-communication.

To be sure, Herder is happy to say that God authorized the autonomy of human language. But Hamann thinks that, in a Promethean act of usurpation, Herder has in point of fact substituted the human for the divine, illegitimately deified human beings, and thereby evacuated language of its prophetic essence as a speech "to the creature through the creature." Another way to look at it would be to say that Herder (anticipating Hegel, on whom he was a well-known influence) took Hamann's notion of divine kenosis too far – to the point that God disappears in the human. In any event, the matter demanded further attention, and so, with characteristic wit, Hamann leaves his readers with the hope that some Don Quixote (i.e., he himself in the guise of the crusading philologist), if he is not long dead, will mount his steed

---

[22] N III, p. 18.

[23] N II, p. 200.

[24] Ibid. *Apocolocyntosis* is the title of Seneca's satire on the deification of the Emperor Claudius, "the Clod," or rather his transmogrification into a "pumpkin"; *apophtheirosis* means "destruction." As Dickson suggests, the term "Galimatias" comes from Montaigne, and has come into English as "meaningless talk or gibberish" (G-D, p. 453).

[25] ZH VII, p. 427.

once more and come to the rescue of the "worthy Dulcinea" of the "higher hypothesis," as that from which the "systems and languages of the old and new Babel" derive their Promethean fire:

> It is our hope that one of our fellow citizens, if he is not entirely decayed in the home of his origin, will yet find some spark from the ashes of his little kitchen stove to fan into a flame, in order to warm up his *doubts* and *oracles* about the content and direction of the academic question and its decision. For what *Dulcinea* could be worthier of a kabbalistic philologist than that of avenging the individuality, authenticity, majesty, wisdom, beauty, fruitfulness, and extravagance of the *"higher hypothesis"* – – from which all the systems and languages of the old and new Babel derive the fire (κοσμον της αδικιας) of their *subterranean, animalistic,* and *human* origin, and from which they may expect either their dissolution or destruction.[26]

THE RETURN OF ARISTOBULUS

At the conclusion of his review Hamann had led us to expect that the author of the *Aesthetica,* i.e., he himself in the guise of the "philologist," would enlighten us with his understanding of the origin of language and come to the defense of the "higher hypothesis." Instead, taking up one of his old masks, Aristobulus (the pseudonym Hamann used in his *Essay on an Academic Question,* and notably, according to 2 Maccabees 1: 10, the name of the teacher of King Ptolemy), he completes his little triptych, which began with his review of Tiedemann, with a supplemental review of his own review of Herder, bearing the plain title "Dispatch" [*Abfertigung*]. The *Dispatch* is a masterpiece of learned wit. It begins with what Aristobulus takes to be a more sensible formulation of the academic question, asking, "whether the first, oldest, original language was imparted to human beings in the same way that language has been propagated until now?"[27] Aristobulus suggests that it is natural to think that the first language was communicated in a manner at least analogous to the way in which language continues to be acquired today, namely, by instruction; whereas the notion that the origin of language bears no analogy to the way that we acquire language today would seem beset by far greater difficulties, requiring a complete renunciation of what is familiar to us. Thus, suddenly, Süßmilch's supernatural hypothesis of divine instruction seems not nearly as ludicrous as Herder had made it out to be. In fact, it now appears to be the more *natural* explanation, whereas Herder's own explanation is not only abstract and speculative, but invariably leads us, Hamann suggests, into a deceptive and wearying labyrinth without any thread of similarity to lead us out. "For what means," Hamann asks, "could possibly help us to attain the least conception of the origin of a phenomenon, if such an origin bears no similarity whatsoever to the ordinary course of nature?"[28] Indeed, we would then be "left without any pole or compass to determine and correct the course of our discoveries."[29]

At this point, Hamann names three possible explanations for the origin of language: instinct, invention, and instruction. The first, he suggests, does not hold up to what we know about the intimate connection between the tongue and the ear, given especially what we know of those born deaf and those rare cases of persons raised

---

[26] N III, p. 19. Cf. Jas. 3: 15 on the two kinds of wisdom.
[27] N III, p. 20.
[28] Ibid.
[29] Ibid.

outside of human society, in whom language would seem lacking. The second explanation, on the other hand, presupposes precisely what it sets out to prove: "Invention and reason already presuppose a language, and can be conceived as little without the latter as *calculation* can be conceived without *numbers*."[30] Thus, once again the most plausible explanation would seem to be instruction, of which Hamann, as Aristobulus, now proposes three possible forms: human, mystical, and animal. The first kind is obviously circular, since it is precisely how the *first* humans came to have language that is in question. The second, that of mystical instruction, would seem to be precisely the kind advocated by Süßmilch, and given the foregoing we would expect that Hamann (Aristobulus) would make a strong case for it. Curiously enough, however, he rejects it as "ambiguous, unphilosphical, unaesthetic, and possessed of ninety-seven defects and deficiencies."[31] (And here we see that Hamann's masks are not always exact representations of his views, but sometimes ironic counterfeits.) This leaves as the only remaining theory that of instruction by animals, which is not so odd a notion, Aristobulus suggests, given that the Egyptians seemed to have worshiped them. And it is precisely this theory that, tongue-in-cheek, he proposes in a hilarious little piece of persiflage, which reduces the proud rationalism of his contemporaries to a "plagiarism" of the "natural light" of animals (which would seem to follow once one denies the higher hypothesis and seeks to replace it with a purely natural explanation):

> What are all the masterpieces of our proud reason but imitations and developments of their blind instinct? What is the borrowed fire of all the beautiful, free, and honored arts but a Promethean *plagiarism* of the original *natural light* of animals? Do we not owe the seed of all knowledge of good and evil, indeed the very philosophical tree of the encyclopedia, to the skepticism of a crafty animal ...?[32]

The most pointed barb here, of course, is Hamann's suggestion that the philosophers of the *Encyclopédie* have taken their instruction, above all, from one animal, namely, the serpent of Genesis – and thus have been taken in by a deceptive form of enlightenment. In the same comical vein, the *Dispatch* then concludes with Hamann, still in the voice of Aristobulus, referring to Hamann (the reviewer of Herder) with respect to the latter's expectation of hearing from Hamann (the anonymous philologist): "In order to send the author of the review contained in the twenty-sixth volume [of the *Königsbergsche gelehrte und politische Zeitung*] packing [*abfertigen*], I cannot view him otherwise than as an alien in Israel, who does not even know that his so-called philologist, living under his taskmasters, has long been transformed into an arch-Apuleian beast of burden ..."[33] In other words, the reviewer should not expect to hear anything from the Hamann, unless, that is, he should speak as an ass.[34] But Aristobulus, speaking as a friend of the philologist who is familiar with his circumstances, nevertheless gives us some sense of how he would respond:

> Instead of entering a competition with an essay of seven parts ... our *pitiful figure* of a countryman would perhaps mutter from the dust of his humble estate: "What do

---

[30] N III, p. 21.

[31] Ibid.

[32] N III, p. 22.

[33] N III, p. 23. Cf. Apuleius, *Metamorphoses*, where Lucius is thus transformed.

[34] As it happens, this is precisely what Hamann does in his *New Apology of the Letter h by Itself* (N III, p. 105), where he speaks in the voice of the letter "just as that mute beast of burden," i.e., like Balaam's ass in Num. 22: 28.

I know of your whole affair? And of what concern is it to me? The dawn, midday, and twilight of all the *beautiful arts* and *sciences,* which one unfortunately! knows by their fruits, have no further influence upon my current happiness except that those merciless sisters interrupt the deep sleep of my rest with allotriocosmic [*sic*] dreams, shift the boundary stone of my expenditures at significant cost to my necessities, limit my bodily attire to a reversible gray *tailcoat,* my diet to watered-down beer and cold cake, and, worst of all, invade even the precious and sweet moments that I should spend babbling and depicting things [*verbildern*] with the stripling of my soul and cooing and smiling over the crib of my little maid. – – Notwithstanding the creed of your anti-Solomonic school masters that the fear of the Lord is the end of wisdom: may it remain of great benefit to me to be *godly* and *content!* – – – The peace that comes from above surpasses all reason – – and the love of *Christ,* the tongues of angels and men. This great *architect* and *cornerstone* of a *system* that will outlast heaven and earth, and of a *patriotism* that overcomes the world, said: "Let your speech be 'yes, yes, no, no; everything else is of the devil' – – herein consists the entire *spirit* of *law* and *social justice,* by whatever names one wants to call them."[35]

In other words, what good have the arts and sciences brought but penury (perhaps from the buying of too many books) and distraction from family life? The key point here, however, is that the philologist, the lover of the Word, has little regard for the many systems that come and go, and still less for those "anti Solomonic," i.e. foolish, teachers of the Enlightenment who have forgotten that the "fear of the Lord" is the beginning, the *principium,* of wisdom (Ps. 111: 10). *Vis-à-vis* the many systems of human invention, therefore, the only system he proposes is one whose foundation and architect is Christ; and it is in this light that any theory of human language and culture must be conceived.

PHILOLOGICAL IDEAS AND DOUBTS

Whereas in his series of reviews (consisting of his review of Tiedemann, his review of Herder, and his review of his own review) Hamann left us with mere hints of his own position and his criticisms of Herder, these are more fully and incisively spelled out in his *Philological Ideas and Doubts concerning an Academic Prize Essay* (*Philologische Einfälle und Zweifel über eine akademische Preisschrift*), which von Balthasar describes as a "devastating persiflage of Herder's enthusiastic naturalism."[36] Written in the voice of the *Magus in Norden,* by now Hamann's most well-known and least disguised sobriquet, it begins with striking epigraphs: from Psalm 120: 4: "It is like a warrior's sharp arrows, like fire from the Juniper tree"; from Pindar: "– – I swear that I did not overstep the line / when I shot forth my swift tongue / like a bronze-tipped spear"; and from Hamann's beloved Horace: "– – Nor would I dare to wring from him the crown / that sits on his head with so much glory."[37] The "sharp arrows" are, of course, aimed at Herder, and the irony of the quotation from Pindar, which is taken from an ode singing the praise of a young victor, is obvious.[38]

The text falls into three parts: some ideas of Hamann's own, some doubts about Herder's *Preisschrift* in the form of a devastating parody, and a highly ironic eulogy

---

[35] N III, pp. 23f. Cf. Prov: 9: 10; Phil. 4: 7; Matt. 5: 37.

[36] Hans Urs von Balthasar, "Laikale Stile," in *Herrlichkeit: Eine Theologische Ästhetik* II/2 (Einsiedeln: Johannes verlag, 1962), p. 613. Cf. von Balthasar, *The Glory of the Lord: A Theological Aesthetics* (San Francisco: Ignatius, 1985), vol. 3, p. 248.

[37] Pindar, *Nemean Odes* VII; Horace, *Satires* I, X, 48–9.

[38] See G-D, p. 190.

addressed to the "victor" of the Berlin games. Hamann begins with an observation about Aristotle's distinction between "voice" and "language" – a distinction, Hamann suggests, that Herder should have been more careful to make – and by means of this distinction wastes no time deconstructing the opening claim of the *Preisschrift* that "already as an animal, man possesses language." Admittedly, this is not Herder's definitive conclusion, but merely his opening statement. It was said, furthermore, as a concession to Condillac, and even in Herder's estimation requires significant qualification. Nevertheless, Hamann suggests, Herder should have consulted Aristotle and not carelessly confused language with the emotional outcries of animals.

That Hamann begins with Aristotle is no coincidence. As Aristotle says in the *Politics*, the human being is unique among living beings in possessing language (λόγον δὲ μόνον ἄνθρωπος ἔχει τῶν ζῴων).[39] Whether one understands *logos* here as "reason" or "language" (it is an ambiguity that defines the whole of Hamann's thought), his use of Aristotle is intended to show that language is what defines the human being as human being, and by extension that any *Sprachtheorie* will invariably be bound up with one's anthropology. The focus of his ideas and doubts concerning the *Preisschrift* is thus, more than anything, Herder's anthropology, and it is in this light that the fundamental differences between them begin to emerge. The further significance of Aristotle in this context is the ironic contrast Hamann intends *vis-à-vis* Herder. Whereas Herder presents his theory as "natural," "well grounded," and even "demonstrative" (at the conclusion of the *Preisschrift* he speaks of his argument as a "proof"), from Hamann's perspective it is in fact quite the opposite: an unnatural, abstract, and speculative brand of "Platonism."

Continuing with Aristotle *vis-à-vis* the more platonic Herder, Hamann begins to spell out his own anthropology as follows:

> With respect to social life the wise Stagyrite considers the human being to be *neutral*. From this I suspect that the true character of our nature consists in the *juridical* [*richterliche*] and *magisterial* [*obrigkeitliche*] dignity of a *political animal*; and that, as a result, the *human being* stands in relation to *animals* like the *prince* to his *subjects*.[40]

Clearly, Hamann has what one might call a "high anthropology." The difference between him and Herder on this point, however, is not evident until Hamann (the more fundamentally Lutheran of the two) goes on to say, "This *dignity*, like all positions of honor, presupposes no *internal worthiness* or *merit* of our nature; on the contrary, like the latter, it is an immediate graced endowment [*Gnadengeschenk*] of the great Giver of all things."[41] To be sure, even here their differences are subtle. For Herder, the clergyman who by 1771 was the court preacher of Bückeburg and by 1776 the General Superintendent of the Lutheran Church in Weimar, would in no way have denied that human dignity has its ultimate source in God. Nevertheless, grace is not a point of emphasis in Herder's "naturalistic" explanation; on the contrary, as an attempt to be "scientific," his anthropology proceeds methodologically *etsi Deus non daretur*. In other words, as Hamann keenly perceived, Herder's *Sprachtheorie* has no explicit need for God, inasmuch as the human being could just as well have invented language *without him*.

[39]   Aristotle, *Politics* I, 2, 1253a.
[40]   N III, p. 37. As Dickson points out (G-D, p. 495), the reference here is to Aristotle's *Historia animalium*. "Neutral," then, refers to the intermediate status of human beings: between social existence (to the point of a lack of individuality) and solitary existence (to the exclusion of any social life).
[41]   N III, pp. 37f.

At first, Hamann and Herder can also seem rather similar in their views of human freedom. As Hamann puts it,

> *Freedom* is the *maximum* and *minimum* of all our natural powers, and both the basic drive and final end of their entire orientation, development, and return. For this reason the human being is determined neither by *instinct* nor by the *sensus communis*, just as a *prince* is determined neither by *ius naturale* nor by the *ius gentium*. Each is his own *lawgiver,* but at the same time the *firstborn* and *nearest* of his *subjects*.[42]

Indeed, at first glance, Hamann's anthropology appears more or less indistinguishable from Herder's own, as when Hamann says that "*Consciousness, attention, abstraction,* and even the *moral conscience* largely appear to be *energies* of our *freedom*."[43] The same is true of the following passage, when he says in paraphrase of Herder's views,

> Freedom involves not only *undetermined powers,* but also the republican privilege of being able to *cooperate* toward their determination. For this reason, as has been said, the *sphere* of the animals determines the direction of all their powers and drives by way of instinct in just as particular and contained a way as contrariwise the perspective of the human being extends toward the *universal* and, so to speak, loses itself in *infinity*.[44]

The difference between them, however, comes down to this: that Herder's doctrine of freedom is, at the end of the day, more genuinely, even enthusiastically *modern,* whereas Hamann's remains fundamentally *theological*.

This difference is apparent, for example, when Hamann says, in reference to the first chapter of James and to Aristotle's *De poetica,* "Without the *perfect law of freedom,* the human being would be utterly incapable of *imitation,* though all *education* and *invention* rest upon it; for the human being is by nature, among all the animals, the greatest *pantomime*."[45] For Hamann, in other words, the point of freedom (and how *unmodern* this sounds!) is *imitation,* specifically, the imitation of the law (Jas. 1: 25), wherein true freedom is exercised and consists, since it is in this way, inspired by the grace of Christ, that one is conformed to and comes to participate in (2 Pet. 1: 4) the freedom of the divine nature. Over against Herder this means that human freedom is determined by imitation, and that imitation therefore retains a certain priority over invention. In this ever so subtle shift of emphasis from invention to imitation lies a fundamental difference between them, which then gets played out in their respective theories of language: for Herder, language is essentially a human *invention,* the result of *Besonnenheit*; for Hamann it is essentially a creative *imitation* of and response to the Word declared in creation (and, as such, always already occurring within a theological context, whether or not the Word is perceived).

We have already seen that Hamann considers some kind of instruction theory more natural and hence more plausible than a theory of invention. A further problem with Herder's theory, in Hamann's view, is that it involves a *petitio principii*. For it answers the question of the origin of language by appealing to some faculty called "reflection," which is presupposed and whose origin is unexplained, but from which

---

[42]   N III, p. 38.
[43]   Ibid.
[44]   N III, pp. 38f.
[45]   N III, p. 38. Cf. Jas. 1: 25: "But he who looks into the *perfect law, the law of liberty,* and perseveres, being no hearer that forgets but a *doer that acts,* he shall be blessed in his *doing*." Hamann's emphasis.

language is nonetheless derived. What is more embarrassing, Hamann points out, is that Herder's supposedly novel theory rests upon a Platonic doctrine of recollection, since for Herder language is always already pre-possessed by reason and merely requires an occasion of recollection to draw it forth. Thus, turning Herder's supposedly naturalist theory on its head, Hamann identifies it with a kind of Platonic idealism. Hamann, on the other hand, standing more firmly in the Aristotelian and empiricist traditions, argues that there is no content to reason prior to engagement with the senses:

> Nothing is in our *understanding* without having previously been in our *senses*: just as there is nothing in our entire body that did not first pass through our own stomach or that of our parents. The *stamina* and *menstrua* of our reason are therefore, most properly understood, *revelations* and *traditions*, which we assimilate as our own, transform into our own humors and powers, and thereby measure up to our vocation partly to *reveal* and partly to *pass on* the *critical* and *archontic* dignity of a *political animal*.[46]

Here in a nutshell we have the anthropological basis of Hamann's later critique of Kant: far from being pure and in possession of its own concepts a priori, reason is the product of history, revelations, and traditions. Accordingly, the archontic dignity of the human being (from *archon*, the Greek word for "ruler") consists not in radically emancipating oneself from history, tradition, and revelation, but in a careful, critical reception of these data, inasmuch as our own thoughts and reflections have been determined by them.

In other words, even if self-governance belongs to the "archontic" dignity of human beings, and even if we must make critical judgments, we should not delude ourselves into thinking that reason or criticism could ever be alchemically purified of the very things by which they are formed. "Our reason," Hamann says, "springs at the very least from this twofold instruction of sensible *revelations* and human *testimonies*."[47] Indeed, as he will later make plain to Kant, there is no such thing as reason apart from "revelations and traditions." And yet, in Hamann's view, this is plainly what the misguided analytical method, the *Scheidekunst*, of Kant's philosophy is all about. Thus he says, pointing out the similarity between the errors of the philosophers and those of the heretics (in theology):

> The philosophers have always given truth a bill of divorce in that they separate what nature has joined together and vice versa, whereby, among other heretics, *psychology* has given rise to its own *Arians, Mohammedans,* and *Socinians,* all of whom want to explain everything on the basis of a *single, positive power* or *entelechy* of the soul.[48]

In other words, inasmuch as it fails to perceive the (ultimately Trinitarian and Christological) mystery of unity-in-difference, following the pattern of earlier heresies, philosophy is wont either to divide and separate what belongs together or, conversely, to combine what should not be combined.[49] In contrast, therefore, to the unlawful divorces and unions which he sees as characteristic of modern thought,

---

[46] N III, p. 39.

[47] Ibid.

[48] N III, p. 40.

[49] In the terms of modern, nuclear physics – its scientific analogue – one could express this as the difference between the atomic (or fission) bomb and the hydrogen (or fusion) bomb – with the one, in keeping with "progress," unleashing an even greater destructive force than the other. Cf. Hamann's statement (ZH VII, p. 158), "What God has joined together, no philosophy can separate; just as little unite, what nature has separated. Divorce and sodomy sin against nature and reason ..."

Hamann proposes anew the mystery of marriage: "Since the *mystery of marriage* between such opposed natures as that of the *external* and *internal* man, or the *body* and *soul,* is great: a *recognition* of multiple distinct, earthly characteristics is certainly required in order to attain to a conception of the *fullness* within the *unity* of our *human nature.*"[50]

Instead, therefore, of dividing philosophy into idealism and realism (or materialism), Hamann sees everything in terms of a mysterious coincidence of opposites. And with this in mind we can begin to appreciate his anthropology, which he presents in terms of the following obscure parable, building upon Paul's statement to the Corinthians, "For we are God's fellow workers; you are God's field, God's building" (1 Cor. 3: 9):

> Man is therefore not only a living *field* but also the *son of the field,* and not only *field* and *seed* (according to the systems of the *materialists* and *idealists*) but also the *king* of the *field,* [who has the power] to cultivate both the good seed and the inimical weeds in his field; for what is a *field* without *seed,* and a *prince* without *land* and *revenues*? These *three* in us are *one,* namely, θεου γεωργιον: just as *three larvae* on the wall are the natural shadow of a single body illuminated by a double light – – –[51]

In other words, the human being is not only the material – the field – that is cultivated, but the product of such cultivation, i.e., man is in some sense his own creation. At the same time, he is not only the material that is cultivated and the material fruit of such cultivation, but also the sower, whose thoughts (ideas), like so many seeds are sown into the matter of his life. Thus, finally, the human being is the king, who has dominion over the field of his life, reaping what he sows (cf. Matt. 25: 14ff.; Gal. 6: 7). And these three aspects, which form a mysterious unity, constitute the peculiar dignity of the human being as the *imago Dei.*

Hamann then concludes his "ideas," i.e., the first section of the work, with an ironic pastiche of Herder's text, which plays on the homonymy between "empirical" and "empyrean" and signals his Aristotelianism versus Herder's Platonism: "Now that I have made myself dizzy, venturing thus far into the empyrean sanctuary of human nature, or perhaps it would be better to say, now that I have spent enough time blowing my peripatetic soap bubbles in front of me: they finally burst halfway to the ground into the following dew drops," i.e., the following condensation of his response to Herder's theory:

> Man *learns* to use and govern all his members and senses, including his ear and tongue, because he *can* learn, *must* learn, and just as gladly *wants* to learn. Consequently, the *origin* of *language* is as natural and human as the origin of all our actions, skills, and arts. And yet, notwithstanding the fact that every apprentice *cooperates* with his instruction according to the proportion of his inclination, ability, and opportunity to learn: properly understood, *learning* is as little a matter of *invention* as it is of mere *recollection.*[52]

Thus Hamann agrees with Herder that the origin of language must have been as natural as all our actions, skills, and arts; where they differ is that for Hamann the origin of language is a matter neither of invention nor recollection, i.e., it is not something spontaneously invented, nor is it something always already in one's possession that one simply has to "remember."

---

[50] N III, p. 40.
[51] Ibid. Hamann evidently means by "larvae" here the larva-like shape of shadows cast on a wall.
[52] N III, p. 41.

Having intimated his own "ideas" about the origin of language, in the second section of the work Hamann begins to express his "doubts" about Herder's theory with typical persiflage. "It would be ludicrous in the extreme," he says, "to contradict a truth that has not only been *firmly proved* but also *crowned*. And so I find myself pleasantly compelled to cure the *fashionable spirit* of my century with the smoke of my doubts."[53] He then proceeds to ask, perhaps legitimately dumbfounded, "*whether the Platonic apologist of the human origin of language was ever serious about proving his theme or whether he ever had any intention of touching upon it?*"[54] For surely Herder cannot have been serious about having delivered a "proof"?

That Hamann thinks he did not, and should never have suggested that he did, is clear from what follows. In a highly ironic pastiche of Herder's language, which mocks Herder's doctrine of reflection, Hamann "singles out" this doctrine "from an entire sea of characteristics," i.e., "errors," saying that "the whole Platonic proof" amounts to a circular argument full of "neither concealed nor subtle nonsense" and of the secret effects of "*arbitrary* terms" and the favorite "catchphrases" of the time.[55] In a masterful stroke of irony he then adds that Herder's "natural" theory must have been the product of divine inspiration, due to a divine "Genesis"; indeed, it must be even more *supernatural* and poetic than the oldest account of the creation of heaven and earth. For, surely, only inspiration would cause this learned author to set himself up "so confidently and so recklessly for such public, earth-shaking, hyperbolic-pleonastic, retaliatory criticism, and to misuse polemical weapons only *to incur wounds and lumps at his own expense,* accomplishing thereby precisely the opposite of what his readers are promised and flatteringly led to expect."[56]

What a lashing! And yet, all of this is merely propaedeutic to the centerpiece of Hamann's criticism, which begins with an array of quotations, interlarded with trenchant commentary, characteristically with Herder's own words turned against him (as is Hamann's "metacritical" custom). For example, after representing Herder's theory of the origin of language – "This first identifiable characteristic of reflection becomes a word of the soul! With it human language is invented!" – he adds the ironic, mocking exclamation, "Eureka!"[57] The core of his criticism, however, is that Herder's entire argument is self-negating. The first part of the *Preisschrift* is intended to show that the human being is not an animal, i.e., not a creature bound by instinct, but a creature of "reflection"; the second part, on the other hand, is dedicated to proving precisely the opposite: that language is instinctive to human beings (and, by implication) that the human being *is* an animal. Thus Hamann says, comically alluding to Revelation 17: 8: "Such an apocalyptic creature as the neo-Platonic human being, who is not a beast but nevertheless is a beast, *can* and *must* be the inventor of language, since no animal *can* invent language, and no God *may*."[58] In other words, Herder naturally comes to this ambiguous conclusion – that the human being is and is not an animal – since he has dogmatically ruled out the supernatural hypothesis, but remains unwilling to say that language is purely a matter of animal instinct.

---

[53]   N III, p. 41.
[54]   Ibid.
[55]   N III, p. 42. As Hamann eventually explains (N III, p. 47), he calls Herder's "proof" Platonic since "it begins with the *neologism* of *Besonnenheit,* as from the 'single point and shining spark of a complete system,' and in the end traces back to a Greek *synonymy* and since the *Platonists* chewed *ad nauseam* over the Λογος ενδιαθετος or ενθυμηματικος and the Λογος προφορικος, the *inner* and *outer* word, like the Swedish goblin-seer [i.e., Swedenborg] *ab intra et extra.*"
[56]   N III, p. 42.
[57]   N III, p. 43.
[58]   Ibid.

In the rest of his "doubts," Hamann continues to highlight the contradiction in Herder's argument. Whereas the first part of Herder's essay makes a strong case for the "*glory* of the *human being*" (whose capacity for reflection makes him *more* than a creature of instinct, and superior to the animals in kind and not just by degree), the second part of the essay, Hamann says, unwittingly destroys it:

> For what does the entire positive (i.e., second) part of the Platonic proof say more positively and explicitly than that the human being thinks and speaks out of *instinct* – – that the *positive power* to *think* and to *speak* are *innate* and *natural* to the human being in an *immediate* way – – that, like the *instinct* of animals, it is forcibly drawn or directed to the *point* of a *characteristic* – that with the first *word* the whole of *language* is invented (and this, in spite of the *law of eternal progress*); – and that the *invention* of language is as essential to the human being as the web to a spider and the honeycomb to the bee – and that nothing more is required than to *place* the human being in the *condition* of reflection, which is *proper* to him, in order to invent that which is already *natural* to him.[59]

In short, the result is utterly nonsensical: the difference between human beings and animals according to the first part of Herder's essay is that human beings possess "reflection," the immediate expression of which is the invention of language, and this is what places human beings above the sphere of animal instinct; the second part of the essay, on the other hand, argues the opposite: that the invention of language is instinctive and a function of what we share with the animals. Resuming the apocalyptic imagery, Hamann then makes his point in the form of a devastating parody of Herder's anthropology, whereby Herder appears as the unwitting creator of an androgynous beast:

> He created him a not-animal and an animal ... High above the animals not by degrees, but by kind of instinct stood the Platonic Androgyne as a non-animal – without instinct. Go, have dominion over the birds of prey and the monsters of the sea; but be mute and dumb! spoke the Andriantoglyph [*sic*] and Protoplast of language – for the moment that you recognize the fruit of your inner and outer instinct, your mouth will be opened and you will be an animal full of instinct, from the outside and the inside, and your non-animal character will wither away like grass. While the Platonic Androgyne was standing there, born mute, in the sleep of hidden powers – behold! in that moment it happened to fall deeper and deeper into its element – into an entire ocean of sensations – into an entire floating dream of images, and to be placed into the condition of reflection and fascination peculiar to it. And behold! in that very moment it let slip the first sound of its external instinct, as a characteristic and verbal communication of its inner instinct. The first word thus arose from external and internal instinct; and the non-animal that was placed above the animals by virtue of its lack of instinct became a creature driven by instinct from within and without, i.e., it became a reflective and language-inventing animal. Hail the inventor of language! Let us shout to it a Salomonic Eureka! (cf. Eccles. 7: 29)[60]

In other words, the whole contradiction turns on the ironic fact that Herder's *Urmensch* is only superior to the animals in kind and not merely by degree as long

---

[59] N III, p. 45.
[60] N III, pp. 46f.

as it does not *instinctively* open its mouth and speak, for then the human being would again be on a level with the animals as a creature of instinct. With consummate irony, Hamann then caps his parody with the following *coup de grace:* "With this divine organon of understanding the entire *Koran* of the *seven* [liberal] arts and the entire *Talmud* of the *four* faculties was invented, and upon this *rock* stands the fortress of the *philosophical faith* of our century, before which all the *gates of oriental poetry* must submit."[61] That is to say, how can this understanding of the origin of language, which rests upon a plain contradiction, possibly serve as a suitable foundation for philosophy, for the sciences, for philology?

What a damning appraisal! But there is more to Hamann's criticism. For, as Hamann perceived, the chief problem with his disciple's seemingly harmless essay was the Promethean attempt of secular reason to write its own genealogy, to establish its own origin. Furthermore, he perceived that, should such an *abstract*, speculative genealogy full-of-holes like Herder's be accepted (should reason claim for itself a purely natural origin and thus a purely secular foundation, however farfetched it may be), then the inspired tradition of the "sure prophetic word" would eventually be forced to submit to the authority and scrutiny of reason (which is precisely what Kant attempted to do). In any event, as Hamann realized, the stakes were exceedingly high – higher than Herder may have realized. And it is in this light, therefore, that one must judge the severity of his criticism.

The final section begins with Hamann ironically saying that, were it worthwhile, he could easily deconstruct [*auseinandersetzen*] further aspects of Herder's *supernatural* [*sic*] proof of the human origin of language – resting entirely, as it does, upon arbitrary assumptions and "erroneous axioms" – but he says that he wants to spare the "apologist" the light in which this would present him.[62] He also gives the (no doubt, facetious) impression that, until this point, he has been ignorant of the fact that the apologist is Herder (who until this point is not mentioned by name). And so, toward the end of his text, as if he had just been made aware of Herder's authorship of the *Preisschrift,* he breaks off his criticism, saying, "*Dearly beloved reader! My name is the Magus in Norden –* – and I make it the last supper and duty of my life to recognize that the crowned Pythian victor is none other than my friend *Herder,* and to embrace and bless him against whom I have until now been fencing blindfolded."[63] Amid ironic gestures of forgiveness, Hamann feigns to understand that, given the academic constraints in competing for the prize, his friend had no choice but to "run aimlessly" and to "box as one beating the air" (1 Cor. 9: 24ff.). Indeed, "he suffered as a *fine* contestant and was justifiably crowned since he fought according to the rules" (cf. 2 Tim. 2: 5). And in a final ironic use of Scripture, he adds (this time in reference to 1 Cor. 3: 10ff. concerning the question of foundations): "Like a *sensible* budgeter of an *unjust* Mammon, he could not do otherwise than build his treatise upon the revelations and traditions of his century, and his proof upon sand, scrap, wood, hay, and stubble – – of course: all of this according to the latest construction methods of his age – Is it his fault …?"[64]

Once again Hamann's point is that his contemporaries think that they are building upon a firm foundation, when in fact (as Herder's essay shows) they are building

---

[61] N III, p. 47.
[62] N III, p. 47.
[63] N III, pp. 48f.
[64] N III, p. 50.

upon sand, scrap, wood, hay, and stubble. They claim to be building upon reason, yet they contradict themselves by feeding their idol with nothing but their own brand of self-aggrandizing *historical faith*. Indeed, herein lies the hypocritical *proton pseudos* of modernity's claims to purity and neutrality, and its corresponding *artificial* separation of reason from faith and tradition. As for Herder, whose *Preisschrift* at least tends in this direction, Hamann ironically comes to his defense, excusing his errors as accommodations to – though they are really symptomatic of – the ills of the age:

> Did he not have to condescend to the critical and archontic impotence of an age, whose politics is no mere *solecism* – nor *Gallionism*, but the *mystery* of the *most holy contradiction*, which dominates the *climate* and is most *active* in *children* – in an age before whose *critical* nose the Hallean [theologian] *Johann Salomo Mathanasius* [i.e., Johann Salamo Semler] can pour out the full measure of his undigested reading, spoiled by acid and gall, indeed, when great men in at least three faculties … nourish and strengthen their *sound reason* by means of what remains [*Str-nt*] of *historical faith* … in a *most Christian* age when an angel of the congregation with a cleft foot can deny the spiritual priesthood and blaspheme the *most holy* vocation with doubly unforgivable lies, in comparison with which all *anacreontic farces* represent genuine *morality* and all the *pythanalogical paralogisms* concerning the origin of language are *gold* and *precious stones* –[65]

In the same vein he continues with terrible praise for his friend and prophetic indignation over the Promethean folly of the age and the unjust policies of its enlightened despot, Frederick, which have left his family penniless:

> In order to rise to the top by way of great victories, my friend *Herder* could not do otherwise than write as a *satyr* for a wicked, adulterous generation that is neither a non-animal [*Unthier*], nor a non-human [*Unmensch*], but a monster [*Ungeheur*] with an *iron* arm, the *belly of an ant*, and the face of *Anubis* – – for a race that denies God and rushes to be rich, and by means of *miscellaneous works* in poetry and prose intends to conquer heaven and earth! – The angel of death and the heir of its filled barns calls it by name (Luke 12: 20) – – in a *tragic comic* century when even a Magus in Europe is not ashamed to run his head against the wall and to whimper in the highest pitch that *elegy* affords: – – *Arithmetique politique rends moi mes 5 écus!*[66]

Hamann asks his readers not to weep over the *Magum in Norden* and his financial straits, however; for should he die, he has left his two children, his "six-month-old muse or grace" and his "three-year-old Apollo" in Herder's good care (Herder was, in point of fact, their godfather). And so he concludes with one final (ironic?) salutation:

> To him, the *worthiest* of all my *friends*, all of whom have not only been *great, faithful, and loving* – but also *countless* – – (go Judas Ἰσκαριωτης, hang yourself and burst!) – in the *north* and Germany – – (for of what concern to me are the *Burgundians, Champagnians, Gasconians,* and *Italians* [*Welsche*]?) – To my *Herder*, the *worthiest* of all my friends in the North and in Germany, I leave my *joy* and my *crown* (Phil. 4: 1) [i.e., his two children], indeed! as truly as I die as a *magus, father,* and *friend!* I leave

---

[65] N III, pp. 50f. By "Gallionism" Hamann refers us to Acts 18: 7ff. and Esther 3: 15, though the overtones of the dominant Francophilia of the day are unmistakable. What is here translated as "what remains," based on Nadler's annotation (N III, p. 428), is in the original text *"Str-nt."* What Hamann intends by this is unclear; according to Nadler, however, it refers to a text of the rationalist Christian Tobias Damm, with whom Hamann engages in his *New Apology of the Letter h.*

[66] N III, pp. 51f.

him the true blood of my heart! May he give you *bread* and *wine* (Lam. 2: 12), but to me no *memorial* of stone. *EXEGI.*[67]

THE CRUSADING KNIGHT'S LAST WILL AND TESTAMENT

The Knight of the Rose-Cross's Last Will and Testament concerning the Divine and Human Origin of Language (*Des Ritters von Rosencreuz letzte Willensmeynung über den göttlichen und menschlichen Ursprung der Sprache*), written around the same time, finally presents Hamann's own views on the origin of language – albeit pseudonymously, its author being a mysterious "Knight of the Rose-Cross," amid some of the most obscure and baffling prose in all of known world literature.[68] It was published in 1772, but backdated by Hamann to 1770, presumably in order to give the impression of its being a contemporaneous essay on the origin of language that was overlooked by the Berlin Academy. Adding to the mystery, the title vignette indicates that the present work is a *"rushed translation"* based on a hieroglyphic *Urschrift* [*Caricatururbilderurschrifft*] made by none other than the "underling" or "handyman" of the "hierophant." Yet the mystery is not impenetrable. For in the title the knight's (i.e., Hamann's) views are plain and upfront: the origin of language is not human *or* divine (as Herder et al. and Süßmilch had, respectively, contended), but at once human *and* divine.

A further clue to Hamann's position is given by the work's first motto from 2 Corinthians 4: 13: "Credidi propter quod locutus sum" ("I believed, therefore I spoke"). Aside from what this says about the rationale behind all of Hamann's publications, it is almost certainly a veiled criticism of Herder, who wrote his *Preisschrift,* as Herder himself suggests, out of ambition.[69] At the same time, however, it indicates that for Hamann the origin of language is not to be conceived in monological but in *dialogical* terms (anticipating the thought of Martin Buber and Ferdinand Ebner), just as, anthropologically speaking, human freedom is properly understood not as an absolute freedom, i.e., as an autonomous self-positing, but rather as the freedom of a creature to respond, having previously been addressed by another.[70] On the one hand, this accords on a purely *horizontal* plane with Aristotle's understanding of the human being not as an "idiot," who must have invented language on his own, but as a political being, for whom language or reasoning is always already a function of membership in society. On the other hand, given Hamann's dialogical understanding of creation in the *Aesthetica,* as the context in which language first arises, it is clear that the notion of "speaking out of faith" also implies a *vertical,* theological dimension. This is supported by the second motto on the title

---

[67] N III, pp. 52f. As Griffith-Dickson notes (G-D, p. 503), "Exegi" refers here to a verse from Horace "I have finished," as in, "I have finished a monument" to Herder.

[68] While the word *Rosencreuz* in the title almost certainly refers to the Lutheran coat-of-arms, which depicts a black cross in a red heart upon a white rose, and thus to Hamann's own Lutheranism (in particular, the Lutheran doctrine of a *communicatio idiomatum* of divine and human natures in Christ), the word is undoubtedly also an allusion to the Rosicrucianism of his contemporary, Johann August Starck. In any case, it refers to the obscure, hermetic quality of Hamann's own writing (as was the case with his "kabbalistic prose" of the *Aesthetica,* just as the present work's authorship by a "knight" is in keeping with the theme of his "philological crusades").

[69] See G-D, p. 177.

[70] See, in this regard especially, Oswald Bayer's theology of human freedom as *Verantwortung,* which is developed largely along Hamannian lines, in *Freiheit als Antwort: Zur theologischen Ethik* (Tübingen: Mohr-Siebeck, 1995).

page verso, which is taken from Plato's *Philebus*: "*It seems to me that a gift of the GODS to men truly came down, mediated in some way by a certain Prometheus together with a most brilliant fire. For the ancients, who are nobler than we are and closer to the GODS, handed down the tradition ...*"[71]

Clearly, to judge from the work's two mottos, Hamann would seem to support the "higher" hypothesis; and certainly he is happy to defend this "worthy Dulcinea" if it should come to making a choice between this and the naturalistic hypothesis. Accordingly, the text proper begins with a theological explanation, indeed a kind of theological syllogism, for the divine origin of language:

> If one assumes God to be the origin of all effects great and small, whether in heaven or on earth, then every numbered hair on our head is just as divine as the Behemoth, that beginning of the ways of God. The spirit of the Mosaic laws extends, therefore, even to the most disgusting secretions of the human corpse. Consequently, everything is divine, and the question of the origin of evil amounts at the end of the day to a game of words and scholastic chatter.[72]

Leaving aside any finer distinctions, say, between primary and secondary causality (as would be crucial in Roman Catholic theology regarding human freedom and the problem of evil), not to mention the audacity of Hamann's imagery, the inference is plain: if God is ultimately the *causa omnium rerum* (as he is in Lutheran and Reformed theology), then obviously God, the Creator, is also the ultimate cause of language. For

> since at least the instruments of language are a gift of *alma mater* nature (which our strong spirits have turned into an idol, promoting an idolatry that is more tasteless and blasphemous than any on the part of the rabble of the pagans and the papists), and since, according to the highest philosophical probability, the Creator of these technical instruments must have intended their implementation: the origin of human language is certainly divine.[73]

In a footnote Hamann then enlists the authority of two Church Fathers to make his point. As Tertullian puts it, "They are said to have *discovered* these necessities of life, not instituted them; before it was discovered, it was, and what was discovered is not attributed to *him* who discovered it, but to him who instituted it"; so too Lactantius, "DEUS et mentis et vocis et linguae artifex."[74]

On the other hand, Hamann says that "everything divine is also human, since the human being can neither act nor suffer except in a way that is analogous to his nature, however simple or complex a machine it may be. This *communicatio* of the divine and human *idiomatum* is a fundamental law and the master key of all our knowledge and the entire visible economy."[75] In other words, however God may have communicated language to human beings, he could not have done otherwise than communicate it according to the nature of the being he created. This is why

[71] N III, p. 26. Original in Latin.
[72] N III, p. 27.
[73] Ibid.
[74] *Apologet. adv. gentes* XI, 5; Inst. VI, 21.
[75] Ibid.

Hamann can affirm Protagoras' maxim that the human being is the *mensura omnium rerum*.[76] Indeed,

> If a higher being, or an angel, as in the case of Balaam's ass, should wish to work through our tongue, all such effects, like the speaking animals in Aesop's fables, must be expressed in a way analogous to human nature; and in this respect the origin of language, not to mention its continuation, cannot be or appear otherwise than as human.[77]

For Hamann, then, a proper understanding of language is neither one-sidedly naturalistic (as was the case with Herder) nor one-sidedly supernatural (as with Süßmilch). Instead, it requires equal attention to both aspects. And it is in this respect that Hamann sees language as an analogue of the *communication idiomatum* of divine and human nature in Christ – whereby the divine is predicated of the human and the human of the divine.

Hamann was well aware, of course, that his argument for the divine aspect of language depends upon faith in a Creator, and that this could no longer be taken for granted – as the French mathematician Laplace famously replied to Napoleon, having been asked why God was never mentioned in his *Mécanique céleste*, "I had no need of that hypothesis."[78] This is not to say that, in Hamann's view, contemporary materialist and mechanistic accounts of origins were somehow more plausible. On the contrary, he grasped that at some point the question of origins cannot be answered otherwise than in mythological or religious terms.[79] For that matter, in Hamann's view, purely materialist explanations would seem to require their own measure – indeed greater measure – of faith. "Our century," he says, "has produced many great souls who revere and appropriate the relics of the Epicurean system in the *Oeuvres philosophiques* of Mr. de la Mettrie in the *Système de la Nature* and the *Evangelie du Jour*; meanwhile, the evolution of the human race from a swamp or slime continues to strike me like a beautifully-painted mask without a brain. The whole work [of creation] reveals no mere potter of plastic forms, but a father of fiery spirits and breathing powers."[80] And if this is true of creation in general, for Hamann it is eminently true of human beings and human language, which is no mere mechanism or product of blind evolution, but a creative testament to our spiritual nature and origin.

But if, on Hamann's view, language cannot be explained in purely materialistic terms as a matter of evolutionary development, culminating in some form of human invention, neither does it drop ready-made from the sky, as Süßmilch's "higher" hypothesis suggested. Instead, Hamann claims, reasonably enough, language, though ultimately of divine origin, is communicated *through human instruction*, in the way that one also learns to eat and walk upright. And in this connection he appeals to the demonstration by the "learned doctor" of Padua, Pietro Moscati, "that the vertical,

---

[76] N III, p. 27.

[77] Ibid.

[78] Quoted in Stephen Barr, *A Student's Guide to Natural Science* (Wilmington: ISI Books, 2006), p. 46.

[79] This is evident today inasmuch as modern cosmology cannot penetrate the veil of the first 10^{-43} seconds following the "big bang." And, one might add, should it one day penetrate this brief period of time, where the laws of space and time no longer hold, even then it would not be able to account for the fact of existence, i.e., why there is something rather than nothing. This is a question any reasonable person would ask but it is not a question that can be answered in scientific terms. This is why modern-day materialists like Richard Dawkins, who confidently espouse a scientific account of evolution as a sufficient explanation of origins, and believe that the question of a creator can henceforth be consigned to the dustbin of pre-scientific inquiry, precisely misunderstand the nature of the philosophical question.

[80] N III, pp. 28f. Cf. Heb. 1: 7.

two-legged gait of human beings" is something both "inherited *and* artificial."[81] "If, therefore," he adds after a long excursus,

> the human being, in accordance with the universal testimony and example of all peoples, times, and places, is not able to learn to walk on two legs, nor able to break the daily bread without the sweat of the brow, nor, least of all, able to meet up with [*treffen*] the masterpiece of the creative brush without the social influence of his attendants and guardians, i.e., as it were, by *iussus* [as something commanded]: how could it ever occur to someone to regard language, *cet art leger, volage, demoniacle* (to speak with Montaigne from *Plato*), as an autonomous invention of human art and wisdom?[82]

But if the *Knight of the Rose-Cross* is concerned primarily with the topic of language, a large and exceedingly obscure portion of the text (even more obscure than usual given fear of censorship) is concerned with something altogether different: on the one hand, Frederick the Great's unjust economic policies (under which Hamann himself suffered), on the other hand, the homosexual lifestyle of his court, which Hamann subjects to truculent satire – "but they harness the horses behind the phaeton."[83] His chief point here is that the "tolerance" of the Prussian state is a parody of paradise, and that its economic policies and lax sexual mores, under the appearance of goodness and benevolence, obstruct the way to the "tree of life" as effectively as the "flaming sword" of Genesis 3: 24:

> The dreamed-up or trumped-up paradise of Sotadian tolerance, which Mahomet [i.e., Frederick], *ex utroque Caesar,* who is just as brash a *latro* as a dissembler, promises to his proselytes and slaves, is nothing but a dead sea of salt, as truly as once was said: *mortua est illa pars, qua quondam Achilles eram!* – No thundering chariot, no flaming sword turning this way and that through the air could more perfectly guard the tree of life than the pestilence of yellow warts along the borders and in the bowels of the State, which soon will be transformed into an *Hotel-Dieu* [i.e., a hospice], where the terrible necessity of poverty teaches us to pray.[84]

Whatever one makes of Hamann's hostility to the Frederickan regime – to understand it one must appreciate his appalling penury as a civil servant, and the conditions of his employment under imported, well-paid French superiors – it could certainly seem that his critique of the homosexuality of Sans Souci is gratuitous and incidental to the topic at hand. In point of fact, however, it is part and parcel of his highly sexualized criticism of the "automatic reason" of the age, which appears bold and innovative, having a semblance of reason to it – "believing themselves to be wise, they became fools" (Rom. 1: 22) – but at the end of the day produces only "dead works of darkness."[85] Indeed, again and again in his works he contrasts

---

[81] N III, p. 28. My emphasis.

[82] N III, p. 31. The French refers to a reference in Montaigne to Plato's *Ion*: κουφον γαρ χρημα ποιητης εστι και πτηνον και ιερον ("for the business [the language] of the poet is a nimble, winged, and sacred thing").

[83] N III, p. 29. A phaeton is a kind of four-wheeled carriage.

[84] N III, p. 30. Sotadian may be a reference to the supposed location of Sodom, but see the note by Kenneth Haynes (*Writings on Philosophy: Johann Georg Hamann*, ed. and trans. Kenneth Haynes (Cambridge: Cambridge University Press, 2007), p. 104) that it is a reference to the "obscene" poet, Sotades; "yellow warts" is a reference to syphilitic warts.

[85] ZH VII, p. 158; Eph. 5: 11.

images of fertility and fruitful intercourse with a sterile and unfruitful rationalism, which out of a misguided sense of purity forgoes "intercourse" with the senses and tradition. As a result, language, which is naturally virile and poetic, is transformed into a muddle of lifeless abstractions and *entia rationis*:

> Our philosophers talk like alchemists of treasures of fruitfulness; to judge from their fields and vineyards, however, one could swear that they do not know how to distinguish weeds from wheat, grapes from thorns, figs from thistles – they take after that charlatan who tried to pass off the *vacuum* of his pocket for the great, beautiful spirit, which, were it possible, would have deceived even the Elus [i.e., the elect]. Admittedly, the confusion of language, whereby they both deceive and are deceived, is a very natural magic of automatic reason, and for jokers of similar blindness transforms itself at little cost into a star of the first magnitude.[86]

What is shocking about this passage, certainly, is Hamann's unabashed, if indirect phallic imagery. His point, in any case, is that automatic reason (i.e., reason in the abstract, alchemically purified of heterogeneous elements) is not truly creative. It puts on airs, but in the end has nothing to show for it. Moreover, in anticipation of the late Wittgenstein, Hamann suggests that the *Aufklärer* are victims of their own misunderstanding of language: they work mischief upon language with their abstract vocabularies, and are deceived by it in turn – namely, into thinking that reason is somehow pure of language (and tradition), and that its concepts are generated "automatically" out of reason a priori.

Hamann then concludes *The Knight of the Rose-Cross* with an intentionally mythological account of the origin of language, the very thing that the Berlin Academy would have found most unacceptable. In part, one can be sure, Hamann took pleasure in the shock value: the *Aufklärer* wanted things to be "clear and distinct," "demythologized," subject to reason and interpretable in its terms. His point, however, is that this is impossible: some things, like the origin of language, can be explained only in poetic terms, as in Genesis. What is most striking about Hamann's account of the origin of language, however, is not that it reflects the pictorial language of Genesis, and leads us back, as it were, into the Garden of Eden, but that the origin of language is presented in explicitly Christological terms. Indeed, Adam's interaction with the world is presented as an interaction with the same Logos, whom the disciples "heard, saw, looked upon, and touched with their hands" (1 John 1: 1). Accordingly, when Adam first speaks, he speaks out of this intimate, even "playful" communion; and he speaks, therefore, both naturally (as a playful response) and prophetically (since his speaking is a participation in the very speaking of God in the Logos). As he puts it:

> Adam was of God; and God himself introduced the firstborn and oldest of our race as the feudal lord and heir of the world prepared by the word of his mouth. Angels, longing to see his heavenly countenance, were the ministers and courtiers of the first monarch. All the children of God rejoiced before the choir of morning stars. All tasted and saw first-hand, in the very act, the friendliness of the master craftsman, who played upon the ground and found his pleasure in the children of men ... Every phenomenon of nature was a word – the sign, symbol, and pledge of a new, secret, inexpressible, but at the

---

[86] N III, p. 31.

same time all the more intimate union, communication, and communion of divine energies and ideas. In the beginning everything that the man heard, saw with his eyes, looked upon, and touched with his hands was a living word; for God was the Word. With this Word in his mouth and in his heart, the origin of language was as natural, so near and easy, as child's play; for human nature remains from the beginning to the end of days as like unto the kingdom of heaven as a leaven, whose meagerness any woman can work into three sacks of flour.[87]

Without succumbing to the Scylla of a fantastic "higher hypothesis" (as represented by Süßmilch) or the Charybdis of an automatic "natural hypothesis" (as proposed by Herder), Hamann presents language as at once fully human ("as natural as child's play") and fully divine (as having its ultimate source in the Creator). And he holds these two aspects together Christologically, seeing language as originally, essentially, and in *ultima intentione* a playful, oracular response to Christ, the incarnate Word.

THE MYSTERY OF LANGUAGE: THE ALPHA AND OMEGA

At the conclusion of *The Knight of the Rose-Cross,* borrowing and transforming a term from Rabelais, Hamann tells his readers that he would continue to "meta-grabolize" if he did not fear that this would weary his readers. He therefore contents himself with having "found and named the element of language – the A and the O – the Word," which is to say that the mystery of language is fundamentally a Christological mystery. As he put it some years later to Jacobi, "For me it is a matter neither of physics nor of theology, but of *language,* the *mother* of reason and its revelations, its A and Ω. It is the double-edged sword of all truths and lies; and do not laugh if I must attack the *matter* from this *angle*. It is my old *lyre*, but by *it all things* are made."[88] When Hamann made this remark late in 1785, he was referring to the angle of his criticism of Kant's philosophy. What is most striking about this statement, however, is not its deconstructive implications (which will be discussed *vis-à-vis* Kant in Part IV), but its double entendre. On the one hand, in light of the Johannine prologue, Hamann certainly means that the world is created by the Word, the Logos: "all things were made through him and without him was not anything made that was made" (1: 3). At the same time, however, he means that the world is the product of human language, that language is *revelatory*, to the point that one can say, "No word, no world." Thus, comprising both moments, language, rather than being a mere instrument, mysteriously touches upon all things: it is the point of intersection between things divine and human; that wherein the divine language of creation first comes to light; and that through which God's nature and will – through so many tongues, through Scripture, and pre-eminently the incarnate Word – is still more intimately known.

In some respects, certainly, we are here very much in proximity to Heidegger's gnomic utterance that "language is the house of being" (and it is not without reason that Heidegger refers to Hamann in this connection).[89] For the world we see and interact with is the world of human language; it is, in some sense, a human construct (which is also why Heidegger, like Hamann, was so sensitive to instrumental tampering

---

[87] N III, p. 32.
[88] ZH VI, p. 108.
[89] Martin Heidegger, *Wegmarken*, 2nd edn. (Frankfurt am Main: Vittorio Klostermann, 1978), p. 311; cf. Heidegger, *Unterwegs zur Sprache*, 9th edn. (Pfullingen: Günther Neske Verlag, 1990), p. 13.

with language). But while we invariably see all things though a linguistic lens, for Hamann we only see and respond to the world aright, in all its cascading glory, when we see all things in light of *the* Word. As he put it years earlier in the London Writings, "our eyes see as sharply as the eagle, receive the light of angels, when we see all things in your Word, loving God!"[90] In other words, for Hamann, we only see the world aright, and we ourselves in turn are only truly creative, when human language is inspired, animated by the Word: when the Word, the truth (John 14: 6), is in our hearts and on our lips, and we speak prophetically, because we see things as they really are – not as they are fashioned and invariably distorted by the reigning ideology of the day.

In this light, it is finally clear why Hamann was so exercised by what was to all appearances a minor academic question on the origin of language, and why he felt compelled to correct Herder's mistakes, even to the point of jeopardizing their friendship. For him, language was everything: it is what miraculously reveals the world, and how, equally miraculously, God reveals himself. It is, on the one hand, a human construct, as natural as "child's play" – but, contra modernity, *not* an "invention" of isolated, "automatic reason." On the other hand, contra postmodernity, far from being an immanent totality or a function of the will to power, it is the "tabernacle" and "chariot [*Merkabah*]-throne" of the Holy Spirit.[91] All of which makes Hamann the first and arguably profoundest modern Christian thinker of language, whose novelty was not lost on the late Schelling when in 1850, toward the end of his life, he renewed the question of the origin of language before the Berlin Academy, taking Hamann's critique of Herder as the starting point of his inquiry.

---

[90] *LS*, p. 131 (N I, pp. 70f.). For a complete discussion of this theme (by a student of Rahner along Rahnerian lines), see Georg Baudler, *"Im Worte Sehen." Das Sprachdenken Johann Georg Hamanns* (Bonn: H. Bouvier Verlag, 1970).
[91] Cf. N III, p. 237.

Part III
Masks and Mystery Writings

7

Life and Writings 1775–1780

If one sought by means of pharisaical criticism to sift out all the Jewish *and* pagan *elements from Christianity: as much would remain of our body after a similar metaphysical severance – namely: a* material nothing *or a* spiritual something, *which, as far as the mechanism of the* sensus communis *is concerned, at bottom amounts to the same thing.*

Hierophantic Letters[1]

Whoever does not enter into the womb of language, which is the DEIPARA *of our* reason, *is not suited for the* spiritual baptism *of a reformation of Church and State.*

Two Mites[2]

The next phase of Hamann's literary production centers upon the figure of Johann August Starck (1741–1816), a student of J. D. Michaelis, who arrived in Königsberg in 1769, quickly made friends with Hamann's publisher, Kanter (in which context Hamann and Starck almost certainly would have met), and before long, through the influence of the Berlin *Aufklärer*, received a full appointment to the theology faculty of the Albertina university of Königsberg. What made Starck so interesting and vexing a figure to Hamann was not only the political intrigue of his appointment, but also, and above all, the odd constellation of ideas he represented. Firstly, as a student of Michaelis, Hamann's old nemesis, he was an advocate for the new brand of rational biblical criticism called "neology," which tended to reduce the content of revelation to the rational terms of a "natural religion" (though in this respect he differed little from other *Aufklärungstheologen*).[3] Secondly, while a prominent clergyman of the Lutheran Church, Starck was simultaneously a crypto-Catholic (having secretly converted in Paris in 1766). Thirdly, to make matters still more interesting, he was an active Freemason and founder of a "clerical society" of modern-day Templars.

HIEROPHANTIC LETTERS

Whatever the extent of Hamann's relationship with Starck may have been up to this point, his curiosity was piqued in 1770 when Kanter published the first edition of Starck's *Apologie des Ordens der Freimauer*; and it is possibly to this work, however indirectly, that the teasing allusion to Rosicrucianism in the title of Hamann's *Knight of the Rose-Cross* from 1772 refers. Their engagement began in earnest, however, in 1774, when Starck held the second of his public lectures immediately prior to his

---

[1] N III, p. 142.

[2] N III, p. 238.

[3] As Schoonhoven notes, the only appreciable difference between the deists and the neologians was that the neologians retained a concept of revelation, but reduced its content to the "natural religion and morality of deism." See *HH* V (*Mysterienschriften*), p. 18.

university appointment, titled "Pagan influences on the Christian religion" (*De tralatitiis ex gentilismo in religionem christianam*). The level of Hamann's interest can be gauged from the fact that, against all custom, he attended Starck's lecture; and his level of vexation, from the fact that he left before it was over.[4] Afterwards, he reported to Herder that Starck "does not have the least understanding of paganism and Christianity."[5] And in his *Prolegomena,* which is cryptically addressed to Kant, he gives a similarly negative assessment:

> That the Sorbonne of O[ur] D[ear] L[ady Albertina] has conferred upon a Roman-apostolic-Catholic heretic and crypto-Jesuit the authority of a chair [*Macht des Hauptes*] and a professorship – and that in [his] old apology the eleutheroteichopoetic [*sic*] mystery, and in the most recent *Semi-libello famoso,* the entire rubbish of which consists in *verbis tralatitiis ex gentilismo praetereaque Nihil,* he claims to have insights into the *Disciplina arcana* of paganism, and *tacite* is allowed to prefer our Roman-apostolic-Catholic mother Church to the nurse's milk of the Augsburg Confession; all of this sticks in my craw.[6]

Aside from Starck's crypto-Catholicism on a Protestant theology faculty, what especially provoked Hamann was his disregard for Luther and the Reformation on his way back to an ostensibly "pure" Christianity untainted by historical accretions – a Christianity that just so happened to coincide with the natural religion of the *Aufklärer*.[7] From Hamann's perspective, the tendentiousness of Starck's "historical retrieval" of the early Church was all too clear, amounting to an illegitimate transposition of Enlightenment ideals onto the early Church. Moreover, it had the pernicious effect of reducing the uniqueness and particularity of the Christian revelation (specifically, its doctrines of the incarnation, the Atonement, and the Trinity) to the terms of a supposedly universal religion of reason.[8] A further insufferable consequence, in Hamann's view, was that Starck's attempted derivation of Christianity from paganism, along with his Masonic contempt for *particular* religions, undermined – if not totally relativized – the significance of Judaism as the "*bodily mother*" of evangelical Christianity (and with it the prophetic, typological dimensions of the Hebrew Bible to which Hamann attached so much importance).[9]

While Starck's views are too complex to be sorted out here, his method was essentially syncretistic, borrowing freely from Jewish, Greek, and Roman religion, all of which he saw as deriving from the wisdom of ancient Egypt. Indeed, the doctrines most essential to Christianity (for Starck these were the belief in one God, the importance of virtue, and the doctrine of the immortality of the soul) could all be derived from paganism. On the other hand, Starck recognized the novelty of Christianity as a *universal* religion, which sought to overcome the "dividing wall" (Eph. 2: 14) between pagans and Jews, and therewith all divisions based on particularity (therein, it seems, lay the seed of his conversion to Catholicism). And thus he came to see Christianity, on account of its universality, as an early version of the "natural religion"

---

[4] *HH* V, p. 18.

[5] *ZH* III, pp. 77f.

[6] *N* III, p. 127. Several things are worth noting here. First, Starck was by no means an orthodox Catholic, but more of a syncretic rationalist. Second, as we shall see in Chapter 13, while Hamann remained a Lutheran, his attitude toward Roman Catholicism underwent a notable change during the last years of his life.

[7] *HH* V, p. 26.

[8] See *ZH* III, p. 78.

[9] See *N* III, p. 305.

of the Enlightenment. Before long, however, in his view, original Christianity was corrupted by both pagan and Jewish influences, specifically, by doctrines regarding the sacraments, celibacy, and cultic worship. And so, in an attempt to harmonize faith and reason, Christianity and the Enlightenment, Starck proposed a second Reformation of Christianity that would restore Christianity to its original "pristine" state, which meant for him a religion fully commensurate with the dictates of sound reason.

Clearly, with his interest in paganism and the early Church, Starck was not your run-of-the-mill *Aufklärer*. As Nadler points out, it would be more accurate to say that he was a Gnostic and "Romantic of the early Church."[10] In any case, wherever his final allegiances lay, he succeeded in convincing Hamann that orthodox Christianity was at stake. Thus, in 1775, in the first of his so-called *Mysterienschriften* and in the guise of an early Christian apologist, "Vettius Epagathus Regiomonticolae" (who would presumably know something more than Starck about the early Church), Hamann responded to the would-be hierophant and reformer in seven *Hierophantic Letters (Hierophantische Briefe)*. The brunt of his response (which applies equally to someone like Harnack) is that it is impossible to separate out all the pagan and Jewish elements from Christianity; any attempt to do so leaves one with a "spiritual something" or "material nothing," which for the "mechanism of the *sensus communis* amounts to the same thing."[11] Accordingly, he defends the *Jewishness* of Christianity against Starck and other *Aufklärungstheologen* who sought to purify Christianity from it. At the same time, he reverses the entire question, claiming that it was not so much that paganism was a corrupting influence on Christianity as that Christianity brought purification and fulfillment to paganism. Moreover, against Starck's proposed purifying, rational "reformation," he points out that purification has already come through Christ, as illustrated by the cleansing of the temple (Mark 11: 15ff.), and during the Reformation through the "strong spirit" of Luther.

Above all, however, he impugns Starck's theism as vapid, abstract, and culturally impotent, in short, as contrary to the vigor and historical power of authentic Christianity – as if Christianity were "nothing but the theism of our own day."[12] He even suggests that Julian the apostate's polytheism would be preferable, given its virulence, to the impotence and ultimate nihilism of Starck's theism, which masquerades as an angel of light (2 Cor. 11: 14). For, though Starck's "Christianity" achieves a common denominator and passes for a so-called "natural" religion, at the end of the day it leaves one with a "spiritual something" that is so vacuous as to be the equivalent of a "material nothing."[13] Finally, in a pun on Starck's name and in an appeal to the strong spirit of Christ, as well as to that of Elijah and Luther, Hamann claims to be the stronger one [*der Stärkere*], namely, given the ease with which he is able to refute Starck's ideas (cf. Luke 11: 21–2). Indeed, he not only makes a show of Starck's historical errors, but unmasks Starck's fundamental lack of faith: his embarrassment at the anointed name "Christian" and his preference – to the honor of the "god" of this world (2 Cor. 4: 4) – for the *empty* name "theist."[14] And yet, in a curious turn of events, Hamann subsequently chose and submitted to Starck as his confessor. As odd as this may seem, it accords entirely with the way that he dealt with his other friends, whether Kant or Herder, Nicolai or Mendelssohn, namely, as someone capable of loving the very person whose intellectual positions he vehemently

[10]   NB, p. 192.
[11]   N III, p. 142.
[12]   N III, p. 144.
[13]   N III, pp. 144, 146.
[14]   N III, pp. 159, 162.

opposed. As he once put it to Nicolai, "Truth is the scale of friendship – and the sword paves the way for the freedom of peace – *hanc veniam petimusque damusque vicissim.*"[15]

In the meantime, Herder had been popularizing Hamann's writings in the western parts of Germany and people began speaking of a "Hamann club." Thus, in 1775 the *Teutsche Merkur* announced Hamann as the leader of a school of the "German Parnassus," which included among its members such luminaries as Klopstock, Herder, Bode, and Goethe.[16] Adding to Hamann's popularity, Nicolai's journal, *Allgemeine Deutsche Bibliothek*, had recently reviewed several of his publications. But along with a wider audience came a greater sense of responsibility. In 1776, therefore, in an effort to clarify some mistaken impressions of his authorship, Hamann penned what Nadler calls his most occasional, but also most timeless, artistic, and intellectually pregnant work, *Doubts and Ideas about a Mixed Review of the* Allgemeine Deutsche Bibliothek (*Zweifel und Einfälle über eine vermischte Nachricht der allgemeinen deutschen Bibliothek*).[17] Indeed, in this work Hamann not only provides a key to his authorial strategies and his continual *Maskenspiel*, but reveals the heart of his authorship as a witness to the mystical body of Christ, from which the subtitle of Nadler's biography, *Der Zeuge des Corpus mysticum,* derives. Other works dating from this period, which I will treat in the following chapters and which Nadler includes among Hamann's "Mystery Writings," are his *Essay of a Sibyl on Marriage* (*Versuch einer Sibylle über die Ehe*), "Aprons of fig leaves" (*Schürze von Feigenblättern*), and the obscurely titled *Konxompax: Fragments of an Apocryphal Sibyl on Apocalyptic Mysteries* (ΚΟΓΞΟΜΠΑΞ. *Fragmente einer apokryphischen Sibylle über apokalyptische Mysterien*), which, among other things, represents the consummation of Hamann's response to Starck.

FAMILY LIFE: PORTRAIT OF A CHRISTIAN SENSUALIST

In other respects, 1776 marked a turning point in Hamann's life. In March his friend Lindner died, having left Hamann the task of auctioning his considerable library. Given his indigence (for reasons already noted), Hamann, though a notorious bibliophile, made a painful financial decision to commit his own library to auction at the same time. Finally, he reasoned, he could make ends meet. Thus began his arduous task of cataloguing a combined total of 3,070 books under the title *Biga bibliothecarum*, according to the following categories: Greek and Latin authors; theological works; philological works; historical works; philosophical and political works; poetry and belletristic literature; and miscellaneous works and manuscripts.[18] And it is to this unfortunate predicament that we have a fair knowledge of Hamann's library. Fortunately, at the last moment, Herder came to the rescue, making a deposit on the core of his library, leaving it intact in his hands, testifying to their continued friendship. Thus, when Herder's letter arrived stating his intention to help him, he responded by calling it a "*DEUS ex machina,*" which brought him comfort and joy as "a decision of providence."[19]

---

[15] ZH II, p. 194. Tr.: "we both ask for this favor and give it in turn."
[16] NB, p. 232.
[17] Ibid.; N III, pp. 171–96.
[18] NB, pp. 263f. The whole of Hamann's catalogue is reproduced in N V, pp. 13–121.
[19] ZH III, p. 255.

Providence came to the rescue again in 1777. Until this time Hamann had been working as a translator for the Customs Administration – the same job that Kant helped to secure for him ten years earlier. Now the superintendent of the customhouse had died, and Hamann petitioned to replace him. Amazingly, given his earlier polemics against Frederick, he found favor with the king (whether or not the king was even aware of him). One contributing factor seems to have been the intercession of a friend, the imperial conductor Johann Friedrich Reichardt; another was the good fortune, at least in this respect, that no one had dared to publish his scathing satire, *Au Salomon de Prusse*. In any case, he succeeded in getting a much better position with fewer responsibilities, affording him even more time for reading and writing.[20] The position also came with an increased salary, derived in part from incidental customs taxes, and so he likens himself during this period to the tax collector of the gospel *in telonio sedens* (Matt. 9: 9).[21] Yet another benefit of the position was that it came with a new house, one that was finally large enough for his family, even though he had to share it with another official. The home came with a spacious garden, two ponds, a sizeable kitchen, space to entertain guests, and three second-floor rooms: one reserved for his brother (whose mental illness had by now left him almost entirely incapacitated); one for Anna Regina and his daughters; and one for Hamann and his son Johann Michael, which functioned simultaneously as a study, a bedroom, and a salon.[22]

Hamann's letters from this period provide a happy picture of his home and family life, including his love for Regina and the children; their family singing and prayers; their anticipation of the postman's arrival; Hamann's late night writing in his sleeping cap by candlelight, listening to the "Prussian" nightingale, which always began its song with the watchman at 10 p.m., stopping punctually at 7 a.m. "à l'heure du Bureau"; and the pleasure he took in his garden, replete with twenty-four fruit trees, into which he ventured every morning, afternoon, and evening "like another Nimrod," hunting for food.[23] In fact, so much did he love his garden that he expressed a wish to retire as Adam began, namely, as a gardener; and so much did he enjoy the pleasures of food that he said of his kitchen, quoting Heraclitus, "Here too *are the gods*."[24] As Nadler put it, "Like all earthly things, the kitchen belonged to the center of his piety."[25] Thus he could say to the concerned Kraus, who had recommended a more modest diet given his weakened condition, "How in the world can you recommend fasting to a *filio thalami* ... Whoever *tastes here* will be given to *see there* how friendly the LOrd [*sic*] of the universe is."[26] Similarly, he said with a positively Christian *joie de vivre* that surpassed that of Nietzsche's paganism (which, after all, was always overcast by fate and, as such, strained by the exertion of the willing of the eternal return),

[20] NB, pp. 273f.

[21] See Arthur Henkel, "In telonio sedens: J. G. Hamann in den jahren 1778–1782," in Reiner Wild (ed.) *Johann Georg Hamann* (Darmstadt: Wissenschaftliche Buchgesellschaft, 1978), pp. 299–313.

[22] NB, p. 275. As for Hamann's room, one of the walls was taken up with books; on another hung a silhouette of Herder flanked by two copper engravings, apparently of the flight of the holy family to Egypt (Matt. 2: 13f.) and the Last Supper; on a third hung three pictures: of Herder, Lavater, and Christoph Kaufmann; above the door hung a picture of Luther.

[23] NB, p. 275. Cf. ZH IV, pp. 196, 384.

[24] ZH IV, p. 401; ZH V, p. 373.

[25] NB, p. 278.

[26] ZH VII, p. 304.

Everywhere is my pasture! ... It is a *blessing* to have more taste for the *present* than for all else that lies here below or beyond; even assuming that everything amounts to a deception or a deception in which there is an element of fiction: nevertheless, I intend to enjoy it as the best *intermezzo* of my journey. The gods are here too – in the kitchen as well as in the temple; in the stall as well as in the palace.[27]

Indeed, rather than Christianity being a life-denying religion, for Hamann it *adds* to the pleasure of this world, even as it prepares one for the next; and for this reason, properly understood, he might legitimately be called a kind of Christian hedonist or sensualist. Summing up his doctrine in this regard, he says to Lavater:

To speak from the bottom of my soul, my entire Christianity ... is a taste for *signs* and for the elements of the water, the bread, and the wine. Here is plenty for hunger and thirst – a fullness that is not merely, like the law, a shadow of *future* goods, but αὐτὴν τὴν εἰκόνα τῶν πραγμάτων, insofar as these things can be made present and visible as through a mirror in an enigma; for the τέλειον lies on the other side. Here our insights and perspectives are fragments, ruins, piece- and patchwork – τότε δὲ πρόσωπον προς πρόσωπον, τότε δὲ ἐπιγνώσομαι καθὼς καὶ ἐπεγνώσθην.[28]

For Hamann, then, even if we see now "in a glass darkly," and faith is fulfilled in eternity, the disposition of a Christian is precisely the opposite of a life-denying flight from the world (as Nietzsche scornfully portrays it). Rather, it requires an *embracing* of this world as God's good creation, in spite of its ills and pains, as if to suggest that whoever cannot enjoy God's gifts here below will not be able to enjoy God himself above. Thus Hamann could say that "all things, even the *Ens entium,* are there for our enjoyment."[29] So much for Nietzsche's prejudiced critique of (Hamannian) Christianity.

During this time, Hamann also became increasingly concerned with his children's education and, to this end, resumed the familiar role of *Hofmeister* in his own home. To his chagrin, his daughters were less inclined to academic subjects, but were well tutored in music, with the oldest, Elisabeth Regina, becoming proficient in Bach's sonatas.[30] Most of Hamann's home schooling was therefore spent on his son, Johann Michael; and given Hamann's own training as a philologist, they spent a considerable amount of time on languages, beginning with Greek and the Gospel of John. At some point they also took to reading the Old Testament in Hebrew, and in 1777 were fortuitously visited by Moses Mendelssohn,[31] who presented Johann Michael with a copy of his edition of *Qoheleth* or Ecclesiastes. In any event, by 1779, when Johann Michael would have been only 10 years old, they were already reading Xenophon; by 1780, Plato; by 1781, the *Iliad* and the *Odyssey*; and eventually they came to Pindar. Then came Latin, beginning with Suetonius, and, last but not least, modern languages, among them, English and French.[32]

---

[27]   ZH VII, p. 339.

[28]   ZH IV, p. 6; cf. 1 Cor. 13: 12: "For now we see in a mirror dimly [or in an enigma], but then we will see face to face. Now I know only in part; then I will know fully, even as I have been fully known."

[29]   ZH V, p. 265.

[30]   NB, p. 292.

[31]   ZH III, pp. 384f.

[32]   NB, p. 289. For a further impression of Hamann's pedagogy, see ZH IV, p. 401.

Given his own employment from seven in the morning to six in the evening, however, Hamann could not undertake his son's education alone, and so he employed in due course several additional tutors, most notably a gifted philologist and theology student named Christian Hill, who eventually replaced Hamann as his children's *Hofmeister*. But Hill, in turn, came to be Hamann's own student, as did others, such as the literary talents Abraham Jakob Penzel and Jakob Brahl, and another budding philologist named Jenisch.[33] Then came even more students, such as the Dutchman, Gysbert Karl Count Hogendorp (who later became an adjutant of Napoleon), and his friend, the Prussian lieutenant Bentevegni. After Johann Michael matriculated at the university in 1783, where he attended Kant's lectures, Hamann then took in at least three more students, who became fast friends of his son: first, Friedrich Ehregott Lindner, the son of his doctor and nephew of his own deceased friend; then Raphael Hippel, a relative of Hamann's friend, the famous author and mayor of Königsberg, Theodor Gottlieb Hippel; and, finally, Ludwig Nicolovius, a friend of Johann Michael's from Kant's lectures, whose parents were recently deceased and who wanted to learn Greek and English. In some cases, Hamann was compensated; in others, he simply acted out of charity. In any case, throughout this period from 1777 to 1785, Hamann's home was teeming with life: it was the picture of a private school and a center of intellectual activity. As Nadler puts it, "his home was his school"; Hamann himself was the "Socrates of his age"; and all his relationships with his students were built upon friendship.[34]

TWO MITES: ON THE TABERNACLE OF LANGUAGE

The last text from this period, which Nadler includes among Hamann's Mystery Writings, is his *Two Mites concerning the Latest German Literature* (*Zwey Scherflein zur neusten Deutschen Litteratur*), which was composed in 1780. Whether or not this text belongs in this category is debatable; for it is not concerned with mysteries per se. Rather, as with Hamann's earlier work, *New Apology of the Letter h* (1773), it is concerned with orthographical reforms of the German language, in this case those that had been proposed by Klopstock in his *Über Sprache und Dichtkunst* (1779). And yet, as we have seen from the *New Apology* and from the *Herderschriften*, few topics were of more concern to Hamann than the *mystery* of language, which he calls "the *mother* of reason and its revelations."[35] By the same token, few things incited fiercer polemic than overbearing "rational" incursions into this sacred matrix. Thus, inasmuch as it represents an attempt to safeguard the mystery of language, Hamann's *Two Mites*, following Nadler, may loosely be classified among his Mystery Writings.

At first sight, *Two Mites*, whose title refers to the gospel story in Luke 21, is almost impenetrable. At one level, this has to do with the typical obscurity of Hamann's allusions (chiefly to Klopstock and to a collection of pedagogical writings by Joachim Heinrich Campe). At another level, the unusual density or *Dicht-ung* of his text should itself be seen as a form of protest against the kind of orthography that would, so to speak, profane the mystery of language, reducing language to a mirror of "reason," and writing to a mirror of "approved" speech. Admittedly, for modern persons, who have come to think of language in instrumental terms, it may be difficult to fathom why Hamann would be so incensed about orthographical reforms,

---

[33]   NB, p. 284.
[34]   NB, p. 294.
[35]   ZH VI, p. 108.

which might seem trivial. From Hamann's perspective, however, as the defender of the poet and poetic genius, such reforms were symbolic of the injustices of reason his entire authorship was intended to combat.[36] Once again, this does not mean that Hamann was against reason or that he was an "irrationalist"; this would be an utterly superficial reading. What he was against was the *injustice* of reason, i.e., reason "overstepping its limits": whether this take the form of "rational" incursions into the sacred matrix of language in order to "clean it up" (as in the orthographical elimination of the terminal h) or impose upon it some kind of "rational" standard; or a Stoic denial of any positive role to the passions (as though human beings would have been better without them); or, in the matter of religion, "rational" eliminations of the supposedly "mythological," "superfluous," "irrational," or at least "incredible" doctrines and contents of the faith (as carried out, for example, in deism, Unitarianism, and Bultmannian existentialism). In short, as Hamann saw it, reason's attempt to "fix the *indeterminate* and to cut out any *excess*," as carried out here with regard to language, was symptomatic of the violence it commits whenever it transgresses its limits.[37]

Hamann's *Two Mites* was therefore no minor skirmish about orthography, but profoundly symbolic of the concerns of his authorship in general and the contest of the age: a contest between a Christian worldview (which allows for and even celebrates a mysterious depth to human language, to human nature, to the world) and a fanatical, puritanical rationalism that would seek to eliminate everything that does not conform to its immanent counsels: whether this be the *"irrational"* arbitrariness of language (as though language were meant to be a mirror of reason), or the passionate *sub-rational* depths of human nature (as though we were meant to be purely rational), or the *super-rational* mysteries of Christianity that could not be envisaged or verified by reason alone. For Hamann all of these things hang together, forming a mysterious set of correspondences. Yet, to his alarm, all of these things were being attacked as things "shameful to reason" by the so-called Enlighteners of his day.

The text begins with the following statement: "The *love of the fatherland* bears a natural relation to its *parties honteuses,* I mean by this, the *mother tongue* and *mother church.*"[38] In other words, patriotism, language, and the Church are the natural bonds of society. The problem with fallen reason, however, is that it separates the first from the second two, which it regards as "shameful parts" or *pudenda.* For example, the dark historical origins, senseless superfluities, and random permutations of tribal tongues are shameful to the ideal of a timeless, universal language of reason; likewise, the plurality of particular creeds, dogmas, and superstitions is shameful to the ideal of a universal, natural religion. As Hamann goes on to point out, however, such an unnatural separation would ultimately bring about the dissolution of society. For "without *language* we would have no reason; without reason, no *religion*; and without these three essential constituents of our nature, neither spirit nor bond of society."[39] Once again, it is clear that Hamann values reason; indeed, reason,

---

[36] For example, reason too, if one thinks of Plato's psychology in book IV of the *Republic*, could conceivably be unjust if it denies its subordination to the good or the divine (which transcends it or is superior to it), or if it should fail to appreciate the proper roles of the lower powers of the soul. To be sure, Plato generally assumes that the appetitive part of the soul is the cause of injustice, whenever, out of a lack of self-control, it does not submit to the guiding voice of reason through the encouragement of the "spirited part." Here, though, we have something akin to the opposite: when reason no longer wisely shepherds the non-rational elements, but instead, failing to recognize their inherent value, tyrannically imposes itself upon them.

[37] N III, pp. 233f.

[38] N III, p. 231.

[39] N III, p. 231.

he says, is an "essential constituent of our nature," and in this regard he stands *with* his contemporaries. What he prophetically warns against, however, is the fanatical separation of reason from language, tradition, and the Church, having foreseen long before Nietzsche's madman that once such secular "reforms" have been carried out, reason will have, theoretically, nothing left to stand on and, practically (i.e., morally), nothing left to guide it.

Accordingly, at one level, the point of Hamann's *Two Mites* is to remind the *Aufklärer* of the natural bonds they unnaturally seeks to dissolve; at another level, it is a prophetic indictment of "reason" for violating its "mother," i.e., for its Procrustean measures to ensure that German pronunciation and writing conform to certain "rational" standards. But, as Hamann points out, repeating his argument in *Doubts and Ideas,* such measures, which claim to be rational, are, in fact, entirely arbitrary, since they can take place only by an arbitrary selection of one particular pronunciation as normative. As a result, such orthographical measures succeed merely in transforming "*laws* into prejudices and *prejudices* ... into laws *sans rime et sans raison.*"[40] Adding to the hypocrisy, the reformers recommend that this norm of spoken German be taken as a standard for writing, whereby writing is made to conform to an arbitrary standard of speech. But, as Hamann points out, "Since our eyes are by nature deaf, and our ears blind," the latter can "scarcely 'serve through substitution as the genetic foundation of a universal orthography.' "[41] In other words, speech cannot serve as the model for writing; the one is not reducible to the other. And to this extent Hamann could be said to anticipate Derrida's distinction between speech and "writing" (*écriture*).[42]

Hamann's *Two Mites,* a mere "widow's offering" (Luke 21: 2), thus contributes far more than meets the eye, to the point of anticipating, by more than a century, many of the concerns of Heidegger (on language and technology) and Derrida (on speech and writing). That being said, the ultimate purpose of his defense of language and writing against an overbearing rationalism (which would reduce language and writing to a mirror of reason) is not to liberate writing from speech-presence, but to reunite language and religion, thereby restoring speech and writing to their original prophetic purpose:

> For as little as the *purpose* of *speech* consists in the mere articulation and modification of blind tones, far less still does the *purpose* of *writing* consist in a counting, weighing, and punctuating of its mute substitutes; all of which amounts to a pharisaical partitioning of mint, dill, and caraway, compared to the true, natural, and higher purpose, which unites both *speech* and *writing* – into a *shekhinah,* tabernacle, and chariot-throne of our sensations, thoughts, and concepts through the audible and visible *signs* of language.[43]

Hamann's point here is that the sensible signs of language – being the tabernacle of human sensations, thoughts, and concepts – have a dignity that rational scribes and Pharisees cannot perceive. Moreover, as he suggestively puts it in reference to Ezekiel's vision (Ezek. 1), beyond its capacity to convey human concepts and sensations,

---

40 N III, p. 242.

41 N III, p. 238.

42 N III, p. 236. Needless to say, comparisons between Hamann and Derrida break down at a certain point; nevertheless, it is interesting, if a mere coincidence, that at one point in his text (p. 236), in a curious adaptation of the Vulgate (2 Cor. 8: 14), Hamann highlights the word *supplementum* and then supplements it with a footnote in French beginning with the word *écriture.*

43 N III, p. 237.

language is also the tabernacle and chariot-throne of the Holy Spirit. In other words, as Hamann himself powerfully experienced through his reading of Scripture, language is the chosen vehicle through which God reveals himself to human beings. Accordingly, given this mysterious capacity of language to convey the divine *in and through the human*, to tamper with it, or to treat it in reductive, pragmatic or instrumental terms, is for Hamann tantamount to sacrilege.

No doubt, to a modern sensibility, which has difficulty conceiving of anything divine, much less finding the divine in something so ordinary and near as the spoken or written word, so exalted a view of language is bound to appear eccentric. From Hamann's fundamentally theological perspective, however, he is perfectly consistent. Indeed, for him it is no big stretch to say that language is (or at least can be) a kind of "sacrament." For, if the pagan intuition affirmed by Paul is correct, namely, that "In him we live and move and have our being" (Acts 17: 28), then how could language possibly be a purely human or purely secular construct impervious to divine inspiration? As he strikingly puts it, on the basis of his profound sense of divine condescension, which assumes everything, even the most mundane aspects of human life, into the workings of providence:

> If the hairs on our head, down to the variation of their color, belong to the *Datis* of divine providence, why should the *straight* and *crooked* lines and strokes of our symbolic and typological (but not hieroglyphic) handwriting not be the counter images and mirror of a *theopneustie* (2 Tim. 3: 16), of an unrecognized central force in which we *live and move and have our being* [?][44]

For Hamann, therefore, given that God knows and makes use precisely of the contingent and seemingly arbitrary, what the orthographers in their *Rechtschreiberei* would eliminate in the name of "right reason" – like the letter h, which, as Hamann ironically puts it, is only a "breath" – may very well be the intended vehicle of divine inspiration.

In any event, as Hamann suggestively puts it, the orthographical reformers are guilty of a proleptic eschatology. For whereas God himself is patient, like the *pater familias* in the parable of the wheat and the tares (Matt. 13: 24–30), they impatiently assume for themselves the right of judgment, which belongs to God alone:

> In such a *spiritual matter* as that of *language*, even in the case of the most plausible and feasible "correction of manifest errors," the economic wisdom, tolerance, and restraint of the *pater familias* in the gospel gives me reason not to be too premature and hasty, but to be hesitating in my zeal [*zaudernd sich zu zauen*] to sort out the weeds and let them grow until the harvest ... since *summum ius* and *summa inuria*, like light and shadow, are inseparable temporal relatives of the *sensible world below*; righteousness without regard to person and physiognomy, on the other hand, is a *regale* of the Last Judge, who will clothe His faithful, patient, and holy lovers ... with pure and beautiful silk; but all poetic illusions and political usurpations of the apocalyptic beast, the lying prophet, and the Babylonian spinster-mother he will bring to light and to nothing, to nothing, to nothing! – by the πνεῦμα of his mouth![45]

The orthographical reformers, then, are like the impatient servants in the Gospel who cannot stand contradiction (in this case ambiguities in speaking and writing), and who would impose upon language an arbitrary but allegedly "rational" standard,

---

44 N III, p. 240.
45 N III, p. 233. Cf. Rev. 17: 5; 19: 8, 15, 21.

usurping, so to speak, the eschatological judgment of Christ. Hamann's profounder point, however, is again that language is a "spiritual matter" and, consequently, beyond the jurisdiction of reason; indeed, *that inspired language, and not reason, is the source of genuine criticism*. For if the πνεῦμα that proceeds from the mouth of Christ is a sword (Rev. 19: 15; cf. Matt. 10: 34), and if the purpose of the Word of God, as the word of eternal life (John 6: 68), is to divide "soul from spirit, joints from marrow," i.e., to effect judgment of the "thoughts and intentions of the heart" (Heb. 4: 12), then the purpose of the language of Christians is to effect a similar "judgment" in those whom they address (in keeping with the original, etymological sense of "criticism," from κρίνειν). Ultimately, however, such "criticism" is effected not by virtue of Christians' own talents and critical powers, though God may make use of them, but by virtue of the Spirit of Christ (Matt. 10: 19–20), who dwells in them (John 14: 17). Accordingly, the language of a Christian, as something holy (1 Pet. 4: 11), should be understood as a vehicle of the continued creative work of the Holy Spirit, who is ever again bringing about a new creation, a transformation of the old, through a "critical" separation of light from darkness (Gen. 1: 4; cf. John 16: 8).

The most important point of Hamann's *Two Mites*, therefore, is that "judgment" and "criticism" belong *not* to reason, as Kant would have it, but to inspired language, whose pre-eminent and authoritative example is Scripture. This is what Hamann himself experienced in London, and this is what his subsequent, inspired, mimetic "authorship" is an attempt to convey. In a nutshell one could say that, for Hamann, *it is not reason that critiques language, but inspired language that critiques reason*, and does so on the basis of an authority *greater* than reason. Indeed, herein lies the essence of the reversal of his "metacritical" thought: his testimony to the potency of language as a vehicle of inspiration and creative divine judgment (and thus to *true* criticism) *vis-à-vis* the ultimate impotence of "rational" language and "criticism" that is divorced from the Logos and *Pneuma* of God. All of which goes to say that Hamann, and not Kant, was the true critic of his age.

But inasmuch as the writing of a Christian is modeled on the "effective Word" of God, for Hamann it is precisely not a direct, but an indirect kind of writing (after the manner of Nathan's parable in 2 Samuel 12), moreover, a writing that is modeled on the kenotic humility of Christ himself; hence titles such as *Two Mites*. And in this regard he speaks of "aesthetic obedience to the Cross," as if to say that such writing will require a certain degree of self-denial and even self-dissimulation. As he puts it *vis-à-vis* the self-certainty of the rational reformers: "Quem penes *arbitrium* est et *ius* et *norma* legendi [whoever has *say* over the *law* and the *standard* of reading] can be disarmed in no other way than μαθήματα παθήματα, by way of a learning through suffering, through aesthetic obedience to the Cross, and can be satisfied only with the *image* and *inscription* of his own *coin*."[46] In other words, "aesthetic obedience to the Cross" requires that one speak or write not for oneself, but for another; not lyrically, but dialectically; not even in one's own tongue, but in another tongue, in this case the "foreign" tongue or dialect of his contemporaries. It requires that one "give to Caesar what is Caesar's" (Matt. 22: 21), which explains Hamann's profligate use of quotation, in order thereby, using his contemporaries' *own words*, to convince and convict them (cf. 1 Sam. 17: 51). And, sure enough, Hamann's *Two Mites* makes abundant use of Klopstock's own words, turning them on their head, so that Klopstock ends up saying the opposite of what he meant to say and is thereby transformed into an unwitting ally in Hamann's "metacritical" crusade.

---

[46] N III, p. 234. Cf. Heb. 5: 8.

8

The Sibyl Speaks: On the Protological and Eschatological Mystery of Marriage

Should I come as a spirit to you, do not be terrified of me.

Essay of a Sibyl on Marriage[1]

... the bride and bridegroom are at the same time God in love with his crea-
tion ... In this way, the union of man and woman reflects the central arcanum
of celestial sexuality.

Czeslaw Milosz[2]

A world without God is a man without a head – without heart, without viscera –
without pudenda.

Hamann to Jacobi[3]

Toward the end of 1774, Hamann's and Kant's and Herder's publisher, Hartknoch, got married; and as a tribute Hamann composed a small work, a mere one and a half printed octavo pages in length, called *Essay of a Sibyl on Marriage* (*Versuch einer Sibylle über die Ehe*), which, given its title, harkening back to the *Sibylline Oracles,* belongs in the category of his "Mystery Writings."[4] For all its brevity, Hamann speaks of this work – his "little embryo" – as a "climacteric monument" of his forty-fifth year, and even requested that Hartknoch provide some gold for the title page.[5] The principal reason why he affords the *Essay* such distinction, however, is the profound importance of sexuality to his authorship; as Nadler puts it, "the language of sex is the technical language of his philosophy."[6] And, true enough, Hamann's writings abound in sexual metaphors: from references to the feckless sterility of the *Aufklärer*, who have forsaken the stamina and *menstrua* of reason (i.e., revelation and tradition), to his shocking self-depiction as the lusty Pan on the title vignette of *Crusades of the Philologist.*[7] Needless to say, he was not oblivious to the possibility that his *Essay* might offend his readers, even his friends, as his correspondence with Matthias Claudius attests:

> Finally, I got some feedback from two friends about the *Sibyl* – The one told me in con-
> fidence that he considered it something *dirty* – The other, who strongly condemned the

---

[1] *Essay of a Sibyl on Marriage*, N III, p. 197.
[2] See Milosz's introduction to Vladimir Solovyov, *War, Progress, and the End of History* (Hudson, NY: Lindisfarne Press, 1990), pp. 8f.
[3] ZH V, p. 326.
[4] N III, pp. 197–203; see ZH III, p. 113; cf. p. 126.
[5] ZH III, pp. 125–6, 128.
[6] NB, p. 246.
[7] See N III, p. 39; N II, p. 137; NB, p. 250.

first saying: *Naturalia non sunt turpia,* wanted to improve it, thinking to have discovered in it something profane. – I admitted to the latter that this accusation seemed to me harsher and worse than the other. I await your opinion about it as well, because I would be glad to have a reason to explain myself … – and since the mystery of the hymen seems to be a suitable example by which to metagrabolize about the nature of the mysteries.[8]

Clearly, Hamann was disturbed by such accusations, since his intention was ultimately not to scandalize his readers, any more than Paul's discourse on the Cross was intended simply to shock the metaphysical sensibility of his Greek audience (cf. 1 Cor. 1: 18ff.); rather, it was to help them to see in the scandal (in the dark depths that are "offensive" and impenetrable to reason) the mystery of divine love. Indeed, at the heart of the "scandal" was his suggestion – in the face of reason's inveterate shame and timidity (Gen. 3: 7) – that the mystery of sex is in some sense a portal to the mysteries of heaven, a mystery that is intimated in paganism and fulfilled in the nuptial reality of Christ and his Church.

THE MYSTERY OF MARRIAGE: A *VERUM SIGNACULUM CREATORIS*

Nevertheless, given the explicitness of Hamann's language and the offense it can cause, the *Essay of a Sibyl on Marriage* requires further explanation. We have already had occasion to discuss Hamann's use of sexual metaphors in the context of the *Aesthetica,* wherein his sexually charged vocabulary was shown to be part of his vehement rejection of the abstract and, in his view, sterile rationalism of the age. Where his contemporaries emphasize the timeless universality of reason, he emphasizes the here and now of the senses and passions; where they flee from embodied life, he revels in it; where they speak of clarity and light – of "clear and distinct" ideas, following Descartes – he speaks of the darkness and creativity of the "hidden" parts. Indeed, avenging the neglect of the senses and the passions at the hands of a colorless, abstract, and essentially asexual rationalism – for which the mystery of sex and gender would seem to be no mystery at all, and in any case irrelevant to a "rational" knowledge of the world – Hamann is in many ways the Dionysus of his age (and, as such, *mutatis mutandis,* a forerunner of Nietzsche).[9] Yet it would be incorrect on this account to see in him the antithesis of the Apollonian spirit, as though he were an irrationalist. On the contrary, as O'Flaherty points out, he always strove to achieve a proper balance of the "Dionyisan" and the "Apollonian," in keeping with his doctrine of the "whole man," which is grounded in turn, as we have seen, in an essentially Christological vision of reality.[10] To put it simply, for Hamann, it is not that reason is at odds with the lower powers of the soul, which must be shut out (as is the tendency with Stoicism); rather, in a way far more continuous with Platonic tradition (and with early Christian apologists such as Justin Martyr or Clement of Alexandria), it is that reason, the passions, and the senses (loosely

---

[8] ZH III, p. 184. See Schoonhoven's explanatory note in *HH* V, p. 168. Hamann's use of the word "metagrabolize" derives from Rabelais's neologism, ματαιογραφοβολιζειν (ματαιος = in vain; γραφειν = to write; βολιζειν = cast the sinker). Thus, to "metagrabolize" means "to write or fish in vain").

[9] In order not to misunderstand Hamann, however, one must be careful here to observe a crucial difference in vocabulary. By "passions" he does not mean, as did the Church Fathers, the various vices or sins (like lust or pride) of a fallen world by which man is enslaved, from which he necessarily "suffers," and which, apart from grace, cannot be redeemed. Rather, he tends to mean profound feelings, like fear, grief, love, and joy.

[10] For Hamann's doctrine of the "whole man," see *JGH,* pp. 34–43.

corresponding to Plato's three powers of the soul) harmoniously come into their own when all together are ruled by Christ.

The chief source of Hamann's anthropology (and with it his understanding of sexuality), however, is Genesis, and what is particularly striking here is his exegetical departure from patristic tradition. For he associates the *imago Dei* not so much with an angelic capacity for rational thought, understood as the *apex mentis,* the "highest" part of the soul, as with a deep-seated creative impulse arising from the depths of human nature, metonymically from the "lower parts," the *pudenda.*[11] Indeed, it is precisely in the hidden *creative* parts of human nature that he sees a mysterious image of the hidden depths of the *Creator* (cf. Ps. 42: 7) – the depths of a God who is no mere *causa sui* of reason, no Platonic "potter of plastic forms," and certainly no Cartesian engineer of the "machine" of the world, but a profoundly creative "father of fiery spirits and breathing powers."[12] Thus, whereas a rationalist or prudish moralist would see in the *pudenda* the darkest, the most "shameful," and certainly the most "sub-divine" aspect of the human being, Hamann sees in them precisely the opposite: the most intimate and most glorious point of contact with the Creator. As he strikingly puts it to Herder, "The *pudenda* strike me as the *only* bond between *creation* and *Creator.*"[13] What is more, inasmuch as they imply the difference of the sexes and point to a procreative "knowledge" of the other in love, the *pudenda* could be said to constitute a *sub-rational* image of the *super-rational* Trinity.[14] Accordingly, in contrast to Augustine's psychological image of *memoria, intellectus,* and *voluntas,* Hamann suggests that the *imago Trinitatis* is to be seen in a concrete reciprocity of *sex, knowledge,* and *life,* which in turn points to an eternal reciprocity in God of life, light, and love.[15]

---

[11]   By "*pudenda,*" in reference to Gen. 3: 7, Hamann means the sexual organs as a metonym for the passions and human creativity. To be sure, compared to interpretations of the *imago Dei* as indicating the dignity of our rational nature, Hamann's own can seem irrational, if not downright antinomian, as if reason is overthrown by the passions. However, Hamann does not reject reason per se; as he says to Jacobi, "*Faith has need of reason* just as reason has need of faith" (ZH VII, p. 165). He simply rejects any exclusively rational understanding of the human being that would fail to appreciate the depths of human creativity. Historically speaking, the importance of this reading of the *imago Dei* lies in its reversal of the standard anthropology of the Enlightenment. For the *pudenda,* which Hamann associates with human creative energies, and which classical and modern anthropologies forcibly *subordinate* to reason, have, for Hamann, a mysterious dignity: though "subordinate" to reason, they are in some sense *superior* to it, inasmuch as they are *deeper* and *darker* than reason can fathom. Accordingly, they are a reflection in the creative, sub-rational depths of the human being of the mysterious depths of the *Creator* who infinitely transcends reason's grasp (as Augustine puts it, *si comprehendis, non est Deus*). In other words, for Hamann, the abyss of the divine will is somehow reflected in the abyss of human creativity. This is not to say that Hamann was a voluntarist. He does not say that God is pure will, as though God were not also the Logos. Nor is he endorsing any nihilistic and ultimately demonic elevation of the passions over reason. On the contrary, reason retains its proper authority so long as it has not become unjust and tyrannical, having cut itself off from the proper source of its authority in the *creative* Logos.
[12]   N III, p. 28. Cf. Heb. 1: 7.
[13]   ZH IV, p. 113.
[14]   Given Hamann's biblical sensibility, it is important to recall that the Hebrew word *yada* can mean both "to know" and "to know sexually," as in such passages as Gen. 4: 1: "Now the man knew his wife and she conceived and bore Cain ..."
[15]   N III, pp. 212f.: "The *hidden parts* of our nature, which are the ground of all taste and enjoyment of the beautiful, the true, and the good, refer, like that tree of God in the middle of the garden to *knowledge* and *life.* Both are the causes as well as the effects of *love.* Their glow is one of fire and a flame of the Lord; for God is *love* and the *life* is the *light* of men. These three are One and witnesses in heaven and on earth." Minimally, what Hamann seems to mean is that knowledge and life are grounded in sexual difference; and that the knowledge of sexual difference is *prior* to the knowledge of good and evil, which is a problem only *after* the Fall. Indeed, only as such, as a postlapsarian problem, does the knowledge of good and evil constitute the "oldest and greatest problem of reason" (N III, p. 212). The truest, most intimate form of knowledge therefore, namely a creative knowledge of the other in love, *does not* begin with the Fall – as though this were in some sense necessary for knowledge. As for life being grounded in sexual difference, this goes without saying. And that these three – life, knowledge, and sexual love – are reciprocally one is for Hamann what makes them together a *vestigium trinitatis.*

Unfortunately, Hamann does not develop his thought in this regard. Nevertheless, it is clear that for Hamann the mystery of the *pudenda* is bound up with the mystery of sexual difference, and that this, in turn, as the mystery of the *creativity* of sexual union-in-difference, is a sacred image of the Creator, a *verum signaculum Creatoris*.[16] Conversely, it is clear that he sees disregard for this mysterious image, this bond between heaven and earth, as a sign of sterility, decadence, and cultural decline; for once sexual union-in-difference is evacuated of transcendent meaning, once it is no longer revered as a mysterious image of the Trinity, the most fundamental bond between Creator and creature is broken.

From this perspective it is easy to see why marriage, the consummate symbol of union-in-difference, is a central topos of Hamann's thought, informing everything from his epistemology to his (at least implicit) metaphysics. Conversely, nothing is more antithetical to his thought and therefore the target of fiercer polemic than the "adulterous" (*ehe-brecherische*) philosophy of his age, which *separates* "what God has joined together" (Matt. 19: 6). Hence Hamann's contrast between the philosophical *Scheidekunst* of the *Aufklärer*, whom he refers to synonymously as *Scheidekünstler,* and his own theological, specifically Christological, *Ehekunst,* which sees all things united, wedded together, in the Word, the *Ars Patris*.[17] So, too, following Christ's almost synonymous usage of the words "evil" and "adulterous" (Matt. 12: 39, 16: 4, etc.), he inveighs against every sundering of concept and intuition, faith and reason, body and soul, matter and spirit, etc. – not to mention the vain meditations, prophylactic skepticisms, and fruitless auto-conceptions of pure, automatic reason.[18] But if Hamann's polemic is motivated by a positive appreciation of the mystery of marriage, it is also inspired by a pro-phetic instinct about where the logic – the *Scheidekunst* – of modernity inevitably leads. For if God is united to his creation according to the *sym-bol* of marriage – this being a mysterious image of the supernatural relationship between Christ and his Church (cf. 5: 32) – the *dia-bolical* logic of modernity, in the sense of a literal "casting asunder," eventually leads to a radical sundering God and world.[19] This, as Hamann saw with foreboding, was the dark other side – the future – of the "Enlightenment," once reason has proudly shut out the supernatural light of the Logos as conveyed through prophetic tradition, pretending it were not in need of it, as though reason could somehow get along without revelation. Indeed, Hamann believed that the aftereffects of the "Enlightenment," of reason cut off from its source, would be a world precisely without reason (!), moreover a culture without genuine inspiration, without life-giving passion, and without fruitful creativity.

---

[16] N III, p. 212.

[17] For references to the *Scheidekunst* of the *Aufklärer* see N I, p. 52; N III, pp. 40, 278, 300; ZH VI, p. 534; ZH VII, p. 158.

[18] In other words, Hamann is wont to diagnose the epistemological and philosophical ills of his age in terms of one or another sexual perversion or profaning of the mystery of marriage.

[19] If the epistemological aspect of this logic is a separation of faith and reason, its social aspect is the so-called "separa-tion of Church and state," in the name of which, as though it were a magical talisman, God is increasingly banished (one might say fanatically purged) from classrooms, constitutions, and any mention in public places. Indeed, no sooner is the phrase "the separation of Church and state" paraded in public discourse – as the ark of the covenant of modern secular reason through which its societal power is conveyed – than one feels mysteriously compelled to bow before it, as though no principle could be more infallible, inviolable, or sacrosanct. The net result of this logic and its attendant social reality – which is none other than a modern manifestation of the *civitas terrena*, with its characteristic contempt for God – is thus the opposite of the nuptial theo-logic of Judaism and Christianity, according to which God is united to his creation in love, dwelling in and among his people (Lev. 26: 11–12; 2 Cor. 6: 16).

As he strikingly put it to Jacobi, "A world without God is a man without a head – without heart, without guts – without *pudenda*."[20]

On the one hand, then, it is out of profound respect for the mystery of marriage as containing some kind of *ultima ratio* that Hamann inveighs against all forms of modern purism. In the *Socratic Memorabilia* he critiqued the puritanical separation of reason from faith; in the *Aesthetica* he critiqued the puritanical separation of reason from the senses and the passions; later he critiques the puritanical separation of reason from language and tradition; and here in the *Essay* he implicitly critiques all of these "acts of separation," which culminate in the separation of God from his creation, as embodying the antithesis of the mystery of marriage (and therein, implicitly, the mystery of Antichrist). On the other hand, he does so because he sees in such secular thinking a withering of human creativity and of the expressly poetic capacities and vocation of the *imago Dei* (cf. Gen. 2: 19), whose creativity is not independent from but rather dependent upon divine inspiration. Indeed, as we have seen, he warns his contemporaries in the *Aesthetica* not to venture "into the metaphysics of the fine arts without being accomplished in the orgies and Eleusinian mysteries,"[21] as if to say that true knowledge necessarily involves a creative, erotic, or ecstatic component, and that no epistemology, metaphysics, or aesthetics can hope to be fruitful without it.[22]

At one level, then, against the *Scheidekunst* and corresponding purisms of modern secular reason, Hamann's intention in the *Essay of a Sibyl on Marriage* is to initiate his contemporaries anew into the creative vitality of the mystery of marriage. At another and profounder level, however, his aim is to prepare them through contemplation of the protological mystery of marriage for the eschatological mystery of Christ and his Church to which it figuratively and prophetically points. For it is precisely his contemporaries' disregard for this first mystery that has rendered them insensate regarding the last. Fittingly, therefore, the text begins with a prophetic address in the voice of a sibyl to Hartknoch and his bride, and through them to Hamann's contemporaries as a whole: "Sensible and blessed bridal pair!, do not stop up your ears, which are open to the magic of harmony, [but] hear the voice of a sibyl, who can prophesy so accurately and so well. Wonderful, like love, and mysterious, like marriage, is my instruction!"[23]

ESSAY OF A SIBYL ON MARRIAGE

The content of the sibyl's instruction is essentially that of the Bible: sexual difference and procreation are constitutive of the image of God (Gen. 1: 26–8).[24] Accordingly, what makes the human being a "*God* of the earth" is his vocation to be "the *creator, self-preserver, and ever-multiplier – semper-Augustus – of his species*."[25] At the same time,

---

[20] ZH V, p. 326. Cf. ZH V, p. 167: "The *pudenda* of our nature are so exactly connected to the chambers of the *heart* and the *brain* that it is impossible to abstract too strictly from so natural a bond." What is striking about Hamann's statement is not so much what it says *before* Nietzsche, namely, that to eliminate God is necessarily to eliminate the human being as well (as the *imago Dei*) and all that this implies, namely, the gradual dissolution of humanism into sentimentality and nihilism, but what it says *contra* Nietzsche: that the elimination of God, rather than liberating human creativity, will have precisely the opposite effect, i.e., the reduction of human beings and human culture to a meaningless and heartless *sterility*.

[21] See N II, p. 208; cf. N III, p. 97. See O'Flaherty's discussion in *JGH*, pp. 38–40.

[22] See *JGH*, p. 39.

[23] N III, p. 199.

[24] See N III, p. 212, where Hamann calls the difference between the sexes a *verum signaculum Creatoris*.

[25] N III, p. 199 *Semper Augustus* is a play on the Latin word *augere*, which means to increase or multiply. It is also, incidentally, the root of such words as "author" and "authority" and, as such, sheds further light on the meaning and intent of Hamann's "authorship."

following Paul (Eph. 5: 32; 1 Cor. 11: 7), Hamann suggests that the union of man and woman in God constitutes a natural image of the Trinity: "'The mystery is great!' – Man is the image and glory *of God,* and the woman is the glory of man' – That is to say: the man relates to *God* as the woman to the man, and where these *Three* are *One,* 'the woman will be blessed through childbearing, and the man will be the body's savior.' "[26] At one level, then, Hamann sees a mystery in the way that man and woman relate to one another within the sacred order, ultimately reflecting the taxis of the Trinity itself. But the further mystery of the *union* of God and human beings is revealed only when these *three* are supernaturally one, when man and woman are one in the triune God (cf. John 17: 22–3), i.e., when the Trinity is *in* the marriage, making the unity-in-difference between man and woman an earthly image of the Trinity itself.

Thus far nothing in the *Essay* could be considered provocative, unless one takes issue with Paul as well. Toward the end of the *Essay,* however, Hamann draws a striking and potentially offensive comparison (even to pious traditionalists) between the fulfillment of virginity through the sexual act, and the fulfillment of pagan virtue through Christ: "Without a *sacrifice* of *innocence,* the *treasure* and *sanctum* of *virginity* will remain unknown, and the entrance to this heavenly virtue [will remain] impenetrable."[27] The obscure allusion here is to the Book of Hebrews, where Christ, the high priest, is described as entering the Holy Place (9: 11–12). Accordingly, with his daring conflation of sexual and redemptive imagery, Hamann means to say that the marital act not only fulfills an essential aspect of the *imago Dei,* but is a sign and veiled prophesy of super-natural redemption through Christ. With imagery still more graphic and potentially offensive he concludes: "Just as the male member unites with its origin, so did he enter whence he came as the body's savior, and like a faithful creator in good works he closed the gap of the place with flesh, in order henceforth to fulfill the oldest *maculatur* of the human race."[28] Understood in light of the many references Hamann adduces, beyond the obvious reference to Gen. 2: 21 (John 3: 31, 8: 14; Eccles. 1: 7; 3: 20; and 1 Pet. 4: 19), it is clear that for him the marital act in some mysterious way images the work of Christ in healing Adam's wound, completing what is otherwise lacking – fixing, as it were, the original "blemish" – in human nature. In any case, the parallel is clear: the earthly union of man and woman (not merely in the abstract but precisely in the ecstasy of sexul love) is an image of the ecstatic, heavenly union of Christ and his Church.

Hamann was well aware, of course, that his little essay might offend pious readers.[29] Thus, already in the motto on the title vignette, he has the sibyl say: "Should

---

[26] N III, pp. 200f.; see 1 Tim. 2: 15; Eph. 5: 23.

[27] N III, p. 202.

[28] N III, pp. 202f. The most obvious sense of *maculatur* is what the Latin would suggest: something that is blemished. For other possible senses of the word, see G-D, pp. 261f.; among them, I take Griffith-Dickson's own interpretation to be the most convincing: "The *Maculatur* is indeed Adam's … 'incompleteness,' his 'missing rib,' his lonely singleness. This longing for another is the oldest '*maculatur*' of the human race, our oldest blemish is our halfness … and it is fulfilled in sexual union."

[29] Thus he writes to Hartknoch: "As for whether you will be able to publish it without offending your conscience, I await your honest confession; let me say in advance, however, that the entire knot consists in that it should be a *scandal* to our moralistic century; and if it is capable of achieving this effect, I will have achieved my purpose" (ZH III, p. 128). By "moralistic" Hamann means not only the *Aufklärer,* who reduce the mystery of Christianity to morality, but also the type of Christian who, in good conscience, follows suit, turning Christianity into a Gnostic and essentially bodiless religion – for which "the crude, physical, earthly quality of Christianity, its fleshliness, its crucifixion and resurrection and *corpus meum* [are] too unrefined." See Hans von Balthasar, *The Glory of the Lord: A Theological Aesthetics* (San Francisco: Ignatius, 1985), vol. 3, p. 240. Such a view, however, only perpetuates the shame of the Fall and thus holds itself, ironically, at a "profane" distance from the original, most fundamental, and most prophetic mystery of human nature, as though it were something tainted and not something which Christ redeemed.

I come as a spirit to you, do not be terrified of me."[30] But if one finds his language offensive, Hamann in turn asks: whence our shame? "Where does it come from that we are ashamed of [our] likeness to *God* as [though it were] theft or robbery? Is this shame not a secret blemish of our nature, and at the same time a mute criticism of its glorious Creator, who alone is wise and greatly to be praised?"[31] He then goes on to say that this shame is not an "innate, universal instinct, as can be seen from the examples of children, savages, and the schools of the cynics; rather it is an inherited custom ..."[32] Accordingly, he concludes that Christianity is not to be confused with moral prudery – if, that is, Christ opened the gates of paradise. On the contrary, those who live in Christ are restored to a primordial innocence that is free from condemnation, and it is in this spirit that he speaks so freely of the mystery of sex.[33] And he must speak of it, inasmuch as for him the mystery of human history and redemption, being the mystery of the mystical body of Christ – of *anthropomorphosis* and *apotheosis* – is ultimately a matter of the connubial mystery of love: of the love of the bridegroom (Christ) for his bride (the Church). Such, to be sure, is the prophetic depth and breadth of the protological mystery of marriage, and so it is hardly surprising that Hamann should see the profaning of the mystery of marriage, and of sexual union-in-difference, as a quasi-eschatological sign.[34]

"APRONS OF FIG LEAVES": ON REASON'S INVETERATE SHAME

Hamann's mysterious fragment from 1778, "Aprons of fig leaves," though thematically similar to the *Essay,* is more than anything a monument to his genius for the obscure.[35] It is concerned with multiple contemporaries, among them, Christoph Martin Wieland, Anton Friedrich Büsching, and Johann Heinrich Voß; but here the ultimate target is Starck, and in particular Starck's *Hephästion,* which in Hamann's mind was unfinished business. What was at issue once again was the significance of paganism (which Starck tended to overvalue) and Judaism (which Starck tended to undercut) in relationship to Christianity. For example, Starck praises the pagan doctrine of the immortality of the soul, and criticizes Judaism for the absence of any such doctrine. Likewise, he praises paganism for having a developed doctrine of the virtues, and criticizes Judaism for being comparatively deficient in this regard.[36] Furthermore, he vigorously rejects typological interpretations of the Hebrew Bible: the very kind of interpretation that for Hamann, ever since his London conversion, attested to their divine inspiration.[37] What was called for, therefore, was not simply a clarification of Christianity's relation to paganism, but a defense of Judaism, whose

---

[30]   N III, p. 197.

[31]   N III, p. 199.

[32]   Ibid.

[33]   Thus he says in the fragment called *Das stellenlose Blatt*: "Innocence knows no difference of good and evil; knows therefore of no disgrace or shame" (N III, p. 213). That this is no proposal for libertinism is clear from what Hamann says elsewhere regarding the law. Indeed, for him, it is precisely by living according to God's law through the law of the Spirit that one discovers the freedom Paul describes (Rom. 8: 2, 21.).

[34]   See NB, p. 201.

[35]   N III, pp. 205–13.

[36]   *HH* V, pp. 167f.

[37]   Ibid.

status as a revealed religion and doctrine of divine election were being attacked in the name of reason and "enlightenment," i.e., in the name of tolerance and a "natural" religion of reason alone. And in this respect, as Nadler points out, "Aprons of fig leaves," though a fragment, forms an important bridge from the Mystery Writings to Hamann's late work *Golgotha and Scheblimini*.[38]

Apart from a critical apparatus many times the length of the text itself, "Aprons of fig leaves" is by all accounts inscrutable; indeed it is the epitomy of what Mendelssohn meant when he called Hamann's style "dark and puzzling."[39] Consider, for example, the ludicrous construction, "allotrioepiscopolypragmatic," or the equally preposterous conglomeration "watrachomyogigantologomachias."[40] Whatever may have accounted for Hamann's exceeding obscurity and philological eccentricity in this work, "Aprons" certainly deserves to be reckoned among the most impenetrable texts in the history of western literature; and one might consider it fortunate for any poor reader who would try to make head or tail of it that it was never finished or published. The work was occasioned by the January 1776 issue of Christoph Martin Wieland's journal, *Teutsche Merkur*, in which Wieland had posed the following question: "Will the efforts of cold-blooded philosophers and Lucianic spirits against what they call enthusiasm and *Schwärmerey* bring about more evil or more good? And to what limits must the anti-Platonists and Luciani hold themselves in order to be useful?"[41] Needless to say, given Hamann's own "enthusiasm," the question demanded his response; and so in 1777, which in his mind came to assume a magical quality (it being 1000 + 777, as well as his own 47th year), he undertook a highly cryptic response in *three parts*. It begins, accordingly, with a *triple* dedication: the first to Wieland; the second to Anton Friedrich Büsching, the editor of the *Wöchentliche Nachrichten* (in which Büsching had published a review of Starck's "pseudo-coptic" *Hephästion*); the third to Johann Heinrich Voß, the editor of the Hamburg journal, *Musen Almanach* (in which Voß had published a comical poem by Hamann's friend Matthias Claudius on

---

[38] N III, p. 451.

[39] See Martin Seils's redaction and explanation of the text in *HH* V, pp. 275ff. At a visual level alone, the 290 footnotes presented here – for a text of a mere 230 or so lines – are already daunting. I include in this reckoning, and in my discussion of the *Schürze*, the fragment which Nadler appended to *Schürze* as *Das stellenlose Blatt*. See N III, p. 213.

[40] N III, pp. 207, 209. As Seils notes (*HH* V, pp. 319, 329), the first is a construction based on the Greek text of 1 Pet. 4: 15; the second is constructed from three Greek words, βατραχομυομαχια = a war between frogs and mice, a legendary Homeric parody of the *Iliad*; Γιγαντομαχια = battle of the giants; Λογομαχια = war of words; hence, altogether, more or less: "a war of words among frogs, mice, and giants." The first part of the "word" is an anagram of the first word of Matthias Claudius' poem, "Wächter und Burgermeister."

[41] See *HH* V, pp. 285ff. The reference here is to Lucian, the second-century cynic and satirist, of whom Wieland was an avid reader and translator. As for the question itself, it was certainly provocative: not only did it aptly summarize the competing intellectual currents of the day, those of rationalism and the *Sturm und Drang*; it also initiated a public debate, which garnered the attention, among others, of Herder, Lessing, Lichtenberg, and Mendelssohn. In the meantime, over the course of 1776, Wieland published the response of an anonymous author in defense of the enthusiasts (which Hamann reports having read ten times with great delight), but not without including in the same issue an "editorial report" in which he sharply criticizes it. For Hamann, this was too much to bear, especially given his suspicion that the anonymous author was none other than his close friend and protégé, Herder; and so he furiously began his response, desperately waiting for an answer from Herder regarding his role in the whole affair. When he finally received Herder's reply, however, and was sorry to learn that he was not the anonymous author after all, his interest abated, he put down his "scorpion whip," as he called it (ZH III, p. 292), and the "Aprons" remained a fragment. As it turned out, the anonymous author was the Swiss pastor and gifted disciple of Lavater, Johann Kaspar Häfeli (1754–1811).

gender in the German language, titled "Wächter und Burgermeister," which was perfectly suited to Hamann's purposes).[42]

Fortunately, one does not have to decode "Aprons of fig leaves" in all its minutiae in order to gather its basic theme, which is in many ways a reprise of the *Essay of a Sibyl on Marriage*. There Hamann's focus was the mystery of marriage; here his focus is the mystery of shame, stemming from his reading of Genesis 3: 7: "Then the eyes of both were opened, and they knew that they were naked; and they sewed fig leaves together and made themselves aprons." This passage, to which the title is an explicit allusion, is significant to Hamann for several reasons. Firstly, it ironizes and highlights the fraudulent nature of everything that in a fallen world passes for "enlightenment" – the kind of "enlightenment" that is grasped at as something within one's reach (cf. Gen. 3: 6), as opposed to the true enlightenment of the Holy Spirit that can be received only through Christ (Luke 24: 3) as a gift from above (cf. John 3: 27). Secondly, it suggests that fallen reason, rather than admitting its fallenness, its guilt – rather than standing the test of its nakedness, and patiently awaiting the redemptive clothing of the Holy Spirit (Luke 24: 49; cf. Gen. 3: 21) – is quick to cover up its poverty like Adam and Eve and boast of its "soundness."[43] Moreover, it highlights the comedy that, even while lacking the illumination of the Holy Spirit, who mediates true judgment (John 14: 8f.), fallen, secular reason nevertheless claims for itself the right of judgment, indeed, as Kant proudly declares in the name of all pseudo-enlightenment, the right to criticize literally everything.[44] Therein for Hamann lies the dark comedy of secular reason, notwithstanding its claims to "enlightenment" – cut off, as it is, from the source of all light and wisdom. Thirdly, it suggests to Hamann the proper method of Christian authorship; for if his rationalistic contemporaries are to be clothed with the "true genius" and "true muse" of the Holy Spirit, they must first be stripped of their pretensions and submit to divine scrutiny; and it is ultimately to this end, as a reminder of eschatological judgment, that his three-part "comedy" is dedicated.[45]

Perhaps the most daring aspect of "Aprons of fig leaves," however, is again what Hamann has to say about sex. And here too he expects to offend the moral sensibility of his age. Thus, in a rather shocking letter to Herder regarding its genesis, he

---

[42] See ZH III, p. 305 (*HH* V, p. 305). The three parts were to be: "Emetic of a vocative" (*Nachhelf eines Vocativs*); "Good Friday penance for Capuchins" (*Charfreytagsbuße für Capuziner*); and "Bridge without supports" (*Brücke ohne Lehne*). By the time he stopped working on it, however, having apparently been reconciled with Wieland (see ZH IV, p. 195), Hamann had only finished the first part, which is based on a quarrel depicted in Claudius' poem between a mayor and a night watchman over the proper gender of the German word "Glocke." In a way that appealed to Hamann's sense of humor, the poem served to reveal the sexual roots of language, which in this case presented a cause of "embarrassment" to the mayor. At the same time, as the title suggests, Hamann means through this comical tale to come to the "assistance" of Wieland, who is himself the "vocative" (the "caller"), whose grammar needs to be corrected or, literally, "purged." As for the second part, we can assume that in it Hamann had planned again to deal with Starck, since the dedication to Büsching is principally concerned with the specious, pseudo-coptic derivation of the name and title of Starck's book, *Hephästion*. The title of the third part, as Hamann's correspondence with Häfeli attests, takes its image from Luther's sermon on the narrow gate (Matt. 7: 13–14). See Martin Luther, *Werke. Kritische Gesamausgabe* (Weimar: H. Böhlaus Nachfolger, 1906–61), vol. 32, p. 502. Cf. ZH IV, p. 201.

[43] As he puts it elsewhere, "Why do we sew for ourselves aprons of fig leaves when garments of skin are prepared for us? Is it perhaps that we would rather not be divested at all, but covered up, so that we will not be found naked?" (N II, p. 362).

[44] "Our age is the true [*eigentliche*] age of criticism, to which everything must submit. Both religion and law-making seek to escape it, the one through its holiness, the other through its majesty" (Kant, *Critique of Pure Reason*, tr. Norman Kemp Smith (New York: St Martin's Press, 1965), A xi, p. 9.

[45] ZH III, p. 292. In this letter to Hartknoch, Hamann goes so far as to say that his *Coemoedia*, should it be finished, should surpass that of "*il Dante, il divino Aretino* [Ariosto] and *el Poeta Christiano* of the mad Roland [the *Song of Roland*]."

writes: "The ideal of my embryo, in case it should be born, will draw upon itself the unavoidable judgment: *He has an unclean spirit*."[46] On the face of it, it is difficult to fathom what Hamann could have meant by such an alarming statement. A second letter to Herder, however, offers a possible explanation. He says that he is "anxious to read [Schlosser's] folk catechism, since no instruction in Christianity seems possible to me without the ... mystery of the Holy Trinity ... In short, what are considered the *pudenda* of religion, and the superstition to *circumcise* them, and the madness even *to cut them out*: herein consists the content of my embryo."[47] What is striking about this passage is, first of all, Hamann's application of the word *pudenda* in reference to the doctrines of revealed religion (e.g., the doctrine of the Trinity, etc.). By this he means not only that the *pudenda* (as a metonym for the creativity of sexual love) and the Trinity are related mysteries, as we have already seen, but that they are all the more intimately related in that, curiously, *each is shameful to fallen reason*. This leads to his second point: the tendency of reason either to "circumcise" these topics, i.e., to make them more rational (as in the Stoic view of sex and the passions, and the Trinitarian heresy of Sabellianism), or, more drastically, to "cut them out" (as in Origen's infamous act and the similarly economical teachings of Unitarianism) – to which scandalous topics, one could certainly add the many miracles of the Gospel or the scandal of the Cross, whose paradox Nietzsche at least understood but Hegel found necessary to translate into speculative terms.[48]

On the one hand, then, by his association of Christian doctrines with the *pudenda*, Hamann means to emphasize the "offensiveness" of Christianity to fallen, secular reason, and to this end he is not afraid to embody the offense in the very language and in the very way in which he writes. (All of which indicates, once again, how fundamentally important Hamann was to Kierkegaard, even if the latter could say in the words of his pseudonym, Climacus, while wholly agreeing with Hamann: "I could not imagine that I, who as a rule am so diffident and fearful, dared to write anything like that."[49]) On the other hand, Hamann means to say that there is something fanatical about fallen, secular reason, namely, its inability to tolerate what falls outside the scope of its understanding and mastery, outside the "limits of reason alone"; for to the very extent that it suffers from such loss of control, to the extent, that is, that it is "maddened by mystery," it is prone to puritanical and fanatical acts of elimination. This begins, as we have seen, with Descartes's experimental self-mutilation in the *Meditations*, whereby reason turns, as it were, against the senses and the phenomenal world, which are uncertain and lie beyond its control. The same logic is evident again in the Stoic attack on the passions, against which Hamann was reacting in the *Aesthetica*; and it continues, as Hamann sees it, when the same fanatical logic is inevitably turned against the "*pudenda*" of revealed religion.[50] Hence the attempt by *Aufklärungstheologen* to cleanse God of all "irrational," historical accretions like the doctrine of the Trinity; and, in a similar vein, anticipating the theology of Rudolf Bultmann, to cleanse Scripture of all "mythological" content. Indeed, in

---

[46] ZH III, pp. 349f.

[47] Ibid.

[48] See Nietzsche, *Beyond Good and Evil*, tr. Walter Kaufmann, in *Basic Writings of Nietzsche* (New York: Modern Library, 1968), §46: "Modern men, obtuse to all Christian nomenclature, no longer feel the gruesome superlative that struck a classical taste in the paradoxical formula 'God on the cross.'"

[49] Kierkegaard, *Philosophical Fragments*, p. 53.

[50] Of course, no work is a better example in this regard – to the point of parody – than Kant's 1793 work, *Religion within the Limits of Reason Alone*; and given how perfectly it embodies the anti-type of Hamann's thought, and how ripe it would have been for his deconstructive genius, it is regrettable that he did not live long enough to respond to it.

accordance with Hamann's axiom that to attack the creative parts of the human being is ultimately to attack the "creative parts" of God, what first befell the "whole man" similarly befalls the "whole God," as the human being is reduced to a mere rational agent (without heart) and God is reduced to a mere monad (without hypostases). Thus, in two fanatical strokes, guided by a purist fantasy, reason enacts a double "castration," which is tantamount to a double elimination, of God and man. This is why Hamann consistently identifies the man of "pure reason" with the figure of a eunuch, and why he considers the rationalist's "god" to be a similarly impotent and ultimately lifeless *ens rationis*.

The positive content of "Aprons of fig leaves," then, and with it Hamann's antidote to the sterility of modernity, is thus a profound respect for the corresponding mysteries of sex and the Trinity, which he sees as corresponding wellsprings of human and divine creativity. Indeed, for Hamann, the flourishing of culture depends precisely on the degree to which these mysteries are regarded not only *as mysteries*, but as *corresponding* mysteries: one profundity, one depth, mirroring the other. If they are profaned by secular reason, on the other hand, i.e., eliminated as mysteries, then the creative bond between heaven and earth will be broken, and culture will degenerate into sterility and nihilism. Thus, whereas the *Aufklärer* disregard the mysteries of sex and the Trinity, Hamann highlights them. But, on the other hand, where prudish pietists would separate them, he combines them – without, however, confusing them. He is, in a word, *shameless*.[51] And so, to the scandal of "our moralistic century," as a form of shock therapy, he not only speaks of God and sex in the same breath, but highlights the very passages in Scripture that would tend to offend well-meaning pietists and rationalists alike. For example, in his opening paragraph against Wieland, in a striking play on the title of Marcus Aurelius' meditations *To Himself* (ΤΩΝ ΕΙΣ ΕΑΥΤΟΝ), he compares the "frosty" "Self in and to itself" (Σεαυτον εν Σεαυτῳ), as the highest ideal of his age, to the "fiery" Son of Man in Ezekiel's vision, "whose *pudenda* are living members, which long for their resolution and transfiguration –"; and then proceeds to highlight the following verse: " 'Upward from what appeared like the loins I saw something that looked like fire enclosed all around; and downward from what looked like the loins I saw something that looked like fire, and there was a splendor all around' "(Ezek. 1: 27).[52] The selection of this verse is typical of Hamann's sensibility. His point, however, is to show up the difference between the "unfruitfulness" of the Enlightenment hero, who *knows* no other, but is wholly "in and to himself" – like the god of Aristotle and Hegel – and the ecstatic potency of God, who so loved the world that he entered into it (John 3: 16), and who in Christ, the Bridegroom, longs to consummate history with his Bride.

[51] It is crucial to observe here, however, that Hamann's "shamelessness" is not that of an antinomianism; for sin remains something of which one should be ashamed. Rather, it is a function of that freedom from condemnation, and return to paradisal innocence, that comes through Christ, the lamb who alone takes away the sin – and the shame – of the world. See Rom. 8: 1.

[52] N III, p. 207.

9

Fragments of an Apocryphal Sibyl: On Rational and Apocalyptic Religion

Natural religion *is for me the same as a* natural *[i.e., universal] language, a real absurdity [Unding], an* ens rationis.

Hamann to Herder[1]

Are not our philosophers the holy seed of Descartes, and our philologists that of Leclerc; and do we not owe it to their common merits in the matter of dogmatics that the spirit of paganism has been dissolved into the basic truths of a natural religion, and that the spirit of Christianity has been dissolved into the same primal matter? Is it not a wonder ... if the pagans become Christians, and those once Christian become pagans, and the end makes its way back into the beginning?

a draft of Konxompax[2]

In the popular imagination, as shaped by modern historiography, the Enlightenment is known as the "age of reason," arising like the sun against the background of the so-called "dark ages," i.e., centuries of superstition and uncritical deference to tradition. Once, so the story goes, reason bowed before "miracles, mystery, and authority" (in the phrase of Dostoevsky's grand inquisitor). Now, no doctrine is regarded as worthy of belief, and no authority worthy of obedience, that cannot endure the scrutiny of rational investigation. As Kant famously and programmatically put it in the preface to the first edition of his *Critique of Pure Reason* in 1781,

> Our age is the true [*eigentliche*] age of criticism, to which everything must submit. Both religion and law-making seek to escape it, the one through its holiness, the other through its majesty. But then they arouse against themselves justified suspicion and cannot claim unfeigned respect, which reason grants only to that which can endure its unfettered and public examination.[3]

And it was precisely on this account that the *Aufklärer* considered themselves modern-day disciples of Socrates, believing that they were merely continuing the same kind of critical questioning of religious and literary tradition that one finds, for example, in the *Republic*.

---

[1] ZH IV, p. 195.

[2] From a draft of *Konxompax*. See Ingemarie Manegold's dissertation, *Johann Georg Hamanns Schrift "Konxompax"* (Heidelberg: Carl Winter Verlag, 1961), p. xxxv, and N III, pp. 215–28. The translations in this chapter are based on Manegold's critical edition.

[3] Kant, *Critique of Pure Reason*, A xii.

But just as Hamann turned the tables on the Enlighteners' conception of Socrates and Socratic dialectic, he also turned the tables on the Enlightenment's *Religionskritik* and corresponding doctrine of religion. On the one hand, in order to do so, he needed merely to point out that whatever we understand by reason is the product of centuries of tradition – that reason is, as it were, nothing other. This being so, the Enlighteners' claims regarding the genealogical purity and automatic self-evidence of reason, upon which their claims to judge tradition rested, were shamelessly hypocritical – as though reason, which is itself a product of tradition and, in any case, inextricable from it, could be set up *against* tradition as an *independent* and authoritative judge of it.[4] On the other hand, Hamann could simply point out that the Enlighteners had simply replaced God with reason, retaining for reason all of the divine attributes hitherto accorded, for example, to Scripture (e.g., "authority, infallibility, perfection, sufficiency, perspicuity, and efficacy"), and even the power of self-interpretation (as Luther put it, *sacra scriptura sui ipsius interpres*).[5] In short, Hamann could claim that the Enlighteners had merely replaced revealed religion with their own idolatrous form of "natural" religion, complete with its own priests, devotees, and superstitions – of which the shrine to the "Goddess of Reason" installed in Notre Dame in Paris during the French revolution is an obvious example. Finally, in view of the fact that many of the *Aufklärer*, like Starck and Lessing, were also Freemasons, he could point out that their supposedly "natural" religion of reason was itself a modern-day "mystery religion" full of its own esoteric and exoteric doctrines.

Accordingly, over against the *apocryphal* Gnosis of reason, which promised a pseudo-enlightenment (Gen. 3: 4), the point of Hamann's "Mystery Writings," was essentially to defend the *apocalyptic* (i.e., revealed) mysteries of the Christian *faith*. And to this extent, inasmuch as he felt himself to be contending with a spurious Gnosis, he in many ways writes as a modern-day Irenaeus or Augustine, whose debate with the *Aufklärer* reprises Irenaeus' debate with the Gnostics and Augustine's debate with the Manicheees. A further point of these writings, accordingly, was to highlight the contrast between Christianity as a *sacramental* religion, which revels in the senses on account of the *incarnation*, and the spurious alchemy of reason's ritual purification from tradition and sense experience. In any case, from Hamann's perspective, the choice was ultimately not between the obscure, irrational teachings of an ancient creed and the plain, universal teachings of reason, as though the one were a matter of dogma and the other a matter of reason, but between the apocalyptic mysteries of Christianity, as plainly *revealed* as Christ on the Cross, and an apocryphal cult of reason, whose *secret, unspoken mystery* is the mystery of nihilism.

---

[4] This is not to say that there is no place for criticism and judgment in human affairs. As Hamann says, the human being is defined by the "critical and archontic dignity of a political animal" (N III, p. 48). The difference between his anthropology and that of the Enlightenment, however, is that, for Hamann, reason is always the judge *and* product of tradition and cannot presume radically to separate itself from the latter without becoming fanatical.

[5] Thus in Kant the self-interpreting power of Scripture is replaced by the self-critique of reason itself. As Oswald Bayer puts it, "In Kant the authority hitherto accorded to Scripture is assumed by the authority of reason. This can easily be shown point by point: *auctoritas, infallibilitas, perfectio, sufficientia, perspicuitas* and *efficacia*, above all the power of self-interpretation, of criticism, of autonomous judgment, and the power to establish norms – all of these effective modes and attributes of Holy Scripture, which can only be effective modes and attributes of the Triune God, are ascribed by Kant to reason – albeit, in the final analysis, not to theoretical, but to practical reason" (*Autorität und Kritik: Zur Hermeneutik und Wissenschaftstheorie* (Tübingen: Mohr-Siebeck, 1991), p. 44). See also Martin Luther, *Werke. Kritische Gesamausgabe* (Weimar: H. Böhlaus Nachfolger, 1906–61), vol. 7, p. 97.

DOUBTS (ABOUT REASON) AND IDEAS
(ABOUT THE MYSTICAL BODY OF CHRIST)

Formally, *Doubts and Ideas about a Mixed Review of the* Allgemeine Deutsche Bibliothek is addressed to Nicolai, i.e., "Cousin Nabal," in the voice of Abigail (1 Sam. 25), and as such represents the conclusion of Hamann's published debate with the famous Berlin *Aufklärer* and editor.[6] But as with all of Hamann's writings, there is much more going on than meets the eye. At one level, like *New Apology of the Letter h*, the work is concerned with orthography, in this case with orthographical guidelines that had been proposed by a certain school teacher named "Martin the lame." As a self-proclaimed reformer of the German language, Martin had recommended the following threefold rule: that one write according to the *best* pronunciation, the *best* German provinces, and the usage of the *best* German authors. As Hamann points out, however, this begs the question of what in each case is to be determined as "best." Moreover, his "rational" attempt at standardization has brought about no "clarification" [*Aufklärung*], but instead "a new Babel of confusions," stemming from his blindness to the "arbitrary maxims" at play in all of reason's allegedly pure deductions.[7]

Another point Hamann makes in this context, anticipating Nietzsche, is that the Enlighteners' muddled philosophy is a consequence of their grammar. Specifically he points out their predilection for the first person, the "beloved I," which lies at the root of their own egological philosophy. In other words, the suggestion is that self-love, and not any genuine universalism, is the real root of their dogmatic rationalism, and that reason, divorced from tradition, will inevitably resolve into the infinitely plastic desires of so many private, self-interested wills. Furthermore, he suggests, it is precisely because they see everything in the first person that they cannot understand the indirect, *kenotic* form of his own authorship, which betrays a curious absence of first-person speech. Thus, contrasting himself with all fashionable authors [*Modescribenten*], who seek to make a name for themselves, he compares his own baldness to the ample hair of Absalom (2 Sam. 14: 26), who was hanged by it (2 Sam. 18: 9).[8]

From questions of orthography, *Doubts and Ideas* thus passes over into questions of style; and here again, just as the former turned out to be surprisingly significant, so too do the latter. To be sure, a rationalist may judge style to be relatively unimportant; for him it has but one purpose: the abstract clarity, and the attainment, as far as possible, of universal intelligibility – in relation to which any stylistic traits peculiar to the individual are either accidental or superfluous. For Hamann, however, it has a far profounder significance, since for him the content of one's philosophy cannot be cannot be separated from the form of one's style any more than one's philosophy can be separated from one's life (or, as we shall see in a later chapter, one's religious convictions can be separated from one's political actions). Indeed, for Hamann, style is not so much a servant of abstract clarity as it is a *direct expression* of the *individuality* of the author. As Goethe once observed, "The principle to which

---

[6] That Nicolai should be addressed as Nabal is hardly flattering, since his name means "fool" (1 Sam. 25: 25), but this should not be taken for a gesture of hostility. Rather it is a case in point of Hamann's hallmark method of "metaschematically" transposing his contemporaries *into* Scripture, wherein they might see themselves and their role in life anew; and to this end, he speaks to Nicolai-Nabal in the voice of his "better half," Abigail.

[7] N III, p. 183.

[8] N III, p. 179.

all Hamann's statements can be referred is this: 'Everything that one sets out to perform, whether by deed, by word, or otherwise, must spring from all one's united powers; everything taken in isolation is worthless.' A magnificent maxim! but hard to follow."[9] From this perspective one can begin to see why for Hamann the question of style manages to touch upon everything. What Goethe failed to point out, however, is that for Hamann the question of style is also and above all a theological question, specifically a Trinitarian question, inasmuch as the Son is, as it were, the "style" or outward expression of the Father (John 1: 18; Heb. 1: 3), and inasmuch as the Father and Son are "one" (John 10: 30). As far as Hamann's own style is concerned, therefore, this means that the Christological content of his authorship should be clothed in an appropriately Christological form, i.e., a form that is initially dark and inscrutable to reason (cf. John 1: 5), a form that will be misunderstood and rejected (John 1: 10–11), a form that will even appear "foolish" and "incomprehensible" (1 Cor. 1: 18ff.), but which nevertheless contains true enlightenment (John 1: 9). Accordingly, in one of his clearest statements about his pyrotechnic style, Hamann says that his words emit an initial smoke, but then, in keeping with the characteristics of fire, burst into flame.[10]

As haphazard as its progression may at first seem, *Doubts and Ideas* thus passes logically from the topic of orthography to the topic of style to the topic of the economy of salvation, since it is here that we see something of the divine "style," and since it is in and through the divine style, i.e., through various kinds of divine self-expression, culminating in Christ (Heb. 1: 1–3), that the truth of God is revealed. But just as the *Aufklärer* cannot appreciate style as an expression of the individual author, neither can they appreciate salvation history as a means of *divine* self-expression. Still less can they see that salvation history is the means by which God chooses to "open our eyes" and heal reason of its inveterate blindness.[11] For, from the outset, they have placed their trust in the purity and soundness of reason, and its ability to discern the truth *apart* from any historical revelation. Indeed, they assume that history has nothing of ultimate significance to convey that could not be arrived at by reason alone, and this is why history cannot help but appear to them as a field full of dry bones (Ezek. 37: 2). And yet, as Hamann incisively points out, "The soundness of reason is the cheapest, most self-authorized, and most shameless self-aggrandizement, whereby everything is presupposed that remains to be proved, and whereby every free investigation of the truth is more brutally barred than by the inerrancy of the Roman Catholic Church."[12] In other words, the *Aufklärer* begin with reason without ever calling reason itself into question, when their starting point, the infallibility of reason, its postlapsarian "soundness," is precisely what is in question (though Kant's *Critique of Pure Reason,* published five years later, could be seen as an attempted response to Hamann's repeated challenge in this regard). Thus Hamann speaks not of reason, but of reason's hypocritical "misuse." And this is why their peremptory critique of the "religion of our *fathers* and our *children*" from an allegedly sound and neutral standpoint, which Hamann calls at once an *Ungrund* and *Übelstand*, yields in the end nothing but "arbitrary principles, sophistries, word games, and empty boasting ..."[13]

---

[9]   Goethe, *Werke* (Weimar, 1890), *Dichtung und Wahrheit,* book XII, p. 108.
[10] N III, p. 188. Cf. Jas. 1: 17, 18; Heb. 12: 29.
[11] Cf. N II, p. 64.
[12] N III, p. 189.
[13] Ibid.

Having called into question his contemporaries' hypocritical claims regarding the purity and soundness of reason – claims that he will utterly demolish in his *Metakritik* of Kant – Hamann then exposes the ultimate *pudenda* of reason, i.e., the shame that it miserably tries to cover up (cf. Gen. 3: 7): namely, that it can neither ground itself, nor lay claim to its own purity or integrity, nor even know anything with certainty except *by faith*. This is the radical point of Hume's skepticism that Hamann brought to bear with singular force upon the self-confident rationalism of his day – paving the way for the existentialist philosophies of the nineteenth century, like those of the late Schelling and Kierkegaard, which similarly recognized that reason cannot get along without certain assumptions. As he puts it,

> Since *faith* belongs to *the natural preconditions* of our cognitive powers and to the *fundamental drives* of our soul; and since every *universal principle* rests upon *good faith*; and since all *abstractions* are necessarily *arbitrary*: the most famous theorists of religion in our time deprive themselves even of their *premises* and *middle terms*, which are indispensable to the genesis of *rational deductions*; they are *ashamed* of their own instruments or make a *mystery* of them, where there can be no *mystery*, and cover the natural shame of their favorite sin like *Adam*.[14]

In other words, what reason shamefully tries to cover over is its dependence upon faith, even though, according to Hamann, it belongs to the "preconditions of our cognitive powers" and is "indispensable to the genesis of rational deductions." Indeed, apart from faith reason cannot even account for the fact of existence, or why, for that matter, there should be any reason at all (a point that is fundamental to the late Schelling's critique of Hegel). For, as Haman goes on to say, "just as all forms of irrationality [*Unvernunft*] presuppose the existence of reason and its misuse: so must all religions have a relation to *faith* in a single, independent, and living *truth*, which, like our *existence*, is older than our *reason* ..."[15] In this regard too, therefore, Hamann speaks of reason's hypocritical "misuse," for not only is it not absolute, it is also eminently *unreasonable*. It is not reason functioning by a faith, which would strengthen its natural light by the light of the Logos (of which it is always a dim reflection), but reason in a priori denial of every dependence, hypocritically and, in Hamann's view, *unnaturally* attempting to run by its own power, *sola ratione*, as it were (without admitting the necessity, as even Plato arguably did, of a kind of *pistis* or *rationis fides*).

At this point in *Doubts and Ideas*, having shown the hypocrisy of the modern doctrine of reason, Hamann proceeds to show why his contemporaries are unable to understand history, specifically, ancient religion. For him reason was never meant to be divorced from faith; nor was it meant to be divorced from history. Rather, faith in what history reveals by way of an inspired tradition was meant precisely to aid reason in discovering the truth. In short, illumined by faith, reason is meant to learn something from history. For Hamann's contemporaries, however, who, in the name of a radical autonomy, have perverted "the natural use of reason" – namely, by divorcing it from faith and historical testimony – history has little to say; it is as dead as the bones in Ezekiel's vision (Ezek. 37). As a result, to the extent that history is not seen with the eyes of faith, to the extent that it does not appear as a living testimony, as a "speech to the creature through the creature," its witness is inevitably

---

[14] N III, p. 190.
[15] N III, p. 191.

distorted and darkened, refashioned according to the tastes and prejudices of the time. Specifically, as Hamann observes, with Starck undoubtedly in mind, the importance of paganism tends to be exaggerated, the importance of Judaism (as anything more than natural religion) tends to be downplayed or denied, and the "day of salvation" in Christ tends to be obscured:

> Because they have forsaken the natural use of reason, they receive in themselves the reward of their error ... and because they study religion from the vantage of the *novels* and *legends* of the self-transfiguration of human nature, they have become vain in their thoughts and their senseless minds are darkened, and since they took themselves to be wise, they became wandering fools or their squires, and lucubrate the nights of paganism brighter and brighter, but the day of salvation, darker and darker – instead of light, cold and frost – neither day nor night.[16]

In other words, having forsaken the "natural use of reason" and embraced in its place an abstract rationality divorced from history and tradition, they *eo ipso* cannot see what nature and history reveal. As Hamann put it years before in the *Socratic Memorabilia*, "Just as nature is given to us to open our eyes, so history [is given] to open our ears."[17] Indeed, for Hamann, such is the ironic effect of the Enlightenment, that those who embrace its doctrines become deaf and blind. They neither see God in nature, nor hear him speaking through history; and that, Hamann suggests, is the self-incurred judgment upon their error: unable to believe in a God who reveals himself historically, they are unable to see Christianity as the fulfillment of human history:

> Thus it comes about that they reject a religion that is in every sense [of the word] universal and fully corresponding to the secret history and nature of the human race, whose spirit and truth contains the very manifold wisdom they seek without recognizing it; and that they attempt to erect an idol out of the dust of the latest teaching and fashion of their winter's day ... that they exchange a *covenantal religion* ... for anti-Socratic, self-flattering shrines [*Galanterie-Schreine*], which outwardly portray a scheme of reason, but inwardly the curse of its decay.[18]

In short, the *Aufklärer* have exchanged the truth of God for a lie (cf. Rom. 1: 25). They have exchanged the *covenantal* religion of Christianity (as based in covenantal Judaism), a religion from above that satisfies the deepest needs and desires of human nature (its need for redemption from sin and its desire for transfiguration), for their own man-made religion, which merely flatters their pride (herein lies the anti-Socratic moment), but conceals the true poverty and moribund condition of what they so proudly call "reason."

Moreover, not only do they not see what is revealed in Christianity; they do not even see what is there to be seen in pagan religion, which would have helped to prepare them for Christianity: "Whence," Hamann asks, "that *mythological* and *poetic* vein running through all religions, their folly and vexing form in the eyes of a heterodox, incompetent, ice-cold, dog-poor philosophy ...[?]"[19] In other words, if religion were reducible to a purely rational content, if it were convertible with philosophy, as the Enlighteners would like to believe, whence that "mythological and poetic

---

[16] N III, pp. 190f. The references are to Rom. 1: 21f. and to *Don Quixote*, which Hamann cites in the original.
[17] N II, p. 64.
[18] N III, p. 191.
[19] N III, p. 192.

vein" running through its history? Does this alone not testify to the fact that the truths of religion transcend reason's grasp, as though nothing but a mythological or poetic form would be suitable to their communication? Indeed, for Hamann it does; and for this reason he cannot countenance for a moment the "heterodox" and ultimately "incompetent" attempts of the *Aufklärer* to reduce religion to the impoverished terms of reason alone.[20]

Undoubtedly, what is most striking and original here, however, is not Hamann's observation that religions tend to be expressed in mythological and poetic forms, or that the Enlighteners would do well to take these forms seriously (inasmuch as they point not to an irrational, but to a super-rational content), but rather the connection he establishes between paganism and Christianity: specifically, the fact that he attributes to pagan religion the same vexing, super-rational, even "foolish" form that for him defines Christian revelation (1 Cor. 1: 18ff). For example, as we have seen in Chapter 2, Hamann compares Zeus' amorous self-emptyings with God's self-emptying in Christ – to the point of the "folly" of death on a Cross (Phil. 2: 6ff.). But if the mythological revelations of paganism share with Christianity a "foolish and vexing" form, for Hamann it is also the case that the former are but dreamlike anticipations of the latter. In other words, though both belong to a single providential economy, they are distinguished from one another as type from fulfillment. Accordingly, for Hamann, paganism's fabulous stories of divine condescension and human deification, of gods becoming men and men becoming gods, are mysterious, but ultimately obscure mythological prefigurations of the *real* story of divine incarnation and human divinization in Christ, i.e., the real story of God becoming man in Jesus of Nazareth (John 1: 14), and of the members of his mystical body, the Church, being transformed "into his likeness from one degree of glory to another" (2 Cor. 3: 18). This, for Hamann, is the truth at the heart of the mystery of religion. As he strikingly puts it in the core passage of *Doubts and Ideas*:

> Among all the revelations of which the human soul is capable, and which it perceives more often in a dream than in a wakeful state, no other has so intimate, intuitive, and fruitful a relationship to all the undetermined capacities, inexhaustible desires, infinite needs and passions of our nature … Indeed, no other *plan* than that which has been revealed by *Christ*, the *head*, and by his *body*, the church, explains the mysteries of that supreme and only *majesty*, which is most hidden [but at the same time] most pressing to communicate itself; and does so in a way that is more analogous to the entire *system* of *nature* and *human society*, and more adequate to the most *arbitrary laws* of sound *reason* and the most *necessary syllogisms* of living *experience*. The mustard seed of *anthropomorphosis* and *apotheosis*, which is hidden in the *hearts* and *mouths* of all religions, is manifest here in the full stature, in the middle of the garden, of a *tree* of *knowledge* and of *life* – all *philosophical* contradictions and the entire *historical* puzzle of our *existence*, the most impenetrable night of its *termini a quo* and *termini ad quem* are resolved by the *original testimony* [*Urkunde*] of the *incarnate* Word. The *spirit* of *prophecy* is of such *testimony* as this, and the reward it promises is "a new name that no one knows except the one who receives it."[21]

---

[20] Needless to say, Hamann's rejection of the Enlighteners' "purely rational" religion applies equally to the "demythologicizing" program of Rudolf Bultmann, which sought to dispense with all mythological form on the way to some pure "existential" content.

[21] N III, p. 192. See Gen. 2: 9; Rev. 2: 17, where Christ, speaking to the Church at Ephesus, mentions a heretical group called the Nicolaitans: "Yet this is to your credit: you hate the works of the Nicolaitans, which I also hate" (Rev. 2: 6). The suggestion here is that Nicolai (-Nabal), the publisher and, in Hamann's view, "heresiarch" of the Berlin Enlightenment, stands in need of a new name, which only Christ can give.

In many ways this passage reveals the heart of Hamann's thought and vision of reality. The mystery of the ages, which is fully revealed in Christianity, is the mystery of anthropomorphosis and apotheosis, i.e., the mystery of God-becoming-man and man-becoming-god, a mystery that takes place in Christ within the crucible of the Church as the *corpus Christi mysticum* (and most centrally, one might say, within the double offering of the Eucharistic sacrifice). And yet, lacking the Spirit, *Aufklärer* have proudly rejected this mystery, having replaced it with their own Pelagian doctrines of *self*-enlightenment and *self*-transformation. But their rejection of it, Hamann goes on to say, is unreasonable:

> If the theorists lack the *Spirit* to believe the fundamental doctrines of Christianity of the *transfiguration* of *humanity* in *divinity* and of *divinity* in humanity through *fatherhood* and *sonship,* and are unable to sing with our Lutheran Church: 'The *fount* of *life* from *Him* does spring / From high in heaven from his *heart* –' if the Nicolaitans are ashamed of the divine *power* and the divine *wisdom* in the *Word* of the *Cross,* and if they stumble upon it: it is nevertheless *unreasonable* in the extreme on this account so wantonly to deny or dismiss truths which, by virtue of their [supernatural] character should be foolish and offensive to the natural man; and it is just as immoral and irresponsible to deprive others of them ...[22]

In the final part of *Doubts and Ideas* Hamann continues his sharp criticism of the *Aufklärer* and what he considers their misuse of reason, pointing out, among other things, that the morality they advocate in the name of "natural religion" is ultimately a cloak for their general hatred of actual historical religions. Moreover, in this regard, he not only prophesies that their project is bankrupt and doomed to fail – since "morality" apart from faith and tradition is groundless and remains to be "invented" – but points to an ultimate harmony in the thinking of these "free spirits" between their hatred of religion and their hatred of man.[23] At bottom, Hamann says, their philosophy is one of "rebellion," and so he goes on to prophesy that their doctrine of "freedom" will be propagated among the people, who, unwilling to wait patiently for the lawgiver's return (i.e., for any final judgment), will begin to make laws for themselves "after the manner of Aaron" (Exod. 32), only now according to the dictates of "sound reason." Indeed, Hamann says that modern secularists, having cut themselves off from the vital source of an inspired tradition, are like the eunuchs(!) Bigthan and Teresh, who conspire before the king's gate (Esther 2: 21). "True reason," on the other hand (NB, true *reason!*), Hamann says is found only through the self-denial and submission of reason, which demonstrates "the *soundness* of its strength in the *practice* and *fulfillment* of the *laws,* without *splitting hairs* over their *fittingness.*"[24] "*But if you judge the law,*" he says, quoting from James, "*you are not a doer* (nor a teacher) *of the law, but a judge*"; and "*If they do this when the wood is green, what will happen when it is dry?*"[25] In other words, Hamann prophetically suggests, if reason should presume to interrogate the law on its own terms, independently of faith and tradition, it will inevitably open the door to nihilism.

---

[22]   N III, pp. 192f.
[23]   N III, p. 193.
[24]   N III, p. 194.
[25]   Ibid. Jas. 4: 11; see also Luke 23: 31.

KONXOMPAX: AN APOCRYPHAL LETTER TO LESSING

Hamann's final attack on Starck was occasioned by two of Starck's works: his *Hephästion*, published in 1775, and the the second edition of his *Apology for the Order of the Freemasons* (*Apologie des Ordens der Frei-Mäuerer*), published in 1778. The latter work was essentially concerned with the same themes, only now in defense of the teachings of modern Freemasonry; and Hamann's *Konxompax: Fragments of an Apocryphal Sibyl on Apocalyptic Mysteries* (ΚΟΓΞΟΜΠΑΞ. *Fragmente einer apokryphischen Sibylle über apokalyptische Mysterien*) was written directly in response to it. The strange title of the work, which was published in 1779, derives from two inscrutable passwords, "konx" (κογξ) and "ompax" (ὄμπαξ), cited by Starck as allegedly spoken by initiates of certain mystery cults.[26]

But *Konxompax* is at the same time directed at several others: Gotthelf Samuel Steinbart, who had written a fashionable book dismissive of Augustine and Anselm, but, more famously, Gotthold Ephraim Lessing, who had recently embroiled Germany in a furious debate over his publication of Reimarus' *Fragments* (1774–8).[27] In fact, the ultimate target of Hamann's own *Fragments* was not so much Steinbart or even Starck, but the far more influential Lessing (whom Hamann personally addresses toward the end of the work and, through Herder and Mendelssohn, still had hopes of befriending). For, as Hamann well realized, what was at issue in the *Fragmentenstreit* was nothing less than the status of Judaism and Christianity as revealed religions, whose legitimacy had been increasingly challenged by the demand of the age for a "natural" and hence universal religion, i.e., a religion founded not upon historical contingencies or notions like "divine election" (and all the prejudice and intolerance this was taken to imply), but upon the necessary, self-evident principles of reason. As Lessing famously put it in *On the Proof of the Spirit and of Power*, "Accidental truths of history can never become the proof of necessary truths of reason."[28] From Hamann's perspective, therefore, the entire historical foundation of Christianity was at stake; and so he writes to Herder in 1778 saying, "You can easily imagine, dearest friend!, that I have no lack of interest in the current crisis in theology."[29]

[26] *HH* V, p. 177. The principal modern source for the term is Hesychius' lexicon of 1668, which Hamann cites in the original edition of *Konxompax*: Κογξ, ὄμπαξ, ἐπιφώνημα τετελεσμένοις, καὶ τῆς δικαστικῆς ψήφου ἦχος, ὡς ὁ τῆς κλεψύδρας, περὶ (παρὰ Martin.) δὲ 'Αττικοῖς, βλόψ. (ὄμπαξ βόμπαξ, Sopingius.). As Hamann also notes, the term is discussed in Jean le Clerc's *Bibliothèque universelle* (1687). Cf. William Warburton's *The Divine Legation of Moses*, vol. 1, pp. 131–252. And in 1795 even Kant briefly discusses the significance of the term in a footnote of his manifesto *Zum ewigen Frieden*. For all his philological skill and months of lexicographical obsession, Hamann could not make head or tail of the word's original meaning. Thus, prompted by the Augustinian, Antonius Georgius' *Alphabetum Tibetanum* (1759, 1762), he tells Herder that he intends to learn Tibetan in order to find an answer and, more generally, to discover in the religion of the "great Lama" a key to the mysteries of paganism. See *HH* V, pp. 184f. Cf. *ZH* IV, pp. 96 and 199f. Thanks to R. Trent Pomplun for helpful conversations regarding these sources.

[27] The principal advocate of orthodoxy in the debate was the Hamburg pastor, Johann Melchior Goeze. Although Hamann considered him, intellectually speaking, Lessing's inferior, he nevertheless confessed to Jacobi that Goeze was in the right. See *ZH* V, p. 274: "Can one honestly pray a Christian Our Father when one is intellectually committed to a pan[the]istic system?"

[28] See Henry Chadwick (ed.) *Lessing's Theological Writings* (Stanford, CA: Stanford University Press, 1957), p. 53.

[29] *ZH* IV, p. 34. Quoted in *HH* V, p. 173.

The result of Hamann's involvement in this debate, *Konxompax,* is one of his most difficult, but also one of his most profound and oddly beautiful writings. It is written in the voice of a sibyl named Adelgunde, ostensibly the same sibyl who spoke in his *Essay on Marriage.* Only now she is concerned with the apocryphal, i.e., *secret,* mysteries of paganism and the apocalyptic, i.e., *revealed,* mysteries of Christianity. On the one hand, her prophecy is directed at would-be hierophants like Starck, who have forsaken the apocalyptic for the apocryphal. On the other hand, it is directed against modern philosophy itself, understood as a kind of modern-day mystery religion in its own right, whose a priori method could be seen as an analogous rite of purification, and whose final mystery is the mystery of nihilism.[30] Indeed, for Hamann, such is the ultimate vanity of the Enlightenment and the worship of "holy reason," once one has turned one's back on the authority of historical revelation and prophetic tradition and – when the claims of reason's self-evidence collapse, as he clearly foresaw – one has nothing left but ideologies or private opinions to fill the void.

But if, on the polemical side, the sibyl denounces the foreseeable results of philosophy divorced from prophetic tradition, this is the flipside of her positive message: that God has revealed himself historically, that reason should heed this fact, and, instead of looking to paganism for apocryphal mysteries, should realize that the mysteries of paganism and Judaism are fulfilled in the apocalyptic mystery of Christianity. And, specifically, recalling *Doubts and Ideas,* she understands this definitive mystery in terms of the mystical body of Christ, according to its double aspect of *anthropomorphosis* and *apotheosis, Menschwerdung* and *Gottwerdung,* incarnation and divinization. Hamann's hope, therefore, is that his contemporaries might see the mystery of Christianity anew. And to this extent, like the *Socratic Memorabilia,* which was an indirect communication to Kant and Berens concerning the matter of faith, *Konxompax* is ultimately an indirect letter to Lessing, whom Hamann very much respected, and a friendly plea for his conversion.

As it turns out, Lessing read Hamann's "letter." It was sent in April, 1779, via Herder in Weimar, who managed to have it published within a month and who immediately sent gift copies at Hamann's behest to Lessing and a number of others, including Matthias Claudius, F. C. Moser, Mendelssohn, Lavater, and, Goethe.[31] Along with the copy he sent to Lessing, Herder included a letter in which he furthered Hamann's request that Lessing continue his unfinished work *Ernst und Falk,* the first parts of which Hamann refers to in *Konxompax.* Lessing's reply to Herder is his only known reference to Hamann, and the only hint we have of his reaction:

> If you send the thing [i.e., the continuation of *Ernst and Falk*] to Hamann, assure him of my greatest respect. At the same time, I would rather have your judgment concerning it than his. For I would not understand him in every respect; at least I would not be able to be certain whether I understood him. His writings seem to be examinations drawn up for those who would claim to be polyhistorians. For they truly require a little knowledge of everything [*Panhistorie*]. It is easy to find someone who wanders; but it is difficult to meet someone who strolls.[32]

---

[30] N III, p. 219.

[31] N III, p. 183.

[32] Lessing, *Werke,* ed. J. Petersen and W. v. Olshausen (Berlin: Deutsches Verlagshaus Bong & Co. [1925]), vol. 18, p. 332, quoted in *HH* V, p. 183.

Lessing's attitude toward Hamann is typical of the greater lights of the age; even if they did not fully understand him, or have much sympathy for his profoundly Christian views, like Kant they nevertheless respected him. As for Goethe's judgment of the work, Herder soon wrote to Hamann to report, "Goethe sends his thanks. He has carefully collected all your writings in a case and has sucked on this one too with great pleasure." As for Herder's own estimation, he tells Hamann, "The more I question your sibyl, and here and there she approaches me, the more dawns on me, especially since I have read Starck's writings one more time. Its core is milk and honey, spices and balm."[33]

Turning now to the text itself, Hamann chose two mottos for the title vignette and a third for the verso. The first is from Proverbs, the second from Apuleius' *Metamorphoses,* and the third from one of Phaedrus' fables. The motto from Proverbs 9: 16–18 is cited in the Vulgate: "To those without sense she says: 'Stolen waters are sweet, and hidden bread is pleasant[!]' But they do not know that the giants are there, and that her guests are in the depths of the underworld" ("Vecordi locuta est: Aquae furtivae dulciores sunt et panis suavior! Et ignoravit, quod ibi sint Gigantes et in profundis inferni convivae eius").[34] These verses are clearly to be read in the context of a comparison between the ways of wisdom and the ways of folly.[35] At the same time, it is doubtless significant that Proverbs is attributed to Solomon, who was revered by the Freemasons in connection with the building of the temple. Indeed, it would be perfectly congruous with Hamann's standard procedure of taking a mutually respected authority and citing this authority in a way that his intended audience would not expect. Accordingly, here the authority of Solomon is used essentially to upbraid his Masonic audience for its foolish obsession with pagan mysteries, when "something greater than Solomon is here!" (Matt. 12: 42).

The second motto comes from Book XI of the *Metamorphoses.* Its context is a description of the cult of Isis and, specifically, Lucius' description of a pagan priest carrying an "image of the supreme deity" in procession: "[its] ineffable subject [being] in any case the higher religion, which must be kept hidden in great silence" ("altioris utcunque et mango silentio tegendae religionis argumentum ineffabile").[36] Notwithstanding Apuleius' paganism, Hamann would seem to mean that Christianity, which his contemporaries have forsaken, is the "higher religion" to which even paganism points.

The third motto comes from Phaedrus, and Hamann (possibly intentionally) provides the wrong reference. It comes from book IV of the fables, but the reference he gives is from the story of the "clown and the peasant" (*scurra et rusticus*) in book V. Since he recorded this reference on three different occasions, and since it accords perfectly with his humorous sensibility, the motto would seem to have an intentional double sense. The cited motto, in reality from book IV, reads in fragmented form as follows: "POETA. PARTICULONI. – – Quare, VIR SANCTISSIME, Si non ingenium, certe brevitatem."[37] Evidently, this is an ironic address to the "most saintly" Starck,

---

[33] ZH IV, p. 83. Cf. ZH V, p. 248, where Herder also mentions Goethe's special regard for Hamann's writings.

[34] N III, p. 215. The exclamation point after the Vulgate quotation is Hamann's.

[35] In his commentary, Schoonhoven puts it even more strongly (*HH* V, p. 191): "In Greek mythology, the giants were a desolate race that stormed Olympus, but were vanquished by the gods. They stand here for the demonic powers contending with the divine. In this first motto the problem is stated as pointedly as possible: either the table of the Lord or the table of demons (1 Cor. 10: 21)."

[36] N III, p. 215.

[37] N III, p. 216.

and an appeal that he appreciate Hamann's work for its "brevity, if not for its intellectual quality." It is also to Starck that the "erroneous" reference from book V would seem to apply. As the story of the "clown and peasant" goes, there was a clown whose act consisted in squealing like a pig while pretending to conceal a pig beneath his clothes; and when it was revealed that there was no pig, he received the crowd's applause. A peasant, who happened to have seen the performance, tries the same thing the following day, this time with a real pig concealed beneath his clothing. The pig squeals and he is laughed off the stage. The point of the parable, then, is that while Starck with his pagan mysteries impersonates the real thing and is applauded for it, Hamann, coming after him, delivers the real thing, the true mystery of Christianity, and is laughed off the stage.[38]

The text proper begins with a satirical gloss of a fragment from Starck's *Apology*:

> Whether or not it is attributable to *historical* circumstance, it nevertheless belongs to the mysteries of the mystery that the *holy fire* of a natural, beatifying religion has been kept hidden so long beneath the *bushel basket* of *Ceres* and the *Thalamus* [i.e., bed] of the *wine-god*, until the genuine descendents of the threshing floor and wine-press have restored it in the form of a *thick liquid* and fulfilled what was originally written in the other book of the Maccabees. (2 Macc. 1: 19–21)[39]

In this one sentence Hamann ingeniously presents Starck's view and supplants it with his own. According to Starck, the "holy fire" of a natural religion has lain dormant for centuries within the ancient mystery religions of paganism, like those of Eleusis and Orpheus, waiting all these years to be recovered by a modern-day hierophant, like Starck himself. By means of his allusion to Luke 11: 33, however ("No one after lighting a lamp puts it in a cellar or under a bushel, but on a stand, that those who enter may use the light"), Hamann implies that what has lain dormant and hidden for so long within the mysteries of paganism is not the holy fire of a natural religion but the holy fire of the Gospel. Thus, by implication, Hamann presents himself *vis-à-vis* Starck as the real hierophant and guardian of the pagan mysteries.

What Hamann criticizes in Starck's supposed recovery of a "natural religion" is not only his circumventing of Christianity on the way back to some allegedly pure teachings of paganism (e.g., regarding the soul's immortality, judgment, and recompense in the afterlife), but also the meager results of his investigation: "The allure of the darkness of the object has also enticed thinking philologists and learned philosophers, and in the end, like the 'honorable Demonax' with his dilemma, found it either a pure *nothing* or an ambiguous *something*, which are opposed to one another like good and evil."[40] Among such persons whom Hamann respected was William Warburton, who held "the whole sixth book of the *Aeneid* to be a description of the *Eleusinian* mysteries," and whose *The Divine Legation of Moses* was to a large

---

[38] See *HH* V, p. 192.

[39] N III, p. 217. Cf. Luke 8: 16.

[40] N III, p. 218. Demonax (*c.* AD 100), a witty Cynic, was allegedly the only Greek to refuse initiation into the Eleusinian mysteries. His dilemma, which served as his excuse, was that if he should approve of the mysteries and find them beneficial, he would proclaim the mysteries to all (thus profaning them); but if he should find them unacceptable or harmful, neither could he fail to express his negative opinion of them. See *HH* V, p. 199.

extent concerned with the subject of pagan hieroglyphics.[41] Hamann's point, therefore, being himself a philologist, is not to denigrate historical or philological research
into paganism as such. Rather, his point is that such research does not yield the kind
of definitive results that Starck thought he had achieved.

The next fragment is pregnant with meaning and contains Hamann's critical
assessment of the transcendental method and ultimate principles of the Enlightenment
(prior to the publication of Kant's *Critique*!). In the foregoing passage Hamann
claimed that modern investigations of paganism (with respect to the discovery of a
natural religion) left one either with "*nothing* or an ambiguous *something*." Now he
attributes the same ambiguous result to the methods of modern philosophy:

> These highest, most universal categories (*nothing* and *something*, *good* and *bad*) are, as
> is well known, the first principles (*Initia*) and final results (τελεται) of all theoretical
> and practical knowledge. It is from their combination and application through the
> intuition [*Anschauen*] of the *one* in the *many* that the extra- and super-sensible or tran-
> scendental light of reason, together with its torchbearer, *true science*, arises (about
> which light, principle, and *logos* our contemporary apostles preach in their *Opusculis
> profligatis* that it enlightens every man that comes into this and that world – by the
> narrow way – through the narrow gate).[42]

Aside from what this passage suggests in advance about Hamann's critique of Kant,
what is most striking is how Hamann reads modern philosophy: not as a pure enterprise based upon reason alone, but as a kind of modern-day mystery religion. Hence,
speaking of modern philosophy, his use of terms such as *initia* and τελεται, both of
which connote "the sacred mysteries"; hence too his contrast between the light of
reason and the light of the Gospel (1: 9); and hence, finally, his contrast between the
"narrow gate" of the Gospel (Matt. 7: 14) and the "narrow" method of modern
transcendentalism. In short, whereas the one is the way to the kingdom of heaven,
the latter is the way to "true science."

To be sure, modern transcendental philosophy is founded upon the notion that its
methods are pure (i.e., pure of the contingencies of time, history, and the senses). In
truth, however, as Hamann points out, its ostensibly pure, scientific methods betray
a curious historical connection to religious method. This is clear from his contrasting
use of "narrow," which is meant to show that, throughout its variants, modern
philosophy's transcendental method involves its own kind of *ascetical* detachment
(as, for example, in Descartes's founding separation from the senses, Kant's even
more rigorous transcendental deduction, and later Husserl's methodological *epoche*),
which leads through a secularized Carmelite "dark night of the senses" (heuristically
guided by a quasi-religious expectation of the reward of a higher *revelation*), beyond
the possibility of deception by the senses, into the *fanum* of pure reason, and from
there into the *sanctum sanctorum* of reason itself, where reason is communicated
to itself in mystical auto-communion and "enlightenment" begins to dawn. As
Schoonhoven puts it, "The sibyl interprets the Enlightenment's striving after reason
as a religion, indeed, as a mystery religion; one must be 'initiated' into it (*Initia*,

---

[41] N III, p. 217. In this context Hamann also refers to the work of John Gilbert Cooper, *The Life of Socrates* (London,
1749), p. 102.

[42] N III, p. 218. Clearly, much that we tend to attribute to Kant's critical philosophy was in fact in the air during this
time. See, for example, Johann August Eberhard's *Von dem Begriff der Philosophie und ihren Teilen*, which Hamann
himself cites in this connection. All of which goes to show that Kant's critical self-examination of reason was by no
means so pure an intellectual exercise as he made it out to be.

τελεται); this is the 'narrow way' and the 'narrow gate' through which everyone must pass in order to participate in the 'true light.' "[43]

The ultimate point, then, of Hamann's comparison is to break down the spurious "wall of separation" erected by the *Aufklärer* between faith and reason, religion and philosophy. For it is not that they have suddenly become "rational," but that they have replaced historical religion with their own pseudo-religion. Thus they deny transcendent revelation, but retain an immanentized version of it qua the mystical revelation of reason to itself (as is especially clear in Kant). Thus they deny spiritual illumination, but their entire self-understanding is conceived in terms of "Enlightenment." Thus they deny worship to a transcendent Reason-Logos, but demand that everything submit to the criticism and binding judgment of secular reason immanently conceived. In short, from Hamann's perspective, they have simply transferred religious categories and metaphors of revelation, initiation, illumination, and authority to a new-fangled mystery religion with its own priests and devotees. And so he continues, "Holy reason! which for them takes the place of a revelation and demands that one reverently bend the knee before reason's syllogisms, however subtle or far-fetched," to which he incisively adds, "whether they crawl on their belly or go on four legs."[44]

Aside from the incisive reminder that the first "enlightenment" was offered by a snake (Gen. 3: 5), the point of this trenchant allusion to Genesis is, firstly, to bring reason back to the context of the Fall. In other words, it is a reminder to the *Aufklärer* that the only reason we know apart from grace is *fallen* reason. Hamann's second and more striking point is that the deductions of postlapsarian reason, far from being pure, can in fact be quite the opposite – to the point of serving "animalistic" ("go on four legs") or even "demonic" ("crawl on their belly") ends.[45] In other words, in their overestimation of reason's soundness, what the *Aufklärer* have failed to appreciate, with potentially fateful consequences, is that reason's operations are intimately connected with human volition and, as such, are profoundly affected by the passions and depravities to which the fallen will is prone.[46] This is why, from Hamann's perspective, it is all too possible for the progressive ideals of secular reason (*liberté, égalité,* and *fraternité*) to degrade into the Reign of Terror; or for the cold, calculating *arithmetique politique* of the Wannsee Conference to conceive a demonic "*Endlösung.*" And so his sibyl gives the following apocalyptic oracle a decade prior to the French Revolution:

> But its [reason's] corpse[s] lie in the street of the great city that is figuratively called Sodom and Egypt, where our LORD [is] crucified, but not yet risen, since no '*accidental truths of history*,' no *physical fact* or *political phenomenon*, 'can ever be a proof of necessary truths of reason,' – for no-nonsense judges [*Biederrichter*] who are thorough and to the point, who understand more than Greek, and who refuse to be fed with any: *Hoc est corpus meum!* or mysteries *sub utraque specie*.[47]

---

[43] *HH* V, pp. 199f.

[44] N III, p. 218. Cf. the fifteenth letter of Mendelssohn's *Briefe über die Empfindungen*. See *HH* V, p. 201.

[45] See *HH* V, p. 201.

[46] For a profound contemporary discussion of this problem, see especially the essays by Reinhard Hütter, Paul Griffiths, and Carver Yu in Reinhard Hütter and Paul Griffiths (eds.) *Reason and the Reasons of Faith* (New York and London: T. & T. Clark, 2005).

[47] N III, p. 218.

What is immediately striking about this passage is Hamann's identification of secular reason with the apocalyptic "beast" in Revelation who "comes up from the bottom-less pit" to kill the "two witnesses, whose bodies "will lie in the street of the great city that is allegorically called Sodom and Egypt, where also their Lord was cruci-fied" (Rev. 11: 8). Accordingly, the apocalyptic contrast here is between secular reason and prophetic witness to the Logos; whereas the latter bears witness to Christ, the former is the counterfeit prophetic voice of "the god of this world" (2 Cor. 4: 4). At the same time, by way of this provocative image, Hamann suggests that the Enlightenment's doctrine of reason will ultimately bring violence to the world and martyrdom to the prophets and saints. As Schoonhoven observes, "It is as though here already the victims of the wars and revolutions of the twentieth century were prophesied."[48]

The second part of the above passage highlights the *metaphysical severance* that serves as the basis and self-justification for secular reason. And it is here, for the first time in the text, that Hamann explicitly refers to Lessing, specifically, to his famous dictum that "Accidental truths of history can never become the proof of necessary truths of reason."[49] This was the "broad ugly ditch" that Lessing was personally unable to get over: he could not see how to connect the accidental truths of history with the timeless truths of reason. This is why Hamann says that for the *Aufklärer*, like Semler and Reimarus, Christ is "crucified" – he is for them a mere historical figure – "but not risen."[50] And this is why, it goes without saying, they cannot make any sense of the resurrected presence of Christ in the Eucharist. In short, their meth-odology, which dispenses with everything contingent and particular on the way to some shrine of "mystical unity," leaves no room for the possibility of any historically mediated revelation.[51]

To be sure, Starck might be considered an exception to this, since he hoped to find in paganism anticipations of modern natural religion; but, as Hamann sees it, Starck's own investigations were guided not by any genuine appreciation of history qua rev-elation, but instead by an a priori commitment to rationalism and a superstitious fascination with the few fragments and phrases of ancient mystery cults that have been "left behind."[52] As Hamann's sibyl puts it, mocking Starck's reverence for the pagan mysteries,

> Since up to the present day of the Lord on which I write, there has been no lack of *pagans* or *mysteries*: My! By the life of Pharaoh!! we have not only a rosary of *"words left behind,"* but, to speak with the wise men of Egypt, *the finger of God!* – a two-part vermin-infested system, which serves as the basis of our capacity for comparison and abstraction, in order artificially to separate *per aquam regis* or by some drier means the *enduring* and *common* from the *contingent* and *particular,* and to penetrate through the multiplicity, which is infinitely composed of the burdensome limits of *space* and *time,* not only to the *shrine* of mystical unity in the universal concept, but also to an intuitive

---

[48] *HH* V, p. 202.

[49] See Chadwick, *Lessing's Theological Writings*, p. 53.

[50] See *HH* V, p. 202. Semler and Reimarus are alluded to in the passage above: Semler, according to Hamann, as being undecided about the "physical fact" of the resurrection, Reimarus as boasting in the *Fragments*, published by Lessing, of his knowledge of Hebrew. See ZH IV, p. 54.

[51] For an excellent treatment of the topic of revelation during the Enlightenment and of how Catholic theologians responded to this particular challenge, see Grant A. Kaplan, *Answering the Enlightenment: The Catholic Recovery of Historical Revelation* (New York: Crossroad Publishing, 2006).

[52] See *HH* V, p. 204.

knowledge or *epopsis* of the universal truth: *that extra- and super-sensible mysteries, like the entire universe beneath the sun, are a deceptive Nothing, an empty Something, in short, subject to the philosophical curse and contradiction of contingency, and will remain such – until the day of the Last Compiler and Smelter – in the power of Elijah!*[53]

Needless to say, this passage requires patient exegesis.[54] The reference to Exodus puts things in context. From the sibyl's perspective, the proliferation of modern-day mystery cults, e.g., the proliferation of Freemasonry, is to be seen as an infestation akin to the third plague upon Egypt. This is just one aspect of the "mysticism" of the Enlightenment. Another is its alchemical method (*aqua regis* was a compound that was used to separate gold from platinum) or "ritual purification" of the necessary from the contingent, the universal from the particular. Yet another is the Gnostic, otherworldly mystagogy driving this "philosophy," which seeks to break free from the senses, the limits of space and time, and every contradiction between the necessary and the contingent. As the sibyl prophesies, however, the only mystery to which modern philosophy will attain by such abstraction is that of a "deceptive nothing" or a "vain something," which amounts to the same thing. In other words, the attempted purisms conducted in the name of reason will succeed only in bringing modern culture to the threshold of nihilism. Hamann's contemporaries would do well, therefore, to heed the sibyl's judgment that such contradictions cannot be swept away in this "in between" time but await an eschatological resolution that only Christ, the real "compiler" (as opposed to Starck) and "smelter," can bring. For Christ, the eschatological judge who baptizes with "refiner's fire" (Mal. 3: 2f.; Matt. 3: 11) and will come again in the "power of Elijah" (the prophet who knew how to distinguish between true religion and idolatry), alone knows precisely what to compile and what to smelt away. Indeed, as he put it in *Doubts and Ideas*, Christ alone resolves "every *philosophical* contradiction and the entire *historical* puzzle of our *existence*."[55]

Thus far, the sibyl has issued her judgment concerning the methods and results of modern philosophy as a modern-day mystery religion, but she has said little in particular about ancient rites, mythologies, and mystery religions – the very things about which she as a pagan prophetess would presumably have something to say. Accordingly, the next sections of the text support her judgment with more specific observations, which draw heavily from Christoph Meiners, *Über die Mysterien der Alten* (1776). First, the sibyl discredits Starck's excessive fascination with the pagan mysteries, suggesting that they were, after all, not genuine revelations of transcendence, but theatrical farces that preyed upon the enthusiasm and superstition of their adherents.[56] Secondly, she points out that the mysteries were really an aspect of folk religion, and that the distinction between the exoteric and esoteric should not be accorded a mysterious significance it did not necessarily have. Thirdly, *Aufklärer* like Starck believe they will find evidence of their own rationalism in the pagan mysteries: evidence, say, of monotheism, the immortality of the soul, and the reward of virtue and punishment of vice. But what doctrines, the sibyl asks, can one find in these mysteries that are not patent aspects of pagan mythology, as in the cult of

---

[53] N III, pp. 218f.
[54] See Schoonhoven's exegesis, *HH* V, pp. 204–7.
[55] See N III, p. 192.
[56] N III, p. 219.

Jupiter *Optimus Maximus* and the legends of Elysium and Tartarus? For that matter, whatever monotheism one can find in these mysteries is undermined by the theurgy they practiced and the demonology they espoused. In sum, what *Aufklärer* like Starck believed that they would find in the ancient mystery religions, little that we know about them, was more than anything a reflection of their interest in things dark, hidden, and esoteric, in short, things *apocryphal*. And with regard to their quixotic view of history, which disregards the real revelation, the *apocalypse*, of Christianity right under their noses in pursuit of spurious hermetic documents of the past (whose untransmitted antiquity by itself is held to be a sufficient sign of their value and credibility), the sibyl has some interesting things to say (especially in light of recent popular interest in Gnostic gospels and the cache of Nag Hammadi, etc.):

> *Theopneustie* and *Vis dialectica* were merely the visible trunk; but the *subterranean root* of the understanding of the mysteries consisted in the safekeeping of secret writings and sacred documents, "which those uninitiated tried in vain to read, because their authors did not write them for those who were uninitiated" – "Not a single one of these apocryphal texts, not even a book of formulas, which could serve the *cognoscenti* in their investigations, has come down to us in our times. Have they been banished from the world by their persecutors" (the dear *fathers* were presumably these murderers!) "or have they been kept from posterity out of jealousy or conscientiousness [Matt. 27: 18, 24] and been buried along with the ruins of the temples" or have they even ascended into heaven along with their originators and authors?[57]

To be sure, for the apocryphal imagination, which operates without a sense of divine providence in matters of textual transmission, and a correspondingly exaggerated sense of intrigue, conspiracy, and subterfuge, the scant remainder of apocryphal texts is taken to imply that valuable wisdom has been lost, and that Church Fathers like the anti-Gnostic Irenaeus are to blame. In response, however, the sibyl says, "*Do not cry!* – over a *complementum artis exorcisticae, cui simile nunquam visum* in Coptic for an adept 'Sphransch and Saben of a sublime, virtuous, and useful society' – with Duke Michel from Egypt [installed] as the head!"[58]

Clearly, Hamann means to paint a ridiculous picture of his contemporaries' interest in hermetic arts. His more important point, however, is that in their obsession with mysteries that have *not* been transmitted (and Hamann is happy to attribute their loss to providence) his contemporaries fail to see the *greatest* mystery of antiquity, the mystery that fulfills all mysteries, the mystery which by virtue of divine providence *has* been transmitted and is recorded in the books of Holy Scripture. Indeed, Hamann's sibyl reminds her modern audience, what could compare to the mysteries of Scripture itself, a book that is "sealed" with "seventy times seven contradictions":

> As if we lacked original documents that *are sealed* (Isa. 29: 11–12), *because one can no longer read* (since Divi Renati Cartesii *Methodus* and B. Joannis Clerici *Ars Critica* have

---

[57] N III, pp. 220f. The first quotation is from Galen, περι της των ἁπλων φαρμακων δυναμεως, book VII, 1. See *HH* V, p. 212.

[58] N III, p. 221. "Do not cry" is also an allusion to Rev. 5: 5. According to Starck's *Apology*, for the Egyptians the "Sphransch" and "Saben" were the supreme prophets, *hierogrammateis*, and interpreters of the mysteries. Duke Michel is a reference to Voltaire's *Essay sur les moeurs et l'esprit des nations*, where the duke is represented as a beggar duke of gypsies. The "supplement on the art of exorcism, the likes of which has never been seen" is an example of the kind of occult interests Hamann is satirizing. See *HH* V, p. 214.

become the *elementary textbooks*, the *Wolffianism* and *Machiavellianism* in sheep's clothing, the deceptive patois of our Gallic *Pedagogue*), and which one *cannot read on account of the seven* seals on the inside and the back or the *seventy times seven* contradictions of the conquering lion and slaughtered [*erwürgten*] lamb – including a beast that was and is not, but nevertheless is.[59]

The problem, in other words, is not a lack of mysteries, but that the *Aufklärer* have either overlooked or perhaps even willfully ignored the mysteries that have been handed down through Sacred Scripture – having been unduly influenced by the philosophical idiom of the Francophile king, Frederick the Great (the "pedagogue"), and the academic language of such texts as Descartes's *Discourse on Method* and Jean le Clerc's *Ars Critica* (the latter had argued, for example, that one should interpret the Scriptures no differently from any classical text).[60] Above all, however, they are illiterate because they have no faith. Having forsaken Christ, they have forsaken the only one who is worthy to break the seals (Rev. 5: 5ff.) and grant an understanding of Scripture's mysterious allegorical contents (Luke 24: 27). Indeed, their prejudicial rationalism, founded upon the principle of non-contradiction, has left them unenlightened regarding the mysterious contradictions of Scripture, such as the Christological paradox of the lion and the lamb *in una persona Christi* – to which Hamann adds the curious contradiction of the Antichrist, who "was and is not and is" (Rev. 17: 8). As a result, they "see what is not there, nor can be," and "do not see what can be touched with one's hands."[61] In other words, they *see* a revelation in the pagan mysteries, where there is none, and *do not see* the revelation that *is* there in Christianity; and this "turns the whole system to night." And so "I worry," the sibyl says, "that the superstitious preachers of natural religion may end up sharing the same fate as the blind Homer – hooked by a valid fisherman's riddle [*Lausangelrätsel*], which he took for the abyss of Euripus!"[62]

In view of the foregoing, however, one must be careful not to misunderstand Hamann's view of paganism. For while he denies any *direct* divine revelation afforded to the pagans, countering Starck's excessive enthusiasm, he by no means excludes paganism from providence (after all, he speaks in the voice of a pagan sibyl and, like Augustine, would presumably wish to affirm her membership in the city of God). On the contrary, as we have seen, he understands paganism according to his typological reading of history as a dream-like anticipation of Christ.[63] But Hamann also realizes that the witness of paganism to Christ is obscure. Indeed, even the allegorical mysteries of the Old Testament can be understood, as Paul puts it in 2 Cor. 3: 14, only when the "veil is taken away," as when Christ himself opened the minds of the disciples "to understand the scriptures" (Luke 24: 45). Accordingly, with an obscure

---

[59] N III, p. 221.

[60] See *HH* V, p. 215.

[61] N III, p. 222. See 1 John 1: 1.

[62] N III. The word *Lausangelrätsel* is based upon the riddle to which Hamann alludes. *Euripus* is the name for any particularly violent strait, but is associated in particular with the deep, in Hamann's description, unfathomable strait between Euboea and Boeotia. According to the biography of Homer attributed to Herodotus, Homer sat down on a rock beside the shore, heard fishermen approaching, and asked them if they had caught anything. They responded with a riddle, "What we caught we left behind; what we did not catch, we are taking with us." Homer, distracted from puzzling over the riddle, which he mistook for something profound, tripped over a stone and died three days later. The answer to the riddle is "lice" [*Läuse*]. See N VI, p. 222; *HH* V, p. 219.

[63] See *HH* V, p. 221.

allusion to Reimarus' *The Aims of Jesus and his Disciples,* the sibyl recasts the entire topic in light of the eschatological parable of the kingdom of God in Matthew 13:

> But *Der Zweck Jesu und seiner Jünger* is like a net that was thrown into the sea in order to catch fish of every kind, and when it [was] full, they drew it ashore, sat down, and put the good ones into the baskets – So it will be at the end of the world, of which all the *grape-harvest* and *crop-harvest festivals of the nations* are fruitful types and eloquent prefigurations: for our entire *Church calendar* is instituted accordingly, in order to familiarize the people in dramatic-symbolic representations and festivities with what the sacred history of the hero, eternal father and prince of peace, who descended to earth from heaven – and ascended into heaven from earth – has preserved for us – to *His Memory!* and as a *sign* of the *contradiction* that he himself endures against himself, in order that we might not grow weary at heart or give up doing the "*deeds*" of His disciples – in a few *baskets* of fragments, like showbread in the sanctuary of the tabernacle in relation to the golden urn that contained the manna.[64]

The first key to the sibyl's difficult imagery is the theme of sorting and dividing. Reimarus was one of the first in what has now become a long succession of liberal theologians to separate the historical Jesus from the Christ of faith, the historical individual from the resurrected God-man; and to this extent his exegesis exemplifies the *Scheidekunst* of the *Aufklärer,* who take the eschatological task of sorting and dividing into their own hands. The imagery of the festive gathering of wheat and grapes is another example of sorting and dividing. From Hamann's perspective, however, these ancient religious festivals are, at the end of the day, obscure prophecies of Christ (John 12: 24) and the eschatological sorting and gathering of souls into the kingdom (Matt. 13: 47). The same is true of the pagan mythology of ascending and descending gods, which Hamann reads as obscure intimations of the *real* descent and ascent of Christ (see Eph. 4: 8–10). Indeed, in this connection the sibyl speaks of the "eternal, mystical, magical, and logical circle of *human deification* and *divine incarnation.*"[65] To be sure, the prophetic witness to Christ, which has been obscurely preserved in the annals of history and the "fragments" of the Gospel, is contradicted by critics such as Reimarus, and this itself is part of the mystery of contradiction, which God willingly suffers. Thus it happens, as a "memorial" and confirmation of the "contradiction," that the "cornerstone of our evangelical and apostolic, historical and dogmatic system becomes, instead of a living bread and *rod,* a stumbling block and rock of offense; the *fish,* a snake; and the *egg,* a scorpion."[66] In other words, rationalistic exegesis does the opposite of faith: it turns the Lord of glory into a mere historical figure, and the fragments of the Gospel into something contemptible. For the eyes of faith, on the other hand, the fragments point to the Lord of glory, whose humanity is the visible sign of his divinity – just as the show bread in the temple is the visible sign and symbol of the heavenly bread, which is hidden behind a veil.

Thus far Hamann's sibyl has elucidated the nature of paganism, satirized Starck's enthusiasm for the occult, and shown that paganism points prophetically not to the

---

[64] *HH* V, p. 222. See Isa. 9: 6; 2 Thess. 3: 13; John 6: 13; Num. 4: 7.

[65] N III, p. 224.

[66] N III, p. 222. Though Schoonhoven reads "*Stab,*" translated here as "rod," in the familiar biblical sense of "staff," it seems to refer to Aaron's "rod," which was preserved in the ark, along with the manna. See Heb. 9: 4. Cf. Luke 11: 11f.

natural religion of the Enlightenment, but to Christianity. Now, incited by G. S. Steinbart's *System der reinen Philosophie oder Glückseeligkeitslehre des Christentums, für die Bedürfnisse seiner aufgeklärten Landsleute und andrer die nach Weisheit fragen eingerichtet* (1778), in the dedication of which Steinbart deferentially cites a letter of Hamann's nemesis, Frederick the Great, she turns her attention to politics; and, picking up a thread from the preceding fragment, she frames her prophecy in terms of the contrast between the "deeds," the works of love, of the disciples and the "great deeds" of the Freemasons,[67] ultimately suggesting an eschatological contrast between two different bodies: a *corpus Christi mysticum* constituted by faith and an *anti-corpus Christi mysticum* constituted by secular reason. Superficially, the "deeds" of these bodies may appear similar. Like the *Aufklärer*, who strive to overcome nationalism and sectarian religious violence in pursuit of the ideal of a universal human fraternity, the disciples gather souls into the kingdom from every nation, tribe, and people (Rev. 7: 9), working toward the eschaton (Matt. 9: 37; 24: 45f.; 25: 14–30), which will bring about a new heaven and a new earth (Isa. 65: 17; 2 Pet. 3: 13; Rev. 21: 1). Their differences, however, are profound. In the case of the *anti-corpus Christi mysticum*, the bond of unity is a universal, secular rationality abstracted from every concrete religious tradition, with no higher authority than reason immanently conceived. In the case of the *corpus Christi mysticum*, the bond of unity is the Spirit of the incarnate Logos, in whom reason (*logos*) analogously participates, but who remains decidedly in-and-*beyond* the human logos, i.e., super-rational; moreover, the Spirit, apart from whose light, the participatory "light" of reason is proportionately darkened (Ps. 36: 9).[68]

In a subsequent fragment Hamann's sibyl sharpens the contrast in a biting satire of the Enlightenment's ideal of a secular, transfigured humanity under the kingship of Frederick the Great, the enlightened despot, who had proposed self-love as the basis and principal means of socio-political transformation, to which the Christian doctrine of "love of neighbor" could in due course be "added":

> The great political *sartorial mystery* of *making* and *transfiguring human beings*, even if a tattered Christendom should be used for the purple underlining of self-love, according to the golden natural law of economy, in order as quickly, dependably, universally, and enduringly, by means of impressions of meteors and antitheses, to *be like Zeus* – or "rather to give a single drive all possible intensive power" – and of what kind? – "a drive that makes all others small and suspicious! and *presents itself as the strongest and the best!*" – – [It is] the old Punic strategy [*Kriegslist*] of widening the narrow gate through the wooden horse of tolerance, in order to draw down the ultimate *palladium* of human nature, so that we can swallow camels in good conscience, and move the Alps by means of a new *fides implicita* in a new covenant of reason, and, by the *grace of God* subject ourselves to all the leaden bulls, which the holy Augustini and Anselmi [issue] from their cells and bordellos as the oracles and products [*Gemächte*] of their undying worm and unquenchable fire.[69]

---

[67] Hamann is alluding here to Lessing's *Ernst und Falk*, where the elusive Falk speaks at some length about the "great deeds" of the Freemasons as the mysterious sign by which *they* are known.

[68] See, for example, Augustine, *In Ioannis tractatus*, XIX, 12: "Si ergo accedendo illuminamini, et recedendo tenebramini: non erat in vobis lumen vestrum, sed in Deo vestro. Accedite, ut resurgatis: si recesseritis, moriemini. Si ergo accedendo vivitis, recedendo morimini; non erat in vobis vita vestra, quae est lux vestra. Ipsa est enim vita vestra, quae est lux vestra. Quoniam apud te est fons vitae, et in lumine tuo videbimus lumen."

[69] N III, p. 223.

To begin unpacking the sibyl's allusions, the phrase "sartorial mystery" takes us all the way back to Genesis 3: 7, human shame, and the attempt to hide it with "aprons of fig leaves." In the present context this means that the cover-up is still going on: the tailors of the Enlightenment are sewing the aprons anew. Rather than awaiting the divine clothing of the Holy Spirit (Luke 24: 49), which alone will bring about real transfiguration, they have taken it upon themselves to re-tailor humanity according to the image of secular reason: all that is needed is that one "grow up" and "put on" reason, in a parody of the disciples growing up by "putting on" Christ (See Eph. 4: 22f.). In doing so, however, the sibyl says, they pervert the natural desire to be like God, "in which the entire *arcanum* ... of the wisdom of reason consists,"[70] falling again into the original sin and *proton pseudos* of wanting to be like God without humbly submitting to God: "This πρόληψις *to be like God* paved the way for all philosophical knowledge and legalistic righteousness ... This ἁρπαγμος was the πρωτον ψευδος of the *original attempt* to derange [*verrücken*] our senses from the simplicity in the *Word* and spoil the peace on earth with the adulterous taste of reason."[71] In other words, by *grasping* after divinity reason not only misses its object – "like a bad marksman," it mistakes "the shadow for the body" – but is deprived of the simplicity of communion with the Logos for which it was made. Moreover, abstracted from the matrix of tradition from below and in rebellion against the paternal wisdom from above, left to its own devices, without any further foundation or guidance, reason invariably kowtows to a "wisdom" that is "earthly, unspiritual," and "devilish" (Jas. 3: 15).[72] For, without a transcendent frame of reference, reason inevitably reduces to an instrument of self-love, and in the interest of the latter, "widens the narrow gate" (cf. Matt. 7: 13) through the "Trojan horse of tolerance." As a result we no longer make sound moral distinctions, but "swallow camels" like Pharisees (Matt. 23: 24), having entrusted our salvation *fide implicita* to a "new covenant of reason," which is promulgated with infernal authority from the "cells and bordellos" of the latest "Church Fathers."[73] In other words, Hamann's sibyl would have us know, the real driving force behind the secular ideals of the Enlightenment is the passions – and desired sexual freedom – of those who promote it. These, she bitterly suggests, are the new "Church Fathers," i.e. the new authorities of the secular age.

The point, then, of the sibyl's trenchant polemic is to clarify the alternatives. On the one hand, there is a tradition of revealed wisdom (from above); on the other hand, there is an anti-tradition of traditionless secular reason (from below). On the one hand, there is a historical, prophetic "covenant of grace" rooted in a historical revelation to the Jews and fulfilled in Christianity; on the other hand, there is an abstract, ahistorical "covenant of reason," which in the name of reason's alleged timelessness, universality, and supreme authority presumes to dispense with any special revelation. And yet, the sibyl asks, prophetically exposing the charade of reason's authority and self-evidence, "What is highly-touted *reason*, with its universality,

---

[70] N III, p. 224.

[71] Ibid. The contrast here is between Adam's grasping after divinity in the garden and the non-grasping after divinity of the Word in Phil. 2: 6f. Though the Word *is* God's sensible self-communication to human beings, reason, rather than being faithfully united to God in the Word, adulterously oversteps this communication. It *grasps* after the divine on its own terms, unable to recognize what is *given*. And this original error, which robs us of peace, is the original source of every legalistic, philosophical, and Gnostic attempt illegitimately to lay hold of the divine.

[72] N III, p. 223.

[73] Among those Hamann means is Steinbart, who explicitly rejected the authority of Augustine and Anselm. See *HH* V, p. 227.

infallibility, and evidence? An *ens rationis,* a stuffed dummy, to which a *flagrant* superstition of unreason ascribes *divine attributes.*"[74] Indeed, she asks, presenting the difference between the two "covenants" – the "covenant" based upon faith in a historical revelation and the "covenant" of modern secular reason – as drastically as possible: "What agreement does Christ have with Lucifer? What does the temple of God have in common with idols? the divine power and wisdom of the *evangelii* with the *eternal rules, Operibus supererogatis* and *Opusculis profligatis* of an earthly, bestial, ghost-like instinct," i.e., a rationality that reduces to the brute instinct of self-love.[75]

To be sure, the sibyl prophesies, the "high priests" and "archons" of this new secular creed will pay lip service to Christ – a "*Samalec to the King of the Jews,*" for they are tolerant – but, unlike Nietzsche, who grasped perfectly well the paradox, they will pass over the contradiction, scandal, and true mystery of the title, which was nailed to the Cross, and therewith "the true idiotism and shibboleth of Pauline hypotheses κατα αποκαλυψιν μυστεριου —"[76] In short, they make light of the mystery of the Cross; it means nothing to them. Moreover, having committed themselves to the "latest revelation" of "*pure* reason," they invariably regard Christ's "sprinkled *blood*" as "impure" and thus "spurn the *Spirit* of grace!"[77] At the end of the day, however, "the whole *Nostrum* of [their] barking in the streets" merely reveals their own *nakedness,* sin, and shame,[78] and for this reason, the sibyl concludes, in defense of Goeze, that "the pulpits are justified in cursing the tree of knowledge, whose foul fruits and bare leaves are useful neither for medicine nor for aprons" (cf. Rev. 22: 2).[79] Such, in sum, is Hamann's view of the famous *Fragmentenstreit.*

The rest of *Konxompax* is concerned more directly with the positive mystery of Christianity in relation to paganism and Judaism. Earlier in the text, as we have seen, the sibyl spoke of the "eternal, mystical, magical, and logical circle of *human deification* and *divine incarnation,*" claiming not only that the history of religion, but that the "whole *Arcanum* of our new-baked theology and philosophy [*Vernunftweisheit*]" was bound up with this mystery.[80] In paganism, according to the sibyl, this mystery was bound up with the mythology of descending gods and ascending heroes, expressing an unconscious longing for the *real historical* incarnation, *descensus ad inferos,* resurrection and ascension of Christ, in whose mystical body humanity is truly transfigured and the dreams of paganism are finally fulfilled. Now, once again, she speaks of "the evangelical mystery that the *human being* is *destined* to be a Συνθρονισμῳ (of a not merely *figurative,* but *bodily* participation in the divine nature)."[81] And again it is clear that from her perspective, speaking as a pagan, the inheritance of paganism points not to a Masonic religion of reason, but to Christianity. Thus, in a pun on his name (cf. Matt. 12: 29), Starck's claims may be

---

[74] N III, p. 223.

[75] Ibid.

[76] Ibid. The word *samalec* is Arabic and means "peace be with you." See *HH* V, p. 228.

[77] N III, p. 225.

[78] Ibid.

[79] Ibid.

[80] N III, p. 224.

[81] Ibid. Συνθρωνισμῳ (here in the dative case), meaning one who "shares the throne (σύνθρονος). The term was applied by the Greek fathers to Christ, who "shares the throne" with the Father, meaning here, by extension, that the human being in Christ is destined to "share the throne" with Christ. See *HH* V, p. 238.

dispensed with: "Away with the *Strong one* [*dem Starken*]," she says, "to the burnt-offering altar of *Diagorus!*"[82]

Having dispensed with Starck's eccentric reading of paganism, the sibyl now presents her own understanding of paganism and Judaism in relation to Christianity. The positive content of paganism, she says, is the richness of its religious sensibility and its dream-like intuition of the twofold mystery of incarnation and deification. Among its shortcomings, however, are its tendency to polytheism and idolatry, its ignorance of the divine name (which is revealed in Judaism), and, in its philosophical variants, its abstract metaphysical conception of the divine as a mere *arché* or *ens entium* – whence Hamann frequently and crassly refers to God in the context of paganism as "the Thing" (*das Ding*). Indeed, the sibyl suggests that after the winds of inspiration had left it, pagan religion degenerated into the original sin of self-deification:

> What befell the *temple of* nature due to polytheism, befell the *temple of the body* due to the mysteries: each became a *tomb* or *thieves' den* [*Mördergrube*] of the *Thing*, whose revealed name is the one unspeakable mystery of *Judaism* – and whose anonymous πρόληψις has brought forth thousands of mythological names, idols, and attributes, all of which flowed together and were either diluted as a result of initiation or, what is more likely, concentrated into the original sin of self-deification [*selbst-abgötterey*].[83]

To be sure, there is something to be valued in paganism's dream of deification – as Christ himself says, " 'ye are gods' " (John 10: 34). The problem, however, is that it tends to become a matter of "*self*-deification." And this is why paganism points to Judaism, which precisely did not miscalculate the difference between God and human beings, and in which the divine name is finally revealed.

Yet, inasmuch as Judaism has developed historically away from its prophetic tradition and thus away from Christianity, it too is incomplete (even if Christianity would be nothing without it); for, on its own terms, it is hard to see how its doctrine of God's radical transcendence can be reconciled with the equally radical possibility of the incarnation or to the possibility of deification (which Christianity shares with paganism). Thus the sibyl suggests that the fulfillment of paganism and Judaism is to be found in Christianity as the "union of these two *tinctures*." As she puts it near the climax of her prophecy, beginning with a transvalued quotation from Lessing's *Ernst und Falk* and concluding with a modified quotation from Colossians 3: 11:

> What, then, should we say of all this mystagogy? "Nothing arbitrary, nothing dispensable, nothing pointless; but Something necessary, which is grounded in the nature of man" and his relationships to the *Ens entium*. But since even this is an *Ens rationis*: the revealed name of the *Thing* κατ' εξοχην became the single mystery of Judaism and the πρόληψις of its unspoken name the thousand-tongued mystery of paganism. The union of these two *tinctures*, however, is the *new man*, according to the image of his Creator – no longer Greek and Jew; circumcised and uncircumcised; barbarian, Scythian; slave, Freemason; αλλα παντα και εν πασι.[84]

---

[82] N III, p. 225. Diagorus, a disciple of Democritus and an atheist, was driven from Athens for his ridicule of the Eleusinian mysteries. See *HH* V, p. 197.

[83] N III, p. 224.

[84] N III, p. 226.

The sibyl's words are clearly intended for Lessing; for instead of "slave and free," she says "slave and Freemason." What is added to the initial quotation from Lessing is also relevant. In *Ernst und Falk* Falk (i.e., Lessing) had said that "Freemasonry is nothing arbitrary, nothing dispensable: but something necessary, which is grounded in the nature of man and civic society," i.e., it has an immanent foundation.[85] Hamann, however, emends Lessing's definition to say that all mystagogy has, to the contrary, a transcendent foundation in man's relationship to the divine.[86] But since the god of paganism is at best an *Ens entium*, and since an *Ens entium* is ultimately something posited on the part of reason as an *Ens rationis*, i.e., what one might call the "god" of onto-theology, paganism itself cries out for a revelation of the "unknown God" (cf. Acts 17: 23), which is precisely what was *given* in Judaism. And, as we shall see, this is precisely why Hamann was so scandalized by Mendelssohn's attempt to naturalize Judaism and pass it off as the epitome of a natural religion of reason. But, once again, as with paganism, Judaism too is incomplete, since it is unable to fulfill either reason's desire for universality or paganism's natural desire for incarnation and deification. What is needed, therefore, and that for which all of "creation waits with eager longing" (Rom. 8: 19), is the "new man" who arises from the "union" of both "tinctures," i.e., the union of paganism and Judaism.[87]

In light of the subsequent fragment it finally becomes clear that the true alchemical mystery, the production of the "new man" (which would satisfy even the dreams for humanity of a Freemason like Lessing) is accomplished through Christ, the king of the Jews, and membership in his mystical body, the Church. This is the apocalyptic mystery of the ages and the crucible of true unity. For it is "not made by human hands" (Heb. 9: 11); it is not a work of social engineering on the part of "enlightened" Freemasons. Rather, it is the work of God:

> This unity of the head as well as the division of the body into its members and its *differentia specifica* is the *mystery of the kingdom of heaven* from its genesis to the apocalypse – the focal point of all parables and types in the entire universe, the *Histoire generale* and *Chronique scandaleuse* of all the customs and families of time; – so that the manifold wisdom of God might be made known to the *majesties* and *faculties* in the high places through His visible house and the invisible community of the firstborn below.[88]

In the London Writings Hamann had expressed a more or less common Baroque sentiment when he affirmed that the "book[s] of nature and history are nothing but *ciphers,* hidden signs."[89] They were signs, to be sure, of divine condescension, but their ultimate significance was not fully resolved. Now it is finally clear that *the* mystery to which all things secretly point is the mystical body of Christ: this is the mystery that is revealed through the lowliness of the Church to the "majesties" and

---

[85] Lessing, *Ernst und Falk*, in *Werke*, ed. H. Kesten (Cologne and Berlin: Kieperheuer & Witsch, 1962), vol. 2, p. 713.

[86] Indeed, as Schoonhoven notes, for Hamann all aspects of human life – reason, will, sexuality, science, art, family, and politics – must be understood in these terms. See *HH* V, p. 246.

[87] The word "tincture," of course, rings of alchemy, as Hamann no doubt intends, and of the process of producing gold, namely, the spiritual gold of the regenerated human spirit.

[88] N III, p. 226.

[89] *LS*, p. 417 (N I, pp. 308f.).

"faculties," i.e., the potentates and academics, of this world. (The allusion to the "principalities and powers" of Ephesians 3: 10 and 6: 12, one will note, could not put the contrast more dramatically.) And it is a mystery that is revealed through the Church in its visible *and* invisible aspect, as if to say that the Church is neither totally visible (as an ultra-Montanism might have it) nor totally invisible (as an ultra-Protestantism might have it). To be sure, it is a visible institution in the world, but "the community of the firstborn" nevertheless remains an invisible reality known only to God.

But again, if the mystery of mysteries, the mystery of the mystical body of Christ, has been revealed, if it is no longer hidden within so many "parables and types," it is also a mystery that is awaiting its final resolution, as suggested by the parable of the wheat and the tares (Matt. 13: 24–30). Indeed, aside from the purification that goes on within the Church (Eph. 5: 27), it is a mystery that is worked out through contradiction (through the suffering of the opposition of the "majesties" and "faculties") and through the "scandalous chronicle" of human history in general. And so, once again, the sibyl casts the unfolding drama in an eschatological light, adding sharp words for the "poetic license" of the age, which is a secular parody of the true freedom of the children of God (Rom. 8: 21). "The entire creation," she says,

> takes part in our *groans* and *lamentations*, since its *redemption* from the bondage of futility, and of misuse and of the stomach (which bondage the creation did not will of its own, but to which it is subject for the sake of the one who will destroy stomach and food and the present bodily and spiritual need to *cover* one's feet, just as the *moral obligation* of our reason ... to *cover* its head *for the sake of the angels* will be abrogated by the *licentiam poeticam* of this philosophical century), because, I say, this *redemption* of *the whole visible nature* from its *swaddling bands* and *chains* depends upon the revelation of Christianity, whose mystery is a pillar and foundation of *truth* and *freedom*.[90]

Leaving aside the more familiar allusions and focusing on the obscure, mysterious center of this prophetic fragment, one will note that Hamann recurs to the mystery of shame; and he does so in order to clarify the manner of its abrogation (as though the mystery of redemption were essentially a matter of redemption *from shame*). This can occur in one of two ways. On the one hand, for those who have repented and are being saved, God will "destroy" the "need to *cover* one's feet," i.e., God will destroy the shame of the Fall with the clothing of the Holy Spirit (of which the clothing with "garments of skin" was a prophetic type). On the other hand, the modern age resolves the mystery of shame – the last reminder to a fallen world that it is fallen and stands in need of redemption – by its own secular abrogation of it. For inasmuch as the modern age does away with the concept of sin (the notion that it is possible for human beings to offend God, or simply to miss the target regarding the fulfillment of their own nature), it also does away with any shame (any guilty conscience) that would arise therefrom. In short, inasmuch as it follows such secular authorities as Freud and Nietzsche, the modern age is "shameless," indeed, "beyond good and evil." Thus does it achieve both its parody of Christian innocence (Rom. 8: 1) and its parody of Christian freedom (Rom. 8: 2; Gal. 5: 1). And yet, as the above passage would seem to suggest, whereas the *via crucis* undertaken by members of the *corpus Christi mysticium*, who have "crucified the flesh with its passions and desires"

---

[90] N III, pp. 226f. See Isa. 6: 2; Rom. 8: 19f.; 1 Cor. 6: 13; Isa. 6: 2; 1 Cor. 11: 4f.; 1 Tim. 3: 15.

(Gal. 5: 24), leads to genuine freedom – "the glorious liberty of the children of God" (Rom. 8: 21) – the modern solution of the *anti-corpus Christi mysticum* leaves one, for all its so-called "freedom," in bondage, the bondage of sin and death, deprived of the energizing life of the Holy Spirit (Rom. 8:11).

In this light, Hamann's allusion to 1 Cor. 11 and Paul's exhortation that women should cover their heads in church begins to make sense. Whereas the "covering of feet" refers to the mystery of shame (Gen. 3: 7), which God abrogates through faith in Christ (Rom. 8: 1), here "covering" is a sign of submission to authority.[91] Hamann is making no statement about whether women should literally cover their heads. Rather, "covering" is here a figure for the "moral obligation" of reason to defer to divine authority – an obligation that is abrogated by the *licentiam poeticam* of the age. In other words, it is another indirect way of saying that secular reason is "shameless": it is reason operating without the fear of God, which is the "beginning of wisdom" (Prov. 9: 10), and so it is fallen, *unjustified,* and devoid of genuine inspiration. As the sibyl says at the conclusion of the fragment, "It is the Spirit, however, that *justifies* and *gives life*. The *flesh* and [a] *book* without spirit is useless."[92]

Given Hamann's allusion to John 6: 63, 2 Corinthians 3: 6, the addition of the word "book," and the immediately following verse from John, "But among you there are some who do not believe" (6: 64), it is clear that the sibyl is now speaking indirectly to Lessing, and that the whole of *Konxompax,* which is more obviously concerned with Starck, is in fact an indirect appeal for Lessing's conversion. Indeed, her real concern all along has been with the publisher of Reimarus' *Fragments,* the author of *On the Proof of the Spirit and of Power,* and his rational (as opposed to spirit-filled) criticism, which presumes to separate the essence of religion from the concrete, historical, inspired letter of Scripture. And the final words of her peroration are sharp: "How then! Should a *sanctimonious* philosophy and a *hypocritical* philology crucify the flesh and eradicate the book because the letter and historical faith in it can be neither a *seal* nor a *key* of the spirit?"[93] In other words, if one assumes, as does Lessing, that the spiritual content of Scripture is something other than the letter and not bound to it, is one then justified in torturing and uprooting the latter, so that one can proceed with one's own views, or even refashion the letter, as reason dictates? This is Lessing's implicit proposal which the sibyl vigorously rejects. For, deprived of the letter, the Bible would then threaten to become objectively meaningless, a reflection of the subjective fancy of the interpreter. This is not to say that Scripture does not have a mystical sense beyond the literal sense; of all people Hamann was a proponent of allegorical-typological exegesis. The key to unlocking Scripture, however, is for Hamann (as we have abundantly seen) not the autonomous light of reason, but the supernatural illumination of the Holy Spirit.

But again, one must be clear, this is not to denigrate reason per se; for earlier in her address the sibyl speaks precisely of the "divine *Adiutoria*[!] of reason and Scripture."[94] Indeed, reason is very much a "helpmeet" of interpretation. The problem, however, is that many take the dim light of "reason alone" as an authoritative guide, and as a result end up replacing the spiritual sense, which is meant to be

---

[91] See ZH II, p. 415.

[92] N III, p. 227. Cf. John 6: 63; 2 Cor. 3: 6.

[93] N III, p. 227.

[94] N III, pp. 224f. *Adiutorium,* or "help[meet]" is the Vulgate's translation of Gen. 2: 18. Here, then, the point is that reason and Scripture go *together* as divine aids, as the two wings, as it were, by which to attain God's purposes for creation.

discovered in the light of the Holy Spirit (cf. Ps. 36: 9), with a "rational" sense, which is *posited* by the individual, unaided by grace, under the influence of a fallen, protean will. Thus the sibyl says, with Lessing and Reimarus no doubt in mind,

> But if the mystical sense of Scripture is replaced by the angel of light, without their knowing the evil they do (Eccles. 5: 1), or distinguishing the body of *the Lord* from the cup and table of demons: to His praise, the internal lies or contradictions of reason will make the truth of God more glorious, but their condemnation is entirely just ... Or should we expect, aside from the *Littera scripta*, another *Regula Lesbia*?[95]

Hamann then adds that this would be Lessing's "necessary answer,"[96] once again suggesting that reason divorced from the letter of Scripture, deprived of any foundation in tradition, in short, with *nothing* left to stand on and no transcendent rule or revelation to guide it, will inevitably succumb to a "bending of the rules" and ultimately to a kind of nihilism. This is the mysterious "other rule," beyond the letter of Scripture and the *regula fidei*, that Hamann's sibyl prophetically tells us to expect.

---

[95] N III, p. 227. See Schoonhoven, *HH* V, p. 255: "*Regula Lesbia*" is a term that can be found in Aristotle, Erasmus, and Luther. In all instances, it means an indefinite rule. Thus Aristotle speaks of housebuilding on Lesbos as following an indeterminate rule for something indeterminate, whereby "the ruler is altered to fit the shape of the stone and does not stay rigid, and the decree is altered to fit the circumstances" (*Nicomachean Ethics,* tr. Joe Sachs, 1137b). In Luther's *Tischreden* it is a flexible rule not bound by any law (*Werke*, vol. 1, p. 557). And in Erasmus' *Adagia*, it is a rule where the factual is not made to suit the rational, but the rule is accommodated to the fact: "non ad rationem factum, sed ratio ad factum accomodatur."

[96] See *HH*, p. 255. Hamann is alluding here ironically to Lessing's "Necessary answer to a very unnecessary question of Head Pastor Goeze" from 1778. Against Goeze, Lessing had disputed that Christianity is founded upon Scripture, and instead claimed that it is founded upon the subsequently formulated *regula fidei*. But this itself, of course, in Lessing's view, being a purely historical foundation, "can never become the proof of necessary truths of reason" (Chadwick, *Lessing's Theological Writings*, p. 53). Thus, either way, according to the terms of Lessing's philosophy, religion is deprived of the possibility of a historical foundation.

Part IV

Metacritique: of Reason, Natural Religion, and Secular Politics

10

Life and Writings 1780–1784

The whole fable of my authorship is a mask, and its silver wedding anniversary, like that of Samson, is intended to show the Philistines their own nakedness, to divest them and transfigure them …

Hamann to Jacobi[1]

Do not worry about adding an ell to me or my stature. The measure of my "greatness" is neither that of a giant nor an angel, no hand broader than that of a common human ell. Please do not paint any moustaches on my life, unless I can still laugh with you, so that the world is not forced to invest and transfigure a rotten sinner with the nimbus of a "saint."

Divestment and Transfiguration[2]

Hamann was now in his fiftieth year, and two works had recently appeared that garnered his interest: Hume's posthumously published *Dialogues concerning Natural Religion* (1779) and another work by Starck, his *Freimüthige Betrachtungen über das Christentum* (1780).[3] As for Starck's "candid observations," they added little to what he had already said elsewhere, and Hamann had not already rejected.[4] Hume's *Dialogues*, on the other hand, Hamann found so much to his liking that midsummer 1780 he began a translation.[5] Whereas earlier he found in Hume an unwitting ally in his attempt to defend the plausibility of faith against the dogmatism of Kant's pre-critical philosophy, he now found in Hume an unsuspecting ally in his battle with the *Aufklärer* over the notion of natural religion. Specifically, Hume lent support to Hamann's attack on a *universal* religion of *reason* and his corresponding attempt to defend Judaism and Christianity as *particular historical revelations* – the very things from which the doctrine of a "natural" religion abstracted. Thus he quickly wrote to Hartknoch about the possibility of publishing the translation: "The dialogue is full of beautiful poetic moments, and I agree with Mr. Green that it is not very dangerous; on the contrary, I am translating it [under the pseudonym] of a *fifty-year-old divine*

---

[1] ZH VI, pp. 331f.

[2] N III, p. 404.

[3] NB, pp. 336ff.

[4] At the time, though he did not know that Starck was the author, Hamann communicated his judgment to Herder: "I received an early copy of the *Freymüthige Betrachtungen* from Hippel … I liked the author better than Bahrt and Steinbart. But, at bottom, it is one and the same προτον ψευδος as in [Lessing's] *The Education of the Human Race* [which also appeared in 1780]. Firstly, *natural religion* is for me the same as *natural language*, a true absurdity [*Unding*], an *ens rationis*. Secondly, what one calls natural religion is to me just as problematic and polemical as revelation. And why [should it be called] *Freymüthigkeit* [i.e., candid], if it [merely] rehashes and refines the true *ton du siècle sub umbra alarum*" (ZH IV, p. 195). In other words, "natural" religion and "natural" language are figments of the imagination because they suppose contents that are miraculously uninformed by particular religions and particular languages, when, for Hamann, there are no other kinds; thus "natural," as used here by Hamann's contemporaries, is in fact an "unnatural" abstraction.

[5] N III, pp. 245–74.

[*Geistlichen*] in *Swabia* for the good of my outspoken *fellow clergy* and *countrymen*, who transform *Judaism* and *Christianity* into nothing but *natural religion ...*"[6] And in the same letter he adds the suggestion that he append the translation with his own contribution to the topic.

In the meantime, however, a competing translation appeared, and Hamann's translation fell by the wayside.[7] (What remained of it, however, was substantial enough to elicit Kant's praise, who would have read it about ten months prior to the publication of the first edition of the *Critique of Pure Reason*.) Hamann still had thoughts of proceeding with his own work on natural religion, but this plan too suddenly changed with the publication of the first *Critique,* whose appearance he had been eagerly awaiting for some time. In fact, Hamann not only mediated its publication with his friend Hartknoch, but on April 6, 1781 surreptitiously obtained the first twenty-eight proof sheets (presumably as a result of his connection with Hartknoch). Four weeks later he obtained another twenty and immediately began writing a response.[8] Thus Hamann was not only the first person to read the *Critique of Pure Reason,* but also the first person to review it, having finished a draft of the review by July 1, three weeks before receiving a copy from Kant himself.[9]

HAMANN'S "TWINS" OF 1784

As a result of these developments, the nature of Hamann's own project on natural religion went through a series of transformations. Initially, he continued to envision an epistolary supplement to Hume's *Dialogues*, which would include his critique of Kant, bearing the title, "Scheblimini: or an epistolary re-reading of a misologist" (*Scheblimini oder epistolarische Nachlese eines Misologen*).[10] Over the course of 1782, however, while awaiting the publication of Kant's *Prolegomena to any Future Metaphysics*, he came across Mendelssohn's reading of Hume, and the shape of his project once again changed. Mendelssohn subsequently became an important inter-locutor and the projected title of the work was now changed to "Scheblimini or an epistolary re-reading of a metacritic." The project was transformed yet again, how-ever, when Mendelssohn's *Jerusalem: or on Religious Power and Judaism* (*Jerusalem oder über religiöse Macht und Judentum*) appeared in 1783, a work that made such an impression on Hamann that he read it as many as three times and immediately conceived a response.[11] Indeed, it affected him so strongly that his planned work split off in two directions, one concerned with Mendelssohn and natural religion, the other with Kant. Thus in 1784 Hamann's "twins" were born: his *Golgotha and Scheblimini* (*Golgotha und Scheblimini*) and his *Metacritique of the Purism of Reason* (*Metakritik über den Purismum der Vernunft*).

These twin texts (the subjects of Chapters 11 and 12) are fundamentally related in that they share Hamann's rejection of a rationality that is separated from language, culture, tradition, and, most importantly, the revelation that is afforded to human beings through them. Whereas in the *Metakritik* he argues that there is no such

---

6   ZH IV, p. 205.
7   NB, p. 344.
8   Quoted in NB, p. 367.
9   ZH VII, pp. 161, 168.
10   N III, pp. 347–407.
11   NB, pp. 347f.

rationality, that the famous *Critique* is built upon an illusion, and that the highest achievement of Kant's transcendental *Scheidekunst* (namely, his so-called "transcendental ideal") is an illusory something that might as well be nothing, in *Golgotha and Scheblimini* he argues that Mendelssohn's political philosophy, inasmuch as it too is divorced from tradition, suffers from similar illusions regarding such *entia rationis* as "natural religion" and "natural rights." To be sure, as we shall see, Mendelssohn's ultimate aim in *Jerusalem* was precisely to provide an "apology" for Judaism and secure the rights of European Jews by demonstrating the universality of its moral precepts and its corresponding compatibility (indeed virtual identity) with the natural religion of the Enlightenment. In Hamann's view, however, the price of Mendelssohn's noble efforts in this regard was far too costly: reducing Judaism to a purely rational religion, he threatened to deny any special revelation to the Jews and the very election of Israel itself.[12]

Hamann had no desire to start a debate with Mendelssohn any more than he wished to publish his *Metakritik* against Kant, which he left in the hands of Herder, intentionally delaying its publication until after his death; both of them were his friends. Mendelssohn, however, had forced his hand: he had called the legitimacy not only of Christianity, but also of Judaism, into question. Indeed, given that for Hamann Christianity stands or falls with Judaism as a revealed religion, presupposing God's covenant with Israel and the testimony of the law and prophets, *Golgotha und Scheblimini* had to be published. In the interest of their friendship, however, he tried to publish the work in Switzerland, hoping that Mendelssohn would suspect its author to be Lavater, his public antagonist, who had already tried to convert him.[13] The attempted ruse never came to anything, however, and it was published in Berlin, the odious center of the German Enlightenment against which his entire authorship was directed. Thus, having heard nothing of its publication for some time, he feared that it had been confiscated by the censors. "My Scheblimini!" he wrote to Hartknoch in August, 1784, "A raging beast has devoured it, an evil beast of a censor has torn it to pieces!"[14]

Hamann's fears were unfounded. *Golgotha und Scheblimini* was published and went on to elicit praise from various circles: from Herder, Goethe, Lavater, Jacobi, and, years later, from Hegel, who judged it to be the most important of Hamann's writings. The other "twin," however, was no less consequential, even if its publication was delayed. For if in *Golgotha und Scheblimini* Hamann deconstructed the notion of a natural religion in order to save Christianity *and* orthodox Judaism, in the *Metakritik* he attacks the palladium of the Enlightenment itself: namely, its confidence in a universal rationality that is allegedly independent of experience, tradition, language, and all the historical contingencies that these entail. But here again, what is ultimately at issue, whether *vis-à-vis* Kant or Mendelssohn, is their shared attempt to sunder reason (and "natural" religion) from tradition and revelation. For, as Hamann feared, one is then left with a civic religion and a secular rationality that is dangerously devoid of content, which is to say that one is left with a culture without historical foundations, poised upon the edge of *nothing* at all – and all that this implies.

---

[12]   See Moses Mendelssohn, *Schriften über Religion und Aufklärung*, ed. Martina Thom (Darmstadt: Wissenschaftliche Buchgesellschaft, 1989), p. 48.

[13]   NB, p. 354. That Hamann did not wish to lose Mendelssohn's friendship is clear, furthermore, from a letter to Herder, in which he happily reports receiving a letter from Mendelssohn, in which the latter assured him of his friendship. See ZH V, p. 351.

[14]   ZH V, p. 180.

HAMANN AND JACOBI

Next to Hamann, Friedrich Heinrich Jacobi (1743–1819) was the one contemporary who most keenly sensed the implicit nihilism lurking in the trajectory of modern philosophy; and it was during the last six years of Hamann's life that a close friendship developed between them – albeit a friendship based upon correspondence at great distance, with Hamann in Königsberg, and Jacobi in Pempelfort, near Düsseldorf. As we have seen thus far, the whole of Hamann's life testifies to an extraordinary capacity for friendship: one need only read his letters to Lindner, to Herder, to "Crispus" (Christian Jacob Kraus), to Hartknoch, and to all the others who populated the almost Edenic paradise of his world.[15] But not even with Herder was Hamann as intimate as he was with Jacobi, whom he came to call his "Jonathan" (or "Jonathan Pollux") and whom he freely addressed in the familiar "Du," even though he would not meet him before the last year of his life!

Their friendship was sparked by Matthias Claudius, who sent Hamann a selection of Jacobi's writings in February, 1782. Before long, Jacobi was sending Hamann everything he wrote, seeking his approbation; and given the frank nature of their communications, Hamann did not withhold his judgments. In fact, at times he could be rather harsh, especially when it came to Jacobi's (in Hamann's view) "ill-considered" philosophy and overly zealous, direct (as opposed to Hamann's *indirect*) remonstrations of his contemporaries.[16] As he once advised him, "Do not mix as a layman in the affairs and official business of the scribes. Be neither their pendant nor pedant – neither their patron nor their sycophant."[17] Nevertheless, Jacobi managed to embroil himself in controversy, often at his own expense, especially in the case of his later debate with Schelling. Thus, in response to receiving one of Jacobi's latest works, Hamann writes, "On the 20th [of April] I received your anxiously awaited present. I devoured the little book, and afterward did not feel well … O My dear Jonathan Pollux! *You do not understand yourself* and are *overly anxious* to make yourself understood and to communicate your sick philosophy to others … Let me be the first to prepare you for the consequences you will draw upon yourself."[18] Needless to say, in light of Hegel's and Schelling's critical and at times scathing treatments of Jacobi, Hamann's judgment proved to be correct.

DIVESTMENT AND TRANSFIGURATION

Over the next few years, spurred by a review of *Golgotha und Scheblimini* in the *Allgemeine deutsche Bibliothek* and by the premature death of Mendelssohn in January 1786, Hamann was conceiving a final literary testament in which he would finally put down his masks and explain himself. The text, which has survived in two drafts, was called "Divestment and transfiguration: a flying letter to nobody, the

---

[15] NB, p. 365.
[16] This applies especially to Jacobi's charge *vis-à-vis* Mendelssohn that Lessing was a Spinozist, which in 1783 ignited the so-called "pantheism controversy" and, in the opinion of some, contributed to Mendelssohn's (Lessing's ardent defender) early death in 1786. For an excellent summary of the controversy, see Frederick C. Beiser, *The Fate of Reason* (Cambridge: Harvard University Press, 1987), pp. 44ff. While Hamann doubtless sympathized with Jacobi's conviction that the purely rational philosophies of the Enlightenment logically end in Spinozism qua fatalism, and that this, in turn, opens the doors to atheism and nihilism, he did not approve of the way Jacobi went about communicating it, which he considered clumsy and ultimately unproductive. See in this regard ZH VII, p. 156.
[17] Quoted in NB, p. 367.
[18] ZH VII, pp. 161, 168.

well-known" (*Entkleidung und Verklärung: Ein Fliegender Brief an Niemand, den Kundbaren*).[19] As with all of Hamann's publications, the title is full of significance. Firstly, it bears a plainly a Christological allusion to the disrobing and resurrection of Christ. Secondly, Hamann is stating his intention finally to put down his many masks and to reveal himself. Thirdly, by the title of this "last" of his texts, he also means to indicate the *eschatological* form of all his writings, namely, his attempt to bring about a critical judgment in his contemporaries, to divest them of their vanity, to lay bare their presuppositions, to show their intellectual nakedness, in order to prepare them by way of a necessary metacritical bath and a confession of Socratic ignorance (cf. 1 Cor. 8: 2–3) for the possibility of transfiguration in Christ. In this respect the title resonates with that of *Golgotha and Scheblimini*, both of which allude to the Christological form of *kenosis* and glorification, which is the archetype of all spiritual growth – "Unless a grain of wheat fall to the ground and die, it remains but a single grain, but if it should die, it bears much fruit" (John 12: 24f.). In London Hamann had experienced this spiritual death and rebirth, beginning with what he described as a *descensus ad inferos* of self-knowledge guided by the critical judgment of the Word of God; the only question for his subsequent authorship (and its method) was how to convey the same thing.

The subtitle is also revealing. "Flying letter," refers both to the occasional nature of his literary productions thus far, but, more importantly, to their prophetic aspect: they are like the flying scroll seen by Zechariah (Zech. 5: 1f.), subject to the purposes of the Holy Spirit, who blows where he wills (John 3: 8). The second part, "Nobody the well-known" (or "Nobody the notorious"), repeats the ironic dedication to the public of Hamann's first work, the *Socratic Memorabilia*, indicating that we have come full circle. Like the *Socratic Memorabilia,* the present work is addressed to a public that is, in a sense, nobody (at least nobody in particular), but is nevertheless "well-known," indeed, "*the highest ideal and idol*" of most authors.[20] As for the motto on the frontispiece, it is a familiar collation of a pagan poet and an Old Testament prophet, in this case Horace and Elijah: "Non fumum ex fulgore, sed ex fumo dare *LUCEM* / Cogitat – – – / – – Conviva fatur – – / *IAM SATIS EST!*" The citation from Horace is a further allusion to Hamann's intended self-clarification, but it alludes more importantly to the sublime, dramatic form of his authorship thus far: "Not smoke from lightning, but from smoke to give *light.*" This, in other words, is what each of his publications sought to achieve: to "enlighten" his contemporaries through the "darkness" of his style (just as the shining Moses received *illuminations* within the *darkness* atop Mount Sinai). As for the citation from 1 Kings 19: 4, it testifies to the fact that, like the prophet Elijah in his struggle against Ahab and Jezebel, Hamann, the *sauvage du nord*, is worn out from his lifelong literary battle, under countless pseudonyms and strategic ruses, with his own king, *Salomon du nord*, i.e., Frederick the Great. Thus the time has finally come to put down his literary weapons and reveal himself: "Now it is enough!"

But while Hamann's purpose in *Entkleidung und Verklärung* is to elucidate the aims of his authorship, even now he does not write in plain prose, nor are his occasionally direct statements about his intentions what one would ordinarily call "elucidations." He is too aware of his audience's erudition not to display his own, and often enough in demonstrations of exquisite and wholly characteristic persiflage.

---

[19] N III, pp. 347–407.
[20] See N III, pp. 352, 360. Hamann refers in this context to Paul's second letter to the Thessalonians, ch. 2, vv. 3–12, alluding to the fact that his entire authorship is conceived in prophetic opposition to Frederick the Great.

As he comically puts it, "With squinting literary critics, who mistake authors for peripatetic trees (Mark 8: 24), I am compelled to speak in the aesthetic language they provide me."[21] He speaks, that is, in their terms, typically using their words, not his own (such is the typical kenotic form he assumes), but with this difference: "that I counter the qualities of their dead filaments with the better qualities of fresh, green wood; their bare, unfruitful, twice-dead and uprooted trees (Jude 12), with those planted by the streams, whose waters flow from the sanctuary, whose fruit serves for food, and whose unwithered leaves serve as medicine for the healing of the peoples" (Ezek. 47: 12; Ps. 1: 3; Rev. 22: 2).[22] Indeed, as he finally and poignantly suggests, he has conducted his prophetic authorship all along under the influence of divine inspiration:

> For how else, with what kind of power, would a meek preacher, who has never had a gift for words (*disertus*), who has a heavy accent and the eloquence of a heavy tongue – how else, but with the refiner's fire and the fuller's soap (Mal. 3: 2), would such a one have dared to mimic the greatest among those born of women in the zeal of Elijah? (Matt. 11: 11) – to provoke the enormous, windy loquacity of Babylonian pyrgotects [i.e., tower builders]? – to demolish the walls of a Punic city of palms in the moon by means of the still, gentle breeze of a persiflage without the assistance of a storm and an earthquake, without the sounding of trumpets and a loud shout (1 Kgs. 19: 11–12; Josh. 6: 5; Isa. 25: 12)? – a man can receive nothing except it be given him from heaven, answered and spoke John the Baptist" (John 3: 27).[23]

In other words, how else could he, by nature possessed of a stammering tongue like Moses, engage in literary warfare with the "enlightened" architects of Babel – with the "enlightened" despot himself, Frederick the Great (cf. 2 Thess. 2: 4ff.) – except by the assistance of the same Spirit who inspired Elijah? Should he be successful, should he bring down the tower of reason, which had been exalted above the throne of God, it would therefore be a victory of divine irony, which "chooses what is foolish in the world to shame the wise," "what is weak in the world to shame the strong," "what is low and despised in the world, things that are not, to reduce to nothing things that are, so that no one might boast in the presence of God" (1 Cor. 1: 27f.). So too, like the prophets, he seeks no laurels; still less does he seek to impress the public with a novel philosophical system that would garner its praise:

> Though there be authors like operatic machines, like insects who are more intelligent than the sages, who construct systems like spiders and theories like the birds [build] nests, busy swarms of bees, who labor to [appease] the taste of the public and [further] its enlightenment with an automatic industriousness that surpasses any imitation on the part of human reason and art: I have never sought to be invested with the honor of such glorified imitations [*Ölgötzen*], or sought to cover my bare head with their laurels, crowns, and horns.[24]

In fact, from Hamann's perspective, the very concept of Christian authorship forbids such intentions (cf. Gal. 1: 10). (As for the reference to philosophical "systems," it is obvious what he would have thought of Hegel – that systematician par excellence.) Instead, he says that, like John the Baptist and all the martyrs, his authorship is poured out for the glory of Christ: "The little stream of my authorship, despised like

---

[21] N III, p. 378.
[22] Ibid.
[23] N III, p. 377.
[24] N III, p. 401.

the waters of Shiloah that flow gently, was poured out for the sake of this king, whose name, like his reputation, is great and unknown."[25]

Herein, then, lies the *ultima ratio* of Hamann's polemic against Mendelssohn's *Jerusalem*: we come to understand that for Hamann Jerusalem is the city of *this particular king*, and that for this reason the city of Jerusalem, which is in a sense *absent*, a figure of the *past* and an anagogical figure of the *future*, must in no way be confused with the "French Babylon" of the *present*.[26] In other words, the problem with Mendelssohn's *Jerusalem* is that he equates a prophetic figure of the past and future with a present-day rational ideal of the Enlightenment, doing away thereby with the spirit of prophecy and the entire Messianic, eschatological dimension of Scripture.[27] But surely, Hamann suggests, no orthodox Jew can presume to "circumcise," i.e., cut out, the past and the future without *ipso facto* denying his faith and succumbing to an *idolatry* of the present. Yet this is precisely what Mendelssohn has unwittingly done:

> He began with the double presence of religious power and Judaism ... and spun out of them ... a brand new Jerusalem, without troubling himself or even asking himself anything about the past and future archetype. This empty construction of poetic plastic seduced his heart and, with the assistance of philosophical abstractions, led him formally to deny and destroy divine credibility and positive truth.[28]

In sum, denying the spirit of prophecy, Mendelssohn made the error of making himself into the creator and architect of his own private city and passing it off as the city of God.[29]

This, then, is what evoked Hamann's spirited rebuttal of Mendelssohn in *Golgotha und Scheblimini*, and also why the heart of *Entkleidung und Verklärung* is dedicated to this one, in his view, central error of modern philosophy: that it divorces the rational "spirit of observation" from the "spirit of prophecy," leaving the dead rump of a dimensionless and idolatrous present. What is more, in its confident reliance upon the rational spirit of observation to the exclusion of the spirit of prophecy – i.e., in its Promethean attempt to control the present, however fleeting, and to establish therein, free of all prophetic, religious interference, a modern secular state – secular reason unwittingly makes the very present disappear, to become *as nothing*. And to this extent, Hamann suggests, throughout its transcendental variants, modern philosophy could justifiably be seen as a kind of anti-prophetic magic:

> The Spirit of observation and the spirit of prophecy are the wings of human genius. To the realm of the first belongs everything present; to the realm of the latter everything absent, the past and the future. The philosophical genius expresses its power in that, by means of abstraction, it labors to make the present absent; and *divests* real objects into naked concepts, into qualities that exist only in thought, into pure appearances and phenomena.[30]

[25] N III, p. 399. See Isa. 8: 6; Job 36: 26.

[26] N III, p. 390.

[27] As Hamann puts it, "Even the casual reader can hardly deny, or put off the observation, that in the Hebrew revelations concerning Jerusalem the most terrifying threats are mixed with the most glorious promises, like the elements in the flood and the pages of the Psalter" (N III, p. 385).

[28] N III, p. 388.

[29] N III. See also Hamann's remark, toward the end of his text (p. 404): "Should I ever again forget your Jerusalem: let everything be forgotten that my right hand has written. Let the quill stick to my thumb if Jerusalem be not my highest joy" (cf. Ps. 137).

[30] N III, pp. 382f.

For Hamann, then, it is *not* that reason, understood here as the "spirit of observation," does not have a dignity in its own right. As this passage adequately shows, he is *not* an irrationalist. What he criticizes is the Enlightenment's unnatural, programmatic separation of reason from the "spirit of prophecy," and the corresponding usurping of this "prophetic spirit" by the present ideologies of secular reason. Positively stated, the "spirit of observation" and the "spirit of prophecy" go together: their union is the *sine qua non* of human genius, inspired creativity, and the flourishing of culture. Their separation, on the other hand, is a sign of cultural decline, the death of art, and imminent nihilism.

From this perspective we can also glimpse the ultimate horizon of Hamann's critique of Kant. For, according to Hamann, this is precisely what Kant's transcendental idealism brings about: a reduction of the world to mere "appearances," to an illusory "something = x" of which, theoretically speaking, we can know nothing at all. Accordingly, Hamann says that in the absence of the prophetic dimension the present inevitably becomes meaningless: "What would the most exact and careful knowledge of the present be without a divine renewal of the past, without a presentiment of things to come [?] ... What a *labyrinth* would the present be for the spirit of observation without the spirit of prophecy and its guiding threads of the past and the future[!]"[31]

Admittedly, like a good magician, Kant (like Descartes) makes the world disappear only to bring it back again, in his case, as the domain of practical reason (pointing the way to Fichte).[32] But as Hamann prophetically realized, because reason is incapable of grounding reality (whether its own reality or that of the external world), it is ultimately powerless to bring back the world it has magically conjured away. This only the prophet or inspired poet can do, who speaks to the dry bones like Ezekiel (Ezek. 37); and so Hamann says, "Poetic genius," i.e., the genius of one inspired by the spirit of prophecy, "expresses its power in that it *transfigures* the visions of the absent past and future into present representations by means of *fiction*."[33] In other words, just as God enlivens creation by his Spirit (Gen. 1: 2; 2: 7), the poet-prophet enlivens the present by a spiritual translation of the past and the future, so that the present stands out not in isolation, but according to the fullness of time (whereby "fiction" is to be understood not in the modern sense of the term, as a kind of fabrication, but as an inspired translation of divine things).

By contrast, the various attempts on the part of secular reason to ground the reality of the present independently of the prophetic spirit, i.e., independently of God, prove in the end to be so many "fictions" in precisely the modern sense of the term – indeed, to be so many unconvincing "magic acts," which can no more establish "the real" than they can establish a secular Jerusalem (which is the objective correlate, so to speak, of secular reason). In sum, Hamann's critique of modernity is that secular reason has forsaken the spirit of prophecy in a misguided attempt to ground itself in itself (*incurvatio in se ipsum!*), whereby it repeats the logic of the Fall, seeking to be God without God – seeking enlightenment without genuine spiritual illumination. As a result, it has forsaken the prophetic temporality (cf. Heidegger!) which alone gives meaning (and substance!) to the present and keeps it from slipping into the void.[34]

---

[31] N III, p. 398. My emphasis.

[32] For more on the "magic" of modernity, as distinct from the prophetic spirit of Christianity, see Eric Vogelin, *Wissenschaft, Politik und Gnosis* (Munich: Kösel Verlag, 1959), pp. 65–85; see also Conor Cunningham, *Genealogy of Nihilism: Philosophies of Nothing and the Difference of Theology* (London: Routledge, 2002). especially pp. 74ff.

[33] N III, p. 384.

[34] For more on the connection to Heidegger and the consequences of modern philosophy for a doctrine of substance – or rather a lack thereof – see the Conclusion in this volume.

In this respect, then, Hamann not only anticipates Heidegger's and, by extension, Derrida's critique of the flattened temporality of every so-called "metaphysics of presence," but also shows their philosophies to be, in the final analysis, secularized prophetic theologies. For, like Hamann, but in secularized terms, they speak "prophetically" in the name of some kind of "absence" (whether this be the "absence" of *Seyn* or the unarrested play of *différance*) against every system of thought that, under the spell of mastery (the spirit of the Babylonian "pyrgotects"), would give unjust, idolatrous primacy to the present (see, for example, Heidegger's *Anaximander Fragment*!). Given, however, that Heidegger's and Derrida's postmodern philosophies ultimately remain *within* the problematic of modernity – indeed, arguably represent its logical conclusion – they are unable to present any clear alternative to it. Hamann, on the other hand, clearly saw the alternative and prophetically intimated it with increasing foreboding over the course of his authorship: either faith in the Logos (as transmitted historically through revelation) or the nihilism of secular reason and its embodiment in the modern nation-state. Accordingly, he ultimately came to see his entire authorship in political terms as a contest between himself, the *Magus in Norden* of "*Grand*-Soucy," writing obscurely amid many cares, and *Solomon du Nord*, the pseudo-philosopher and "enlightened" despot of Sans Souci.[35]

At the conclusion of the first draft of *Entkleidung und Verklärung,* Hamann provides a final testament to his friends and benefactors concerning the prophetic nature of his authorship. Turning to them, he says, "Have mercy on me, have mercy on me, you friends of mine, for the hand of God has rested on me too. Were it not for your good deeds and the pleasure they provided, my life would have been similar to that of Job and Lazarus. May our common comfort at our departure be the hope of seeing one another again in the true fatherland of all aliens and pilgrims and brothers of this world."[36] To which he adds:

> The dead need neither placard nor reward. You household divinities of the living, do not humble me by folly and vanity; do not exalt one who is dead by making an idol of me. Do not worry about adding an ell to me or my stature. The measure of my "greatness" is neither that of a giant nor an angel, no hand broader than that of a common human ell. Please do not paint any moustaches on my life, unless I can still laugh with you, so that the world is not forced to invest and transfigure a rotten sinner with the nimbus of a "saint." I would rather divest myself and spread out my hands like a swimmer (Isa. 25: 11), in order to swim across the gently flowing water of the past or submerge myself in it.[37]

As it happens, though Jacobi and Franz Buchholtz (a wealthy Catholic patron from Münster, who had entrusted himself to Hamann as a "spiritual son") had hoped to publish it, *Entkleidung und Verklärung* was never finished. At a certain point, Hamann simply ran out of steam. Or perhaps this too was part of his point: that the sum of our knowledge and work in this life is "fragments" (cf. 1 Cor. 13: 12), which God alone, in the spirit of John 6: 9ff., can turn into a meaningful whole. Still, his friends (Jacobi, Herder, Hippel, and Kraus, among others) and a growing number of wealthy admirers in Münster had hopes that he would produce a complete edition of his "sibylline leaves," and encouraged him to this end. And they had good reason

---

[35] See NB, p. 378.
[36] N III, p. 404.
[37] Ibid.

for doing so. As Nadler puts it, Hamann had become "to his age more the subject of legend than of *lectio*, and his influence was more the result of his *mythos* than his *logos*."[38] In other words, an edition of his works had become necessary if they were to communicate to their own and to the next generation, beyond Hamann's alluring persona, the specific content of his wisdom.

"METACRITICAL TUBS"?

Undoubtedly, the suggestion of producing a complete edition struck Hamann as vain and fundamentally incongruous with the pseudonymous, occasional, and self-denying nature of everything he wrote. Nevertheless, he remained open to the idea; and given his obsession with titles he was soon corresponding with Herder about it.[39] Their correspondence about this matter is utterly comical and representative of Hamann's general sense of humor. He proposed the ludicrous title, "Bathhouse quackeries" [*Saalbadereien*], and the still more absurd title for the initial volume: "First little tub" [*Erstes Wannchen*].[40] In truth, however, the title conveys precisely what Hamann had understood his entire authorship to be: a humble, "metacritical" washing of the feet of his age, in fidelity to the memory of his father's occupation and Christ's mandate in the Gospel (John 13: 12f.). Needless to say, Herder found the title unsuitable and insisted that Hamann come up with a new one:

> As much as I am excited about the collection of your writings, dearest H., I completely disapprove of the title = *Saalbadereien*, whatever reasons you may wish to advance in its behalf. I beg you, for the sake of our friendship, give it up to me: for your *Socratic Memorabilia*, etc. truly do not belong under this heading, which, as a matter of fact, [would] disturb the effect of the book and obstruct its pure and true perspective.[41]

Herder then added, in joking reference to his ecclesiastical authority as superintendent general of the Lutheran Church in Weimar, "I impose upon it [i.e., the title] a formal and solemn interdict ..."[42]

Hamann's response was tellingly slow: "So you do not want *Saalbadereyen* – then how about "Little tubs" [*Wannchen*], say, "Little metacritical tubs," or something to that effect?"[43] Clearly, Hamann could not let go of the image; his father's tub, he reminds Herder, is "as holy to him as the [midwife's] stool of Socrates' mother was to Socrates."[44] In a letter to Jacobi he explains himself further: " 'Little metacritical tubs' – this means as much as to wash the feet = *medios terminus progressus* of our

---

[38] NB, p. 370.

[39] For Hamann the title was the "Orphic egg" and "tabernacle" of his muse, the "minimum of a mustard seed" from which his "elastic" texts developed and to which they returned. See N III, p. 372.

[40] ZH V, p. 204. The term "Saalbadereien" is almost impossible to translate. At one level, it suggests the act of giving someone a bath in a bathing salon (which was precisely the occupation of Hamann's father); it also implies the word "Salbader," which can mean both a "babbler" as well as a "quack doctor," who cures patients with salves. Thus, "Saalbadereien" suggests the curative methods of a babbling quack doctor in a bathing salon. For more on this term, see Oswald Bayer and Christian Knudsen, *Kreuz und Kritik* (Tübingen: Mohr-Siebeck, 1983), pp. 137f.

[41] ZH V, p. 248.

[42] Ibid.

[43] ZH V, p. 350.

[44] Ibid.

enlightened century."[45] Herder found this second proposal equally problematic and pointed out that the Prussian penchant for diminutives, as exhibited in the title, was not only provincial but would invariably elicit ridicule.[46] In reply, Hamann thanked him for his advice, but insisted on keeping the title, at least for the time being, adding, "The provincial, like the individual, belongs to the character of my baroque taste, which I will never be able to deny."[47] Such was the difference between the idiosyncratic, provincial Hamann (the German Socrates) and his famous cosmopolitan disciple, Herder (the German Plato).

Unfortunately, though his friends kept pressing him about it, the planned edition came to nothing. For one thing, at this point in his life Hamann was simply not up to the task of organizing his occasional tracts into a coherent whole. As he put it to Johann George Scheffner, who was prepared to help him: "It has truly been an Herculean labor for me to go through what I wrote between [17]59 and [17]83, since everything refers to the actual situation of my life, to moments, to mistaken, cockeyed, withered impressions that I am no longer able to renew."[48] Aside from the practical difficulties, however, there were other reservations, stemming partly from his humility, partly from a sense of the pointlessness of publishing works so occasional, so obscure, and so unintelligible (after so many years) even to himself:

> I no longer understand myself, quite differently from then; some [writings I understand] better, some worse. What one does not understand, one is inclined to leave unread – and so it should also remain *unwritten* – still less should it be *published again* ... My name and reputation are of no account; as a matter of conscience, however, I can expect neither a publisher nor the public to read such unintelligible stuff. 'God understands me,' says Sancho Panza, if I am not mistaken; but I would at least like to understand myself ... It is impossible that everyone should understand the same amount; and yet, each [understands] something, according to the measure he himself possesses and I am neither able nor [presuming] to give.[49]

The edition was therefore almost destined to run aground. As Hamann himself realized, none would have been satisfactory without a massive textual apparatus, which would explain all the obscure occasions and allusions of his writings, much of which he himself could no longer explain. Indeed, what was the point of producing an edition no one could possibly understand? But even if the edition was an absurdity from the start – as Hamann alone may have grasped – his friends' drive to publish his writings, which would not come to fruition until well into the next century, had begun.

---

[45] ZH V, p. 331. By *medios terminus progressus* Hamann means the middle term of Aristotle's syllogism in the *Prior Analytics* 25b, 32–7. Here, however, faced with the overblown claims of the *Aufklärer* and the unsoundness of their deductions, Hamann means to say that a metacritical washing of feet has become a necessary step in sound reasoning.

[46] ZH V, p. 362.

[47] ZH V, p. 403.

[48] ZH V, p. 358. Cf. Hamann's remark to Buchholtz (quoted in NB, p. 374) "What I have published consists of mere text, of coincidental *auditis, visis, lectis* and *oblitis*, without the notes necessary to understand it."

[49] ZH V, p. 358.

11

Hamann's *Metacritique* of Kant: Deconstructing the Transcendental Dream

Jordani Bruni Principium coincidentiae oppositorum *is worth more to me than all Kantian criticism.*

Hamann to Herder[1]

Were I as eloquent as Demosthenes, I would have to do no more than repeat a single phrase three times. Reason is language, Λόγος. This is the marrow-bone on which I gnaw, and I will gnaw myself to death on it. For me there remains a darkness over this deep: I am still waiting for an a apocalyptic angel with a key to this abyss.

Hamann to Herder[2]

Experience and revelation are one and the same and indispensable crutches or wings of our reason, if it is not to remain lame and creep along. The senses and history are the foundation and ground – however deceptive the former, and naïve the latter: I nevertheless prefer them to all ethereal castles.

Hamann to Jacobi[3]

In *The Fate of Reason*, which addresses a series of thinkers and controversies that are often ignored in broader surveys but are nevertheless crucial to the development of post-Kantian philosophy, Frederick Beiser notes that "Hamann's thought is often striking for its modernity, its foreshadowing of contemporary themes."[4] However much this applies to other aspects of Hamann's thought, it is most certainly true of his understanding of the relationship between reason and language. Indeed, in Hamann one encounters arguably the first *linguistic turn* in the history of ideas, in the sense of a thoroughgoing reflection on the cultural and linguistic determinations of thought itself.[5] This is not to deny earlier philosophical treatments of language, from Plato's *Cratylus* to Locke's *Essay concerning Human Understanding*, which Hamann knew and drew upon. But with Hamann the subversive implications of a

---

[1] ZH IV, p. 462. As we now know, the term *coincidentia oppositorum* is original not to Giordano Bruno, but to Nicholas of Cusa.

[2] ZH V, p. 177.

[3] ZH V, p. 265.

[4] Frederick C. Beiser, *The Fate of Reason: German Philosophy from Kant to Fichte* (Cambridge. MA: Harvard University Press, 1987), p. 17.

[5] Ibid.

philosophy of language are for the first time forcefully brought to bear against the rationalism of the Continental tradition. For example, long before such notions became commonplace (the Enlightenment was defined by the pursuit of an abstract rationality and criterion of truth), Hamann contended that "*language* and *writing* are the inescapable *organs* and conditions of all human learning, more essential and absolute than light to seeing and sound to hearing"; that "invention and reason already presuppose a language, and can be conceived as little without the latter as *arithmetic* can be conceived without *numbers*"; and, perhaps more novel still, that "not only the whole capacity to think depends upon language ... but [that] language is also the center of the misunderstanding of reason with itself."[6]

For Hamann, therefore, the chief problem with Kant's philosophy is a failure seriously to consider the ways in which reason is always already affected by the *impure* historical and cultural operations of language – though it is the most obvious and necessary condition for the possibility of any cognitive experience! Thus he says, "With me it is not so much the question: What is reason? but rather: What is language? And this I take to be the ground of all the paralogisms and antinomies of which the former is accused."[7] But, according to Hamann, not only does Kant not get to the bottom of reason's antinomies; his lack of attention to the role of language (however transcendentally he might attempt to escape from it) inevitably leads him to be *deceived* by it. As Hamann strikingly puts it to Jacobi, "The *adiutorium* of language is the seducer of our understanding, and will always be so until we come back home to the beginning and origin ..."[8] In other words, language is at once the indispensable helper *and* seducer of understanding: on the one hand, there is no philosophy without it, inasmuch as it lies at the basis of all thought; on the other hand, philosophers will be seduced by it as long as they have not inquired into its mysterious origin and appreciated the ways one can be deceived by it.

But, of course, for Hamann this is where philosophy also runs up against its limit; for the origin of language (and hence too the origin of reason) is impenetrable to reason and can be approached only mythologically (as we saw in Chapter 6). Indeed, for Hamann this is precisely where the whole of philosophy, understood as a quest for certainty, comes to a grinding halt. This is where reason stands before an abyss; this is where it must recognize its own inadequacy and incompleteness; in short, this is where it can proceed no further except by some kind of faith. In any case, this is what calls the bluff on all philosophical claims to have attained a purely rational, logical, or formal foundation (whether through Descartes's *cogito*, or Kant's transcendental deduction, or Schelling's intellectual intuition, or Fichte's "I = I," or Husserl's "phenomenological reduction," or Russell's logical atomism). But neither, following Hamann, can one presume to attain a purely material, "factual" foundation, as in the positivism of the Vienna Circle or the crass materialism of much modern science, since it is through language, in its simultaneously material *and* formal aspects, that we have cognitive experience of anything at all.

If, therefore, philosophy is not to be hypocritical (in the case of a rarefied idealism) or fall victim to reductivism (in the case of a crass materialism), it must, according to Hamann, "await the apocalyptic angel with a key to this abyss."[9] But, as Hamann sees it, this is precisely what Kant does not do. Instead he either ignores the problem

---

[6] N III, pp. 130, 21, 286.

[7] ZH V, p. 264.

[8] ZH VII, p. 173.

[9] ZH V, p. 177.

of language's influence, in which case he unwittingly plunges into the abyss, or he proleptically attempts to vault the abyss by means of transcendental concepts a priori. Either way, his philosophy is marked by a fanciful flight from and beyond the question of language. As Hamann puts it, "What is sought in oriental cisterns lies in the *sensu communi* of the use of language; this key transforms our best and worst [*wüst*] philosophers into senseless mystics."[10]

But if language can be deceptive (to the point of turning so rigorous and sober a philosopher as Kant into a "senseless mystic"), for Hamann it is also the vehicle of revelation and supernatural wisdom (to the point of transforming "the simplest Galileans and fishermen into the profoundest experts and heralds of a wisdom that is not earthly, human, and devilish, but a secret, hidden wisdom of God, which God ordained before the foundation of the world for our glory ...").[11] In short, language can both deceive and reveal; it can turn philosophers into fools and fishermen into saints. Accordingly, Hamann suggests that the science of sciences would in some sense be a science of language; for without language there would be neither physics nor theology, i.e., neither any knowledge of nature nor knowledge of God, nor indeed any science at all. As he puts it to Jacobi: "For me it is a matter neither of physics nor of theology, but of *language,* the *mother* of reason and its revelations, it is the double-edged sword of all truths and lies; and do not laugh if I must attack the matter from this angle. It is my old lyre, but by *it all things* are made."[12]

Earlier we saw how Hamann appropriated the Lutheran doctrine of *sola fide* for a penetrating critique of modern philosophy; now, toward the end of his life, he appropriates the logos theology of John's gospel for similar purposes. Whereas in the *Socratic Memorabilia* he used Hume to show the dependence of reason upon faith, here he shows the dependence of reason upon the word (in both the ordinary and Johannine senses of the term). The novelty of Hamann's argument in this regard would eventually have a profound effect on the shape of twentieth-century philosophy. Indeed, one could easily argue that the thematic importance of language and textuality to postmodern philosophy has its roots in Hamann's theologically inspired "linguistic turn" – to the point that one could legitimately see him as a herald not only of the late Heidegger but also of the late Wittgenstein. Even Hamann himself seems to have recognized that his ideas were ahead of their time; as he put it to Jacobi, "*I do not know if you understand me ... It is not yet a matter for the rooftops.*"[13]

Hamann's insights concerning language did not go unnoticed by the next generation, however. As we saw in Chapter 6, Schelling renewed Hamann's reflections on the origin of language before the Berlin Academy in 1850. Hegel, too, took note of Hamann's insights in this regard, especially his spiritual understanding of language as involving a mysterious *coincidentia oppositorum* of the sensible and the intelligible, from which the rationality of the *Aufklärer* was an unnatural abstraction. As he put it in his review, "It is wonderful to see how in Hamann the concrete Idea ferments and turns itself against the divisions of reflection ... Hamann places himself in the middle of the problem of reason and proposes its solution; and he conceives it in terms of *language.*"[14] In other words, whereas Kant's philosophy divided the phenomenal from the noumenal, the sensible from the intelligible, and subsequent to

---

[10] ZH V, p. 95.
[11] Ibid. Cf. Jas. 3: 15f.
[12] ZH VI, p. 108; cf. John 1: 3.
[13] ZH V, p. 95.
[14] Hegel, *Berliner Schriften 1818–1831*, in *Werke* (Frankfurt am Main: Suhrkamp, 1970), vol. 11, p. 326.

"this unnatural and unholy divorce" (in Hamann's phrase) could offer only a tenuous connection by means of synthetic judgments a priori, Hamann repeatedly points out that the actual living unity of these elements, which reason subsequently sunders, is already *given* in language.

Whatever Hegel ultimately made of Hamann's view of language, given the problems bequeathed to him and Schelling by Kant's dualisms, Hamann's intensely Christological, anti-dualistic philosophy must be seen as a formative, if background, influence on German Idealism. Indeed, given that Hamann conceives of the overcoming of Kant's dualisms precisely in terms of "spirit," one can even find in his thought, *mutatis mutandis,* anticipations of Hegel's *Geist.* Consider, for example, Hamann's statement to Herder regarding the abstract religion of the *Aufklärer* and their inability to see the operations of a *transcendent* God *in* history and the contingencies of human affairs:

> It seems to me that the transition from the divine to the human is always susceptible to a similar misunderstanding [*Misbrauch*]. Both extremes must be absolutely united in order to explain the whole, ουσια του σωματος and εξουσια του αξιωματος. Through this union the book becomes holy, as a man becomes a prince. A κοινονια without transubstantiation – neither body, nor shadow; but *Geist.*[15]

Whatever the extent of Hegel's familiarity with Hamann may have been prior to the first edition of his writings (which Hegel himself reviewed in 1828) such statements show that Hamann stands in the background not only of German Idealism's attempt to overcome Kant's dualisms, but also of its attempted recuperation of history. And for this reason, as Beiser points out, Hamann's *Metacritique* "has a strong claim to be the starting point of post-Kantian philosophy."[16]

In any case, Hamann merits consideration as the first, undoubtedly the most novel, and to this day perhaps the most incisive critic of Kant's philosophy.[17] To this end, in the rest of this chapter I will examine first Hamann's review of the first edition of Kant's *Critique of Pure Reason,* which was penned on July 1, 1781, shortly after receiving the proofs from Hartknoch. It was never published, however, as Hamann explained to Herder, because of his friendship with Kant: "since I [consider] the author an old friend and I almost have to say, my benefactor, since I owe my first post almost entirely to him."[18] I will then turn to Hamann's *Metakritik über den Purismum der Vernunft,* which Hamann conveyed in a final form to Herder on September 15, 1784, had thoughts of publishing, but ultimately withheld from publication for the same reason.[19]

---

[15] ZH IV, p. 254. Evidently, Hamann was fundamentally Lutheran in his understanding of Eucharistic doctrine.

[16] Ibid., p. 39. As Beiser puts it (*The Fate of Reason*, p. 43), "the history of post-Kantian philosophy largely consists in the quest for the unifying principle behind Kant's dualisms; and there are almost as many principles as there are philosophers: language in Hamann, representation in Reinhold, the will in Fichte, the indifference point in Schelling, religion in Schleiermacher, and spirit in Hegel. But this search begins with Hamann."

[17] The landmark study in this regard is Oswald Bayer's *Verunft ist Sprache: Hamanns Metakritik Kants* (*HMK*). For the most important treatment in English, see G-D, pp. 270–318.

[18] ZH IV, p. 317. For all their intellectual and personal differences, Hamann clearly held Kant in high regard; Kant was also gracious enough to allow Hamann's son to attend his lectures free of charge. Thus, as Hamann put it to Herder, "Leaving aside the *old Adam* of his authorship, he is a genuinely obliging, selfless and, at bottom, good and noble-hearted man of [many] talents and merits" (ZH V, p. 432).

[19] The *Metakritik* was not published until 1800 by Friedrich Theodor Rink, a Königsberg philosophy professor and Kantian, in a volume titled, *Mancherley zur Geschichte der metacritischen Invasion. Nebst einem Fragment einer ältern Metacritik von Johann George Hamann, genannt der Magus in Norden, und einigen Auffsätzen, die Kantsche Philosophie betreffend.* By pointing out his indebtedness to Hamann, Rink was hoping to discredit Herder's own two-part *Metakritik* of Kant, which was published in 1799. See *HMK*, pp. 199f.

TRANSCENDENTAL "MYSTIQUE": THE FIRST REVIEW
OF THE *CRITIQUE OF PURE REASON*

In his preface to the first edition of the *Critique of Pure Reason,* Kant proposes a new way to address the mutually opposing problems of skepticism and dogmatism, as well as a third problem of "indifference" [*Indifferentismus*], which he calls "the mother of chaos and night."[20] Out of this "chaos" and "night" he dramatically proposes to bring about order and "enlightenment," indeed to revolutionize the sciences by finally giving them a firm footing through a self-critique of reason:

> It is a call to reason to undertake anew the most difficult of all its tasks, namely, that of self-knowledge, and to institute a tribunal which will assure to reason its lawful claims, and dismiss all groundless pretensions, not by despotic decrees, but in accordance with its own eternal and unalterable laws. This tribunal is no other than the *critique of pure reason.* I do not mean by this a critique of books and systems, but of the faculty of reason in general, in respect of all knowledge after which it may strive *independently of all experience.*[21]

To be sure, there is something admirable in Kant's intentions, especially given the dubious inheritance of Wolffian metaphysics, on the one hand, and the threat of skepticism, on the other. Indeed, in the interest of "saving" reason, Hamann and Kant both perceived the need to give reason a much needed "critical" (Kant) or "metacritical" (Hamann) bath that would alert reason to its limitations, beyond which it could not confidently tread. The all-important difference between them, however, is that whereas for Hamann the salvation of reason lies in the light of faith and reason's ordering to revelation, which *gives* to reason the material of its reflections, Kant believes that reason can "save itself" by its own self-critical power. In short, Kant is philosophically a Pelagian, who believes that reason is sufficient, in need neither of the subjective grace of faith nor the objective grace of revelation, and as such able to determine its own immutable laws a priori, independently of all custom and experience.

For Hamann, however, this "auto-referentiality" of reason, its purported independence of experience, tradition, and language (and all the historical contingencies that these imply) is the *proton pseudos* of Kant's philosophy; and in this respect Kant himself is sorely in need of a *meta*critical bath. To be sure, Kant explicitly says that he does not mean "a critique of books and systems," i.e., a critique in the traditional sense of the term, but rather a pure, philosophical critique of "the faculty of reason in general." But again, this is precisely what Hamann disputes: the notion that Kant is not an embodied critic, who is part of a tradition of interpretation, but an abstract being with access to a realm of pure thought. Indeed, for Hamann, as we shall see, there is no such thing as "pure reason" or reason *in abstracto,* but only reason within a tradition of interpretation. As he puts it, "Children become adults, maidens become brides, and readers become authors. Most books thus give a true impression of the abilities and inclinations with which one has read and is able to read."[22] For Hamann, therefore, Kant's *authorship* reveals nothing so glorious as a self-clarification

---

[20] Kant, *Critique of Pure Reason,* tr. Norman Kemp Smith (New York: St Martin's Press, 1965), p. 9 (A x).
[21] Ibid. (A xi–xii). Cf. p. 60 (B 27): "Still less may the reader here expect a critique of books and systems of pure reason; we are concerned only with the critique of the faculty of pure reason itself."
[22] N II, p. 341.

of reason and its timeless laws, but simply how well Immanuel Kant, a professor in Königsberg, who lives just down the road, was able to read (i.e., assimilate a *prior* tradition) and write (in response to it).[23] Accordingly, rather than introducing the historic *Critique* as a timeless oracle (which Kant claims will "decide as to the possibility or impossibility of metaphysics in general, and determine its sources, its extent, and its limits – all in accordance with principles"), Hamann treats it quite consciously as the subject of a *literary* review.

Hamann begins his review with a *footnote* from Kant's preface. "Our age," Kant says, "is the true [*eigentliche*] age of criticism, to which everything must submit. Both religion and law-making seek to escape it, the one through its holiness, the other through its majesty. But then they arouse against themselves justified suspicion and cannot claim unfeigned respect, which reason grants only to that which can endure its unfettered and public examination."[24] The fact that Hamann draws attention to this seemingly incidental remark is highly significant – aside from what it says about his proto-deconstructionist reading habits. For what he wants to emphasize is the *under-stated*, but subversive *subtext* of Kant's *Critique*. To be sure, Kant's *stated* concern is to show the errors to which reason, abstracted from experience, is prone, and to ensure that it no longer go chasing after *entia rationis*. Such is the meaning of the *genetivus objectivus* of the book's teasing title: Kant offers a critique *of* reason, its native dialectic, and its tendency to metaphysical illusion – the same kind of things he earlier criticized in *Dreams of a Spirit-Seer* (1766) with regard to Swedenborg.[25] What Hamann brings to light in view of this footnote, however, is the *genetivus subjectivus* in Kant's title, which indicates that his internal critique *of* reason is ultimately undertaken for the sake of a radical political critique *on the part of* reason. In other words, Kant's aim is precisely to re-establish reason upon a sure foundation, free of internal contradictions, so that it can be reinstated as an independent judge of legal and religious tradition. Such, as Hamann immediately perceived, are the revolutionary political implications of Kant's seemingly abstruse, philosophical work. Should his critique *of* reason be successful, then all the previous claims of tradition would suddenly be forced to submit *to* rational scrutiny. What is more, should these claims of tradition before the court of reason fail the test (i.e., the test of secular reason now clarified and exalted beyond the contingencies of tradition, *impossible* though this be), then earlier tradition could no longer hope to receive any political sanction or *public* approbation. To be sure, earlier tradition – however defining of a people or a culture, however attested by prophets and saints, however fruitful in works of charity – might be retained *privately* by individuals as a matter *subjective* opinion; but, according to the dictates of "sound reason," it would henceforth be denied any *objective* or binding validity in matters of state or public policy.

Admittedly, if one reads Kant's *Critique* simply as a work of theoretical philosophy, it easily gives the impression of impartial neutrality, of being a purely rational investigation conducted in the ether of *pure* thought, with Kant, the new Moses, entering into the heavenly tabernacle of thought itself and relaying to the profane crowd the heavenly, i.e., transcendental, architecture of what he has seen. For Hamann, however, what is everywhere implied but *understated*, as this footnote

---

[23] Interestingly, in this respect, Hamann applauds Descartes's *Discours de la méthode* since Descartes relates his thought-experiment in the form of a story of his own understanding. See Oswald Bayer, *Autorität und Kritik: Zur Hermeneutik und Wissenschaftstheorie* (Tübingen: Mohr-Siebeck, 1991), pp. 39–42, 67–71, 89–97.

[24] *Critique of Pure Reason* A xii.

[25] *Critique of Pure Reason*, B 350ff.

reveals, is that Kant's allegedly pure philosophy is ultimately a highly sophisticated rhetorical effort on behalf of a far more worldly and therefore *impure* motive: namely, the furthering of a tendentious political program, whose popular acceptance depends upon strategic metaphors (like "enlightenment"), a catchy slogan (*sapere aude!*), an abstract mystagogy (called the "transcendental method") by which to impress the vulgar with a sense of mystery, and an accompanying myth of a universal rationality to which all have equal and immediate access. Should Kant be successful, Hamann wryly observes, his "magical" philosophy, which purports suddenly to resolve two thousand years of philosophical disputation, stands to be received like a "new revelation," "holier than religion and more majestic than the law":

> Knowledge that is not concerned with the objects themselves, but with concepts of objects *a priori* is called *transcendental*, and the *Critique of Pure Reason* is the complete idea of a *transcendental philosophy*. Under this new name an aged [*verjährte*] metaphysics is transformed overnight from a *two-thousand-year-old battlefield* of endless disputations into a *systematically ordered inventory of all our possessions by pure reason* – and propels itself on the wings of a rather abstract *genealogy* and *heraldry* to the monarchic dignity and Olympian hope "to see itself as unique among the sciences, their absolute fulfillment ... without the means of magic arts" or *magical talismans*, as the wise *Helvetius* says – "but rather all from principles" – – holier than those of religion and more majestic than those of the law.[26]

Hamann's sarcasm is, of course, thick. He cannot help but smile at Kant's presumption to have suddenly resolved two thousand years of metaphysical disputation, as if he were not a function of this tradition himself. Nor can he help but satirically clip "the wings" of its "rather abstract genealogy," which he elsewhere likens incredulously to Melchizedek, "without father, without mother, without race")[27] – as if thought could be accessed apart from the tradition of its forms. Indeed, in view of Kant's stupendous, but ultimately naïve claim suddenly, i.e., "magically," to have solved the historical problems of metaphysics, Hamann suggests that Kant's philosophy is itself a kind of "magic act," despite Kant's explicit repudiation of "magical devices, in which I am no adept."[28]

Among Hamann's initial charges, then, is that Kant turns out to be an unwitting magician; which is another way of saying that, like all magic acts, the *Critique* is based upon an illusion. This is true, on the one hand, of Kant's claims suddenly to have resolved the inherited problems of philosophy, as if the *Critique* would no sooner be published than philosophical disputation would come to an end. It is true, on the other hand, inasmuch as Kant "assimilates appearances and concepts, the elements of all our knowledge, 'to a transcendental something = x, about which we know and can know nothing as soon as it is isolated from the data of the senses.'"[29] In other words, like a good magician, Kant makes things disappear: he brings the phenomenal world to a transcendental *vanishing point* that is the object of thought alone, a pure transcendental noema = x.[30] To be sure, by means of his "transcendental

---

[26] N III, p. 277. Cf. *Critique of Pure Reason*, A xii, xx. Hamann is referring here to Claude Adrien Helvétius' *De l'Homme* in *Oeuvres completes* (London, 1777), vol. 3, p. 143. See *HMK*, p. 99.

[27] N III, p. 133.

[28] *Critique of Pure Reason*, A xiii.

[29] *Critique of Pure Reason*, A 250.

[30] For more on Kant as a magician, see Conor Cunningham, *Genealogy of Nihilism: Philosophies of Nothing and the Difference of Theology* (London: Routledge, 2002).

object," Kant seeks precisely to unite the two sources of knowledge: sensibility and understanding.[31] From Hamann's perspective, however, the magical result of Kant's purist philosophy, his "mystical inclination to empty form," is that "the whole *content*" of the *Critique* is "nothing but form *without content.*"[32] Indeed, in light of Hamann's corresponding claims in *Konxompax,* the result of Kant's transcendental magic is nothing as glorious as Kant intends, but the conjuring of a ghastly two-faced phantom: either "a *deceptive Nothing*" or an "*empty Something,*" either "a *material Nothing* or an *intellectual Something,*" which "for the mechanism of the *Sensus communis* amounts to the same thing."[33] Therein lies, as we shall see, the theoretical connection between Kant's philosophy (abstracted from all particular content, whether of the senses or tradition) and the problem of nihilism.

Admittedly, few readers would think to describe Kant's sober *Critique* as a magical or mystical treatise. For that matter, at one point in the *Critique* (A 314) Kant explicitly rejects Plato's "mystical deduction" of the Ideas. And yet, Hamann contends, "*Without knowing it,* [Kant] raves more hopelessly about space and time than Plato [about] the intelligible world."[34] Indeed, from his perspective, the entire *Critique* can be read as a *mystagogical* treatise. This is evident, firstly, with regard to Kant's transcendental method, which proceeds by way of an ascetical detachment from the senses and ordinary experience in order to contemplate the denuded form of things, the "transcendental object," which is stripped of every particular content and determination. It is evident, secondly, with regard to the even more sublime mystagogy whereby Kant himself as the hierophant of "pure reason," having cleansed himself of the contamination of the senses, passes through the apparent contradictions of the parologisms and antinomies of the "transcendental dialectic" to the "*ideal* of its mystical *unity,*" i.e., to God "as the regulative principle of [pure reason's] entire constitutive schematism and ethereal edifice."[35] Indeed, following Hamann, the very structure of Kant's *Critique* could be said to mirror the mystagogy of the temple cult, proceeding by way of an ever more inward progression from the forms of intuition, which concern the "outer court" of sensibility, to the "sanctuary" of the transcendental categories of the understanding, to the *sanctum sanctorum* of the regulative ideas of reason itself.

In any case, as Hamann reads it, the *Critique* is a kind of "magical mystery" *tour de force*; and one can only imagine Kant's dumbfounded reaction when Hamann personally confronted him with this charge.[36] As he related the occasion to Herder, "He [Kant] was very intimate with me, despite the fact that last time I made him a bit bemused by approving of his *Critique* but rejecting the mysticism contained in it. He had no idea how he got to be a mystic."[37] Importantly, this is not to deny the legitimacy and seriousness of Kant's questions. In the same context, for example, Hamann says that the *Critique* constitutes "a new leap from Locke's *tabula rasa* to *formas* and *matrices innatas,*" adding: "Both err, and both are right: but *in what* and *to what extent?*"[38] Clearly, therefore, he recognizes the philosophical problem

---

[31] See *HMK*, p. 95.

[32] *HMK*, p. 111. My emphasis.

[33] N III, p. 219; cf. N III, p. 142.

[34] N III, p. 293.

[35] Ibid.

[36] See G-D, p. 289.

[37] ZH IV, p. 355.

[38] ZH IV, p. 294.

involved, namely, the age-old dialectic between sensibility and understanding, empiricism and rationalism, realism and idealism, etc. At the same time, however – and here is his positive contribution to this endless debate – he sees this inveterate dialectic as arising in the form of a problem only once the natural unity of opposites, of material and formal elements, is not perceived in the miracle of *language*. In short, for Hamann, the problems attending Kant's *Critique* ultimately stem from a misunderstanding of language. "Here," he says, "language and artifice are really the *Deipara* of pure scholastic reason."[39]

Another difficulty that Hamann identifies in the *Critique* is what he considers a certain amount of intellectual dishonesty regarding the role of faith, resuming his earlier argument with Kant in the *Socratic Memorabilia*. On the one hand, he calls Kant the "Prussian Hume," presumably given how much of Hume's skepticism Kant had in fact assimilated; but he suggests that Hume is preferable in that he "at least dignified the *principium* of *faith* and incorporated it into his system," whereas "our countryman keeps *blustering about causality* without considering it. This doesn't strike me as honest."[40] In other words, Hamann applauds Hume for recognizing that some kind of faith, i.e., some kind of trusting of the senses, is required even for the most ordinary experience. As he put it to Kant some twenty years earlier, in what may have been Kant's first exposure to Hume: "The Attic philosopher Hume has need of faith if he should eat an egg and drink a glass of water."[41] But it is precisely this that Hamann finds missing in Kant. To be sure, Kant claims to be making room precisely *for* faith by marking off reason's proper limits. Hamann's point, however, is that faith cannot be bracketed out even for methodological purposes, since it is involved from the outset in all our reasoning. What is more, as Hamann profoundly grasped, the very attempt to separate reason from faith (and from the testimony of history and the senses) is ultimately inimical to reason itself, since reason is suddenly forced to do what it cannot, however much, like Sisyphus, it might try: namely, ground itself.[42] The result, as Hamann foresaw, is a crisis of reason, which, having now to bear the weight of so impossible a task, is tempted in one of two ways to commit theoretical suicide: either by embracing nihilism (and filling the void with noble lies of the will to power) or by capitulating to the service of purely immanent, pragmatic technological ends.

But again, this is not to say that Hamann did not respect the rigor of Kant's investigations or grant a certain legitimacy to his questions:

> To be sure, the decision as to the mere possibility or impossibility of metaphysics continues to depend upon the multifaceted and unexhausted question: *What* and *how much* can understanding and reason know independently of all experience? How much can I possibly hope to achieve with reason when deprived of all the material and assistance of experience? Is there such a thing as human knowledge apart from all experience – forms apart from all matter?[43]

---

[39] ZH IV, p. 294. In other words, Kant's "pure reason" is ultimately a function of language: the problems it addresses are *produced* by an abstraction *from* language, and the answers it *provides* are, in turn, a misuse and distortion *of* language.

[40] Ibid.

[41] ZH I, p. 379.

[42] Thus arose the post-Kantian enterprise to do just this in Fichte and Hegel. At the end of the era of German Idealism, Schelling realized that the effort was futile and called for a new beginning: what he called a "positive" philosophy. But by then it was too late; philosophy was already heading toward Nietzsche and the prospect of nihilism.

[43] N III, pp. 277f. As Bayer points out (*HMK*, p. 105), Hamann was no strict empiricist. As he puts it to Jacobi (ZH VII, p. 165): "Is knowledge possible apart from rational principles? – just as little as *sensus sine intellectu*. Composite beings are not capable of simple sensation[s], and still less simple [i.e., immediate, intuitive] knowledge. In human nature, sensibility can as little be separated from reason, as reason can be separated from sensibility."

Hamann points out, however, that Kant's philosophy is really not all that novel; moreover, he calls into question Kant's fascination with the analytic method as such, as if *this* were the purpose of reason, as if dividing things into their constitutive parts, and then trying to put them back together again, were the road to certain, infallible knowledge:

> Is there really a mystery hidden in the *differentia specifica* of analytic and synthetic judgments that did not occur to any of the ancients? Are *prius* and *posterius*, analysis and synthesis, not natural correlates and accidental opposites – both, however, like the *receptivity* of the subject to the *predicate*, grounded in the *spontaneity* of our concepts? Are not *ideae matrices* and *ideae innatae* the children of one *spirit*? Do not *sensibility* and *understanding*, the two branches of human knowledge, spring from a common, but unrecognized root, so that by means of the former objects are *given,* and by means of the latter, they are *thought* (understood and comprehended): what is the purpose of so violent and unauthorized a separation of what nature has joined together? Will not this dichotomy or division cause both branches to break off from their transcendental root and wither?[44]

Although he does not develop his point here, the common root to which Hamann refers is once again language, logos, which miraculously unites concepts and intuitions, understanding and sensibility. And it is in view of this natural wonder (which, in turn, for Hamann is a sign of the supernatural wonder of the *communicatio idiomatum* of the divine and human natures in Christ, the incarnate Logos) that Hamann asks Kant: why so violently divide and partition what nature, through language, brings together? What will it achieve? Will it not lead to a withering of both sensibility and understanding?

In keeping with his thoroughly Christological perspective, the force of Hamann's criticism here stems from his nuptial vision of reality (as was discussed in Chapter 8) and the words of Christ in the Gospel, "Let no one separate what God has joined together" (Mark 10: 9).[45] Indeed, here is the root of his criticism of Kant's analytic method and of the *Scheidekunst* of the age. As Bayer notes,

> Hamann's contemporaries are 'adulterers' first and foremost as '*Scheidekünstler.*' They understand themselves ... to be following a method similar to that of chemistry, namely, a method that 'separates the empirical from the rational,' the *a priori* from the *aposteriori*, the separation of accidental historical truths from the necessary truths of reason, the separation of Jesus from the Christ, the separation of the human from the divine quality of the Bible.[46]

To Kant's *Scheidekunst,* therefore, "Hamann opposes his *Ehekunst,*" i.e., his Christological "art of marriage."[47] And it is ultimately on these grounds, in view of his fundamentally Christian outlook – in view of the protological mystery of marriage,

---

[44] N III, p. 278.

[45] Cf. Hamann's remark to Jacobi (ZH VII, p. 158): "What God has joined together, no philosophy can separate; just as little unite, what nature has separated. Divorce and sodomy sin against nature and reason [–] the elemental philosophical forms of original sin, dead works of darkness [–] with the *Organis* of our internal and external life, our physical being = nature and metaphysical being = reason."

[46] Oswald Bayer, "Die Geschichten der Vernunft sind die Kritik ihrer Reinheit," in *Acta des vierten Internationalen Hamann-Kolloquiums* (Frankfurt am Main: Peter Lang, 1987), pp. 60f.

[47] HMK, p. 106.

the central mystery of the hypostatic union, and the eschatological mystery of Christ and his Church – that Hamann could say to Herder, "*Jordani Bruni Principium coincidentiae oppositorum* is worth more to me than all Kantian criticism."[48]

Thus far we have discussed the following angles of Hamann's criticism: Kant's *eschatological* presumption suddenly to have resolved the history of metaphysical disputation, the *prejudice* of his revolutionary politics, his transcendental magic and its *spectral* consequences, his ascetical, *mystagogical,* quasi-religious method, his profound *underestimation* of the role of language and tradition as the matrices of reason, his *disingenuous* bracketing of faith, his incipient *nihilism*, and, finally, his problematic *privileging* of analysis over what Griffith-Dickson rightly calls Hamann's "relationalism." All of which is stated with a shocking degree of concision. But there is more: in addition to Kant's *puritanism*, there is the implicit *Gnosticism* or *Manichaeism* of his quasi-alchemical method. As Hamann describes it, for Kant "Experience and matter represent what is *common,* and the *purity* that is sought is to be found by their separation; the remaining *form* is, so to speak, the *virginal earth* of a future system of pure (speculative) reason under the title: *Metaphysics of Nature,* of which the present *Critique* is merely the propaedeutic."[49]

But as Hamann metacritically points out, the *Critique* is precisely *not* pure; it itself is a product of tradition, and he exposes the hypocrisy, saying, "But since the whole content can be nothing but form without content, was none more expedient than the product [*Gemächte*] of the scholastic art form, and was no schematism purer than the synthesis of the syllogistic apodictic tripod?"[50] In other words, the supposed purity of Kant's principles notwithstanding (whose miraculous birthing apart from any impregnation by experience or tradition Hamann equates with a kind of parthenogenesis), Kant has borrowed not only from Aristotle's logic, but even from the scholastic tradition he rejects.[51] This is why in general Hamann accuses the tradition of modern philosophy, beginning with Descartes, of blatant hypocrisy: it claims to be laying a new foundation for the sciences, but it does so disingenuously, building with the materials of the philosophies that preceded it. And herein, Hamann suggests (with his crass use of the word *Gemächte,* which refers to genitalia), one can see the embarrassing *pudenda* of "pure reason" and of the *Critique* in general: the dark, shameful parts, i.e., the unacknowledged dependence upon tradition, which Kant has covered up. Thus, once again we see the importance of shame as a topos of Hamann's authorship: at almost every turn he is embarrassing the *Aufklärer* about what they would rather hide, exposing their secret reliance upon the contingencies of history and tradition even as they speak of reason's virginal purity, necessity, and universality. This is why he cannot help but view the Enlightenment as an extravagant charade: the *Aufklärer* parade reason like a shrine through the streets, even as they attempt to cover up its secret poverty, limitations, and nakedness. And it is this that Hamann's authorship is intended therapeutically-metacritically to uncover and expose. For, applying what he learned from Socrates and Paul, it is through the recognition of reason's ignorance and weakness – indeed the recognition of its

---

[48]   ZH IV, p. 462.

[49]   N III, p. 278. Cf. *Critique of Pure Reason*, B 25.

[50]   N III, p. 278.

[51]   Cf. N III, p. 133: "Given that one can in no way become an author without a censor and publisher, except, that is, after the manner of Melchizedek, without father, without mother, without race – I must now be a *philosopher* and remain speechless in the face of 'this, this new age …' "

fallenness – that true knowledge begins. Only then, in light of such self-knowledge, which leads to humility, can reason be enlightened.

In this context, however, by the *"pudenda* of pure reason" Hamann specifically means the paralogisms and antinomies, i.e., the inveterate and seemingly insuperable self-contradictions to which reason is prone and which Kant treats in his transcendental dialectic. These are the source of reason's shame, which, as a matter of necessity, in order to meet the demands of science, Kant must somehow overcome:

> But since *formal purity,* without content or object, is bound "through no fault of its own" to degenerate into hypocrisy [*Scheinheiligkeit*]: the actual purpose of the *transcendental dialectic* is to transfigure the true *pudenda* of pure reason, which constitute an hereditary defect as unrecognized as it is incurable, namely, its *paralogisms* with respect to the psychological *ego* and its *antinomies* with respect to all *cosmological ideas per thesin et antithesin,* which bears comparison to that odd battle described in an old Church hymn: where one death was devoured by the other [*wie ein Tod den andern fraß*].[52]

To be sure, Kant himself candidly admits that the paralogisms and antinomies are, so to speak, the "shameful parts" of pure reason: "It is something distressing and depressing that there should be any such thing as an antithetics of pure reason, and that the latter, which is supposed to be the supreme court adjudicating all conflicts, should end up in conflict with itself" (A 740). What Hamann criticizes in this regard, however, is not Kant's identification of the dialectic, but, as Bayer points out, Kant's *naturalization* of the dialectic.[53] In other words, for Hamann the dialectic of reason is indicative of a real *hamartiological* problem; it is bound up with the fact of reason's fallenness. But this is precisely what Kant whitewashes – as indeed he must if any critique of tradition *on the part of reason,* in the name of secular reason, is ever to be considered reliable or authoritative. Thus Kant speaks of the dialectic as an inevitable, even a natural "illusion" (A 297). Moreover, it is clear that for him it is *merely* an illusion, i.e., it is not really a problem, but only an *apparent* problem. Indeed, Kant not only covers up the shame of reason's fallenness, doing away with the question of sin, but, as Hamann points out, effectively "transfigures" it. In other words, he does in the name of reason what only God can do: he absolves reason of any guilt and reinvests it with glory, as though it had never been fallen. This is why Hamann contrasts Kant's "transcendental dialectic" (and its hypocritical attempt to transfigure reason's shame through reason apart from faith) with the true glorification that comes by way of the *genuine* dialectic of Christ's death overcoming death.

In the final section of his review Hamann reiterates a striking point of far-reaching consequence for his entire attitude toward the Enlightenment, which he made to Kant more than twenty years earlier, namely, that the purpose of reason is analogous to Paul's understanding of the law as a "pedagogue to Christ" (cf. Gal. 3: 24): "The *transcendental method* defines the formal conditions of a complete system of pure reason, and is concerned with its *discipline,* which constitutes a superb parallel to the Pauline theory of the *discipline* of the *law* ..."[54] In other words, for Hamann neither the disciplinary self-critique of reason nor the external discipline of the law is complete in itself: just as the law reveals our moral weakness and inability to fulfill

---

[52] N III, pp. 278f. The verse to which Hamann refers is from Luther's Easter hymn, "Christ lag in Todesbanden."
[53] *HMK,* p. 118.
[54] N III, p. 279.

it, the purpose of reason and its self-critique is to reveal our ignorance and the prospect of intellectual futility apart from faith. Neither reason nor the law, therefore, being fundamentally incomplete, can be considered a definitive revelation. Rather, for Hamann the purpose of each is that of a *praeparatio evangelica*. As he put it to Jacobi, "I am so sick and tired of repeating that it goes with the philosopher[s] as it does with the Jews; neither know what *reason* is, or the *law*, or why they have been given: for the knowledge of sin and ignorance – not of grace and truth, which must be *historically revealed* and cannot be gained by reasoning about it, inheriting it, or earning it."[55]

The review then concludes as it begins, with reservations about the extent of Kant's achievement. As we have already seen, Kant claims to have navigated and overcome the dialectic between the Scylla of skepticism and the Charybdis of dogmatism. Indeed, by means of his critical philosophy he claims not only to have avoided these opposing dangers, but to have brought "enlightenment" out of the quasi-despair and "*indifference*" [*Indifferentismus*] of the age, which he calls the "mother of chaos and night" (A x), and thereby to have inaugurated a new era of confidence in the sciences. We have also seen why Hamann considers Kant's critical philosophy misguided: instead of demonstrating reason's need for faith and revelation, Kant has hypocritically covered over and "transfigured" reason's shame and thereby inflated the very pride that bars the path to true knowledge.[56] Now, in reference to Kant's conclusion (A 856), Hamann gives the following wry assessment: "The *critical path* alone remained open. – This new footpath seems just as unsuitable for a military highway [*Heerstraße*] as a tightrope for a common footpath."[57] In other words, the *Critique* is not going to make Kant into a conquering hero. It will hardly command such popular appeal. And so he adds that the happiness of an author consists " 'in being known by *all*, praised by *some*,' " and – "as the *maximum* of authentic authorship and criticism" – "in being understood by *bloody few*."[58] Needless to say, Hamann's judgment was correct. Thus, in view of the "aesthetic length" of the *Critique* (i.e., the sheer bulk of its pages and the immense labor put into it), anticipating the meager results and ultimate pointlessness of all his friend's efforts, he concludes with a fitting two-part quotation, first from Persius and then from Virgil, "O quantum est in rebus inane! sunt lacrumae rerum."[59] The fact that the first part of the quotation appeared some twenty years earlier as an epigraph to the *Socratic Memorabilia* is significant. It means that Hamann's debate with Kant has come full circle, but that sadly nothing has changed.

THE *METACRITIQUE:* A BRIEF HISTORY OF THE PURISMS OF REASON

In the meantime, with his review left unpublished out of respect for Kant, Hamann was still churning over the *Critique* and had begun drafting what was to become one of his most important and consequential works, his *Metakritik über den Purismum der Vernunft*. We have already seen that Hamann took issue with Kant's "puritanical" streak; and, in point of fact, as the title would suggest, much of the *Metakritik* is concerned precisely with a series of dubious "purisms" upon which Kant's entire

---

[55] ZH V, p. 326.
[56] Cf. N III, p. 189, where Hamann says in *Doubts and Ideas*, in reference to Seneca, *Epistula* LIII, that he aims at that "*Stoic wisdom* that interchangeably unites the *imbecillitatem* Hominis and the *securitatem Dei*" [*sic*]. Cf. ZH VII, p. 339.
[57] N III, p. 279.
[58] N III, p. 280.
[59] Persius, *Satires* I, 1; *Aeneid* I, 459f.

system of thought, in Hamann's view, depended. The meaning of the word "meta-critique," a term that is original to Hamann and by various byways has entered the postmodern vocabulary, is less obvious. On the one hand, according to the etymological sense of μετά, it means that the work is essentially an "after"-word to Kant's *Critique* – just as Aristotle's *Metaphysics* was originally so titled because it comes "after" his *Physics*. And doubtless Hamann intends us to understand his *Metakritik* in this way, namely, as a literary *supplement* to what he viewed as a *contingent, historical* work. Thus Hamann suggests elsewhere that his kind of criticism, his metacriticism, is that of a "re-reading" (*Nach-lese*) or "parody" (*Nach-Spott*) or "post-lude" (*Nach-Spiel*).[60] On the other hand, playing on the traditional connotation of Aristotle's *Metaphysics*, *Metakritik* also carries the sense of that which goes "beyond" the *Critique* in the sense of "surpassing" it.

Among the proximate causes of the *Metakritik* was another review of the *Critique* that was published in Göttingen in 1782 and pointed out the connection between Kant and Berkeley.[61] Hamann apparently approved of the review, since it is in view of the historical *dependence* of Kant's purportedly *a priori* philosophy upon Berkeley's earlier idealism, that the *Metakritik* begins: " 'A great philosopher has asserted that universal and abstract ideas are nothing but particular ones, which are bound, however, to a certain word that gives them a greater compass or range of meaning and, at the same time, in view of particular things, reminds us of them.' "[62] Hamann goes on to say, "*Hume* takes this claim of the Eleatic, mystical, and raving [*schwärmenden*] bishop of Cloyne, *George Berkeley*, to be one of the *greatest* and most *prized discoveries* that have been made in the republic of letters of our time."[63] As Bayer points out, it is no coincidence that Hamann begins with a quotation, as conventional as this might seem; for his very act of quotation is meant to demonstrate that thought is never pure, as Kant alleges is possible, but always situated within a given tradition to which it responds. This, one could say, is Hamann's first metacritical point. Thus he says, "It seems to me, first of all, that the new skepticism owes the old idealism infinitely more than this fortuitous and particular occasion would give us to understand in passing, and that, without *Berkeley*, *Hume* would hardly have become the *great philosopher* that the *Critique*, from a position of similar indebtedness, alleges him to be."[64] Hamann makes the same point more simply to Herder, "So much is certain: that without *Berkeley* there would have been no *Hume*, just as, without the latter, there would have been no *Kant*."[65] The way Hamann puts it in the *Metakritik*, however, is revealing: for the striking series of modifying terms, e.g., "fortuitous," "particular," "occasional," "in passing," are all meant to highlight the contrast between his understanding of the life of the intellect (as a function of the historical contingencies of our *Sitz im Leben*) and Kant's understanding of intellectual activity (as something conducted in the ether of pure, necessary, universal concepts).

Hamann's second metacritical point is also implied in his opening statement, where he signals his empiricism, nominalistic bent,[66] and corresponding attention to

---

[60] As noted in *HMK*, p. 210. Cf. ZH IV, p. 340; N III, p. 401; N II, p. 83.

[61] See *HMK*, p. 216.

[62] N III, p. 283. The "great philosopher" to whom Hamann refers is Berkeley; not possessing the work in question, however, his quotation is really a pastiche of Berkeley derived from Hume's *Treatise of Human Nature*.

[63] N III, p. 283.

[64] Ibid.

[65] ZH IV, p. 376.

[66] See, for example, ZH VII, p. 172, where Hamann says to Jacobi, "A universal word is an empty wine-skin, which in any given moment is modified differently and, being stretched beyond its capacity and able to contain absolutely no more air, bursts; and is it really worth it to haggle over such worthless salt and hollow skin without content?"

the role of language. Universal, abstract ideas, he says, are in reality particular ideas inextricably bound to language. Indeed, for Hamann *language* – a contingent, historical, a posteriori phenomenon – could be considered a kind of transcendental a priori category to the extent that we cannot think apart from it. Abstract terms, on the other hand, insofar as they are held to be independent of language or transcendentally pure, constitute, in his view, a misunderstanding and misuse of ordinary language.[67] As he puts it to Jacobi, "Being, faith, and reason [abstractly conceived] are mere relations, which may not be treated absolutely; they are not things, but pure scholastic conceptions, signs for understanding, not admiring, aids to rouse, not to hold our attention."[68] In any case, while abstract terms may have an important role to play *within* language, for Hamann, they cannot in any ultimate sense be isolated from it.

In a sense, one could argue this connects Hamann to the linguistics of Saussure and, later, to post-structuralism; what saves language from arbitrary and ultimately meaningless "play," however, is the way in which Hamann grounds it theologically. Indeed, for Hamann, language is never *merely* language: it is also a *revelation*. Moreover, as his reference above to "a certain word" would suggest, language, logos, is that which mysteriously unites both the particular and the universal, forming a mysterious analogy to the Logos who, in becoming flesh, united the human and the divine. As he puts it to Jacobi, language, poetic language in particular, is the mysterious site where a "transference and *communicatio idiomatum*" takes place between "the spiritual and the material," between spatial "extension" and comprehended "meaning," between the "corporeal" and the "intelligible."[69] Thus, contra Kant, in reference to Hume's statement about Berkeley, he says that the "*important discovery*" of our time, which is "plainly revealed," is none other than the ordinary use of language.

From these two metacritical points we can see where Hamann is going. What Kant does not adequately appreciate is that tradition and language are constitutive of reason; as a result, he does not see how fundamentally this fact calls into question the alleged purity of his investigations. To be sure, Kant presumes to have laid bare the timeless transcendental structure of thought; from Hamann's perspective, however, Kant (an existing human being, who leads the life of a professor, happens to be a personal friend, and lives just a few blocks away) has merely written a novel of his own understanding, which is informed a priori by his reading and assimilation of the preceding history of philosophy. In short, according to Hamann, we have *no pure, immediate access* to transcendental structures of reality. Nor do we have any pure immediate access to something called "reason." On the contrary, how we reason and what we reason about is inseparable

---

[67] As O'Flaherty argues, the origin of abstractions lies in a confusion regarding the role of relational terms: "The most important clues to a deeper understanding of the language philosophy are to be found in Hamann's linking of abstractions with relations, in his assumption of the reality of relations between real objects (but not between abstract entities)." See "The quarrel of reason with itself," in *Neue Zeitschrift für Systematische Theologie und Religionsphilosophie* 30 (1988), p. 286. See also James C. O'Flaherty, *Unity and Language: A Study in the Philosophy of Johann Georg Hamann* (Chapel Hill: University of North Carolina Press, 1952), p. 48. O'Flaherty has done the most to develop Hamann's insights in relation to analytic philosophy; a letter from his correspondence with Bertrand Russell well sums up his conclusions: "It seems possible to prove, on philological and logical grounds, that prepositions and other relational words are the archetypes of abstractions ... Therefore all genuine abstract terminology is relational terminology." Russell expressed his agreement in a letter to O'Flaherty of December 2, 1954.

[68] ZH VII, p. 173 (O'Flaherty's translation). Cf. ZH VII, p. 166, to Jacobi: "The affirmation of *existence per se* – [This is] the most abstract relation, which does not warrant being viewed and reckoned as belonging to *things*, much less as being a *particular thing*; and yet, [it is] the *talisman* of Your philosophy and Your *superstitious belief* in *verba praetereaquae nihil* are the idols of Your concepts ..." For all of their agreement on matters of faith, one of the principal differences between Hamann and Jacobi, therefore, was Hamann's impatience with the abstract nature of Jacobi's philosophy.

[69] ZH VII, p. 158. Quoted in *HMK*, p. 225.

from, and largely a product of, language and tradition. This is Hamann's fundamental metacritical and, one might say, "deconstructive" point. The fact that Kant proceeds as if this were not so – as if there really is some region of thought that can be accessed in purity apart from all experience – is for Hamann the hypocritical *proton pseudos* that undermines the foundation of his philosophy right from the start.[70]

After reviewing the shaky pillars of Kant's philosophy – from the alleged possibility of transcendental knowledge a priori, to the alleged possibility of pure forms of intuition, to his supposedly "powerful distinction" between analytic and synthetic judgments – Hamann proceeds to explicate the history of the "purisms" upon which Kant's mystical induction to the shrine of pure reason depends, as if to emphasize that Kant's allegedly pure reason is precisely not pure, but a function of history, which it hypocritically seeks to escape.[71] "The *first* purification of philosophy," he says, "consisted in the partly misunderstood, partly unsuccessful attempt to make reason independent of all tradition and faith in it."[72] Clearly, this kind of purification applies to Kant, but it is not especially peculiar to him: it is the hallmark of modern philosophy since Descartes and traces back at least to Plato's anamnestic doctrine of knowledge. In any case, in Hamann's view, this is where the history of philosophy went wrong, since there is no such thing as a tradition-free standpoint; to suggest otherwise is sheer hypocrisy. By the same token, because some amount of faith is always involved in any philosophizing, inasmuch as one inevitably reasons in light of certain presuppositions, it is just as hypocritical to deny some measure of faith in philosophy (as we have seen).

"The *second* purification," Hamann says, "is more transcendent and comes to nothing less than an independence from experience and its everyday induction."[73] And this is the historical purification that he associates more properly with Kant's transcendental deduction:

> For after reason, over a period of 2000 years, sought – one knows not what? – *beyond* experience, it not only suddenly comes to *despair* over the progressive course of its predecessors, but with just as much *defiance* promises to its impatient contemporaries [that it will produce] in only a short time that universal and infallible *philosopher's stone*, necessary for *catholicism* and *despotism*, to which *religion* will straightway submit its *holiness* and *lawgiving* its majesty ...[74]

As Bayer points out, Kant claims in his *Prolegomena* that his philosophy stands in relation to scholastic metaphysics as "chemistry to alchemy" (A 190), and thus implicitly distances himself from the fabled pursuit of the philosopher's stone.[75] As Hamann suggests here, however, echoing the criticisms of his review, Kant's philosophy nevertheless has a magical, indeed an alchemical quality to it.

It is "alchemical," firstly, as regards its objective. For Kant, too, quixotically seeks a kind of "philosopher's stone" (in this case, a purely rational, universal, transcendental language, abstracted from all particular languages, which would serve as a

---

[70] Thus Hamann goes on to say in ironic allusion to 1 Cor. 2: 9: "Among the *secret mysteries*, whose task – not to mention their solution – has supposedly never entered a philosopher's heart, is the possibility of having human knowledge of objects of experience *without* and *before* all experience and, following from this, the possibility of a sensible intuition *before* all sensation of an object" (N III, p. 283).

[71] See *HMK*, p. 241. The phrase "powerful distinction" comes from Kant's *Prolegomena* (A 40), which appeared in 1783.

[72] N III, p. 284.

[73] Ibid.

[74] Ibid.

[75] *HMK*, p. 257.

sure foundation for the sciences); and in this connection, Hamann describes Kant's philosophy as an attempt to produce the "chemical tree of Diana," which, for the alchemists, is said to result from the crystallization of silver.[76] The latent irony in Hamann's use of this term, according to Bayer, is that Diana, who is alchemically identified with silver, is also the goddess of the moon, and thus symbolizes for Hamann the pale, borrowed, and – because it is made absolute – idolatrous light of the Enlightenment.[77] By this term Hamann means, furthermore, metaschematically to identify Kant's philosophy with the cult of Artemis encountered by Paul in Ephesus; and Kant himself with Paul's chief antagonist in the affair, Demetrius, "a silversmith who made silver shrines of Artemis" and made a profitable business from it (Acts 19: 24ff.). In other words, as in the *Socratic Memorabilia*, Hamann means to say that Kant's philosophy is involved in a subtle but personally profitable form of idolatry. Thus he once again assumes the prophetic mantle, speaking to Kant as Daniel did to Belshazzar, a worshiper of the gods of silver, etc. (Dan. 5: 23), in interpretation of the writing on the wall: "Woe to the tyrants if *God* should see to them! To what purpose do they still ask about him? *Mene, mene, tekel* [is said] to the sophists! Their divisional coin [*Scheidemünze*] will be found too light and their discount house [*Wechselbank*] will be destroyed."[78]

Kant's philosophy is "alchemical," secondly, because its transcendental method involves a similar process of purification; the only difference here is that the "dross," which must be separated in order to attain the "philosopher's stone" is phenomenal experience. And finally, it is a "magical" process, inasmuch as, though the alchemists insist that the process of a rebirth is a "most long" one (*longissima via*), Kant's *renovatio* is promised, as it were, overnight.[79] As Hamann puts it, the "dew of a pure natural language must be reborn from the *dawn* of the promised imminent revolution and enlightenment."[80] Hamann, however, is not among those anxiously anticipating the fulfillment of this promise, which he likens to the arrival, not of enlightenment, but of a "new Lucifer," who "masquerades as an angel of light" (2 Cor. 11: 14). Instead, he sees Kant's philosophy as a pseudo-eschatology facilitated by yet another illegitimate and deceived "grasping" after a "tree of knowledge" (cf. Gen. 3: 6), which he prophetically likens in this context to the fig tree of the gospel that is cursed by Christ, because it will bear no fruit (Mark 11: 13).[81]

According to Hamann, however, neither of the preceding "purisms" is quite as quixotic and absurd as the third and final historical purism: "The *third,* most refined, and, as it were, *empyrean* [sic] purism is conducted with regard even to *language,* the only (first and last) *organon* and criterion of reason, which has no other credentials than *tradition* and *usum.*"[82] Hamann is borrowing here from the *Night Thoughts* by

---

[76] N III, p. 287. See *HMK*, pp. 342f.

[77] *HMK*, pp. 343f.

[78] N III, p. 284. Thus, once again, Hamann identifies language, and the "wealth of human knowledge," with a form of currency. See N II, p. 129. The implied background of this prophetic rebuke is Matthew 12: 36–7, out of respect for which Hamann, who wrote only *opuscula*, speaks to his son of the "evangelical law of economy": "My dear child, let the *evangelical law of economy* be commended to you in speaking and writing: Taking account of every *vain, superfluous* word – and *economy of style.* In these two mystical words lies the whole art of thinking and living" (ZH V, p. 88).

[79] N III, p. 284. See Mircea Eliade, *The Forge and the Crucible*, 2nd edn. (Chicago: University of Chicago Press, 1978), p. 163.

[80] N III, p. 287.

[81] Ibid.

[82] N III, p. 284. As Bayer notes (*HMK*, p. 271), in this passage Hamann is directly contradicting Kant. See *Prolegomena* A 45. In this extract, words enclosed in parentheses indicate a subsequent emendation by Hamann inserted to the original text.

Edward Young.[83] As he says to Herder, "All chatter about reason is pure wind; *language* is its *organon* and criterion! as Young says. *Tradition* is the second element."[84] In a similar vein he says to Jacobi, "I hold myself now to the visible *element*, to the *organon* or *criterion* – I mean *language*. Were there no Word, there would be no reason – no world. Here is the source of *creation* and *government*."[85] While we should doubtless hear the theological overtones in such a statement (cf. John 1: 3), the essential point here and throughout the *Metakritik* is that reason *depends* upon language (and tradition) and can in no conceivable way be separated from it. As Griffith-Dickson puts it, "Not only is reason helpless and unable to operate without language (language is reason's *organon*), but reason without language is not even *reasonable*: i.e., coherent, able to make sense, articulate (language is reason's *criterion*)."[86]

Kant, however, would seem to ignore this fact. Thus Hamann likens his own stupefaction *vis-à-vis* Kant's philosophy to the speechlessness of the ancient philosopher Simonides, who, day after day, upon being asked by the tyrant Hieron to give an explanation of the nature and existence of God, each time gave no answer except to ask for twice as much time to consider the matter as the day before.[87] As he originally put it in a draft,

> I had the same experience with pure reason as that philosopher did with its ideal. The more profoundly he considered it, the more speechless he became. According to its discoveries, there is a land *this side* of experience, and *beyond* [it], nothing but mist. A *reason* without *experience* seems just as impossible as a *reason* without *language*. *Tradition* and *language* are the true elements of reason.[88]

Similarly, in the final version of the *Metakritik,* he says, "One has just about the same experience with this *idol* [i.e., pure reason] as that ancient philosopher had with the *ideal* of reason. The longer one thinks about it, the more profoundly (and inwardly) one falls silent and loses all desire to speak."[89]

Aside from Hamann's prophetic charge that pure reason is an idol, what is easily overlooked in all of this, is that, with his sequence of historical purifications, Hamann has just proved his point: he has given a *history* (or *genealogy*) of *pure reason*. In other words, that there should be such a thing as a history or development of reason proves that reason is precisely *not* pure and never has been, but is invariably and fundamentally shaped by history and tradition. By the same token, this is what makes Kant's curious postscript to the *Critique* (A 852–6), titled "The history of pure reason," so odd, standing at the conclusion of his text like an

---

[83] Edward Young, *Night Thoughts, Or the Complaint and the Consolation,* illustrated by William Blake (Mineola, NY: Dover, 1975), p. 35: "Had thought been all, sweet speech had been denied; Speech, thought's canal! speech thought's criterion too!"

[84] ZH V, p. 108.

[85] ZH V, p. 95. As Bayer notes (*HMK,* p. 265), this letter forms an especially important parallel to the *Metakritik.* Cf. ZH VII, p. 49.

[86] G-D, p. 284.

[87] See Cicero, *De natura deorum,* (Stuttgart: B. G. Teubner, 1980), Book I, 22, p. 23. The same story is related in Hume's *Dialogues.*

[88] From draft A, reprinted in *HMK,* p. 157; or Bayer, "Hamann's Metakritik im ersten Entwurf," *Kantstudien* 81 (1990), p. 437. The "ideal of pure reason" is Kant's own phrase for God as the "object of a transcendental theology" (*Critique of Pure Reason* A 580).

[89] N III, p. 284.

ironic bookend, subverting his entire argument up to that point, which had depended upon the genesis of pure concepts a priori (A 86). As Kant curiously puts it, "This title stands here merely to designate a lacuna within the system that still needs to be filled out in the future" (A 852). This task was, of course, taken up by Hegel. Hamann, however, was the first to pick up on the idea and metacritically, by means of Kant's own words (his standard metacritical device), shake his philosophy to the foundations.

THE "GENEALOGICAL PRIORITY" OF LANGUAGE

The next section of the *Metakritik* makes similarly subversive use of Kant's own words. At the beginning of his "transcendental logic," Kant speaks of intuitions and concepts – specifically, "receptivity of impressions" and "spontaneity of concepts" – as the two sources of human knowledge (A 50). What Hamann sees as missing in Kant's all-too-neat-and-tidy distinction, however, is any mention of the role of language. Indeed, this is what makes the clarity of Kant's distinction a deception, concealing a deeper confusion, since one cannot adequately treat the subject of concepts without *also* inquiring into the relationship between concepts and language. Thus, reintroducing the question of language, Hamann strikingly emends Kant's famous formula as follows:

> *Receptivity* of *language* and *spontaneity* of *concepts!* – From this twofold source of ambiguity, pure reason fashions all the elements of its self-righteousness [*Rechthaberei*], skepticism [*Zweifelsucht*], and criticism [*Kunstrichterschaft*]; produces from its thrice-old leaven, by means of an analysis that is just as arbitrary as its synthesis, new phenomena and meteors of the changing horizon; creates signs and wonders – creating all things, destroying all things – with the mercurial magic wand of its mouth or with the cloven goose quill between the three syllogistic fingers of its Herculean fist –[90]

What can easily get lost here amid the humorous declamations of Hamann's highly allusive imagistic style is the incisiveness of his philosophical point: that Kant's philosophy rests upon an unacknowledged *ambiguity* between language (an impure product of history and culture) and concepts (upon whose alleged purity Kant's transcendentalism depends). Kant claims that the concepts of the understanding are a *spontaneous* contribution to human knowledge, by which the objects of intuition are *thought* (A 50). But are these concepts not always also *received* through language? Are they not historical and cultural *acquisitions*? Indeed, for Hamann, they are; and this is why there is no such thing as a purely spontaneous concept that is not something, as it were, "impurely" received. As Paul puts it, "What do you have that you did not receive?" (1 Cor. 4: 7). In Hamann's view, therefore, the *proton pseudos* of Kant's philosophy lies in what it assumes (namely, the purity of the concepts of the understanding) and the root *ambiguity* (between language and concepts) it fails to see. And it is on the basis of this shaky foundation that Kant magically produces false signs and wonders.

---

[90] N III, pp. 284f. As Bayer notes (*HMK*, p. 283), Hamann's reference to "thrice-old leaven" is an allusion to 1 Cor. 5: 7. As for "mercurial magic wand of its mouth" (following *HMK*, pp. 287f.), Hamann is again alluding to the impatience of Kant's *Critique* as well as the messianic "rod of his mouth" of Isa. 11: 4; as for the "cloven goose quill," "cloven" suggests the devilish effects to which Kant's abuse of language can lead; and by the "three syllogistic fingers of its Herculean fist" we may understand Kant's syllogistic sensibility and the compulsory force with which it is applied.

With his identification of an underlying ambiguity that subverts Kant's tidy distinctions, and therewith, arguably, the entire foundation of his critical philosophy, Hamann's metacritical reading of the *Critique* thus figures *mutatis mutandis* as a herald of postmodern "deconstruction." Indeed, in Hamann too one will find an eye for fundamental ambiguities, controlling metaphors, unintended consequences, an attention to footnotes, marginalia, and the play and deceptions of language. So, too, in addition to his proto-deconstructionist reading habits (and as a result of them), one will find in Hamann, not unlike Derrida, a prophetic humbling, if not humiliation, of all proud and ostensibly complete systems of thought. An example of this can be seen in the following section, where Hamann draws attention to the etymological ambiguity and "hereditary defect" borne by the name "metaphysics." By this he means not only the obscurity and historical contingency of the word's origin, i.e., the ambiguous sense of μετά in connection with Aristotle's *Metaphysics,* but the comical irony that "meta" (whether read as "after" or "beyond") is a "pre-fix." As he puts it, "The name *metaphysics* is already infected with this hereditary defect and leprosy of ambiguity, which cannot be improved, much less transfigured by going back to its birthplace, which consists in the arbitrary synthesis of a Greek *prefix.*"[91] In other words, on account of its name, even so sublime a science as metaphysics is always already determined by historical ambiguities and spatial metaphors from *this side* of experience.

But if metaphysics cannot claim any methodological purity, then neither can Kant's refurbished critical philosophy. For the very terms "a priori" and "a posteriori," upon which his supposedly "transcendental" philosophy depends, are always already determined by spatial metaphors of "before" and "behind"; and it is Kant's blindness to this spatial metaphoricity running through the pages of his allegedly pure *Critique* – a blindness that is most transparent in his use of the term "transcendental topic" (A 268) – that, in Hamann's view, constitutes the "*hysteron-proteron*" of his philosophy:

> But even if one grants that the transcendental topic depends even less upon the empirical distinction between *behind* and *beyond* than *a priori* and *a posteriori* depend upon a *hysteron proteron*: the birthmark of the name [metaphysics] nevertheless extends from the forehead to the viscera of the entire science, and its terminology is related to all the other languages of the arts, fields, mountains, and schools as mercury to the other metals.[92]

In other words, while Kant's supposedly pure "transcendental topic" depends upon *empirical* spatial distinctions, his similarly rarefied distinction between a priori and a posteriori depends all the more upon a *hysteron proteron,* by which Hamann means not only Aristotle's term for a logical fallacy, but an abiding ambiguity (between the "former" and "latter," between the a priori and a posteriori). For one can easily reverse the priority and say that Kant has things, as it were, "*ass-backwards,*"[93] that is, that what we know a posteriori is, in fact, *prior* to anything we might presume to know a priori. Indeed, according to Hamann, it is this ambiguity (like the ambiguity in the concept of metaphysics), which affects the whole of Kant's allegedly "pure" *Critique.* As a result, Kant's abstract philosophical terminology compares

---

[91] N III, p. 285.

[92] Ibid. The term *hysteron-proteron*, which essentially means putting the cart before the horse, as in the case of an invalid syllogism, comes from Aristotle's *Analytica priora* 64b, where we see, within what appears to be a pristine logic, yet another example of recourse to spatial metaphors – as though one could not do logic without them.

[93] N III, p. 280.

unfavorably to the "languages of the arts, the fields, the mountains, and schools," where words have definite meanings determined by use; indeed, in this respect, given its slippery, indefinite quality, Kant's vocabulary is like liquid mercury (another allusion to Kant's "alchemy") in relation to the other solid metals.[94]

As Hamann observes, however, Kant is at home neither with ambiguities, nor with the metaphorical indeterminacies of language, nor indeed with matter – in short, much of the stuff of earthly existence. Accordingly, he sees in Kant's philosophy a kind of Gnosticism, a kind of escapist, life-denying sensibility (one could even say a kind of pathology) for which the senses, history, language, and experience itself are all in some sense unclean – and, in any case, unclean vehicles of truth:

> To be sure, from so many *analytic* judgments one should infer a *Gnostic* hatred of matter, or also a *mystical* love of form; that being said, the synthesis of the *predicate* with the *subject,* wherein at the same time the actual *object* of *pure reason* consists, has no other mediating concept before and behind it than an old, cold prejudice for mathematics, whose apodictic certainty rests primarily upon a, so to speak, kyriological description of the simplest sensible intuition and, consequently, the ease of proving and representing its syntheses and their possibility in manifest constructions or symbolic forms and similitudes, by whose sensibility any possible *misunderstanding* is automatically ruled out.[95]

What is striking here is that Hamann brings the age-old philosophical quest for mathematical certainty down to earth, relating the *desideratum* of certainty to the "kyriological description of the simplest sensible intuition." The curious term "kyriological" is familiar from his *Aesthetica*. Deriving from a work by Johann Georg Wachter, which catalogues the stages of pre-alphabetical writing, it refers to the simplest, most primitive, and universally intelligible kind of signification.[96] In this context, therefore, Hamann means that even mathematical certainty in some sense depends upon, and cannot help but reproduce in examples, the kind of intuitive certainty we associate with simple sensation. The same is true of geometry, which cannot help but determine and figure "the *ideality* of its concepts of points without parts, of lines and surfaces … by means of empirical signs and images."[97] Thus Hamann adds, comically reducing the quest for certainty to absurdity, "Finally, it goes without saying that if mathematics can claim the distinction of nobility on account of its universal and necessary trustworthiness, then even human reason would have to be considered inferior to the infallible and unerring *instinct* of the insects."[98]

For Hamann, then, the basic problem with Kant's transcendentalism – a problem that it shares with metaphysics – is that it does not sufficiently appreciate the empirical dimension of human knowledge, but instead abstracts from it and from the appropriate use of ordinary language. As a result, we are left with nothing ("an indeterminate something = x") but what "transcendental superstition" posits in its place:

> Metaphysics misuses the signs of language and figures of speech by transforming them into nothing but hieroglyphs and types of ideal relations, and by means of this learned nonsense

[94] See *HMK*, p. 294.
[95] N III, p. 285.
[96] Johann Georg Wachter, *Naturae et scripturae concordia commentario de literis ac numeris primaevis* (1752). As Bayer notes (*HMK*, p. 301), Wachter borrows from Clement of Alexandria's description of Egyptian hieroglyphics in the *Stromateis* (Book V, §20).
[97] N III, p. 285.
[98] N III, p. 285. Cf. *Critique of Pure Reason* A xv.

works the *straightforwardness* [*Biderkeit*] of language into such a senseless, rutted, unsteady, indeterminate something = x, that nothing remains but a windy soughing, a magical play of shadows, at most, as the wise Helvetius says, the talisman and rosary of a transcendental superstition regarding *entia rationis*, their empty skins and slogans.[99]

Of course, Kant himself recognizes the problem of *entia rationis*, i.e., conceptual objects that have no correspondence to reality (e.g., chimeras and unicorns).[100] As Hamann sees it, however, this is the inevitable result of Kant's own philosophy. For, after clearing away the empirical, phenomenal world, all that is left is a "something = nothing," i.e., whatever we might now on the basis of reason alone posit in its place. To be sure, for their part, Descartes and Kant believed that the integrity of the world, having been theoretically destroyed and depleted of all immediate value, could be rationally and thus credibly restored. Hamann, however, did not share their faith in the creative power of "*automatic* reason"; in this regard, what Nietzsche aptly said a century later was but an echo of what Hamann had already prophesied: "All possible superstitions are posited into the void."[101]

Having made several penetrating criticisms of Kant's general method, midway through his *Metakritik* Hamann picks out a weak spot in Kant's preface (A xvii), where Kant excuses himself for not treating the question that, in Hamann's view, is most fundamental, namely: "how is the *ability* to think possible?" Kant admits that this question is of "great importance," but, as Hamann observes, he carefully sidesteps it, saying that it is *inessential* to his primary purpose, which is to answer the "primary" and "abiding" question, "what and how much can understanding and reason know independently of all experience?" In reply, Hamann asks: "So, a primary question remains: *how is the ability to think possible?* – the ability to think *right* and *left*, *before* and *without*, *with* and *beyond* experience?"[102] In short, Hamann reverses the priority of Kant's questions. "How is the ability to think possible?" That is the primary question, which Kant leaves unanswered – and with good reason since the purity of his *Critique* depends upon him *not* attempting to answer it. Hamann, on the other hand, answers it, knowing very well its implications for Kant's thought. In what amounts to his central claim, which turns Kant's philosophy on its head, he says that "no deduction is required to prove the genealogical priority of *language*."[103] In other words, for Hamann language, with all its a posteriori qualities, is *prior* to reason. But not only is language prior to reason, according to Hamann it is also the source of the conceptual confusion by which reason is plagued – not least of all regarding its own nature and purpose. Thus he says, "Not only does the entire ability to think rests upon language ... but language is also the *center of the misunderstanding of reason with itself* ..."[104]

Upon declaring the genealogical priority of language, Hamann then makes another provocative substitution for a standard set of terms in Kant's vocabulary. Whereas in his transcendental aesthetic Kant famously speaks of time and space as the pure forms of intuition a priori (A 22), Hamann now says, "*Sounds* and *letters* are therefore the pure forms *a priori*, in which we encounter nothing that belongs to sensation or to the concept of an object, and which are the true aesthetic elements of all human

---

[99] N III, p. 285.
[100] Thus he defines an *ens rationis* as an "empty concept without an object." See *Critique of Pure Reason* A 292.
[101] *KSA*, vol. 7, p. 466.
[102] N III, p. 286.
[103] Ibid.
[104] Ibid.

knowledge and reason."[105] Needless to say, from Kant's perspective, sounds and letters do not qualify in any sense as "pure forms *a priori*." On the contrary, for him they belong squarely within the, so to speak, "impure" realm of everyday experience. For Hamann, however, the contradiction is fully intended: sounds and letters may not be "pure" in any Kantian sense; nevertheless, as the *aesthetic* medium of language, upon which the entire capacity to think depends, they are the indispensable elements of all human knowledge. This is not to say that Hamann denies the legitimacy of such concepts as space and time; what he rejects is Kant's transcendental attempt to disassociate them as "pure forms" from the concrete, sensible, and artistic experience from which they, in his view, originally derive:

> The oldest language was music, and, next to the felt rhythm of the beat [*Pulsschlag*] and the breath in the nose, [it constituted] the original bodily archetype of all measure of time [*Zeitmaß*] and its (numerical) proportions. The oldest script was *painting* and *drawing* and, as such, was just as soon occupied with the *economy* of *space*, its limitation and determination through figures. Thus, through the overflowing and persistent influence of the two noblest senses, sight and hearing, upon the entire sphere of understanding, the concepts of *time* and *space* came to be as universal and necessary as light and air for the eye, ear, and voice, such that space and time, even if they are not *ideae innatae*, nevertheless seem to be at least *matrices* of all intuitive [*anschaulichen*] knowledge.[106]

This passage clearly recalls the *Aesthetica,* where Hamann says, "Poetry is the mother-tongue of the human race; just as gardening is older than the cultivated field; painting – than writing; song – than declamation; parables – than syllogisms; barter – than trade."[107] Here again, therefore, Hamann's point is that the knowledge of the sciences derives from a more basic, more *artistic* origin; and that modern philosophy is somehow – and especially – out of touch with this primordial estate.

The final sections of the *Metakritik* repeat and drive home the point that Hamann initially made in his review: that Kant's philosophy "violently" and "illegitimately" divides into discrete elements – "those that are completely *a priori* in our power [*Gewalt*]" and "those that can be taken only *a posteriori* from experience" (A 843) – what nature, through the miracle of language, has purposefully joined together. One could say much here about the puritanical and implicitly violent tendency of modern epistemology in general, of which Kant is but one example: how knowledge is not the result of a peaceful conjugal fruitfulness – in the sense of Adam "knew" Eve (Gen. 4: 1), or in the sense of a "coincidence of opposites," as one finds in Franz von Baader – but demands a fanatical excision of heterogeneous elements and a scrupulously guarded maintenance of one's "personal property" (in Kant's case, the "property of reason" being what is uncontaminated by phenomenal experience and can be said to be "completely *a priori* in our power").[108] Indeed, in this respect, modern epistemology is characterized precisely by the opposite of a nuptial, Christological vision: whereas the former presumes to find

---

[105] N III, p. 286.

[106] Ibid.

[107] N II, p. 197.

[108] Among German words for power, for example, none carries more overtones of violence than Kant's word of choice, "*Gewalt*." As Hans Urs von Balthasar observes, knowledge is here understood "as a form of domination, as a categorical ordering of phenomenal matter, without consideration of what it is that 'appears' (since this in itself is unknowable) or *why* anything should appear at all." See *The Glory of the Lord: A Theological Aesthetics*, vol. 5: *The Realm of Metaphysics in the Modern Age* (San Francisco: Ignatius Press, 1989), p. 483.

certainty in what it can grasp and control by way a methodological *ars dominandi,* the latter finds *life* by following the true path or method (John 14: 6), whose *kenotic, non-grasping* pattern is laid down by Paul in the so-called Christological hymn of Philippians 2: 6f. Indeed, the contrast goes all the way back to the two trees in the garden (Gen. 2: 9), one of which, one could argue, is a type of the Cross. Thus Hamann says that modern philosophy is always barking up the wrong tree, grasping at the wrong fruit. As he puts it to Jacobi, "By the tree of knowledge we are deprived of the tree of life – and should not the latter be dearer to us than the former[?] – we who are always following the example of the *old Adam* ... [refusing] to become *children* like the *new Adam,* [who] assumed flesh and blood and took upon himself the Cross."[109]

No doubt such statements have provided fodder for those who would see Hamann as an "irrationalist." But as we have seen throughout, Hamann is in no sense an enemy of reason, but only of what he perceives to be its misuse: the kind of "reason," falsely so called, which presumes to find "certainty" through a method of endless "dividing and conquering," thereby repeating the logic of the Fall, which bars the path to the "tree of life." Whereas "the reason of the schools" is divided into idealism and realism, "true reason," Hamann says, "knows nothing of such fictional distinctions," but is animated by the vision of a profounder unity. As he put it to Jacobi:

> *Faith* has need of *reason* just as much as reason needs faith. *Philosophy* is composed of *idealism* and *realism*: just as our *nature* is composed of body and soul ... The *reason of the schools* is divided into idealism and realism, [but] right and authentic reason knows nothing of this fictional distinction, which is not grounded in the *nature of the matter* and contradicts the *unity* that lies at the basis of all our concepts, or at least *should*.[110]

It should go without saying, therefore, that Hamann was no irrationalist. On the contrary, foreseeing the collapse of the *autonomous* "reason" of the Enlightenment, his authorship was in large part a prophetic attempt to save reason from theoretical self-destruction and call his contemporaries back from the road to nihilism. This is why he consistently emphasized reason's dependence upon faith and tradition. From this statement it is also clear that he stands in the background of German Idealism, which begins by trying to overcome the dualisms left by Kant's philosophy. As he put it, again to Jacobi, "It is pure idealism to separate *faith* and *sensation* from *thought. Fellowship* [*Geselligkeit*] is the true *principium* of reason and language, by which our sensations and conceptions are modified. This and that philosophy always separates things that in no way can be separated. Things without relations, relations without things."[111]

LANGUAGE AS A SACRAMENT

In view of the foregoing it is clear that, from Hamann's perspective, Kant erred in "separating what nature had joined together," leaving an insuperable divide between faith and reason, the ideal and the real. But it is also clear that Hamann would not have endorsed German Idealism's *rational* attempt to unite, *from an idealist perspective,* what Kant had divided. Instead, he overcomes the dualism (which for him is an

---

[109] ZH V, p. 265; cf. Hamann's letter to Thomas Wizenmann, "By the tree of knowledge we are deprived of the fruit of life, and the former is no *means* to the enjoyment of this ultimate *end* and *beginning* (ZH VI, p. 492).

[110] ZH VII, p. 165.

[111] ZH VII, p. 174.

unreal abstraction to begin with) simply by pointing to the "sacrament of language."[112] At the conclusion of *The Knight of the Rose-Cross* he had said, "I would *metagrabolize* still longer and more broadly and more deeply," but "I content myself with having found and named the element of language – the A and the O – the Word."[113] Now, at the conclusion of the *Metakritik,* he says much the same, only now attributing the "metagrabolizing" to Kant: "What the transcendental philosophy has metagrabolized, I have for the sake of the weak reader interpreted with regard to the sacrament of language, the letters of its elements, [and] the spirit of its institution, and I leave it to each to unfold the balled fist into a flat hand."[114] In other words, the problems that Kant attempted in vain to solve after hundreds of pages of his *Critique,* namely, how subjective conditions of thought can have objective validity (A 89) or how an intuition of an object can be subsumed under something as generically different as a concept (A 137), Hamann says that he has succinctly answered by referring the "weak reader"[115] to the sacrament of language.[116]

We have already seen in earlier chapters that for Hamann language is something profoundly spiritual. As he put it in *Two Mites,* language is a "*shekhinah,* tabernacle, and chariot-throne of our sensations, thoughts, and concepts."[117] Here, however, the sacramental nature of language is understood more specifically in terms of its natural union of the logical and aesthetic aspects of experience:

> Words have, therefore, an *aesthetic* and *logical* capacity. As visible and audible objects they and their elements belong to *sensibility* and *intuition* [*Anschauung*], but according to the spirit of their *institution* and *significance,* to *understanding* and *concepts.* Consequently, words are both pure and empirical *intuitions,* as well as pure and empirical *concepts: empirical,* since the sensation of sight or hearing is caused by them; *pure,* insofar as their significance is determined by nothing that belongs to these sensations. Words, as indefinite objects of empirical intuitions are therefore called, according to the textbook of pure reason, aesthetic *phenomena* [*Erscheinungen*]: consequently, according to the never-ending story of the antithetical parallelism, words, as indefinite objects of empirical concepts, are critical *phenomena,* ghosts, non-words [*Nicht- oder Unwörter*], and become definite objects for the understanding only through their institution and the meaning of their use. This meaning and its definition arises, as those with worldly experience will tell you, from the connection of a word-sign, which is *a priori* arbitrary and indifferent, but *a posteriori* necessary and indispensable, with the intuition of the object itself, and through this repeated connection none other than the concept is communicated to, impressed upon, and incarnated in the understanding by means of a word-sign as by way of the intuition itself.[118]

What is immediately striking about this extremely dense passage is Hamann's subversive use of Kant's terms, in keeping with what he earlier identified as the

---

[112] N III, p. 289.

[113] N III, p. 32. See Bayer's discussion, *HMK,* p. 414. The word "metagrabolize" [*matagrabolisiren*] is a Hamannian concoction that derives from Rabelais's *Gargantua and Pantagruel,* ch. 18, and may roughly be translated from the Greek (ματαιογραφοβολιξειν) as "to sound out nothing in writing," i.e., to write a lot about nothing.

[114] N III, p. 289.

[115] The phrase "weak reader" should not be taken pejoratively, but, as usual with Hamann, ironically: the "weak reader," i.e., the reader who is dependent upon the senses and unsuited for the pure ether of Kant's transcendental philosophy, like Hamann himself, is, in fact, Christologically, the "stronger" reader. Cf. 2 Cor. 12: 10: "for whenever I am weak, then I am strong."

[116] See *HMK,* p. 358.

[117] N III, p. 237.

[118] N III, p. 288.

hysteron proteron of Kant's philosophy: the necessary categories that for Kant are established a priori are for Hamann established a posteriori by tradition and use. Equally striking is how he combines a priori and a posteriori elements in the event of language. Accordingly, the mediation between understanding and sensibility is attributed here not to the schematic work of the imagination, nor to synthetic concepts a priori, but to language, which unites the "*a priori* but arbitrary" (the sign) with the "*a posteriori* but necessary" (institution and use) and thereby – by way of a sensible intuition – facilitates conceptual understanding.[119]

To be sure, this kind of union may be paradoxical to reason (cf. 1 Cor. 1: 18ff.). For Hamann, however, as we have seen, notwithstanding its potential seductions, language, logos, is ultimately analogous to the hypostatic union of the incarnate Logos and a marvelous exchange of properties or idioms. As he puts it, contrasting his own Christological understanding of ordinary language, as the answer to the internal contradictions of reason, with the deceptive enlightenment of Kant's *Critique*:

> Without, however, waiting for the visitation of a new Lucifer emerging from on high, or grasping afoul at the fig tree of the *great goddess Diana!*, the wicked snake of the ordinary language of the people, which is close to the heart, provides the most beautiful likeness to the hypostatic union of sensible and intelligible [*verständlichen*] natures, to the mutual *communicatio idiomatum* of their powers, to the synthetic mystery of both corresponding and contradicting figures a priori and a posteriori, together with the transubstantiation of subjective conditions and subsumptions into objective predicates and attributes by means of the copula or a command or an expletive [*Macht- oder Flickwort*] to drive away boredom and to fill out the empty space in periodic Galimathias [*sic*] per *thesin* and *arsin*.[120]

In other words, the most suitable analogy to the mystery of language is the mystery of the *communicatio idiomatum* (ἀντίδοσις τῶν ἰδιομάτων) of the divine and human natures of Christ.[121] The same union is also suggested by Hamann's use of the word "transubstantiation." Here, however, the union of the formal and the material, concept and intuition, is accomplished not by any special words of institution, much less by anything so needlessly sophisticated as synthetic concepts a priori, but by something as trivial as a copula or a command or even an expletive. For, as Bayer points out, what Kant seeks to solve by ascending the heights of pure reason, Hamann finds already given, and wondrously so, amid the trivialities of everyday language.[122]

Such, then, is the abiding theoretical difference between them: whereas Hamann approaches everything from a Christological perspective – in terms of a *communicatio idiomatum* of faith and reason, idealism and realism, form and matter, concept and intuition, Christ and his Church, in short, in terms of marriage or, as he also puts it, following Cusa and Bruno, a *coincidentia oppositorum* – Kant, seeking a definitive, certain, logical, Archimedean standpoint, a Δος μοι που στω, by means of his "critical

---

[119] See G-D, p. 301.

[120] N III, p. 288. As we have already seen, for Hamann language can be deceptive. As Bayer notes (*HMK*, p. 352), the "wicked snake" [*Busenschlange*] is a reference to Aesop's fable of the farmer who, upon finding a frozen snake and trying to warm it up by holding it close to himself, was bitten by it (*Corpus Fabularum Aesopicarum*, V, 2). "*Per thesin and arsin*," according to Bayer (*HMK*, p. 361), is a reference to the "rising and falling" rhythm of language. Cf. ZH I, p. 366.

[121] See *HMK*, p. 354. The term is not original to Chalcedon, but arises later, e.g., in Leontius of Jerusalem's *Contra Monophysitas*.

[122] See *HMK*, p. 359.

idealism," recoils from the muddier, liquid notion of marriage (the ultimate transcendental, one could say) and from any genuine notion of reciprocity into the cold, frozen "tower and logical construction of pure reason."[123] Indeed, therein, according to Hamann, lies the *proton pseudos* of the *Critique*: that it seeks "to produce the form of an empirical intuition without [reference] to its object or sign, out of the pure and empty quality of our external and internal frame of mind."[124] *Vis-à-vis* his old friend, therefore, who *dreams* of pure reason, he says:

> Oh, if I had the *action* of a *Demosthenes* and his triune energy of eloquence, or the mimic art that is yet to come without the panegyric-sounding gong of an angelic tongue! I would open the reader's eyes so that he might see – hosts of intuitions rising into the fortress of pure understanding and hosts of concepts descending into the deep abyss of the most felt sensibility upon a ladder that no dreamer would dream of – and the round dance of these armies [*Mahanaim*] or two hosts of reason – the secret and vexing chronicle of their love affair and rape – and the entire theogony of all the forms of giants and heroes of the Shulammite and muse, in the mythology of light and darkness – up to the play of forms of an old *Baubo* with herself – *inaudita specie solaminis*, as Saint *Arnobius* says – and a new *immaculate* virgin, but one that is not likely to be any *mother of God*, as Saint *Anselm* held her to be.[125]

In other words, Hamann would help Kant to see that, just as angels were descending and ascending Jacob's ladder (Gen. 28: 11f.), foreshadowing Christ's "descent into the lower parts of the earth" and "ascent above all heavens" (Eph. 4: 9–10), so too language is the site of a "marvelous exchange," a "ladder" with "intuitions rising" and "concepts descending" upon it. Therein, in a Christological understanding of language, which unites both formal and material elements, lies the solution to the age-old dialectic between empiricism and rationalism, realism and idealism. But there is more to the passage. For if the "love affair" between concepts and intuitions is consummated in a Christological understanding of language, the history of their "relationship" (i.e., the history of philosophy) has more often than not been a "vexing chronicle" marked by one forcing itself upon the other, of one gaining the advantage at the expense of the other.[126] The most recent and distressing chapter in this "vexing chronicle," however, is represented by Kant's "automatic reason." As Kant himself puts it, "Pure reason is in fact occupied with nothing but itself and can have no other concern …"[127] In Hamann's view this exhibits, metaphorically speaking, a different kind of sexual perversion: that of reason, represented here as the old Baubo, turned in upon itself in a form of auto-affection – from which "auto-play" the concepts of the understanding are produced by a kind of parthenogenesis a priori.[128]

A final point we may take away from the above passage, following Bayer, is that, inspired by "pure reason," his "Shulammite" (S. of S. 6: 13) and "muse," Kant has

---

[123] N III, p. 289.

[124] See *HMK*, p. 359.

[125] N III, p. 287.

[126] Here again one will note that Hamann is not simply an empiricist, just as he is not an irrationalist: instead what he seeks is a genuine union of empiricism and idealism, just as he seeks a genuine union of faith and reason.

[127] *Critique of Pure Reason* A 680. Admittedly, Kant said this in the context of his treatment of the transcendental dialectic; nevertheless, it applies to Kant's understanding of how reason in general operates.

[128] The lewd story of Baubo, a legendary woman from Eleusis, who tried to impress Demeter by sexually gratifying herself in front of her is related by Arnobius, *Adversus nationes*, book V, 25. For a thorough account of this and other sources, see *HMK*, pp. 370f.

unwittingly produced his own mythology, inasmuch as the *Critique* arises out of "indifference," which Kant calls the "mother of chaos and night" (A x). In any case, the "logos" of Kant's philosophy is in no way as pure as he feigns: as a philosophy of "enlightenment" arising out of "chaos and night," not only is his *Critique* shot through with ancient metaphors of light and darkness, but these themselves are employed as part of a story – a mythological, Olympian story – of reason's triumph over "indifference." In short, what Hamann metacritically exposes and Kant's philosophy hypo-critically conceals is an inevitable correlation of logos and *mythos*. Accordingly, for Hamann there is no such thing as a human *logos* that is free from *mythos*, no more than there is a logos that is free from experience, from tradition, from an implicit faith (be it merely a faith in the trustworthiness of the senses or reason itself, or the tradition in which one's own "reason" is formed), and, last but not least, from the historical, cultural, and profoundly metaphorical play of language. That Hamann was reluctant to communicate these metacritical insights to Kant is understandable: they are the same insights that, like so many well-positioned explosives, eventually set off by postmodern critics, brought the entire structure of his philosophy crumbling down.

The final sentence of the *Metakritik* contains an obscure but pregnant reference to Hamann's other twin of 1784, *Golgotha and Scheblimini*, which was about to be born: "But the entire wall of separation between Judaism and paganism is perhaps [the result of] a similar idealism. The Jew has the word and the sign; the pagan, reason and its wisdom – (The consequence was a μεταβασις εις αλλο γενος, the noblest part of which is planted in little Golgotha)."[129] In other words, on the face of it, there would seem to be a dialectical opposition between paganism and Judaism: whereas Judaism begins with *faith*, revelation ("word and sign") and the accidental facts of history, paganism (i.e., pagan philosophers and their modern-day heirs, the *Aufklärer*) begins with the "eternal truths of *reason*." And these radically different and seemingly irreconcilable points of departure constitute the "wall of separation" (or "the broad ugly ditch") that *Aufklärer* like Lessing cannot get over. But, Hamann suggests, this "entire wall of separation" – and with it the entire "wall of separation" between Church and state – is perhaps the result of a similarly bogus idealism. In other words, it too is an illusion based upon the same bogus claims he has just deconstructed in the *Metakritik* regarding the purported timelessness, purity, and ahistoricitiy of the truths of reason. Thus, any ultimate opposition or dialectic between paganism (qua the quest for the eternal truths of reason) and Judaism (qua historical revelation) collapses. And when, under metacritical leverage, it finally does, when it finally gives way, as Hamann fully intends, the result is a *metabasis eis allo genos*, i.e., a categorical leap into Christianity, to which paganism (qua reason) and Judaism (qua the law) respectively point, and in which both are fulfilled.

---

[129] N III, p. 289.

Metacritical Politics:
On Mendelssohn's *Jerusalem*
and the Modern Secular State

If I forget you, O Jerusalem, let my right hand wither! Let my tongue cleave to the roof of my mouth, if I do not remember you, if I do not set Jerusalem above my highest joy!

Ps. 137: 5–6[1]

A week ago today I received [Lessing's] Education of the Human Race *... At bottom, it is the same old leaven of our modish philosophy: prejudice against Judaism – and ignorance of the true spirit of the Reformation.*

Hamann to Herder[2]

In Hegel's judgment, the last of Hamann's published writings, bearing the mysterious title *Golgotha and Scheblimini,* was his most significant, and from Hegel's perspective, it is easy to see why.[3] For just as in the *Metakritik* Hamann radically called into question the *Scheidekunst* of Kant's theoretical philosophy, in particular Kant's fundamental separation of reason from experience, language, history, and tradition, here he radically challenges a similar *Scheidekunst* in Mendelssohn's political philosophy. Specifically, he challenges Mendelssohn's basic distinction between private convictions [*Gesinnungen*] and public actions [*Handlungen*] – anticipating Hegel's own attempt in the *Philosophy of Right* to overcome the Enlightenment's characteristic separation of internal morality from external legality.[4] Furthermore, in *Golgotha and Schleblimini* Hamann suggests that Christianity overcomes the dialectic between Judaism (understood as a particular, historical religion based upon revelation) and pagan philosophy (inasmuch as the latter places no trust in the "accidental" and dubitable data of the senses and history, but seeks a foundation in the universal, abstract principles of reason). For the universality that Judaism lacks, inasmuch as it is bound to a particular people, is fulfilled through Christianity's proclamation of Christ as a light to the Gentiles (Isa. 42: 6); whereas what paganism desires but lacks, namely, a deifying knowledge (*gnosis*) of the "unknown God" (Acts 17: 23), is historically given through the self-revelation of the one true God to Israel, culminating in the transforming, indeed divinizing knowledge of God's glory in the face of Christ (2 Cor. 4: 6). Thus, broadly speaking, as much as paganism and Judaism (like Athens and Jerusalem as types of reason and revelation) might at first be

---

[1] Cf. ZH VII, p. 475.
[2] ZH IV, p. 192.
[3] Hegel, "Hamanns Schriften" in *Werke* (Frankfurt am Main: Suhrkamp Verlag, 1970), vol. 11, p. 321.
[4] See Oswald Bayer, *Zeitgenosse im Widerspruch: Johann Georg Hamann als radiklaer Aufklärer* (Munich: Piper Verlag, 1988), p. 193.

opposed, they also point to one another; and to this extent they point beyond themselves to Christianity.

Whether or not one subscribes to Hegel's view of history, which is ultimately alien to Hamann's own, *Golgotha and Scheblimini* is without question one of Hamann's most important works.[5] As Hamann puts it, it contains "the true content of my entire authorship, which is nothing but an *evangelical Lutheranism in petto*."[6] Written at the apex of the Enlightenment, in view of the rise of the modern secular state and the corresponding collapse of Christendom, it also contains his most important contribution to political theology, treating such topics as natural law, human rights and duties, and the relationship between Church and state. What is perhaps most significant in this regard is that Hamann challenges the modern relegation of religion to the private sphere of subjective feeling, the intended or unintended consequence of which is that revealed truth (indeed truth itself) need have no objective, legal, or public manifestation. The result of such a dubious "wall of separation," in Hamann's view, is that the state is turned into a "body without spirit and life ... and the church into a ghost without flesh and bones."[7]

Its brevity notwithstanding, *Golgotha and Scheblimini* also bears comparison to Augustine's *City of God*. For, as with the *City of God*, it is concerned with the unfolding of world history, the relationship of paganism and Judaism to Christianity, and the prophetic significance of Jerusalem. The only difference in this respect is that Hamann defends Jerusalem as an anagogical reality not against Roman critics or Greek philosophers, but against the rationalists of the German Enlightenment centered in Berlin, who, in the name of a secular state threatened to gut history in general, the history of Israel in particular, and even Jerusalem itself, the city of God, of any prophetic significance. Indeed, inasmuch as *Golgotha and Scheblimini* defends Jerusalem as a metonym for the spirit of prophecy against secular reason, it is here that we see the proper conclusion of his "philological crusade."

Occasioned by the publication in 1783 of Mendelssohn's *Jerusalem, or on Religious Power and Judaism* (*Jerusalem oder über religiöse Macht und Judentum*), *Golgotha and Scheblimini* is of interest, finally, as an example of friendly but vigorous modern Jewish–Christian dialogue, represented in this case by two friends – one the most important Jewish philosopher of the Enlightenment, the other, arguably its profoundest Christian prophet and critic. As Alexander Altmann, the dean of Mendelssohn scholars, has noted, "The most severe but also the most brilliant opposition to *Jerusalem* came from Johann Georg Hamann, the 'Magus of the North,' who seized the opportunity of delivering a well-aimed blow not merely to Mendelssohn, for whom he had a great deal of affection, but to the whole school of the Berlin Enlightenment ..."[8] In fact, *Golgotha* is not only a penetrating metacritique of *Jerusalem,* but follows its argument so closely as to be unintelligible apart from it. As Herder observed, "You have never written a work that so clearly ... follows your opponent step by step."[9]

As for *Jerusalem,* it is the first great modern apology for the rights of European Jews, which makes Mendelssohn, in the words of Simon Rawidowicz, the "first

---

[5] For a comparative study of Hamann and Hegel in this regard, including a study of Hegel's review of Hamann and the only translation of *Golgotha and Scheblimini* thus far in English, see Stephen Dunning, *The Tongues of Men: Hegel and Hamann on Religious Language and History* (Missoula, MT: Scholars Press, 1979).

[6] ZH VI, p. 466.

[7] N III, p. 303.

[8] *Jerusalem,* tr. Allan Arkush, with an introduction and commentary by Alexander Altmann (Hanover and London: University Press of New England, 1983), p. 27.

[9] ZH V, pp. 191f.

bridge-builder between Judaism and the world."[10] Indeed, as Hermann Cohen similarly observed, *Jerusalem* "is the theoretical expression of the great practical influence Mendelssohn had upon German Jewry and, through the latter, upon the Jews of the whole world."[11] But if *Jerusalem* was written on behalf of diaspora Jews in the modern world, its intended audience was the intellectual elite of the German Enlightenment, with whom it found a ready reception. Kant, for example, though in other respects a critic of Mendelssohn's philosophy, seems to have considered the work irrefutable.[12] Above all, however, Mendelssohn had enjoyed strong support from Lessing, a close friend, whose *Nathan der Weise* was not only an appeal for tolerance and religious freedom, but an indirect tribute to Mendelssohn himself, whom Lessing described to Michaelis upon first meeting him as a "second Spinoza, who will lack nothing with respect to complete parity but the errors of the first."[13]

Given the nobility of Mendelssohn's aims, and given that *Golgotha and Scheblimini* is essentially a point-by-point deconstruction of his arguments, Hamann can appear prima facie to be on the wrong side in this debate. If one is not to misjudge him, however, one must realize that in the opening of *Jerusalem* Mendelssohn had thrown down the gauntlet, criticizing Catholics for their uncritical obedience to the "despotism" of their Church, and Protestants for being confused rebels lacking any coherent ecclesiology.[14] One must also keep in mind that Hamann did not even spare Herder when he felt that truth was at stake or that a serious error had been made. As he put it to Nicolai, "Truth is the scale of friendship – and the sword paves the way for the freedom of peace – *hanc veniam petimusque damusque vicissim.*"[15] For that matter, as he later reported to Jacobi, Mendelssohn was not even his chief target, but rather the critics of Berlin-Babel.[16]

That being said, given Hamann's typically passionate, energetic, and declamatory style, Herder, though in complete agreement, was concerned that Mendelssohn might mistake his intentions. As he put it to Hamann,

> Either what you have depicted is the pure old faith or there is none. Likewise, in the principles of this so-called philosophy I agree with you completely ... when I read these general philosophical debates, it is as if I am hearing someone talk about a dream, for neither natural right nor state and society exist anywhere in such philosophical purity and clarity, etc. etc. In the meantime, I am anxious to see how Mendelssohn will take up the matter or understand it. I am certain that he can understand you: for he has understood you in the case of more obscure works; nor do I harbor any doubt about his love of the truth ... I earnestly hope that he will give an answer – not for myself, since I am satisfied with your work, but for others and for the development of things that are really the most important of all our philosophical endeavor[s]. I also hope that Mendelssohn will not take your enthusiasm in the matter personally: for it seems to me that here too the energy of your writing speaks for itself.[17]

---

[10] Quoted in *HH* VII, pp. 32f.

[11] *HH* VII, pp. 24f.

[12] ZH VI, p. 228.

[13] Letter to Michaelis, October 16, 1754, quoted in Moses Mendelssohn, *Schriften über Religion und Aufklärung*, ed. Martina Thom (Darmstadt: Wissenschaftliche Buchgesellschaft, 1989), p. 7.

[14] See *Jerusalem*, p. 34.

[15] ZH II, p. 194. Tr.: "we both ask for this favor and give it in turn." Cf. Prov. 27: 17.

[16] ZH VI, p. 227.

[17] ZH V, pp. 191f.

Herder had good reason to be concerned. Dealing with Mendelssohn, even in an honest intellectual debate, was a sensitive matter. He had been publicly proselytized by Lavater in 1769, and had been attacked from several quarters by less worthy intellectuals for less worthy motives. And for his part Hamann certainly had no desire to alienate a friend whose company in 1777 he described as the only joy of his summer.[18] Why Hamann's rebuttal of *Jerusalem* must not be taken or misrepresented as the product of anti-Semitism, why his polemic remained within the context of friendship, and why indeed *Golgotha and Scheblimini* deserves to be regarded as an important touchstone in the history of modern Jewish–Christian dialogue, will therefore require some explanation.

Provisionally, let it suffice to say that Hamann's "more penetrating genius," in Hegel's phrase, recognized that something more was at stake than the issue of human rights or the equality of European Jews.[19] This was not the issue, though, as we shall see, Hamann was profoundly suspicious of the language of rights in general – not whether they should be conferred, but whence they should be derived. Rather, what Hamann detected in the language of tolerance, rights, and religious freedom in Mendelssohn and on the part of the *Aufklärer* in general was an implicit atheism – inasmuch, namely, as their advocacy of "natural religion" was tantamount to "no particular religion," and inasmuch as a sphere of rights claimed by reason apart from God *ipso facto* created the space for an autonomous secular counter-kingdom, an anti-Jerusalem, so to speak, devoid of any transcendent obligation to a transcendent God. Moreover, he detected right within the language of tolerance, at least on the part of other *Aufklärer* – from the explicitly atheist to the liberal Christians – an implicit anti-Semitism, indeed, a prejudice against Judaism as profound as their prejudice against the Roman Catholic Church. For according to their doctrine of progress, the particularity of Israel's claim to divine election – not to mention its scriptures, which were notoriously lampooned by Voltaire[20] – represented an affront and impediment to the dream of a secular society built not upon historical doctrines and creeds, much less upon superstitious notions of divine election, but upon the "sound universal principles" of reason.

To be sure, Judaism could be "tolerated"; like all particular religions, it too could be assimilated – but only if it relinquished any claims of binding significance for the world at large, i.e., if it denied that it possessed a transcendent revelation with moral and political implications for all human beings. In short, it could keep its commandments for itself, as merely one religion among others, but it must deny its own prophetic self-understanding as a "covenant to the people, a light to the nations" (Isa. 42: 6) and submit to the last Nebuchadnezzar of the religiously indifferent modern secular state. To orthodox Jews and Christians, for whom God's self-revelation to Israel is not reducible to tribal mythology, but an objective, historical initiative with implications for the entire world, such conditions might well seem intolerable. But this was the price that Mendelssohn was apparently willing to pay: in order to secure the rights of European Jews, he sacrificed his faith on the altar of the secular state, presenting it as little more than a religion of reason, i.e., the kind of religion that reason could have come up with *even if no revelation had been given*. In short, Mendelssohn threatened to collapse faith into reason, moreover, to deny not only the prophetic, revelatory character of his faith, but even the notion of Israel's election – all out of political expedience.

---

18 ZH III, pp. 384f.
19 Hegel, "Hamann's Schriften," p. 325.
20 See Voltaire, *Sermon of the Fifty*, ed. J. A. R. Séguin (New York: R. Paxton, 1962).

In Hamann's view, however, this was tantamount to a wholesale betrayal of the spirit of Judaism. If Judaism is not merely a religion of reason and not merely a product of human culture, i.e., if it is not merely an immanent phenomenon, but a *prophetic* religion based upon the historical *self-revelation* of a transcendent God – a God who is no tribal deity but the Creator of the universe – then what is revealed in Judaism can *in no conceivable way* be treated as one religion among others, all of which, in the name of an indifferent pluralism, are equally important and equally meaningless. No, if Judaism is a revealed religion and its scriptures are divinely inspired, then its prophetic implications for the world at large, even for the modern state, cannot be ignored (cf. Wisd. 18: 4). Thus, irony of ironies, Hamann, a Christian, ends up a passionate defender of Judaism against Mendelssohn, a would-be defender of the Jews, who, in Hamann's view, unwittingly "put a stumbling block before the people of Israel, so that they would eat food sacrificed to idols" (Rev. 2: 14) – in this case the secular principles of the modern state. And in this respect Hamann could hyperbolically accuse Mendelssohn, notwithstanding his noble defense of the rights of Jews, of being a "*fellow believer* in the spirit and essence of pagan, naturalistic, atheistic fanaticism."[21]

A SYNOPSIS OF MENDELSSOHN'S *JERUSALEM*

Given that *Golgotha and Scheblimini* is essentially a metacritical "mosaic" of *Jerusalem,* as Hamann puts it, punning on Mendelssohn's name, a brief synopsis of Mendelssohn's important text is indispensable.[22] As a plea for religious tolerance on behalf of European Jews, *Jerusalem* stands consciously in a tradition of earlier apologies like that of Menasseh ben Israel's *The Vindication of the Jews* (1656), which was translated from English into German and published, along with an important preface by Mendelssohn himself, in 1782. What distinguishes it from earlier apologies, however, is, firstly, Mendelssohn's use of the principles of modern political philosophy in order to establish a theory of natural rights and therewith the basis for his doctrine of a separation of Church and state; secondly, whereas earlier apologies sought to secure an autonomous and essentially insular space for Jews within the modern state (whereby Jews would remain subject to their own theocratic laws), Mendelssohn argues in *Jerusalem,* curiously enough, *not* for the autonomy of a theocratic Jewish community, but for the dismantling of all theocratic law (specifically the rabbis' so-called *Bannrecht* or "right of excommunication") and for the freedom of conscience of all individuals, including Jews, as equal members of the modern state.[23]

That Hamann would have been sympathetic to Mendelssohn's plea for "civil admission" one can assume from their friendship, as well as from his prophetic denunciation of the persecution of Jews more than twenty years earlier in the London Writings.[24] What was principally at issue for Hamann, therefore, was neither the question of rights per se, nor the specific question of rights for European Jews – very

---

[21] N III, p. 315.

[22] N III, p. 319.

[23] See Allan Arkush, "The Jewish response to modernity," Bradley lecture delivered at Boston College, October 1996. As it happens, Mendelssohn had personal reasons for making his argument, since he himself narrowly escaped excommunication by the rabbis. See Alexander Altmann, *Mendelssohn: A Biographical Study* (London: Routledge & Kegan Paul, 1973), p. 455.

[24] *LS,* p. 425 (N I, p. 319): "Has Jesus ceased to be the king of the Jews. Has the inscription on his cross been changed? Do we not persecute him in his people?"

concerned though he was about the way in which rights in general are derived. Rather, what concerned him were the secularizing implications of Mendelssohn's argument, beginning with the work's provocative title. For by "religious power" Mendelssohn meant not only the theocratic power retained by the rabbis, which he sought to abolish, but ecclesiastical law (*Kirchenrecht*) of any kind, including that of the Lutheran Church. In other words, Mendelssohn's argument demanded a stricter separation of Church and state (in this case, the ties between the Lutheran Church and the Prussian state) – and therewith the disestablishment of the last remnants of Christendom.

It is important to note, however, that Mendelssohn did not endorse the kind of fanatical separation of Church and state that goes along with a certain reading of the "establishment clause" of the United States Constitution – the kind of reading that appeals to a proverbial "wall of separation" and makes the government de facto committed to agnosticism as the "established" religion of state. In reality, Mendelssohn's views in this matter are rather complex, as is evident from his admirable attempt to navigate between the Scylla of Hobbesean despotism and the Charybdis of Lockean individualism.[25] Indeed, for Mendelssohn, precisely because the state cannot be indifferent to the attainment of human happiness, which consists in the acquisition of virtue (following more or less the whole of ancient moral reflection), and since the common good of human beings "includes the present as well as the future, the spiritual as well as the earthly," the one being "inseparable from the other," it would be "neither in keeping with the truth nor advantageous to man's welfare to sever the temporal so neatly from the eternal."[26] The problem, however, as Hamann saw it, was that Mendelssohn's own philosophy was full of contradictions. On the one hand, as in the above passage, he says that the temporal and the eternal should not be strictly separated. On the other hand, as in the following passage, he strictly segregates state and Church into public and private spheres: whereas the former belongs to the realm of objective action [*Handlungen*], the latter – and with it the entire question of man's relationship to God – belongs to a merely private realm of subjective conviction [*Gesinnungen*]:

> Now, two things belong to the true fulfillment of our duties: *action* and *conviction*. Action accomplishes what duty demands, and conviction causes that action to proceed from the proper source, that is, from pure motives. Hence actions and convictions belong to the perfection of man, and society should, as far as possible, *take care of both* by collective efforts, that is, it should direct the actions of its members toward the common good, and cause convictions which lead to these actions. The one is the *government*, the other the *education* of societal man. To both man is led by *reasons;* to actions by *reasons that motivate the will* [*Beweggründe*], and to convictions by *reasons that persuade by their truth* [*Wahrheitsgründe*]. Society should therefore establish both through public institutions in such a way that they will be in accord with the common good.[27]

To be sure, Mendelssohn's distinction seems harmless enough: whereas the "Church" is concerned with *education* regarding eternal principles and man's relationship to

---

[25] The problem with Hobbes, Mendelssohn contends, is that he fails to do justice to natural law as a source of societal obligations, which would mitigate the need to regulate societal behavior by sovereign power. The problem with Locke, on the other hand, is that the state cannot be indifferent to man's eternal destiny, since this temporal life is a preparation for eternity. See *Jerusalem*, p. 37.

[26] *Jerusalem*, pp. 39f.

[27] *Jerusalem*, p. 40.

the Creator, the "state" is concerned with *government,* intra-societal relationships, and the compelling reasons of law. Indeed, by today's standards, Mendelssohn's view of the relationship between Church and state might even be considered conservative. For, rather than denying a public role to religion, he would seem to advocate it: "Public institutions for the formation [*Bildung*] of man that concern his relations with God I call *church;* those that concern his relations with man I call *state.*"[28] Moreover, according to Mendelssohn's ideal, Church and state are so mutually supportive that the strong arm of the law is brought to bear when public religion has failed to convince the public that justice has an internal worth, that integrity in one's business affairs is conducive to an eternal happiness; that the true knowledge of the Creator can involve no hatred of man; and that one's duties toward one's fellow man, not to mention one's obligations toward the state, are simultaneously duties towards God.[29]

So wherein lay the rub? To understand Hamann's criticisms one must read between the lines. One must observe, firstly, that by "Church" Mendelssohn does not mean any one religion in particular, but at once churches, synagogues, and mosques (thus already implying the relativizing of the Lutheran Church). One must also observe that when Mendelssohn speaks of the Church as a "public institution," he does not mean that the Church or the doctrines of any particular religious body should have any objective bearing upon the laws of the state. Rather, whatever *churches, synagogues, or mosques* espouse in public is of relevance *only* to the sphere of private subjective feeling (however much the state may hope that the convictions inspired by religious institutions will make people better citizens). Thus, while Mendelssohn speaks of a harmony between Church and state, he undermines it with his sharp distinction between a *private* sphere of privately-held doctrines and a *public* sphere of rights and actions. Indeed, even Mendelssohn himself admits: "The state will therefore be content, if need be, with mechanical deeds [*toten Handlungen*], with works without spirit, with conformity of action without conformity in thought."[30] To be sure, this is not the case for religious persons, who know "no act without conviction, no work without spirit, no conformity in deed without conformity in the mind."[31] And there is even a poetic quality to Mendelssohn's distinction of spheres, as when he says, "The state treats man as the *immortal son of the earth;* religion treats him as the *image of his Creator.*"[32] But note – and this is crucial to observe here – for Menedelssohn there is nothing about the state qua state that necessitates its being concerned with such things as God or even "reasons of truth" – not to mention any need to be concerned with revelation. And in this regard, notwithstanding the authority Mendelssohn cedes to the state to suppress atheism in the face of imminent moral collapse, his own *Jerusalem,* in Hamann's view, ironically paved the way for an essentially God-less, truth-less, secular state. *Therein* lay the rub – not to mention Hamann's own, very different vision of Jerusalem as based upon the hypostatic *union* of the divine and human in Christ.

If the first problem, then, was too strict a separation between convictions and actions, doctrines and rights, Church and state, the second problem, and the one closer to Hamann's heart, was Mendelssohn's blurring of the distinction between

---

28 *Jerusalem,* p. 41.
29 *Jerusalem,* p. 43.
30 *Jerusalem,* p. 44.
31 Ibid.
32 *Jerusalem,* p. 70.

revealed and natural religion. To be sure, here again Mendelssohn's intentions are noble: he wants to safeguard against the kind of religious violence that arises from a perceived conflict between divine and human right – and in our own day, what could be more relevant? His solution, however, rather than observing an analogical relation between the love of God and the love of neighbor (see Matt. 22: 36–40), is to reduce the one to the other: the cultic worship of a *transcendent* God to an *immanent* civic duty to man, in short, religion to ethics. As he puts it, "In the system of human duties, those toward God form, in reality, no special division. Rather, all of men's duties are obligations toward God."[33] The problem with this is not that human duties are ennobled with religious significance, but that religion, according to Mendelssohn, has *no other* duties. Indeed, he says,

> it only gives those same duties and obligations a more exalted *sanction*. God does not need our assistance. He desires no *service* from us, no sacrifice of our rights for his benefit, no renunciation of our independence for his advantage. His rights can never come into conflict [or deviate from] ours. He wants only what is best for us, what is best for every single individual ...[34]

In sum, according to the terms of Mendelssohn's philosophy, faith can never conflict with reason, since God does not ask of anyone anything pertaining to salvation that reason itself does not already prescribe.

To be sure, in support of his argument Mendelssohn could appeal to reason's divine origin, which in his view put it on an equal footing – to say the least – with Scripture and historical revelation.[35] As Altmann puts it, "Reason, to Mendelssohn, was divine. It sufficed for the ultimate happiness of all men. As a philosopher, he required no revelation to teach him universal truths," even while, "as a Jew, he recognized the fact of revelation and lived by its laws. He saw no conflict between the two parts of his being."[36] And, true enough, given their common source, one might grant that *ultimately* reason and revelation cannot contradict one another. From Hamann's perspective, however, the postlapsarian soundness of reason and its ability to decipher the text of nature – to read off, as it were, a clear and distinct set of natural rights – is precisely what is in question. Indeed, precisely because reason is in need of healing, and suffers from "volitional depravity," it is dependent upon the historical revelation provided by Scripture, whose "unwithered leaves serve as medicine for the healing of the peoples" (cf. Ezek. 47: 12; Ps. 1: 3; Rev. 22: 2).[37] In other words, from Hamann's perspective, like Kant, Mendelssohn failed to appreciate the predicament of sin, its effect upon reason, and the corresponding need for revelation. Furthermore, given Mendelssohn's reduction of faith to reason, religious duty to civic duty, in short, religion to ethics, the pertinent question was whether he had not forsaken the core beliefs of his own tradition. For it is one thing to say that Mosaic law is in many respects convertible with natural law and, as such, rational. It is another thing to say that Abraham, the father of *faith* – who did not lean on his own understanding (cf. Prov. 3: 5), *believed* in the irrational promise when Sarah laughed at it, and, willing to

---

[33] *Jerusalem*, p. 59.

[34] *Jerusalem*, pp. 59f.

[35] *Jerusalem*, p. 87; cf. p. 130.

[36] See Altmann, *Mendelssohn*, p. 200.

[37] N III, p. 378. See Paul Griffiths's essay in Paul Griffiths and Reinhard Hütter (eds.) *Reason and the Reasons of Faith* (London and New York: T. & T. Clark, 2005).

sacrifice his son, with knife in hand, continued to believe that God could raise the dead (Heb. 11: 19) – was in any way a portrait of the Enlightenment hero.

As it happens, Hamann was not the first to respond to *Jerusalem,* or to charge Mendelssohn with contradicting his own faith. This had already been done by August Friedrich Cranz, a one-time theology and law student, in an anonymous tract titled, *The Searching for Light and Right,* which included a postscript by another critic, David Ernst Mörschel.[38] Specifically, Cranz (and Mörschel) pointed out the discrepancy between Mendelssohn's professed Judaism and his concerted effort to undermine its theocratic foundations, specifically, Menedelssohn's suggestion that being Jewish did not entail membership in a theocratic polity administered by ecclesiastical laws – including the possibility of excommunication (*herem*). Being a liberal Protestant and self-styled "Voltaire," Cranz could not claim to speak for orthodox Christianity, which he sought rather to undermine.[39] Nevertheless, he saw in the contradictions of Mendelssohn's position an opportunity to propose his conversion to Christianity – not to orthodox Christianity, but to a liberal version of it, like that of Reimarus and the "rational worshippers of God." For the latter are bound to no religious authorities, particular institutions (from which one could be "excommunicated"), or ceremonial observances, much less to particular plots of land, but worship God, as Cranz suggestively put it in reference to the words of the Gospel, "neither on this mountain, nor in Jerusalem," but "in spirit and in truth" (John 4: 21, 23).

Although Mendelssohn had other reasons for writing *Jerusalem,* the need to respond to the anonymous "searcher" was doubtless among them. Indeed, according to Altmann, "the avowed object of the work was to show the compatibility of Mendelssohn's political liberalism and his loyal adherence to the faith of his fathers, which he now calls 'Judaism.'"[40] And to this end, as Altmann points out, given Cranz's suggestion to convert in light of John 4: 21 and Christ's reference to Jerusalem, the title itself is significant: it is a defiant statement of Mendelssohn's commitment to Judaism, as enshrined in the image of Jerusalem. Whether or not Mendelssohn succeeded in making his case, the second part of *Jerusalem* directly takes up Cranz's challenge. It begins with a reference to a work by Christian Wilhelm von Dohm, a Christian, which the latter had graciously and secretly undertaken at Mendelssohn's behest. Mendelssohn's mention of Dohm and his collaboration with him was strategic. Instead of directly challenging ecclesiastical law, be it Jewish or Christian, he could claim merely to be following up on questions that Dohm himself had raised: "Mr. Dohm's excellent work *On the Civil Improvement of the Jews* led to the inquiry: *To what extent should a naturalized colony be permitted to retain its own jurisdiction in ecclesiastical and civil matters in general and the right of excommunication and expulsion in particular?*"[41] Mendelssohn's answer is clear: no religious body, neither the Christian Church nor a naturalized religious community such as his own Jewish community, should have any such jurisdiction. For "according to the principles of sound reason, *whose divinity we must all acknowledge,* neither state nor church [is] authorized to assume any right in matters of faith other than the right to teach, any power other than the power to persuade, any discipline other than the discipline of reason and principles."[42] In short, religion is to be free of coercion,

[38] Altmann, *Mendelssohn*, pp. 510ff.
[39] Ibid.
[40] Altmann, *Mendelssohn*, p. 514.
[41] *Jeruslaem*, p. 77.
[42] Ibid. My emphasis.

a matter of conscience, and in order to ensure this Mendelssohn cedes all temporal power and authority to the state.

From Hamann's perspective, it was bad enough that Mendelssohn makes the same error as all the *Aufklärer* of divinizing fallen reason, naively trusting the soundness of its deductions and operations, as if no fall had earlier occurred. Adding to his consternation, Mendelssohn goes on to offer a tribute to Hamann's arch-nemesis, Frederick the Great. Mendelssohn praises the "wise regent" for his tolerance, *excuses him* for preserving "the privileges of external religion he found installed," and then makes a political statement of profound import: "It will, perhaps, still take centuries of culture and preparation before men understand that privileges on account of religion are neither lawful nor, actually, useful and that it would therefore be a veritable boon totally to abolish all civil discrimination on account of religion."[43] What is more, having paid tribute to Nebuchadnezzar, he proceeds to praise those who have upheld his attack on the "idol"! of ecclesiastical law: those who have seen the wisdom of separating matters of doctrine from matters of right (since rights, for Mendelssohn, do not need to rest upon any revealed truths, say, the biblical doctrine of the *imago Dei*, but only upon those that reason by itself can establish).[44] To be sure, for Mendelssohn *personally*, a rational faith in the Creator gives these rights a higher sanction. As for the state itself and its system of laws, however, it is administered strictly according to secular terms, i.e., irrespective of God's existence or anything that this might imply.[45]

But how does any of this square with the fact that ancient Israel was obviously a theocracy? For "What are the laws of Moses" if not "a system of religious government, of the power and right of religion?"[46] Indeed, as Cranz incontrovertibly pointed out, "The whole ecclesiastical system of Moses did not consist only of teaching and instruction in duties but was at the same time connected with the strictest ecclesiastical laws."[47] Thus, Cranz could boldly say,

> Ecclesiastical law, armed with power has always been one of the principal cornerstones of the Jewish religion itself, and a primary article in the creedal system of your fathers. How, then, can you, my dear Mr. Mendelssohn, remain an adherent of the faith of your fathers and shake the entire structure by removing its cornerstones, when you contest the ecclesiastical law that has been given through Moses and purports to be founded on divine revelation[?][48]

Clearly, Mendelssohn had a lot of explaining to do – not least to his own Jewish community. "This objection," he says, "cuts me to the heart. I must admit that the notions given here of Judaism, except for some indiscretion in the terms used, are taken to be correct even by many of my coreligionists."[49]

---

[43] *Jeruslaem*, p. 79.

[44] Of course, precisely herein lies the problem, since secular reason alone, apart from the support of revelation, cannot even establish the dignity of the human person. Hence the 50 million abortions in America since *Roe* v. *Wade*. Hence the eugenics and sterilization programs that persisted in America well into the twentieth century. Hence too the readiness with which the aged are "euthanized." Yet all of this is possible, even predictable, once the secular state, trusting in the meager light of fallen reason, having disavowed the need for grace and the guidance of revelation, no longer looks to a transcendent *good*, but instead kowtows to the idol of popular *opinion*.

[45] For Mendelssohn, there would seem to be only one exception to this: when the society has become so corrupt and decadent as to require state suppression of atheism. Indeed, he suggests that the state must be on guard *equally* against atheism and fanaticism. See *Jerusalem*, pp. 62f.

[46] See *Jerusalem*, p. 84.

[47] *Jerusalem*, p. 85.

[48] Ibid.

[49] Ibid.

Mendelssohn's response to Cranz is revealing. First, he repudiates the notion that, in the case of a conflict between faith and reason, he would forthwith side with the latter and abandon the former:

> Now if this were the truth, and I were convinced of it, I would, indeed, shamefully retract my propositions and bring reason into captivity under the yoke of [faith] – but no! Why should I dissimulate? Authority can humble but not instruct; it can suppress reason but not put it in fetters. Were it true that the word of God so manifestly contradicted my reason, the most I could do would be to impose silence upon my reason. But my unrefuted arguments would, nevertheless, reappear in the most secret recesses of my heart, be transformed into disquieting doubts, and the doubts would resolve themselves into childlike prayers, into fervent supplications for illumination. I would call out with the Psalmist: *Lord, send me Thy light, Thy truth / that they may guide and bring me / unto Thy holy mountains, unto Thy dwelling place!* [Ps. 43: 3].[50]

In no sense, therefore, does Mendelssohn mean to overthrow his own religion. On the contrary, here, one could argue, in this appeal to the real Jerusalem, and for the light to reach it, he remains more genuinely Jewish than his contemporary liberal Protestants remained genuinely Christian. Yet it would be a far cry to say that Mendelssohn represented Jewish orthodoxy. This is clear from the shockingly diminished importance of historical revelation not only to his philosophy, but to his faith. Thus, while he admits in response to Mörschel's criticism that "a true Christian or Jew should hesitate before he calls his house of prayer 'reason's house of devotion,'" he says "I must, however, also do justice to his searching eye. What he saw was, in part, not wrong. It is true that I *recognize no eternal truths other than those that are not merely comprehensible to human reason but can also be demonstrated and verified by human powers.*"[51]

The problems with such a statement, from a theological perspective (whether Jewish or Christian), are plain. On the one hand, it *devalues the faith* of Abraham, which led him to follow God *against all reasoning* – the very faith that is the foundation of God's covenant with Israel and of all "righteousness" (Gen. 15: 6; Rom. 4: 3). On the other hand, inasmuch as it shifts the burden of proof to reason (the burden of proving, say, God's existence, the immortality of the soul, and just recompense in the afterlife), it *burdens reason* with a task greater than it can bear. Regarding the first problem, Hamann keenly perceived that a devaluation of faith and a corresponding exaggeration of reason's powers would in the end destroy reason itself – inasmuch as secular reason, unable to sustain its pretensions to certainty, could not forestall collapse into nihilism. Regarding the second, he saw that, in his radical attempt to defend his orthodoxy, Mendelssohn ended up denying that Judaism is, in any real sense of the term, a revealed religion. As Mendelssohn himself puts it:

> Yet Mr. Mörschel is misled by an incorrect conception of Judaism when he supposes that I cannot maintain this without departing from the religion of my fathers. On the contrary, I consider this an essential point of the Jewish religion and believe that this doctrine constitutes a characteristic difference between it and the Christian one. To say

---

[50] *Jerusalem*, pp. 85f.
[51] *Jerusalem*, p. 89.

it briefly: *I believe that Judaism knows of no revealed religion in the sense in which Christians understand this term.*[52]

Of course, the all-important question here is what exactly Mendelssohn understands by revelation, which he explains in greater detail in the following passage. "The Israelites," he says,

> possess a divine *legislation* – laws, commandments, ordinances, rules of life, instruction in the will of God as to how they should conduct themselves in order to attain temporal and eternal felicity. Propositions and prescriptions of this kind were revealed to them by Moses in a miraculous and supernatural manner, but not doctrinal opinions, no saving truths, no universal propositions of reason. These the Eternal reveals to us and to all other men, at all times, through *nature* and *thing [Sache]*, but never through *word* and *script*.[53]

In other words, for Mendelssohn, whatever was revealed to Israel through Moses and the prophets is of no consequence to the human race as a whole, and certainly nothing of salvific importance (not even to Jews), inasmuch as one's eternal destiny does not rest upon a historical communication or a transcendent revelation, but upon truths of reason that are immanently and immediately accessible to all people at all times.

Whether or not this accords with the spirit of orthodox Judaism, it is clear that Mendelssohn has applied to Judaism Lessing's distinction between the "accidental truths of history" and the "eternal truths of reason" – to the greatly diminished importance of the former. For while eternal truths rest solidly upon reason, "in historical matters, the authority and credibility of the narrator constitute the only evidence."[54] To be sure, Mendelssohn does not deny that God has revealed some things by such means. The eternal truths of reason, however, which "are useful for men's salvation and felicity, are taught by God *in a manner more appropriate to the Deity; not by sounds or written characters, which are comprehensible here and there, to this or that individual, but through creation itself, and its internal relations, which are legible and comprehensible to all men.*"[55] Thus, whatever was revealed to Moses, whatever is special about Israel, is for Mendelssohn of *secondary* importance and at best analogous to what is plain to all persons at all times by means of natural religion; for "no testimonies and authorities can upset any established truth of reason, or place a doubtful one beyond doubt and suspicion."[56] Indeed, he says, "Judaism boasts of no *exclusive* revelation of eternal truths that are indispensable to salvation, of no revealed religion in the sense in which this term is usually understood."[57] Thus, for Mendelssohn, historical truth, including even the revelation of the Torah, adds nothing of consequence to what one can know by way of reason alone. To be sure, like Mendelssohn himself, observant Jews might continue to live by the law, but Mendelssohn's own philosophy leaves them no clear reason for doing so.

Such is Mendelssohn's response to Cranz's and Mörschel's objection that Judaism is a *revealed* religion. But what of the corresponding objection that Judaism is, in its

---

[52] *Jerusalem*, p. 90. My emphasis.

[53] Ibid.

[54] *Jerusalem*, p. 93.

[55] Ibid. My emphasis.

[56] *Jerusalem*, p. 99.

[57] *Jerusalem*, p. 97. As a fitting example of his reduction of religion to philosophy, Mendelssohn translates the divine name revealed to Moses (Ezek. 3: 14) simply as "the Eternal One," whom presumably anyone at any time could have known *apart* from any special revelation.

origins, obviously "a hierocracy, an ecclesiastical government, a priestly state, a theocracy"? Mendelssohn's reply, which is consistent with rabbinical teaching, is that such a constitution has ceased with the destruction of the second temple: "This constitution existed only once; call it the *Mosaic constitution,* by its proper name. It has disappeared, and only the Omniscient knows among what people and in what century something similar will again be seen."[58] As a consequence, "religious offenses were no longer crimes against the state; and the religion, as religion, knows of no punishment, no other penalty than the one the remorseful sinner *voluntarily* imposes on himself. It knows of no coercion, uses only the staff [called] *gentleness,* and affects only mind and heart."[59] Thus, in his final peroration – after a legalistic, anti-Pauline, and unmistakably anti-Lutheran reading of Christianity, which doubtless provoked Hamann's sensibilities – Mendelssohn concludes that the state should not be involved in or lend its authority to a so-called *Glaubensvereinigung,* or make any laws that pertain to matters of faith and conscience.

Such are the rudiments of Mendelssohn's *Jerusalem.* The question, from Hamann's perspective, however, was whether *this* Jerusalem bore any similarity to that of Scripture, or whether, in building upon the foundation of reason – to the virtual neglect, if not denial, of the spirit of prophecy – Mendelssohn had not at the end of the day, in deed if not intent, reduced the future city of the king, the primary prophetic object of the Jewish and Christian anagogical imagination, to a mere "ideal of reason," to a cipher for the Enlighteners' secular dream of a rational, bourgeois, cosmopolitan utopia.

GOLGOTHA AND SCHEBLIMINI: BY A PREACHER IN THE DESERT

With regard to Hamann's authorship hitherto, the title of his last published work, along with his last published pseudonym, is in itself a kind of apocalypse. After years of cryptic masks and *Versteckspiele,* the inner core and theme of his authorship from the time of his London conversion – namely, the Christological coincidence of majesty and abasement, glory and *kenosis, exaltatio* and *exinanitio* – is now explicitly stated in a final variant, *Golgotha and Scheblimini.* The word "Golgotha" is familiar enough: it comes from the Gospel and means "the place of the skull" (Matt. 27: 33), or, when translated from the Latin *calvarius* (skull), "Calvary." As such, it signifies the folly of the depth of divine condescension manifest in Christ on the Cross, which is a "stumbling block to Jews [i.e., adherents of the law] and foolishness to Greeks [i.e., adherents of reason], but to those whom God has called, both Jews and Greeks, Christ the power of God and the wisdom of God" (1 Cor. 1: 23–4).

The word "Scheblimini" is more obscure, being a transliteration of the Hebrew from Psalm 110: 1, which may be translated "Sit at my right hand." But its connection to "Golgotha" is plain, having long been understood in connection with the prophetic testimony of Scripture regarding the humiliation and exaltation of the Son of God. As such, it picks up on the same prophetic theme that one can find throughout Scripture, one example of which is the story of Joseph: from his being a most-beloved son, to his rejected claims of authority, to his being sent to his brothers, to the conspiracy of his brothers against him, to his being stripped of his robe of glory, to his *descent* into a pit (though not to die), to his being forsaken by his brothers and handed over to foreigners,

---

[58] *Jerusalem,* p. 131.
[59] *Jerusalem,* p. 130.

to his *ascension* to the right hand of Pharaoh with authority over all of Egypt. The chief difference here is that the testimony to the Son's glorification, which is hidden beneath the letter of the Torah, is now presented in terms of an implicitly intra-Trinitarian conversation between the Father and the Son: "Sit at my right hand, till I make your enemies your footstool" (Ps. 110: 1).

Golgotha and Scheblimini, then, are code names for Christ, "the *great king* of the desecrated city" of Jerusalem.[60] And they go together, moreover, each representing Christ in a unique way, inasmuch as Golgotha represents the law – i.e., simultaneously its abrogation (cf. Col. 2: 14) and fulfillment (Phil. 2: 8) – and Scheblimini represents the spirit of prophecy. In short, together they stand for the law and the prophets. As Hamann puts it in a series of clarifications from *Divestment and Transfiguration*: "*Golgotha* was the final triumph of the extraordinary giving of the law [*außerordentlichen Gesetzgebung*] over the lawgiver himself, and the wood of his Cross, planted on this hill, is the banner of *Christendom*."[61] The word "Scheblimini," on the other hand, is the secret, prophetic heart of the outward mystery of Golgotha:

> The word *Scheblimini* contains the virtue and the power of the one and only name that is exalted above all names (apart from which the human race can seek and find no salvation and blessedness), the hidden treasure within all the extraordinary giving of the law, and all the mythological revelations of religion, the pearl of great price between the two oyster shells of Judaism and paganism, the mystery of their natural economy and elemental uniformity, the only key to the development and resolution of the problem and enigma stretching from the invisible nothing through all the universe, ever-present to the senses, to its conclusion and dissolution. Seers, epopts, and witnesses of the passion and glory were subsequently equipped and sent out to all nations and creatures with the extravagant evangelical sermon: *All authority in heaven and earth has been given to ME* – with the royal words of promise: *Behold, I am with you always, to the end of the age!*[62]

In other words, just as Scheblimini is hidden within Golgotha, the majesty of Christ is the prophetic secret, the treasure hidden all along in the field, beneath the *Knechtsgestalt* of the Torah. Indeed, for Hamann, Christ is not only the key to Scripture (cf. Luke 24: 25–7), but the ultimate meaning of creation and history; he is the Alpha and Omega to which both Judaism and paganism – the one by way of the law and prophets, the other, more obscurely, by way of its myths.

But if Scheblimini is a codeword for the prophetic testimony to Christ and his glory, for Hamann it is also a codeword for the spirit of the Reformation and for the "familiar spirit" of Luther, "the German Elijah":

> In a Socratic mood, *Luther,* the German Elijah … baptized the familiar spirit of his aging [*verjährt*] Reformation with the kabbalistic name Scheblimini, which I dared to claim for myself and placed next to Golgotha in order to comfort Rachel of any Christian-Protestant reader, who is crying in the desert of her lonelines, with the symbolic connection between the earthly crown of thorns and the heavenly crown of stars, and the relationship mediated in the form of the Cross between the opposing natures of the deepest abasement and the loftiest exaltation.[63]

---

[60] N III, p. 319.

[61] N III, pp. 403f.

[62] N III, p. 405f. See Phil. 2: 9; Matt. 13: 44; 28: 18.

[63] Ibid. Hamann's source concerning Luther's supposed "familiar spirit" was a biographical account of Luther published by Friedrich Siegemund Keil in 1753, the seventeenth chapter of which was titled, "Whether doctor Luther had a familiar spirit?" Keil defends Luther on this point saying that his so-called "Scheblimini," who equipped and protected him, was none other than God himself. See *HE* VII, pp. 19f. See also ZH II, pp. 194, 201.

On the one hand, we see here the pastoral intent of Hamann's work, namely, to encourage the members of the Lutheran Church *in via* by reminding them of the mysterious coincidence in Christ of lowliness and glory. On the other hand, this passage provides a clue to the whole of Hamann's mimetic "cruciform" authorship: whereas the outward humility, folly, and (to rationalists) sheer incomprehensibility of his self-denying style mirrors the humility, apparent folly, and incomprehensibility (to Jews and Greeks) of Christ's self-sacrifice on the Cross (Golgotha), the inner sublimity of his inspired, prophetic message shares in the power and the glory of the Spirit of the resurrection (Scheblimini). In short, we come to understand that the only thing that can make sense of Hamann's writings is Christ – in the double aspect of majesty and abasement, of a glory hidden from the "wise and learned" beneath a rejected outward form. And, in a final clarification, we come to see that "Scheblimini," as a codeword for the spirit of the Reformation (and the content of his own authorship), stands for a renewal and quickening of the one Christian Church: "Golgotha and Scheblimini were thus pure types of Christianity and Lutheranism … which covered the hidden testimony of my authorship and its Ark like the cherubim at both ends of the Mercy Seat, covering it from the eyes of the Samaritans, the Philistines, and the rollicking crowd at Shechem."[64]

Hamann's final pseudonym is similarly apocalyptic, revealing the intention of his authorship hitherto. He speaks not in his own voice, but like John the Baptist, in "the voice of one crying in the wilderness" (Mark 1: 3; Matt. 3: 3). He stands, that is, with the last of the prophets giving testimony to Christ. As he put it as early as 1758, whoever "is called to be a preacher in the desert must clothe himself in camel's hair and live from locusts and wild honey."[65] And, true to form, this is exactly what Hamann did: living on the meager income of a civil servant, he imitated the rough exterior of John the Baptist through what is by all accounts a course, rebarbative style (*stylus atrox*), in order to deflect attention away from himself to Christ. As for the meaning of "desert" or "wilderness," as Schreiner observes, it signals several things – aside, that is, from Hamann's intention, following the Baptist, to "prepare the way for the king of our hearts and desires."[66] Firstly, it means that Hamann's prophetic vocation has left him isolated, as von Balthasar put it, "out of joint" with his age; secondly, that Hamann felt himself to be living in the shadow of "Berlin-Babel" amid the spiritual devastation or wasteland brought about by the *philosophi acediosi* (i.e., rationalist intellectuals suffering from the vice of spiritual boredom) of the Enlightenment.[67]

The two mottos on the title vignette are similarly significant, representing, respectively, the law and the prophets; this is the common ground he shares with Mendelssohn and on the basis of which he argues. As such, they are like "two olive trees or two torches before the threshold."[68] The first comes from Moses' blessing of Levi in Deuteronomy 33: 9–10, notably in Mendelssohn's translation, where Moses praises Levi for his unyielding fidelity to his faith. The bitter irony here lies in the suggestion that Mendelssohn has not done the same and held true to *his* faith. The second, whose significance *vis-à-vis* Mendelssohn is likewise transparent, comes from Jeremiah 23: 15, this time in Luther's translation: "I am going to make them eat wormwood, and give them poisoned water to drink; for from the prophets of *Jerusalem* hypocrisy has spread throughout the land."[69]

[64] N III, p. 407.
[65] ZH I, p. 267. Quoted in *HH* VII, p. 51.
[66] ZH I, p. 421.
[67] *HH* VII, p. 52.
[68] N III, p. 481.
[69] N III, p. 291. Hamann's emphasis.

BUILT UPON SAND: THE BABEL OF MODERN
NATURAL RIGHTS

Already in view of the mottos to *Gologotha and Scheblimini,* Hamann's primary charge is clear: however unwittingly, Mendelssohn is a false prophet who speaks not for the real Jerusalem, the shared object of the Jewish and Christian anagogical imagination, but for the ersatz Jerusalem of a modern secular utopia. As we have seen throughout his writings, however, Hamann does not simply declaim; he is not a fanatic. On the contrary, his peculiar style of metacriticism (which one might call proto-deconstructionist) characteristically engages his interlocutors on their own terms, in order to let these terms, so confidently espoused, unravel on their own. And such is the case here, where the terms of Mendelssohn's *Jerusalem* are those of modern political philosophy and, in particular, the language of natural rights. Accordingly, mirroring the first part of *Jerusalem,* the first part of *Golgotha and Scheblimini* is little more than a metacritical reflection upon Mendelssohn's philosophy of right. As Hamann puts it in the opening of the work, alluding to the story of the rich man and Lazarus (Luke 16: 26–31), in order to underscore the distance between them, especially regarding how they understand the law and the prophets: "But since a great divide is fixed between our religious and philosophical principles: fairness demands that the author be compared only with himself and with no other but the measure that he himself provides."[70]

Hamann's initial round of questioning concerns Mendelssohn's positing of a separate realm of nature that is supposedly prior to society – much along the lines of Derrida's later critique of the naturalism of Rousseau – from which a doctrine of human rights could in some way be derived. From Hamann's perspective, the positing of a realm of "pure nature" apart from societal influence is fallacious from the start, since there is no realm of nature we could ever encounter that is not at the same time *also* the product of our linguistic (and therefore societal) interaction with it. In other words, for Hamann the world we encounter is always already a world determined by language and society; and so the posited distinction, upon which Mendelssohn's entire argument depends, collapses under metacritical scrutiny. Interestingly, Hamann then compares Mendelssohn's error to the dogmatic error of positing a state of pure nature in opposition to a state of grace:

> Herr Mendelssohn *believes* in a state of nature, which he partially presupposes and partially opposes to society, in the way the dogmatists oppose [the state of nature] to a state of grace. I will grant him and every dogmatist his conviction, even if I can neither form a right conception of this hypothesis, nor make any use of it, common as it is among the majority of the *literati* [*Buchstabenmänner*] of our century. And I fare with the social contract no better![71]

In other words, Hamann believes that Rousseau's social contract is founded upon a similarly fictitious notion of a pure state of nature – a notion that is just as fictional, and ideal, as the notion of "pure reason." To be sure, the social contract is said to be a postulate of reason, but as Hamann points out, the assumption of a state of pure nature, from which Rousseau's doctrine of rights is derived, is taken *on faith.* Accordingly, given how little modern political philosophy is able to establish a

---

[70] N III, p. 293.
[71] Ibid. My emphasis.

convincing system of rights apart from faith and tradition – unless its rights be based upon popular fictions – Hamann suggests that he and Mendelssohn might look with more confidence past the *uncertainties* of reason to the prophetic light of their common scriptures. Indeed, should they not have more confidence in the "contract" between God and Abraham, which was based not upon reason but upon *faith* in God's promise? As he puts it, "The divine and eternal covenant with Abraham and his seed must therefore be all the more important to both of us on account of the blessing promised and sworn to all peoples of the earth on the basis of the original testimony of this celebrated contract."[72] Thus, right away Hamann appeals to Mendelssohn's faith, claiming that the historical revelation afforded to the Jews – contrary to Mendelssohn's supplanting of it by his supersessionist doctrine of reason – is of *universal* significance to all people.[73] Surely, Hamann rhetorically suggests, this is the only "social contract" – and not any contract founded on purely secular terms – to which a Jew or Christian can in good conscience be committed.

Hamann continues his interrogation of Mendelssohn's "speculative" and ultimately "fruitless" theory of natural right (now with regard to its application to the distinction between Church and state), saying that it is like the legendary "golden hip" of Pythagoras, whose metal must be proved.[74] Admittedly, on the face of it, Mendelssohn's theory seems rather and plausible sensible: the highest moral categories are wisdom and goodness, and these, in turn, form the basis of justice: "Whatever must be done in accordance with the laws of wisdom and goodness, or the opposite of which would be contrary to the laws of wisdom or goodness, is called *morally necessary*," and "wisdom combined with goodness is called *justice*."[75] Rights are then said to follow from the "law of justice," which is invested in the holder of a right either in a "perfect" or an "imperfect" way. Perfect rights include, above all, "the right ... to the enjoyment of [the] means of attaining felicity."[76] "This right constitutes man's *natural liberty*" and is a proper good.[77] Other goods "to which a man has an exclusive right are: (1) his own capacities; (2) whatever he produces by means of those capacities or advances by his care ...; (3) goods of nature, which he has connected with the products of his industry. These goods constitute his *natural property*."[78] Natural rights are thus founded upon a posited state of nature that is somehow connected to the laws of wisdom and goodness, and this, in turn, upon man's entrance into society, yields an additional set of perfect and imperfect duties. The former are compulsory, negative in character, and essentially have to do with *not* impeding another's perfect rights; the latter Mendelssohn calls "duties of conscience." And here is where his distinction between Church and state comes into play: whereas the Church is concerned with "imperfect duties of conscience," the state is concerned only with such perfect duties as not to injure or "*act against the perfect right of another*."[79] In short, the state is concerned merely with civic obedience and the tolerance of others; the formation of conscience, on the other hand, is a strictly private affair left to one's own discretion.

Admittedly, to any citizen of a modern western democracy, Mendelssohn's philosophy of right cannot help but seem persuasive. As Hamann keenly perceived,

---

[72] N III, p. 293.
[73] Cf. *HH* VII, p. 58.
[74] N III, p. 294; cf. *Jerusalem*, p. 81.
[75] *Jerusalem*, p. 46.
[76] *Jerusalem*, p. 54.
[77] *Jerusalem*, p. 52.
[78] *Jerusalem*, p. 57.
[79] *Jerusalem*, p. 49.

however, no state-sponsored doctrine of right can be sufficiently grounded apart from religious tradition, i.e., explicitly apart from the Church, on the basis of reason alone. Nor can such "rational" attempts to construct a doctrine of right claim to be scientific. On the contrary, as Hamann immediately recognized, for all its philosophical pretense, the modern language of rights has something inherently mythological about it. Thus he challenges the notion of a pure state of nature within which human rights (according to the evangel of the *Aufklärer*) are supposedly hidden like a treasure in a field merely waiting to be unearthed by reason and claimed as one's own. So too he points out the tendency of the *Aufklärer* to hypostatize certain words and treat them as real entities, when, in fact, one should realize that "state, religion, and freedom of conscience are, at least initially, three *words*, which upon first impression can mean everything or rather nothing, and thus relate to other words like the indeterminacy of man to the determinacy of animals."[80] In short, a lot more depends upon how one is using language and what specific meaning one gives to terms than Mendelssohn admits. Hamann's more incisive proto-Nietzschean point, however, is that Mendelssohn's language of rights is ultimately indistinguishable from a language of power. For though "*power* and *right*" are supposedly "heterogeneous concepts," "*capacity, means* and *goods* nevertheless seem to be too closely related to the concept of *power* that they should sooner or later not amount to the same thing."[81] To be sure, Mendelssohn grounds human rights in the "laws of wisdom and goodness," but since these laws are given no further explanation, no further grounding in divine revelation (as in Hamann's view would seem to be required), any set of rights founded upon them cannot help but appear as an arbitrary self-interested positing of what Nietzsche would call the "will to power."

Following Hamann, then, we may summarize the major problems with Mendelssohn's theory of right thus far as follows. Firstly, it is dependent upon a largely imagined reality called "a state of nature" from which a set of rights (and a corresponding doctrine of religion) could subsequently be derived; and if this pure "state of nature" cannot withstand metacritical (or deconstructive) scrutiny, then neither can the set of rights Mendelssohn claims to derive from it. Secondly, inasmuch as the fundamental right in this theory is the right to preside over the means to personal happiness, it rests upon the principle of self-love, which is the foundation, for Augustine, of the *civitas terrena*. Thirdly, lacking any foundation in revelation, his theory raises the question of whether the "laws of wisdom and goodness" are not entirely plastic, i.e., ultimately conformable to the various wills of those who interpret them.[82] To be sure, in cases of "collision" between self-love and benevolence (i.e., duties merely of conscience), Mendelssohn appeals to the law of justice, "which appears," as Hamann puts it, "out of the brain of the theorist like a *dea ex machina* [*Maschinenpallas*]."[83] But here again, what this justice might look like is left to the individual himself to determine.[84] Thus Hamann concludes, "What an expenditure of mystical laws in order to come up with a meager right of nature that is hardly worth mentioning and is neither adequate to the state of society nor suitable to the matter of Judaism!" – to which he adds, alluding to Nehemiah's rebuilding of the

---

[80] N III, p. 294.
[81] Ibid.
[82] N III, p. 295.
[83] N III, p. 296. Justice is introduced by Mendelssohn, furthermore, to balance the scales between the perfect *right* to a positive appropriation of means to personal happiness and a passive dependence upon the perfect *duty* of non-interference on the part of others.
[84] *Jerusalem*, pp. 52ff.

walls of Jerusalem, " 'Let them build,' an Ammonite would say, 'Let them build; if foxes should jump upon their stone walls, they would tear them down' " (Neh. 4: 3).[85] In other words, the walls of Mendelssohn's *Jerusalem*, inasmuch as they are built upon a purely secular foundation, without any grounding in divine revelation, cannot be trusted to stand.

But what exactly is this secular foundation? As we saw in the last chapter, in the name of *Wissenschaft*, this dubious foundation was formed by Kant's strict segregation of reason from faith, experience, tradition, and historical revelation. Similarly, *vis-à-vis* Lessing, it consisted in the sharp and dubious distinction between the eternal truths of reason and the accidental facts of history. Now, in the matter of politics, it consists in Mendelssohn's fundamental and for Hamann equally dubious distinction between a realm of external actions and a realm of internal convictions: whereas the former belong to a realm of perfect rights supposedly derivable by *reason* from nature, the latter belong to a realm of imperfect duties of conscience, which may be commended by *historical* doctrines, but carry no binding obligation. This is what makes it possible to be a member of Mendelssohn's *Jerusalem*, in full possession of rights, without believing in this or that doctrine, without believing in God, or, for that matter, without believing anything – so long as one observes the perfect duties of tolerance and non-interference with the self-interest of others.

What this means in practice is illustrated by Mendelssohn's response to a reviewer from the *Göttingsche Anzeigen*, who had presented him with the following interesting case regarding circumcision:

> The Jewish community in Berlin appoints a person who is to circumcise its male children according to the law of its religion. This person receives, by agreement, certain rights to such and such an income, to a particular rank in the community, etc. After a while, he has doubts concerning the doctrine or law of circumcision; he refuses to fulfill the contract. Does he still retain the rights he has acquired by contract?[86]

Leaving aside the reviewer's ignorance of Jewish custom, according to which no remuneration is given for such a service, Mendelssohn's answer is revealing. He asks, "What is this example … supposed to prove? Surely, not that, according to reason, rights over persons and goods are connected with doctrinal opinions, and are based on them? Or that positive laws and contracts can render such a right possible?"[87] In other words, for Mendelssohn, rights are *not* connected to doctrines, nor do they rest upon positive laws and contracts. As for the specifics of the case, Mendelssohn replies that the unbelieving circumciser "would enjoy his income and rank *not because he approves of the doctrinal opinion, but because of the operation he performs* in place of the fathers of the families. Now, if his conscience prevents him from continuing in this labor, he will, of course, have to give up the reward previously stipulated."[88]

---

[85] N III, p. 296.

[86] *Jerusalem*, p. 82.

[87] Ibid.

[88] Ibid. To apply Mendelssohn's doctrine to a Christian frame of reference, this would entail that the Church would be obligated not only to retain, but to remunerate an atheist priest, so long as he continued to perform his official duties – *ex opere operato*! Here, however, it is no longer a question of the sanctity of the priest, as in the Donatist controversy, but of the more basic question of whether or not he believes in what he is doing.

Admittedly, we may find nothing wrong with Mendelssohn's answer, especially to the extent that we have accepted the modern *Scheidekunst* upon which it is founded. From Hamann's perspective, however, there is a fundamental hypocrisy here, which runs through Kant's epistemology, Mendelssohn's politics, and indeed the whole of the Enlightenment, namely, an artificial but nevertheless dogmatic separation of reason from traditional doctrines. For whatever we mean by reason or rights is inseparable from the history and development of concepts: "If a connection between the physical and the moral cannot be denied, and if the various modifications of writing and types of designation have necessarily affected the development and improvement of concepts, opinions, and knowledge in various ways, then I do not know why it should be difficult to conceive of a connection between doctrines and one's moral capacity."[89] At the same time, Hamann, unlike Mendelssohn, affirms that perfect rights *can* follow from positive laws and contracts, since for him rights do not derive from nature anyway, but from a revealed contract between God and human beings. "If there is a *social contract*," he says, "then there is also a *natural* one, which is more authentic and older, and upon whose conditions the social contract necessarily depends."[90] According to this contract, which Hamann calls "natural," as opposed to an artificial contract drawn up by reason alone, "all *natural property* again becomes conventional, and the human being in the state of nature is made *dependent* upon its laws, i.e., positively obligated to act according to precisely the same laws to which all of nature, and especially man, owes its thanks for the preservation of existence and for the use of all the means and goods that belong to it."[91]

As obscure as Hamann's point may be, we can at least discern this basic difference between his and Mendelssohn's conception of right: whereas for Mendelssohn, rights are, as it were, pre-possessed by *reason* and *claimed* by *independents* in the manner of *private property*, for Hamann, they are something *received* in *faith* from the Creator by *dependents* as a covenantal *gift*. In short, for Hamann, the liturgical offering of oneself, one's labor, and one's possessions to God is *prior* to right. Hence, as one who bears duties toward God and nature within this sacral economy, the human being has neither "an exclusive right to, and odious monopoly upon, his abilities, nor to the products of these abilities, nor to the unfruitful mule of his industry and the sadder cases of the bastards of his usurping violence against the *creature* that is subject to his vanity against its will."[92] In other words, as Hamann suggestively puts it, Mendelssohn's theory amounts to a ringing endorsement of the fallen order described by Paul (Rom. 8: 20). And for this reason, he cannot help but conclude that his friend's theory is supremely *unjust*, since it terminates willy-nilly in the concupiscence of the individual will:

> In short, for all the extolling of the laws of wisdom and goodness, the law of justice and the law of reason dissolve into the most gracious will and *bon plaisir* of that Roman puppet player and virtuoso, and into his swansong: *Heu quantus artifex pereo!* – Your end has come, and, in your cupidity, the thread of your life is cut![93]

---

[89] N III, p. 298.
[90] N III, p. 299.
[91] Ibid.
[92] Ibid.
[93] Ibid. The first allusion here is to the demise of the "great artist" Nero, the second is to Jer. 51: 13.

By implication, therefore, Hamann prophetically suggests that the same end is reserved for Mendelssohn's *Jerusalem*, inasmuch as it is founded not upon faith in the God of Israel, but upon secular principles, which reduce to the arbitrary "good pleasure" of those who posit them.[94]

The prophetic instinct of Hamann in this regard speaks for itself. For just as the rationalism of the Enlightenment over the course of a century gradually gave way to nihilism, so too conceptions of "nature," "natures," and "natural law," *without the backing of revelation*, have gradually given way to the voluntarism of "personal choice" and the arbitrariness that this implies – all of which can be traced back to Kant's Copernican turn away from the ordered cosmos to the individual subject as the creator of any order or meaning. Against, therefore, the radical autonomy and implicit egocentrism of Mendelssohn's theory of right – "in the state of nature, *to me, and to me alone,* appertains the right to decide whether, to what extent, when, for whose benefit, and under what conditions I am obliged to exercise beneficence"[95] – Hamann says, echoing Psalm 115 and using Mendelssohn's own better words against him, "The moral capacity to make use of things as *means* is subordinated not to *man himself,* not to *him alone,* but to those laws of wisdom and goodness that we encounter shining forth from the immeasurable realm of nature."[96] In other words, "not to us, O Lord, not to us, but to thy name be the glory" (Ps. 115: 1). Thus Hamann can say, echoing John the Baptist (John 3: 27), that even happiness is not a personal right, but rather a gift: "Man has neither a physical nor a moral capacity for any other happiness than that which is *given* to him. All the means that he would employ in order to attain a happiness that is not given and bestowed amount to [nothing but] a great affront to nature and a willful injustice."[97] Indeed, he goes so far as to suggest that the pursuit of personal happiness is the index and spark of a "hellish rebellion."[98] And it is precisely this spirit of self-interest that Hamann sees embodied in the regime of Frederick the Great, the philosopher of Sans Souci and architect of "Berlin-Babel," the very one lauded as the representative king of Mendelssohn's *Jerusalem*:

> Not for any *Solomon,* whom the God of the Jews endowed with exceedingly great wisdom and understanding, and a confident heart, like the sand of the seashore; not [even] for any *Nebuchadnezzar,* to whom the God of the Jews gave the wild animals ... that they should serve him: but only for a philosopher without cares and without shame, only for a *Nimrod* in the state of nature would it be appropriate to exclaim, with the emphasis of a horned brow: "To *me* and to *me alone* appertains the right to decide *whether,* to what extent, when, for whose benefit, and under what conditions I am *obliged to exercise beneficence.*"[99]

Here, as elsewhere, even if he does not say so explicitly for fear of censorship, Hamann takes aim at the "shameless" mores of Frderick's court. What is easily overlooked, however, is that Hamann draws a connection between Frederick's libertinism and his laissez-faire approach to social justice, which resulted in a "lack of care" about the penury of civil servants like Hamann himself. Thus Hamann satirically says,

---

[94] Cf. Schreiner's commentary, *HH* VII, p. 76.
[95] *Jerusalem*, p. 48. My emphasis.
[96] N III, p. 299.
[97] Ibid. Cf. John 3: 27. My emphasis.
[98] N III, p. 299.
[99] N III, pp. 299f. See 1 Kgs. 4: 29; Jer. 27: 6; Gen. 10: 8f.

If the ego, even in the state of nature can be so unjust and immodest, and if every human being has the same right to *me!* and *me alone!* – let us be of good cheer about the *We by the grace of God* [i.e., the royal "we" of Frederick's court], and thankful for the crumbs that it leaves to dependent orphans [*Waysen*] after its hunting dogs and lapdogs, greyhounds and bulldogs have been fed![100]

The first part of *Golgotha and Scheblimini* concludes with criticism of Mendelssohn's *Jerusalem* on two main counts. The first criticism has to do with the conceptual confusion and ambiguity Hamann finds throughout the text, as when he says in reference to Isaiah 22: 1 that *Jerusalem* is "a *valley of vision* full of indefinite and vacillating concepts," and that, on this account, Mendelssohn should not be so quick to boast of "greater enlightenment [or clarification]!"[101] As we have seen, this is a common metacriticism on Hamann's part: that his contemporaries, though they claim to be *Aufklärer,* are in fact far more confused than they realize. His second criticism concerns the problematic implications of Mendelssohn's dualism between Church and state, doctrines and rights, convictions and actions. And he makes his criticism once again in the form of a metacritical "mosaic" of Moses' own words, emended here and there for metacritical effect, moreover, by appealing to a common scriptural reference, namely, the famous example of Solomon in 1 Kings 3, who precisely did not divide the living child asunder:

> In fact, one sees here a confusion of concepts, and it is in the most *precise* sense as little in keeping with the truth, as it is bearable for the best of readers, if one opposes *state* and *church*, and *separates internal* happiness from *external* peace and security *as sharply* as the *temporal* from the *eternal*. The child of the one mother was smothered by this mother herself while she was sleeping, and the living child that remained wriggles under the raised sword of the Solomonic executioner, charged with dividing it into two, *half to one and half to the other*.[102]

The irony Hamann would have us see here is that, while Mendelssohn's own concepts are muddled and confused, he nevertheless proposes the strictest separation of Church and state. This is what makes Jerusalem, at a purely philosophical level, unbearable for "the best of readers" – whether by this Hamann means the most generous readers or simply the most perceptive. His further point, as the allusion to Solomon makes clear, is that too strict a separation of Church and state, doctrines and rights, convictions and actions, morals and laws will ultimately have a deadening effect – whether one is talking about political zombies, who can believe one thing but vote for another,[103] or whether one is talking about the state as a whole, which threatens to become an equally lifeless entity, a mere aggregate of individuals united and animated by nothing nobler than the duty to tolerate one another.

To be sure, in all fairness, one must observe that Mendelssohn at one point says that both actions and convictions belong to the true fulfillment of our duties and the perfection of man.[104] The problem, however, is that his *Scheidekunst,* having dissected the

---

[100] N III, p. 300. The word here for orphan, *Waise,* is undoubtedly an homonymous allusion to Hamann himself as the " 'Weise' (i.e., Magus) of the North."

[101] N III, p. 302.

[102] Ibid.

[103] Thus, for example, in our own day many politicians can claim to be *personally* against abortion, and may even be legitimately horrified at the thought of unwarranted late-term abortions, but like the passing priest and Levite, having uncritically accepted the modern, mind-boggling separation of convictions and actions, feel no responsibility to do anything about it.

[104] *Jerusalem*, p. 40.

living unity, can no longer restore it or bring it back to life. Thus, quoting Mendelssohn's better half back to him, Hamann says, "*Actions* and *convictions* belong to the true fulfillment of our duties and to the perfection of man. State and church have both as their object."[105] And then he draws what he takes to be the obvious conclusion:

> Therefore, actions without convictions, and convictions without actions, are a halving of whole and living duties into two dead halves. If *motivating reasons* should no longer be *reasons of truth*, and *reasons of truth* are no longer suitable for *reasons of action*; if the essence [of the state] is a matter of necessary understanding, [but] the reality is a matter of the arbitrary will: all divine and human *unity* terminates in convictions and actions. The state becomes a body without spirit and life – carrion for eagles! The church becomes a ghost, without flesh and bones – a scarecrow [*Popanz*] for sparrows.[106]

In other words, if the state is no longer motivated by truth, but instead becomes motivated by popular opinion, the only truth left, then the state will be emptied of spirit and life, human unity will dissolve into the *agon* of so many wills to power, and the Church will be deprived of any *visible* manifestation. As a result, Hamann says, however unintentionally, Mendelssohn not only contradicts his own understanding of Judaism, but ends up siding with Hobbes in his understanding of the state purely in terms of power, i.e., as having a merely regulative function to ensure "external peace and security":

> Nevertheless, the theorist [Mendelssohn] is of the opinion that, when it comes down to it, the state can be as little concerned with the convictions of its subjects as dear God should be concerned with their actions, whereby he not only contradicts his own *scheme* of Judaism, but again shows his agreement with Hobbes by making the greatest happiness a matter of external peace and security, come how it may, and perfectly frightful though it be, like that evening peace in a fortress, which would pass [into enemy hands] during the night, with the result that, like Jeremiah says, "they sleep an eternal sleep from which they will never wake."[107]

The reference here is to the opening of *Jerusalem,* where Mendelssohn says something similar about the relative security of despotism, which "prevails in the evening in a fortress, which is to be taken by storm during the night."[108] Hamann's point is that the same holds true here: Mendelssohn's *Jerusalem* will likewise fall. For while its arguments may appear sound, they are easily refuted; and those who trust in them are deceived – doomed (in this case) to a certain spiritual death. In sum, as Hamann sees it, *this* Jerusalem will fall since it is built not upon faith, but upon reason; since its hope is not in the God of Israel, but in the fickle benevolence of the religiously indifferent modern state; and since its theorist has admitted the Trojan horse of alien, secular principles and forgotten the prophetic testimony to Jerusalem's true king and defender (cf. Ps. 127: 1).

DEFENDING JUDAISM AGAINST SECULAR REASON, OR THE REAL CONTENT OF THE REAL JERUSALEM

Looking back on the first part of *Golgotha and Scheblimini,* we may now say, broadly speaking, that it is concerned with the law, not so much with Mosaic law,

---

[105] N III, p. 303.
[106] Ibid. Cf. Luke 17: 37.
[107] Ibid.
[108] *Jerusalem*, p. 34.

as with Mendelssohn's *supplanting* of Mosaic law by the eternal "law of reason" – a development one might describe as a kind of secular supersessionism, whereby Judaism is superseded in this case not by Christianity, but by the secular principles of modernity. We have also seen that Hamann considered this to be a betrayal of the true spirit of Judaism, whereby Jerusalem comes to land "beneath the meridian of Babel."[109] Now, in the second part of *Golgotha and Scheblimini*, it becomes clear that for Hamann the true spirit of Judaism, which Mendelssohn virtually ignores, is the spirit of prophecy, upon which even the law itself depends and apart from which the law degenerates into uninspired legalism. Accordingly, in the second part of the work the focus shifts away from modern political theory and the secular foundations of Mendelssohn's *Jerusalem* toward what Hamann takes to be the real foundation of the *real* Jerusalem, namely, the prophetic witness of Judaism as a prophetic witness to Christ. Thus, whereas the first part is chiefly metacritical or deconstructive, the second part contains Hamann's positive, constructive understanding of the relationship between Judaism and Christianity.

Early in the second part of *Jerusalem*, in reply to the anonymous "searcher" who had suggested his conversion to Christianity, Mendelssohn had wryly and astutely pointed out that if, as "the searcher" had suggested, Mendelssohn had in fact undermined the foundations of his own faith, then this cannot bode well for Christianity, which is built upon it: "If it be true that the cornerstones of my house are dislodged, and the structure threatens to collapse, do I act wisely if I remove my belongings from the lower to the upper floor for safety? Am I more secure there? Now Christianity, as you know, is built upon Judaism, and if the latter falls, it must necessarily collapse with it into *one* heap of ruins."[110] From Hamann's perspective, no truer words could have been spoken. For Hamann himself declares Judaism to be "the *bodily mother* of our *evangelical Christianity,* just as the *Roman papacy* is the *bodily mother* of our *German Lutheranism.*"[111] At the same time, the anonymous searcher was no doubt right, in Hamann's view, that Mendelssohn had "dislodged" the "cornerstones" of his house, having turned it into a "temple of reason." What was necessary, therefore, from Hamann's perspective, was to defend the *real* Jerusalem by pointing out the errors in Mendelssohn's own, and thereby place Judaism itself back on a sure foundation – thus saving at once Judaism and Christianity as the first and second floors of a single building.[112]

Hamann begins his defense of Judaism by applying to *Jerusalem* the same metacritical leverage Mendelssohn applied to Kant's *Critique*. Like Kant and Lessing, Mendelssohn builds his philosophy (and his religion) upon the "eternal truths" of reason, since these are held to be more certain than any "accidental truths" of history and tradition. As Mendelssohn puts it – his reasoning having been informed by the *authority* of Plato and a *traditional* Platonic prejudice against the senses – "The senses cannot convince ... of the truth. In historical matters, the authority and credibility of the narrator constitute the only evidence. Without testimony we cannot be convinced of any historical truth. Without authority, the truth of history vanishes

---

[109] N III, p. 302.
[110] *Jerusalem*, p. 87.
[111] N III, p. 356.
[112] N III, p. 303.

along with the event itself."[113] To this Hamann replies once again by metaschematically using Mendelssohn's own words against him:

> Since I too know of no other *eternal truths* than those that are *unceasingly temporal,*
> I do not need to go so far as to ascend [*versteigen*] into the cabinet of the divine under-
> standing, nor into the sanctuary of the divine will; nor do I need to tarry over the distinction
> between *direct revelation* through *word* and *scripture,* which is understandable only *here*
> and *now,* and *indirect revelation* through *thing* (nature) and *concept,* which, being written
> on the soul, is supposed to be legible and intelligible at all times and in all places.[114]

In other words, Hamann rejects the opposition between a general revelation through nature and reason and a direct and specific revelation through Scripture and tradition, because for him *there are no eternal truths to which we have access apart from historical, linguistic mediation.* Indeed, from his metacritical perspective, *there is no reason,* nor any purely natural knowledge, apart from the historical contingencies of language and a given oral and textual tradition.[115] Accordingly, for Hamann, the entire project of secular modernity, which is built upon a strict separation of the "eternal truths of reason" from the "accidental, merely historical truths of tradition," is built upon a bogus distinction.

It is with a healthy suspicion of all rational systems and secular political agendas, therefore, which presume to get along without tradition, that Hamann once again turns Mendelssohn's own words against him, saying: " 'That we should again and again resist all theory and hypotheses, and want to speak of facts, to hear nothing but of facts, and yet should have the least regard for facts precisely where they matter most!' "[116] For his part, Mendelssohn made this statement in criticism of those who would place their faith merely in facts. Hamann, however, repeats this statement to Mendelssohn to remind him that Judaism and Christianity rest precisely upon facts, upon historical events and revelations, and that being a Jew or a Christian is not about transcending them in the name of reason, but about taking these historical facts, transmitted by the authority of tradition, on *faith* as matters of *eternal significance.*[117] As Hamann puts it,

> The characteristic difference between Judaism and Christianity has to do therefore nei-
> ther with *direct nor with indirect revelation,* in the sense that the latter is taken by Jews
> and naturalists – – nor with *eternal truths* and *doctrines* – – nor with *ceremonial* and
> *moral laws:* but merely with *temporal truths of history,* which took place at a particular
> time and will never return – *facts* that came *true* through a connection of cause and
> effect at a particular point in time and space.[118]

For Hamann, therefore, Judaism and Christianity rest not upon rational assent to abstract, universal principles, but upon facts, historical events and recorded

---

[113] *Jerusalem,* p. 93.

[114] N III, pp. 303f. One will take note here how Hamann reverses Mendelssohn's prioritization of nature and reason over oral and written tradition. Mendelssohn thought the former to be a direct revelation, the latter to be indirect. To Hamann, however, it is the other way round. See *Jerusalem,* p. 39.

[115] This need not mean that Hamann denies a limited natural knowledge of God "written on their hearts" (Rom. 2: 15). One would simply need to say that, for Hamann, there is no such knowledge in an *unnatural,* pre-linguistic, ahistorical vacuum.

[116] N III, p. 304; cf. *Jerusalem,* p. 96.

[117] It is worth noting here that this reversal of Lessing's and Mendelssohn's rationalism – which not only overcomes the rationally insuperable distance between the historical and the eternal, but makes a historical testimony the point of departure for an eternal salvation – anticipates one of the fundamental points of Kierkegaard's philosophy.

[118] N III, p. 304; cf. *Jerusalem,* p. 91.

testimonies, which are handed down by authority and appeal to *faith*.[119] To be sure, as Mendelssohn points out, underscoring the unreliability of historical truth, such facts "must be confirmed by authority," without which "the truth of history vanishes along with the event itself."[120] And therein, for Mendelssohn, lies the need for a more certain, rational-philosophical foundation. Hamann's point, however, is that Judaism and Christianity rest not accidentally, but fundamentally upon faith, and therefore must not be confused with philosophy or a "natural religion" of reason. Nor does this make them poorly founded, as Mendelssohn suggests. On the contrary, whereas the *Aufklärer* build castles in the air on the basis of an abstract rationality that is artificially divorced from history and tradition – a rationality that is, ultimately, a matter of human speculation – Judaism and Christianity, for all their undeniable historicality and dependence upon facts, rest upon the "sure prophetic Word" (2 Pet. 1: 19), which transcends history and embraces all of history, since what is historically revealed through God's prophetic Word has its origin not in time, but in eternity (cf. Ps 119: 89, 160):

> Christianity *believes*, that is to say, not in the *doctrines of philosophy*, which are nothing but an alphabetic scribbling of human speculation, and subject to the fluctuating cycles of moon and fashion! – not in *images* and the *worship of images!* – not in *the worship of animals and heroes!* – not in *symbolic elements* and *passwords* or in some black figures obscurely painted by the invisible hand on the white wall! – not in *Pythagorean-Platonic numbers!!!* – not in the passing shadows of *actions* and *ceremonies* that will *not remain* and *not endure*, which are thought to possess a secret power and inexplicable *magic!* – – not in any *laws*, which must be followed even without *faith*, as the theorist somewhere says, notwithstanding his Epicurean-Stoic hairsplitting about *faith* and *knowledge!* – – No, Christianity knows of and recognizes no other *bonds of faith* than the sure *prophetic Word* as recorded in the *most ancient documents of the human race* and in the *holy scriptures of authentic Judaism*, without *Samaritan* segregation and apocryphal *Mishnah*.[121]

Hamann's first point is clear: Christian faith must not be confused with the reason of the philosophers, especially not with any form of transcendental or numerological mysticism; nor with the worship of images or animals or folk heroes; nor with a kind of ancient mystery rite *à la* Freemasonry; nor with a merely legalistic observance of the law, bereft of faith and the spirit of prophecy. His second point is that Christianity rests upon Judaism – not upon post-Christian rabbinical Judaism, which he sees as a deviation from true Judaism, but upon pre-Christian Judaism.[122] And in view of

---

[119] Note: this is not to exclude reason, but rather to provide it with new data, directing its attention to the facts of history qua revelation, thus providing reason with a point of departure for truly *metaphysical* thought, past the immanent, anamnestic logic of what reason always already knows – a knowledge that, alas, can be all too banal – to a knowledge that can be imparted only gradually, in keeping with the gift of the infinite to the finite, in the form of a progressive self-revelation of God through the Holy Spirit (1 Cor. 2: 6ff.). But this "metaphysics" (in Rosenzweig's sense of this term), "beyond" the banalities of reason, cannot be undertaken – this "super"-natural knowledge of God cannot be received – except by beginning with *faith* in a historical testimony.

[120] N III, p. 304; cf. *Jerusalem*, p. 93.

[121] N III, p. 306. Cf. Dan. 5: 5ff. By "Samaritan segregation," Hamann presumably means either the separation of the law from the spirit of prophecy or Israel's forsaking of its implicit universalism, i.e., its call through its prophetic witness to bring light and healing to the Gentiles.

[122] Given that Hamann's theology of Israel is essentially that of Paul (Rom. 9–11), one could say that "authentic Judaism" continues to apply to the "remnant" of Israel, which will be "grafted back in" (Rom. 11: 23), to the extent that it retains an openness to the Messiah in his glory – now as a matter of *eschatological* expectation – such that, for all their differences, Jews and Christians remain eschatologically united (*vis-à-vis* the immanent contentedness of the secular age) in their shared longing for the appearance of Christ.

this sacred testimony he says that the Jews are "a race instructed in divine things, anointed, and called and chosen [as God's] possession before all other peoples of the earth."[123] Indeed, he says that Christianity is wholly dependent upon their authoritative witness:

> This characteristic difference between Judaism and Christianity is a matter of *historical truths* not only of *past* but also of *future times*, which are prophesied and declared in advance by the spirit of a providence that is as universal as it is particular, and which by their very nature cannot be received in any other way than by *faith*. Jewish authority alone gives them the authenticity they require; these memorabilia of earlier and later times were confirmed by *miracles*, preserved by the *credibility* of witnesses and those who took care to pass on the tradition, and supported by the *evidence* of actual fulfillments, which are sufficient to place *faith* beyond all Talmudic and dialectical doubts and reservations. The *revealed* religion of Christianity is therefore rightly and with good reason called *faith*, trust, confidence, assured and childlike trust in divine pledges and promises, and in the glorious progression of its life as it unfolds itself in representations from one degree of glory to another, until a complete revelation and apocalypse in the fullness of a vision face to face of the mystery which was hidden in the beginning and was *believed:* just as father *Abraham* believed the Eternal One, rejoiced that he would see His day, and was glad; for he did not doubt the promise of God through unbelief, but was strong in faith and *gave God the glory*. And for this reason it was also credited to him as *righteousness* [*zum Verdienst*].[124]

Such is the profound bond and basis of fellowship between Jews and Christians. At the same time, however, Hamann again makes it clear that for him Talmudic Judaism represents a departure from authentic Judaism – at least to the extent that it has forsaken the spirit of prophecy that once animated it, and become merely a matter of ritual observance of the Law. Thus he points out, again connecting the righteousness of Abraham to his visionary faith in Christ, that "Righteous Abraham was given the *promise*, but no law, as the sign of the covenant [to be enacted] through his flesh."[125]

In further support of his point that Judaism and Christianity are religions not of reason, nor of legalistic observance, but of faith, Hamann appeals to the example of Moses, the lawgiver himself, who was explicitly denied passage to the Promised Land because of *a lack of it* (Deut. 32: 51f.). And in this connection he relates Moses' fate to that of Judaism, namely, to the extent that personal messianic faith disappears into mere legalism (or, in Mendelssohn's case, into mere reason), and one is no longer attentive to the prophetic spirit by which the law itself was first inspired and written. The consequence of this uncoupling of the law from the spirit of faith and prophecy, he says, is that the "hieroglyphic customs" and "symbolic ceremonies" of the law itself – like the "symbolic actions"[126] of one's own life – are deprived of their mystical sense and reference:

> But the lawgiver *Moses* was flatly denied entrance into the Promised Land; and due to a similar sin of unbelief in the spirit of grace and truth, which should have been preserved in hieroglyphic customs, symbolic ceremonies, and actions of weighty significance until the time of the revival, outpouring, and anointing [of the Holy Spirit], this

---

[123] N III, p. 306. Cf. 1 Pet. 2: 4.
[124] N III, p. 305. See 2 Cor. 3: 18; Exod. 33: 11; Rom. 4: 22.
[125] N III, p. 307.
[126] N II, p. 139: "Human life seems to consist in a series of symbolic actions ..."

earthly vehicle of a temporal, figurative, and dramatic legislation and offering of animal sacrifices, degenerated into the corrupted, deadly creeping poison of a childish, literalist, idolatrous superstition. Accordingly, the entire *Moses*, together with all the *prophets* is the *rock* of the Christian faith; and the *cornerstone*, chosen and precious, which the builders rejected, has become to them also the head of the corner, but in the manner of a stumbling block, a rock of offense, so that out of unbelief they stumble on the *Word* upon which their entire edifice depends.[127]

Admittedly, Hamann's description of what happens to Judaism once it is no longer animated by a living faith and by the same prophetic spirit that originally inspired its scriptures is harsh. His point, however, is that just as Christianity cannot stand without Judaism, so too Judaism cannot be fulfilled apart from Christianity; indeed, for him they are *reciprocally foundational* as *archē* and *telos* of a single providential economy.

For his part, certainly, Mendelssohn was perfectly able to affirm his faith, and continued to abide by the law. The all-important question that Hamann poses to Jews and Christians, however, is what one makes of their shared testimony. When Mendelssohn reads the Hebrew Bible, he finds nothing of ultimate consequence (i.e., of eternal significance) that he did not already know by way of reason. Thus he can sincerely say that "Judaism knows of no revelation in the sense that this term is usually understood."[128] When Hamann reads the Hebrew Bible, on the other hand, he discovers along with the Church Fathers a prophetic testimony to Christ that is far more mysterious than anything that reason alone could ever have recorded or fathom. Weary, therefore, with Mendelssohn's reduction of Judaism to the terms of reason, Hamann ironically states his agreement with him that "Judaism knows of no revelation," i.e., no *ultimate* revelation, but is like the showbread of the sanctuary, a mere index or type of the mystery itself:

> I have neither hunger for the *showbread*, nor leisure and strength for *labyrinthine walks* and *peripatetic labyrinths*, but get to the point and state my complete agreement with Herr Mendelssohn when he says that Judaism knows of no *revealed* religion, in the sense, namely, that he himself understands this term, i.e., that God actually made known to them and entrusted to them, through word and scripture, nothing other than the sensible vehicle of the *mystery*, the shadow of *future goods*, not the essence of the goods themselves, the actual communication of which God reserved for a higher mediator, high priest, prophet and king than Moses, Aaron, David, and Solomon. – Just as Moses himself, for this reason, did not know that his face had a shining brightness that struck the people with fear: so too the whole giving of the law on the part of this divine minister was a mere veil and curtain of the religion of the old covenant, which to this day remains veiled, wrapped, and sealed.[129]

Hamann's point here at the end of his authorship is reminiscent of its beginning in the *Socratic Memorabilia*. Indeed, in a sense we have come full circle. There one of his main points was that nature and history are books that are "sealed" to reason, but open to the eyes of faith. Now his point is that God's election of Israel and the prophetic testimony of its scriptures – in which God has recorded as in an enigma the mysteries of his kingdom – are similarly unintelligible apart from faith in Christ. As Hamann already put it in the *Aesthetica,* quoting Augustine, "If you read the

[127] N III, p. 305.
[128] *Jerusalem*, p. 90.
[129] N III, p. 304.

prophetic books without understanding *Christ*, what exceedingly insipid and fatuous things you will find! But if you perceive Christ in them, what you read will not only be to your taste, but will also intoxicate you."[130] Now Hamann claims that this applies not only to the Hebrew Bible, but to the entire symbolic economy of the history of Israel:

> The whole mythology of the Hebrew economy was nothing but a *type* of a more transcendental history, the *horoscope* of a heavenly hero, by whose appearance everything is already completed and remains to be completed that is written in their law and their prophets: "They will pass away, but *you* endure; they will all wear out like a garment; when *you* change them, they will be changed like clothing."[131]

Granted, Hamann speaks similarly of pre-Christian pagan mythology as a dream-like anticipation of Christ. But for him the revelation afforded to the Jews is something far more sublime, because it is a revelation given not obscurely through a poet like Homer, and passed on in the form of folklore, but written directly into the very history of Israel, no longer in dreams and riddles but in reality:

> For what are all the *miracula speciosa* of an *Odyssey* and an *Iliad* and their heroes compared to the simple but richly significant phenomena of the patriarchs' venerable walk [with God]? What is the gentle loving soul of the blind Maeonian minstrel compared to the spirit of Moses, which glows *a priori* and *a posteriori* with its own deeds and lofty inspirations![132]

Thus, while there is an analogical community between paganism and Judaism, inasmuch as both point to Christ, for Hamann it is also the case that divine revelation moves with increasing profundity and clarity from the former toward the latter. As he puts it toward the end of his work, summarizing in an inspiring coda his lofty understanding of Judaism as a prophetic testament to Jesus:

> According to the analogy of its ceremonial law, the entire history of the Jewish people seems to be a living *primer* to all *historical literature in heaven*, on and *under the earth*, which awakens the mind and heart – – – a progressive, diamond-like index pointing to the Jubilees and plans of divine government, spanning the whole of creation from its *beginning* to its *end*, and the prophetic enigma of a theocracy is reflected in the fragments of this shattered vessel, like the sun "in the droplet on the grass, which tarries not for men, nor waits for the sons of men" [Mic. 5: 7]: for *yesterday* the dew of the Lord was only on *Gideon's* fleece, and it was dry over all the earth; *today* the dew is over the whole earth, and is dry only on the fleece [cf. Judg. 6: 36–40] – Not only the entire history of Judaism was *prophecy*; but more than all the other nations to which one perhaps cannot deny the *analogy* of a similar, dark intimation and presentiment, its *spirit* was concerned with the *ideal* of a savior and king, a man of power and wonders, a lion's whelp, whose lineage according to the flesh was from the tribe of *Judah*, but whose procession from above should be from the *bosom of the Father*. Moses, the Psalms, and prophets are full of winks and glimpses, pointing to the appearance of a *meteor* that is more than a pillar of cloud and fire, a *star* arising out of *Jacob*, a *sun* of justice with healing beneath its wings! – to a sign of contradiction in the ambiguous figure of his person, his message of

---

[130] N II, p. 212. The quotation is from Augustine's commentary on John, *In Ioannis tractatus*, IX, 3.
[131] N III, p. 308. Cf. Ps. 102: 26f. Note: by calling the Hebrew economy "mythological," Hamann does not mean that the history of Israel is fictional, but that, as the *historical poetry* of God, it is figurative in the manner of an obscure revelation.
[132] N III, p. 309.

peace and joy, his works and sorrows, his obedience unto death, indeed, death on a cross! and his exaltation from the dust of the earth of a *worm* to the throne of a glory that cannot be moved – – to the *kingdom of heaven,* which this *David, Solomon,* and *Son of Man* would plant and bring to fulfillment in a *city* that has a foundation, whose master builder and creator is God, to a *Jerusalem* above, which is *free* and the mother of us all, to a new heaven and a new earth, without sea and temple within –.[133]

Indeed, seen in light of Christ, the history of Israel becomes so significant as to be nothing less than the living poetry of God's gradual self-revelation, culminating in the "face to face" of Christ himself: a historical mirror, full of *facts,* which are anything but accidental, in which are gradually revealed according to divine providence the eternal mysteries of the kingdom of heaven.

As we have seen, following Lessing, Mendelssohn had sharply distinguished between the "eternal truths of reason" and the "accidental facts of history." Hamann, however, as we have also seen, completely rejects any such strict and dubious separation, and now it is fully clear why. For here, *in and among* the facts of the history of Israel, the eternal Logos and archetype of all reason is revealed. Thus, against Mendelssohn, who would transform Judaism into an *abstract* religion of reason, and contemporary *Aufklärungstheologen,* who would do the same with Christianity, he says: "These *temporal* and *eternal* truths of history concerning the king of the Jews, the angel of their covenant, the firstborn and head of his church, are the A and Ω, the ground and summit of the *wings* of our *faith* ..."[134] Conversely, unbelief, he says, following Luther, "is the only sin against the *spirit* of the true religion, whose heart is in heaven, and whose heaven is in the heart."[135] To which he adds, emphasizing the difference between a legalistic righteousness, what Luther calls "works righteousness," and the righteousness that comes by faith:

> The secret of Christian godliness consists not in *services, sacrifices,* and *vows, which God demands of human beings,* but rather in *promises, fulfillments,* and *sacrifices* that *God has made* and *accomplished* for the greatest good of human beings: not in the *noblest* and *greatest commandment* that he *imposed,* but in the *greatest good* that he *gave:* not in *laws* and *moral instructions,* which touch merely upon *human convictions* and *human actions,* but in the execution of divine *judgments* through *divine deeds, works,* and *institutions* for the salvation of the whole world.[136]

The references to "actions" and "convictions" make it clear that Hamann again has Mendelssohn in mind. His point here, accordingly, is that Mendelssohn's *Jerusalem* is more than anything about human rights and duties, whereas Hamann's Christianity is more than anything about what God has done (see John 3: 16) and the edifice God has built (1 Pet. 2: 6). Indeed, inasmuch as God is banished into the interiority of private conviction, according to Mendelssohn's founding separation of convictions and actions, the net result of his *Jerusalem* is that human works are, ironically, all that is left. In other words, God is not an actor in this Jerusalem; whereas for Hamann the emphasis remains on the divine works and judgments that God accomplishes in and through human beings.

---

[133] N III, p. 311. References, among others, are to Gen. 49: 10; Rev. 5: 5; Heb. 7: 14; John 1: 18; Exod. 13: 21; Deut. 24: 17; Mal. 3: 20; Luke 2: 34; Isa. 52: 7, 53: 3, 11; Phil. 2: 8; Ps. 22: 7; 110: 1; Job 25: 6; Heb. 11: 10; Gal. 4: 26; Rev. 21: 1, 22.

[134] N III, p. 311.

[135] N III, p. 312.

[136] Ibid.

At this point, it almost goes without saying that Hamann rejects any strict separation of Church and state – as if the notion of a purely secular state, independent of divine judgment, were not a complete illusion; as if the vacuum created by God's eviction from the state would not be filled by some kind of idol – in this case, the idol of secular reason. Now, at the end of *Golgotha and Scheblimini*, he sharpens his criticism of Mendelssohn's strict separation of spheres, taking aim, specifically, at the dubious natural religion that would serve as the basis of Mendelssohn's "church." The main problem here, Hamann points out, is that a natural religion cannot bridge the gap between God and human beings, as Mendelssohn intends, since there is an "infinite disproportion" between them; in other words, a natural religion cannot legitimately relate to God, because in order to be known, God would have to reveal himself. Nor, for that matter, can it hope to overcome the distance created by human sin. No, the double "disproportion," at once natural (due to the qualitative distance between the Creator and creation) and culpable (due to sin), can be overcome only through divine condescension (the first disproportion through Christ's incarnation, the second through his Cross).

But if Mendelssohn's natural religion is unable to establish a proper relation between God and human beings, as Hamann points out, then his public sphere of intra-societal human relationships will also be affected and left unredeemed. Indeed, here too a "disproportion" will persist:

> Given the *infinite disproportion* of man to God, "public educational institutions, which refer to the relation of man to God," are simply absurd propositions in dried-up words that infect the inner humors the more a speculative creature imbibes them. Firstly, in order to remove the *infinite disproportion* and dispense with it, before one can speak of relations, which are supposed to serve as a relational ground for public institutions, man must either come to have a share in the *divine nature*, or the deity must taken on *flesh and blood*. The *Jews* seized parity through the palladium of their *divine law*, and the *naturalists* through their *divine reason*: as a result, there remains for the Christians and for *Nicodemus* no other mediating concept than to believe with one's whole heart, with one's whole soul, with one's whole mind: *For God so loved the world* – – This faith is the victory that has overcome the world.[137]

Aside from anticipating the dialectical theologies of Kierkegaard, Gogarten, and the early Barth (though here, one will note, the dialectic is not exacerbated but *overcome* by the incarnation), as Schreiner observes, this passage holds a key to Hamann's typology of history. As Hamann put it as early as the London Writings, "In its concepts of blessedness, the human race divides into two groups, of which the first seeks to *inherit it,* and the other seeks to *acquire it.* The Jews said: it is owed to us; we are Abraham's children. The pagans demanded deification as the reward for their virtues and deeds."[138] In Hamann's view, neither of these claims is adequate to the "infinite disproportion" between God and human beings. For just as the law of the Jews achieves its elenchtic purpose by exposing human sin and frailty (instantiating thereby the infinite distance between God and human beings), the reason of the pagans achieves its purpose by convicting us of ignorance (as we saw in the *Socratic Memorabilia*). In short, each prepares us for what only God can give: ontologically, the grace that heals our nature from sin; noetically, the faith that enlightens the darkness of ignorance. Herein, and not in what we might claim for ourselves as something

---

[137] N III, pp. 312f. Cf. *Jerusalem*, p. 58, and John 3: 16; 16: 33.
[138] N I, p. 47. Quoted in *HH* VII, p. 142.

owed, whether through inheritance or through virtuous works, lies the secret of "Christian godliness." As Schreiner observes, this does not mean that Greek and Jew (representing reason and the law) are typological errors in the script of world history. On the contrary, they are part of God's providential design: they are the crucible, so to speak, out of which the "new man" is born. [139]

In his peroration, Hamann then concludes with an apostrophe to his "devout reader," saying, "before I give you my parting blessing, allow me, an old *Marius,* to rest for a while upon the rubble of this philosophical-political *Jerusalem*" [140] (alluding to the ease with which he took this city, just as the old Marius easily took Rome) – adding some final criticisms, essentially amounting to the charge that Mendelssohn has abandoned his own Jewish faith and adopted an "adulterous *psilosophy*" [sic]. [141] Indeed, he goes so far as to accuse him of having "unfortunately! been seduced by the loose doctrine of the *Greeks* and the statutes of the *world* into becoming a circumcised *fellow believer* in the spirit and essence of pagan, naturalistic, atheistic fanaticism." [142] Simply put, he accuses Mendelssohn of having surrendered his faith to philosophy and mistaken Athens for Jerusalem. Finally, as in the *Metakritik,* Hamann indicates the Christological root of his criticism of Mendelssohn's *Scheidekunst,* i.e., Mendelssohn's metaphysical separation of reason from history, eternity from time:

> No one who *denies* the Son has the Father, and whoever does not honor the Son does not honor the Father. But whoever sees the Son, sees the Father. *He* and the *Son* are *One in being* [*ein Einiges Wesen*], admitting not the least political or metaphysical division or multiplicity; and no one has seen God; the only Son, who is in the bosom of the Father, has made known his fullness of grace and truth. [143]

In other words, what Mendelssohn divides – the rational and the historical, the eternal and the temporal – are for Hamann united in Christ. Here is his ultimate answer to Mendelssohn and the *Aufklärer* in general.

And yet, interestingly enough, Hamann does not fault Mendelssohn for not being a Christian; as far as we know he never tried directly to convert him. Rather, what he regretted was that his friend, having sacrificed the prophetic faith of his ancestors to the reason of the philosophers, was no longer even identifiable as a Jew. For therein lay the possibility of genuine conversation and rapprochement between them. Thus he sharply says, in words he may later have regretted, "It is certainly sad not to know what one is, and almost ludicrous to be precisely the opposite of what one wants and intends to be." [144] Indeed, he suggests that Hume, though a skeptic, was ironically closer to the true, prophetic spirit of Judaism, inasmuch as at the conclusion of the *Dialogues* the "Pharisee" Philo, rather than contenting himself with the uncertainties of natural religion regarding the "darkness of the *unknown object,*" like the "hypocrite" Cleanthes, at least longs to be relieved of the "disgrace of such crass ignorance" through the "Jewish anachronism" of an "adventitious instructor." [145]

---

[139] *HH* VII, p. 143.
[140] N III, p. 315.
[141] N III, p. 316. For more on this neologism, see Chapter 13.
[142] N III, p. 315.
[143] Ibid. Cf. 1 John 2: 23; John 5: 23; 14: 9; 12: 45; 10: 30; 1: 18.
[144] N III, p. 315.
[145] N III, p. 316; David Hume, *Dialogues Concerning Natural Religion* (Indianapolis: Hackett, 1998), p. 89.

PROSPECT FOR JEWISH–CHRISTIAN DIALOGUE

On the one hand, one might consider it unfortunate, given the prospects it might have held for Jewish–Christian dialogue, that Mendelssohn made no reply to Hamann's criticisms. On the other hand, as Altmann has suggested, citing Hamann's cryptic style and apocalyptic imagery as "the very antithesis of Mendelssohn's lucid and graceful presentation," there is perhaps no real possibility of debate between them, but "only a clash of two worlds."[146] Indeed, given how thoroughly they differed, in substance and in style, it is a virtual wonder of providence that they could be friends. And yet, their friendship itself is perhaps reason enough why they should be in dialogue, and why contemporary dialogue between Jews and Christians could benefit from their unfinished debate.

While it is true that Hamann's criticisms were harsh – he was not one to compromise when he felt the truth was at stake – his goodwill toward Mendelssohn, whom he calls "my old friend," is evident from his regret over having accused him of "atheistic fanaticism" and his grief over his premature death in 1786.[147] In a revealing letter to Jacobi, he writes:

> All day Thursday I was turning over the sudden death of poor Mendelssohn and could find no peace, always regretting that I did not write to him before his end, as on more than one occasion I was prepared to do, and explain to him that my *Gologotha* was directed more at the Berlin critics than at him … and that my profession of the truth against them would not have made me his adversary if I had expressed myself fully or had completed what I intended to write. Mendelssohn seems to have expected as much from me, to judge from the little he said to others and to Hill and from Biester's letters to Kraus, who defended me I don't know how. Out of my own pride I perhaps inferred his own, and thought that if he took my friendship seriously, he could just as well take the first step as I.[148]

Clearly, Hamann was troubled about the way things ended, and in the rest of the letter alternately defends and recriminates himself. On the one hand, he worries that he misunderstood Mendelssohn and treated him unfairly, even quoting parts of *Jerusalem* with approval; he also contemplates a trip to visit Mendelssohn's family to express his condolences and, like an old friend, to repeat to Mendelssohn's son what he refers to as "the final admonitions of the father," namely, "to be on guard against the *pestilent mistress* [i.e., presumably the seductions of secular reason unenlightened by revelation], to stay true to *Moses and the prophets,* and to prefer their testimony to all mathematical and metaphysical speculations," i.e., all systems of thought based upon reason alone, to the neglect or disregard of revelation and prophesy.[149] On the other hand, he suggests that he understood Mendelssohn correctly and had no other choice in the matter. As he puts it to Jacobi, the problem seems to have come down to this: that "Mendelssohn's religion was, at the end of the day, nothing but philosophy."[150]

---

[146] Introduction to *Jerusalem*, p. 28.
[147] ZH IV, p. 270.
[148] ZH VI, p. 227.
[149] Ibid. Cf. ZH VI, p. 230. In any event, in light of Rev. 17: 5, where Babylon is identified as the "mother of harlots," what these phrases indicate is an idolatrous, seductive counterfeit of the real kingdom of the real Jerusalem.
[150] ZH VII, p. 39.

Part V

A Final Journey:
Hamann's Last Will and Testament

13

Life and Writings 1785–1788

At one moment he has the appearance of one who cannot count to three;
the next moment he overflows with genius and fire.

Friedrich Leopold of Stolberg[1]

On one occasion in particular I was fortunate enough to catch sight of him,
and I saw through his appearance an exalted picture of Christian greatness in
the form of rags and tatters [Lumpengestalt], a picture of strength in weakness,
which inspired my soul but also humbled it, given that I saw the divide that
still lay between me and this great man.

Princess Amalia Gallitzin[2]

For some time now, since the mid-1780s, Hamann had been planning a trip. For one thing, he and Jacobi, who had long been correspondents, had hoped to meet one another; and so the first leg of the trip would take him to Pempelfort, Jacobi's estate near Düsseldorf. For another thing, he owed a visit to the so-called "Münster circle," a distant "fan club," consisting, curiously enough, largely of Catholics, who providentially provided him with financial support out of the blue just when he most needed it. And, last but not least, he longed to see Herder in Weimar, with the added expectation of finally meeting Goethe. In December 1785, however, he had suffered a mild stroke, and his health was in decline. Consequently, if he was to undertake so long a journey, he could not do so at this point without the company of Johann Michael, his 20-year-old son, and Gottlob Emmanuel Lindner, his "doctor Raphael," lifelong friend, and brother of Johann Gotthelf Lindner. There was also the problem of leave and the question of how to ensure the continued financial support of his family. Hamann was not yet retired and could scarcely afford to do so without a sufficient pension. Thus, in 1786 he petitioned Berlin, but was given only one month's leave, hardly enough time for travel so far. Waiting for a better opportunity, the following April he again put in a request to Berlin.[3] This time things were more auspicious: his arch-nemesis, Frederick the Great, had died, and the heavens seemed to open. His letter, though, was rather daring: in order to make his leave seem more feasible, he alerted his superiors to the relative unimportance of his position. The response was foreseeable: his position was officially terminated. After some wrangling, however, and notable interventions on his behalf, he was eventually given a respectable pension at half his yearly salary. It was, in any case, enough. The road to Münster was now finally open, and on June 21, 1787 he boarded the coach with his son, never to return.

---

[1] Friedrich Leopold Graf zu Stolberg, *Briefe*, ed. J. Behrens (Neumünster, 1966), p. 188, cited in ZH VI, p. xii.

[2] C. H. Gildemeister, *Johann Georg Hamann's des Magus in Norden: Leben und Schriften*, vol. 6: *Hamann Studien* (Gotha: F. A. Perthes, 1857–73), p. 14.

[3] NB, pp. 419f.

THE MÜNSTER CIRCLE

Of all the periods of Hamann's life after his conversion, it is this last period that offers the clearest picture of his spiritual stature; for now, having finally set aside his public masks and pseudonyms, he is exclusively among friends. It also tells us the most about his ecumenical spirit as a devout Lutheran, having had little exposure to Catholicism, entering at the end of his life into a circle of devout Catholics. Chief among them, and the founder of the "Münster circle," was the priest and statesman, Franz Friedrich von Fürstenberg (1728–1810), who as vicar-general ran the city for many years while the prince bishop of Münster was otherwise occupied as Elector of Cologne. During this time he introduced many landmark educational reforms, which were notable for their combination of intellectual and spiritual formation, and were later widely introduced across Germany.[4] Others in the circle included the poet, historian, and collaborating reformer, Anton Matthias Sprickmann; the priest, Bernhard Overberg; the priest and theologian, Johann Michael Sailer (whose devotional works helped to ferment a Catholic renewal during this time); and the young nobleman, Franz Kaspar Buchholtz, Herr von Welbergen, who had connections to Lavater in Switzerland. At the periphery were Jacobi in Pempelfort, along with his promising protégé, Thomas Wizenmann; Matthias Claudius in Wandsbeck, who had first put Hamann in touch with Jacobi; and the German translator of the *Zend-Avesta*, Johann Friedrich Kleuker in Osnabrück, with whom Hamann had been in correspondence since 1776, and whose translation had made a notable impact upon Herder.[5]

Eventually, however, the circle came to be centered on a woman of great charm, learning, and spiritual depth, who in her day was considered the female counter-part of Goethe: the Princess Amalia von Gallitzin (1748–1806).[6] Born into a noble family, she met and married the Russian Prince Gallitzin in Aachen, and, subse-quent to his appointment as ambassador to the Netherlands, accompanied him to The Hague. Soon, however, she was overcome by the emptiness of her circum-stances and withdrew from social life to pursue her own education and spiritual growth, doing so initially with the help of none other than Denis Diderot.[7] Thereafter she was tutored for several years by the Dutch philosopher, Franz Hemsterhuys, who introduced her to the writings of Plato. Then, in 1780, evi-dently separated from her husband, and having heard of Fürstenberg's reforms, she moved to Münster for the sake of the education of her two children, continu-ing her own education with Fürstenberg and others. Before long she came to be the central figure of this broadening intellectual circle, and Fürstenberg, Sprickmann, and Hemsterhuys were accompanying her in her travels, which included, among other things, a trip to see Goethe in 1785. Yet all her searching and education had left her wanting, to the point that she doubted God's existence and the immortality of the soul. Indeed, she reached such a low point that even the charms of Goethe could not cheer her, though he ardently sought her confidence, apparently confessing that she alone possessed the key to his heart.[8] Although up to this point she had

---

[4] NB, pp. 421f.
[5] NB, p. 320.
[6] See Gildemeister, *Hamann Studien*, p. 10.
[7] NB, p. 422.
[8] Gildemeister, *Hamann Studien*, p. 10.

warned Fürstenberg not to make any attempts to convert her, amid her despair she began to consider returning to the Catholic Church (her mother had been a Catholic), and in 1786 she formally did so.[9] As she notes in her journals, however, any solace she found upon returning to the Church was offset by intense introspection: "I perceived for the first time how vanity and pride had gradually taken hold of my soul. With this discovery any previous joy I had had in myself was gone."[10] To judge from other entries it seems that her soul had become the site of a joyless tension between her own sense of sinfulness and her own fervent desire for personal perfection.

As providence would have it, the German Diotima was about to meet the German Socrates, albeit in a reversal of roles. On one occasion, when in the company of Jacobi and Kleuker, she heard them speaking about Hamann, and she came to be interested in his writings. For his part, Jacobi tried to dissuade her – which is not surprising given that he himself had great trouble understanding them – but Kleuker suggested that she might at least try the *Socratic Memorabilia*.[11] Their advice, it seems, only increased her curiosity, and before long she had borrowed a number of Hamann's writings from Buchholtz, who several years before had entrusted himself to Hamann as his "spiritual son." She was so impressed with the *Socratic Memorabilia* that she wrote directly to Hamann, pledging her support and urging him if possible to make a trip to Münster. Hamann was already prepared in spirit to make the trip, but it was because of her persistent efforts to intercede with the new king, Friedrich Wilhelm II, on his behalf, that he actually did.[12]

The journey took almost a month. Their first major stop was in Berlin, where Hamann and his son stayed with his friend, the director of the Royal Symphony, Johann Friedrich Reichardt, whom Hamann praises for his hospitality; and it was here that they met up with the younger Lindner, who accompanied them the rest of the way, passing through Magdeburg, Braunschweig, and Bielefeld. Finally, with swollen feet, an omen of deteriorating health, Hamann arrived in Münster with Lindner and Johann Michael on July 16, 1787. Their reception at Buchholtz's home was a joyful occasion, but Hamann soon took ill and was confined to bed. As he described it to Jacobi, however, the exceptional care and hospitality he received from Buchholtz and his wife made him feel as if he was in "the bosom of Abraham"; and on the third day he was well enough to receive visitors.[13] Among the first was the princess, whom he described as a "wonder of her sex."[14] A few days later he finally met Jacobi and, upon recovering, followed him back to Pempelfort, which he compared to "Elysium." It was from Pempelfort, for example, that he wrote to Kraus, "Whoever tastes *here* will be given to *see there* how friendly the LOrd [sic] of the universe is."[15] And in the same letter, he says, "If you only knew with what delicacies, treasures, books, and papers I am surrounded here, and how, like a new Tantalus, I am forced to see and smell more than I can enjoy ..."[16]

---

[9] NB, p. 424.
[10] Gildemeister, *Hamann Studien*, p. 12.
[11] NB, p. 424.
[12] NB, pp. 424f.
[13] ZH VII, p. 251.
[14] ZH VII, p. 303.
[15] ZH VII, p. 304.
[16] ZH, p. 305.

THE "DICTATORS OF PURE REASON"

By November Hamann had returned to Münster, where he continued to spend his time with the princess and her circle, traveling with them from time to time. By December, however, he once again fell ill, but with Lindner's help once again recovered. While convalescing he began drafting a final work, which was directed at his old nemesis Starck and three Berlin *Aufklärer*: Johann Erich Biester, Friedrich Gedike, and Friedrich Nicolai. Appropriately, in light of his recovery, he penned as his last pseudonym "Ahasverus Lazarus Elias Redivivus," and as his last comical title, "Neither *to* nor *about* the most recent Triumvirate of the universal French Jezebel and its strong, and even stronger Dictator; but *for* at least XCV hidden readers whom God knows and understands better than I do."[17] Aside from the reference to Starck as the strong [*starck*] dictator and the prophetic denunciation of Nicolai and the two other *Aufklärer* for consorting with the "French Jezebel" (which in Hamann's vocabulary is always a codeword for the French Enlightenment and its *philosophes*), it is hard to say what Hamann had in mind. In the background, however, was an ironic shift in alliances: Nicolai and the others had suddenly declared themselves defenders of Protestantism against Starck, whom they accused of being a Jesuit; and Starck, in turn, appealed to his Lutheran orthodoxy.[18] It was just the kind of occasion, full of irony and hypocrisy, that Hamann found irresistible and to which he could not help but respond, even if he got no further than three mottos and a couple of entries. The first is a cento from Romans 2: 1, 28–9, pointing out the hypocrisy of the Triumvirate: "Therefore you have no excuse, O man! – For a person is not [a Jew] who is one outwardly – but rather one who is [a Jew] inwardly – and – of the heart, in spirit not in letter, and the praise [one] receives is not from men but from God."[19] The second is from Elihu in the book of Job (32: 21–2): "I will not show partiality to any person or compare GOD to man; for I do not know how long I shall live or whether my Maker will take me away over a trifle."[20] The third is from a hymn of Paul Gerhard, "O love! love! You are strong!," which is yet another ironic pun on Starck's name. All of which demonstrates Hamann's typical combination of the comical and the prophetic.

The rest of the draft contains no more than some ideas for a title page and a few fragments; nevertheless, they contain *in nuce* the summa of his authorship. The title vignette, for example, was intended to satirize the good will of the Triumvirate in taking up the cause of Protestantism against Starck by depicting an empty altar dedicated to the "unknown goddess of pure doctrine and reason." The suggestion here was that any attempt to defend Protestantism from the standpoint of the Enlightenment and "pure reason" will not advance the cause of Protestantism (or Christianity in general), but instead lead to its evacuation of any objective content. In other words, thinking to upbraid Starck, the Triumvirate would succeed only in reducing Protestantism to paganism (as Starck himself had done), inasmuch as paganism's greatest contemplative achievement was a divine "Something," and an altar with the inscription, "to an unknown God" (Acts 17: 23). Indeed, such an effort would succeed only in returning the Christian culture of Europe to paganism – not to a paganism

---

[17] N IV, p. 460.

[18] NB, p. 427.

[19] Ibid.

[20] Ibid. Given that Hamann's translation of this passage differs from Luther's (as well as from the standard English translations), I have translated Hamann's own, apparently loose translation from the Hebrew.

longing for its fulfillment in Christianity (since this possibility has now been stripped away by the "dictators" of pure reason), but a post-Christian paganism that has nothing left to embrace but nihilism. Hamann then explains that his entire authorship hitherto had been directed against these "dictators of pure reason":

> I too was once in the Arcadia of literature and mixed with the legions of anonymous and pseudonymous authors, attempted with small pamphlets, with suspicions and insights, to labor against the dictators of pure doctrine and reason – against the demagogues of Ephesian tabernacles and minters of miracles. I too sacrificed hecatombs to nobody, the well-known, as one of my brothers called the Attic public of our enlightened century – not, however, in the form of fatted young bulls and oxen, but in consecrated wafers, in *petits pâtés*, and fine flat cakes; not in great sacks of the going currency, but in λεπτοις of commemorative coins, in *urceis* of broken shards, not, though, in any bulging *amphoris* of well-traveled and well-read minters of legends.[21]

In other words, Hamann too made offerings to the reading public, not, however, to receive its praise, still less to become a celebrity – for him the very notion of Christian authorship precluded such desires – but rather to confound its prejudices and, if possible, to overthrow the dictators of pure reason. And he sought to do so not through any standard kind of writing, but through little pills, bitter to the taste of the time, which, like an emetic, were meant to induce vomiting on the part of the *Aufklärer*, in order that, purified of *unclear* thinking, they might be prepared for the meat of the gospel he hoped to convey.

PORTRAIT OF A CHRISTIAN: GREATNESS IN *KNECHTSGESTALT*

During the last months of his life, from winter to spring 1788, for all his caveats about being a "rotten sinner" (following Paul), we finally begin to see something of Hamann's true spiritual stature, which had been hidden for so many years beneath so many pseudonyms in "aesthetic obedience to the Cross."[22] Indeed, only now, having exhausted himself in an authorship that is quite possibly the most rigorously Christian of modern times – both in its content and in its self-denying *form* – do we begin to see the spiritual fruit of his life in a gathering harvest of spiritual sons and daughters, in providential confirmation, as it were, of the logic of the Gospel (John 12: 24). Buchholtz, for one, considered himself a "spiritual son"; Jacobi (though much closer in age) called him the "father of his heart"; and around the same time a young man named Druffel wrote to thank him for "breaking the chains of his soul," adding how marvelous it was to see Christ in a man and, more amazingly still, one apparently unaware of his own spiritual greatness.[23] And then there was the princess herself, who essentially became Hamann's spiritual daughter. To be sure, there was Hemsterhuys; there was Fürstenberg; there was Jacobi, and even Goethe, each of whom played a role in her life. But it was Hamann, she says, who opened her eyes and taught her "true humility and devotion":

> Finally, Hamann came and showed me the heaven of true humility and devotion – childlikeness before God. He enthralled me with the religion of Christ, beyond anything I had

[21] N IV, pp. 460–1.
[22] N III, p. 234.
[23] ZH VII, pp. 249, 355.

previously come to see in it; for he allowed me to see from the most sublime vantage, in his own person, a living portrait of its true followers. To him alone ... it was given to remove the thickest incrustation from my eyes. Moreover, he alone saw crust there in the first place. All my other friends, Fürstenberg included, saw my strong drive for perfection as the most lovable thing about me, indeed, as something beautiful and worthy of admiration. Far, therefore, from seeing something wrong in this constant sentiment, I clung to it like a cushion in the face of threatening dejection. But Hamann saw pride in it, and told me so. With this explanation he tore the skin from my bones; I felt like a lame person who had been robbed of her only crutch, but I loved and revered him too deeply not to take his explanation to heart. Indeed, I loved him more than ever before on account of his paternal harshness; I seriously turned over in my soul what he had said, and found it to be true. Thereafter we came increasingly to confide in one another.[24]

In short, Hamann conveyed to her Luther's understanding of grace, affording precisely that sense of liberation that Luther himself experienced upon reading Paul's Letter to the Romans, and which John Wesley, in turn, experienced upon reading Luther. He conveyed the one, purest insight that Lutheranism could offer to one breaking under the weight of her own perfectionism: that sanctification is ultimately the work of God. And he explained his point on one occasion by way of a poignant agricultural metaphor taken, ironically enough, given Luther's prejudices against it, from the Letter of James: "If I sow a seed in the earth, I do not remain standing there, straining to hear it and to see whether it is growing or not; rather I sow it and leave it in order to do more sowing, and I leave the growth and development to God."[25] The princess was strongly affected by Hamann's point: "In my inmost being I felt touched and struck by this sublime maxim – as if a bright light had entered my soul and all of a sudden illuminated an obscure presentiment I had long since felt."[26]

Above all, however, what convinced her of the truth of Hamann's words was the example of his life, having seen in him, as in a moving picture, the humility of a true follower of Christ. "In Welbergen," she writes, "I experienced many enlightening moments in view of Hamann's self-deprecation, which at times appeared to me almost exaggerated; on one occasion in particular I was fortunate enough to catch sight of him, and I saw through his appearance an exalted picture of Christian greatness in the form of rags and tatters [*Lumpengestalt*], a picture of strength in weakness, which inspired my soul but also humbled it, given that I saw the divide that still lay between me and this great man."[27] In other words, she saw in Hamann precisely a reflection of what Hamann saw and described throughout his authorship as the kenotic *form* – the Gestalt – of divine revelation: in creation, in Scripture, and, above all, in Christ. Specifically, regarding his appearing in the "form of a servant," she observes,

This humbling effect was not the result of pride; for no figure could have been more offensive to pride than this one, which in every sense of the word was that of a true *Knechtsgestalt* – one implying, to put it briefly, a complete inversion, whereby man

[24] Gildemeister, *Hamann Studien*, p. 13.
[25] Ibid., p. 17. Cf. Jas. 5: 7.
[26] Gildemeister, *Hamann Studien*, p. 17.
[27] Gildemeister, *Hamann Studien*, p. 14.

bears inwardly what he tends to wear *outwardly*, and turns to the *outside* what he tends to hide inwardly. O, he alone is wholly a *Christian*, who can do this completely.[28]

She then adds, in a wonderful tribute to Hamann (the Lutheran) and Fürstenberg (the Catholic):

> It has been dawning on me more and more that Hamann is the *truest Christian* I have ever seen ... He avoids nothing so much as presenting himself as virtuous, *learned*, and knowing. His humility is as unaffected as Fürstenberg's righteousness. For just as the latter tends to defend even his enemies, so that even his audience is really convinced, the former shows forth his own *real weaknesses*, moreover, he never and in no way hides them, so that those who see him are likewise *truly* convinced. For nothing is so offensive to him as hypocrisy, and even *humility* can be hypocritical if it is unconvincing; in which case it is only a more subtle, worse, and therefore Satanic hypocrisy. He speaks of his *pride*, but *shows* himself to be humble.[29]

Clearly, Hamann spoke powerfully through his humility, through his "weakness" (cf. 2 Cor. 12: 10). But again, for him such speaking through humility, through apparent "weakness," is first and foremost a perfection of God himself – a perfection that he perceived, from the time of his illumination in London, in creation, in Christ, and in Scripture (and, as such, as an attribute proper to all the persons of the Trinity).

Amazingly, amid so many persons of such great intellect – from Kant in Königsberg, to Herder and Goethe in Weimar, to Jacobi and the other members of the Münster circle – the princess alone seemed to grasp the *raison d'être* of Hamann's "symbolic existence."[30] Fittingly, therefore, he communicated to no one as directly as to her the "Alpha and Omega of his entire philosophy."[31] Once again he refers to James 5: 7: "Be patient, therefore, brothers, until the coming of the Lord. The farmer waits for the precious crop from the earth, being patient with it until it receives the early and the late rains," adding, in reference to the parable of the sower (Mark 4: 1–20; Matt. 13: 1–23) that this can be understood only in light of two conditions that are presupposed. The first is that one has made "the appropriate preparations for his field in accordance with the *various properties* of the *soil*"; the second is that one has "accepted the same *good* and *pure* seed" (Matt. 13: 24).[32] Hamann admits that this parable may seem trite to today's philosophers, who no longer appreciate the symbolic connection between natural and moral laws. For him, however, this parable contains nothing less than the logic of his symbolic existence and authorship. For just as his life is one long preparation (cf. Jas. 5: 8), so too his published works are attempts to prepare the hearts of his intended readers, always with a keen sense of the various properties of their own manner of thought, for the seed of the Word of God.

In practice, this meant disabusing them of their prejudices through a healthy dose of learned ignorance, so that they might begin to see, by an application of this

---

[28] Gildemeister, *Hamann Studien*, p. 14.
[29] Ibid.
[30] Cf. N II, p. 139.
[31] ZH VII, p. 376.
[32] Ibid.

"universal remedy," what reason alone cannot. As for the "*good* and *pure* seed," it is none other than the "sure prophetic word" of revelation (2 Pet. 1: 19), which for Hamann is more trustworthy, indeed more logical, than any rationality divorced from it, since it comes directly from the Logos. As he puts it,

> We have in the logical, pure milk of the Gospel a sure prophetic word, whose light disperses the darkness of our fate until the day will dawn and the morning star will rise. We have a mediator who speaks on our behalf, who has ransomed us from futile ways with paternal care, and whose blood speaks better things than that of the first martyr and saint [i.e., Abel].[33]

Then, he says to the princess, "Trust Him, that He will bring to light and richly reward every *work* of *faith*, every *work* of *love*, and the *patience* of our *hope*. This is the Alpha and Omega of my entire philosophy ... I know nothing more, nor is there anything more I wish to know."[34]

UNA SANCTA ECCLESIA

Although Hamann's exposure to Catholicism was very limited before he arrived in Münster, by the end of 1786 through Buchholtz (the first Catholic he really knew) he had begun to be acquainted with some contemporary Catholic authors and with the ecumenical movement of the time. Thus he read a book by Johann Nikolaus Masius, which made a proposal for unification of the Churches, ostensibly under Rome, and was not ill-disposed toward it.[35] After all, Hamann himself affirms the one *corpus Christi mysticum*, to which all Christians belong, and even confesses to Jacobi that he is a Catholic as regards the liturgical celebration of Mary and the apostles.[36] At the same time, however, he clearly signals that unification is something only God can bring about. As he put it in a letter to Masius,

> Faith in one Christian Church, like faith in its invisible but omnipresent Head, can bring comfort even to its smallest member, as much on account of the deficiencies and imperfections of every external fellowship as on account of one's natural and personal shortcomings. Let it be left, therefore, to the discretion of the good shepherd to gather his scattered flock and to fulfill the glorious promise [of John 10: 16]: γενησεται μια ποιμην, εἰς ποιμην.[37]

But even if the *una sancta* remained for Hamann an eschatological hope, the last months of his life were a kind of deposit on its reality – a telling testament, amid visible disunity, to the Church's underlying invisible unity (just as the saints of different confessions tend to recognize one another). Indeed, it is striking to see how much Hamann (a dyed-in-the-wool Lutheran) and his new friends (zealous Catholics) loved one another (John 13: 34f.), to the point that Hamann could almost seem Catholic (devouring Catholic devotional books), and they themselves, to Hamann, could seem almost Lutheran. Thus Hamann reports reading, of all people, Francis de Sales, a saint of the Counter-Reformation, and falling in love with the prayer book

---

[33] ZH VII, p. 376. Cf. 1 Pet. 1: 18.
[34] ZH VII, p. 376. In the margin of the letter Hamann refers to 2 Thess. 1: 3.
[35] NB, p. 430.
[36] ZH VI, p. 252.
[37] ZH VII, pp. 51f.

of Johann Michael Sailer, which he admired for its "Lutheran" piety and began to use for his daily devotions: "If Luther had not had the courage to be a heretic, Sailer would not have been able to write such a beautiful prayer book, which I read every morning for my edification."[38] And, what is yet more intriguing, on at least one occasion he seems to have received the Catholic Eucharist.[39]

A CRYPTIC FINAL TESTAMENT

By the middle of May, 1788, Hamann's life was hurtling toward its end. He had been away from Königsberg for nearly a year now and was anxious to return home, albeit via Weimar, where he still hoped to see Herder and Goethe. Yet he seems to have realized that his health might not allow it. On May 17 he therefore penned a text that was to be his final literary testament, his so-called "final page" – an extremely dense, cryptic monument to his self-understanding as a Christian author.[40] The text, which is largely a cento of biblical passages from the Vulgate, interlarded with French and Greek references, reads verbatim in the version Hamann transcribed to Jacobi as follows:

> Si. q. Sages de ce monde sont parvenus par leurs Etudes dela Nature (speculum in aenigmate) à la vision d'un Etre des Etres de raison, d'un Maximum personifié: Dieu a revelé (facie ad faciem) l'humanité de Sa vertu et de sa Sagesse dans les Origines etymologiques de l'Evangile Judaeis Scandalum; Graecis Stultitiam 1 Cor. 1.23.24. XIII. – Vetera transierunt ecce facta sunt omnia nova 2 Cor. V 17 per EUM qui dixit: Ego sum A et Ω Apoc. XXI.6. Prophetiae evacuabunt[ur], Linguae cessabunt, Scientia destruetur, evacuabitur quod ex part[e] est – Non est *Judaeus* neque *Graecus*: non est servus neque liber: non est masculus neque femina. OMNES – UNUS Gal. III.28. DEUS erat verbum – et vita erat lux hominum, quam tenebrae non comprehenderunt et mundus per IPSUM factus non cognovit, Ip[se] *didicit* ex iis quae *passus* est Ebr. V.8. παθηματα, vera μαθηματα et *Magna Moralia* Sicuti aliquando – ita et nunc – Rm. XI.30, 31. L'hypocrite renversé, le Sophiste arctique, Philologus Seminiverbius Act. XVII.18. Π. et Ψ. λοσοφος cruci (furci) fer, Metacriticus bonae spei et *voluntatis,* Pierre à deux poles – et parfois fungens vice cotis, exsors ipse secandi – à Munster ce 17 May la veille du Dimanche de la S. Trinité 88.[41]

In a postscript Hamann then adds at the end of the letter that he failed to include two things, presumably of great significance to his authorship: the saying of Sancho Panza, "God understands me!" and the verse from 1 Corinthians [4]: 9–10, about being a "spectacle to the world," and a "fool for Christ's sake."[42] Needless to say, this cryptic monument is strikingly dense, even compared to his other works. Indeed, just when we are hoping to receive a final self-clarification, to rise to some understanding of his work, Hamann plunges us once again, and even deeper, into the familiar obscurity of his style. Yet, word for word, it also contains – again in the form of a nutshell – the very logic of his life and thought. And for this reason, and for the light it may retrospectively shed on his notoriously difficult writings, it warrants brief consideration.

---

[38] ZH VII, pp. 445, 461.

[39] NB, p. 431.

[40] Originally, the "final page" was a continuation of an entry in the *Stammbuch* of the princess's daughter, made in October 1787. For the definitive critical edition, see Oswald Bayer and Christian Knudsen, *Kreuz und Kritik: Johann Georg Hamanns Letztes Blatt* (Tübingen: Mohr-Siebeck, 1983), henceforth cited as *Kreuz und Kritik.*

[41] ZH VII, p. 482 (*Kreuz und Kritik*, pp. 62f.). Alternate versions of the text (in the form of earlier drafts) can be found in Nadler (N III, p. 410; N IV, p. 462).

[42] ZH VII, p. 482. In the original letter to Jacobi, Hamann forgot to include the chapter citation from 1 Corinthians; in light of other manuscripts, Bayer and Knudsen have shown the chapter to be the fourth. See *Kreuz und Kritik,* p. 147.

Following Bayer and Knudsen, one might divide the text into five parts. The first part refers to the *Etudes de la Nature* of the French natural philosopher, Jacques Henri Bernardin de Saint-Pierre (b. 1737), and more or less summarizes Hamann's view of the relation between reason and revelation: that reason, unenlightened by grace, can attain nothing more than a metaphysical concept of an *ens entium*, and is incapable of affirming, much less discovering for itself, the proper content of Christian revelation, which is a "stumbling block to Jews and foolishness to Greeks" (1 Cor. 1: 23). The second part affirms that Christ is the Alpha and the Omega, the principle and end of the new creation (2 Cor. 5: 17); that to live in Christ is to live "between the times," between Fall and eschaton, when prophecies, tongues, and knowledge will finally end in love (1 Cor. 13: 8–10); and that Christ is the principle of unity, in whom all are one (Gal. 3: 28).[43] The third part states the proper content of Christian revelation: that the Son of God became incarnate in Christ and that this was inscrutable to reason (John 1: 1–14). It also suggests that if reason is to become wise, it must "suffer" revelation and its own "weakness," following the pattern presented in Christ. Indeed, for Hamann, Christ is the model of all true learning in that he "learned ... through what he suffered" (Heb. 5: 8).[44] The same is true of ethics (as indicated by the allusion to Aristotle's *Magna moralia*), which likewise consists in the principle of "learning through suffering" (and hence in a Lutheran reversal of Aristotle, for whom virtue is cultivated precisely through action). In other words, for fallen human beings, just as authentic reasoning begins with the suffering of reason's "insufficiency" and a corresponding recognition of one's need for the light of faith and the guidance of revelation, true moral learning begins with the suffering of one's moral weakness and a corresponding recognition of one's need for grace. The fourth part is an implicit acknowledgment that Hamann himself has learned through suffering: that he too, in the words of Paul, was once disobedient, and that he too was shown mercy – precisely so that he, in turn, might be merciful toward others (Rom. 11: 30–1). This is why Hamann is averse to even the slightest appearance of hypocrisy.

Indeed, the whole of Hamann's authorship can be understood as one protracted balancing act, whose sudden movements (which made him appear to his rationalist audience either as a haphazard thinker or a holy fool) are but an index of the narrow path he took (cf. Matt. 7: 13): attempting by indirect means to disabuse the *Aufklärer* of their vanity and hypocrisy (e.g., their blindness with regard to their own reliance upon tradition and the inexorable nihilistic consequences of their attempted severance from it) without resorting to direct, edifying discourses of the kind Kierkegaard eventually wrote. Add to this Hamann's peculiar "economy of style" in light of Christ's words in Matthew 12: 36 – "I tell you, on the day of judgment you will have

---

[43] The reference to Galatians picks up on an earlier quotation from Saint-Pierre, which Hamann transcribed in his first *Stammbuch* entry on October 17, 1787, and which read: "Les Sexes se denaturant, les hommes s'effeminent et les femmes s'hommassent." Hamann's quotation from Galatians is thus meant to answer the modern erasure of sexual difference. Accordingly, what he seems to mean is not a univocal sameness, which would abolish genuine difference, but a nuptial, Christological union of the sexes, without division or confusion, mirroring the union of the divine and human natures of Christ. See *Kreuz und Kritik*, pp. 21, 97–100.

[44] Thus, for Hamann, the passage from Hebrews corresponds with the ancient Greek pairing παθήματα – μαθήματα, which appears in Greek literature as early as Herodotus. As Bayer and Knudsen point out, however, the meaning of the Greek pairing is reversed in Christianity: whereas in Attic tragedy, the protagonist suffers on account of his presumptuous proximity to the gods, in Christianity God suffers on account of his loving proximity to human beings. Whereas the former is a function of hubris, the latter is a function of *kenosis*, the central motif, both at the level of form and content, of Hamann's authorship. See *Kreuz und Kritik*, pp. 109f.

to give an account for every careless word you utter, for by your words you will be justified, and by your words you will be condemned" – and the result is a collection of writings that to this day are not only *sui generis* but doubtless some of the oddest and most fantastic in all of western literature.[45]

The fifth part is the most inscrutable, comprising a list of cryptic self-descriptions that are meant to convey the secret meaning of Hamann's authorship: *L'hypocrite renversé, le Sophiste arctique, Philologus Seminiverbius,* Π. et Ψ. λοσοφος *cruci (furci) fer, Metacriticus bonae spei et voluntatis, Pierre à deux poles.* To understand the first phrase, it is helpful first of all to recall Hamann's frequent criticisms of the "hypocritical" rationality of his contemporaries, as when Kant speaks of the "purity" of reason. Indeed, in this respect, Hamann's entire authorship is precisely an attempt to "reverse the hypocrisy," to overturn his contemporaries' arguments, and to do so, if possible, with their very own words. At the same time, however, this phrase carries implications for Hamann himself, as is suggested by contemporary usage of the phrase by Bolingbroke, among others, to describe the character of Jonathan Swift. In the words of Thomas Sheridan,

> It was this strangely assumed character, this new species of *hypocrisy reversed,* as Lord Bolingbroke justly termed it, which prevented his appearing in that amiable light, to which he was entitled from the benevolence of his heart, except to a chosen few. In his friendships he was warm, zealous, constant, and perhaps no man ever contracted such a number with so judicious and happy a selection. We find him everywhere extolled for his pre-eminence in this first and rarest of virtues, by his numerous correspondents; among whom were many the most distinguished of that age for talents and worth.[46]

It is striking how much this applies to Hamann himself, down to his extraordinary capacity for friendships. It is even more striking given what Sheridan says about Swift's "peculiar cast of mind, which made him not only conceal these qualities [namely good-will, love of mankind, friendship, liberality, charity, good-nature] from the public eye, but often disguise them under the appearance of their contraries."[47] Indeed, by virtue of his own humility (which is patterned on the humility of God), Hamann too was an "inverted hypocrite," intentionally disguising his own good nature, in Luther's phrase, *sub contrario.* As he put it to E. F. Lindner, "To appear worse than one actually is, [and] actually to be better than one seems. I consider this to be a duty and an art."[48] For Hamann, it is a duty above all because God himself is wont to appear under disguises, bereft of glory, and even *sub contrario,* as in the paradoxical formula, "God on the Cross." Accordingly, what he means by *l'hypocrite renversé* corresponds exactly with what he earlier called "aesthetic obedience to the Cross," whose meaning is now finally made clear: it indicates a method of purgation, a spiritual discipline, whereby a Christian learns to invite the good and drive out the bad by willingly suffering disfigurement, following the example of Christ.[49]

---

[45] See again his letter to his son, ZH V, p. 88: "My dear child, I commend to you the *evangelical law of economy* in speaking and writing: Accounting for every *vain, superfluous* word – and *economy of style*. In these two mystical words lies the whole art of thinking and living. Everything that Desmosthenes was thinking of when he repeated a single word three times is for me contained in the two words *economy* and *style*." Cf. ZH V, p. 177.

[46] Thomas Sheridan, *The Life of the Rev. Dr. Jonathan Swift, Dean of St. Patrick's, Dublin* (1784), p. 430; quoted in *Kreuz und Kritik*, pp. 122f. My emphasis.

[47] Sheridan, *Life,* p. 429.

[48] ZH V, p. 43.

[49] Ibid. Cf. N III, p. 234.

In keeping with this interpretation, no sooner does Hamann call himself a "reverse" or "inverted" hypocrite than he enacts what he means by calling himself *le Sophiste arctique*. On the face of it, this makes no sense. Why would Hamann, the Socrates of Königsberg, call himself a Sophist, when his entire authorship was conceived precisely in opposition to the sophistry of the *Aufkärer*? In light of his previous self-designation, however, as well as his stated desire at the conclusion of *Entkleidung und Verklärung* not to be venerated as a saint ("do not paint any moustaches on my life"), his meaning is clear. Out of humility or "aesthetic obedience" to the Cross, he would rather be known as *le Sophiste arctique* than as the *Magus in Norden* – in radical imitation of Christ, who knew no sin but became sin (2 Cor. 5: 21), who was "the righteousness of God" (2 Pet. 1: 1), but was counted "a friend of publicans and sinners" (Matt. 11: 19), in short, who willingly appeared *sub contrario*. Accordingly, *le Sophiste arctique* points to Hamann's next self-designation, *Philologus Seminiverbius*. Recalling one of his earliest pseudonyms, Hamann means that he is not only a lover of words and languages, but a lover of Christ, the incarnate Logos. Moreover, as a servant of Christ, he willingly appears to his contemporaries, through his *Autorhandlungen*, like Paul did to the Athenians, namely, as a "babbler" [*seminiverbius*], whose words they cannot understand (cf. Acts 17: 18).

The next self-designation, Π. et Ψ. λοσοφος, is more obscure. It bears a similarity, of course, to the word "philosopher." But if Hamann conjures up this word, he does so intentionally in order to write over it and recode it with a dialectical pairing of two neologisms, which derive from the Greek noun πίλος ("felt covering") and the Greek adjective ψιλος ("bare," "naked," "stripped," "uncovered," etc.). It is an odd pairing, to be sure, but in light of his other writings his meaning would seem to be as follows. The term "philosopher," which appears *sous rature*, is supplanted with a dialectical cipher for a new kind of philosopher, who has discovered a higher, genuinely spiritual wisdom: the wisdom of "divestment and transfiguration," *Entkleidung und Verklärung*. This new kind of philosopher has grasped the prophetic logos of Genesis 3 that we are clothed "with garments of skin," understood as a type of the "clothing" of the Holy Spirit (Luke 24: 49; Acts 1: 8), not by pitiful attempts to cover over or excuse our sin and nakedness (which only highlight our sinfulness and nakedness and make it all the more ridiculous), but by confessing our sin *coram Deo* and submitting to divine judgment – at which point, having been clothed with the Comforter (Matt. 5: 4), we may look forward in hope to that final clothing in immortality (1 Cor. 15: 53; 2 Cor. 5: 2–5).[50] In other words, for Hamann, being divested of pretensions (*Entkleidung*) and being transfigured (*Verklärung*) go hand in hand. Accordingly, what the term Π. et Ψ. λοσοφος attempts to convey is nothing less than the logic of the Gospel and the kingdom of God, which is demonstrated in Christ (John 12: 24; Phil. 2: 6ff.) and faithfully enacted by that truest of philosophers, the publican: "I tell you, this man went down to his home justified rather than the other [the Pharisee]; for all who exalt themselves will be humbled, but all who humble themselves will be exalted" (Luke 18: 14; cf. 14: 14).

The term *cruci (furci) fer* follows from this; for anyone who would follow Christ and attempt to live out the logic of the incarnate Logos will invariably be

---

[50] For an alternative reading of this dialectic as one between *psilosophy* [*sic*] qua the purely rational philosophy of the "spirit of observation" and *pilosophy* [*sic*] qua the poetic wisdom of the "spirit of prophecy," see *Kreuz und Kritik*, p. 133. According to this reading, the spirit of observation (when purified of the spirit of prophecy) leaves things bare, devoid of any ultimate meaning, whereas the spirit of prophecy transfigures them, i.e., clothes them.

a "crucifer," one who "bears his own cross" (Luke 14: 27); indeed, should the *imitatio Christi* be carried to its logical conclusion, the disciple will appear as a "rogue" (*furcifer*) locked in a "pillory" (*furca*) subject to public ridicule (Luke 23: 11, 36). And yet, as difficult as this cross may be to bear, Hamann goes on to call himself the *Metacriticus bonae spei*, the "metacritic of good hope," in reference to Paul's statement to the Thessalonians: "Now may our Lord Jesus Christ himself and God our Father, who loved us and through grace gave us eternal comfort and *good hope*, comfort your hearts and strengthen them in every good work and word" (2 Thess. 2: 16–17). For Christ is resurrected, and "if we have been united with him in a death like his, we will certainly be united with him in a resurrection like his" (Rom. 6: 5).

As Bayer and Knudsen have pointed out, however, this self-designation implies yet another sense of hope, namely, the hope that Hamann holds out for those he critiques.[51] This is manifest in that, as a metacritic, he never criticizes his opponents directly, but always indirectly – if possible through their own words – so that it is never, or at least ideally never, he himself who passes judgment (since this always carries with it the danger of hypocrisy). Rather, it is his opponents who pass judgment on themselves when they are indirectly confronted, like David through Nathan's parable (2 Sam. 12: 1–15), with the incongruities and hypocrisies of their own positions. Therein lies the essence of Hamann's metacriticism as a "metaschematism."[52] Accordingly, his metacriticism might be described as a kind of *merciful* deconstruction, which leaves his interlocutors room to think freely. Indeed, for Hamann, the art of metacriticism consists precisely in kenotically disappearing behind one's communications in order to allow one's interlocutors to appropriate all the more freely what has been said (again imitating what he took to be the form, the "style," of divine self-communication and revelation). As he put it in a draft of *Entkleidung und Verklärung*: "Just as every man, when confronted with the light of truth, is both his own lawgiver and judge: so too every author (and his book) is the judge of himself (itself). The *lectio* of a true critic consists merely in dissolving the text of his older brother into its elements, without violently or uncharitably interfering with his ability to consent."[53]

Thus, Hamann is a metacritic in at least two senses: firstly, he does not force any system of his own upon his opponent; instead, he is merely an "after-reader" (μετά in the sense of "after") who speaks in the language of what he reads, in order by a kind of Socratic-Christian dialectic to induce greater clarity from within. Secondly, unlike a hypo-critical reader, he does not presume to be "above" or "beyond" criticism (ὑπέρ in the sense of "above" or "beyond"); rather, as a metacritic (μετά in the sense of "with" or "besides" or "in the company of"), he stands "with" those he critiques, inasmuch as all human criticism is ultimately subject to the judgment of

---

[51] See *Kreuz und Kritik*, pp. 143ff.

[52] For more on the latter term, see Chapter 2.

[53] Quoted in *Kreuz und Kritik*, pp. 145f. To be sure, for Hamann, "metacriticism" implies a dissolution or "shaking up" of the text at hand, a rigorous undermining of its self-certainties; and in this respect he might be considered a forerunner of Derrida. But it is not, therefore, a negative, merciless, postmodern deconstruction, i.e., a dissolution of the meaning of a text to no ultimate purpose – except to demonstrate the absence of any final, identifiable meaning or significance. Rather, Hamann undertakes his metacriticism precisely in the *good hope* that by "divesting" his intended readers of their pretensions they might come to recognize the poverty of their own positions; and that by suffering this *docta ignorantia* they might be made more open to faith and possibly be "transfigured" by the reception of the new and greater light it brings.

Christ (2 Cor. 5: 10). And therein lies the abiding difference between him and Kant, who famously claims that "everything must submit" to *our* reason, to *our Critique*.[54] From Hamann's perspective, however, such a claim could not help but strike him as a deluded, secular inversion of reality; for there is ultimately but one critic whose judgment matters, one "Meta-critic." And this is why, living in the "age of criticism" as in "the days of Noah" (Matt. 24: 36ff.), blissfully oblivious to any higher criticism, any higher judgment, Hamann conducts his authorship under an eschatological sign.

Then, in the final version of the "final page," he adds and even emphasizes that he is not only a metacritic of "good hope" but also a metacritic of "good *will*." On the one hand, this would suggest that he conducts his metacritical readings with "good will" toward his opponents. As he put it to Nicolai, arguably the ringleader of the Berlin *Aufklärer*, "Truth is the scale of friendship – and the sword paves the way for the freedom of peace – *hanc veniam petimusque damusque vicissim.*"[55] On the other hand, it in all likelihood refers to himself as a metacritic of this concept in Kant's moral philosophy, which Hamann had already identified as an "idol" in tandem with "pure reason." As he put it to Herder with regard to Kant's *Grundlegung zur Metaphysik der Sitten*, "Instead of *pure reason,* here the talk is of another chimera and idol, that of the *good will.*"[56] And, similarly, he says to Jacobi, "What a good pendant the *good will* makes to *pure reason.* Do not both deserve a millstone around the neck? God's mercy is the only religion by which we are blessed."[57] In other words, just as he did with his *Critique,* which transferred the right of judgment from God to reason, Kant has here seductively and idolatrously shifted the foundation of morals from the will of God to the "good will" of man. For Hamann, on the other hand, this foundation is to be found precisely in *God's* "good will" (Luke 2: 14) – declared in a revelation of which we can be more certain than any chimera of reason – since it is "God's kindness that leads us to repentance" (Rom. 2: 4), and from repentance to a moral life.

Hamann's final self-designation, *Pierre à deux poles*, likewise requires some decoding. Perhaps the first thing to observe is that it carries an implicit eschatological reference. It refers to the fact that Hamann lives consciously "between the times," i.e., between the "two poles" of Fall and eschaton.[58] In other words, we are not living in the age of the "bright morning star" (Rev. 22: 16), but in the age of shadows and expectation, the age of "already but not yet." Accordingly, we possess in this present state no clear vision, but know "only in part" "through a glass darkly" (1 Cor. 13: 9, 12). This is why Hamann's favorite temporal metaphor, which he typically opposes to the Enlightenment, is "twilight." Thus, it was in the twilight hours, "*entre chien et loup,*" as he often dated his letters, that he did most of his work. At the same time, *Pierre à deux poles* is also a fitting description of Hamann himself, whom Schelling once described (on the basis of Hamann's writings) as "a true πᾶν of harmony and discord, light and darkness, spiritualism and materialism."[59]

---

[54] See Kant, *Critique of Pure Reason*, A xii.

[55] ZH II, p. 194. Tr.: "we both ask for this favor and give it in turn."

[56] ZH V, p. 418. See *Kreuz und Kritik*, p. 145.

[57] ZH VI, p. 440.

[58] See *Kreuz und Kritik*, pp. 149ff.

[59] F. W. J. Schelling, *Sämtliche Werke*, ed. K. F. A. Schelling (Stuttgart and Augsburg: J. G. Cotta'scher Verlag, 1856–61), I, vol. 10, p. 171.

Indeed, even those who knew him personally describe him as a living coincidence of opposites. As the *Sturm und Drang* poet, Friedrich Leopold, Count of Stolberg related upon first meeting him:

> Finally Hamann came, a very interesting and extraordinary man. At one moment he has the appearance of one who cannot count to three; the next moment he overflows with genius and fire. So child-like by nature, at times so colorfully simple, and yet so deep, so genuinely philosophical – and with such warmth, naivety, openness, and estrangement from everything that is called the *world*, that I came to find him very endearing and interesting.[60]

In short, to those who knew him, Hamann seems to have exhibited a coincidence of "idiocy and profundity."[61] All of which accords with what Hamann communicated to Jacobi in 1787, "All is *good* – all is *vanity*! What joy is mine, that I am able to feel with equal intensity both the *imbecillitatem hominis* and the *securitatem* DEI."[62] Ultimately, therefore, *Pierre à deux poles* would seem to suggest Hamann's understanding of Christianity itself in terms of a super-rational coincidence of opposites: from Paul's wisdom and folly, strength and weakness, even being and nothingness (1 Cor. 1: 27–8), to Luther's dialectic of sin and righteousness (*simul iustus et peccator*), to his own dialectical vision of divine glory and *kenosis*, majesty and abasement – to the point that Paul could see wisdom *in* folly, strength *in* weakness, and Hamann could see the glory of God *in* his humility, etc. Seen in this light the reference to Peter also begins to make sense; for Peter too exhibits a striking contrast. He is the greatest of the apostles precisely because he knows that he has the least to boast about. Thus, as much as it may say about Hamann, *Pierre à deux poles* is ultimately a cipher for the paradoxical logic of the kingdom: that "the least among all of you is the greatest" (Luke 9: 48).

Hamann then makes an addition in French and Latin (the Latin being a citation from Horace's *Ars poetica*), "et parfois fungens vice cotis, exsors ipse secandi," which can be translated as follows: "And sometimes functioning in place of a whetstone, which has no share in what is to be cut." In other words, Hamann once again indicates that he does not engage in direct polemic. Instead, he understands his authorship as an abrasive whetstone – alternatively, himself as a Socratic gadfly – for others to sharpen their critical thinking (cf. Prov. 27: 17), and, if possible, to be disabused of their misconceptions.

Finally, there is Hamann's dating of the text, which, as Bayer and Knudsen point out, is no mere technicality. Indeed, with Hamann, nothing is without significance, not the least dot or iota. He dates it, "à Munster ce 17 May la veille du Dimanche de la S. Trinité 88," the eve of the feast of the Trinity. On the face of it, it is unclear what special significance this might have; but in the context of Hamann's entire life and authorship *against* the Enlightenment, it says everything. It says that his is not a philosophy of the dawn, much less of the day, when all is clear, but again a philosophy of the evening – of twilight. It says that (unlike Kant) he does not presume to occupy a definitive eschatological perspective (from which, like Kant, to issue an

---

[60] Stolberg, *Briefe*, p. 188, cited in ZH VI, p. xii.

[61] *Kreuz und Kritik*, p. 149.

[62] ZH VII, p. 339; cf. N III, p. 189, where he says (in the voice of Abigail) that he aims at that "*stoic wisdom* that interchangeably unites the *imbecillitatem Hominis* and the *securitatem Dei*."

"authoritative" critique of all metaphysics and religious tradition). Rather, for Hamann, this is precisely the πρῶτον ψεῦδος of Kant's philosophy, which makes his and the Enlightenment's critique of Christianity illegitimate from the start. Thus, Hamann is, ironically, more honest about the limitations of reason than Kant is: unlike Kant he knows that he knows "only in part" and does not presume to know more than this – enough, say, to usurp divine judgment in the name of "reason alone." And so, unlike Kant's "hypo-critical" philosophy, his "meta-critical" philosophy is not a philosophy of the "dawn," but a sober philosophy of the *veille*, of expectation and "good hope." Finally, as a philosophy of the "eve of the Sunday of the feast of the Trinity," it is, as Bayer and Knudsen put it, a philosophy in expectation of that "eternal Sunday," in which all time is fulfilled in the triune God.[63]

Of course, given the peculiar form and content of his writings, not to mention the intellectual prejudices of the age, Hamann knew that he would be misunderstood, either as an "enthusiast" or as an "irrationalist." Thus, in his letter to Jacobi he appends two final references: one to Sancho Panza, the comical squire and side-kick of Don Quixote, who on several occasions in Cervantes's text exclaims, "God understands me!";[64] and one to Paul, which he had jotted down just a few days before, "we have become a spectacle to the world, to angels and to mortals. We are fools for the sake of *Christ*, but you are wise in Christ. We are weak, but you are strong" (1 Cor. 4: 9–10).[65] Clearly, Hamann takes this verse to apply to himself; for he too has become a fool for Christ. A few days later, in what amounts to a final clarification of his authorship, he says something similar to Jacobi: "O dearest Jonathan! How little we would be able to guess the truth if there were no *children* and *fools* in the world" – to which he adds, more or less summarizing his opinion of the Enlightenment, "the blindness [of an enthusiast] is of more use to me than the most splendid enlightenment of the so-called *beaux-esprits* and *esprits forts,* who, despite their moral appearance, are in my eyes lying apostles clothed in an angelic form."[66]

THE JOURNEY HOME

By the end of May, Hamann had begun making plans to head back to Königsberg, and in the meantime wrote a letter to his eldest daughter, Elisabeth Regina, which would be his last letter to his family. It is a final testament of his love for Anna Regina and their children, in which he expresses his eagerness to see them again. It also testifies to his role in his children's spiritual life and to his tenderness as a father. "Have God before your eyes and in your heart," he tells his daughter, "and you will be able to resist all temptations; to this end, in accordance with his holy

---

[63] *Kreuz und Kritik*, p. 154.

[64] Cf. Hamann's remark to Herder of 1781, "Sancho Panza's transcendental philosophy is as salutary to me as the Samaritan's oil and wine" (ZH IV, p. 340); and his letter to Jacobi from March, 1788, only a few months prior to composing the "final page": "May this honest squire of an errant knight be forgiven everything if he lets so many sighs escape against his knowledge and will — in fear that he does not understand himself and, what is worse, that he will be misunderstood by impatient critics. At least [I can say that] I live [full of] good hope in the *conviction* that I am *truly* understood by God" (ZH VII, p. 419). In light of these remarks, the first of which was made shortly after Hamann had reviewed Kant's *Critique of Pure Reason*, it is clear that he is implicitly stating his opposition to Kant's *transcendental* philosophy. Whereas the latter purports to find security for philosophy and for himself by delimiting what one can know on the basis of reason alone ("What can I know?", "What should I do?", "What can I hope for?"), Hamann's "*transcendental* philosophy" is founded not on what *we* can understand (about ourselves or the world) on the basis of reason alone (meager as this is), but rather on what *God knows and understands about us.*

[65] N IV, p. 461. Hamann's emphasis.

[66] ZH VII, pp. 485f.

counsel, God can use friends as well as foes in order to confirm us in the good and decisively establish us against all evil, so that we may finally obtain the victory to his glory and our salvation, which he alone knows [to work out] and is in his fatherly hands."[67] Hamann's manner is typical of his letters to his family, which are, as one would expect, generically different from all his other writings, even his letters to his friends. For here one sees what the world did not: a Christian father communicating with his children in plain and simple terms. In conclusion he sends his greetings to all of them, asking Elisabeth to kiss her dear mother, whom he has not forgotten, in expectation of his return.

Though writing, like walking, had now become quite difficult – Sprickmann would take him by the arm for turns in the princess's garden – on the first of June Hamann wrote his last substantial letter, this time to "Crispus" Jacob Kraus, his long-time friend, and colleague of Kant, at the university of Königsberg. In it he relates the blessings of his life in Münster:

> [My] circle is limited to that of Frantz and Jonathan Jacobi. Frantz, Diotima, Pericles, Sprickmann constitute my entire *Universum*. ... What a last supper providence has stored up for me at the end of my toilsome and delightful life! ... With what emotion I now say with Virgil's shepherd: *DEUS nobis haec otia fecit*! Not once has his providence neglected anything, no! What he does and allows comes to a good end. All is well that ends well.[68]

Clearly, Hamann had a sense that the end was near, but he was still optimistic. Thus, while staying with Buchholtz, he continued making his plans. He and his son would leave for home on June 20, exactly a year after they first left Königsberg. They would travel first to Pempelfort to say farewell to Jacobi, and from there they would set out for Weimar, at long last, to see Herder. On June 19 all seemed well – at least well enough. Buchholtz and his wife went ahead to Pempelfort, where they planned to meet up the following day, and Hamann spent the morning with the princess. He was weak, but not alarmingly so. As the princess described it,

> I spent the last morning with the blessed, the one and only [Hamann ...]. He was very weak, but in a way that I had seen him before, and in his own estimation it was due to the disquiet of the last few weeks, so that he and I both believed that as soon as he set foot in the coach to Düsseldorf everything would change and he would make a wonderful and speedy recovery, as he had done so many times in the past. He was continually on the verge of sleep, but he spoke a lot, although he seemed to find it difficult and I kept trying to restrain him. His pipe, which had been prepared with a case that very morning, gave him a childlike pleasure; and he especially enjoyed the fact that my name was inscribed on it along with the year. He then said with tears in his eyes, "So you want me to remember you always; well now, at any rate, I have enough stuff for that." I said: "Pray occasionally for your daughter, and when you write to me, don't call me Your Highness." He: "No, I would rather also call you Amalie; as for my prayers, they are not worth anything, but we all have an Advocate who constantly intercedes for us with unceasing sighs." I: "Today, when Hans [Johann Michael] goes, you will be alone; do you want Mikeln, Pois and ..." He: "No, I do not need anything, and I am never alone; you too will never be alone; we have One who is constantly with us and in us" (with tears). I fell on his hands with unspeakable sorrow and kissed them for a long time. – He: "You humble me, dear Amalie."[69]

---

[67] ZH VII, p. 495.
[68] ZH VII, pp. 501f.
[69] Quoted in Gildemeister, *Hamann Studien*, pp. 20–1.

The princess goes on to say that they spoke a lot about their favorite subject, the Bible, and in the course of their conversation came to the topic of worthy and unworthy communion. Hamann responded with an interpretation of the parable of the wedding banquet in Matthew 22: "Everything has to be given to us to communicate worthily, just as the wedding garment, according to ancient custom, was given to the wedding guests. The only thing we can add is our will."[70] By ten o'clock the princess had to leave, but was overcome with an "indescribable fear" concerning Hamann's condition. He assured her, and asked her not to say good-bye, expecting to see her in only a few days at Jacobi's residence in Düsseldorf. By this time his son was present (evidently more of a realist than his father) and harshly contradicted him; to which Hamann gently responded, "My dear little son, you do not know any better; I want to err, *errare humanum est.*"[71]

After a few worried moments, the princess left and made arrangements for Hamann's departure the following day. Early the next morning she returned to check on him, found him asleep with "an indescribable, gentle smile" on his face, and left again confident that he would recover.[72] In truth, however, Hamann was on the brink of death, and by the time he awoke he could hardly speak. Still, he insisted on making the trip. Fürstenberg, who soon arrived with the doctors, persuaded him to stay at least one more night, and the princess, hearing the news, quickly returned to spend the day with him. Late that evening, still hopeful, she dispatched a message to Jacobi, alerting him of Hamann's condition, but by then it was too late. Early the next morning, on June 21, he still recognized his son and Fürstenberg, but by the time the princess arrived he was unconscious. The doctors tried to dissuade her from seeing him, but she insisted that she had to see "the dear saint" one more time. A few hours later, in the company of Fürstenberg, the princess, and his son, he died "with eyes fixed toward heaven."[73]

The pertinent question at this point was where Hamann should be buried: in Catholic Münster or Protestant Düsseldorf? Hamann himself seems to have made no decision in this regard. The princess, however, had a fitting solution: she suggested that he be buried beneath the bower in her garden. There, only a month before, on May 22, she and Hamann had had a conversation that left an indelible impression. As she relates it, Hamann spoke "inimitably" of divine folly according to 1 Corinthians 1, "with a fullness of feeling that could only be expressed by one who felt it personally."[74] So Fürstenberg and Overberg, both Catholic priests, wrapped his body in woolen cloths and brought him to the princess's residence, where, on the evening of June 21, 1788, he received an official, presumably Catholic burial. That very evening Hemsterhuys arrived from The Hague, but the princess was in no mood for his "highfalutin Hellenism"; she was too absorbed in the memory of her true Socrates and his "child-like sublime simplicity." As she put it, "The good man could in no way guess that Hamann's elevated simplicity, which appeared contemptible (to philosophers of his kind), had taught me more about internal dignity than all of Hemsterhuys's ... philosophical, and otherwise beautiful writings."[75] Yet Hemsterhuys

---

[70] Gildemeister, *Hamann Studien*, p. 21.

[71] Ibid.

[72] NB, p. 450.

[73] NB, p. 451; Gildemeister, *Hamann Studien*, p. 23.

[74] NB, p. 452; Gildemeister, *Hamann Studien*, p. 23.

[75] Gildemeister, *Hamann Studien*, pp. 22f. As the princess noted early the following year, "Whenever my soul is empty and all tangled up, it is Hamann's memory that most readily brings fullness and freedom. ... I am now collating Hamann's writings on the Old Testament, during which the hours fly by like minutes; it is a commentary full of marvelous perspectives and insights! O dear blessed one, what a source of pleasure and blessing you have already been to me. Surely God has taken you into his kingdom, with whose ways you were familiar and in whose steps you so faithfully walked. *Ora pro nobis.*"

himself was not lacking in admiration, for it was he who prepared Hamann's tombstone. At first he proposed that it be engraved with the words *"philosopho theologo."* Jacobi, however, had the final word. It would read instead, more simply and more appropriately, *"viro christiano"*; and, fittingly, on the reverse side they inscribed the verses from 1 Corinthians 1: 23, 25 that Hamann had earlier extolled to the princess on that very spot.

Conclusion

After Postmodernity: Hamann before the Postmodern Triumvirate

Do not be alarmed my dear friend! ... If the natural man has 5 senses, the Christian is an instrument of 10 strings. And without passions more similar to sounding brass than a new man.

Hamann to J. G. Lindner[1]

Wie mag der Schöpfer nicht in seiner Allmacht lachen,
Wenn sich das Nichts zu Was und Ihn zu Nichts will machen!

Hamann to Jacobi[2]

Reason *and* writing *[Schrift]* *are fundamentally* one and the same = *language of God. My wish and the* punctum saliens *of my little authorship is to put this theme in a* nutshell ...

Hamann to Jacobi[3]

In view of the previous chapters, and the picture of Hamann's life and writings that emerges from them, we are finally in a position to summarize and bring into sharper focus the content of his "post-secular vision." Though ultimately of a piece, tracing back to his conversion in London, we may roughly divide this vision into its metacritical-deconstructive and positive-constructive aspects – the former being essentially philosophical, the latter essentially theological in character. With regard to the first aspect, Hamann's "penetrating genius" (in Hegel's words) helps us to see past the veneer of the Enlightenment as a self-sustaining system of thought to its fallacious assumptions and unintended consequences – ultimately, to the black hole that he saw lurking behind its attempts to base everything from art and religion to morality and politics upon a secular foundation of "reason alone."[4] In this respect Hamann figures as a prophet, having foreseen that the Enlightenment, having stripped away the supports of faith and tradition, standing upon nothing but a highly suspect doctrine of reason, would end in nihilism – understood here, firstly, as the absence of all theoretical foundations and, in due course, as the absence of all moral foundations. In short, Hamann foresaw where modernity would end and postmodernity would begin. In the following, therefore, my initial concern will be to show how his meta-criticism compares with postmodern thought, which is in many ways heir to his insights, even though it does not share his theological perspective. Thereafter I will attempt to summarize some of the positive-constructive aspects of his vision.

[1] ZH I, p. 339.
[2] ZH VI, p. 277 (Hamann is citing a traditional Prussian saying).
[3] ZH VI, p. 296.
[4] See *JGH*, pp. 150–68.

HAMANN AND POSTMODERNITY

Aside from the obvious anachronism, the first thing to be noted regarding Hamann and postmodernity is that any comparison between them quickly breaks down given an internal inconsistency on the part of "postmodernity" itself – inasmuch as post-modernity is not truly "post-modern," but in reality modernity's logical conclusion, and to this extent no real alternative to modernity after all.[5] Indeed, whereas moder-nity, behind the veneer of sound reason, is latently nihilistic, postmodernity, at least in its philosophical forms, simply makes explicit the nihilism that was implied by modernity's founding separation of reason from faith and tradition all along. For present purposes, therefore, I will focus chiefly on those aspects of postmodernity, broadly understood, which might more legitimately be considered innovations upon modernity (and thus give some merit to the prefix "post"), but which Hamann antic-ipated two centuries before.

Assuming that "postmodernity" can be treated as a more or less fixed constella-tion of ideas, the most obvious points of connection to Hamann are the following. Firstly, implicitly following Hamann, postmodernity rejects all systems of thought that are believed to have an eternal validity apart from the contingencies of lan-guage, history, and culture – as though reason were not inevitably shaped by them. As Hamann put it to Jacobi, in reference to Kant, "A *mask* or a *misunderstanding* (of language and reason) plainly lies at the basis [of his philosophy]; but it is hard and perhaps impossible to uncover it if one [has already] *accepted* [his] *conceptual assumptions.*" In other words, Kant is either disingenuous in avoiding the question of language, or he has failed to grasp the ways reason is influenced by it. Moreover, in failing to acknowledge the role of faith in his assumptions, he has effectively barred the path of honest philosophical investigation. Thus Hamann adds in the same letter, a "System is in itself already an obstacle to truth."[6] The same thought is echoed by Nietzsche a century later: "I distrust all systematicians. The will to [a] system [betrays] a lack of honesty."[7]

Secondly, following from this, postmodernity is heir to Hamann's "linguistic turn," i.e., his insight that reason is essentially a function of language and, as such, bound to the historical, cultural, and metaphorical contingencies from which modern philosophy – under the cover of so many similar transcendental guises, from Descartes to Husserl – deludedly sought to escape. As Nietzsche declares, recognizing the delusion, "We have to cease to think if we refuse to do it in the prison-house of language ..."[8] Indeed, anticipating Nietzsche and even the late Wittgenstein, Hamann affirms not only that language presents a limit condition for reason, for thought itself, but also that language is the chief source of philosophy's congenital errors and deceptions.[9] "No deduction," he says in the *Metacritique*, "is required to prove the genealogical priority of *language* ... Not only the entire ability to think rests upon language ... but language is also the *center of the misunderstanding of reason with itself* ..."[10]

---

[5] Nowhere is this continuity more obvious than in postmodernity's hyper-modern doctrine of the radical autonomy of the individual, understood now in the absence of all rational and traditional norms as a pure function of the will to power.

[6] ZH VI, p. 276.

[7] KSA, vol. 6, p. 63.

[8] Cited as the epigraph to Fredric Jameson, *The Prison-House of Language: A Critical Account of Structuralism and Russian Formalism* (Princeton, NJ: Princeton University Press, 1972); see Nietzsche, *Ueber Wahrheit und Lüge im aus-sermoralischen Sinne*, KSA, vol. 1, pp. 875ff.; KSA, vol. 3, p. 592.

[9] N III, p. 288.

[10] N III, p. 286.

Thirdly, postmodernity follows Hamann in thinking through the radical consequences of this linguistic turn for metaphysics. As Hamann put it to Jacobi as early as 1784:

> Metaphysics has its scholastic and courtly language; I am suspicious of both … Hence I nigh suspect that our entire philosophy consists more of language than of reason, and of the misunderstandings of countless words, the prosopopoeia of the most arbitrary abstractions, the antitheses της ψευδωνυμου γνωσεως; indeed, even the most common figures of speech of the *Sensus communis* have given rise to an entire world of questions, the posing and answering of which are equally baseless.[11]

Long before postmodernity, therefore, Hamann clearly grasped that an understanding of the linguistic mediation of thought not only spells fateful consequences for the modern doctrine of reason (radically calling into question its ideological claims to purity and autonomy), but also challenges the very possibility of metaphysics – that is, the possibility of a science that could transcend the "epistemic limit condition" of language.[12] As Katie Terezakis incisively puts it, "The strength of Hamann's linguistic 'metacritique' of Kant lies in his reckoning with the unreservedly immanent character of language, as the genetically prior, shared root of sensibility and understanding, and thus as the ideal and real boundary of subjective consciousness."[13]

Whether this commits him to a wholesale "rejection of ontology and theology," as Terezakis suggests, is a question that will be taken up in what follows *vis-à-vis* Derrida's, for lack of a better word, "linguistic idealism." For now, one might simply say that, if one accepts the radical terms of Hamann's "immanent linguistic perspective" – this being the inevetable consequence of his metacritique of Kant – then the possibility of metaphysics, theology, indeed of any confidence in truth as such depends upon his corresponding doctrine of divine condescension [*Herunterlassung*], which was discussed at length in Chapter 2. In other words, for Hamann, the possibility of metaphysics and theology (of the knowledge of God and super-sensible truths) depends upon an equally radical "immanence of the Word," the Logos, who "condescends to the blindness of Adam,"[14] presents himself according to Adam's limited senses and capacities, and thus kenotically breaks through any epistemic limit conditions (and the concomitant skepticism) to which we would otherwise be subject. In short, it depends upon a theology of grace, which makes up for the fallenness of reason. So too, finally, it depends upon language not being a Gnostic "prison-house," to which we are miserably confined, but upon it being at once human *and* divine as the sacramental medium of God's self-communication "to the creature through the creature."[15] In any event, as Terezakis's reading of Hamann shows, when postmodern authors boldly proclaim the "end of reason" or the "end of metaphysics" – inasmuch as reason is a function of language and metaphysics, ironically, cannot get "beyond" it – they are, *mutatis mutandis*, consciously or not, doing so from a Hamannian perspective.

---

[11] ZH V, p. 272; cf. p. 470: "Since Adam's fall, all *gnosis* is suspicious to me, like a forbidden fruit."

[12] See Katie Terezakis, *The Immanent Word: the Turn to Language in German Philosophy, 1759–1801* (New York and London: Routledge, 2007), p. 4.

[13] Ibid.

[14] *LS*, p. 77 (N I, p. 18).

[15] N II, p. 198.

There are, then, profound similarities between Hamann and postmodernity. Indeed, one could argue that postmodernity commences – once it is recognized that the theoretical foundations of the Enlightenment have, in fact, collapsed, i.e., once it is realized that we can no longer return to a naïve confidence in reason's power to establish its own principles a priori – precisely by accepting the terms of Hamann's *Metacritique* and what Terezakis rightly calls his "immanent linguistic perspective."[16] At the same time, however, there are crucial differences between them, stemming most obviously from the fact that Hamann was a Christian thinker, whereas postmodern thought is typically – if not essentially – a secular, post-Enlightenment continuation of modern unbelief.

As was intimated above, this difference appears, firstly, in their respective views of language. For here one is presented with a clear alternative: Is language a Gnostic "prison-house" in which thought is trapped because it cannot get outside the infinite regress of signification to some definitive "transcendental signified" that could bestow meaning upon what is otherwise a "bad infinite" of meaningless "supplementation"? Or is it a sacramental medium of divine self-communication, whose infinite regress is an image of God's own infinity and whose metaphorical richness is a foretaste of divine plenitude? In short, is language a purely human construct, or is it also – in and through human creativity and self-expression – a vehicle of divine self-revelation? Clearly, these are two radically different options: whereas the former forecloses the possibility of metaphysics and theology, the latter very much holds it open, once one is able to affirm that language comes from God and, as such, is capable of revealing God.[17]

Secondly, while Hamann too speaks of reason's "end," namely, in learned ignorance, as we have seen, his metacritique serves a higher "elenchtic" purpose, namely, the salvation of reason by ordination to faith – in which respect his metacritical understanding of reason and its *telos* precisely mirrors Paul's understanding of the purpose of the law as a pedagogue to Christ (Gal. 3: 24). Postmodern deconstruction, on the other hand, serves no ostensible purpose except that of reducing metaphysical notions of permanence, order, presence, identity, and reason to nothing but the endless play of interpretation and ultimate (in)difference. Indeed, whereas Hamann's metacritique is meant ultimately to save reason from theoretical suicide, i.e., from nihilistic auto-destruction, by pointing reason past its own dialectical uncertainties to the bedrock of an inspired tradition, postmodern deconstruction leaves reason foundering in the very abyss – and even celebrates the abyss and loss of meaning – from which Hamann would save it. In sum, whereas Hamann applies metacritical leverage to secular reason in order to lead true reason from pride to faith as its necessary support and perfecting light, postmodern deconstruction leads reason irredeemably to its own destruction, with no other prospect to embrace but some form of nihilism.

Thirdly, to name but one last difference, whereas postmodernism rejects all "metanarratives," Hamann objects only to systems of merely human origin, built upon the sands of human speculation, and happily embraces the inspired "system"

---

[16] Terezakis, *The Immanent Word*, p. 4.

[17] This is why too much has been made in theology about the so-called "problem" of religious language. To be sure, out of reverence for divine transcendence and aseity, one must not fail to observe an analogical interval between our words about God and the divine nature they would signify; but neither should one, out of false humility, presume to short-circuit the paths of divine condescension, as though God were not able to reveal himself precisely in and through what is most proximate and familiar to us.

and "metanarrative," the narrative of narratives, prophetically foreshadowed in the Torah, foretold by the prophets, and proclaimed by the apostles, martyrs, and saints, of the salvation of the world – Jew first, then Greek (Rom. 1: 16) – through faith in Jesus Christ, the "great *architect* and *cornerstone* of a *system* that will outlast heaven and earth ..."[18].

One is free, of course, to turn aside from the authority of a two-thousand-year old tradition to some other authority, be it some modern or postmodern author or one-self (as narrow a base of wisdom as this may be); one is free to shut out the super-natural light of prophetic testimony and place one's faith solely in the natural light of one's own reasoning (though this light becomes dimmer and less "natural" to the degree that one has turned away from its source).[19] Hamann's point, however, is that, if one does so, one should not be so deceived as to think that, in rejecting pro-phetic tradition, one thereby stands upon a firm "rational" foundation, as if a die-hard secularist is somehow more rational, and more "grounded" than a person of faith. On the contrary, it is perhaps Hamann's most fundamental insight that there is *more* certainty in the prophetic tradition of the "sure prophetic word" (2 Pet. 1: 19) – which holds that certain persons have actually been inspired by God to communi-cate divine things – and that this unanimous tradition of prophets, apostles, and martyrs provides a firmer foundation for human culture than the speculative mytho-logies of those inspired by reason alone. As Hamann strikingly puts it, "Whoever does not believe Moses and the prophets will therefore always become a poet, with-out his knowing it or intending it ..."[20] Indeed, for Hamann, such is the poetic end of the Enlightenment: that reason apart from faith not only conjures up the void of nihilism, but is ultimately indistinguishable from the speculative and ideological fictions required to fill it. A century later, and therefore less prophetically, Nietzsche similarly describes the poetic fate of philosophy and its various attempts to ground reality by way of reason, when he says, "All possible superstitions are posited into the void."[21]

But if Hamann and Nietzsche are right – if secular reason, unable to establish any definitive ground, reduces to one or another form of speculative mythology, whose final ground is the will to power – one is ultimately left with the following choice. Either one affirms the nihilism with Nietzsche, absurdly believing that meaning can be created *ex nihilo* by "strong spirits," "overmen," who have enough creative power to shape a culture and endow it with meaning in view of the darkness and formlessness they uniquely perceive; or, with Hamann, one similarly perceives the threat of darkness and formlessness, i.e., the nihilism, lurking behind secular reason, but affirms that God has always already come to the rescue of reason, made himself known, and sought to shape human culture and destiny through the "strong spirits"

---

[18] N III, p. 23.

[19] According to Augustine's doctrine of illumination, not only do we reason by the light of the Logos, "which enlightens everyone" (John 1: 9), we reason all the better the more we are illuminated by him, that is, the more we are turned toward him and the light of his face. Conversely, we reason all the more poorly the more we turn away from him: "If, then, by approaching you are illuminated and by withdrawing you are darkened, your light is not in you but in your God" ("si ergo accedendo illuminamini et recedendo tenebramini; non erat in vobis lumen vestrum, sed in Deo vestro") (*In evangelium Ioannis tractatus centum viginti quattuor*, 19, 12). The same holds true at an ontological level that holds true here at a noetic level: for in turning away from God not only does one turn away from the source of all intellectual light and reason, but also from the source of all being.

[20] N II, p. 64.

[21] See "Nachgelassene Fragmente" in *KSA*, vol. 7, p. 466.

of an inspired tradition. In short, *after the Enlightenment,* the fundamental option comes down to one or another form of secular postmodernity or a post-secular theology: whereas the former has nothing left to believe in except ideology or self-interest, having rejected both the universal rationality of the *Aufklärer* and the *unam, sanctam ecclesiam catholicam,* authoritatively attested by prophets, apostles, martyrs, and saints, the latter similarly sees through the inflated claims of the Enlightenment, but believes that a genuine reason-sustaining, reason-inspiring, and indeed reason-furthering revelation has, in fact, occurred.[22]

To be sure, one might continue to dream that there is a third possibility; one might continue to believe that reason can perhaps yet save itself and that the grand secular attempt to construct a sure foundation for science and morals by means of reason alone (in a modern version of the story of Babel) is not altogether bankrupt. Thus, for example, one might look in hope to the last-ditch efforts of our last philosophers to secure the tower with some form of ethics based upon some form of "pragmatic," "communitarian," or "communicative" rationality. But if one has once stood with Hamann and Nietzsche and seen the futility of all such attempts, then the same choice inexorably reappears: either one capitulates to postmodernity, which can save neither reason, nor meaning, nor morality, nor even, as we shall see, the substance of the phenomena themselves; or one admits the possibility of enlightenment from another source, enlightenment not in the form of an auto-illumination, not in the form of a "self-kindled fire" (Wisd. 17: 6), but as a gift that flows down from above, "from the Father of lights" (Jas. 1: 17), and is experienced from within (by all who come to Christ) like a torrent of living water (John 7: 37–9). This, for Hamann and the saints, is real enlightenment; and this is why Augustine speaks so limpidly of "drinking the light of God."[23]

But if Hamann's metacritique forecloses the possibility of a return to the Enlightenment, it does so also – and here is the catch for theology – for any return to a *neo*-scholasticism (which is to be distinguished in important respects from much of the scholasticism of the Middle Ages) that would attempt to isolate reason and faith, nature and grace, into airtight compartments, believing (not unlike some of the religiously-minded of the *Aufklärer*) that reason apart from faith can infallibly establish not only certain metaphysical principles, but also the theological origin and end of all things.[24] In other words, Hamann's metacritique cuts both ways: while it deflates the Enlightenment's overblown doctrine of reason, depriving the *Aufklärer* of many of their most cherished illusions (including their dream of a secular utopia based upon reason), it also demands a far more modest estimation of the possibilities of a purely rational metaphysics or a purely natural (or philosophical) theology. Granted, following Descartes, the father of the modern project, one might wish that reason alone – uninformed by faith, and unenlightened by prophetic testimony – *could* infallibly establish the existence of God and the immortality of the soul, or that it could perfectly descry the limits of natural law and thereby lend the force of certainty to the gentle promptings of conscience. Indeed, one might very well *want*

---

[22]   See along these lines Phillip Blond (ed.) *Post-Secular Philosophy: Between Philosophy and Theology* (London and New York: Routledge, 1998), especially Blond's introduction, pp. 1–66.

[23]   See, for example, Augustine, *De moribus ecclesiae catholicae* I, §11.

[24]   While it is not the place here to develop a genealogy of secular reason, following John Milbank, the modern doctrine of reason could be said to derive ultimately not from the humanism of the Renaissance, but from late medieval distinctions between philosophy and theology, which ceded to philosophy (and to reason) far greater capacities than the Augustinian and, later, Lutheran traditions allowed, each of which remained more profoundly impressed by the degree to which reason is affected by the fallenness of the will.

to believe that reason can provide a certain foundation and common ground for theology to negotiate with an increasingly secular world. For Hamann, however, given that the postlapsarian soundness of reason is precisely what is in question, reason alone, apart from grace and the light of faith, cannot be expected *adequately* do so.

This is not to say that reason can do nothing. It can give demonstrations like Aquinas's "five ways"; it can by all means show the *reasonableness* of God's existence, the immortality of the soul, etc., as even Kant himself contends (who for this reason is no radical secularist). But, *pace* Anselm (and following Aquinas), it cannot make these things self-evident, to the point that their contrary would imply a contradiction. This is evident enough in that "rational" persons can reason very differently about many things, often coming to opposite conclusions, which would seem to attest once again (as we saw in Chapter 11) to an inveterate dialectic of reason.[25] Finding common ground is complicated further given that reason itself is an analogical term: given that we reason well to the degree that we are enlightened by the Logos (the primary analogate), and poorly to the degree that, owing to our own turning away, we are not. In short, there is no guaranteeing that two persons or parties will be reasoning with the same degree of light. Finally, reason will not suffice as a common ground in the marketplace of ideas, inasmuch as for Hamann, faith, being a gift of God and generically different from reason, "cannot be communicated like merchandise."[26] Indeed, as Hamann experienced with Kant, in matters of faith not all reasoning persons – and, often enough, not even the most "rational" of philosophers – can be reasoned with.[27] And this is precisely why he did not attempt to communicate with Kant or his contemporaries in discursive terms, but wrote prophetically in the peculiar way that he did.

Admittedly, Hamann's metacritique is radical – it cuts to the quick of modern and neo-scholastic rationalism, leaving no room either for Kantian illusions about "pure reason" or for theological illusions about reason being a firm and irrefragable springboard to faith. On the one hand, it demolishes secular foundations (forcing upon secularists the recognition that they have none); on the other hand, it tempers the confidence one might have in reason as an apologetic resource. Its virtue, however, is that it brings enlightenment about the fate of reason, which the Enlightenment had obscured. Wasting no time with illusions about what reason can deliver in terms of foundations, it prophetically forces one to recognize the alternative: either illumination (the sustaining and perfecting of reason by the light of faith) or nihilism. Such is the fundamental option *after* the Enlightenment. Granted, illumination comes in degrees; and nihilism is a final destination. The question that Hamann poses, however, is this: Should one not know what road one is on? Should one not know that the ultimate noetic consequence of reason divorced from faith (in prophetic tradition) is nihilism – much as one should know that the ultimate ontological consequence of sin is death? This would seem to be a rather simple, almost obvious question; in the age of secular reason, however, which for the most part is content with illusions about the sufficiency of reason, it is the kind of question that makes Hamann, in Bayer's words, a "radical Enlightener."

[25] See, for example, Alasdair MacIntyre's discussion of rival moral arguments in *After Virtue*, 2nd edn. (Notre Dame, IN: Notre Dame Press, 1984), pp. 6ff.

[26] ZH VII, p. 176.

[27] See ZH I, p. 370, where Hamann is speaking precisely of his relationship with Kant: "The question remains, whether in all the world it is possible for a person who is awake to convince a person who is dreaming, so long, namely, as he is asleep, that he is asleep? No – Even if God himself spoke with him, he is compelled to send the word of power in advance and to allow for its fulfillment: 'Awake, O sleeper ...'" Cf. Eph. 5: 14.

Anticipating the collapse of secular reason, Hamann thus brings us to a decidedly postmodern crossroads, at which point one can take the road of faith, which, as an inspired tradition attests, leads to ever greater enlightenment; or one can take the road of postmodern unbelief, which leads to nihilism. Simply put, the alternative is one between Hamann and postmodernity. But inasmuch as the various strains of postmodern philosophy are in one way or another permutations of the thought of Nietzsche, Heidegger, and Derrida – and inasmuch as Hamann both anticipates and offers an alternative to each of them – the alternative could also be presented in more personal and concrete terms as one between this reigning "postmodern triumvirate" and Hamann, perhaps the first postmodern prophet. Accordingly, the immediate task will be to see by way of a series of brief vignettes how Hamann compares with each of these thinkers in order, if possible, to get past them – to get *beyond* postmodernity to the positive-constructive possibilities his thought holds for a post-secular theology.

HAMANN BEFORE NIETZSCHE

Although Nietzsche had little to say about Hamann – he quotes him only once, approvingly, in his unfinished work from 1873, *Die Philosophie im Zeitalter der Griechen*[28] – Hamann in many ways represents his alter ego, the kind of path he *might* have taken had he remained a Lutheran. Indeed, Nietzsche's silence about Hamann becomes all the more intriguing, given a number of striking similarities between them, the most obvious being that both were first and foremost philologists well versed in the languages and literature of antiquity, and only secondarily philosophers. Accordingly, possessed of a keen sense of the connections among thought, language, and the genealogy of concepts, neither could for a moment countenance something as fabulous as "pure reason." As Nietzsche put it, clearly following the import of Hamann's *Metakritik*, "Let us beware ... of the dangerous old conceptual fables introduced by a 'pure, timeless subject of knowledge without will and without pain; let us beware of the tentacles of such contradictory concepts as 'pure reason,' 'absolute spirit,' 'knowledge in itself.' "[29] For this reason too, both reject every sharp binary distinction between philosophy and poetry, logic and aesthetics, as well as every devaluing of human creativity that would follow from it – as though logic and philosophy belonged to a privileged and invisible realm of truth, but poetry and art to the fallen world of appearances; as though knowledge were not affected by "our own creative modality" or creativity were not itself a kind of knowing.[30] In short, both understand truth as inherently poetic.[31]

This being so, inasmuch as for Hamann and Nietzsche thought is not prior to language but formed, shaped, and in some sense *made* by it, we should not be surprised that both were exceedingly, even obsessively concerned with their styles. As Hamann put it, quoting Buffon, "Le style est l'homme même."[32] So too, keenly

---

[28]   *KSA*, vol. 1, p. 811; cf. N II, p. 65. See Chapter 3, n. 40.

[29]   Nietzsche, *Genealogy of Morals* III, §12; *KSA*, vol. 5, p. 365. Cited by Johannes von Lüpke in Oswald Bayer (ed.) *Johann Georg Hamann. 'Der hellste Kopf seiner Zeit'* (Tübingen: Attempto Verlag, 1998), p. 203. Cf. Hamann's parable to Kant about the *ghostliness* of truth apart from the data of history and the senses, ZH I, p. 381.

[30]   See John Milbank, "The theological critique of philosophy in Hamann and Jacobi," in John Milbank, Catherine Pickstock, and Graham Ward (eds.) *Radical Orthodoxy: A New Theology* (London: Routledge, 1999), p. 29.

[31]   In Nietzsche's case this is true inasmuch as we alone give meaning to the world, creating it *ex nihilo*; in Hamann's case, because God himself is a poet, because creation itself is a kind of poetry, and because human language, as an interaction with the world, is fundamentally an analogous poetic construction – whereby Adam, as the image of the divine poet, is allowed, so to speak, to finish the poetry of creation (cf. Gen. 2: 19).

[32]   N IV, p. 424.

aware of how much a culture is a product of its language, its manner of speaking, both were profoundly concerned about the impoverishment of language at the hands of orthographical "correctness" – to which one might today add the potentially enervating effects of "political" correctness. Thus Hamann says, "The purification of a language strips it of its wealth, just as too strict a correctness strips it of its strength and manhood."[33] Likewise, Nietzsche declares: "The poverty of language corresponds to the poverty of opinions ..."; "I demand a more powerful and attractive language"; "a doctrine of style that would see to what is correct and conventional, would be the last thing *we* need ..."[34]

But it is not only orthographical correctness that robs language of its power; for both of them the same effect is associated with philosophical abstractions. "Δος μοι που στω –" Hamann says, "just no purified and abstract and empty words; these I avoid like deep still water and slick ice."[35] Or as Nietzsche puts it, expressing his particular distaste for the abstraction "appearance": "The word appearance [*Erscheinung*] contains many seductions, which is why I do everything possible to avoid it ..."[36] Accordingly, over against their contemporaries, both write in a radically different style: a style that is unmistakably prophetic and declamatory, full of passion and aphoristic energy; a style that is meant not to inform, but to effect something, to bring about some form of awakening, to help people – for both of them always "the few" – to see something new. And for this reason their styles might legitimately be described as sublime, flashing, in Hamann's words, with "monosyllabic lightning," or thundering, as Nietzsche puts it, "with a hammer"[37] – in the attempt to awaken the "sleepwalkers" of the age either (in Hamann's case) from a feckless and sterile rationalism or (in Nietzsche's case) from a mindless, quotidian nihilism (both of which, as both of them strikingly perceived, amount to the same thing).

To this end, therefore, as an antidote to the sterility of the modern age – the age of secular reason and Nietzsche's "last men" – both appeal to the cult of genius, freely invoking Dionysus in their cause.[38] Moreover, both write in a characteristically dithyrambic style, inveighing against the neglect of the senses, the passions, and aesthetic concerns generally at the hands of what they perceive to be an effete, decadent, excessively "Apollonian," and ultimately life-denying rationalism. In sum, both of them view this kind of rationality, the rationality of the Enlightenment, as a "castration" of our creative powers.[39] Hence Hamann's repeated identification of the *Aufklärer* with *castrati*; hence his lampooning of the Stoics and his impugning of Origen's supposed self-mutilation; hence Nietzsche's incessant complaints about sterility, decadence, hatred of the body, and *ressentiment* against life.[40]

---

[33] N II, p. 136.

[34] *KSA*, vol. 7, pp. 830, 833.

[35] ZH V, p. 266. The phrase, "give me a place to stand," is attributed to Archimedes (in the sense of an Archimedean point).

[36] *KSA*, vol. 1, p. 884

[37] See *Götzen-Dämmerung oder Wie man mit dem Hammer philosophirt* (*KSA*, vol. 6, pp. 55ff.).

[38] As Hamann puts it in the *Aesthetica*, quoting Tibullus, "*Come Bacchus! with your sweet grapes dangling from your horns* ..." (N II, p. 201); similarly Nietzsche calls himself "the last disciple of the philosopher Dionysus" (*KSA*, vol. 6, p. 160; cf. p. 258). Along with the cult of genius, the nineteenth century saw a general renewal of interest in the Dionysian in poetry and philosophy. But all of this arguably begins with Hamann and ends with Nietzsche. See Max L. Baeumer, "Die Romantische Epiphanie des Dionysos," in *Monatshefte 57/5* (October 1965), pp. 225–36.

[39] See in this regard James C. O'Flaherty, "The concept of knowledge in Hamann's *Sokratische Denkwürdigkeiten* and Nietzsche's *Die Geburt der Tragödie*," in *The Quarrel of Reason with Itself: Essays on Hamann, Michaelis, Lessing, Nietzsche* (Columbia, SC: Camden House, 1988), pp. 148ff.

[40] See especially Hamann's *Wolken* (N II, p. 97) or the *Aesthetica* (N II, p. 208).

Following from this, a further similarity is that both tend to see the history of philosophy as the history of a pathology: from Plato's *Phaedo* (with its Gnostic doctrine of the soul's incarceration in the body), to Descartes's fantasy of self-mutilation in the *Meditations* (the perverse founding gesture of modern philosophy), to the transcendental method of Kant's critical philosophy (which abstracts from the world of the senses as though it were something "unclean" and, in any event, an impediment to the "purity" of reason's investigations) – a tradition whose last notable instantiation can be seen, *mutatis mutandis,* in the "phenomenological reduction" of Husserl's increasingly transcendental phenomenology. In short, they tend to see this tradition of thought, which methodologically abstracts from the senses, the passions, and our own "creative modality,"[41] either in terms of a puritanical illness or a "Gnostic hatred of matter" worthy of contempt.[42] To be sure, such methodological abstraction is never an end in itself, but always undertaken in the hope of attaining a more certain foundation in some *topos noetos* – whether this be a realm of forms (in Plato), clear and distinct ideas (in Descartes), or pure concepts a priori (in Kant). For the senses, after all, can deceive; and because they *can* deceive it would seem imperative, according to this tradition, to proceed methodologically as though they are *fundamentally* deceptive and cannot be trusted. To Hamann and Nietzsche, however, this very notion was itself the original deception – the idea that the world of the senses is essentially a fallen world of appearances, containing and revealing no inherent truth, and that truth, therefore, must be sought elsewhere, "meta-physically." Indeed, because neither of them believed that any such foundations were available to us – certainly not by reason alone – they tended to see such intellectual exercises as a misuse of reason in the first place, moreover, as an empty "love of form" or a nihilistic fascination with the void, which Nietzsche calls a "will to nothing."[43]

Aside from its pathological aspects, however, and aside from the plain philosophical error they saw in it, Hamann and Nietzsche rejected the metaphysical impulse on several other counts. Firstly, regarding its moral (or nihilistic) implications, they realized that the net result of the purisms of reason, i.e., the net result of its methodological abstraction from the senses and the "accidents" of history (and tradition), would be no certain foundation for the sciences and morality but, on the contrary, the creation of a moral vacuum with nothing to fill it.[44] In other words, such methodological abstraction would conjure up the specter of nihilism without being able to conjure it away. For, as they uniquely seem to have perceived, morality can no longer be sustained once reason *alone* is left to vouch for it – once historical tradition is hastily and unreasonably dismissed as capable of transmitting a supersensible revelation, and one is subsequently left with the mere *assumption* (which turns out to be an appalling error) that reason is not dependent upon history and tradition and is therefore able to attain moral and theoretical certainty on its own terms.[45]

---

[41] See Milbank, "The theological critique of philosophy," p. 29.

[42] See N III, p. 285; and see Nietzsche, *Genealogy of Morals* III, §§4, 28; *KSA*, vol. 5, pp. 343, 412.

[43] N III, p. 285.

[44] For Nietzsche's understanding of nihilism, see especially *KSA*, vol. 12, pp. 211ff. See also *KSA*, vol. 6, p. 72.

[45] For what is required is precisely a theoretical ground *beyond* the immanent dianoetic certainties of mathematics, which not even Plato could hope to disclose apart from certain stories and myths, i.e., apart from a form of sensible, parabolic mediation.

Secondly, in addition to the problematic nihilism they saw in the metaphysical impulse of pure reason, Hamann and Nietzsche were both profoundly concerned about its enervating aesthetic consequences. For Nietzsche, of course, this has to do with the fact that for him, this world, the world of the senses, is the only world that there is. Thus any form of metaphysics is in his view a deception. It is especially the case, however, inasmuch as for Nietzsche truth is not only bound up with human creativity (as in some sense it also is for Hamann), but essentially a human creation. To seek truth elsewhere – in another world – is therefore, for Nietzsche, to fail to appreciate the creative source (ultimately in the *Wille zur Macht*) from which it springs. For Hamann, on the other hand, the aesthetic problem of "pure reason" lies chiefly in that it forecloses the possibility of genuine religious perception. In other words, it forecloses the possibility of religio-aesthetic experience, the possibility, that is, of "tasting and seeing" (Ps. 34: 8) the Lord *in* his works.

For both of them, in any case, the aesthetic consequences of "pure reason" were just as problematic and debilitating as its moral consequences. After all, this was precisely what Hamann's *Aesthetica* was meant to show: that a purely rational approach to things *deadens* our senses to the kenotic language of God, missing the very movement by which God is always already *adapted* to the senses; as a result, we no longer synaesthetically *hear* the Word in what we *see*, whether in creation, in Christ, or in Scripture. Thus he speaks elsewhere of the "πρωτον ψευδος of the *original attempt* to derange [*verrücken*] our senses from the simplicity in the Word and to spoil peace on earth with the adulterous taste of reason."[46] In other words, the "Enlightenment" of the modern age is merely a refurbished version of the first lie (Gen. 3: 4–7), which instead of providing enlightenment precisely deadened our senses to a perception of God in creation. To be sure, there is nothing like this in Nietzsche. For him the senses do not reveal anything but nature and, behind that, the *metaphysicum* of the will to power. But he too was enough of a sensualist to say something strikingly similar: that " 'Reason' … causes us to falsify [or adulterate] the testimony of the senses."[47]

For all their similarities, however, there are, needless to say, profound differences between them, among them their radically different views of Socrates,[48] their different understandings of the cause of nihilism, and their radically different valuations of it. For Hamann, nihilism is a function of reason's abstraction from the senses, history, and tradition, since God is made known precisely through these means and apart from them one is left with nothing but what reason can dream up to fill the void. For Nietzsche, on the other hand, while it is certainly connected to this process of abstraction, nihilism is ultimately bound up with belief in transcendence as such. Moreover, for Nietzsche, all the shrieks and cries of his madman notwithstanding, nihilism is not only a crisis, but also an opportunity, a "night of indifference" out of which the "overman" will arise. But above all and most obviously, it is with regard to Christianity – what was most dear to Hamann and most loathed by Nietzsche – that their stark and insuperable differences appear. Indeed, what difference could be

---

[46] N III, pp. 378, 223.
[47] *KSA*, vol. 6, p. 75;
[48] See, for example, O'Flaherty, "The concept of knowledge," pp. 145–61.

more drastic? Hamann writes as a servant and prophet of Christ; Nietzsche, as a self-declared prophet of Antichrist – and thus with profound antipathy and bitter *ressentiment* towards everything Christian. Moreover, Nietzsche clings to the illusion that Christianity is essentially a Gnostic, life-denying religion, wholly identifiable with Buddhism or the world-weariness of Plato's *Phaedo*, and that, on this account, "Dionysus" and "the Crucified," the terms of his imaginary debate, cannot be reconciled.[49]

No doubt, Nietzsche could find support for his prejudices among certain Christian ascetics. In view of Hamann's life and doctrine, however, Nietzsche's standard criticism of Christianity as an otherworldly, life-denying religion is simply unconvincing. For quite the opposite of causing him to fly away from the world, Hamann's profoundly kenotic, incarnational, and anti-Gnostic understanding of Christianity leads him precisely to find God *in the world*. Indeed, from a perspective opened up precisely through the Cross, which reveals the depths of divine love, Hamann sees God's glory, as it were, always "coming down," disguised in the most ordinary experiences, in the most "minor circumstances" and "common events" of human life.[50] As he put it shortly after his conversion, "Every *phoenomenon* [sic] of natural and civic life, every appearance of the visible world is nothing but a *wall* behind which He stands, a *window* through which He sees, a *trellis* through which He peers; He watches our coquetries just like the king of the Philistines."[51] What is so striking in all of this, given Nietzsche's prejudices, is that, according to Hamann's theological vision, it is precisely divine humility (a virtue Nietzsche loathed) as seen in the Cross (to Nietzsche the scandal *par excellence*) that endows this world with a shocking degree of significance, transforming it from a world of mere phenomena into a world of "phoenomena," i.e., from a world of mere appearances (which to an unredeemed man can appear dubious) into a continual synaesthetic experience of God speaking "to the creature through the creature." Thus he could say, again on the heels of his conversion, "God makes the voice of clay, earth and ash as pleasant, as melodious, as the jubilation of the Cherubim and Seraphim."[52] Indeed, in an almost Blakean turn of phrase, he says, "God is where the flower is."[53] This is the summa of his aesthetics. But it is not one that is immediately accessible. Rather, as his *Aesthetica* makes clear, it depends upon a restoration of the senses in Christ, the giver of sight (John 9), in whom the spiritual and the physical are perfectly joined, and in whom, therefore, one sees the mystery of all things.

In any event, one finds in Hamann not a trace of otherworldly melancholy, but to the end a jubilant, life-affirming pleasure in this world. Thus, instead of wishing for an early departure from life, he says to Jacobi:

> Everywhere is my pasture! ... It is a *blessing* to have more taste for the *present* than for all else that lies here below or beyond; even were everything a deception or a deception

---

[49] See the conclusion of Nietzsche, *Ecce Homo*, in *KSA*, vol. 6, p. 374.

[50] See *LS*, p. 95 (N I, p. 36): "One has to be amazed to see how God enters into all minor circumstances and prefers to reveal his kingdom in common events of human life rather than in rare and extraordinary ones." As for the role of the cross in Hamann's aesthetics, which strikingly reintroduces the lost glory of a *theologia gloriae* into Luther's *theologia crucis*, so that God's glory appears more than anywhere here, in the cross, see *ZH* I, p. 395: "the one on the Cross is the key to all divine attributes, *especially that of omnipresence*." My emphasis.

[51] *ZH* I, p. 352; cf. Gen. 26: 8.

[52] *LS*, p. 188 (N I, p. 127).

[53] *ZH* I, p. 395.

in which there is an element of fiction: nevertheless, I intend to enjoy it as the best *intermezzo* of my journey. The gods are here too – in the kitchen as well as in the temple; in the stall as well as in the palace.[54]

And to Kraus, who had innocently recommended a more modest diet, given his failing health, he similarly responds: "How in the world can you recommend fasting to a *filio thalami* [i.e. a son of the palace] ... Whoever *tastes here* will be given to *see there* how friendly the *Lord* of the universe is."[55] Indeed, Hamann's *this*-worldliness goes so far that he could say to Herder, "The older I get, the more wisdom I find in the saying: *Quae supra nos, nihil ad nos.*"[56]

The difference between Hamann and Nietzsche thus comes down to two radically different conceptions of Christianity: whereas Nietzsche sees Christianity in terms of a Gnostic flight from the world and a nihilistic denial of life (disregarding centuries of Christian anti-Gnostic polemic), Hamann sees it in the kenotic light of the incarnation ("for God *so loved the world* ...") and even the Cross as justifying what one might describe, rightly understood, as a radical Christian *worldliness*.[57] "In the Cross," he says to Reichardt, "lies a great *enjoyment* of our existence ..."[58] Indeed, for Hamann, it is precisely through the "fresh green wood" of the Cross that Christ breaks open the gates of paradise, enabling one to return to the senses, to revel in them, and to enjoy this world anew with a genuine freedom and childlikeness (Rom. 8: 15–16; Gal. 4: 6–7) that Nietzsche could only parody in his dream of the "overman."[59] Thus Hamann says to Jacobi against the latter's tendency to otherworldliness, precisely because of the fruits already gained by Christ: "The first commandment is: you *should eat* (Gen. 2); and the last: come, everything is prepared. Eat, my dear ones, and drink, my friends, and be intoxicated."[60] To be sure, Nietzsche sees Christianity almost exclusively in terms of self-denial; for Hamann, however, even the call to take up one's cross is ultimately, and precisely, about sharing in the joys of Christ. Thus, whereas Nietzsche presumes to oppose Dionysus *to* Christ, for Hamann Dionysus is nothing but a mythological prefiguration *of* Christ, the real Dionysus and true wine-bringer (John 2: 1ff.; Acts 2: 13), who through the gift of the Holy Spirit (John 4: 10–14) brings peace (John 14: 27; 20: 21), joy (Rom. 14: 17), abundant life (John 10: 10), and – as many a saint has reported – even intoxication. As he puts it, commenting on the Song of Songs, "I sit beneath the shadow of the one

---

[54] ZH VII, p. 339.

[55] ZH VII, p. 304.

[56] ZH IV, p. 385. Translation: "Those things that lie above us are as nothing to us." Importantly, Hamann can affirm this saying not because God is not transcendent, but because in his view the *transcendent* God is always "coming down," saturating immanence with the kenotic presence of transcendence. To put it another way, this saying is a way of affirming with Luther a *theologia crucis*, as opposed to a *theologia gloriae*, which would attempt to seek God apart from his self-revelation "to the creature through the creature."

[57] By this, one must be clear, is meant not a love of the world in the sense of Jas. 4: 4 or a love of the present fallen order, which is subject to "the god of this world" (2 Cor. 4: 4; cf. 1 John 1: 15f.; 5: 19) and "hates" the disciples, who are "not of the world" (John 15: 18f.; 17: 14), but a love of the world, even amid its fallenness, in the sense that it remains God's good creation and God continually speaks to us through it and through the most ordinary events of human life.

[58] ZH IV, p. 391.

[59] N III, p. 378.

[60] ZH V, p. 275. See Oswald Bayer and Christian Knudsen, *Kreuz und Kritik: Johann Georg Hamanns Letztes Blatt* (Tübingen: Mohr-Siebeck, 1983), pp. 92f.

I desire, says my muse, and his fruit is sweet to my taste. He leads me into the *wine cellar*, and his banner over me is love. He delights me with *flowers*, and refreshes me with *apples*."[61]

Of course, postmodern epigones of Nietzsche, to whom such experiences are alien, are wont to repeat the tired refrain that any belief in transcendence devalues this world as *this* world (when, in fact, it is the other way around: that unbelief and the denial of transcendence makes this world trivial and ultimately meaningless). To Hamann, however, for reasons we have seen, belief in transcendence does not subtract but precisely *adds* to human pleasure. Accordingly, he could say to Jacobi, "everything ... even the *Ens entium* is there for our enjoyment ..."[62] More than anything, however, such postmodern criticisms are a sign of an impoverished imagination: an inability to imagine that human beings, as even the pagans intuited, are made for something greater than this world can afford. "If [the soul]," Hamann says,

> in comparison with God, is itself nothing but a breath of God, how great must we become through him, how blessed in him ... [when one thinks of how] the limits of our members and organs of sense, with their sensations, compare to the flight of which our souls even now are already capable, what excessive imaginations must we have of a being – that is to be One in God, as the Father is in the Son, and the Son in the Father (John 17: 21).[63]

This, one could say, is Hamann's version of the "overman," of which Nietzsche's doctrine of a creative apotheosis is a mere shadow. In the tradition of the Church, (as was discussed at greater length in Chapter 2), it is called "deification in Christ"[64] – which is something more real and more powerful than the aesthetical self-transformations of Nietzsche's disciples. As Hamann puts it, prophetically,

> with two porcelain eyes they cannot tell the difference between blind artists and children of light ... and will never experience the dawn of a refreshing day as long as they cannot believe in a resurrection of the flesh, because they already go about transfiguring their own lowly bodies in this life through beautiful arts, so that they assume a clarity similar to glowworms, which have a light in their hind quarters, which is a beam from the evening star.[65]

In other words, after the first pseudo-enlightenment (Gen. 3: 7) and now a second, such is the meager result of our own attempts to remake and re-tailor ourselves apart from Christ, the "true light that enlightens every man" (John 1: 9), whose "face shone like the sun" and whose garments were "dazzling white" (Matt. 17: 1ff.); and who promises similarly to clothe those who believe in him (Luke 24: 29; cf. Matt. 22: 11–12), who eagerly await his appearing when they will "be like him" (1 John 3: 2), shining like stars, differing in glory (1 Cor. 15: 40f.).

---

[61] ZH I, p. 410; cf. S. of S. 2: 3–5.

[62] ZH V, p. 265.

[63] LS, p. 370 (N I, p. 268).

[64] See Panayiotis Nellas, *Deification in Christ* (Crestwood, NY: SVS Press, 1987).

[65] N II, p. 347. "The beam from the evening star" is a reference to the Greek myth in which Zeus approaches a young girl in the form of a beetle and then makes love to her. Catching him in the act, Hera exacts punishment by transforming the girl into a worm with the added glow of a beam from the evening star. See Martin Seils, *Johann Georg Hamann: Eine Auswahl aus seinen Schriften* (Wuppertal: Brockhaus Verlag, 1987), p. 386.

In sum, in view of the foregoing, Hamann was perhaps the one Christian Nietzsche *had* to ignore, precisely because he was the kind of person he otherwise admired: full of passion and energy, full of inspiration and creativity, full of good cheer and life-affirming joy. To be sure, after Nietzsche there have been many secular prophets of pure immanence, Lyotard and Deleuze among them, who claim more radically to affirm this world, because they have resolutely denied any other, as though being a lover of this world requires the rejection of transcendence. One might even grant that such claims have a point if one has misunderstood Christianity as a kind of dour puritanism or joyless asceticism, and has no conception of what it might mean to rejoice in the Holy Spirit (Luke 10: 21; cf. Rom. 14: 17; Eph. 5: 18). In view of Hamann, however, this Christian *Dionysus*, how emptily such arguments ring.

HAMANN BEFORE HEIDEGGER

If Hamann anticipates and presents a compelling Christian alternative to Nietzsche, he stands in a similar relation, though for different reasons, to Heidegger. Of course, given the increasing distance in time, and given that many of Hamann's ideas had already worked their way into the German philosophical tradition, the connections between them are obscure and difficult to trace; but they are nevertheless there, just as Hamann stands in the background of the whole post-Kantian philosophical tradition. Indeed, closer investigation reveals many striking similarities: from their existential critique of modern philosophy; to their critique of historicism, instrumental reason, and the abstract God of metaphysics; to their reflections on language, temporality, and the nature of poetry qua revelation.

Of course, in the matter of existentialism Heidegger could draw upon Kierkegaard, among others. But as we have seen, Kierkegaard in turn draws upon Hamann, who is arguably the original source of the "existential turn" in the history of German philosophy. In *Doubts and Ideas,* for example, Hamann says that "our *existence* is older than our *reason*" and that "the ground of religion lies in our *whole existence* and outside the sphere of our cognitive powers, all of which taken together constitute the most arbitrary and abstract mode of our existence."[66] So too he counsels the brooding Jacobi "not to forget the noble *sum* for the *cogito*."[67] And calling into question the epistemological starting point of modern philosophy in Descartes, he says, "Not *Cogito; ergo sum,* but vice versa, and more Hebraic: *Est; ergo cogito,* and with the inversion of such a simple principle perhaps the whole system might receive a new language and direction."[68] In other words, he wishes to undo what he considers to be the ὕστερον πρότερον of modern philosophy, beginning with Descartes, which gave primacy to the thinking subject, and give priority back to being, to the revelation of the "I Am" (Exod. 3: 14), as the *precondition* of thought. In this respect, the only difference between him and Heidegger is that Heidegger strips being of any theological determination, as though possessed of an allergy for anything Hebraic in origin.

Before Heidegger, therefore, Hamann criticizes the modern transcendental turn away from the things in their appearing (as though there were something inherently suspicious about them) into the fortress of pure reason (as though its lonely cogitations, divorced from intercourse with the senses, were somehow more certain); and

---

[66] N III, p. 191.
[67] ZH VI, p. 230.
[68] ZH V, p. 448.

to this extent he shares Heidegger's criticism of modern epistemology and humanism for making man, specifically, the "rightness of thought," the "measure of all things."[69] Indeed, both of them recognize that inasmuch as modern epistemology begins with the *logical* conditions for the *possibility* of experience, thought is inevitably alienated from the *actuality* – the being – of what appears. As Hamann put it as early as 1764, rejecting in advance the wisdom of Kant's critical turn, "the wisdom of the world has begun to transform itself from a universal science of the possible into a universal ignorance of the real."[70] In other words, inasmuch as being can appear only as an object of transcendental consciousness – in Kant's case, ultimately in terms of a transcendental unity of apperception – being cannot appear qua being, but is always already strapped to one or another synthetic operation of the modern subject. As a result, Heidegger observes, ontology is assimilated into "transcendental philosophy," and the question of the being of beings, if it is even raised, is treated as a subset of logic.[71]

Admittedly, Hamann is not concerned as is Heidegger with the "forgetfulness" of the ontological difference between being and beings, *Sein* and *Seiendes*. Nevertheless, he anticipates Heidegger's critique of the subjective starting point of modern philosophy to the extent that the latter transforms being, and ultimately the being of God, into a mere "ideal of pure reason," thereby evacuating being of any objective content and foreclosing the possibility of any self-revelation of God as Being. As he gnomically put it to Jacobi:

> Being is indeed the *one* and the *all* of every thing. But the Tὸ ὄν of the old metaphysics has unfortunately! been transformed into an ideal of pure reason, whose being and non-being cannot be made out by it. Original *being* [*Seyn*] is truth; communicated being is grace. Non-being [is] a lack, moreover, an illusion ... on account of which manifold nothing [any] unity and center is lost from view.[72]

That is to say, because we have no access to original being apart from the gift of the self-communication of Being itself (as occurs through nature and the grace of an inspired tradition), attempts to envision being or truth *apart* from what is given, i.e., by means of reason alone, inevitably plunge reason into an abyss in which it can make nothing out. As Hamann similarly says to Herder, "The A and Ω [i.e., God as *principium et finis*] amounts at bottom to nothing but an *ideal of pure reason,* whereby one gains an infinite field of play for the most arbitrary imaginations or, to put it differently, all truth is transformed into raving nonsense" [*Schwärmerei*].[73] In other words, as a consequence of Kant's transcendentalism, for which God is at the end of the day merely a regulative fiction of "pure reason," truth becomes whatever speculative mythology is posited into the void – a void that reason itself creates, having presumptuously begun with itself as its own *principium,* and not with God or the objectivity of the gift of being.

But this does not mean that Hamann advocates a return to classical metaphysics any more than Heidegger does. To be sure, for Hamann, classical metaphysics may

---

[69] For Heidegger, however, this criticism applies not only to modern philosophy, but includes the entire history of metaphysics. See "Platons Lehre von der Wahrheit," in *Wegmarken*, 2nd edn. (Frankfurt am Main: Vittorio Klostermann, 1978), pp. 201–36.

[70] N IV, p. 271.

[71] Heidegger, "Kants These über das Sein," in *Wegmarken*, pp. 455f.

[72] ZH V, p. 271.

[73] ZH VI, p. 339.

be preferable to the modern metaphysics of subjectivity, inasmuch as it at least has an objective "thing," crude conception though this be, as the *principium et finis* of its reflections, whereas Kant's transcendental idealism leaves one with a transcendental something = *x*, which, as Hamann suggests, might as well be nothing.[74] In the absence of revelation, however, the God of metaphysics and natural theology is itself an abstraction, a mere *ens entium*, in any case, as Heidegger rightly observes, not the kind of God before whom one can "make music or dance."[75] As Hamann puts it, recalling Pascal's distinction between the God of the philosophers and the God of Abraham, Isaac, and Jacob, between the "god" of Plato and the God of the Bible, God is "no potter of plastic forms, but a father of fiery spirits and breathing powers."[76] And to this extent, in the name of the God of the Bible, not to mention his aversion to abstractions like *causa sui*, Hamann could be said, *mutatis mutandis*, to share Heidegger's critique of metaphysics.

But if, on the face of it, Hamann's metacritique of "pure reason" and Heidegger's "destruction" of metaphysics seem purely negative in character (as though Hamann were simply against reason or Heidegger were simply against metaphysics), one must be clear that, properly speaking, each is carried out with the positive intention of recovering some kind of *revelation* of which human language is capable but which a veneer of abstract terms and metaphysical concepts has obscured. Thus, in a rhetorical aside, lamenting the stultifying effects of modern rationalism, Hamann writes: "As if we lacked original documents that *are sealed* (Isa. 29: 11–12), *because one can no longer read* (since Divi Renati Cartesii *Methodus* and B. Joannis Clerici *Ars Critica* have become the *elementary textbooks,* the *Wolffianism* and *Machiavellianism* in sheep's clothing, the deceptive *patois* of our Gallic *Pedagogue*) ..."[77] In other words, just as merely rational exegesis deadens one's sensibility to the mysteries of Scripture, which remain "sealed" against profane readings, so too a merely rational approach to reality cannot make out the text of nature or the "dialect" of God in his works. The same holds true for both Hamann and Heidegger of merely rational or historicist approaches to history, which fundamentally misconceive the nature of history qua revelation and, consequently, through their own readings of history, obscure any revelation that has occurred or may be occurring through it. Indeed, in such cases, as Hamann points out, when "the spirit of observation" is divorced from "the spirit of prophecy" (in Heidegger's terms, "authentic temporality"), any understanding of history as revelation (or of *Geschichte* as the destiny or *Geschick* of being) is *ipso facto* lost from view. Thus he asks, anticipating Heidegger's emphasis upon authentic temporality as the key to an authentic understanding of Being: "Can one understand the past without for a moment understanding the present? – – And who would presume to derive adequate conceptions of the present without a knowledge of the future? The future determines the present, and the present the past, just as the end determines the nature and use of means."[78]

Thus, as we saw in Chapter 10, Hamann too is concerned about a merely rational-scientific mode of cognition, barren of any prophetic-poetic dimension, which isolates the present as an abstract moment subject to one's control, failing thereby to see the present authentically in light of the past and future. And along these lines he even

---

[74] Cf. *Konxompax*, N III, p. 226.

[75] See Heidegger, "Die onto-theo-logische Verfassung der Metaphysik," in *Identität und Differenz*, 10th edn. (Stuttgart: Günther Neske Verlag, 1957), p. 64.

[76] N II, p. 28.

[77] N III, p. 221.

[78] N II, p. 175.

anticipates Heidegger's concerns about modern technology. As he put it in the *Aesthetica*, identifying a dialectic at the heart of modern secular reason: "Every creature will alternately become your sacrificial offering and your idol."[79] In other words, in the absence of a prophetic understanding of nature and history, nature will be treated either as a means to an end (as in modern technology) or idolatrously worshiped as an end in itself (as in the case of modern pantheistic or "new age" spiritualities). In any event, once it is treated as an immanent totality and thereby subjected to futility (cf. Rom. 8: 20), nature no longer reveals anything beyond itself; it is no longer perceived as a "speech to the creature through the creature," but like a mute idol falls eerily silent (cf. Ps. 19: 1).

Of course, the content of the revelation Hamann and Heidegger respectively seek to recover could not be more different: in Hamann's case it is the revelation of the triune God; in Heidegger's case it is the revelation of *Sein als Nichts*. But even here there are striking similarities as regards the kenotic form in which revelation is understood to take place. Thus, for Hamann, it is central to Christianity that God, the Son, appears *sub contrario* in *Knechtsgestalt*; that the Holy Spirit likewise does not appear in glory but is similarly hidden to the eyes of reason beneath the clothing – the "rags" – of the Old Testament; and that the Father too does not appear directly, but instead appears "as nothing" in his self-revelation in creation.[80] In short, for Hamann, as we have abundantly seen, the form of divine self-revelation is essentially kenotic. And, curiously enough, something similar can be said of Heidegger, for whom Being [*Sein*] not only appears in relation to beings as "nothing," but, following an almost Christological logic, "empties itself" and "nihilates" itself in beings as the condition for the possibility of anything – the world of beings [*Seiendes*] – appearing at all. All of which makes Heidegger in certain *formal* respects a "Christian philosopher" – despite his claims to the purity of his own philosophy as a fundamental ontology (as though his own thought were not somehow and, in fact, profoundly influenced by the very Christianity he rejected) and his explicit rejection of the notion of a Christian philosopher as a *contradictio in adjecto*.[81]

A further similarity between them, which more than any other suggests an influx of Hamann's ideas, is the extraordinary importance both attach to language as the medium of our experience of the world. For Heidegger it is the "house of being"; for Hamann it is "the *mother* of reason and its revelations, its A and Ω," indeed, that by which "all things are made" (cf. John 1: 3).[82] It is not surprising, therefore, that Heidegger quotes Hamann precisely in this connection. The quotation, which we have already adduced, comes from a letter to Herder:

> If I were as eloquent as Demosthenes, I would have to do no more than repeat a single phrase three times. Reason is language, Λόγος. This is the marrowbone on which I gnaw, and will gnaw myself to death on it. For me there remains a darkness over this deep: I am still waiting for an a apocalyptic angel with a key to this abyss.[83]

---

[79] N II, p. 206.

[80] N II, p. 204.

[81] In this respect, Heidegger repeats the same hypocritical pretensions to philosophical purity that Hamann criticized in Kant. The only difference here is that Heidegger's allegedly pure philosophy is more of a heterodox theology: from his early existential analysis of the "fallenness" of *das man*, to his doctrine of the *kenosis* of Being in beings (as a surrogate account of creation), to his "eschatology" of the "poet-shepherds" awaiting the "advent" of being (cf. Luke 2: 8), to his own favorite prophets, like Hölderlin and Trakl. Indeed, the whole of his philosophy, one could argue, is formally a secularized theology, and by no means a clear alternative to theology itself.

[82] Heidegger, *Wegmarken*, p. 311; ZH VI, p. 108.

[83] ZH V, p. 177.

Heidegger reads this as follows: "For Hamann this abyss consists in that reason is language. Hamann comes back to language in the very attempt to say what reason is. This view of language plunges into the depth of an abyss. Does this consist merely in that reason rests upon language, or is even language itself the abyss?"[84] In other words, as Heidegger recognized, once one has seen the implications of language for reason, like Hamann has, once one has, so to speak, gone down into the waters of language as into a kind of metacritical baptism, one cannot simply go on reasoning in the same old way – the way the *Aufklärer* and modern-day rationalists do. One cannot simply go on pretending that thought is pure and that language is its instrument. Rather, having seen this abyss, one must recognize that thought is, in some sense, the product of language, which is prior to reason and therefore ultimately inscrutable to reason. This is why Hamann could not take Kant's otherwise impressive philosophy seriously; and why Heidegger's philosophy, beginning with his early lectures on Hölderlin, is largely an extended meditation on the mysterious relationship between language and being.

But if Hamann and Heidegger are generically similar with regard to the importance they attach to language in general, they are similar yet again with regard to the specific emphasis they place upon the connection between revelation and poetry. Indeed, for them poetic language is a unique site of revelation; it reveals our "being-in-the-world" and establishes our "dwelling" in it in a way that reason alone, for all its searching for foundations, cannot (the difference here being that with Hamann the revelatory power of poetry is attributed, above all, to Scripture, whereas in Heidegger it is attributed to Hölderlin and Trakl, etc.). And, finally, to note but one last similarity, given the importance each attaches to the revelatory power of language, it almost goes without saying that for both of them language should not be tampered with. Indeed, it would be difficult to find two thinkers who had a more elevated view of language and, like guardians of this "temple," this "sacred matrix," were more hostile to profane incursions (whether in the name of reason or utility) on the part of modern orthography.

For all their similarities, however, the differences between Hamann and Heidegger are equally obvious (as was also the case with Nietzsche). For the one is a post-secular Christian; the other is a post-Christian philosopher. This difference is manifest above all in their respective understandings of revelation: whereas Hamann seeks to recover a super-rational sense of the self-revelation of the triune God in creation, Christ, and Scripture, Heidegger seeks a revelation (of being qua being) that is unencumbered not only by metaphysical pre- and misconceptions, but by anything that theology might legitimately have to say about it. In other words, according to Heidegger, in his attempt to keep ontology "pure" (analogously to the way in which Kant sought to keep epistemology "pure"), the only way to do philosophy is to stop thinking theologically. To be sure, Heidegger retains for his pure, philosophical ontology a formally theological notion of revelation (under new terms such as *Lichtung* and *Unverborgenheit*, etc.); he also retains a formally Christological conception of being qua *kenosis*; he even retains a formally evangelical notion of the "poet-shepherds" who await the advent of being – not to mention his "inspired canon" of German poets in which their experiences of being are recorded. Nevertheless, according to Heidegger, the one-time Jesuit novice, one must radically and resolutely sunder any connection between being and God. As a result, his *Sein* cannot be identified with any Creator or with any divine attribute

---

[84] Heidegger, "Die Sprache," in *Unterwegs zur Sprache*, 9th edn. (Pfullingen: Günther Neske Verlag, 1990), p. 13.

(be it as simple as "oneness" or as elevated as "goodness"), since such impositions would adulterate the "purity" of our experience of "being as such." Thus, as a matter of philosophical "rigor," Heidegger's *Sein* is, strictly speaking, neither creative nor good; indeed, as he himself says, it is nothing at all – *nothing* but the being *of beings*.[85] Thus it comes about that for Heidegger, the anti-Augustine, paradoxically "Nothing" really "Is"; and that this "Nothing" becomes the source of ethics, revelation, and poetic inspiration. Such is the odd, uncompelling, and, in view of the horrors of the twentieth century, ethically chilling result of Heidegger's attempt to purify philosophy of theology, whereby he essentially repeats in the realm of ontology the same fundamental error Hamann identified at the heart of Kant's epistemology, thereby bringing the history of philosophy (divorced from theology) to its explicitly nihilistic conclusion.[86]

HAMANN BEFORE DERRIDA

The last member of what I have dubbed the "postmodern triumvirate" is Jacques Derrida, who warrants consideration given his influence during the last decades of the twentieth century and his clear continuity with Nietzsche and Heidegger. One could even say, modifying one of Hamann's observations, that without Nietzsche there would have been no Heidegger, and without Heidegger no Derrida.[87] Whatever connection there might be between Hamann and Derrida, however, is even less obvious than it was with Heidegger, and, in any case, far more indirect. The point of comparing them here, therefore, is not to establish any clear lines of influence, but merely to highlight some of the ways in which Hamann anticipates and presents a theological alternative to his thought. And to this end we have already covered much ground; for what connects Hamann to Derrida is to a great extent what connects him to postmodern thought in general: from his suspicion of metaphysics and all allegedly "pure thought," to his corresponding emphasis upon the metaphorical play of language, to his novel, proto-deconstructionist metacriticism.

Among the most obvious differences between Hamann and Derrida is a difference in basic vocabulary. Whereas Hamann critiques the notion of "pure reason," Derrida critiques the notion of "pure speech"; whereas Hamann calls attention to the metacritical implications of language, Derrida calls attention to the "differential trace structure" of "writing" or *différance*. Yet their fundamental metacritical or deconstructive point is strikingly similar. For just as Hamann's metacritique dissolves the pretensions of "pure reason" into language and tradition, Derrida's deconstruction dissolves every metaphysical pretension to stability and presence into the iterability of "writing." In short, both of them deny the immediacy of truth or meaning that the "purity of reason" and the "purity of speech" are respectively thought to provide. Nor is there any substantial difference between the way they use the terms "pure reason" and "pure speech." For the purest form of "speech," as understood by Rousseau et al., namely, an "absolute hearing-oneself-speak," is none other than an

---

[85] For further criticism of Heidegger in this regard, see John R. Betz, "Beyond the sublime: the aesthetics of the analogy of Being (Part One)," *Modern Theology* 21 (July 2005), pp. 367–411.

[86] See Heidegger's *Phenomenology and Theology* (1927), in *Wegmarken*, pp. 45ff., where he conveniently classifies theology as a "positive" science *of faith* (more or less along the lines of Schleiermacher), and not according to theology's traditional self-understanding as a science *of revelation*, since this would call into question his tendentious distinction between the subjectivity of faith and the objectivity of his own fundamental ontology.

[87] Cf. ZH IV, p. 376: "So much is certain: that without *Berkeley* there would have been no *Hume*, just as, without the latter, there would have been no *Kant*."

internal monologue, without intermediary, of reason with itself.[88] Indeed, it is precisely this "monological" conceit of western philosophy – the notion of a logical apprehension of truth in the inner chambers of the soul apart from any external or aesthetic mediation of sounds and letters, in short, the notion of knowledge through the immediacy of the concept – that Hamann and Derrida are both at pains to deconstruct. And to this extent one could easily make the case that postmodernity begins with Hamann's assault upon the unmediated self-certainty of the modern subject.

Beyond a similarity with regard to *what* they critique, a further similarity can be seen in how they carry out their criticism. And in this regard, precisely because they deny any pure philosophical access to truth apart from the contingencies of language and a textual tradition, both make an explicit point of reading philosophical texts as *literary* critics. More specifically, whether one call it "metacriticism" or "deconstruction," each proceeds by close reading, by drawing out the ambiguities in a given text, and by highlighting the indeterminate, aleatory, and "abject" elements, e.g., the senses, history, language, a textual tradition, that much of the history of philosophy – in its quixotic quest for transcendental purity, apodictic certainty, and epistemological mastery over what is, in Kant's phrase, "completely *a priori* in our power [*Gewalt*]"[89] – has either blindly overlooked, willfully ignored, or hypocritically denied. And for Hamann, as we have seen, next to the role of faith in our conceptions, there has been no greater blindness in the history of philosophy than its lack of attention to the question of language and its influence upon what we call "reason." Indeed, for Hamann, not only is language the "mother" of reason (and as such an "original supplement" to reason), it is also why reason cannot presume to attain any firm conceptual footing or totalizing grasp. It is an abyss, Hamann says, to which reason lacks the key.[90] Thus, when, therefore, Derrida says that "we *think only in signs*," he is saying nothing new, but merely repeating what Hamann argued several centuries before.[91]

Something similar could be said of Derrida's call for a science of writing or a "grammatology." As Hamann presciently put it to Jacobi in 1784, "We still lack a *grammar* of reason, like that of writing, and of their common elements ..."[92] And again, in 1787, "Do you now understand, dearest Pollux, my *language-principium of reason* and that, with Luther, I make the whole of φφy [i.e., philosophy] into a *grammar*, into a textbook of our knowledge, into an algebra and construction according to equations and abstract signs, which mean *nothing per se,* and everything possible and real *per analogiam?*"[93] In other words, following Luther, for whom theology is essentially a grammar of Scripture (i.e., of inspired language), philosophy should be understood analogously as a grammar, a science, of language as such, whose signs mean nothing in themselves but "everything possible and real" according to their relative position within a given semiotic system. Even as early as 1759 Hamann was thinking along these lines. Anticipating Saussure, he says, "Words, like numbers, receive their value from the positions in which they stand, and, like money, the determinations and relations of their meanings change according to place and time."[94]

---

[88] Jacques Derrida, *Of Grammatology*, tr. Gayatri Chakravorty Spivak (Baltimore, MD: Johns Hopkins University Press, 1974), p. 89.
[89] Kant, *Critique of Pure Reason*, B 871.
[90] ZH V, p. 177.
[91] Derrida, *Of Grammatology*, p. 50.
[92] ZH V, p. 272.
[93] ZH VII, p. 169.
[94] N II, p. 71.

Of course, what Hamann means by a grammar of language is only remotely analogous to what Derrida means by "grammatology." Nevertheless, he clearly points in this direction inasmuch as he understands meaning to be a function of the relation of words within a given cultural-linguistic system. Thus, for Hamann, even so weighty (or empty) a concept as "being" has no significance in and of itself, but only as a relational term within a linguistic network. As he strikingly put it to Jacobi, "Is *being* or *being itself* a real object! No, but rather the most universal *relation* ..."[95] The same is true for Derrida. Quoting Valéry, he says, "Whatever the words may be – Ideas or Being or Noumenon or Cogito or Ego – they are all *ciphers,* the meaning of which is determined solely by the context ..."[96] In sum, for Hamann and Derrida, there is no single concept, taken in isolation, whose univocal meaning could arrest the endless supplementarity and polysemous play of language. And to this extent Hamann could even be said to anticipate Derrida's critique of "logocentrism"; that is, his critique of the metaphysical attempt metaphysically to stop the flux and ground the play of language by means of a highest, all-controlling concept.

Admittedly, to deny that reason can establish a stabilizing metaphysical ground or presence might seem at first theologically untenable. From Hamann's radical orthodox perspective, however, rather than undermining faith, this presents no crisis of meaning at all – and Derrida could not have spoken more truly or, unwittingly, more prophetically – given that we can as little reason as we can know God apart from the "original supplement" of the Word (in both senses of the word!). In other words, when Derrida says, "in the beginning was the supplement," with Hamann all Christians can say, "quite so!," "In the beginning was the Word" (John 1: 1). Thus, curiously enough, at the "end" of the story of philosophy, when philosophy seems to have run its course with nowhere else to go, and one might conceivably despair over the "end of reason," postmodern philosophy picks up precisely by affirming the supplementarity of the word, logos, which is the most fundamental doctrine of the Christian faith.

Another striking similarity is that for Hamann, as for Derrida, writing is more than a derivative representation of speech. "Letters," Hamann explicitly says, "are not simply signs of *articulated tones* ..."[97] In fact, as we have seen, his *New Apology of the Letter h* is precisely an attempt to say that written language is not reducible to a representation of speech, but carries within it an obscure supplementary sign. And of course, to name but one last similarity, there is the example of Hamann's own inimitable writing, his *bricolage,* full of fragments, clipped quotations, meta-schematic insertions, elliptical allusions, cryptic jokes and puns, and meanings that none of his contemporaries (or, for that matter, any finite reader) could ever hope exhaustively to determine or understand. Indeed, given their endless associative links and their defiance of any single significance, the elusive nature of Hamann's texts epitomizes what Derrida means by the "iterability" and "supplementarity" of "writing." All of which makes one wish that Derrida had had something to say about him.

The all-important difference between them, however, turns upon how one understands Derrida's famous phrase that "there is nothing outside the text" (*il n'y a pas de hors-texte*).[98] On the face of it, this means just what Hamann affirms, namely, that we always experience the world through the medium of language, and that we

[95]   ZH VII, p. 169.
[96]   Jacques Derrida, *Margins of Philosophy*, tr. Alan Bass (Chicago: University of Chicago Press, 1982), p. 292.
[97]   N III, p. 93.
[98]   Derrida, *Of Grammatology*, p. 158.

have no access to truth apart from it. In short, we can never get "beyond language." In Derrida's usage, however, "text" means not only language in the generic sense, but also language in the more specific sense of "writing" qua *différance*; and to this extent his phrase carries with it the further anti-metaphysical connotation that there is no self-identical, self-present truth – and by implication no metaphysical or theological foundation – "outside of the text" of *différance*. In other words, it carries with it the more radical *metaphysical* claim – as it would have to be, since it is a claim about what is "beyond" our experience – that there really is "*nothing* outside the text," i.e., no God or metaphysical foundation, no "transcendental signified," in short, no Archimedean point that is "out there" independent of language that could serve to ground the play of language. Such is the implied (or explicit) nihilism of the phrase, "there is nothing outside the text."

Granted, within Derrida's textual world there is a simulacrum of transcendence, an *in infinitum* of endless supplementation, but there is no real, positive *infinitum* – no real transcendent *infinitum* of which the metaphorical richness of language, taken as a whole, is a reflection, and to which the surging repetitions of prayer aspire. Instead, everything terminates here in a "bad infinite," to use Hegel's phrase, which, at the end of the day, is not even truly infinite, as it curves in upon itself into the circuit of pure immanence. Indeed, according to Derrida's own terms – in the absence of any real opening to transcendence through religious language, and despite his language of "non-finite" supplementation – "there is nothing outside the text" ultimately signifies "a closed system of signs, which only refer to other signs without ever meeting up with [a] referent."[99] And to this extent language is for Derrida undeniably a kind of "prison-house," since there is nothing else beyond it or outside it.

Thus far we have seen that the phrase "there is nothing outside the text" has at least two radical meanings. The first is its implicit (or explicit) nihilism; the second is that language is hereby made into a closed, immanent totality, a "prison-house" from which there is no escape. But this is not all. For in a still more radical and arguably still more perverse meaning of the phrase, just as there is nothing outside the text, neither are there are any "things" within it. Indeed, the entire point of Derrida's *différance* (as a highest concept and simultaneously a nihilistic ontology) is to deny any point of contact with "substances" that we could call "real" or any "things" that would "match up" with our words for them, according to a traditional correspondence or designative theory of truth. Thus, as even a friend of Derrida like Geoffrey Bennington has pointed out, we are here only one step away from a "ghostly" idealism – in the sense that, for Derrida, there is nothing outside our linguistic experience that is really "there" that we could call "real," or in the sense that "there has never been anything but writing," and an endless chain of "supplements" and "substitutive significations" all along.[100] For his part, Derrida would seem blithely unconcerned about the ghastly consequences of his position, i.e., the way in which *différance* makes things and real persons "disappear," forced, as it were, by a dark, spectral magic to relinquish any claims to reality and vanish like ghosts, torn from any embodiment, into an endless chain of signification, where

---

[99] Geoffrey Bennington, *Jacques Derrida* (Chicago: University of Chicago Press, 1993), p. 99.
[100] Ibid.; Derrida, *Of Grammatology*, p. 159. Bennington, it should be noted, does not think that Derrida necessarily ends up as a linguistic "idealist" or "relativist," though how this is so is not entirely clear. See his *Jacques Derrida*, pp. 101ff.

nothing is ultimately significant.[101] "To risk meaning nothing," he says, "is to start to play, and first to enter into the play of *différance* which prevents any word, any concept, any major enunciation from coming to summarize and to govern from the theological presence of a center the movement and textual spacing of differences."[102] Far, therefore, from recoiling at the nihilistic implications of his thought, Derrida celebrates them; for it is the condition of "play," "that writing literally mean nothing."[103]

Needless to say, understood according to its ultimate implications, Derrida's maxim is incompatible with any form of orthodox theology, even if one were to try to understand it in terms of a radical apophaticism, since this still implies a real God who cannot be "positioned." Whereas God, the Creator *ex nihilo*, calls things that are not that they might be, the demon of *différance* – refusing to acknowledge any Creator – would return all things to the Nothing from which they came, and of which (according to this view) they are, ever so fleetingly, a reflection. Accordingly, beginning with Nietzsche's inversion of the "real world" and Heidegger's anti-Augustinianism, we see in Derrida the logical conclusion of postmodern nihilism. For Nietzsche, there remained the *metaphysicum* of the will to power, and with it a kind of naturalism; for Heidegger, Nothing really is, but paradoxically still reveals itself; for Derrida, who dispenses with Heidegger's nonsense of revelation, nothing means anything and everything, indeed, the point of language and life is precisely to mean nothing and worship nothing. Thus, to return to our comparison, while Hamann and Derrida are profoundly similar in the way they critique "pure reason" and "pure speech," and while Hamann's practice of metacriticism prefigures many aspects of Derrida's deconstruction, their positive views of the nature and purpose of language are at the end of the day radically different – stemming ultimately from Hamann's faith and Derrida's unbelief.

At this point, let us briefly sketch their views of language as follows. For Hamann, as we have seen, language is originally and essentially a *playful* response to the speaking of the Word in creation, even if this origin is now so obscure that it can be presented only in mythological terms. "With this Word in his mouth and in his heart," Hamann says, "the origin of language was as natural, so near and easy, as child's play."[104] Accordingly, for Hamann, language is *essentially* a dialogical religious phenomenon, and, especially in its poetic forms (which retain something of this original, creative "playfulness") bears traces of the "original supplement" of the Word. Indeed, for Hamann, when language is truly inspired, it is never merely human, but at once something human *and* divine, a poetic construct, *but also* – in and through the creative signs of language – a revelation. Therein for Hamann lies both the extraordinary dignity of the human being qua linguistic being and the highest expression of our capacities as the *imago Dei*: that our own words have the capacity to be revelatory not only of things human, but also of things divine. In short, he says, "We are all capable of being prophets."[105]

For Derrida, on the other hand, language has no outside, no beginning or end, no ultimate significance, and nothing is ultimately communicated through it. It is, in a word, pointless – pointless dissemination without the possibility of any real communion

---

[101] See Conor Cunningham, *Genealogy of Nihilism: Philosophies of Nothing and the Difference of Theology* (London: Routledge, 2002).

[102] Jacques Derrida, *Positions*, tr. and annotated by Alan Bass (Chicago: University of Chicago Press, 1981), p. 14.

[103] Ibid.

[104] N III, p. 32.

[105] N III, p. 417 (N I, p. 308).

or redeeming communication, since *différance* also deconstructs the notion of any "persons," i.e., any subjective identities, who could be "present" to one another to begin with. Of course, there is a semblance of similarity here in that, in a parody of Hamann's view of original and redeemed language as a kind of innocent, "playful" response to the Logos, Derrida similarly wants to understand language in terms of play. But it is a "playful" response precisely to Nothing – a play that, in a parody of paradise, is supposedly prior to "the alternative of presence and absence."[106] And this is the closest that Derrida comes to a kind of "redemptive return."[107] But, as Milbank points out, for Derrrida this play cannot help but remain intrinsically violent, inasmuch as language is essentially a "mechanism for concealment."[108] This is not to deny Derrida's point that language is always already marked by a "trace structure," or that one sign always supplements another. The question, rather, is how one interprets this structure. And to this extent one is presented with what amounts to a metaphysical choice (inasmuch as one is still making claims about the "nature" of language, which cannot be determined rationally): either, following Hamann, language is *essentially* prophetic and revelatory, and absence is not taken as something dark and sinister but as a positive excess of what graciously gives and presents itself to be thought or perceived; or, following Derrida, language is *essentially* governed by the violence of occultation, inasmuch one sign can be present only at the expense of another.

The choice between Hamann and Derrida becomes still more radical when one considers what each of them means by "writing." For Derrida, for writing to be writing, it cannot have any element of speech or living presence to it. It must in a sense be dead.[109] For Hamann, on the other hand, speech and writing go together – the one enlivens the other. This is *not* to say that writing is merely a written representation of speech: "For," as Hamann declares, "as little as the *purpose* of *speech* consists in the mere articulation and modifications of blind tones, still less does the *purpose* of *writing* consist in the counting, weighing, and punctuating of its mute substitutes ..."[110] Rather, for Hamann, "the true, natural and higher purpose" of language unites "both *speech* and *writing* – into a *shekhinah*, tabernacle and chariot-throne of our sensations, thoughts, and concepts through the audible and visible *signs* of language."[111] In other words, language is a tabernacle of God's glory; it is the ark, as it were, of God's covenant with human beings, the *Merkabah*-throne upon which the effective Word, who condescends to speak "to the creature through the creature," sits and moves. Thus Peter, who understood something about inspiration, says, "If anyone speaks, he should do it as one speaking the very words of God" (1 Pet. 4: 11).

But again, to emphasize the divine aspect of human language is not to deny that language is a free human construction, and therefore full of contingent signs, poetic metaphoricity, and polysemous supplementation. For as we have seen throughout,

---

[106] See especially Jacques Derrida, *Writing and Difference*, tr. Alan Bass (Chicago: University of Chicago Press, 1978), pp. 289ff. The perverse implication here is that only atheists truly know how to play, when in fact their "play," in order to overcome their secret despair, involves a Nietzschean affirmation of the pointlessness of their own existence.

[107] John Milbank, *The Word Made Strange: Theology, Language, Culture* (Oxford: Blackwell, 1997), p. 61.

[108] Ibid. At the same time, Derrida's understanding of language can be seen as a linguistic application of Heidegger's violent ontology. See, for example, "Der Ursprung des Kunstwerkes," in *Holzwege*, 6th edn. (Frankfurt am Main: Vittorio Klostermann, 1980), p. 41.

[109] See Catherine Pickstock, *After Writing: On the Liturgical Consummation of Philosophy* (Oxford: Blackwell, 1998).

[110] N III, p. 237.

[111] Ibid.

Hamann understands language precisely in Christological terms, and thus as being something at once human (a free poetic construct) and divine (as a vehicle of divine inspiration). Indeed, for Hamann, just as Christ fully (and not docetically) assumes human nature, the Holy Spirit analogously assumes human language – not superficially, therefore (as a corresponding docetic understanding of divine inspiration would have it), but profoundly, to the point of appropriating the very creativity, individuality, eccentricity, and personality of the prophets and authors of Scripture. In fact, for Hamann, just as God condescends in salvation history to make use of unsuspecting and fallible instruments (e.g., Moses, Gideon, Peter, and Paul) so too even our errors, the "crooked lines" of our "symbolic writing," can be vehicles of divine inspiration. As he strikingly puts it,

> If the hairs of our head, down to the variation of their color, belong to the *Datis* of divine providence, why should the *straight* and *crooked* lines and strokes of our symbolic and typological (but not hieroglyphic) handwriting not be the counter images and mirror of a *theopneustie* (2 Tim. 3: 16), of an unrecognized central force in which we *live and move and have our being* [?][112]

For all their similarities, the choice between Hamann and Derrida is now finally clear. Either, following Derrida, language is essentially, for all its non-finite supplementarity, a purely immanent construct that reveals nothing outside it; or, following Hamann, language is essentially a prophetic revelation of transcendence, of the divine *in and through* the human, including all the contingency and indeterminacy, creativity and eccentricity of human language that this implies. But perhaps more to the point, the choice between them really comes down to a final variant of the alternative between illumination and nihilism. And it is a choice that is all the more pressing inasmuch as, after the Enlightenment, the problem of reason, following Hamann and now Derrida, has come down to the problem of language. In short, it comes down to a choice between inspired and uninspired language: either language inspired by the Holy Spirit in response to the Logos, or language inspired by Nothing at all.

A CONCLUDING POSTSCRIPT TO POSTMODERNITY

Thus far we have discussed the "metacritical-deconstructive" aspects of what I have called Hamann's post-secular vision. We have seen how he radically reduces the problem of reason to the problem of language and thereby sets the stage for postmodernity. We have also seen how he not only anticipates but presents a genuine alternative to postmodern thought in its most prominent guises. Now, finally, we are in a position to summarize the "positive-constructive" aspects of his vision, looking ahead to the possibilities it offers for a post-secular theology – a kind of theology that would hope to get not only beyond the Enlightenment, but beyond postmodernity as well. Admittedly it would seem to be one thing to get past the secular reason of the Enlightenment, which Hamann rather easily did – at least in so far as he demolished its foundations. It would seem to be another thing to get past "postmodernity." And yet, for reasons we have already seen – inasmuch as the nihilism of postmodernity is but the flipside and inevitable result of the "pure reason" of modernity – there is arguably little difference between them. Indeed, postmodernity merely

---

112 N III, p. 240. Cf. Acts 17: 28.

makes explicit what was implied by the modern severance of reason from prophetic tradition (and from the superior light communicated through it). But to this extent, precisely because of its continuity with the Enlightenment, postmodernity can help us to see what was at stake in Hamann's debate with his contemporaries all along, namely, a radical choice between illumination and nihilism (as the respective destinies of faith and secular reason).

Specifically, one might summarize Hamann's relevance to a post-secular theology in terms of the following insights. Firstly, and perhaps most importantly, he recognized that reason cannot stand on its own, i.e., it cannot attain any moral or epistemological certainty, beyond, say, the sphere of analytic and mathematical judgments, but will inevitably collapse into nihilism apart from the backing of faith and the inspiration of prophetic tradition. In short, as Hamann perceived, reason qua secular reason has no foundation; it can neither ground itself nor provide any stable ground for human culture. On the contrary, far from being able to do without faith, reason needs faith and the authority of a prophetic tradition to tell it what it is: to tell it that its light is not merely a random consequence of material causes, or merely pragmatic and instrumental, or merely a function of the will to power, but a participation in and reflection of the light of a transcendent Logos, which allows for varying degrees of luminosity. This is in no way to endorse fideism, which would be the opposite error; for, as Hamann, himself says, "*Faith* has just as much need of reason as the latter of the former."[113] Rather, it is to say that the *Scheidekunst* of modernity, its foundational separation of reason from faith and tradition succeeds only in undermining reason itself and accelerating the advent of nihilism. For reason, according to Hamann, was never meant to be "alone," separated from faith and separated from prophetic tradition – no more than man was meant to be separated from woman (Gen. 2: 18) or man from God. And this is why Hamann's attitude toward the Enlightenment – and the ultimate vapidity of its secular rationality – could be summed up in the phrase, "*ob fugam vacui.*"[114]

Secondly, as a corollary, Hamann recognized that reason apart from faith cannot even establish the substance or veracity of the phenomenal world. Indeed, as John Milbank and Conor Cunningham have pointed out, the various attempts of modern philosophy, beginning with Descartes, to start with reason and subsequently establish the external world upon reason alone – starting with what the modern subject can "clearly and distinctly" grasp – not only made the world illusory, but cannot prevent the phenomenal world from, as it were, dissolving and vanishing before our eyes.[115] On the contrary, such mad attempts to "save the phenomena" by reason alone only accelerate their disappearance – which is precisely why Descartes, having first doubted the phenomena, desperately needs God to bring them back again. But if Descartes's thought-experiment makes the world suspicious in a way that it never was before, in the absence of his *Deus ex machina,* postmodern atheism, as we have seen, leaves us with a world that is even more ghostly, a world haunted by phantasms lacking any substance at all. As Lyotard candidly puts it, "Modernity, in whatever age it appears, cannot exist without a shattering of belief and without discovery of the 'lack of reality' of reality …"[116] And true enough, whether owing to the modern *suspension* of

---

[113] ZH VII, p. 165.

[114] ZH III, p. 45.

[115] See Milbank, "Theological critique," pp. 25f.; Cunningham, *Genealogy of Nihilism.*

[116] Jean-François Lyotard, *The Postmodern Condition: A Report on Knowledge,* tr. Geoff Bennington and Brian Massumi (Minneapolis: University of Minnesota Press, 1993), p. 77.

faith or the postmodern *absence* of faith (whether through Descartes's doubt, Kant's transcendental idealism, Husserl's phenomenological reduction, Heidegger's nihilistic ontology, or Derrida's *différance*), the spectral *unreality* of things is now what appears. In Hamann's striking words, "What a Nothing, smoke, what a pestilent Nothing are [our days] in our eyes when reason counts them!" But "What an All, what a treasure, what an eternity, when they are counted by faith ..."[117] Thus, for Hamann, faith not only saves the phenomenal world from ultimate vanity and insignificance, but, positively stated, is the key that allows us to perceive here, in this world, even in the most fleeting of appearances, the weight of God's glory and the traces of his providence.

A third Hamannian insight, which follows from this, and which postmodern authors would rather ignore, is that faith alone provides a foundation for genuine aesthetic experience – indeed, a genuine *sensuality*. For apart from faith, when reason is left with the impossible task of grounding reality, things tend to become *mere* appearances, and to this extent they tend to lack any real depth that could hold one's interest or inspire further desire. But, of course, this is precisely the nature of aesthetic experience: that beautiful things display a mysterious depth that cannot be reduced to the thing itself. In other words, in works of art, and supremely in the artwork of creation, there is always something *more* to see. And this, in turn, as Gregory of Nyassa points out in the *Life of Moses*, says something about the nature of genuine religious experience: namely, that, once one has experienced the *divine* beauty, and intimated something of its depth, one's desire for God is never exhausted (se Ps. 105: 4). Thus for Hamann (as for Gregory of Nyassa), religion and aesthetic experience naturally go together, the one providing the basis for the full, sensual enjoyment of the other. As Milbank observes, here "worship of God and the celebration of corporeality and sensual beauty absolutely require each other"[118] – so much so that for Hamann only the believer can truly and profoundly enjoy the world as it was meant to be enjoyed. Otherwise, in the absence of a transcendent depth, "if we take things as *only* finite, their solidity paradoxically vanishes. Equally, certain apparently real properties of things, like colours, being not fully comprehensible by reason, will tend to vanish also."[119] Thus Hamann could say in criticism of his contemporaries, who have taken the Word out of the world, "All the colors of the most beautiful world grow pale as soon as you extinguish that light, the firstborn of creation."[120] Indeed, as Milbank strikingly puts it, for Hamann "we only *see* things when they *speak* to us," i.e., "we cannot have sight if we are deaf."[121] Consequently, those who perceive things apart from faith are for Hamann (as for Bonaventure) ultimately deaf and blind. Moreover, they are mute, since, not hearing and therefore not seeing, they do not respond – they do not use their native tongue and linguistic creativity – by glorifying "Him who made heaven and earth, the sea and the fountains of water!" (Rev. 14: 7).[122]

A fourth insight, which follows from this, is that for Hamann not only do we not really *know* apart from faith, or truly *perceive* apart from faith, or truly *enjoy* the fullness of aesthetic experience apart from faith, we also do not truly *create* apart

---

[117] *LS*, p. 131 (N I, pp. 70f.).
[118] Milbank, "Theological critique," p. 26.
[119] Milbank, "Theological critique," pp. 26f.
[120] N II, p. 206. Cf. Col. 1: 15; 2 Cor. 4: 6: John 1: 3.
[121] Milbank, "Theological critique," p. 27.
[122] N II, p. 217.

from faith, inasmuch as, apart from faith in Christ, we lack the poetic inspiration that comes from the Creator Spirit. To be sure, there is such a thing as art without God or an aestheticism of "art for art's sake." From Hamann's perspective, however, true genius and true creativity come from divine inspiration. As he drastically puts it, thinking of the decadent sterility of a culture without faith, which has lost its will to create or even procreate and no longer "feels" the creative analogy between God and the *imago Dei*: "A world without God is a man without a head – without heart, without viscera – without *creative* parts [*pudenda*]."[123] In short, the modern world, insofar as it is a secular world, having nothing greater worth living for, is not only mindless, heartless and gutless, but also – having denied any analogy to the *Creator* – impotent.

A final insight, which follows from the others, given its aesthetical and poetical aspects, is that, if it is not to be fallen but redeemed, human language too is dependent upon faith, whereby our own words by divine inspiration become tabernacles of "divine energies and ideas."[124] Indeed, for Hamann, as we have seen, language is a kind of "sacrament," inasmuch as it is in and through the visible and audible signs of language that God kenotically conveys himself to the world through what is, to the eyes of reason alone, a merely human construct.[125] To be sure, postmodernists tend to see in language nothing but the will to power or merely an interminable chain of signification, but this is because they are not seeing *the* supplement of the Word in the words of human language. In short, they are missing Hamann's most fundamental point: that the *transcendent* God is kenotically hidden *within* language – just as he is kenotically hidden within creation, just as he is kenotically hidden within human history, just as he is kenotically hidden within the humanity of Christ, and just as the Holy Spirit is kenotically hidden within the "rags" of Scripture. In sum, on the basis of this vision of the *kenosis* of transcendence, which is able to find the *transcendent God in* this world under the various guises of his love, Hamann points the way to a theological recovery of nature, history, language, and art, opening our eyes and ears to a more refined perception of the "original supplement" of the Word, speaking in and through them.

Of course, it may be impossible to recover Hamann's thought in its entirety. But given that his understanding of reason's historical and cultural-linguistic embodiment has prevailed, given that his prophecies about secular reason ending in nihilism have been fulfilled, given, moreover, the richness of his theological aesthetics – his vision of a world full of God's abasing glory – is it not time to heed the voice of this prophet? In this regard the sober counsel of Friedrich Schlegel given two centuries ago is just as relevant today: "With Kantianism we have wasted years that ... will never return. This immensely *wise* and profound thinker, this seer, we did not recognize and heed."[126]

---

123 ZH V, p. 326. My emphasis.
124 See N III, p. 32.
125 N III, p. 289.
126 Friedrich Schlegel, *Deutsches Museum* III, in *Kritische Neuausgabe*, ed. Hans Eichner (Munich: Verlag Ferdinand, Schöningh, 1961), vol. 6, p. 628.

Biblical Index

APOCRYPHA

Index

CPSIA information can be obtained
at www.ICGtesting.com
Printed in the USA
FSOW04n2049020517
33817FS